EIGHTH EDITION

Introductory Foods

EIGHTH EDITION

Introductory Foods

MARION BENNION

FORMER PROFESSOR OF FOOD SCIENCE AND NUTRITION
BRIGHAM YOUNG UNIVERSITY

MACMILLAN PUBLISHING COMPANY

NEW YORK

Collier Macmillan Publishers

London

Copyright © 1985, Macmillan Publishing Company, a division of Macmillan, Inc.

PRINTED IN THE UNITED STATES OF AMERICA

Earlier edition copyright © 1980 by Macmillan Publishing Company

Macmillan Publishing Company
866 Third Avenue, New York, New York 10022

Collier Macmillan Canada, Inc.

Library of Congress Cataloging in Publication Data

Bennion, Marion,
  Introductory foods.

  Includes index.
  1. Food. 2. Cookery. I. Title.
TX354.B46 1985   641.3   84-23370
ISBN 0-02-308180-5

Printing: 1 2 3 4 5 6 7 8   Year: 5 6 7 8 9 0 1 2

ISBN 0-02-308180-5

Preface

Introductory Foods has been a widely used text for beginning college foods courses for more than 40 years, the first four editions being authored by Osee Hughes of Ohio State University. During that time, tremendous changes have occurred in food science and technology, as well as in the rest of the world around us, thereby markedly affecting both the content and approach to the teaching of introductory foods courses.

The eighth edition of this text is in keeping with the tradition established by the preceding editions as it attempts to keep abreast of changing trends in the teaching of introductory foods. A number of specific changes and a general updating have been made in the text, although the basic format remains essentially the same. The first four chapters have been completely reorganized and revised and include a separate chapter on food economics and convenience. Most of the information on measuring ingredients is now incorporated into a new chapter entitled "Weights and Measures." A short chapter entitled "Heat Transfer and Use of Water in Cookery" has also been added. Because the home use of microwave ranges continues to expand, information on microwave cookery has been incorporated into several chapters, including those on meats and vegetables, and discussed along with other methods of cooking these food products. However, a separate chapter entitled "Microwave Cooking" discusses some of the general principles of this method of food preparation. A chapter entitled "Sweeteners and Sugar Cookery" includes some discussion of artificial sweeteners, as well as the basic principles of sugar crystallization in candies. The chapter entitled

"Frozen Desserts" follows the discussion of sugar cookery to emphasize the common thread of crystallization. The discussion of batters and doughs has been divided into several chapters, including a general discussion chapter, "Batters and Doughs" followed by "Quick Breads," "Yeast Breads," "Cakes and Cookies," and "Pastry." A separate chapter entitled "Gels and Gelatin" has also been included with an introductory discussion of gel formation. The chapter on food preservation has been divided into four chapters, including "Canning," "Preservation of Food by Freezing," "Drying and Pickling," and "Fruit Jellies and Preserves." The chapter on meal planning has not been included in the eighth edition because it was felt that one chapter cannot do justice to this important area. Many excellent texts on meal management are available and an entire course is often devoted to this subject. The emphasis of this text is on food preparation.

The color photographs that were included in the seventh edition are retained. Additional black and white photographs and drawings have been included to emphasize points made in the discussion.

The sequence of chapters is not meant to set the order in which the subjects are presented in class. The chapters are written so that they can be used in any sequence. Cross references are made throughout to other sections of the book where similar or related discussions occur. An attempt has been made to minimize duplication of material in various chapters.

This text is written for the beginning student of foods who has not yet taken college chemistry. However, some high school background in science will help the student to more readily grasp the various principles of food preparation that are presented. The text should still be valuable for use with students who have had some college chemistry or are taking a concurrent chemistry course. A laboratory session often accompanies an introductory foods course. This text may be used with any of several excellent laboratory manuals that have been published.

M. B.

Contents

1

Food Choices and Quality

The food choices that people make and the development of their habits concerning food are influenced by many interacting factors [1]. However, for most persons, and under ordinary circumstances, foods must be palatable or have appetite appeal if they are to be eaten. A food is palatable to an individual if it is acceptable and agreeable to the taste.

The various sensory impressions or sensations, including odor, taste, mouth-feel or touch, and appearance of food, are all involved in an individual's judgment of palatability and quality. A taste or liking for many different types of foods may be acquired. The person who would learn to prepare foods with high appetite appeal must learn to taste discriminatingly in order to evaluate the quality and the intensity of the sensations received. People vary in their capacities to experience flavors and odors. But sensitivities to pleasurable experiences with food may be heightened as one learns more about food characteristics and quality.

Humans, as biological beings, require food to sustain life. Humans eat to satisfy hunger and to meet a basic drive for food. But a person is also a social being. Humans have learned to live and work together and have organized themselves into societies. As human in-

Factors Affecting Patterns of Eating

fants grow and develop they are incorporated into this society through varied experiences, and some of these experiences involve food. A person's pattern of eating is formed from infancy onward in a network of interrelationships with other human beings. The pattern begins with the family and is modified as a child grows into adulthood and travels in ever-widening circles of contact with others [16]. Contrary to the popular belief that dietary patterns are very stable and unyielding to change, patterns of eating by individuals and families are in a dynamic, continuous process of change as their economic, social, and technological environments change [4]. The term *culture* is used to describe a way of life in which there are common customs or rules for behavior and in which there is a common understanding among members of the group. The culture in which one develops determines, to a large extent, one's food patterns or habits. Foods are eaten in combination with other foods in ways that are determined and continued by the culture.

Food patterns may markedly differ from one culture to another. Grasshoppers, baked mouse, or roast dog may be delicacies in some parts of the world, whereas it would be unthinkable for humans to consume them in other areas. Eggs may be a staple breakfast food in certain cultures, whereas in others it is taboo for at least some members of the group to eat them. Not everyone in a cultural group eats exactly alike, however. Within a culture, individual preferences differ and subgroups develop. Families tend to develop their own distinctive food patterns, and even individuals within a family have personal food preferences. Differences both between and among cultural groups may be found in not only what specific foods are eaten but in the number of meals eaten each day, the way the food is served, and the utensils used in the service. Each culture passes on its food habits and patterns through training children from infancy so that each child knows what is acceptable and not acceptable and patterns become familiar [7].

The geography of an area and variations in climate influence the types of food that are usually grown and are readily available. This, in turn, affects the eating patterns of people in this area. Examples are the widespread use of pinto beans and chili peppers in the southwestern United States and the extensive use of seafood in coastal areas. The influence of diverse ethnic groups, such as Mexican, Chinese, Italian, Scandinavian, and others, is also seen in geographical areas where these groups have predominated. Each group has developed a cuisine with its distinctive combination of flavorings for basic foodstuffs [13].

Economics can be a powerful factor in changing dietary patterns although these changes may be transitory in some cases. When family food budgets are restricted because of financial problems, less expensive foods must make up a larger share of the menus offered.

Knowledge of nutrition and the effects of various diets on health encourages many of those responsible for food purchasing and preparation to adjust food patterns in accordance with suggestions from various governmental and professional agencies. Dietary guidelines have been suggested by the U.S. Departments of Agriculture and Health and Human Services [12]. These guidelines recommend that fewer fats, fewer sugars, and less salt be consumed and that more starch- and fiber-containing foods be added to the diet.

Food also has significance in relation to religious beliefs and practices. The types of foods chosen, the complete omission of certain foods, and the frequency of eating other foods may be dictated by religious preferences.

The growth of the food industry and technological developments that keep an ever-increasing supply of convenience-type foods on the market affect the purchasing habits of the consumer and the types of family meals served. Advertising through the media of television, radio, newspapers, and magazines makes sure that the consumer knows about new types of foods that are available and is enticed to try them. The development of technological expertise in food preservation extends the seasons of food availability. Refrigeration and freezing processing within the home make possible patterns of eating that cannot exist in a technologically developing society in which methods for keeping fresh foods are not available. The type of equipment available for food preparation, such as modern ranges and microwave ovens, markedly affects patterns of eating. The proliferation of food vending machines in technologically developed countries also helps to mold food habits. The ready availability of fast-food restaurants is changing the eating patterns of many individuals. An increasingly larger share of the U.S. consumer food dollar is being spent for meals away from home. Much of modern society has become oriented toward science and technology. The development of the science of nutrition has increased our confidence in the ability to provide foods that supply adequate nutrients for health. Developments in food technology may influence even the social aspects of food as they decrease individual family members' reliance on each other for providing prepared food to eat. Perhaps the impact of technology has had an influence in stimulating the "back to nature" movement in food. Organic home gardening is becoming popular among some groups in which so-called natural or unprocessed foods are emphasized. More, rather than less, food preparation is done at home by those who are part of this movement.

With all of these technological influences, it is important that the meanings of food, other than merely the biological ones, be considered (Figure 1-1). Food means security. Infants learn about security when mothers respond to their crying by giving them food. Familiar foods bring back memories of home and family and make one feel

1-1 *Food has many meanings. It does more than physically sustain life.*

Food means home and security with a steaming bowl of lamb stew. (Courtesy of Lamb Education Center)

Mexican women chat while they dry chili peppers. (Photograph by Kay Franz)

A brother and sister can get to know each other over ice cream cones. (Photograph by Roger P. Smith)

Eating spaghetti requires real concentration.

secure. The feeling of being full and physically satisfied and knowing that there is more food available for other meals brings security. Food is the symbol of hospitality and is used to show that one cares about others and is a friend. Gifts of food are given both in times of happiness and sorrow. Certain foods show status. Beefsteak has status in the United States. Polished white rice has status over brown rice in some countries. Foods commonly eaten by blacks in the southern United States—collards, turnip greens, fat pork, and certain fish—were for a long time not acceptable to whites because of status. Now this has changed, and "soul food" is served in prestigious restaurants. The study of foods should help one to appreciate the food patterns of other cultures and to gain understanding of them. Fascinating experiences await the adventurer who learns to enjoy the foods of many different ethnic or cultural groups.

Flavor

Thousands of flavor sensations are experienced in a lifetime. Flavor is a complex quality, involving an integration of sensations from the olfactory center in the nasal cavity, the taste buds on the tongue, and various pressure and movement sensors in the mouth. In a broad sense, the appearance of a food and even the sound of crunching such crisp foods as raw carrots and celery may be part of the overall flavor complex. Sometimes the words *flavor* and *taste* are used synonymously. It is generally accepted, however, that there are only four primary taste sensations involving the taste buds on the tongue: sweet, sour, bitter, and salty.

Taste buds are found in small elevations, called papillae, on the surface of the tongue (Figure 1-2). The actual taste sensations are produced when bitter, salty, sweet, or acid substances in solution contact taste receptors in the taste pore leading to the taste bud. Figure 1-2 shows a diagram of a taste bud. A message is sent to the brain from the taste cells by way of nerve fibers with their endings present in the taste cells. The brain interprets and identifies the specific taste.

Much of what we call taste is a combination of odor and taste sensations. Some foods with an intense aroma, such as well-prepared coffee or fresh, ripe pineapple, may affect the olfactory center more than the taste receptors. The olfactory center is found at the top of the nasal cavity as shown in Figure 1-3. In order to stimulate the olfactory center, substances must be in gaseous form. The gaseous molecules enter the nose as food is placed in the mouth and are drawn toward the olfactory center where they stimulate nerve endings. Nerve impulses are thus sent to the brain to be interpreted. The sense of smell is estimated to be about ten thousand times as sensitive as the sense of taste in detecting minute concentrations and it can differentiate hundreds, or possibly thousands, of distinct odors.

Temperature may affect the blending of primary tastes as well as other factors contributing to flavor. Within the temperature range

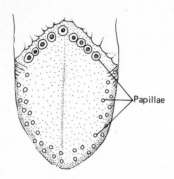

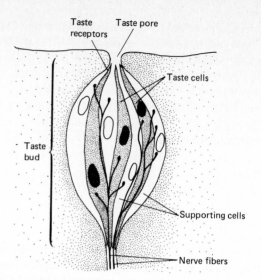

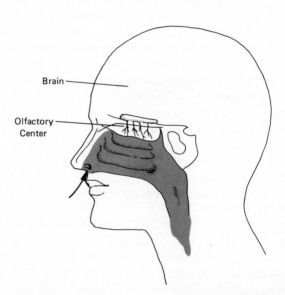

1-2 *The tongue showing papillae on its surface. Taste buds are located on the sides and at the base of many of the papillae.*

Diagram of an individual taste bud containing: tiny taste receptors that come in contact with the substance being tasted; taste cells; and nerve fibers that carry the message from the taste bud to the brain for interpretation.

1-3 *Gaseous molecules enter the nose and stimulate the olfactory center from which nerve fibers send messages to the brain concerning the odor of food.*

at which most food is eaten, from ice cream to hot chocolate, there are marked changes in the apparent intensity of some of the primary tastes. At higher temperatures the same amount of sugar will seem sweeter than at lower temperatures. Just the reverse seems to be true of salty tastes. Sourness is less affected by change in temperature. Extremes of temperature may cause actual pain or injury to body tissues. A substance such as menthol feels cool; it sensitizes certain receptors in the mouth and throat so that they exaggerate the feeling of coolness. Other substances in foods such as hot peppers irritate the mucous membranes lining the mouth and give a biting or hot sensation.

Countless numbers of molecules contribute to our perception of odor or aroma and taste. Many of the odorous substances in food may occur in such vanishingly small concentrations that it is difficult to show that they are even present. With the development of analytical tools such as the gas chromatograph, which is shown in Figure 1-4, the chemist has been able to separate, isolate, and identify many of the molecules that are responsible for aroma and taste in such foods as onions, strawberries, and beef. However, continuing research in the field of flavor is necessary to learn more about flavor molecules and how the flavor of food is perceived by the human. The aroma and taste of food seem to be the complex results of many simultaneous responses to odor and taste stimuli.

Some flavors occur preformed in foods as they are served. For example, strawberries, peaches, and other fresh fruits each contain a unique flavor bouquet composed of many volatile substances that stimulate the nasal olfactory center in combination with sweet and acid components that stimulate the taste buds. Raw vegetables, meats, and fish also present characteristic flavors. The flavor of raw meat and fish is appreciated by some, whereas others prefer the change in flavor that occurs when these products are cooked.

Cooked flavor is often formed from nonflavorful substances, sometimes called precursors, that are present in the raw food. The chemical changes that occur during heating in the presence of air may be very complex and are not completely understood for most foods. Different flavors are produced when foods such as meat are cooked in water than when they are roasted in an oven where they are surrounded by dry heat. Some cooked flavor precursors are present in the lean portion of meats such as beef, pork, and lamb, whereas other precursors are present in the fat. The tantalizing odors developed during the baking of bread are additional examples of flavor substances produced by heating. Many of the volatile substances that waft from the oven where bread is baking are initially the products of yeast fermentation. Crust formation occurs as the outer layers of the bread are dehydrated and subjected to very high temper-

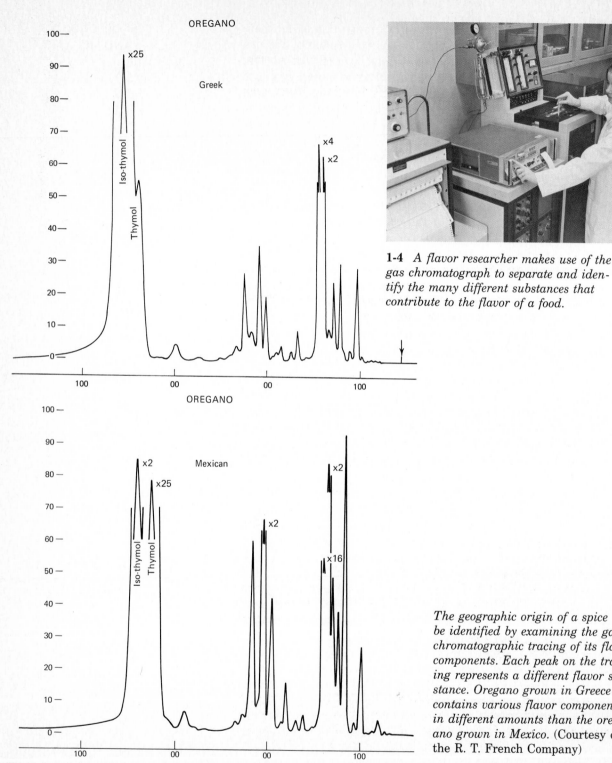

OREGANO

Greek

x25

Iso-thymol

Thymol

x4
x2

100—
90—
80—
70—
60—
50—
40—
30—
20—
10—
0—

100   00   00   100

1-4 *A flavor researcher makes use of the gas chromatograph to separate and identify the many different substances that contribute to the flavor of a food.*

OREGANO

Mexican

x2
x25

Iso-thymol
Thymol

x2

x2

x16

100—
90—
80—
70—
60—
50—
40—
30—
20—
10—
0—

100   00   00   100

The geographic origin of a spice may be identified by examining the gas chromatographic tracing of its flavor components. Each peak on the tracing represents a different flavor substance. Oregano grown in Greece contains various flavor components in different amounts than the oregano grown in Mexico. (Courtesy of the R. T. French Company) atures. Browning of the crust contributes to both a pleasing appearance and a pleasant flavor.

A knowledge of flavor chemistry and ways of simulating natural flavors is especially important as the world population increases and new protein foods are required. The protein may be derived from soybeans, fish meal, or algae, but it will have no nutritional value if it is not eaten by the people who need it. It must be flavored so that it will be acceptable and sought after. The flavor chemist, in order to successfully apply the science of flavor to the development of new products and the improvement of old ones, must know what substances are responsible for the acceptable flavor and the mechanism by which people eating the food will experience flavor [2, 5, 11].

Texture and Appearance

The physical properties of foods, including texture, consistency, and shape, involve the sense of touch or feeling. This is called the tactile sense. When food is contacted, pressure and movement receptors on the skin and muscles of the mouth and tongue are stimulated. Sensations of smoothness, stickiness, graininess, brittleness, fibrous qualities, or lumpy characteristics may be detected. Terms describing extremes of texture and consistency may include *dry* or *moist, solid* or *fluid, thick* or *thin, rough* or *smooth, coarse* or *fine, tough* or *tender, hard* or *soft,* and *compact* or *porous.*

The eye appeal of foods is contributed by such qualities as color, form, size, and arrangement or design. Without an attractive appearance, many foods are rejected without being tasted. The commercial vendor of prepared foods regards appearance as being extremely important.

The proper use of seasonings and flavoring materials greatly enhances the natural flavors of other foods. The appeal to the senses from a prepared dish entices one to eat and enjoy it. Flavorful food, therefore, is always the ultimate goal of the cook.

Salt and Pepper

Salt and pepper are basic seasoning substances that should be used to heighten the taste of a food without changing it or adding their own flavors [10]. Optimal amounts to be added will vary with the food product being prepared and with the preferences of the per-

Seasoning and Flavoring Materials

sons who will consume the food. For most cooked dishes, the seasonings should be added in small increments, with a tasting after each addition, until the most desirable taste is achieved.

Salt is a crystalline substance with the chemical name of sodium chloride (NaCl). It is obtained from salt beds or extracted from brine and is purified before being marketed for food use. An anticaking agent may be added to it and it may be iodized for nutritional purposes. The usual amount of salt consumed varies from one population to another as well as from one individual to another. Because of the possible relationships between a high sodium intake and hypertension (high blood pressure), governmental and professional organizations have encouraged Americans to reduce their intakes of salt. A number of individuals are following low sodium diets for specific health purposes. The judicious use of herbs and spices, as well as fresh lemon juice, may make foods acceptable with little or no added salt [9] as the reduction of dietary sodium becomes necessary or desirable.

Black pepper is the dried unripe berry of a climbing vine. White pepper is the kernel of the ripe berry. Red peppers, native to the Americas, come from crushed red pepper pods and include cayenne pepper. Red peppers are "hot" but also have their own distinctive flavors. Peppers in the ground form are often used to season food without altering the natural flavor of the food. However, certain cuisines use peppers in amounts large enough to convey their own distinctive flavors.

Monosodium Glutamate

Monosodium glutamate (MSG) is a crystalline material that looks something like salt. It occurs naturally in a variety of foods and may be produced from wheat gluten or corn protein and also from sugar beet molasses in a fermentation process [3]. MSG has come into general use, both commercially and in the home, as a seasoning substance. Although this substance is generally considered to be a flavor enhancer or intensifier, bringing out the flavors of other foods, it may also add its own flavor to foods when used in sufficiently large amounts. It seems to have the greatest flavor effect in low acid foods (pH from 5.0 to 6.5) such as vegetables, meats, poultry, and fish.

A group of compounds called *5'-ribonucleotides* has been reported to act synergistically with MSG. Synergism refers to cooperative action among two or more substances so that the total effect of the mixture is greater than the sum of the individual effects. Even a very small amount of the ribonucleotides increases the flavor-enhancing properties of MSG. Some of the 5'-ribonucleotides have been recommended as flavor enhancers by themselves and are being used commercially in Japan.

In the past, there has been controversy over the safety of the widespread use of MSG in foods. Extensive study of its effects on a variety of animal species, however, has lead to the conclusion that, in the amounts commonly used, there is no hazard to the public health [3]. Probably 1 to 2 percent of the adult population may react negatively to large doses of MSG with symptoms such as tingling, warmth, and a feeling of pressure in the upper part of the body [6, 14]. Although MSG is commonly used in a number of manufactured food products, processed foods marketed primarily for babies and small children do not now include this flavor substance as an ingredient.

Spices and Herbs

The history of the use of spices and herbs is a fascinating one. In ancient times, spices were valued for many nonfood purposes, such as ingredients in ointments, cosmetics, embalming preservatives, and medicines. After the first century A.D. spices were increasingly utilized as condiments in food. Spices were so important, costly, and scarce that wars were fought for them. The United States is now the world's largest importer of spices and herbs, which come from the Orient, the Mediterranean area, and Central and South America.

The term *spice* is often used to cover a wide variety of dried aromatic vegetable products that are used in building the flavors of prepared foods. True spices are defined as parts of aromatic plants, such as bark, roots, buds, flowers, fruits, and seeds, that are grown in the tropics. Examples of spices include allspice, anise, caraway, cardamom, cayenne pepper, cinnamon, cloves, cumin, ginger, mace, nutmeg, paprika, pepper, and tumeric. Some spices are sweet, some are spicy sweet, and some are "hot." Herbs are usually leaves of plants that grow in a temperate climate. Examples of herbs are basil, bay leaves, marjoram, mint, oregano, rosemary, sage, savory, tarragon, and thyme. Seeds used in cooking may sometimes be classified separately since they come from plants cultivated in both tropical and temperate regions. Examples of seeds include caraway, celery, and dill. Spice blends are mixtures of several true spices, herbs, seeds, and dehydrated vegetables for use in food preparation. They include curry powder, chili powder, poultry seasoning, and mixed pickling spice. In practical use it is difficult to separate spices and herbs [15]. They are both commonly used as flavor builders in the cooking process so that their separate flavors merge indistinguishably with the total flavor as it develops. Some herbs and spices, however, have very distinctive flavors and, when used in quantities large enough to taste, become major flavors for prepared foods rather than blending into the total flavor. These special flavored spices and herbs include basil, which has a warm sweet flavor that blends well with tomato dishes; oregano, with a strong bittersweet taste commonly associated with spaghetti sauce; tarragon and its licorice-like flavor; and sage, with a pungent, fragrant flavor that permeates many stuffings for poultry or meat. Some herbs and spices are shown in Figure 1-5. The description and use for a number of herbs and spices are given in Table 1-1.

Spices are sold whole or in ground forms. Flavor strength and quality are quite well preserved in the whole spice but are gradually lost during long storage. Flavor is much more readily lost from the ground spices. Herbs also tend to lose flavor during storage. Neither ground spices nor herbs should be purchased in quantity for usual use. Both spices and herbs should be stored in a cool, dry place in airtight containers. Under favorable conditions they should keep their aroma and flavor for several months. Since ground spices release their flavor immediately when added to prepared dishes, they should usually be used near the end of the cooking period. Whole spices are added at the beginning of long cooking periods so that their full flavor can be extracted. They may be tied in a cheesecloth

1-5 *Many herbs and spices may be judiciously used in seasoning to enhance the flavor of food.* (FPG)

Table 1-1 *The Uses of Some Spices and Herbs*

Spices and Herbs	Description	Uses
Allspice	Dried berry of tree grown in West Indies and Latin America; reminiscent of several spices.	Whole, in pickling, meats, fish; ground, in baking, puddings, relishes.
Anise	Dried greenish-brown seed of annual herb grown in many temperate and warm climates; strong licoricelike flavor.	Whole or ground, in cookies, candies, sweet pickles, beverages.
Basil or sweet basil	Dried leaves and tender stems from annual spicy herb of mint family.	In tomato paste and tomato dishes, vegetables, chicken, fish.
Bay leaves (Laurel)	Dried green leaves of evergreen member of laurel family; herbaceous, spicy, pungent flavor.	In bouillons, meats, fish, poultry, vegetables.
Caraway seed	Fruit of biennial herb of the parsley family; long, curved seeds tapered at each end; sweet, biting, acrid, pleasant flavor.	In rye breads, cakes, cheese, soups, vegetables.
Cardamom	Fruit of herbaceous, tropical perennial from ginger family; whole fruit or hulled seeds used; sweet, pungent, highly aromatic; tiny brown seeds.	Whole, in pickling; ground, in breads, pastry.
Cayenne pepper	Ripe, dried pods of plants of the genus Capsicum, known as chili peppers; may blend several varieties for desired strength; hot.	In pickles, relishes, hot sauces, spiced meats.
Cinnamon	Bark of aromatic evergreen tree; most cinnamon in U.S. is cassia from same family; pungent, sweet flavor.	Sticks, in pickling, beverages; ground, in baked products.
Cloves	Dried flower buds from evergreen of myrtle family; sweet, pungent, strong flavor.	Whole, in studding ham, pickling, beverages; ground, in puddings, baked products.
Cumin	Seedlike fruit of small annual herb of parsley family; hot, bitter, strongly aromatic.	Whole, in pickles, soups, meats; ground, in curry and chili powders.
Ginger	Rhizome (underground stem) of perennial tropical plant; warm, fragrant, pungent flavor.	Whole, in pickling, chutneys; ground, in gingerbread, cookies, puddings, beverages.
Mace	Scarlet, netlike membrane between nutmeg shell and outer husk; strongly aromatic, nutmeglike flavor.	Whole, in pickling, fish sauces; ground, in baked products, stewed fruits.
Marjoram	Leaves and tender tops from bushy perennial of mint family; mild, sweet-minty flavor.	In stews, soups, poultry, fish.
Nutmeg	Kernel of fruit of evergreen nutmeg tree; sweet, warm, highly spicy flavor.	Ground, in sauces, custards, puddings, baked products, vegetables, fruits.
Oregano	Leaves of hardy perennial; strong, aromatic flavor.	In tomato dishes, pizza, meats, omelets, soups, eggs.
Rosemary	Narrow leaves of small evergreen shrub of mint family; sweet, fresh flavor.	In stews, soups, vegetables.
Saffron	Dried stigmas of crocuslike flower; bright yellow; most expensive spice.	In baked products, rice dishes.
Sage	Leaves of hardy evergreen shrub of mint family; pungent, camphoraceous, fragrant flavor.	In sausages, poultry seasonings, fish, salads.
Savory	Herb of the mint family; inexpensive.	In meats, fish sauces, chicken, eggs.
Tarragon	Leaves of perennial plant; minty, aniselike flavor.	In salad dressings, vegetables, meats, fish.
Thyme	Leaves and stems from perennial shrub of mint family; warm, aromatic, pungent flavor.	In fish, meat, poultry, vegetables, fresh tomatoes.
Turmeric	Rhizomes from tropical perennial herb; orange-yellow color; mild peppery, mustardlike flavor.	In curry powder, prepared mustard, meats, dressings, salads.

bag so that they can be easily removed. Whole herbs should be crumbled before use to release flavor. Toasting of seeds may enhance their flavor.

Flavor Extracts

Extracts and essential oils from aromatic plants, dissolved in alcohol, are often used in the flavoring of baked products, puddings, sauces, and confections. These include extracts of vanilla, lemon, orange, and almond and oils such as peppermint and wintergreen. These are used in small amounts but add their own distinctive flavors to the final products. These flavorings should be stored in tightly closed containers and put in a cool place to avoid loss of volatile substances.

Browning Reactions

Several types of browning that may occur during food preparation affect palatability. Some of the changes associated with browning are detrimental to the quality of the food while others are beneficial. A type of browning or darkening that is undesirable is that which occurs on the cut surfaces of such fresh fruits and vegetables as bananas, apples, peaches, and potatoes when they are exposed to air. This type of darkening is sometimes called *enzymatic oxidative browning* for it requires oxygen from the air and enzymes, which are present in the plant tissue itself. The enzymes catalyze (increase the speed at which the reaction occurs) the addition of oxygen to certain substances already present in the plant tissue, producing brown colored compounds. Enzymatic oxidative browning and ways to control it are discussed in Chapter 8, Fruits and Fruit Preparation, p. 141.

Another type of browning that occurs in a variety of food products involves neither enzymes nor oxygen from the air and, therefore, is sometimes called *nonenzymatic nonoxidative browning*. This process has also been named, after the Frenchman who first described it, the *Maillard reaction*. The browning of baked products such as bread has been attributed chiefly to the Maillard reaction. The brown color of caramel candy is also the result of a browning reaction of the Maillard type. Browning is encouraged in baked products and in caramels and is desirable for both flavor and appearance. Examples of products in which the Maillard reaction is undesirable are the browning of dried milk and eggs stored for relatively long periods of time. When browning occurs in these products, they not only become less attractive but they are more difficult to rehydrate and the nutritive value of their protein is decreased.

The Maillard or nonenzymatic browning reaction involves, as a first step, the combination of a sugar with the amino group of a protein. A series of additional complex chemical reactions then follows and eventually a brown color results. Thus, any food that contains both sugars, such as glucose, and proteins may be susceptible to browning of the Maillard type if it is stored for long periods of time or is subjected to very high temperatures.

Table sugar, or sucrose, does not participate in the Maillard reaction. However, browning is produced in yet another way when table sugar is heated to high temperatures. This change in sugar is called *caramelization.*

Sensory Evaluation of Food

When the quality of a food is judged or evaluated by the use of the senses (taste, smell, sight, touch, and hearing), it is said to be a sensory or subjective or *organoleptic* evaluation. Since food is prepared for the primary purpose of being eaten and enjoyed through the senses, sensory evaluation is most appropriate. No machine has yet been devised that can totally substitute for the human senses in evaluating the quality of human food. However, even with the use of human subjects to evaluate the flavor of food, the process is not always easy.

Flavor perceptions are difficult to describe verbally. In food research, small groups of trained individuals, called tasting or judging panels, are commonly used to determine differences among food samples [8]. These panels often consist of from five to fifteen individuals who have had experience testing the particular food products being evaluated. In the food industry, judging panels are often used to check the quality of a manufactured food and to assure that the desired quality is constantly maintained. It may sometimes be desirable to do a complete analysis of all of the flavor components in a particular food. Such a flavor profile of the food may be determined by a panel of trained tasters working together. The aroma and taste are studied separately in completing the total flavor analysis. Various types of scoring, ranking, or difference tests are used with judging panels.

Another type of organoleptic evaluation involves the ascertaining of consumer opinions about new food products that are to be marketed. The foods may be sampled by several hundred potential consumers and their preferences noted. Data from these types of evaluations are valuable to companies as they perfect their products and plan marketing strategies.

Although the beginning student of food science is not likely to be involved as a member of a formal judging panel, the ability should be developed to describe and evaluate the aroma, taste, texture, and appearance of the food being prepared.

The character of the taste or aroma may be described using a wide variety of terms. Often the terms used to describe the flavor of a food indicate that the flavor is similar to that of some other familiar food product. For example, a prepared cereal may be described as being nutty, starchy, haylike, floury, oily, or buttery. The primary tastes—sweet, sour, salt, and bitter—are relatively easy to describe. Other terms used to describe flavors in foods include caramel, stale, rancid, metallic, cardboardlike, musty, fragrant, flowery, fruity, sharp, pungent, tart, chalky, branny, burnt, spicy, astringent, sulfury, diacetyl (butterlike), malt, effervescent, earthy, chemical, putrid, yeasty, fishy, grassy, bland, toasted, and aftertaste. The student of foods should accept the challenge to find new descriptive words for flavor evaluation.

In addition to a description of the character of the taste or aroma, the intensity of the flavor note should be described. It may be weak, moderate, or strong or some place in between. In cases where preference is being measured without a description of the flavor, a hedonic scale indicates how much one likes or dislikes a food product. Descriptive terms used in this scale may range from "Like Extremely Well" to "Dislike Intensely."

Objective Evaluation of Food

Objective evaluation of food involves the use of laboratory instruments to determine certain characteristics that may be related to eating quality. Examples of objective measurements that may be made in the laboratory include the use of a viscometer to measure viscosity (thickness or consistency) of a tomato paste or a starch-thickened pudding; a gelometer to measure the firmness or strength of a gelatin gel or a fruit jelly; a pH meter to measure the acidity of lemon juice; a color difference meter to measure the color of tomato catsup; a compressimeter to measure the compressibility or softness of a slice of bread; a shear or cutting apparatus to measure the tenderness of a piece of meat; and a Kjeldahl apparatus to chemically measure the amount of nitrogen (protein) in a sample of wheat flour. The Instron Universal testing machine can be adapted to measure the texture of a variety of foods (see Figure 1-6). These types of tests do not directly involve the human senses and are not considered to be subjective.

The use of judging panels to evaluate food is often time-consuming and expensive. Therefore, the use of laboratory instruments that will give useful information with less time and expense is desirable whenever the information thus collected correlates well with sensory characteristics. Objective tests can usually be reproduced with reasonable precision. Sensory and objective methods complement each other in the overall evaluation of the quality of a food product.

1-6 *A variety of instruments are used for the objective measurement of food quality.*

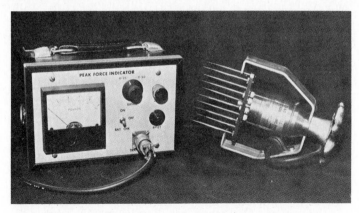

The Armour Tenderometer gives an indication of meat tenderness when the needles on the probe are pushed into raw muscle. (Reproduced from "Objective Methods for Food Evaluation," 1976, with permission from the National Academy Press, Washington, D.C. 20418.)

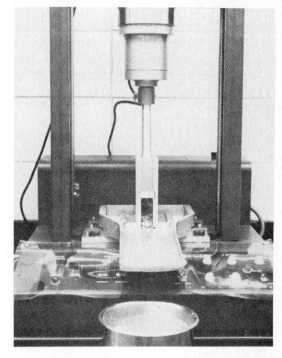

A setup for measuring texture in a soy protein product uses an Instron Universal Testing Machine (Model TM-M) with an extrusion cell and plunger. (Reprinted from *Food Technology.* 1977. **31** 95 (no. 4). Copyright © by Institute of Food Technologists.)

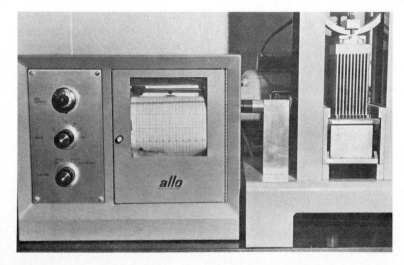

The Kramer Shear Press may be used to measure the texture of many different foods. A small rectangular box holds the food sample and narrow moving bars probe through it. (Reproduced from "Objective Methods for Food Evaluation," 1976, with permission from the National Academy Press, Washington, D.C. 20418.)

Study Questions

1. a. What is meant by palatability?
   b. Why is it important for the student of food science to be able to evaluate the palatability and quality of foods?
2. Discuss at least six factors that are likely to affect the kind of eating patterns that develop in an individual.
3. a. Define and distinguish among the terms flavor, taste, and odor.
   b. List four primary tastes.
4. Briefly describe how the eating of food produces the sensations of taste and smell in the human.
5. Give examples of:
   a. Flavors that occur preformed in foods.
   b. Flavors that are produced by heating.
6. What effect does the temperature of a food have on your perception of its flavor? Discuss this.
7. Of what practical importance to humanity is research on flavor chemistry?
8. Give an example of how the appearance of a food may influence your evaluation of its flavor or other quality characteristics.
9. Which human sense perceives the texture and consistency of a food?
10. Describe the basic roles of salt and pepper when properly used in seasoning foods.
11. What is a flavor enhancer? Give an example.
12. a. What are spices and herbs? Give several examples.
    b. Explain the reasons for using spices and herbs in food preparation.
13. Food quality may be evaluated by sensory (subjective) or objective methods.
    a. Give examples of each type of evaluation.
    b. Describe several situations or conditions under which quality evaluation of specific food products may be desirable or necessary.
14. Give examples of two general types of browning or darkening that may affect the quality of certain food products.

References

1. Brown, E. L. 1976. Factors influencing food choices and intake. *Geriatrics* **31,** 89.
2. Hall, R. L., and E. J. Merwin. 1981. The role of flavors in food processing. *Food Technology* **35,** 46 (no. 6).
3. Institute of Food Technologists' Expert Panel on Food Safety & Nutrition and the Committee on Public Information. 1980. Monosodium glutamate (MSG). *Food Technology* **34,** 49 (no. 10).
4. Jerome, N. W. 1982. Dietary patterning and change: A continuous process. *Contemporary Nutrition* (General Mills Nutrition Department) **7,** (no. 6).
5. Kazeniac, S. J. 1977. Flavor trends in new foods. *Food Technology* **31,** 26 (no. 1).
6. Kerr, G. R., M. Wu-Lee, M. El-Lozy, R. McGandy, and F. J. Stare. 1979. Prevalence of the "Chinese restaurant syndrome." *Journal of the American Dietetic Association* **75,** 29.

7. Lowenberg, M. E. 1974. The development of food patterns. *Journal of the American Dietetic Association* **65,** 263.

8. Martin, S. L. 1973. Selection and training of sensory judges. *Food Technology* **27,** 22 (no. 11).

9. Miller, R. W. How to ignore salt and still please the palate. *Department of Health and Human Services Publication* No. (FDA) 82-2165. Washington, DC: Department of Health and Human Services, 1983.

10. Mizer, D. A., and M. Porter. *Food Preparation for the Professional.* New York: Harper & Row, Publishers, Inc., 1978.

11. Moskowitz, H. R., and J. W. Chandler. 1978. Consumer perceptions, attitudes, and trade-offs regarding flavor and other product characteristics. *Food Technology* **32,** 34 (no. 11).

12. *Nutrition and your health.* Home and Garden Bulletin No. 232. Washington, DC: Departments of Agriculture and Health and Human Services, 1980.

13. Pangborn, R. M. 1975. Cross-cultural aspects of flavor preferences. *Food Technology* **29,** 34 (no. 6).

14. Reif-Lehrer, L. 1977. A questionnaire study of the prevalence of Chinese restaurant syndrome. *Federation Proceedings* **36,** 1617.

15. Rosengarten, F., Jr. *The Book of Spices.* Wynnewood, PA: Livingston Publishing Company, 1969.

16. Zifferblatt, S. M., C. S. Wilbur, and J. L. Pinsky. 1980. Understanding food habits. *Journal of the American Dietetic Association* **76,** 9.

2

Food Economics and Convenience

Economics has been defined as the efficient use of resources to achieve a desired goal [24]. Food economics is thus concerned with wisely using all resources, which may include money, time, knowledge, skills, equipment, and human values, that are available, to obtain food that will contribute to the well being of individuals and families. There are wide variations in food preferences and purchasing practices of families at all income levels. Each family is unique and may strive to achieve its economic goals in an individual manner. However, there are similarities among various groups.

In recent years, many consumer groups have been organized as more people have become interested in food safety and nutritional quality as well as cost of food. The word *consumerism* has become widely used, chiefly in relation to the activities of organized consumer groups. We are all consumers. Throughout our lives we are concerned with exchanging money for goods and services. The responsibility for spending a family's income is tremendous, and, with the cost of food making up such a major proportion of this expenditure, the responsibility for food purchasing is a major one. Today's consumers occupy a key position in the economic world. The actions and attitudes of consumers are closely watched by producers of market goods and their influence is being felt in the legislative arena. The consumer needs a knowledge of many trends and factors that affect the cost and quality of food in order to meet the challenges of the economic world.

What and how much people eat is of interest to many who work in the various fields of food and nutrition. Information on food consumption may be obtained in different ways. One method is to measure the quantities of foods that "disappear" into the nation's food distribution system. These quantities are arrived at by taking data on the amount of food produced, the amount imported into the country, and the beginning-of-the-year inventories. From this total is subtracted the amount of food exported, used by the military, and found in year-end inventories. The U.S. Department of Agriculture (USDA) has periodically collected such data for up to 350 foods and has published estimates on the nutrient content, on a per capita basis, of the national food supply since 1909 [31]. These studies, including 1980 data, indicate an increased use since 1909 of meat, poultry, and fish; dairy products; fats and oils; fruits and vegetables; and sugar and other sweeteners. They also show decreased use of eggs, potatoes, and grain products. The use of dry legumes, nuts, coffee, and tea has remained stable at a relatively low level.

Another method for collecting information on food consumption was used by the USDA in their Nationwide Food Consumption Survey of 1977–78 [9, 10, 23]. This was their sixth national survey since 1936. Information was collected by interviews and records kept by members of approximately 15,000 households, including about 34,000 individuals, in the 48 adjoining states. The average nutrient content of the food consumed generally appeared to be adequate when compared with Recommended Dietary Allowances. Calcium and vitamin B_6 were the nutrients most often found to be below recommended levels.

The survey revealed some interesting relationships in regard to the money value of food [21]. Although there were wide individual variations, averages showed that as the income of households increased, the money value of food used at home and the amount of money spent for food eaten away from home both increased. This relationship would probably be expected. However, the proportion of the food dollar spent for food eaten away from home was different for different income levels. The percentage of the food dollar spent for "eating out" averaged 14 percent for households with below $5,000 yearly incomes, but was 29 percent for households with more than $20,000 annual incomes. For all income groups, the average share of the food dollar spent for food purchased and eaten away from home was 24 cents or 24 percent. In the previous 1965 USDA survey, that share was only 17 percent. The trend toward more "eating out" by American families is clearly shown in Figure 2-1.

The number of members in the household affects the amount of food money spent per person. Although the total amount of money spent for food increased as the size of the household increased, the money value *per household member* decreased. Households with

Food at home*   Meals away from
                             home
                                  Snacks away
                                  from home

13¢

4¢

83¢

1965

Food at home*   Meals away from
                             home
                                      Snacks
                                      away
                                      from
                                      home

19¢

5¢

76¢

1977**

2-1 *The U.S. household food dollar—a comparison between 1965 and 1977.* (Courtesy of the U.S. Department of Agriculture)

*Value of all food used at home
**USDA Nationwide Food Consumption Survey, 48 States, Spring 1977 (Preliminary)

only one member averaged $26 per week in food expense while households of six or more members weekly used food valued at $16 per member. Savings can be made by purchasing and preparing food in larger quantities.

Generally, the groups of households that used food at home with the lowest monetary value received the most nutrient return per dollar spent. These were the southern, nonmetropolitan, and low-income households and those with more than five members. Apparently, many of them were making wise choices when purchasing food.

Another USDA study [26] has shown that, as income increases, a greater share of the at-home food dollar goes for bakery products, beef, veal, fruits, and vegetables. Less is spent on cereal products, pork, poultry, dairy products, and fats and oils.

Consumer Food Waste

Trends toward increasing food prices, coupled with growing concerns about conservation of resources, have focused attention on food loss or waste. It is important to know how much food is generally being wasted by consumers in order to attack this problem sensibly and try to change wasteful practices.

What is food waste? Different definitions may be used. In a broad sense, however, any food that was once useable but has since been discarded and not eaten by humans may be considered waste. Food eaten by animals and birds that are household pets may be counted as waste if this food was originally prepared for human consumption [16].

Food loss may occur at different stages of the handling and preparation process. As food is taken home from the market and transferred to cabinets, refrigerators, and freezers it should be handled so that no loss occurs. While food is in storage, waste may result from microbial spoilage, contamination by insects and rodents, breaking of containers, and spilling. If food is stored too long, particularly with improper packaging, it may be discarded simply because it is not fresh or has dried out. More waste may occur during preparation as a result of discarding edible portions of the food before cooking, improper cooking procedures such as scorching or overcooking, preparing too much for the number of people to be served, and spoilage because of inappropriate holding of the food before service. Lack of utilization of leftovers creates additional waste. Plate waste, or food left on plates by individual diners, accounts for a significant portion of total food loss.

It is difficult to measure the food wasted by households but a few major attempts have been made [16]. A study of garbage discarded by 200 to 300 households suggested that about 10 percent of food, by weight, was wasted in these homes. Measurement of plate waste from feeding school children showed that overall waste was about 24 percent of the weight of food served. A USDA food consumption study has suggested that about 35 percent of the total calories of food brought into the home are wasted. This figure may be larger than estimates by weight of food because excess fat on meat is often discarded and fat contains a very large proportion of calories. In any case, consumer food waste in the United States is probably substantial.

Rising food prices have been a reality in the United States for more than a decade as illustrated in Figure 2-2. The cost of food has risen

Some Factors Influencing Food Costs

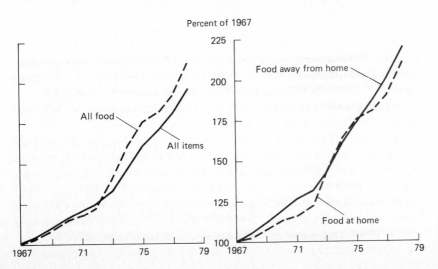

2-2 *Change in consumer food prices.* (Courtesy of the U.S. Department of Agriculture)

even more than the Consumer Price Index for all goods and services. In addition to the general effects of inflation, a number of factors affect the rising cost of food [11].

Crop Production and Availability

Producing food is costly. Farmers must make a substantial investment in property and equipment to even begin producing crops. Farmers have become more and more dependent on such things as fuel to operate the equipment, fertilizers, herbicides, and insecticides which they must purchase. Farm wages and machinery costs have risen substantially in recent years.

Poor weather conditions often reduce the size of the crops of fruits, vegetables, and grains. The weather is not controllable, and efficient management of commodity production thus becomes very difficult. Costs rise when there are crop shortages.

Trade Policies

Export sales of grains and legumes to other countries affect the prices of these commodities in the United States. Safeguards need to be established to limit wide fluctuations due to variable export sales.

Food Processing and Packaging

Much of the food appearing on the supermarket shelves has been processed to some degree. Even the trimming of retail meat cuts and the packaging of fresh vegetables is a type of processing, though minimal, that increases the cost of the food items offered to the consumer. Examples of highly processed foods include fabricated breakfast cereals, meat substitutes produced from textured vegetable proteins, and frozen ready-to-eat entrees of various descriptions.

Food processing, as well as food production, is costly. A large investment in equipment and facilities is essential. Labor costs are high. The increased cost of raw food commodities is passed on to the consumer by the food processor. Packaging materials and labeling to meet governmental regulations are additional costs and are sometimes substantial in proportion to the cost of the food itself. Advertising and marketing expenses are also reflected in the cost of the food to the consumer. Highly advertised brands are generally more expensive than less advertised and generic products.

Technological developments have made possible many new food

products scarcely dreamed of a century ago. New foods, once they are developed, require extensive promotional campaigns and test marketing procedures. A large proportion of new processed food products are not successful in the marketplace, and losses are sustained by the manufacturing company. These losses must be made up in other areas of operation and may be reflected in higher food costs at the consumer level.

Many of today's foods have built-in "maid service" with partial or complete preparation having been accomplished before the food is purchased. These so-called convenience foods must include the costs of preparation in their sale price. These types of food are discussed in more detail later in the chapter.

Marketing

Most food in the United States is marketed through retail grocery stores. There are a number of different types of food stores. These include specialty stores, such as bakeries and fish markets, that offer only one type of food; supermarkets, which are departmentalized stores doing a large volume of business; convenience stores, which are miniature supermarkets often open on a 24-hour basis; food cooperatives, which are groups of consumers organized to purchase food on a wholesale basis; and combination stores, that combine a supermarket with other nonfood operations such as pharmacy and clothing.

The supermarket handles most of the retail food business. Services offered, pricing policies, and cost of marketing differ among stores. Prices are influenced by services offered. The consumer should evaluate the markets in terms of desired services and benefits. Factors to consider in this evaluation may include:

1. Quality and variety of merchandise carried
2. Layout and organization of the market
3. Pricing policies, such as specials, discounting, advertising, price on shelf in lieu of pricing individual items, availability of store brands and generic or unbranded products, coupons, trading stamps, and games
4. Location of market
5. Sanitation
6. Customer services, such as bagging, carry-out, computer-assisted checkout, home economics information

Shopping Aids. Food manufacturers and retailers offer the consumer a number of conveniences to facilitate efficient shopping for food. These include unit pricing, open date labeling, nutrition labeling, and computerized checkout systems. Some of these aids involve additional labor and skill in producing and/or marketing food products and may thus increase the cost of food to the consumer.

Unit Pricing. The cost per pound or ounce for products sold by weight and the cost per quart, pint, or fluid ounce for products sold by volume is printed on a label that is usually attached to the edge of the shelf where the products are displayed. This allows the shopper to compare prices per unit for different size packages of the same product. The most economical size to buy can thus be readily determined. Unit pricing is mandatory in some states but voluntary in others.

Open Date Labeling. A date-code is placed on packaged food products for the customer to read and interpret. The date may appear in different forms on different packages. It may represent (1) the last recommended day of retail sale, (2) the end of the period of optimum quality, or (3) the date of processing or final packaging. Open date labeling provides some information for the shopper but the conditions, particularly of temperature, under which the products are handled and stored greatly affect the quality change and hence the significance of the date printed on them.

Nutrition Labeling. In the early 1970s the U.S. Food and Drug Administration (FDA) completed a major revision of regulations concerning the labeling of food. An important part of this revision was the publication of detailed regulations governing nutrition labeling. This is a relatively new era in food labeling practice [12, 22, 27]. The purpose of nutrition labeling is to help consumers choose diets that are well balanced and health-promoting and to do this at the lowest cost. Nutrition labeling allows for the voluntary declaration of nutrition information, in addition to required product information such as net weight, ingredient declaration, and the manufacturer's or distributor's name and address. Although it is generally voluntary, if nutrition labeling is included it must meet specified requirements for substance and format. Nutrition labeling is mandatory for products that contain added nutrients or for products on which nutrition claims are made. FDA is presently proposing that it be given legislative authority to, in addition, require nutrition labeling for food which has a significant role in the diet, or a potential for misleading the public when the information is not provided, or otherwise has public health significance [17].

Required nutrition information includes, at a minimum, the grams of protein, fat, and carbohydrate, and the number of kilocalories in a specified serving of the product, and the percentage of the "U.S. RDA" for protein, vitamins A and C, thiamin, riboflavin, niacin, calcium, and iron in that serving or portion. Other essential vitamins and minerals may be listed according to regulations governing their declaration. Regulations have also been written to cover the listing of fat, fatty acids, and cholesterol on labels. Examples of nutrition labels are shown in Figure 2-3. U.S. RDAs were developed by FDA as a replacement for the outdated Minimum Daily Requirements that were previously used in labeling foods such as breakfast cereals and food supplements. The U.S. RDAs are based on the Recommended Dietary Allowances published by the Food and Nutrition Board of the National Academy of Sciences—National Research Council, but have been selected for easier and more uniform application to the population as a whole. The U.S. RDAs are listed in Table 2-1. Nutrition labeling gives consumers much more information about the foods they buy than they would have without this service. For those on diets that have been modi-

Nutrition Information
(Per Serving)
Serving Size = 8 Oz.
Servings per Container = 1

Calories	560	Fat (Percent	
Protein	23 Grams	of Calories	
Carbohydrate	43 Grams	53%)	33 Grams
		Polyunsaturated*	2 Grams
		Saturated	9 Grams
		Cholesterol* (20 MG/100 G)	40 Milligrams
		Sodium (365 MG/100 G)	830 Milligrams

Percentage of U.S. Recommended Daily Allowances (U.S. RDA)

Protein	35	Riboflavin	15
Vitamin A	35	Niacin	25
Vitamin C (Ascorbic Acid)	10	Calcium	2
Thiamine (Vitamin B_1)	15	Iron	25

Information on fat and cholesterol content is provided for individuals who, on the advice of a physician, are modifying their total dietary intake of fat and cholesterol.

Nutrition Information
Serving Size = 1/7 of 9'' Pie
Servings per Container = 7

Calories	350
Protein	3 Grams
Carbohydrate	51 Grams
Fat	15 Grams

Percentage of U.S. Recommended Daily Allowances (U.S. RDA)

Protein	4
Vitamin A	0
Vitamin C	2
Thiamine	2
Riboflavin	2
Niacin	2
Calcium	0
Iron	2

2-3 *Examples of nutrition labels showing required information.* (Courtesy of the U.S. Department of Health and Human Services, Food and Drug Administration)

Table 2-1 *U.S. Recommended Daily Allowances (U.S. RDA)**

Protein	
Protein quality equal to or greater than casein	45 grams
Protein quality less than casein	65 grams
Vitamin A	5,000 International Units
Vitamin C (ascorbic acid)	60 milligrams
Thiamin (vitamin B_1)	1.5 milligrams
Riboflavin (vitamin B_2)	1.7 milligrams
Niacin	20 milligrams
Calcium	1.0 gram
Iron	18 milligrams
Vitamin D	400 International Units
Vitamin E (tocopherol)	30 International Units
Vitamin B_6	2.0 milligrams
Folic acid (folacin)	0.4 milligrams
Vitamin B_{12}	6 micrograms
Phosphorus	1.0 gram
Iodine	150 micrograms
Magnesium	400 milligrams
Zinc	15 milligrams
Copper	2 milligrams
Biotin	0.3 milligrams
Pantothenic acid	10 milligrams

*Used for labeling purposes only; taken from the 1968 Recommended Dietary Allowances.

fied for reasons of health, nutrition labeling is especially helpful. This information is also valuable to professional nutritionists and home economists. However, much nutrition education for the typical consumer is necessary if the consumer is to make effective use of the labeling. Suggestions have been made for simplifying the format in which nutrition information is presented. Cost to the food manufacturers who choose to provide nutrition labeling may be appreciable since they are required to do laboratory analyses of samples of their foods for nutrient content. This expense eventually affects the cost of the food to the customer [25].

Computerized Checkout Systems. A computer-assisted electronic cash register system may be installed in a supermarket when the volume of business justifies it. The cost of the items in the customer's shopping cart can then be tabulated by using a laser optical scanner to read Universal Product Code (UPC) symbols which are affixed to each food package. The scanner is connected to a computer that then retrieves the necessary information from its storage and prints the name and price of each item on a screen for the customer to see. It also prints this information on the sales receipt. The computer must be properly programmed at all times with the current price information. The Universal Product Code symbol contains a series of dark lines and spaces of varying widths as shown in Figure 2-4. The left half of the symbol identifies the manufacturer and the right half identifies the product. A large proportion of the items on supermarket shelves carry a UPC symbol.

Use of the computerized system allows pricing of items to be done on the display shelves only and not on each individual product, although some consumer and union groups have objected to the elimination of individual package pricing. It also speeds up checkout time and reduces errors at the cash register. The consumer has a meaningful record of purchases. Inventory control for the retailer is improved.

Manufacturer identification number   Item code

2-4 *Universal Product Code.*

Convenience Foods

Convenience foods have been defined as fully or partially prepared foods for which significant preparation time, culinary skills, or energy use have been transferred from the homemaker's kitchen to the food processor and distributor [28]. Most of the foods in a modern supermarket have had some preparation treatment and thus, in a sense, are convenience foods. However, as commonly used, this term applies to foods that have had a comparatively large amount of processing or market services done on them and may be served with a minimum of effort and skill. These types of foods may also be called service ready foods, prefabricated foods, ready-prepared foods, or efficiency foods. Many different processes are used by the food industry in the production of convenience foods. These processes include dehydrating the food to variable moisture levels by freeze-drying and other methods; compressing the food to decrease bulk; precooking and freezing; and using various flexible packaging materials.

Recently a flexible package or pouch that will withstand the high temperatures required for heat processing of low-acid foods such as meats and vegetables has been developed [30]. This package, commonly called the retort pouch, can replace the tin can in some cases, particularly for foods that require reheating since they may be heated right in the pouch. In addition to improving food quality, in many respects, the retort pouch makes possible a substantial saving in the energy used for processing and transporting the finished products.

The production of convenience foods actually began many years ago with the development of canning. A number of canned products are now well-established convenience foods. With the widespread availability and use of home freezers, many frozen convenience foods entered the market. Dehydrated convenience items are also plentiful. The real convenience food era probably began in the 1950s. The development of certain convenience foods sometimes seems to have a snowballing effect. For example, potato flakes were developed by the Eastern Regional Research Laboratory, U.S. Department of Agriculture, to encourage a wider use of potatoes. The marketing of potato flakes and granules for making instant mashed potatoes has been followed by numerous other commercial potato products, such as frozen scalloped, hashed brown, and French fried potatoes that require only a brief heating period and a wide variety of packaged dehydrated potato mixes containing convenient sauce and seasoning packets. The quality of these potato products in relation to the prepared fresh product may vary, depending on both the type of product and the manufacturer. Many of them have been very well accepted and have become established convenience foods [19]. If new products are not well accepted, which is true in many cases, they disappear from the market in a short period of time.

Some convenience foods are designed for the snack shelf, but the majority are for regular use in food preparation in the home and in institutions. Many cookbooks reflect the convenience food market as convenience items are included in recipes. Convenience foods offer storage and transportation savings to industry as well as to the homemaker. Dehydrated fruit and tomato juices, which can be shipped and stored without refrigeration and reconstituted with water before use, are examples of great savings in transportation costs and storage space. Even prior to the manufacture of commercial flour mixes, many homemakers prepared, in quantity, their own biscuit and other mixes to be stored in the refrigerator ready for instant use. Some homemakers continue to do this. Industry, however, has the advantage of knowing about and being able to obtain and use ingredients that are well suited to prolonged storage. The standardization of products and suitable packaging are also factors in the retention of desirable qualities in stored foods.

Convenience Foods in Space

Travel into space brings special demands for food. Convenience-type foods have been developed to meet the demanding specifications on weight, volume, and ease of preparation [2]. Since the astronauts have much work and experimentation to do in space, the time required to eat must be kept to a minimum. Special demands for stability during storage are put on foods that go into space. They must be stable for several months at temperatures up to 38° C (100° F). Their packaging must be flexible and able to withstand extremes of pressure, humidity, temperature, and vibration that could cause breakage or cracking. Packages of food must also be convenient to handle.

Many changes have been made in space foods since space exploration began. Much had to be learned about how foods could be handled in a state of weightlessness. During the Mercury flights it was learned that man could chew and swallow while weightless. First

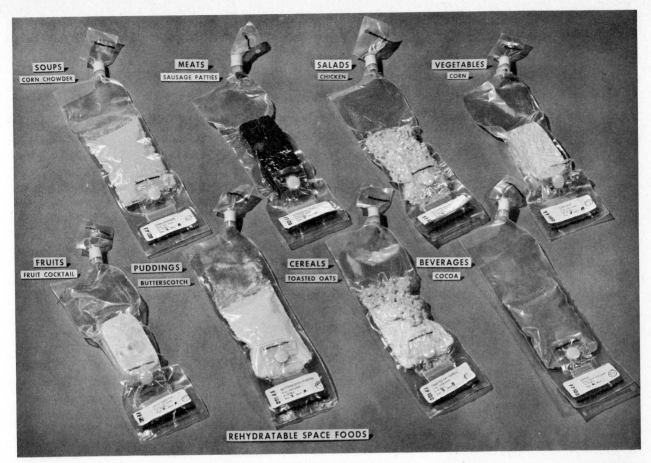

2-5 *Foods for space travel have included bite-size portions and rehydratable items.* (Courtesy of U.S. Army)

space foods were either pureed so they could be forced into the mouth through tubes or they were compressed into compact, bite-sized pieces that were coated to avoid any loose crumbs that would float in zero gravity (see Figure 2-5). During the Apollo flights a spoon, rather than a tube, was used to eat moist foods. During the Skylab program astronauts had knives and forks available to them and ate from a food tray with cavities to hold containers of food. Beverages were still sent as dry powders and were rehydrated by putting water through a one-way valve into a special container.

A new era in the exploration of space began with the space shuttle, Columbia. The shuttle is shaped like an airplane and is designed to take off from the ground, use a reusable rocket system, enter the earth orbit for a number of days, and then return to earth, landing like an airplane.

31

It can carry up to seven persons, and a galley has been designed for their food service needs. The galley has hot and cold water and an oven, but no food freezers or refrigerators. Food packaging is simplified to some degree over that used for previous space ventures. The food includes dehydrated, thermostabilized, irradiated, and intermediate-moisture items. Many foods are dehydrated because water is produced onboard as a by-product of the spacecraft fuel cells [3].

Testing of space foods and development of packages to contain them continues. Spin-offs from these studies may provide the consumer with improvements in convenience foods used at home.

Cost of Convenience

How much does convenience cost? In making cost comparisons between various convenience foods and similar home-prepared products some difficulties may be encountered. The proportions of ingredients contained in convenience foods are not identified on the labels and, therefore, home-prepared products may not contain the same amounts of component ingredients. However, a number of cost comparisons have been made with these limitations in mind.

Five frozen-prepared plate dinners (TV dinners) and 12 frozen entrees, such as lasagna, chicken à la king, cheese pizza, fried chicken, and crabcakes, were purchased in the Washington, D.C. area and compared with home-prepared foods [18]. The frozen dinners cost from 13 percent to 105 percent more than the comparable home-prepared products. Frozen entrees were also more expensive than the home-prepared items with the exception of crabcakes and deviled crab. These dishes, however, contained substantially less crabmeat than the home-prepared products. The cost increases ranged from 9 percent for chicken pie to 127 percent for lasagna.

On another occasion, frozen plate dinners and skillet-dinner mixes, both low- and high-cost brands, were purchased in the Washington, D.C. area and compared with similar home-prepared products [6]. A fried chicken dinner with a breast and drumstick cost 20 percent more and the dinner with a wing and back section cost 55 percent more than comparable home-prepared chicken dinners. A frozen meat loaf dinner cost 69 percent more than one made at home.

Each of the three skillet dinners made from the low-cost brand was *less* expensive than the home-prepared dish. The high-cost brands were from 11 to 33 percent *more* expensive than the home-prepared products on a one-cup serving basis.

A major study to provide more information about 166 convenience foods considered not only the cost of food but also, for 41 products, the cost of fuel used in preparation and, for 115 products, the cost of the homemaker's time [28, 29]. Food cost comparisons were based on price information from supermarkets in Philadelphia, Milwaukee, San Francisco-Oakland, and New Orleans. Table 2-2 shows the number of convenience foods that were more expensive, less expensive, or approximately the same cost as their home-prepared counterparts when only the cost of the food was considered. Fifty-nine percent of the 166 convenience foods were at least 1 cent more expensive than their home-prepared or fresh counterpart; about 25 percent were at least 1 cent less expensive; and about 16 percent cost approximately the same as their counterparts.

When the cost of fuel used and the homemaker's time, calculated at the minimum wage rate, were added to the food cost for forty-one convenience products, nearly one-half the convenience items were at least 1 cent *less* expensive than their home version.

Consumer Reports periodically evaluates convenience foods and compares them with similar homemade products. In a comparison of fried chicken they found that homemade chicken cost 9 cents per edible ounce; frozen prepared chicken cost from 12 to 21 cents per edible ounce; and fast-food restaurant fried chicken cost 23 to 29 cents per edible ounce [13].

Some convenience baked products are more costly than equal amounts of similar products prepared from home recipes. Using prices from three Washington, D.C. supermarkets, cost comparisons were made for biscuits, sugar cookies, pancakes, and yeast rolls made from basic ingredients and from several convenience forms.

Table 2-2 *Number of Convenience Products More or Less Expensive Than Fresh or Home-prepared Foods by Product Category**

Product Category	Number More Expensive by at Least 1 Cent	Number Less Expensive by at Least 1 Cent	Number Within 1 Cent
Beef	9	2	0
Pork	3	0	0
Poultry	10	1	0
Finfish and shellfish	7	8	0
Pizza, rice, and spaghetti	7	2	2
Vegetables	18	13	6
Fruits	12	5	4
Dairy and eggs	3	0	0
Baked goods and desserts	27	9	9
Baby foods	1	2	0
Coffee and tea	1	0	5

*Total number of products evaluated was 166.

From Traub, L. G., and D. D. Odland, 1978. Convenience foods vs. home-prepared: Costs, yield, and quality. *National Food Review* (September), U.S. Department of Agriculture.

Biscuits made from a mix with added milk and pancakes made from a mix with added water cost slightly less than similar products made from basic ingredients. Biscuits from refrigerated cans; sugar cookies from a mix with egg added; sugar cookies from a refrigerated roll of dough, pancakes from a mix with added egg, oil, and milk; and yeast rolls frozen or made from a mix with added water cost slightly more than similar products made from basic ingredients. Pancakes that were frozen and ready for the toaster and yeast rolls that were ready-to-eat or brown-and-serve cost two to four times as much as did similar products made from basic ingredients [5].

It may be concluded that most convenience products have a higher food cost than home-prepared products. However, when fuel and time costs are also considered, the total cost for many of them may be less than the homemade counterpart.

Quality of Convenience Foods

The quality characteristics of convenience foods vary widely but some compare quite favorably with home-prepared products. Twenty-two convenience foods and their home-prepared counterparts were evaluated by a trained taste panel [29]. A five-point evaluation scale was used with five being the optimum score. All home-prepared foods and about 80 percent of the convenience products rated four points or higher in overall quality. However, compared to their corresponding convenience products, nineteen of twenty-two home-prepared foods rated higher in texture; eighteen rated higher in appearance and overall quality; and fifteen rated higher in flavor.

Forty-three frozen pizzas were evaluated by a *Consumer Reports* panel [14]. The majority of them were rated as fair and a few as good. Most of them were rated low because of hard, dry, or soggy crusts. A similar report was made on frozen pot pies with only seven of thirty-three pies rated as good. Most were rated fair and a few were rated poor [15]. However, half of twenty-four canned or frozen beef stew samples were rated good by a sensory panel [1].

A *Consumer Reports* panel also evaluated a wide variety of cakes made from commercial mixes. A few cakes were rated very good. Most of the rest were "undistinguished" with artificial flavorings predominating. In spite of these ratings, the panel felt that a flavorful frosting could cover up many of the defects in the cakes [4].

Nutritive Value

It is certainly important for the consumer to consider the nutritive value of convenience items and how this may differ from the nutritional contribution made by corresponding home-prepared ones. The USDA reported that commercially prepared foods of the meat, fish, poultry, and cheese group generally had lower fat, protein, and calorie values and higher ash and carbohydrate contents than did corresponding home-prepared foods [20].

The ascorbic acid content of dehydrated potato products is usually substantially lower than that of fresh cooked potatoes. Instant potatoes may be fortified with ascorbic acid to make them comparable to the fresh product. Many canned and dehydrated soups that are presently being marketed contain very low amounts of protein or other nutrients. Soups made at home will vary greatly in the amount and type of ingredients used and thus in nutritional value so comparisons with commercial soups are difficult to make. Extra ingredients may be added to purchased soups to make them more hearty. The consumer should be aware of what is being purchased nutritionally when buying various types of soups.

Convenience

Reduced preparation time and effort is probably a major consideration for many in the purchase of convenience foods. Not only are preparation tasks decreased but cleanup chores, such as dishwashing, may also be substantially reduced. Lack of culinary skill may also contribute to the decision to purchase. The variety of dishes served at home may be greatly expanded in households with inexperienced cooks.

In a USDA report on ninety-five items of meat, fish, poultry, and cheese, the active preparation time for home-prepared foods ranged from less than 1 minute to 54 minutes. Over half of the home-prepared foods, however, required more than 25 minutes. Less than 10 minutes of active preparation time was needed for preparing four servings of most of the convenience foods [20].

From annual supermarket sales figures it is obvious that households rely heavily on convenience foods. They are undoubtedly here to stay (Figure 2-6). Some of them, such as frozen orange juice and gelatin or pudding mixes, have become so well established and widely used that they are probably not considered as convenience foods in the same sense as frozen entrees. There are both advantages and disadvantages to the use of convenience foods. Personal preferences will vary from one household to another. Decisions to purchase one or another food form should be made with consideration of convenience, amount of time saved, cost, quality, one's ability to prepare food, cooking equipment and storage space available, and concerns regarding nutrition and health.

2-6 *A wide variety of convenience foods is commonly available on the market.*

Basic Mixes Prepared at Home

Mixes of all varieties are numbered among the many convenience foods found today on supermarket shelves. These mixes include a large number of dry flour mixes for preparing such items as cakes, cookies, gingerbread, brownies, piecrusts, muffins, cornbread, coffee cakes, biscuits, pancakes, and hot rolls. They also include many seasoning mixes such as taco mix, meat loaf mix, and a variety of salad dressing mixes. Pudding mixes and canned fruit pie fillings are among a number of additional products that are available. The average homemaker utilizes many commercially prepared mixes.

Although commercial mixes are convenient and time saving, do-it-yourself mixes prepared at home may also provide convenience. Considerable time may be saved by making mixes because the basic ingredients for a large number of prepared items are mixed at one time. The time for preparing the mix may also be scheduled during less busy periods, thus making more effective use of time.

Eliason, Harward, and Westover [7, 8] have published two cookbooks concerned with how to make your own mixes. They have suggested that the convenience of cooking with mixes may be combined with the quality advantages of cooking "from scratch" when mixes are made at home. They have presented recipes for many mixes, including three types of master mixes from each of which several recipes may be prepared. One type consists of dry mixes that contain only dry ingredients with no shortening. These may be stored at room temperature for 6 to 8 months. Examples of this type of mix include hot roll mix, pancake mix, and pudding mix.

Another type of master mix includes semidry mixes which contain vegetable shortening, butter, or margarine. Because of the fat content, these mixes keep for shorter periods of time than do the dry mixes. If stored in a cool, dry place they should keep well for 10 to 12 weeks. Examples of this type are basic cake mix, cornmeal mix, muffin mix, oatmeal mix, and gingerbread mix.

The third type of master mix is a freezer-refrigerator mix which is moist and more perishable than the other master mixes. These mixes require freezer or refrigerator storage in well-sealed containers and keep well for about 3 months. Examples are braised beef cube mix, chicken mix, Mexican meat mix, and moist piecrust mix.

In addition to the master mixes from which several recipes can be prepared, special mixes designed primarily for one recipe are outlined in the cookbook. Examples of special mixes include hot chocolate mix, fruit slush mix, chicken-flavored rice mix, various salad dressing mixes, chicken coating mix, seasoned bread crumb mix, various dip mixes, and spaghetti seasoning mix.

Study Questions

1. Describe two different methods that have been used by the U.S. Department of Agriculture (USDA) to obtain information on what and how much food is eaten in America. Evaluate the advantages and inaccuracies that may be associated with each method.
2. According to USDA surveys:
   a. How does family income affect "eating out?"
   b. What has been the trend toward "eating out" since 1965?
   c. What effect does size of household have on the amount of money spent for food by the household and per person?
   d. As income increases, what types of foods are generally used more and what types are used less frequently?
3. What is food waste and how may food be wasted at the household level?
4. List at least six factors that are likely to influence food cost to the consumer and briefly explain how they exert their influence.
5. Describe what is meant by unit pricing and open date labeling and explain their possible usefulness to the consumer.
6. What is required when a food product is given nutrition labeling and what is the purpose of this type of labeling?
7. Define the term convenience foods and give several examples.
8. Explain how the widespread availability of convenience foods may affect food preparation techniques used in the home.
9. Convenience foods are sometimes compared with similar home-prepared products. Discuss how they generally compare in:
   a. Cost: both food cost alone and cost which includes energy use and homemaker's time
   b. Eating quality
   c. Nutritive value
   d. Preparation time and effort
10. Discuss advantages and disadvantages for making your own mixes at home.

References

1. Beef stews, 1981. *Consumer Reports* **46,** 267.
2. Bourland, C. T., M. F. Fohey, R. M. Rapp, and R. L. Sauer. 1982. Space shuttle food package development. *Food Technology* **36,** 38 (no. 9).
3. Bourland, C. T., R. M. Rapp, and M. C. Smith, Jr. 1977. Space shuttle food system. *Food Technology* **31,** 40 (no. 9).
4. Cake mixes. 1982. *Consumer Reports* **47,** 120.
5. Collier, L., and D. Odland. 1975. Convenience and the cost of baked products. *Family Economics Review* (U.S. Department of Agriculture) 14. (Spring).
6. Cromwell, C., and D. Odland. 1974. Convenience and the cost of plate dinners and skillet main dishes. *Family Economics Review* (U.S. Department of Agriculture) 10. (Summer).
7. Eliason, K., N. Harward, and M. Westover. *Make-A-Mix Cookery*. Tucson, AZ: H. P. Books, 1978.
8. Eliason, K., N Harward, and M. Westover. *More Make-A-Mix Cookery*. Tucson, AZ: H. P. Books, 1980.
9. *Food and Nutrient Intakes of Individuals in 1 Day in the United States, Spring 1977*. Nationwide Food Consumption Survey 1977–78 Preliminary Report No. 2. Washington, DC: U.S. Department of Agriculture, September 1980.
10. *Food Consumption: Households in the United States, Spring 1977*. Nationwide Food Consumption Survey 1977–78, Report No. H-1. Washington, DC: U.S. Department of Agriculture, September 1982.
11. *Food Prices in Perspective: A Summary Analysis*. National Economic Analysis Division; Economics, Statistics, and Cooperatives Service, ESCS-53. Washington, DC: U.S. Department of Agriculture, April 1979.
12. Forbes, A. L. 1978. Nutrition labeling from the government point of view. *Food Technology* **32,** 37 (no. 12).
13. Fried chicken. 1982. *Consumer Reports* **47,** 362.
14. Frozen pizza. 1980. *Consumer Reports* **45,** 25.
15. Frozen pot pies. 1981. *Consumer Reports* **46,** 555.
16. Gallo, A. E. Consumer food waste in the United States. *National Food Review* NFR-12, p. 13. Washington, DC: U.S. Department of Agriculture. Fall 1980.
17. Hutt, P. B., and A. E. Sloan. FDA issues tentative positions on food labeling and nutrition issues. *Nutrition Policy Issues* No. 8. Minneapolis, MN: Nutrition and Governmental Relations Departments, General Mills, Inc. February 1980.
18. Isom, P. 1979. Frozen-prepared plate dinners and entrees—cost vs. convenience. *Family Economics Review* (U.S. Department of Agriculture) 18. (Summer).
19. Jerome, N. W. 1978. Prepared frozen dinners—modern staple emergency meals? *Food Technology* **32,** 48 (no. 11).
20. *Meat, Fish, Poultry, and Cheese: Home Preparation Time, Yield, and Composition of Various Market Forms*. Home Economics Research Report No. 30. Washington, DC: Agricultural Research Service, U.S. Department of Agriculture, 1965.

21. *Money Value of Food Used by Households in the United States, Spring 1977.* Nationwide Food Consumption Survey 1977–78 Preliminary Report No. 1. Washington, DC: U.S. Department of Agriculture, August 1979.
22. Moore, J. L., and P. F. Wendt. 1973. Nutrition labeling—A summary and evaluation. *Journal of Nutrition Education* **5,** 121.
23. *Nutrient Levels in Food Used by Households in the United States, Spring 1977.* Nationwide Food Consumption Survey 1977–78 Preliminary Report No. 3. Washington, DC: U.S. Department of Agriculture, January 1981.
24. Paarlberg, D. 1977. Food and economics. *Journal of The American Dietetic Association* **71,** 107.
25. Rusoff, I. I. 1978. Nutrition labeling from the industrial point of view. *Food Technology* **32,** 32 (no. 12).
26. Salathe, L. E. *Household Expenditure Patterns in the United States.* Economics, Statistics, and Cooperatives Service Technical Bulletin No. 1603. Washington, DC: U.S. Department of Agriculture, April 1979.
27. Schrayer, D. W. 1978. Consumer response to nutrition labeling. *Food Technology* **32,** 42 (no. 12).
28. Traub, L. G., and D. D. Odland. *Convenience Foods and Home-prepared Foods.* Agricultural Economic Report No. 429. Washington, DC: U.S. Department of Agriculture, 1979.
29. Traub, L. G., and D. D. Odland. Convenience foods vs. home-prepared: Costs, yield, and quality. *National Food Review* NFR-4, p. 30. Washington, DC: U.S. Department of Agriculture. September 1978.
30. Tuomy, J. M., and R. Young. 1982. Retort-pouch packaging of muscle foods for the Armed Forces. *Food Technology* **36,** 68 (no. 2).
31. Welsh, S. O., and R. M. Marston. 1982. Review of trends in food use in the United States, 1909 to 1980. *Journal of The American Dietetic Association* **81,** 120.

3

Food Safety and Standards

Food Safety

Many people in the United States appear to be concerned about the safety of their food supply. However, rational scientific discussions of food safety are infrequently held. Instead the discussions are often of an emotional nature.

There are several different hazards that are associated with the food supply. Some of these hazards are more important than others in terms of how much illness is generally involved, but all of them must be controlled. The most common problem with food results from infections and intoxications by the presence and/or growth of certain microorganisms, usually bacteria but sometimes also molds and animal parasites. Food infections result when microbes that can cause illness (*pathogens*) are present, usually in large numbers, in the food that is eaten. Food intoxications occur when microbes have grown and produced a toxin in the food and the toxin-laden food is consumed.

A second hazard is contaminants in the environment, such as industrial chemicals and pesticide residues, that may be present in foods. Toxic substances that are naturally present in foods that are commonly eaten represent a third hazard. A fourth hazard, one that has caused the least amount of documented illness because of the strict testing procedures required, is the use of chemical additives or food additives in food processing and preservation.

Foodborne Infections and Intoxications

Tremendous technological progress has been made in recent years in the entire system of food processing and distribution. Improved methods of preservation have been developed, and techniques for the chemical and bacteriological identification of injurious agents in food have been improved. In spite of such progress, foodborne infections and food intoxications appear to be fairly common and create a great deal of unnecessary human misery. The more a food is handled and the longer it is held, the greater is the opportunity for problems to arise. Changes in the food-processing, distribution, and storage system that allow food to be held for comparatively long periods of time before it is consumed have actually increased the potential danger of microbial contamination and growth. Everyone along the food-handling chain—the processor, the packager, the wholesaler, the retailer, and the consumer—needs to recognize the potential health hazards and to know how to prevent them. Many meals are eaten away from home in restaurants and other food-service establishments. Personnel in the food-service industry must constantly strive for microbial quality and safety in the food that is served to the public. Governmental agencies are closely surveying sanitary practices in the food and food-service industries and many food companies have their own microbiology laboratories.

Foodborne outbreaks of illness in the United States and other countries are inadequately reported. When such outbreaks are reported, the information on them is often incomplete and does not allow a specific cause to be assigned to the incident. In order to increase knowledge about foodborne illness and its effective control, a better system of reporting and investigating is essential. Many causative microbial agents of foodborne illness have been recognized and should be searched for when outbreaks occur [10].

The consumer should recognize that poor food-handling practices in the home may cause illness among family members even though the food was safe to eat when it was purchased or first prepared. The homemaker who is interested in the health of the family needs to become familiar with possible sources of contamination for food and with effective methods of caring for food to keep it safe and wholesome. A considerable number of outbreaks of food infections and intoxications are caused by not following simple rules of sanitation in the kitchen, such as washing hands before handling food, putting clean bandages on cuts and sores before working with food, keeping pets away from food that is being prepared, and maintaining the proper temperature when holding food [7, 16].

Animal Parasites. In certain parts of the world infection by such parasites as tapeworms, roundworms, and certain species of protozoa may be common problems and foods or water may be carriers of these infecting agents. In the United States these problems are rare. A small percentage of pork produced in this country may be infected with *Trichinella spiralis,* a nematode worm that can cause trichinosis in man. Symptoms of trichinosis are given in Table 3-1. The incidence of trichinosis in the United States has declined in the last two decades but continues to average between 100 and 150 cases a year [24].

The U.S. Department of Agriculture (USDA) has recommended a procedure for processing pork products so that any trichinae present will be destroyed in the processing. Thorough cooking of fresh pork to an internal temperature of at least 58° C (137° F) should also ensure the destruction of any trichinae that might possibly be present.

Pathogenic Microorganisms. Some pathogenic microorganisms may be carried by food even though they do not grow in the food itself. Other pathogenic microorganisms are able to grow in foods under certain conditions of temperature and other environmental factors. The contamination of foods by pathogens may occur through food handlers, air, soil, water, flies, roaches, rodents, and from animals producing milk or being used for meat. Food utensils used for eating, drinking, or food preparation may become contaminated when used by persons who are carrying potential disease-producing organisms.

A significant public health problem is the contamination of food by *Salmonella* bacteria. There are more than one thousand two hundred known strains of *Salmonella* and all are capable of causing infection in man. Certain species of *Salmonella* may grow in foods to attain high numbers and produce an acute gastrointestinal disorder when the food is consumed. An estimated two million Americans suffer from *Salmonella* gastroenteritis each year, with at least half the cases attributable to contaminated food.

The primary signs and symptoms of salmonellosis are nausea, diarrhea, abdominal pain, and fever. These symptoms usually appear within 12 to 18 hours after the contaminated food has been eaten. In most cases, recovery occurs within 2 or 3 days. However, some individuals develop complications that persist for weeks or even months. Although information on mortality from salmonellosis is incomplete, death may sometimes occur with this disease, especially among the very young, the aged, and the infirm. A summary of the major factors involved in salmonellosis is found in Table 3-1.

Salmonella microorganisms have been found in a wide variety of foods, and animals may harbor the organism. Raw poultry, meat, eggs, and dairy products are among the foods most frequently found to contain *Salmonella*. Actually, the main health hazard to man lies in the constant introduction of contaminated animal products into

Table 3-1. *Food Infections and Intoxications**

Disease	Cause	Incubation Time (Hours)	Symptoms	Mortality	Involved
Salmonellosis	Infection with *Salmonella* species	12 to 24	Nausea, diarrhea, abdominal pain, fever. Headache, chills, prostration.	1%	Meat, poultry, and egg products.
Trichinosis	Infestation of *Trichinella spiralis*	48	Nausea, vomiting, diarrhea, sweating, loss of appetite. Later, muscular pains.	1 to 30%	Raw pork or pork products.
Staphylococcus poisoning	Toxin produced by certain strains of *Staphylococcus aureus*	1 to 6	Severe vomiting, diarrhea, abdominal cramping.	Essentially zero	Custard- or cream-filled baked goods, ham, tongue, poultry, dressing, gravy, eggs, potato salad, cream sauces, sandwich fillings.
Botulism	Toxin produced by *Clostridium botulinum*	12 to 36	Nausea, vomiting, diarrhea, fatigue, dizziness, headache, dry mouth, double vision, muscle paralysis, respiratory failure.	20 to 60%	Low- or medium-acid canned foods; meats, sausage, fish, and other seafood.

*From [8, 9].

the food supply. It is not unusual to find 25 percent of a particular lot of broiler chickens to be carrying *Salmonella* [8]. Turkeys and swine and cracked eggs may be contaminated with the microorganisms. During slaughtering, microorganisms may be spread from one carcass to another. Humans who have had salmonellosis may carry the infecting organisms in their digestive tracts for some time after the symptoms of the disease have disappeared and may contaminate foods that they handle improperly.

The specific foods most commonly involved in the development of salmonellosis are various kinds of meat and poultry products; eggs and foods made with eggs, such as cream or custard fillings; milk and milk products such as ice cream, cream, and custard-filled confectionery; fish and shellfish. The most vulnerable foods are those that are lightly cooked and subject to much handling, especially if they are unrefrigerated for long periods of time.

The consumer cannot control the contamination of animal products with *Salmonella* organisms if this occurs before the food is brought into the kitchen. Proper cooking and careful handling practices after the products have been received, therefore, are the sole protection against illness. Thorough cooking destroys the microorganisms. Poultry should be cooked to a well-done stage. Commercial pasteurization of milk before drying and of eggs before freezing or drying destroys *Salmonella* organisms. The proper storage of foods controls the growth of *Salmonella*. Fresh meats, poultry, and eggs should be stored in the refrigerator at 1.7° to 4.4° C (35° to 40° F) or in the freezer −18° C (0° F). Cooked meat or poultry and leftovers should be tightly covered and stored immediately in the refrigerator or freezer. Perishable foods should be kept chilled when they are carried on a trip or a picnic. Cutting boards used for cutting up raw poultry should be disinfected by washing with a dilute solution of sodium hypochlorite (household bleach) before being used for the cutting of other foods, such as the slicing of potatoes for salad. This prevents cross-contamination from one infected food to a noninfected item.

Other bacteria that may be involved in food infections include microorganisms of the *Shigella* species and certain strains of *Escherichia coli*.

To help protect family members from foodborne illness, strict cleanliness should be stressed for anyone who handles food. All dishes and equipment used in food preparation should be carefully cleaned. Machine-washed dishes both in the home and in commercial foodservice establishments may be almost if not entirely sterile because of the use of hot water and strong sanitizing agents that is possible in machine washing. In homes where infectious diseases exist, it is important to keep all dishes used by patients separate from other dishes until they are sterilized.

Precautions should always be taken in preparing, cooking, and storing foods. Cold foods should be kept cold (below 5° C or 41° F), and hot foods should be kept hot (above 60° C or 140° F) if kept for any length of time. It is also important to assure adequate heating in cooked foods so that microorganisms are destroyed and to avoid cross-contamination between raw and cooked foods.

Food Toxins. Whereas salmonellosis results from the ingestion of large numbers of the microorganisms themselves, other types of illness may result from consumption of toxins produced by the microorganisms. Certain strains of *Staphylococcus aureus* produce a potent toxin that is recognized as a common cause of food poisoning. It is called an *enterotoxin* because it produces gastroenteritis or inflammation of the lining of the stomach and intestines. The symptoms of staphylococcal poisoning, severe vomiting and diarrhea, appear between 1 and 6 hours after the food is consumed, and usually disappear a few hours later. Complete recovery normally takes 1 or 2 days. The mortality rate for this type of food poisoning is essentially zero but it could be fatal in severely malnourished infants or in infirm adults [8].

The food-poisoning strains of *Staphylococcus aureus* may be present in the nasal passages of many individuals. Boils and some wounds may also be infected with them. Food may be contaminated with these potentially dangerous organisms when transfer occurs from the nasal passage or a sore on the hands of the food handler to the food being prepared.

If foods contaminated with staphylococcal organisms cool very slowly or are held without refrigeration, the staphylococcus microorganisms may grow and then produce a toxin that is responsible for the gastrointestinal symptoms which occur when the food is consumed. The symptoms occur relatively quickly since the toxin is preformed.

The staphylococcal toxin, once it has formed in the food, is not easily inactivated or destroyed. Since it is stable toward heat and may withstand boiling for 20 to 60 minutes, it is important to prevent the formation of the toxin. This can be done by the hygienic handling of food during preparation and by proper storage conditions. Staphylococci usually get into food from persons handling the food. The hands of the person handling food should thus be washed before the food is prepared, and if the person uses a handkerchief, the hands should be washed again in order to avoid transfer of organisms from the nasal passages to the food. Rubber or plastic gloves should be worn by the food preparer if cuts or sores are present on the hands. This not only keeps bacteria from getting into the cuts but also prevents staphylococcus organisms from being transferred to the food from the cuts. Staphylococcus organisms grow in a wide variety of foods including roast fowl, baked ham, tuna, egg products, potato salad, and custard- or cream-filled baked goods. These foods, in particular, should be held in a refrigerator at a temperature of 1.7° to 4.4° C (35° to 40° F). Failure to refrigerate foods that have been contaminated with the microorganisms, thus allowing toxin to form, is the usual reason for an outbreak of the disease. The toxin does not necessarily affect the taste of the product and individuals consuming such foods are not aware that they are eating "spoiled" food. The number of cases of *Staphylococcus aureus* food poisoning in this country are not known. Cases are usually not reported unless they occur in large groups of people, such as at conventions or picnics. A large proportion of all cases of food poisoning are probably of this type and many of us encounter it several times during our lives. Table 3-1 summarizes the major factors involved in staphylococcal food poisoning.

Another microorganism involved in food poisoning is *Clostridium perfringens*. The symptoms associated with this type of food poisoning include severe abdominal cramps and a pronounced diarrhea. Nausea and vomiting are rare. The symptoms appear 8 to 12 hours after eating the contaminated food and the illness lasts no more than 24 hours. It is usually not serious. Foods responsible include beef, chicken, turkey, stews, meat pies, and gravy that have been mishandled. These foods may be cooled too slowly after cooking or kept several hours without refrigeration or kept on a serving line steam table at a temperature below 55° C (131° F) for an extended period of time. *C. perfringens* organisms multiply rapidly under these conditions.

The mechanism causing illness seems to involve the ingestion of large numbers of live vegetative cells of *C. perfringens*. These cells then form encapsulating spores in the intestinal tract and release an enterotoxin. The toxin produces the characteristic symptoms [12].

Botulinum food poisoning is the most feared of all foodborne diseases. At one time the death rate from this disease was 50 to 60 percent of those contracting the disease. In recent years, however, the mortality has dropped to about 20 percent. This is probably the result of early diagnosis and improved treatment of the illness. Botulism is a condition that results from the action of a potent toxin on the neurological system of the body, producing paralysis. The toxin is produced by the bacterium *Clostridium botulinum*. Symptoms include nausea, vomiting, diarrhea, double vision, difficulty in swallowing, inability to talk, and finally respiratory paralysis. The signs of disease usually appear about 12 to 36 hours after eating food that contains the active toxin [8].

Clostridium botulinum is a spore-forming bacterium that grows and elaborates toxin only in the absence of free oxygen. It is thus said to be *anaerobic*. The organism itself is nonpathogenic, but the toxin that it produces in such foods as inadequately heated canned meats, low-acid vegetables, and some processed fish is one of the most potent known. Toxin production may also be a problem in such foods as fresh mushrooms in tight plastic bags and baked potatoes wrapped in foil and left at room temperature overnight. Spoiled foods containing the toxin may have off odors and gas and appear to be soft and disintegrated. However, cases of botulism have been reported from eating foods that had little or no abnormal appearance or odor. Because of this, and because the toxin can be inactivated, a recommendation has been made that all low-acid home-canned foods, particularly vegetables and meats, be boiled for 10 to 15 minutes before being tasted.

The extent of botulism outbreaks in the U.S. due to commercially canned foods has been very small considering that more than 10 billion cans of commercially processed low-acid canned foods are consumed each year. There have been approximately ten times more outbreaks involving home-canned than commercially canned foods. From 1899 to 1981, 522 outbreaks of botulism were reported involving home-canned foods and 55 outbreaks involving commercially canned foods. Since 1973 there have been only six incidents with botulism toxin in commercially canned products. These have involved peppers, marinated mushrooms, tuna, beef stew, and salmon. In some cases the problem was with use of imperfect cans [23]. Some outbreaks in recent years have also involved vacuum-packed smoked fish.

Inadequate processing of home-canned foods that are low in acid, particularly vegetables and meats, creates the greatest problem in regard to botulism. If spores of this bacterium are present, boiling will not destroy them unless the solution is sufficiently acid or unless boiling is continued for 6 to 10 hours. Various strains of the organisms vary in their temperature relations, but low-acid foods are never safe unless they are heated at temperatures considerably above the boiling point of water (100° C or 212° F). It is recommended that temperatures no lower than 114° to 119° C (237° to 246° F) be used for low-acid vegetables. These temperatures can be achieved by processing in a pressure cooker at 10 to 15 pounds pressure. Low-acid foods should never be processed in a boiling water bath. Because the botulinum toxin is so deadly, recommended procedures should always be carefully followed in the home canning of low-acid foods to guard against any possibility of the toxin's developing.

It was discovered in 1960 that toxins produced by molds growing on cereal grains were responsible for the deaths of thousands of young turkeys who were fed the grain. These toxins were called *aflatoxins* since it was found that they had been produced by certain strains of *Aspergillus flavus*. Aflatoxins have been detected in peanuts and cottonseed and in the meals made from them. Other toxins produced by molds have also been identified and are generally called *mycotoxins*. These toxins are capable of causing damage to humans if mold-contaminated foods are eaten over a period of time [1].

Environmental Contaminants

Toxic substances may contaminate the environment in which people, plants, and animals live. These substances include both inorganic elements, such as arsenic, cadmium, mercury, and lead, and organic substances, such as various chemicals used in pesticides. When contaminants persist in the environment, they may accumulate along the food chain in amounts that are toxic to humans when various animals and plants are consumed. For example, fish taken from water contaminated by the industrial use of mercury contain high levels of mercury which may cause illness if consumed in large amounts [19].

Metals may enter foods from certain utensils. Galvanized containers are not suitable for foods because the zinc used for galvanizing is toxic. Cadmium and brass are also undesirable metals for use as food containers. Tin-coated cans are used in food processing, but only very small amounts of tin are generally found in most foods. However, acid fruits and fruit juices packed in unlacquered tin-coated cans and stored in the opened cans in the refrigerator may contain enough tin to depress the intestinal absorption of zinc when several servings of the fruit are consumed [11]. Food stored in opened tin-coated cans may also change in color or develop a metallic taste. Small quantities of aluminum are dissolved from utensils in many cooking processes. This is apparently not harmful, but scientists are continuing to study the effects of aluminum in the diet. The element copper is nutritionally essential yet certain salts of copper are toxic. Cooking green-colored foods in copper containers to get bright green color is no longer practiced because of the danger of toxicity.

Pesticide spray residues on agricultural products, such as fresh fruits and vegetables, represent chemical additives to food that occur incidentally and are sometimes called *incidental additives.* The Food and Drug Administration sets tolerances for residue levels on agricultural products in an effort to protect the public against the improper use of pesticides. Pesticides are widely used in the intensified agriculture practiced in our modern civilization. They are intentionally added to agriculture crops although they are not intended to become part of the consumed food. Pesticides may also get into foods unintentionally as they move through soil, water, and air in the environment. Pesticides aid in preventing food destruction during growth and storage. However, they also constitute hazards if misused. Public education programs are useful for increasing the public's awareness of the dangers while recognizing the value of pesticides in agricultural production. Fresh farm products, such as fruits and vegetables, should always be washed well before they are eaten.

Naturally Occurring Toxic Substances in Foods

Certain plants and animals may contain natural constituents that are toxic and produce gastrointestinal disturbances or even death when these foods are consumed in sufficient quantities. Poisonous varieties of mushrooms, mistaken for edible kinds, are a well-known example of toxic plants. Oxalic acid is a constituent of plants such as rhubarb greens, spinach, and beet tops. In large amounts these may be responsible for oxalic acid poisoning in certain individuals. Solanin is a water-soluble toxin that may develop in potatoes during sprouting or exposure to the sun. It is present principally in the skin and in the green-colored portion directly under the skin, which may be removed by paring. Some tropical fish contain poisonous substances. Ocean mussels and clams may contain a poisonous alkaloid at certain seasons of the year. Doubtless many foods contain small amounts of substances that could cause toxicity if eaten in excess, but the amounts of oxalic acid, solanin, and several other toxins in some foods have not been shown to be toxic in the amounts usually eaten, hence the toxins represent only minor hazards [3, 15].

Food Additives

The use of chemical additives in foods is not new, but their roles have become more prominent in recent years as the production of processed convenience foods has increased. At the same time, several issues concerning their safety have been raised, particularly by consumer groups. A serious responsibility is placed on both the food industry and appropriate governmental agencies to assure the safety of any substance that is added to foods either directly or indirectly.

What is a food additive? Under a broad definition it is any substance that becomes part of a food product either when added *intentionally* or when it *incidentally* becomes part of the food. Examples of incidental additives are pesticide residues that may remain on farm produce and substances that may migrate from the packaging material into a food. In either of these cases the amount of additive involved is extremely small [5, 17].

There is also a legal definition of a food additive which includes only those substances that must receive special approval from the Food and Drug Administration after they have been thoroughly tested for safety and before they can be used in food. In addition to these specially tested and approved additives, the Food and Drug Administration maintains an official list of other substances added to foods that are "generally recognized as safe" (by experts in the field) for human consumption. This list is commonly called the *GRAS* list. Although GRAS substances do not need the special clearance for safety that is required for legally defined food additives, they are constantly being evaluated for safety by the Food and Drug Administration on a case-by-case basis. Occasionally substances are removed from the GRAS list as more sensitive methods for evaluation of safety are developed. An example is the removal in 1970 of the artificial sweetener cyclamate. The safety of another GRAS substance, the artificial sweetener saccharin, was also questioned in the late 1970s. A Congressional moratorium has allowed saccharin to continue in use while more conclusive safety research is completed. Aspartame, a new artificial sweetener, is discussed in

Chapter 15, Sweeteners and Sugar Cookery, p. 363. The use of the sulfites, also GRAS substances, for maintaining the color of fresh fruits and vegetables has been questioned because some people have adverse reactions to them.

Justifiable Uses. An additive is intentionally used for one or more of the following general purposes.

1. To maintain or improve nutritional quality. Vitamins and minerals are used to fortify some foods when these nutrients may have been lost in processing or when they might be otherwise lacking in the usual diet.
2. To enhance the keeping quality with consequent reduction in food waste. Freshness may be maintained by the use of additives to retard spoilage, preserve natural color and flavor, and retard the development of rancid odors in fats.
3. To enhance the attractiveness of foods. Many additives will make food look and taste better. Natural and synthetic flavoring agents, colors, and flavor enhancers serve this purpose.
4. To provide essential aids in processing or preparation. A large variety of additives are used to give body and texture to foods as stabilizers or thickeners; to distribute water soluble and fat soluble particles evenly together as emulsifiers; to control the acidity or alkalinity; to retain moisture as humectants; to leaven or make rise many baked products; to prevent caking or lumping; and to perform other functions.

Legislation. The Food and Drug Administration administers the Food, Drug, and Cosmetic Act. Several provisions of this law govern the use of additives in food entering interstate commerce. State and local governments are responsible for the safety of foods produced and sold within the state.

Harvey Wiley, who was chief U.S. Department of Agriculture chemist, was an early pioneer in the struggle for adequate legislation to protect the public's food supply. His efforts led to the passage of the first Pure Food and Drug Act in 1906. The act was completely revised in 1938 and renamed the Federal Food, Drug, and Cosmetic Act. Among other things, the 1938 law required truthful labeling of additives. Several amendments to the Food, Drug, and Cosmetic Act have been passed to strengthen the law and keep up with changes in food technology and medical science.

The Miller Pesticide Amendment of 1954 established a procedure for setting safe tolerances for pesticide residues on fresh fruits, vegetables, and other raw agricultural commodities. The 1958 Food Additives Amendment was designed to protect the public by requiring approval of new additives *before* they could be used in foods. The responsibility for proving the safety of additives was placed upon the manufacturer. A company must file a petition with the Food and

Drug Administration showing the results of extensive tests for safety and the Food and Drug Administration must approve the additive as safe before it can be marketed. The Food and Drug Administration also prescribes the types of foods in which the additive can be used and specifies labeling directions.

FOOD SAFETY *51*

The Color Additives Amendment of 1960 covers all coloring substances added to foods. Additives in meat and poultry products are the responsibility of the Food Safety and Inspection Service in the U.S. Department of Agriculture.

The Food Additives Amendment and the Color Additives Amendment include a clause called the Delaney Clause, named after the Congressman who sponsored it. This clause prohibits the approval and use of any food additive that is found to induce cancer when ingested by man or animal. This clause has created a great deal of discussion and disagreement among members of the food industry, officials of the Food and Drug Administration, and certain consumer groups. Some feel that the clause should be strictly enforced, whereas others suggest that an additive requiring extremely large amounts to produce any adverse effects in test animals may still be safe for use in the human food supply under specified circumstances. There is no way in which the absolute safety of a legally defined food additive or a GRAS substance can be guaranteed. Clearance through the Food and Drug Administration should assure that the risk of adverse effects is minimal. Constant testing and reevaluation of these substances by the government and the food industry is essential [6, 20].

The consumer should be alert to the problems and issues involved in the evaluation and use of food additives. The use of additives improves or extends the shelf life of many foods and reduces distribution costs, increases the aesthetic qualities of some foods, and improves the nutritional value of certain processed foods with enrichment or fortification. If an additive is hazardous to health, in the amounts that might reasonably be consumed by a human being, there is no question: it must not be used. There is an area in between, however, where issues about safety versus palatability and cost are much less clear-cut. It is in this area that much controversy lies. Industry and governmental groups, and consumer groups as well, continue to discuss ways to evaluate benefit versus risk for the use of food additives.

Additives Used in Processing. Every additive must serve a useful purpose in food. Additives cannot be used to conceal damage or spoilage or to deceive the consumer. There are many different, specific functions for food additives but most of them may be grouped into classes. Some of the more important classes or types of additives are listed here. Examples of additives in use for each class are given in Table 3-2.

Table 3-2. *Examples of Food Additives in Use for Various Types of Additives*

Type or Class	Additives	Foods in Which Used
Nutrients	Thiamin Niacin Riboflavin Iron	Flour, breads, and cereals in enrichment process
	Ascorbic acid	Fruit juices, fruit drinks, and dehydrated potatoes
Antioxidants	Butylated hydroxyanisole (BHA) Butylated hydroxytoluene (BHT) Tertiary butylated hydroxyquinone (TBHQ)	Animal fats as lard, ready-to-eat cereals, crackers, potato chips to retard rancidity
	Ascorbic acid	Frozen peaches and apples to prevent browning
Antimicrobial agents	Propionates	Bread to retard molding and development of "rope"
	Benzoates	Carbonated beverages, fruit drinks, and margarine
Coloring agents	Beta-carotene	Margarine, butter, and cheese
	Certified colors as Citrus Red No. 2	Skins of oranges
	Red No. 3, Green No. 3, and Yellow No. 6	Candies, cereals, soft drinks, and bakery goods
Flavoring agents	Benzaldehyde	Almond flavoring
	Vanilla	Ice cream, baked goods, and candies
	Monosodium glutamate (MSG)	Soups, Chinese foods as flavor enhancer
Emulsifiers	Mono- and diglycerides	Margarines and shortenings
	Lecithin	Bakery products, chocolate, and frozen desserts
Stabilizers and thickeners	Alginates	Ice cream
	Carrageenan	Evaporated milk, sour cream, and cheese foods
	Pectin	Fruit jellies, confections, and sherbets
	Modified starches	Puddings and pie fillings
Sequestrants	Ethylenediamine tetraacetic acid (EDTA)	Wine and cider

Type or Class	Additives	Foods in Which Used
Humectants	Glycerine Sorbitol	Marshmallows, flaked coconut, and cake icings
Anticaking agents	Calcium silicate Magnesium carbonate	Table salt, powdered sugar, and baking powder
Bleaching and maturing agents	Chlorine	Cake flour
	Chlorine dioxide Benzoyl peroxide (bleaches only)	All purpose flour
Acids, alkalies, and buffers	Citric acid and its salts	Soft drinks
	Acetic acid Sodium bicarbonate Sodium hydroxide	Process cheese Baking powders Dutch processed cocoa Pretzels (glazing)
Nonnutritive sweeteners	Aspartame	Lemonade and cocoa mixes and ready-to-eat cereals
	Saccharin (used with warning label)	Soft drinks, punch mixes, and dietetic foods

Nutrient Supplements. Vitamins and minerals are added to some processed foods to restore or improve their nutritive value.

Antioxidants (preservatives). Fatty foods are particularly susceptible to spoilage as rancidity develops with unpleasant off odors. Some antioxidants retard the development of rancidity. Another type of antioxidant may prevent enzymatic oxidative browning in fresh fruits and vegetables. The use of sulfites on fresh fruits and vegetables has been questioned because a number of adverse reactions after consumption of treated foods have been reported. Asthmatics appear to be particularly susceptible.

Antimicrobial Agents (preservatives). Some preservatives are used to prevent or inhibit microbial growth.

Coloring Agents. Proper use of color makes foods more visually appealing and corrects for natural variations and irregularities.

Flavoring Materials. A wide variety of natural extractives, essential oils, and synthetic flavorings are used in processed foods. This makes up the largest group of intentional additives.

Emulsifiers. These substances are widely used to mix fat and water soluble substances uniformly together in the making and stabilizing of emulsions. They are also used to stabilize foams and suspensions.

Stabilizers and Thickeners. Texture and body are important characteristics of many foods. A variety of substances is used to achieve desired smoothness and consistency.

Sequestrants. Sequestrants are used to bind (chelate) small amounts of metals such as iron and copper which may have undesirable effects on flavor or appearance.

Humectants and Anticaking Agents. Humectants are used to retain moisture and keep certain foods soft. Some additives are added to finely powdered or crystalline foods to prevent caking as moisture is absorbed.

Bleaching and Maturing Agents. The baking properties of wheat flours are improved by use of certain oxidizing agents. Many of them also have a bleaching effect.

Acids, Alkalis, and Buffers. The acidity or alkalinity is very important in many processed foods. Acids, alkalis, and buffers are therefore used to adjust and control the pH (measurement of degree of acidity or alkalinity). The alkaline salt, sodium bicarbonate or baking soda, is also used to produce carbon dioxide gas in baked products.

Nonnutritive Sweeteners. Sugar substitutes are used in foods designed for persons who must or wish to restrict their intake of ordinary sweets.

Food Standards

The government plays an important role in assuring food quality by setting standards for various food products. In performing this function the government is attempting to implement the constitutional mandate to promote the general welfare. Standard setting involves several agencies of the federal government. Some of the standards are mandatory while others are voluntary. The Food and Drug Administration in the Department of Health and Human Services is required to establish a food standard when it is needed to promote honesty and fair dealing in the interest of consumers. Three kinds of standards have been set—standards of identity, standards of fill of container, and standards of minimum quality. The U.S. Department of Agriculture has set standards for grading agricultural products and also participates in the setting of some standards of identity. The U.S. Department of Commerce, National Marine Fisheries Service, has set grade standards for fish and shellfish [6, 13, 22].

Standard setting for foods was not always as it is today. During the 1800s there were no official national food standards in the United States. Each buyer of food had to be on the alert for poor food quality. As the volume of the buying and selling of food increased, it became apparent that some order was necessary. There was need for a uniform language to describe quality and establish prices. The first official standards were issued for farm products when a cotton standard was established in 1909. The first food grade standards were set in 1917 for potatoes. In 1946, Congress enacted the Agricultural Marketing Act which gave the U.S. Department of Agriculture its authority to standardize food quality grades and to establish a voluntary grading program.

In our rapidly shrinking world, international trade in food is accelerating. This has created a need for international standards to safeguard the consumer's health and ensure fair food trade practices. The Codex Alimentarius Commission was established in 1963 by the Food and Agriculture Organization and the World Health Organization of the United Nations. This commission administers programs dealing with the setting of international food standards and the evaluation of food additives and pesticide residues.

Standards of Identity

Standards of identity aid in determining adulteration and mislabeling of foods. They define of what a food product must consist if it is to be legally labeled and sold by its common or usual name. For example, the standard of identity for mayonnaise specifies the ingredients that it must contain—including oil, egg, and an acid component—and requires that at least 65 percent oil be included in the finished dressing. If these requirements are not met, the product cannot be labeled "mayonnaise" but must be labeled "imitation" or some other term to indicate that it does not meet the standard. Standards of identity protect against deception and ensure the basic nutritional value of foods.

Standards of identity are only set after many public hearings and much discussion. They have been established for a number of products, including bakery and cereal products, cacao products, canned fruits and vegetables, fruit butters and preserves, fish and shellfish, eggs and egg products, margarine, nut products, dressings for foods, cheeses and cheese products, milk and cream, frozen desserts, macaroni and noodle products, and tomato products.

If a standard of identity has been established for a food product, a listing of ingredients on the label is not presently required. Some consumers might benefit from these label declarations of ingredients since they do not have ready access to the legal standards of identity. Perhaps in the future the listing will be made mandatory as federal legislation is changed.

The U.S. Department of Agriculture establishes composition, preparation, and labeling requirements for certain meat and poultry products. The requirements may cover only the meat content of a product (standard of composition). For example, the minimum percentage of beef that beef stew must contain is 25 percent. Or the specifications may go further to establish a standard of identity.

Standards of Fill of Container

Standards for fill of container state, for certain processed foods, how full a food container must be. These standards aim at avoiding deception for the consumer. They are needed especially for products that are made up of a number of pieces packed in a liquid, such as various canned vegetables, or for products, such as nuts, that shake down after filling.

Standards of Minimum Quality

The Food and Drug Administration has set standards of quality for a number of canned fruits and vegetables. These are regulatory and specify minimum requirements for such characteristics as tenderness, color, and freedom from defects. If a food does not meet the minimum standard, it must be labeled "Below Standard in Quality; Good Food—Not High Grade." Other words may be substituted for the second part of the statement to show in what respect the product is substandard, such as "Below Standard in Quality; Excessively Broken." The consumer seldom sees a product with a substandard label at retail stores.

Grading

Grading services for foods offer an official certification that a particular product meets a predetermined standard of quality. These services are offered for meat, poultry, eggs, dairy products, some fish, nuts, rice, and fresh fruits and vegetables. The grading of each of these products is discussed in more detail in other chapters. Only a general discussion of grading and inspection is given here.

Grading is voluntary, unless it is required on a local level or for a particular industry program, and is provided for a fee that is paid by the one requesting the grading services. Grade standards for many foods were originally established to aid wholesale trading, but more recently many consumer grades have become useful. Consumer grades are designed to apply to small units of food that would usually be sold in a retail market. Grades indicate the quality of the food at the time it was graded and do not allow for changes in quality that may occur during handling and storage. Graded foods offer the consumer a choice of quality and enable the consumer to pick the one that is most suitable for the intended use. Grade standards are defined to cover the entire range of quality of a food product. Some products are more variable in quality than are other products and, therefore, may require more grades. For example, there are eight grades for beef, but only three for chicken. Most federal grades for consumers are preceded by the letters U.S. and are enclosed in a shield-shaped mark (Figure 3-1).

Since grade standards for various products were developed one at a time, there is variance in the naming systems. For instance, the top quality grade for cantaloupes is U.S. Fancy; for beets it is U.S. No. 1; for carrots it is U.S. Grade A; and for celery it is U.S. Extra No. 1. U.S. Grades A, B, and C are used on poultry and on canned fruits and vegetables. Grades for meat are very different. To help achieve a more uniform grading system, the U.S. Department of Agriculture issued in 1976 a policy statement that when standards for fresh fruits, vegetables, and nuts are issued, revised, or amended, only the classifications U.S. Fancy, Grades 1, 2 and 3 may be used.

Even though a product may have been officially graded, the law still does not require that a designation of grade appears on the label. If the grade shield is used on a food product, however, it must have been officially graded.

Foods are "inspected" by the grader when a grade is determined, or it might be said that they are "inspected for grade." However, the term *inspection* has different meanings when applied to various commodities. The U.S. Department of Agriculture administers an inspection program for meat and poultry, which is mandatory for meat and poultry sold in interstate commerce and for that sold in those states that do not have an inspection program of their own that is equal to the federal program. This inspection is for wholesomeness and proper labeling; it is not for grading. The meat and poultry must be from healthy animals or birds, be processed under strict sanitary conditions, and must be truthfully labeled. All meat

3-1 *Shield-shaped marks used by the U.S. Department of Agriculture in grading food products. From left to right are the symbols used on butter, instant nonfat dry milk, eggs, poultry, fresh fruits and vegetables, and meat.* (Courtesy of the U.S. Department of Agriculture)

| Butter | Instant nonfat dry milk | Eggs | Poultry | Fresh fruits & vegetables | Meat |

and poultry must be inspected before it can be graded. The inspection is for wholesomeness; the grading is for quality.

Food grading should be an aid to shoppers in effectively buying to meet their needs and desires. However, the results of two national surveys [2, 21] involving the questioning of a sample of U.S. households in both 1970 and 1980 showed that, although there was a general awareness of the food grading program and its purpose, only 10 to 25 percent of the respondents knew specific details. The 1980 respondents were less knowledgeable about the system and more often confused regarding grading versus inspection than were their 1970 counterparts. These consumers would find the system more useful if it were simpler, more uniform, and if information about it were more readily available. More consumer education concerning food quality standards and grades would be helpful.

Labeling

The Food and Drug Administration shares responsibility with the Federal Trade Commission for enforcing fair packaging and labeling legislation. The U.S. Department of Agriculture is also involved for some foods. This legislation requires complete information to be prominently presented on food labels. The label must tell the name of the product, its form, the net contents for weight, and the name and place of business of the manufacturer, packer, or distributor. The term *imitation* must be used if the product is nutritionally inferior to the established food that it resembles. If the product is as nutritious as the established food, it may be given a new name rather than use the word *imitation*. Ingredients must be listed for foods for which a standard of identity has not been established and are listed in descending order of predominance by weight. Colors and flavors do not have to be listed by name but artificial flavors must be so designated [18].

In the 1970s a number of changes were made in labeling requirements. Regulations governing nutrition labeling were formulated. (Nutrition labeling is discussed in Chapter 2.) An "information panel" was established for mandatory information, such as a statement of ingredients for nonstandardized foods and, if it is shown, nutrition labeling information. A minimum type size for mandatory information was specified. The principal thrust of the labeling changes was to provide greater information to consumers, particularly about the nutritional characteristics of food.

Recently efforts have been made by the Food and Drug Administration, the U.S. Department of Agriculture, and the Federal Trade Commission to further streamline and modernize federal food labeling policy. Public hearings have been held. The policy objectives include full ingredient labeling of standardized foods, greater use of quantitative ingredient labeling that specifies amounts, nutrition labeling for more foods, and clarification of certain labeling terms and concepts [14].

Study Questions

1. Name four general types of hazards that are associated with food.
2. Explain the difference between a food infection and a food intoxication. Give examples of each.
3. For each of the types of food poisoning listed below:
   a. Indicate if it is an infection or an intoxication.
   b. List the usual symptoms.
   c. Describe the usual mortality.
   d. List the types of foods most likely to be involved in each type of food poisoning:
      Trichinosis.
      Salmonellosis.
      Staphylococcal poisoning.
      Clostridium perfringens poisoning.
      Botulism.
4. Why is it important that food handlers observe appropriate sanitary procedures when working with food? Explain.
5. Describe examples of food-related illness resulting from:
   a. Environmental contaminants
   b. Naturally occurring toxicants
   c. Mycotoxins
6. a. Define food additives in a general sense.
   b. What is the legal definition of food additives?
   c. What are GRAS substances?
   d. Give examples of intentional and incidental food additives.
7. Describe four justifiable uses for food additives.
8. Discuss implications for foods resulting from each of the following federal laws or amendments:
   a. 1906 Pure Food and Drug Act
   b. 1938 Federal Food, Drug, and Cosmetic Act
   c. 1954 Miller Pesticide Amendment
   d. 1958 Food Additives Amendment
   e. 1960 Color Additives Amendment
9. What is the Delaney Clause and why is it important to both the food processor and the consumer?
10. How can a consumer know that a food additive is safe? Discuss this.
11. List at least eight different types or groups of food additives and give examples of specific additives for each group. Also, indicate the foods in which these additives are generally used.
12. Which agencies of the federal government are particularly involved in setting standards for food and how are they involved? Discuss.

13. Distinguish among each of the following types of standards:
    a. Standards of identity
    b. Standards of fill of container
    c. Standards of minimum quality
    d. U.S. grade standards
14. How is grading of food products useful to the wholesaler, the retailer, and the consumer? Discuss this.
15. What information must be listed on a food label?

References

1. Campbell, T. C., and L. Stoloff. 1974. Implication of mycotoxins for human health. *Journal of Agricultural and Food Chemistry* **22,** 1006.
2. *Consumers' Knowledge and Use of Government Grades for Selected Food Items.* Marketing Research Report No. 876. Washington, DC: U.S. Department of Agriculture, 1970.
3. Crocco, S. 1981. Potato sprouts and greening potatoes: Potential toxic reaction. *Journal of the American Medical Association* **245,** 625.
4. *Federal Food Standards.* FSQS-19. Washington, DC: U.S. Department of Agriculture, March 1981.
5. *Food Additives.* FSQS-32. Washington, DC: U.S. Department of Agriculture, August 1980.
6. Food and Nutrition Board, Assembly of Life Sciences. *Risk Assessment/ Safety Evaluation of Food Chemicals.* Washington, DC: National Academy Press, 1980.
7. *Food Safety for the Family.* Food Safety and Inspection Service. Washington, DC: U.S. Department of Agriculture, 1982.
8. Foster, E. M. 1978. Foodborne hazards of microbial origin. *Federation Proceedings* **37,** 2577.
9. Frazier, W. C., and D. C. Westhoff. *Food Microbiology,* 3rd ed. New York: McGraw-Hill Book Company, 1978.
10. Gilchrist, A. *Foodborne Disease and Food Safety.* Monroe, Wisconsin: American Medical Association, 1981.
11. Greger, J. L., and M. Baier. 1981. Tin and iron content of canned and bottled foods. *Journal of Food Science* **46,** 1751.
12. Hatheway, C. L., D. N. Whaley, and V. R. Dowell, Jr. 1980. Epidemiological aspects of *Clostridium perfringens* foodborne illness. *Food Technology* **34,** 77 (no. 4).
13. Hutt, P. B. 1977. Balanced government regulation of consumer products. *Food Technology* **31,** 58 (no. 1).
14. Hutt, P. B., and A. E. Sloan. Proposed new legislation on food labeling and nutrition. *Nutrition Policy Issues* no. 7. Minneapolis, MN: Nutrition and Governmental Relations Departments, General Mills, Inc. November 1979.
15. Institute of Food Technologists' Expert Panel on Food Safety and Nutrition and the Committee on Public Information. 1975. Naturally occurring toxicants in foods. *Food Technology* **29,** 67 (no. 3).
16. *Keeping Food Safe to Eat.* Home and Garden Bulletin No. 162. Washington, DC: U.S. Department of Agriculture, 1978.

17. Lehmann, P. More than you ever thought you would know about food additives. *Department of Health and Human Services Publication* No. (FDA) 82-2160. Washington, DC: Department of Health and Human Services, February 1982.

18. Morrison, M. 1977. A consumer's guide to food labels. *Department of Health and Human Services Publications* No. (FDA) 77-2083 (June).

19. Munro, I. C., and S. M. Charbonneau. 1978. Environmental contaminants. *Federation Proceedings* **37,** 2582.

20. Oser, B. L. 1978. Benefit/risk: Whose? What? How much? *Food Technology* **32,** 55 (no. 8).

21. Reidy, K. Solving the mysteries of the food grading system. *National Food Review* NFR-12, p. 19. Washington, DC: U.S. Department of Agriculture. Fall 1980.

22. Sackett, I. D., Jr. 1982. Quality inspection activities of the National Marine Fisheries Service. *Food Technology* **36,** 91 (no. 6).

23. Schaffner, R. M. 1982. Government's role in preventing foodborne botulism. *Food Technology* **36,** 87 (no. 12).

24. Schantz, P. M. 1983. Trichinosis in the United States—1947–1981. *Food Technology* **37,** 83 (no. 3).

4
Food Composition and Nutrition

Most foods are complex substances and contain many different chemical molecules oriented in a variety of ways. It is obvious, simply by visual observation, that some food products are not homogeneous. The casual examination of a sliced tomato, for example, reveals skin, seeds, and soft tissues, each with different structures. Even foods that appear homogeneous, such as cheddar cheese, contain many different substances.

A determination of the chemical composition of a food may be made in the laboratory. Water, carbohydrates, fats, and proteins are the chemical substances that are found in foods in largest amounts. Enzymes are special types of proteins that are found in small amounts in unprocessed plant and animal tissues. Minerals, vitamins, acids, and many flavor substances are present in foods in very small amounts.

Some knowledge of the individual chemical substances in a food is important to the student of food science because changes may occur in these components as a food is processed and prepared. For example, water is removed in large quantities from fruits, vegetables, or meats when they are dehydrated. Fat melts and is found in the drippings when meat is roasted. Oil and water or vinegar separate from each other when the emulsion in mayonnaise is broken. Addition of fresh pineapple to a gelatin mixture prevents setting of the gelatin because the gelatin, which is a protein, is broken down to peptides or amino acids by an enzyme in the pineapple.

Another reason for knowing about the component parts of foods is to gain a better understanding of what happens to foods when they are eaten. The aim of this chapter is to provide some information on the major and minor components of foods for those students who would like to know a little more about the chemistry of food and for those who have not studied basic nutrition prior to the study of food preparation.

Specific Nutrients in Foods

Metabolic processes (all of the chemical changes) that occur in the cells of the healthy human body are complex, orderly, and efficient. A great variety of chemical compounds are involved in these reactions of metabolism. Those chemical compounds that come into the body as food and participate in metabolic processes are called nutrients. Nutrients that are essential for life and health include proteins that contain specific amino acids, fats that contain specific fatty acids, carbohydrates, several vitamins, many mineral elements, and water [1, 2, 6]. Proteins, fats, carbohydrates, and water are also important in determining the quality characteristics of prepared foods.

A food may be defined as any substance that, when taken into the body, will perform one or more of the following functions: (1) build new tissues and maintain or repair old body tissues; (2) provide energy; and (3) regulate body processes. Table 4-1 shows the groups of nutrients that are important for each of these body functions. The principal constituents of foods used for the building and maintenance of tissues are proteins, minerals, and water. Vitamins play an important role, probably regulatory, in growth processes but enter also into the structure of some body components, such as the visual-purple pigment of the eye.

Common foods are mixtures of nutrients. Some highly processed foods, such as table sugar, shortenings, and oils, provide a single nutrient, and in some foods one or two nutrients predominate. Generally, however, each food may be expected to contribute to the diet

Table 4-1 *Nutrients Important for Body Functions*

Nutrients for Building	Nutrients for Energy	Nutrients for Regulating Body Processes
Proteins	Carbohydrates	Minerals
Minerals	Fats	Vitamins
Vitamins	Proteins	Water
Water		Bulk or fiber
		Some proteins contribute material for certain regulatory substances.

in several ways. The nutrients in foods are affected by various practices of handling and preparation. Procedures should be used that will best conserve the essential nutrients in foods so that they will actually be consumed and nourish the body [3].

Water

All foods contain water. It is present in amounts ranging from 1 to 2 percent to 98 percent, although most foods contain intermediate amounts. Examples of foods that are high in water are fresh vegetables and juicy fruits. Lettuce contains 95 percent water and watermelon has about 93 percent. Crackers, which are examples of low-moisture foods, usually contain only 2 to 4 percent water.

Water is an important building and regulating substance in the body. Here it acts as a solvent, carrying other substances in solution and allowing chemical reactions to take place between substances that are dissolved. Water is needed for the building of every kind of body tissue. It plays an important role in regulating body temperature because it aids in transporting heat and in losing heat from the body by evaporation from the skin. Water is essential for the elimination of waste from the body by way of both the kidneys and the intestines.

Carbohydrates

Carbohydrates, which are composed of the elements carbon, hydrogen, and oxygen, are either sugars or more complex substances, such as starch, which are formed by combining many sugars together. The simplest sugar carbohydrates are called *monosaccharides; saccharide* referring to their sweetness and *mono* to the fact that they are a single unit. Three simple sugars or monosaccharides that are of importance in food preparation are glucose, fructose, and galactose. The chemical structures for these sugars in cyclic form are shown in Figure 4-1. Glucose is also called *dextrose,* and *levulose* is another name for fructose.

Glucose is the most widely distributed monosaccharide in foods and is present in at least small amounts in all fruits and vegetables. It is a major component of corn syrup, which is produced by breaking down the complex starch molecule. Crystalline glucose, as well as corn syrup, is widely used in bakery products and in other manufactured foods. Glucose is also present in honey along with relatively large amounts of fructose, which is the sweetest sugar.

In recent years a high fructose corn syrup has been developed by employing an enzyme that changes glucose to fructose. This syrup is

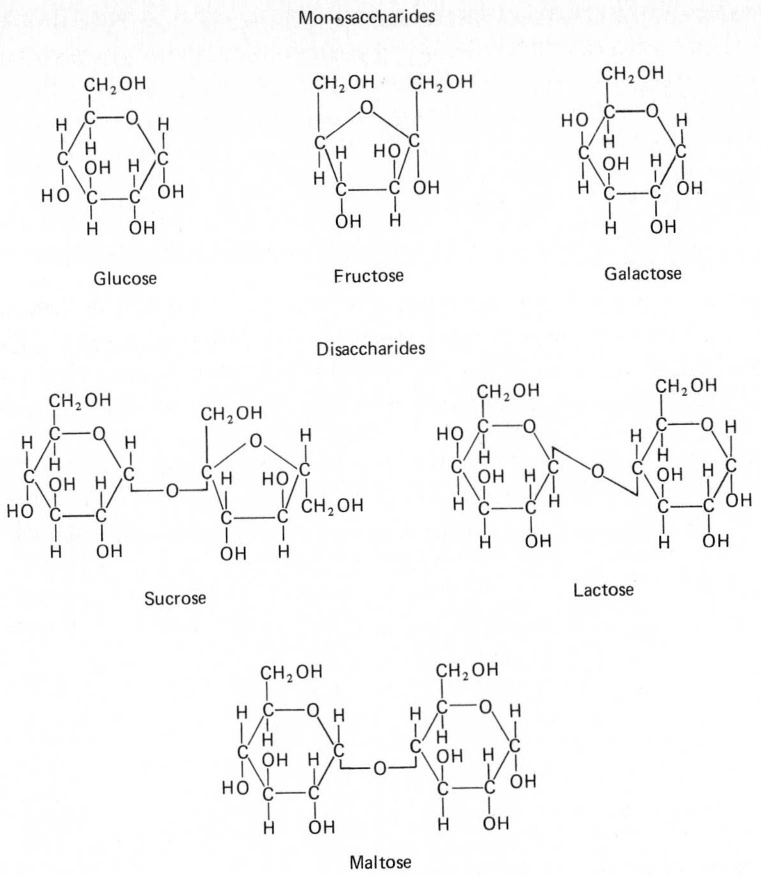

Monosaccharides

CH$_2$OH

Glucose

CH$_2$OH CH$_2$OH

Fructose

CH$_2$OH

Galactose

Disaccharides

CH$_2$OH

CH$_2$OH

Sucrose

CH$_2$OH

CH$_2$OH

Lactose

CH$_2$OH

CH$_2$OH

Maltose

now being used in the food industry. Galactose, which is generally not found free in natural food products, is however, one of the building blocks of milk sugar (lactose) and is formed when milk products are fermented. Therefore, yogurt and aged cheeses may contain galactose.

Monosaccharides are the building blocks for disaccharides and polysaccharides. Disaccharides consist of two monosaccharides linked together. The disaccharides of particular interest in the study of foods are sucrose, lactose, and maltose. The chemical structures for these disaccharides are shown in Figure 4-1. Sucrose is table sugar and is widely used in crystalline form for food preparation. It is usually extracted from sugar cane or the sugar beet. Sucrose is composed of one molecule of glucose and one molecule of fructose. These two monosaccharides are linked together through their most reactive groups, the aldehyde group of glucose and the ketone group of fructose.

65

Lactose, commonly called milk sugar, is found naturally only in milk and milk products. The two monosaccharides that make up lactose are glucose and galactose. Maltose consists of two glucose molecules joined together. It is produced when the polysaccharide starch is broken down to simpler substances. The common sources and products of breakdown or hydrolysis for sugars are summarized in Table 4-2. Polysaccharides are complex carbohydrates containing hundreds or thousands of monosaccharide units linked together in various ways. Linkages may produce long, straight chains in some cases and branched-type molecules in other cases. Starch, a polysaccharide found in plant tissues, is composed of many glucose units linked together. The properties of starch are discussed in Chapter 17, Cereals and Starch. Dextrins, which are intermediate in size

Table 4-2 *Sugars, Their Sources and Products of Hydrolysis*

Sugar	Common Sources	Products of Hydrolysis
Monosaccharides, $C_6H_{12}O_6$:		
Glucose or dextrose	Fruit and plant juices. Often present with other sugars. Honey. Formed by hydrolysis of sucrose, lactose, and maltose. A practically pure crystalline form known as *Cerelose* is obtained from cornstarch.	
Fructose or levulose	Fruit and plant juices. Often present with other sugars. Honey. Formed by hydrolysis of sucrose.	
Galactose	Does not occur free in nature. Formed by hydrolysis of lactose or galactans.	
Dissaccharides, $C_{12}H_{22}O_{11}$:		
Sucrose	Often present with other sugars. In many fruits and vegetables. Sugar cane and sugar beet are rich sources. Sugar maple and sugar palm.	One molecule each of glucose and fructose. A mixture of equal amounts of glucose and fructose is called *invert sugar*.
Lactose	Milk.	One molecule each of glucose and galactose.
Maltose	Malted or germinated grains. Formed by hydrolysis of starch.	One molecule yields two molecules of glucose.

between starch and maltose, are polysaccharides produced by the partial breakdown of starch. They are formed from starch when corn syrup is made, when bread is toasted, and when flour is browned. They have less thickening power than starch.

Glycogen is a branched polysaccharide composed entirely of glucose molecules. It is sometimes called animal starch and is stored in the liver.

Pectic substances are plant polysaccharides that contain galacturonic acid, a sugar acid, as their building block. The use of pectic substances in making jelly is discussed in Chapter 30, Fruit Jellies and Preserves.

Pectic substances are one component of a complex mixture generally called plant fiber. Other polysaccharides that are part of the fiber complex are cellulose and hemicelluloses. Cellulose contains many glucose units linked together as does starch. However, the glucose molecules in cellulose are linked in a different way than are the glucose units in starch, and form long, strong fibers in the cellulose molecule. Hemicelluloses are mixtures of polysaccharides that have various monosaccharide building blocks. They play important structural roles in plant tissues, along with cellulose, as they are concentrated in the cell walls. The branny layers of cereal grains and fresh fruits and vegetables contain relatively large amounts of fiber.

Fiber is not digestible by the human since no enzymes are present in the human digestive tract that can break down or hydrolyze the polysaccharide molecules that make up fiber. Fiber, sometimes called bulk, is necessary for regular and efficient elimination. In recent years, it has been suggested that adequate amounts of dietary fiber are particularly important in the prevention and/or treatment of diseases of the large intestine or colon, such as diverticulitis and cancer of the colon. The chief function of nutritive or digestible carbohydrates in the diet is to supply energy.

A group of substances called vegetable gums or *hydrocolloids* are chiefly polysaccharides and are performing increasingly important functions in food processing. This group includes (1) seaweed extracts, such as agar, alginates, and carrageenan; (2) plant seed gums such as guar gum and locust bean gum; (3) plant exudates such as gum arabic, gum tragacanth, and gum karaya; (4) modified materials such as methyl cellulose and sodium carboxymethyl cellulose; and (5) microbial derivatives such as xanthan gum. These gums are used in processed foods for such purposes as the retention of water, the reduction of evaporation rates, the modification of ice crystal formation, and the production of changes in consistency or flow characteristics. The production of dietetic foods often requires the ingenious use of hydrocolloids.

Some foods that are classified as largely carbohydrate are the following.

Sugars	Honey	Dried fruits
Syrups	Candies	Legumes
Molasses	Jellies and jams	Cereal products

Fats

Fats are composed of the same elements as are carbohydrates, that is, carbon, hydrogen, and oxygen. However, fats have much more carbon and hydrogen and much less oxygen than do carbohydrates. Because of this, fats are a more concentrated source of energy. The oxidation of 1 gram of pure fat in the body produces 9 kilocalories whereas the oxidation of 1 gram of pure carbohydrate yields only 4 kilocalories. One gram of protein also yields 4 kilocalories when protein is used by the body cells for energy. In a broad classification, all fatlike substances are called *lipids*. The lipids that are found in largest amount in foods, which are called *triglycerides* or neutral fats, are made up of an alcohol called *glycerol* and three fatty acids. Glycerol has three carbon atoms and three hydroxyl groups (—OH). Fatty acids are commonly composed of long chains of carbon atoms with an organic acid group ($-\overset{\overset{\textstyle O}{\|}}{C}-OH$) on the end. However, some foods such as butter contain a number of short chain fatty acids. The fatty acids are joined to the glycerol molecule by what is called an *ester linkage,* as shown in the following, where R represents the chain of carbon atoms.

$$
\begin{array}{ccc}
\begin{array}{c}
H \\
| \\
H-C-OH \\
| \\
H-C-OH \\
| \\
H-C-OH \\
| \\
H
\end{array}
&
+ \; 3\; R-\overset{\overset{\textstyle O}{\|}}{C}-OH \; \longrightarrow
&
\begin{array}{c}
H \quad\;\; O \\
| \quad\;\; \| \\
H-C-O-C-R \\
| \quad\quad\;\; O \\
| \quad\quad\;\; \| \\
H-C-O-C-R \\
| \quad\quad\;\; O \\
| \quad\quad\;\; \| \\
H-C-O-C-R \\
| \\
H
\end{array}
\\
\text{glycerol} & \text{fatty acid} & \text{triglyceride}
\end{array}
$$

A number of different fatty acids are combined in the triglycerides that are commonly found in foods. Some of these fatty acids are holding all of the hydrogen that they can hold on the carbon chains. There are no double bonds between carbon atoms. These types of fatty acids are called *saturated.* Other fatty acids contain double bonds between some carbon atoms and are *unsaturated* in terms of the amount of hydrogen that they contain. Examples of saturated fatty acids include butyric acid, which is present in butter, and stearic acid, which is a major component of beef fat. Palmitic acid is widely distributed in meat fats, vegetable oils, and cocoa butter.

$$CH_3CH_2CH_2COOH \quad \text{(Butyric acid) (4 carbon atoms)}$$

$$CH_3CH_2CH_2CH_2CH_2CH_2CH_2CH_2CH_2CH_2CH_2CH_2CH_2CH_2CH_2CH_2CH_2COOH \quad \text{(Stearic acid) (18 carbon atoms)}$$

$$CH_3CH_2CH_2CH_2CH_2CH_2CH_2CH_2CH_2CH_2CH_2CH_2CH_2CH_2CH_2COOH \quad \text{(Palmitic acid) (16 carbon atoms)}$$

Saturated Fatty Acids

Oleic acid contains one double bond. Linoleic, linolenic, and arachidonic acids contain, two, three, and four double bonds, respectively. Fatty acids with more than one double bond are often called *polyunsaturated.*

$$CH_3CH_2CH_2CH_2CH_2CH_2CH_2CH_2CH{=}CHCH_2CH_2CH_2CH_2CH_2CH_2CH_2COOH \quad \text{(Oleic acid) (18 carbon atoms)}$$

$$CH_3CH_2CH_2CH_2CH_2CH{=}CHCH_2CH{=}CHCH_2CH_2CH_2CH_2CH_2CH_2COOH \quad \text{(Linoleic acid) (18 carbon atoms)}$$

Unsaturated Fatty Acids

Good food sources of linoleic acid include seed oils from corn, cottonseeds, and soybeans (50 to 53 percent linoleic acid), and special margarines and peanut oil (20 to 30 percent). Corn oil contains more than six times as much linoleic acid as olive oil, and chicken fat contains up to ten times as much as the fat of ruminant animals such as cattle. The fat from an avocado is about 10 percent linoleate.

The body is not able to make linoleic acid with its two double bonds. Linoleic acid is, therefore, considered to be an essential fatty acid for both infants and adults since it must be obtained in the diet. Skin lesions and poor growth have been reported in infants receiving a diet limited in fat, and these symptoms disappeared after adding a source of linoleic acid to the diet. It has been suggested by the Food and Nutrition Board of the National Research Council— National Academy of Sciences that a linoleic acid intake equivalent to 2 percent of the total dietary kilocalories for adults and 3 percent for infants is probably satisfactory to avoid any deficiency. The average American diet apparently meets this recommendation.

A great deal of research has been reported on the roles of dietary fats in the production and control of coronary heart disease. Although undoubtedly many factors are involved and the final answers are not known, it appears that diets that are relatively low in total fat as well as diets containing a high proportion of vegetable fat, rich in polyunsaturated fatty acids, lower the level of cholesterol in the blood of many individuals who have an elevated level. Saturated fats tend to produce an elevation of blood cholesterol. A substantially elevated blood cholesterol level appears to be one factor that is associated with a high incidence of coronary heart disease and is commonly listed as an important "risk factor" for this disease. However, several other risk factors are associated with the development of coronary heart disease and the precise role of dietary fat needs additional clarification.

Foods high in fat include the following: (See also Table 14-1).

Butter	Margarine	Cheese
Cream	Hydrogenated shortening	Nuts
Lard	Deep-fat fried foods	Fat meats
Oils	Chocolate	

Fats play several important roles in food preparation. They are important tenderizing agents in baked products. Oils are major components of salad dressings and mayonnaise. Fats may be heated to high temperatures and act as a medium of heat transfer in the frying of foods. High fat products such as butter and margarine are used as table spreads. The properties and processing of fats are discussed in Chapter 14, Fats and Emulsions.

Proteins

Proteins are unique because, in addition to containing the elements carbon, hydrogen, and oxygen, they also contain nitrogen. Sulfur is often present in proteins. Proteins are large molecules made up of small amino acid molecules joined together in a special linkage called a *peptide* linkage. These linkages produce long chains that then coil or bend into shapes that are characteristic for a particular protein. Some proteins are generally round or globular in shape whereas others are long and fibrous.

Approximately twenty amino acids are commonly included in the structure of proteins. All of these amino acids have an amino group

$(-NH_2)$ and an acid group $(-\overset{\overset{\displaystyle O}{\|}}{C}-OH)$. The remainder of the molecule differs specifically for each amino acid. A general formula for amino acids is written as follows, with the R representing a side chain of variable structure.

$$
\begin{array}{c}
O \\
\| \\
C-OH \\
| \\
H_2N-C-H \\
| \\
R
\end{array}
$$

The side chains or R groups on a protein give it its particular characteristics. Some of them have short carbon chains, some contain sulfur, some have additional amino or acid groups, and some have a cyclic structure. A few of the side chain structures are shown in Table 4-3.

Amino acids are joined together through the amino and acid groups to form protein molecules. The following hypothetical protein molecule shows several amino acids joined together by peptide linkage.

$$H_2N-CH-CO-NH-CH-CO-NH-CH-CO-(NH-CH-CO)_n-NH-CH-COOH$$

CH_2	CH_3	$(CH_2)_4$	R	CH_2
C_6H_5		NH_2		OH
Phenylalanine	Alanine	Lysine		Serine

Eight amino acids are called nutritionally essential for tissue maintenance in the adult human, in the sense that the diet must furnish them in suitable amounts. These essential amino acids are isoleucine, leucine, lysine, methionine, phenylalanine, threonine, tryptophan, and valine. Two additional amino acids, histidine and arginine, were found to be essential for the growth of rats. From early studies, histidine did not appear to be necessary for the maintenance of nitrogen balance in adult humans, but some later research suggested that it is an essential amino acid for this group. Histidine has been shown to be essential in the diet of infants. Arginine can be made in the human body but there is still some controversy as to whether or not it can be made rapidly enough under all conditions. The other amino acids, called nonessential, may be synthesized in the body if sources of nitrogen are available.

The balance of essential amino acids in a protein will determine

Table 4-3 *Side Chain (R) Groups for Selected Amino Acids*

Amino Acid	Structure for Side Chain (R Group)
Glycine	—H
Alanine	$-CH_3$
Serine	$-CH_2OH$
Cysteine	$-CH_2-SH$
Glutamic acid	$-CH_2-CH_2-\overset{\displaystyle O}{\overset{\|}{C}}-OH$
Lysine	$-CH_2-CH_2-CH_2-CH_2-NH_2$
Methionine	$-CH_2-CH_2-S-CH_3$
Tyrosine	$-CH_2-CH\underset{CH=CH}{\overset{CH-CH}{\diagup\diagdown}}C-OH$

the biological value of that protein. Proteins of high biological value contain adequate amounts of the essential amino acids to promote the normal growth of animals, whereas those of low biological value do not. Because the amino acid requirement for growth is more rigid than that for the maintenance of tissues, some proteins that are inadequate for growth may function satisfactorily for maintenance or repair. Specific examples of proteins of high biological value are those found in milk, cheese, eggs, meat, and fish. Vegetable sources of protein are often lacking to some degree in one or more of the essential amino acids and have a lower score for biological value. In addition, the total amount of protein compared to the total calories found in certain vegetable products, such as cereal grains, is relatively low. Table 4-4 lists several food proteins along with their source and biological value.

The world's supply of protein is more limited than is the world's supply of calories. Protein malnutrition, especially in young children, is found in many parts of the world, and is more prevalent in those areas where plant foods of relatively low protein content, such as rice and cassava root, make up the major part of the diet. The supplementary value of proteins is of importance on a practical basis. Cereals are more valuable in the diet if they are combined with even a small amount of milk, which furnishes amino acids that cereals lack. Cereals are also supplemented by legumes; for example, the peanut butter sandwich contains a better protein mixture than each component alone.

Table 4-4 *Sources and Qualitative Values of Some Common Proteins*

Protein	Source	Biological Value
Casein	Milk or cheese	High
Lactalbumin	Milk or cheese	High
Ovovitellin	Egg yolk	High
Ovalbumin	Egg white	High
Myosin	Lean meat	High
Gelatin	Formed by hydrolysis from certain animal tissues	Low
Gliadin	Wheat	Low
Glutenin	Wheat	High
Hordein	Barley	Low
Prolamin	Rye	Low
Glutelin	Corn	High
Zein	Corn	Low
Glycinin	Soybean	High
Legumelin	Soybean	Low
Legumin	Peas and beans	Low
Phaseolin	Navy beans	Low
Excelsin	Brazil nut	High

Protein is present in many foods in varying amounts. It is an essential substance for living cells and, therefore, both plant and animal tissues contain protein. Foods that are relatively high in protein include meats, fish, poultry, eggs, cheese, milk, nuts, and dry legumes. Even after dry legumes are rehydrated and cooked, they may make an excellent contribution to dietary protein requirements. Cereal grains contain lesser amounts of protein; however, in the quantities of cereal grains that are often consumed, they make an important contribution to protein needs.

Amino groups act as bases or alkalis whereas carboxyl groups act as acids. Since both of these groups are present on the same amino acid or protein structure, amino acids and proteins may act as either acids or bases, and are said to be *amphoteric*. This is an important characteristic for many aspects of food preparation where the degree of acidity or alkalinity affects the quality of a food product. Proteins may combine with either acid or base within a limited range and resist any change in acidity. Because of this characteristic, they are called *buffers*.

Denaturation of Protein. Protein molecules undergo changes in their structures when they are subjected to various conditions of food preparation and processing. If the protein molecule unfolds to some degree yet still retains all of the peptide linkages between the amino acids that make up the molecule, it is said to be *denatured*. The process of denaturation is illustrated in Figure 4-2. Some of the properties of the protein change when it is denatured. For example, the denatured protein usually becomes less soluble. The degree of denaturation may be limited or it may be extensive. If the conditions causing denaturation persist, additional changes may occur in the protein. The unfolded parts of the molecule recombine in different ways to produce a new molecular shape and protein molecules may bond together to form a continuous network. The term *coagulation* has been used to describe some of the later stages of protein denaturation in which denatured protein molecules bind together and produce a gel or a solid mass. The coagulation of egg white upon heating is an example of this process.

Since heat denatures proteins, cooking produces these types of changes in food proteins. An example is the roasting of meat, which denatures the meat proteins. Proteins may also be denatured by

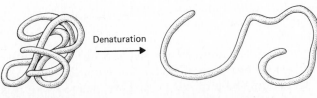

Native State   Denatured State

4-2 *Denaturation of a protein involves an unfolding of the molecule.*

mechanical beating. As an example, when egg whites are whipped to produce a foam, denaturation and coagulation of the egg white proteins occur. Changing the degree of acidity, changing the concentration of mineral salts, and freezing may also cause denaturation.

Enzymes in Foods. Enzymes, which are protein molecules with a special function, are produced by living cells and act as catalysts. A *catalyst* is a substance that increases the rate of a chemical reaction without being itself used up in the reaction. Enzymes catalyze a wide range of reactions in living matter, from the digestion of foods in the digestive tract of animals to most of the complex processes occurring in plant and animal metabolism. Enzymes and enzymatic action in foods are mentioned frequently throughout the text.

Enzymes may be classified into groups according to the type of reaction they catalyze. For example, some enzymes catalyze hydrolysis reactions (*hydrolytic enzymes*) and some catalyze oxidation-reduction reactions. Hydrolysis is a chemical reaction that involves breaking or cleaving a chemical bond within a molecule. Water plays an essential role in this reaction and the hydrogen and oxygen atoms of water are added to the two new molecules formed. Within the classification of hydrolytic enzymes, some are designated *proteases,* or *proteinases,* because they hydrolyze or digest proteins; they are designated *lipases* when they hydrolyze fats, and *amylases* when they act upon starch. *Sucrase* breaks down sucrose into two simpler sugars. Some enzymes that catalyze oxidation-reduction reactions are commonly called *oxidases* or *dehydrogenases.*

Some hydrolytic enzymes occur in plant tissues and have importance in food preparation. For example, the enzyme bromelin, which occurs in pineapple, is a protease and causes gelatin (a protein product) to liquefy if fresh or frozen uncooked pineapple is added to gelatin. It is necessary to destroy bromelin by heating the pineapple before adding it to a gelatin mixture if the gelatin is to set. Bromelin has been used as a meat tenderizer because of its proteolytic action. Papain, which is obtained from the papaya plant, also acts upon proteins to hydrolyze them. It forms the basis of some tenderizing compounds applied to less tender meats. Enzymes used as meat tenderizers do not penetrate very far into the meat and may tenderize only on the surface. Certain oxidases in plant tissues are involved in the darkening of cut or bruised surfaces of many fresh fruits and vegetables.

Enzyme activity may be destroyed by heating because the enzymes are proteins and are denatured or coagulated at high temperatures. Blanching vegetables before freezing helps control enzyme activity. There are optimum conditions of acidity and temperature for the reactions of enzymes in foods. Changing these conditions by various degrees may help to control enzyme action when this is desirable.

Minerals

Carbon, hydrogen, oxygen, and nitrogen make up about 96 percent of the human body composition. The remaining 4 percent is composed of mineral elements or inorganic nutrients. Minerals are needed in the body for hard tissues, such as bones and teeth, and also for soft tissues and body fluids. Not all minerals that have been found in the body are known to be essential, but many have been definitely shown to be necessary. Minerals may act as building materials in both hard and soft tissues of the body and also as body regulators.

Calcium and phosphorus are fundamental to the building of strong healthy bones and teeth and also have other important functions in the body. Calcium is necessary for the normal contractility of muscles and the clotting of blood. Magnesium is an activator for a number of enzymes that work in the body. Potassium is found in constant amounts in lean body tissue and is important in muscle contraction. Sodium is an important element in the regulation of body water and acid-base balance. Chlorine has a special function in forming hydrochloric acid in the stomach. Phosphorus plays a vital role as a component of high energy compounds in body metabolism and is an important building element in nervous tissue. Without the necessary concentration of minerals in the body fluids the heart does not beat normally, muscles and nerves do not perform their important functions, and numerous other growth and regulatory processes are impaired.

A number of essential minerals are classified as trace elements because they are necessary in very small amounts. Iron, zinc, and manganese are required in milligram quantities. Other trace elements are needed in microgram amounts. Essential trace elements for higher animals include, in addition to iron, zinc, and manganese, iodine, fluorine, copper, cobalt, chromium, selenium, nickel, molybdenum, tin, vanadium, and silicon. Various roles are played by the essential trace elements in the body. More research is needed to clarify many of these roles although some are being intensively studied in humans. Without iron, not enough hemoglobin can be synthesized and one type of anemia develops. Without copper, iron is not properly utilized for the building of hemoglobin. Without iodine, the thyroid gland cannot produce thyroxine and function normally. Without zinc, wounds do not heal normally. Without chromium, the body's mechanisms for regulating blood glucose levels do not seem to operate properly.

Cobalt is a necessary element in vitamin B_{12}. Zinc is part of the hormone insulin, which is important in carbohydrate metabolism, and also plays an important role in certain enzyme reactions. Fluorine (in the form of fluoride) presents a problem because it is very

Table 4-5 *Important Sources of Calcium, Phosphorus, and Iron*

Calcium	Phosphorus	Iron
Milk	Meat, fish, and poultry	Lean meats
Cheese	Milk	Liver
Green leaves*	Cheese	Kidney
Carrots	Dried legumes	Egg yolk
Molasses	Whole-grain cereals	Dried legumes
	Eggs	Green leaves
		Other green-colored vegetables
		Molasses
		Whole-grain cereals
		Enriched white cereals

* Except beet greens, spinach, and chard.

unevenly distributed in nature. The natural waters of some areas contain enough fluoride to cause serious mottling of the enamel of the teeth. There is evidence, however, that smaller concentrations of fluoride are beneficial to sound tooth structure, and the fluoridation of fluoride-deficient water supplies has been rather widely adopted as a public health measure.

Iodine is probably supplied in adequate amounts by foods produced in nongoitrous regions where sufficient iodine is present in the soil. In goitrous regions, however, iodized salt should be used to prevent simple goiter. Seafoods are a dependable dietary source of iodine. Sodium and chlorine are not likely to be lacking in the diet because of the amount of common salt that is usually consumed. The consumption of calcium may be low unless foods are carefully chosen to include it.

Table 4-5 shows some common foods that are dependable sources of calcium, phosphorus, and iron. Without milk or milk products in suitable amounts, it is difficult to get sufficient calcium to meet the Recommended Dietary Allowance. Good vegetable and fruit sources of calcium are few and are often not eaten in sufficient quantity to provide the calcium needed.

Potassium, magnesium, and copper, along with several other minerals, are thought to be provided in a dietary that includes ample amounts of the minerals listed in Table 4-5 from the food sources shown there. Sulfur is closely related to protein intake, and the body's requirement for sulfur is thought to be met if the protein intake is adequate.

Vitamins

Vitamins are organic chemical compounds that are required in the diet in only very small amounts but are vital for normal growth and health. The early differentiation of vitamins was by letters of the alphabet, but as chemical identification has become clear, the tendency is to use the chemical name instead.

Vitamins are primarily regulatory substances. As a group they promote growth and the maintenance of health and vigor. They bring about these effects usually by their roles as catalysts in chemical reactions throughout the body. This helps to explain why vitamins are needed in such very small amounts and yet are vital to life. If they are lacking completely or are very deficient in the diet, definite dietary-deficiency diseases result. Less pronounced deficiencies may cause vague and less easily recognized conditions that may be responsible for a lack of optimum growth, health, and vigor. Many vitamins are available in concentrated forms, but for a normal, healthy individual a variety of foods remains the recommended source of vitamins. With the very concentrated vitamin capsules available it is possible to get too much of certain fat soluble vitamins, such as vitamins A and D, which results in toxic effects in the body.

Vitamin A. Vitamin A is an alcohol that can be formed in the bodies of animals from yellow and orange pigments, known as *carotenes* and *xanthophylls,* which are found in plants. The vitamin A value of foods includes the vitamin as such plus any pigments that are precursors of the vitamin. Plants contain the precursors rather than the preformed vitamin. In animal foods such as whole milk and butterfat both substances may be present. In plant tissues, the intensity of yellow or green color indicates the presence of carotenes and, therefore, the vitamin A value. In green-colored vegetables carotenes are always present although chlorophyll (green pigment) may mask their presence. Vitamin A and carotenes are fat soluble, and hence are not dissolved in cooking waters to any appreciable degree. In most cooking processes they are relatively stable but may be destroyed by oxidation in the presence of air. Vitamin A is important in human nutrition for the maintenance of sound epithelial tissues which aid in resistance to infection; for the synthesis of visual purple, the pigment that is deficient in night blindness, and the maintenance of normal vision; for growth; and for normal tooth development. Vitamin A is stored in the body so that symptoms from its deficiency usually develop rather slowly. Important animal sources of vitamin A are liver, butterfat, and egg yolk. It is usually added to margarine. Important plant sources of vitamin A value are the deep green and yellow vegetables.

Vitamin D. Vitamin D is necessary for the normal calcification of bones and teeth. It is essential for calcium absorption and utilization. Severe deficiency of this vitamin results in the disease *rickets* in infants and children. The vitamin is fat soluble and is little affected by ordinary food processing. Few foods are significant sources of the vitamin; however, certain sterols (fatlike substances) in the skin may be changed into active vitamin D by exposure to ultraviolet light. Hence, this vitamin has been called the *"sunshine vitamin."* Milk is usually fortified with Vitamin D.

Vitamin E. Vitamin E refers to a group of compounds called tocopherols. It is fat soluble and is required for normal reproduction in rats and for the prevention of muscular dystrophy in several animals. All of the functions of vitamin E in the human body have not been fully determined. Humans do require the vitamin for the prevention of certain blood disorders. Vitamin E appears to act in the body as an antioxidant, controlling unwanted oxidation in the cells. It also acts as an antioxidant in foods such as vegetable oils where it is naturally present. Whole grains are a source of vitamin E.

B Complex Vitamins. Thiamin (vitamin B_1) belongs to the water-soluble vitamin B complex. It is widely distributed in both plant and animal foods but often in low concentration. Fresh fruits, vegetables, and milk, although not rich sources of thiamin, may contribute important amounts if eaten in the quantities recommended for good nutrition. Enriched and whole grains, organ meats, pork, legumes, eggs, and nuts are important sources of thiamin in the diet. Because thiamin is water soluble it tends to be dissolved in cooking waters. It also tends to be destroyed in an alkaline medium. The longer the time of heating and the greater the alkalinity, the greater is the extent of inactivation. Nutritionally, thiamin prevents or cures *beriberi*, a multiple neuritis. It is essential for maintaining healthy nerve tissue, helps keep a normal appetite, and aids digestive functions, including good muscle tone and motility in the digestive tract. As with most members of the B complex group, thiamin plays an important role as part of a coenzyme in cell metabolism. It is essential for the utilization of carbohydrates for energy in the body.

Riboflavin (vitamin B_2) is a greenish-yellow, fluorescent, somewhat water-soluble vitamin of the B complex. Its stability is greatly affected by light, but it is much more resistant to destruction by heat than is thiamin. It may be destroyed by being heated in an alkaline solution, however. Riboflavin is widely distributed in plant and animal tissue. Because it is formed in the leaves of plants, green leafy vegetables are a good source of the vitamin. Seeds are rather low in riboflavin. Milk, when consumed in the recommended amounts, supplies a substantial part of the daily riboflavin allowance. Other important food sources are eggs, enriched and whole grain cereals, lean meat, and cheese. Riboflavin is part of several coenzymes that are active in energy metabolism in living cells, so it is essential for general health at all ages. It is necessary for growth and reproduction. A deficiency of riboflavin may result in *cheilosis* (fissures and cracks in the angles of the mouth), in skin lesions, and in burning and sensitivity of the eyes. Deficiency symptoms in man have been found to be less specific than in many animals.

Niacin is also a member of the B complex and is water soluble but very resistant to heat and oxidation. Little is lost in cooking unless the cooking water is discarded. It was discovered in 1937 that niacin prevents or cures *pellagra,* a disease characterized by a severe skin rash, diarrhea, and nervous disorders. The amino acid tryptophan is a precursor of niacin because the body can change it into niacin. Recommended dietary allowances for niacin are expressed in terms of niacin equivalents, which include tryptophan. Animal protein foods of high biological value (that is, those that contain adequate amounts of essential amino acids) contain tryptophan. Lean meat, fish, and poultry are good sources of both niacin and tryptophan. Enriched or whole grains, legumes, and nuts are also important sources of niacin. Niacin is part of a coenzyme that plays an essential role in oxidation-reduction reactions of living cells.

Other B complex vitamins include vitamin B_6 (pyridoxine), pantothenic acid, folacin, and vitamin B_{12} (cobalamin). Vitamin B_6 is important in a number of enzyme systems in the body. Pantothenic acid is part of coenzyme A, a most important substance in body metabolism. Lack of folacin in man results in gastrointestinal disturbances and a macrocytic anemia, an anemia characterized by the presence of many large immature red blood cells. Vitamin B_{12} is effective in the treatment of pernicious anemia.

Ascorbic Acid. Ascorbic acid (vitamin C) is a water-soluble vitamin that is easily destroyed in aqueous solutions exposed to heat in the presence of air and alkali. It is the most unstable of the known vitamins and the most easily lost in cooking. Important sources of this vitamin include citrus fruits, cantaloupes, strawberries, tomatoes, green peppers, and raw cabbage. Nutritionally it is necessary for the prevention of *scurvy,* a disease affecting many tissues. Ascorbic acid is necessary for the proper formation of collagen in the body, a protein important in the formation of bone, skin, and supportive tissues. This vitamin plays a role in producing substances that cement body cells together and promotes normal healing of wounds or injured tissues. It also functions in some way to protect the body against infections and bacterial toxins. Table 4-6 summarizes functions and major food sources of vitamins.

The Relation of Food to Health

Good health is a major factor in our happiness and our ability to work productively. The science of nutrition has uncovered many proofs that food is a vital tool in building strong bodies and promoting good health. Modern nutrition is a part of preventive medicine.

Table 4-6 *Important Functions and Food Sources of Vitamins*

Vitamin	Major Functions	Good Food Sources
Vitamin A	Maintenance of epithelial tissues Synthesis of visual purple for seeing in the dark Promotion of normal growth, especially bones	Butter Whole milk Cream Egg yolk Green leaves Other green vegetables Apricots Yellow vegetables Tomato Liver Cod, halibut, and other fish-liver oils
Vitamin D	Control of absorption and utilization of calcium for bones and teeth Prevention of rickets	Cod and other fish-liver oils Body oils of certain fish Egg yolk Vitamin-D-fortified milk
Vitamin E	Control of unwanted oxidations Prevention of certain anemias	Vegetable oils Whole grains Wheat germ Walnuts
Thiamin	Maintenance of nerve tissue Maintenance of normal appetite and muscle tone in digestive tract Prevention of beriberi Utilization of carbohydrate as part of coenzyme in cell metabolism	Pork Liver Kidney Heart Lean meats Whole-grain products Enriched white cereals Wheat germ Bran, prepared Dried yeast Legumes Nuts Egg yolk Chard Spinach
Riboflavin	Utilization of energy foods as component of coenzyme in metabolism	Milk Egg Liver Green leaves Lean meat Kidney Enriched white cereals Legumes Buds (broccoli) Dark meat of poultry Whole grains

Table 4-6 *Important Functions and Food Sources of Vitamins (continued)*

Vitamin	Major Functions	Good Food Sources
Niacin	Normal cell metabolism by acting as part of coenzyme	Liver Chicken breast Lean meats Kidney Fish Dried yeast Enriched white cereals Peanuts Whole grains
Ascorbic Acid	Formation of collagen for structural integrity of bones, teeth, and skin Promotion of normal wound healing Control of intercellular cementing of capillary walls to prevent hemorrhaging Provision for increased need of this vitamin in fevers and infections	Citrus fruits Tomatoes (fresh or canned) Raw cabbage Strawberries Peas Raw green leaves Broccoli Green and Red peppers Potato Cantaloupe

Individuals who are in a state of good nutrition are well fortified to resist infection, can look forward to a long life span, and show such signs of proper nourishment as vitality, abundant energy, and buoyant spirits.

The United States produces an abundance of good food that is generally available to most of its citizens. Although a large proportion of our population would seem to be fairly adequately nourished, there is still much room for improvement in food habits. The degenerative diseases of middle and later life may well be related to dietary habits that have developed from childhood. Overnutrition, or obesity, is a form of malnutrition that is associated with an increased incidence of various chronic diseases.

Food is, of course, only one of the factors affecting growth and health. We know that lasting good health is impossible without good nutrition, but we also know that not all well-fed persons are healthy. Many other factors, such as heredity, various disease conditions, environmental stress, general habits of living, rest and recreation, emotional problems, and exposure to infections, play a part in the maintenance of normal health and may sometimes counterbalance the effects of a good diet. As discussed in Chapter 1, food has many meanings in addition to its role in sustaining life and nourishing the body. But finally, all of the roles of food are channeled into its major purpose of providing for life and health.

In recent years there has been a renewed interest in nutrition and

4-3 *Good nutrition and proper exercise contribute to the building of strong, healthy bodies.* (Photographs by Roger P. Smith)

nutrition education among some consumers and consumer groups in the United States, as well as among food and nutrition professionals. The use of nutrition labeling on food products is one indication of this interest. Studies on marketing influences would seem to indicate that food advertising on television has a marked influence on the buying practices of families. An interest in "health, organic, and natural foods" is part of the renewed interest in nutrition among consumers. Congressional hearings have been held on these subjects in an effort to define some of the terms and investigate the feasibility of developing regulations that would ensure consumer protection in marketing. There is much controversy about "health" foods among consumers. Certainly many palatable and nutritious dishes may be prepared with foods purchased at either health food stores or supermarkets providing that proper choices are made. A well-balanced nutritious diet may be secured by many different combinations of foods that satisfy the desires of many different individuals.

Guides to Meeting Nutrient Needs

The Food and Nutrition Board of the National Research Council, National Academy of Sciences periodically publishes recommended dietary allowances for many nutrients [5]. Their publication also includes estimated safe and adequate daily dietary intakes of some vitamins and minerals for which less research information is available. The recommended allowances are set for healthy persons living in the United States and include a margin of safety to cover the widely varying individual needs of members of the population. These standards serve as a goal for good nutrition and are most effectively applied in evaluating the dietary intake of population groups.

Since food is our source of nutrients, nutritionists often start with foods when they teach people about nutrition. Foods have been grouped together on the basis of the major nutrients that they supply. Nutrients do not work alone but are interrelated in many processes involved in nourishing the body. Various foods, both within and between food groups, supplement each other in providing all of the necessary nutrients. Foods that are mixtures, such as stews, soups, casserole dishes, and certain bakery products, fit into food groups on the basis of the basic ingredients they contain.

Food groupings and patterns of eating that provide an adequate diet will vary in many parts of the world. However, there are basic similarities among the common food groupings used in many nations of the world. Most groupings will include vegetables and fruits; cereals and breads or foods high in energy nutrients such as starch; and foods high in protein such as meat, fish, poultry, eggs, cheese, dry beans and peas, lentils, and nuts. In the United States, a daily food guide has been presented through the U.S. Department of Agriculture and has been adapted by various groups concerned with nutrition education [4, 7]. The food groups and recommended amounts in this daily guide are as follows:

1. Milk group: some milk for everyone
   Children under 9 . . . . .2 to 3 cups
   Children 9 to 12 . . . . .3 or more cups
   Teenagers. . . . . .4 or more cups
   Adults. . . . . .2 or more cups
2. Meat or Alternates group: 2 or more servings
   Beef, veal, pork, lamb, poultry, fish, eggs
   As alternates, use dry beans, dry peas, nuts
3. Vegetable-Fruit group: 4 or more servings, including:
   A citrus fruit or other fruit or vegetable important for vitamin C
   A dark-green or deep-yellow vegetable for vitamin A at least every other day
   Other vegetables and fruits, including potatoes
4. Bread-Cereal group: 4 or more servings
   Whole grain, enriched, or restored
5. Plus other foods as needed to complete meals and to provide additional food energy and other food values.

Figure 4-4 illustrates the four food groups as adapted by the National Dairy Council. The milk group is our major source of calcium. It also provides high quality protein, riboflavin, phosphorus, and

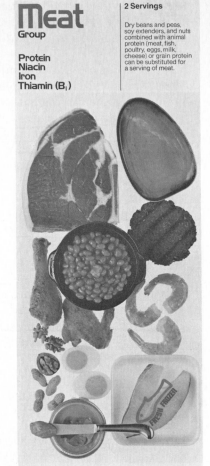

4-4 *A guide for use in choosing an adequate diet.* (Courtesy of National Dairy Council)

vitamin A (carried by the butterfat). The meat or meat alternates group supplies high quality protein, iron, phosphorus, thiamin, riboflavin, niacin, other B vitamins, and trace minerals. Vegetables and fruits contribute many vitamins and minerals. The food guide emphasizes vegetables and fruits that are valuable sources of ascorbic acid (vitamin C) and vitamin A. This food group also provides fiber that promotes motility and health of the digestive tract. The bread and cereal group furnishes worthwhile amounts of protein, iron, several of the B vitamins, and carbohydrates for energy. Suggested choices from these food groups should supply a normal healthy indi-

Fruit-Vegetable

Group

Vitamins A and C

Dark green, leafy, or orange vegetables and fruit are recommended 3 or 4 times weekly for vitamin A. Citrus fruit is recommended daily for vitamin C.

4 Servings

Grain

Group

4 Servings

Whole grain, fortified, or enriched grain products are recommended.

Carbohydrate
Thiamin (B₁)
Iron
Niacin

Foods and condiments such as these complement but do not replace foods from the four groups.

Amounts should be determined by individual caloric needs.

Others

Carbohydrate
Fats

---

vidual with most of the recommended daily allowances of essential nutrients except calories. Additional amounts of the four groups, supplemented with other foods such as fats and oils, can make up the needed calories while supplying additional vitamins and minerals as well. Empty calories, food contributing calories only, should be used in only limited quantities in most dietaries.

Good food adds to the joy of living, by both its contribution to buoyant health and the pleasure of eating. Food, appropriately prepared, looks good and tastes good and is good for us. With the development of a greater variety of manufactured and convenience foods and their availability to the consumer, it is important that both the food scientist and consumer carefully consider the nutritional adequacy of the consumer's usual diet patterns.

Study Questions

1. The chemical composition of food may be determined in the laboratory. List the major components and the minor components that are present in foods.
2. a. What are nutrients? List six groups of essential nutrients.
   b. What is a food?
3. Describe three important functions of water:
   a. In food preparation
   b. In body processes
4. a. What are carbohydrates?
   b. In the following list of carbohydrates, indicate which are monosaccharides, which are disaccharides, and which are polysaccharides:

   (1) Starch   (6) Fructose (levulose)
   (2) Glucose (dextrose)   (7) Galactose
   (3) Lactose   (8) Dextrins
   (4) Cellulose   (9) Glycogen
   (5) Maltose   (10) Sucrose

   c. Identify the monosaccharide building blocks for each of the disaccharides and polysaccharides listed in question b.
   d. Give several examples of vegetable gums and describe some of their uses in food processing.
5. a. Describe in words the chemical structure of a triglyceride.
   b. Distinguish among saturated, unsaturated, and polyunsaturated fatty acids.
   c. For each of the fatty acids listed below, indicate if it is saturated, monounsaturated, or polyunsaturated:

   (1) Palmitic acid
   (2) Linoleic acid
   (3) Butyric acid
   (4) Stearic acid
   (5) Oleic acid

   d. Name the fatty acid that is essential for both infants and adults and must be supplied in the diet.
   e. In the list of foods given below, check those that are rich sources of fat:

Whipped cream	Lard	Pork spareribs
Spinach	Walnuts	Potato chips
Pinto beans	Cheddar cheese	Shortening
Corn tortillas	Chocolate	White bread
Margarine	Corn oil	Apples

6. a. What chemical groups characterize amino acids?

b. How are amino acids joined to make proteins?

c. What is meant by the "side chains" or "R" groups of a protein? Explain why proteins may act as buffers in foods.

d. What is an essential amino acid and how many amino acids are so designated for the human adult?

e. From the following list of amino acids, identify those that are nutritionally essential:

Methionine	Cystine	Alanine
Isoleucine	Serine	Phenylalanine
Leucine	Tyrosine	Glycine
Lysine	Glutamic acid	Valine
Threonine	Tryptophan	

f. Explain the meaning of biological value in relation to proteins. Why do some protein foods, such as eggs and milk, have high biological value while others, such as kidney beans and wheat flour, have lower biological value?

g. How can proteins supplement each other to improve the net nutritional value? Explain this.

7. Describe what probably happens when a protein is denatured and list at least four treatments, likely to be applied to foods, that can cause protein denaturation.

8. Explain what probably happens when proteins are coagulated and describe some examples from foods of coagulation.

9. What are enzymes? Explain why they are of importance in:

a. Body metabolism

b. Food processing and preparation

10. For each of the following minerals and vitamins, describe the major functions in the body and list significant food sources:

a. Calcium

b. Phosphorus

c. Iron

d. Vitamin A

e. Vitamin D

f. Thiamin

g. Riboflavin

h. Niacin

i. Ascorbic acid (vitamin C)

11. Foods have been divided into various groups to produce a daily guide for good eating.

a. Explain why food groups are commonly used to teach people about good nutrition.

b. Describe the food groups presented by the U.S. Department of Agriculture, including suggested amounts in each group.

c. Indicate the major nutrients supplied by each of the food groups described in question b.

References

1. Briggs, G. M. and D. H. Calloway. *Bogert's Nutrition and Physical Fitness,* 10th ed. Philadelphia: W. B. Saunders Co., 1984.
2. Clydesdale, F. M. and F. J. Francis. *Food, Nutrition, and You.* Englewood Cliffs, NJ: Prentice-Hall, Inc., 1977.
3. *Conserving the Nutritive Values in Foods.* Home and Garden Bulletin No. 90. Washington, DC: U.S. Department of Agriculture, 1980.
4. *Food.* Home and Garden Bulletin No. 228. Washington, DC: U.S. Department of Agriculture, 1979.
5. Food and Nutrition Board. *Recommended Dietary Allowances,* 9th ed. Washington, DC: National Academy of Sciences—National Research Council, 1980.
6. Hamilton, E. M. N. and E. N. Whitney. *Nutrition Concepts and Controversies.* St. Paul, MN: West Publishing Co., 1982.
7. *Nutrition. Food at Work for You.* Reprinted from Home and Garden Bulletin No. 1, Family Fare, Separate 1. Washington, DC: U.S. Department of Agriculture, 1978.

Weights and Measures

Correct proportions of ingredients contribute to success in the preparation of a number of food products. These proportions are best achieved when the measuring or weighing of each individual ingredient in a recipe is done accurately and consistently. In the United States, recipes generally call for volume measurements whereas in other countries ingredients may be more commonly weighed than measured. A change in the United States from the English system of weights and measures to the metric system has been recommended. Use of the metric system will affect food preparation generally by encouraging the weighing in grams or kilograms of solid ingredients and the measuring in milliliters of liquids [5].Weighing is usually more accurate than measuring, particularly when it involves ingredients, such as flour, that may pack down [4]. The volume of chopped foods, such as minced onions, will also vary depending upon the fineness and uniformity of chopping.

The Metric System

The metric system of weights and measurements was introduced to the world by France during the French revolution and is presently being used by most nations of the world to express length, mass, volume, and temperature. This system is based on multiples of ten. Various prefixes are combined with the basic unit of weight (gram), the basic unit of volume (liter), and the basic unit of length (meter) to indicate the designated amounts. Prefixes and symbols for weight, volume, and length are shown in Table 5-1.

Table 5-1 *The Metric System*

	Prefix	Weight	Symbol	Volume	Symbol	Length	Symbol
0.001	milli	milligram	mg	milliliter	ml	millimeter	mm
0.01	centi	centigram	cg	centiliter	cl	centimeter	cm
0.1	deci	decigram	dg	deciliter	dl	decimeter	dm
1.0		gram	g	liter	l	meter	m
10	deka	dekagram	dag	dekaliter	dal	dekameter	dam
100	hecto	hectogram	hg	hectoliter	hl	hectometer	hm
1000	kilo	kilogram	kg	kiloliter	kl	kilometer	km

A scale or balance is used to measure weight in grams. Metric scales may become a common item of food preparation equipment for the home. While the conversion from the English avoirdupois system of weights and measures to the metric system is taking place, both measurements will likely be used. Information on conversion of English to metric and vice versa is found in Appendix A.

Measuring Equipment

The standard measuring cup is of a half-pint or 8 fluid-ounce capacity. This is equal to approximately 237 milliliters. Subdivisions are marked on many cups for measuring ¼, ½, ¾, ⅓, and ⅔ cup. The majority of cups do not show smaller subdivisions (see Figure 5-1). Measuring cups often are marked with both milliliter and cup designations.

5-1 *Household measuring utensils include a glass cup for measuring liquids, fractional cup measures for measuring dry ingredients, and measuring spoons.*

Individual cups for fractional measurements as well as full-cup measurements are also available. The fractional cups, if standardized, permit more nearly accurate measurements of dry ingredients than can be obtained in the single cup with subdivisions.

Measuring spoons are commonly available in sets that measure 1 tablespoon, 1 teaspoon, ½ teaspoon, and ¼ teaspoon. One tablespoon measures 1/16 cup; there are 16 tablespoons in 1 cup. Three teaspoons are equal to 1 tablespoon.

The American Home Economics Association and the American Standards Association have published a set of standards and tolerances for household measuring utensils [2]. A deviation of 5 percent from the precise measure indicated on the measuring cup or spoon is allowed. Not all measuring utensils on the market meet the tolerance of 5 percent, however.

How to Measure Staple Foods

Even though accurate measuring equipment is available, measuring problems still exist. Inaccuracies may occur through the manner in which the equipment is used. Most recipes will allow small deviations in the amounts of ingredients used, which result from differences in measuring techniques, and acceptable products are still produced. However, the quality of some products, such as shortened cakes, may be adversely affected by different methods for measuring the flour [3]. Accurate and consistent measurement of ingredients is very important in producing uniform products of high quality time after time [1]. Some common measurements and symbols used in food preparation are found in Appendix A.

Flour

Flour should be sifted once before it is measured. Sifting should be done shortly before it is measured because sifted flour may tend to pack on standing. The quantity of flour sifted at one time should be fairly small so that it will not pack because of its own weight. Graham or whole wheat flours are usually not sifted before they are measured because the bran particles may be sifted out. Finely milled whole wheat flour may be sifted, however. Instantized flour, which contains agglomerated particles of quite uniform size, does not require sifting before being measured.

After the flour is sifted, it is lightly filled into the cup with a spoon until it is heaping full. The filled cup is then leveled with the straight edge of a knife. It is important not to shake or tap the cup while it is being filled, as either will cause packing of the flour.

Quantities of less than 1 cup should be measured in smaller fractional cups.

In measuring with a tablespoon or teaspoon, the spoon should be heaped full by dipping into the flour and then leveled with the straight edge of a knife. Half spoonfuls should be measured by cutting in half lengthwise and scraping out half. Quarter spoonfuls are measured by cutting a half spoonful crosswise into two portions as nearly equal as possible and scraping out half.

Liquid

In measuring liquid, a cup that extends above the largest measure mark should be used. The cup is placed on a flat surface and filled to the measure mark. The eye should be at the measure mark level when reading contents.

Fat

Solid fats should be removed from the refrigerator long enough before they are measured so that they will be plastic. Very hard fats are difficult to measure accurately except in the case of cubes of butter or margarine that have measurements marked on the wrapper. In this case they may be cut, as marked, with a sharp knife. For measuring in a cup, the plastic fat should be pressed into the cup so that the air spaces are forced out. The cup or fractional cup is then leveled with a straight edge. For measurements up to ¼ cup, level tablespoons may be used. As an alternative, a water displacement method may be used if the water that clings to the fat will not affect the product. Cold water is poured into a cup up to the measure that will equal 1 cup when added to the amount of fat to be measured. Enough fat is then added to bring the water up to 1 cup when the fat is completely submerged in the water. The water is then drained off.

Sugar

For measuring granulated sugar, the cup is filled as for flour. Sifting is omitted, however.

In measuring brown sugar, any lumps should first be rolled out before the sugar is pressed firmly into the cup. Measured in this way, 1 cup of brown sugar is approximately equal in weight to 1 cup of granulated sugar.

In measuring confectioners' or powdered sugar, sifting is followed by spooning the sugar into a cup as for flour. One cup of confectioners' sugar is slightly heavier than ½ cup of granulated sugar. About 1¾ cups of confectioners' sugar is equal in weight to 1 cup granulated sugar.

Syrup or Molasses

The cup or fractional cup should be placed upon a flat surface and filled completely full. Because of the thickness of the liquid, it may tend to round up higher than level full. It should be cut off level with the straight edge of a knife. Spoonfuls may be measured by pouring syrup into the spoon and cutting off level with the edge of a knife. Care should be taken to keep syrups, as well as fats, from sticking to the outside of the measuring cup or spoon.

A recipe is considered standardized only after it has been tried, evaluated for quality, and any necessary adaptations or adjustments have been made. The equipment, types of ingredients available, and skills of the person preparing the recipe differ from one situation to another. Therefore, each recipe must be adapted and standardized for use in a particular situation. Once a recipe has been standardized for a particular setting, it is useful in making out market orders and in calculating food costs. Recipes that are standardized for inclusion in cookbooks generally use the methods for measuring ingredients that have been outlined in the previous section of this chapter.

Standardization of Recipes

1. Discuss why accurate measurements are important in the preparation of quality food products.
2. What is one of the most basic differences between the metric and the English system of weights and measures? Name the basic unit of length, of volume, and of weight for the metric system.
3. What type of measuring cups should be used to measure liquids? What type should be used to measure dry ingredients?
4. How many tablespoons are there in 1 cup? How many teaspoons are there in 1 tablespoon?
5. Describe appropriate procedures for measuring flour, liquid, solid fat, sugar, and syrups.
6. What is a standardized recipe? What advantages are there to the use of standardized recipes?

Study Questions

References

1. American Home Economics Association. *Handbook of Food Preparation.* Washington, DC: American Home Economics Association, 1980.
2. American Standards Association. *American Standard Dimensions, Tolerances, and Terminology for Home Cooking and Baking Utensils.* New York: American Standards Association, Inc., 1963.
3. Arlin, M. L., M. M. Nielsen, and F. T. Hall. 1964. The effect of different methods of flour measurement on the quality of plain two-egg cakes. *Journal of Home Economics* **56,** 399.
4. Matthews, R. H., and O. M. Batcher. 1963. Sifted versus unsifted flour. *Journal of Home Economics* **55,** 123.
5. Miller, B. S., and H. B. Trimbo. 1972. Use of metric measurements in food preparation. *Journal of Home Economics* **64,** 20.

6

Heat Transfer and Use of Water in Cookery

Water plays several important roles in food preparation, affecting both the sensory characteristics of food [4] and the processes by which foods are cooked. Water is a unique molecule and often its unusual characteristics are taken for granted.

The Nature of Water

Water is a small molecule containing two hydrogen atoms and one oxygen atom (H_2O). However, the water molecule does not behave in the same manner as do most other molecules of the same size with regard to boiling point, freezing point, and vapor pressure. This is chiefly because of what is called its *polar* nature [2]. Although the hydrogen and oxygen atoms of water are joined together by strong bonds called *covalent bonds,* the positive and negative charges are not evenly distributed over the whole molecule. Figure 6-1 shows a representation of a water molecule with a negative (−) charge on the oxygen side and positive (+) charges on the hydrogen sides. The water molecule then has positive and negative poles and may be said to be dipolar. Since opposite charges attract each other, the negative part of one water molecule is attracted to the positive part of another water molecule, causing these molecules to cluster together as demonstrated in Figure 6-2. Because water molecules are attracted to each other, additional energy is necessary to separate

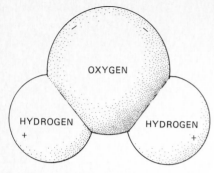

6-1 *The water molecule is called a dipolar molecule because part of it is positively charged and another part is negatively charged.*

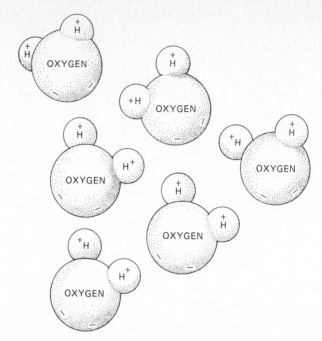

6-2 *Water molecules cluster together because the positive charge on one molecule is attracted to the negative charge on another molecule, forming a weak bond.*

them from each other and to change their state from liquid to gaseous molecules of water vapor. Therefore, the vapor pressure over the surface of liquid water is less and consequently the boiling point is higher than might be expected for such a small molecule. The boiling point of water is discussed in connection with boiling sugar solutions on pp. 363–364.

Uses of Water in Food Preparation

Water has been called a universal solvent, indicating that it can dissolve many different substances. It acts as a solvent or a dispersing medium for most of the chemical substances in foods. For example, many of the flavor molecules in beverages such as coffee and tea are dissolved in water; sugars are dissolved in fruit juices and in syrups; and starch granules may be dispersed in cold water and swell when heated in the making of gravies and starch-thickened puddings. Certain chemical changes are promoted by water, such as the reaction of baking powder when dry ingredients are moistened.

In cooking, water is an important medium for applying heat. It may be used for this purpose both in its liquid form as hot or boiling water and in its vapor form as steam. When water boils, the forces of attraction discussed above are overcome and the water molecules become gaseous. They leave the container in bubbles of steam. At sea level, the temperature of boiling water is 100° C (212° F). Making water boil very rapidly does not increase this temperature. Steam that is not under pressure has the same temperature as boiling water. However, a certain amount of energy, called *latent heat* or *heat of vaporization* is necessary to change the state of water from its liquid form to its vapor form as steam. This heat is absorbed by the steam but does not register on a thermometer. When steam condenses on a cooler surface and returns to its liquid form, the latent heat is released to the atmosphere.

Water also performs an important function as a cleansing agent both for food itself and for utensils and equipment used in the preparation and serving of food. It removes soil particles and many microorganisms as well. Cleaning agents, such as soaps and detergents, increase the cleaning capacity of water.

Water Hardness

Water may be soft or hard. Water is said to be hard when it contains various mineral salts. There are two general types of hard water. One is called *temporarily hard water* because the calcium, magnesium, and iron bicarbonates that it contains are precipitated as insoluble carbonates when the water is boiled. These mineral deposits may accumulate in kettles used over a long period of time primarily for boiling water. *Permanently hard water* contains calcium, magnesium, and iron sulfates that do not precipitate out on boiling. They form insoluble salts with soap and decrease its cleaning capacity. The mineral salts may also have various effects in food preparation. For example, calcium retards the softening and rehydration of dried beans and peas during soaking and cooking. Hard water is often fairly alkaline and may thus affect the color of some of the pigments in cooked vegetables. Water that is naturally soft contains very few mineral salts.

Hard water may be softened by several different processes. In one method, water-softening agents, such as washing soda and polyphosphates, may be added to water to precipitate the calcium and magnesium salts. Another method uses an ion exchange process in which calcium and magnesium ions are exchanged for sodium ions. A resinous material may be contained in a water-softening tank through which the hard water flows. Sodium ions held by the resin are exchanged for calcium and magnesium in the hard water until the resin has exhausted its sodium supply. At this point, the resin may be recharged with sodium by flushing it with a strong salt solution. Water softened in this manner is high in sodium.

Heat Transfer in Cooking

Heat is a form of energy in matter related to the rapid movement of molecules within the substance. This movement of molecules is called kinetic energy. Temperature is a measure of the intensity of the heat produced. Thermometers are often used to determine specific temperatures. Various thermometers used in cooking are described in Appendix B. All substances with a temperature greater than absolute zero possess some heat and heat is constantly being transferred from one substance to another. Heat tends to move from a warmer material to a cooler one.

Conventional cooking results when heat is transferred to foods. Heat energy may be transferred from its source to the food by (1) conduction, (2) radiation, and (3) convection currents [3]. In most cases of cooking, more than one method of transferring heat is involved. When microwaves are used for cooking, heat is generated in a different fashion than with conventional heating. Microwave cooking is discussed in Chapter 25, Microwave Cooking, p. 526.

Conduction

When heating occurs by conduction, heat is transmitted from one molecule or particle to the next one that is in direct contact with it. Heat moves from the heated coil of an electric unit to the saucepan that is placed on it and from the saucepan to the first layer of food or water that is in contact with the bottom and sides of the pan. Heat is then conducted throughout the mass of food. Fat, which can be heated to much higher temperatures than can water, may be used as a medium for conducting heat from the pan to the food in the frying process. Some materials are better conductors than others. Metals are generally good conductors, particularly copper and aluminum, although stainless steel does not conduct heat uniformly. Water is a better conductor than is air. Wood is a poor conductor of heat.

Radiation

Energy may be transmitted as waves or rays that travel very rapidly through space. These rays go directly from their source to the food without assistance from any material in between. When the radiant energy reaches the surface of the food it is absorbed and produces heat by increasing the vibration of the molecules in the food. This heat then travels to the center of the food mass by conduction as described above. The broiling of foods and the use of a toaster are examples of radiant heating. Radiant energy is also used in baking. Dark, dull pans readily absorb radiant energy while bright, shiny pans reflect it. Ovenproof glass dishes transmit radiant energy.

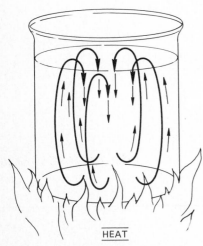

6-3 *When liquids and gases are heated they become lighter or less dense and rise, whereas cooler molecules of the liquid or gas move to the bottom of a container or closed compartment. These movements create convection currents that aid in distributing heat throughout the liquid or gas.*

Convection Currents

When gases and liquids are heated they become lighter or less dense and tend to rise. The colder portions of these gases and liquids are more dense and move to the bottom to replace the heated portions. Circular convection currents are thus set up, as illustrated in Figure 6-3. They move the molecules around in their enclosed space and tend to distribute the heat more uniformly throughout. Convection currents aid in cooking only when gases and liquids are involved. Examples where this is useful include cooking in a saucepan or other container where food particles are dispersed in water, such as soup; deep fat frying; and baking in an oven.

Thermometer Scales

Two thermometer scales may be used to indicate the temperature of a substance. Using the Fahrenheit scale (F), water at sea level freezes at 32° F and boils at 212° F. This scale has been commonly used in the United States in previous years. With emphasis being placed on changing to the metric system of weights and measures, the Celsius (or Centigrade) scale (C) is being used. Using this scale for the same measurement, water freezes at 0° and boils at 100°. The usual room temperature of 72° F is 22° on the Celsius scale. While the two scales are in use, it is sometimes necessary to convert from one to the other. Formulas that may be used for the conversion, as well as a partial conversion chart, are found in Appendix B. Conversion tables may also be found in Reference 1.

Study Questions

1. Describe some unique characteristics of the water molecule.
2. Describe three important uses of water in food preparation.
3. a. Name two types of hard water and the types of mineral salts contained in each.
   b. Describe two methods for softening permanently hard water.
4. Describe how heat is transferred in food preparation by:
   a. Conduction
   b. Radiation
   c. Convection currents
5. Compare the Fahrenheit and Celsius thermometer scales.

References

1. American Home Economics Association. *Handbook of Food Preparation.* Washington, DC: American Home Economics Association, 1980.

2. Buswell, A. M. and W. H. Rodebush. 1956. Water. *Scientific American* **194,** 2 (no. 4).
3. Charley, H. *Food Science,* 2nd ed. New York: John Wiley & Sons, 1982.
4. Katz, E. E. and T. P. Labuza. 1981. Effect of water activity on the sensory crispness and mechanical deformation of snack food products. *Journal of Food Science* **46,** 403.

Vegetables and Vegetable Preparation

Vegetables are plants or parts of plants that are used as food. So broad a definition includes all fruits, nuts, and cereals that, although of vegetable origin, are not commonly classed as vegetables. The term *vegetable* has through usage come to apply in a more narrow sense to those plants or parts of plants that are served either raw or cooked as part of the main course of a meal. Sweet corn and rice are two examples of cereals that, through usage, are sometimes given the place of vegetables on the table.

Various parts of plants are used as food and vary in their water, protein, carbohydrate, vitamin, and mineral content. Although technically some parts of plants may be grouped under more than one heading, Table 7-1 shows the usual classification of the parts of plants that are commonly used as vegetables.

Composition and Nutritive Value

The functions of the various parts of a plant influence the composition and nutritional value. For example, the leaf is an actively working or metabolizing part of a plant and does not generally store energy nutrients. It is low in energy value but high in many vitamins that function in metabolism. The root and seed act more as storage depots for starch and protein.

Vegetables as a group may be depended upon to contribute indi-

Table 7-1 *Parts of Plants Commonly Used as Vegetables*

Leaves	Seeds	Roots	Tubers	Bulbs	Flowers	Fruits	Stems and Shoots
Beet greens	Beans, dry	Beet	Artichoke	Garlic	Artichoke	Cucumber	Asparagus
Brussels sprouts	Corn (a seed of	Carrot	(Jerusalem)	Leek	(French	Eggplant	Celery (a
Cabbage	the grass family	Parsnip	Potato (Irish)	Onion	or Globe)	Okra	leaf stem)
Chard	frequently	Potato		Shallot	Broccoli	Pepper	Kohlrabi
Chinese cabbage	served as a	(sweet)			Cauliflower	Pumpkin	
Collards	vegetable)	Radish				Snap beans	
Dandelion	Lentils	Rutabaga				Squash	
Endive	Peas	Salsify				Tomato	
Kale		Turnip					
Lettuce							
Mustard							
Parsley							
Spinach							
Turnip greens							
Watercress							

gestible fiber, minerals, and vitamins to the diet. Potatoes and sweet potatoes supply starch and sugars while many dried legumes are high in both starch and protein.

Most fresh vegetables furnish about 25 kilocalories for an average serving but some leaves and stems, such as lettuce and celery, are lower than this in caloric value and some roots, such as carrots and beets, and seeds, such as peas, furnish 35 to 50 kilocalories per average serving.

The principal carbohydrate that is available as a source of energy is starch, although some vegetables, such as sweet potatoes, carrots, onions, parsnips, and beets, contain 5 percent or more sugar. Vegetables probably do more than any other group of foods, excepting fruits, to add appetizing texture, color, and flavor to the daily food supply. The composition and nutritive value of selected vegetables is given in Appendix C. In spite of the apparently desirable characteristics of vegetables, they are not always favorite items on the menu. From a report of factors affecting fruit and vegetable acceptance by students it was concluded that children's rejection of some vegetables may be based on prejudice, related to such factors as early negative conditioning and faulty generalization from a single unfavorable attribute such as texture, color, shape, or fortuitous associations [43].

Some fresh vegetables, depending partly on the way they are trimmed for marketing, may have a relatively high percentage of refuse or waste parts that are thrown away. Table 7-2 shows the percentage of refuse from some commonly used vegetables.

Vegetable	Source	Percentage
Asparagus	Butt ends	44
Beans, snap	Ends, strings, trimmings	12
Beets, without tops	Parings	30
Broccoli	Tough stalks, trimmings	22
Brussels sprouts, fair quality	Trimmings, outer leaves	26
Cabbage	Outer leaves, core	21
Carrots, without tops**	Scrapings	18
Cauliflower, untrimmed	Jacket leaves, inner leaves, stalk, base, core	61
Celery	Leaves, root ends, trimmings	25
Chard, Swiss, good quality	Tough stem ends, damaged leaves	8
Corn, sweet, with husk	Husk, silk, cob, trimmings	64
Without husk	Cob	45
Cucumber, pared**	Parings, ends, bruised spots	27
Lettuce, crisphead varieties		
Good quality	Core	5
Fair quality	Coarse leaves, core	26
Onions	Skins, ends	9
Peas, green	Pods	62
Potatoes**	Parings, trimmings	19
Spinach, trimmed (packaged)		
Good quality	No refuse	0
Fair quality	Damaged leaves, trimmings	8
Squash, winter	Cavity contents, rind, stem ends, trimmings	29
Tomato, peeled	Skins, hard cores, stem ends, trimmings	12

Table 7-2 *Refuse from Vegetables**

*From *Composition of Foods*. Revised 1963. *Agriculture Handbook* No. 8. Agricultural Research Service, U.S. Department of Agriculture.
**Refuse will be considerably less if vegetables are not pared or scraped.

The Leaf Vegetables

The leaf vegetables (Figure 7-1) are high in water and low in carbohydrates. They contain only small amounts of protein and little or no fat. Their chief nutritive contributions to the diet are in minerals and vitamins. Leaves, in general, are important sources of iron, vitamin A value, riboflavin, and ascorbic acid. The greener the leaf, the higher is its vitamin A value. The bleached inner leaves of plants that form compact heads and bleached celery leaves contribute little vitamin A value. Green leaves are also one of the better

7-1 *Leaf vegetables.* (Courtesy of Burpee Seeds)

Swiss chard

Chinese cabbage

Spinach

Brussels sprouts

Cabbage

vegetable sources of calcium but most of the calcium in spinach, chard, and beet greens is combined with oxalic acid in the plant and is not available for absorption from the digestive tract.

The Vegetable-Fruits

Some of the vegetable-fruits (Figure 7-2), such as winter squash, contain about 15 percent carbohydrate and 80 to 82 percent water. This is comparable to many of the sweet fleshy fruits in carbohydrate content. However, many other vegetable-fruits, such as cucumbers, peppers, and tomatoes, contain less carbohydrate and more water with water levels of 93 to 94 percent. Tomatoes and green peppers are rich sources of ascorbic acid. Pumpkin and squash as well as tomatoes and green peppers contain carotenoid pigments, which are precursors of vitamin A. String beans, green and red peppers, and okra may be classified as vegetable-fruits but they are also seed pods.

Flowers, Buds, and Stems

Flowers, buds, and stems (Figure 7-3) are, in general, high in water and low in carbohydrates. Broccoli has been shown to be a particularly nutritious green vegetable in terms of its vitamin and mineral content. It is one of the richest vegetable sources of ascorbic acid with even the stems containing enough of the vitamin so that, where possible, the stems should be pared and used. Broccoli is also a good source of vitamin A value and contributes some riboflavin, calcium, and iron. The leaves of broccoli have four times as much calcium as the flower buds and twice as much vitamin A value and riboflavin. Cauliflower is a good source of ascorbic acid. Green asparagus contributes vitamin A value.

Bulbs, Roots, and Tubers

Onions and leeks are examples of bulbs (Figure 7-4) which are enlargements above the roots. The potato is an example of a tuber which is an enlarged underground stem. The bulb, root, and tuber vegetables (Color Plate II) are, in general, higher in carbohydrate and lower in water content than leaves, stems, and flowers. Most of the carbohydrate in potatoes is in the form of starch. Sweet potatoes also contain a fairly large amount of starch but have more sugar than white potatoes. Because of the quantities of potatoes usually consumed, they make valuable dietary contributions of kilocalories

7-2 *Vegetable-fruits. To aid in identifying squash, four types are shown.* (Courtesy of Burpee Seeds; eggplant, courtesy of Western Growers Association)

Hubbard squash

Zucchini squash

Summer squash

Summer crookneck squash

Green peppers

Okra

Cucumbers

Eggplant

7-3 *Flowers and stems used as veg-etables.* (Courtesy of Burpee Seeds)

Kohlrabi

Celery

Broccoli

108

Cauliflower

and ascorbic acid. Yellow sweet potatoes contribute vitamin A value, as do carrots.

Seeds

The legumes are seeds of the Leguminosae family and include many varieties of beans, peas, soybeans, and lentils (Figure 7-5). They are used in both the green or fresh state and in the mature or dried state, where the water content is very low. There is more protein in the dried legumes than in any other vegetable group, and they may be used as alternates for meat in meal planning. Although the biological quality of the protein in many of the legumes is substantially less than that of meat, fish, and poultry, when supplemented with the protein from other foods legumes may make a valuable contribution to the body's protein requirement. Corn, although a cereal product, is commonly used as a vegetable in the United States. It is relatively high in carbohydrate, chiefly starch.

The sprouting of soybean and mung bean seeds was developed by the Chinese centuries ago. Sprouts from many different seeds have become popular as vegetables in recent years. The sprouts of some seeds provide significant sources of ascorbic acid, thiamin, riboflavin, and some minerals [13]. Sprouts are often used in fresh vegetable salads.

Purple-top yellow rutabaga   *Parsnips*

Leeks

Beets, carrots, and turnips

7-4 *Roots and bulbs used as vegetables.* (Courtesy of Burpee Seeds; beets, carrots, and turnips, courtesy of U.S. Department of Agriculture)

110

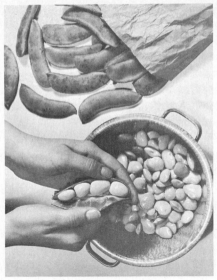

Sweet corn   *Lima beans*   *Green peas*

7-5 *Seed vegetables.* (Courtesy of Burpee Seeds; lima beans, courtesy of U.S. Department of Agriculture)

Color

The bright colors of many vegetables contribute much to their appeal. The colors result from the various pigments contained in the tissues. These pigments may undergo changes during cooking that make them less attractive. Vegetables are classified into four groups, depending on the predominant colors: green, yellow-orange, red, and white. Specific groups of plant pigments are responsible for these colors. The chlorophylls are green pigments; the carotenoids are yellow and orange (and some pink or red) in color; the anthocyanins are red, purple, or blue in color; and the anthoxanthins are creamy white to colorless. Anthocyanins and anthoxanthins have many similarities in chemical structure and are called flavonoid pigments.

Chlorophyll plays an important role in photosynthesis, in which the plant uses the energy of the sun's rays along with gases from the air to synthesize carbohydrates. Chlorophyll is concentrated in the green leaves, where it is present in tiny bodies called chloroplasts. It is mostly insoluble in water. When chlorophyll comes in contact with acids, which may be liberated during the cooking of vegetables, it chemically changes to a compound called *pheophytin,* which is a dull olive-green color. In canned vegetables, which have been subjected to prolonged periods of heating at high temperatures, essentially all of the chlorophyll has been changed to the olive-green pheophytin. In the presence of baking soda, which is alkaline in nature, chlorophyll changes to a bright green compound called *chlorophyllin.* Addition of soda to vegetables is not recommended, however, because of adverse nutritional and textural changes (see p. 122).

Carotenoids, like chlorophyll, are insoluble in water. They are present with chlorophyll in the chloroplasts of green leaves, and in the autumn when the chlorophyll disappears, the yellow color can usually be seen. Carotenoids constitute a group of similar pigments, some of which are called *carotenes*. Three of the carotene pigments, alpha-, beta-, and gamma-carotene, are found in relatively large amounts in carrots. Other carotenoids, which contain some oxygen, are called *xanthophylls*. Cryptoxanthin is a xanthophyll that is found in many yellow vegetables. The red pigment of tomatoes, named *lycopene,* is a carotenoid. Some of the carotenoid pigments, including alpha-, beta-, and gamma-carotene and cryptoxanthin, may be changed into vitamin A in the body and, therefore, contribute substantially to the vitamin A value of the diet. Carotenoid pigments may lose some of their yellow color when exposed to air because they are susceptible to oxidation. This may occur in dehydrated vegetables such as carrots. The presence of alkali has little effect on the color of the carotenoid pigments, but acid may produce a somewhat lighter orange color because of a chemical change (see p. 123).

The flavonoid pigments are water soluble and are found in the cell sap. The pigments in the anthocyanin group of flavonoids are usually red in an acid medium and change to blues and purples as the pH, a scale which gives an indication of the degree of acidity, becomes more alkaline.

Red cabbage contains anthocyanins and is easily changed in color when it comes in contact with even weak acids or alkalies. When cut with a nonstainless steel knife, red cabbage reveals another property of anthocyanins—their ability to combine with metals to form salts of various colors. The use of lacquered tin for canning red fruits and vegetables prevents the bluish-red or violet color that comes from the combination of anthocyanin pigment with tin or iron. The salts of iron combined with anthocyanins are more blue than those formed with tin.

The pigments in the root tissue of red beets have some properties similar to those of anthocyanins but they contain nitrogen and are called *betalains* [42]. Some of these pigments are purplish red while others are yellow and somewhat resemble the anthoxanthins. Beets lose much pigment and become pale when they are pared and sliced before cooking because the pigments are very soluble in water and bleed from the tissues.

The anthoxanthin pigments change from white or colorless to yellowish colors as the pH increases from acidic to alkaline ranges. These pigments are widely distributed in plants and often occur

Table 7-3 *The Solubility in Water and the Effect of Various Factors on the Color of Plant Pigments*

Name of Pigment	Color	Solubility in Water	Effect of Acid	Effect of Alkali	Effect of Pro-longed Heating
Chlorophylls	Green	Slightly	Changes to olive-green (pheophytin)	Intensifies green (chlorophyllin)	Olive-green color (pheophytin)
Carotenoids	Yellow and orange; some red or pink	Slightly	Less intense color	Little effect	Color may be less intense[a]
Anthocyanins	Red, purple, and blue	Very soluble	Red	Purple or blue	Little effect
Anthoxanthins	White or colorless	Very soluble	White	Yellow	Darkens if excessive[a]

[a]Heating *usually* produces little effect.

with anthocyanins. They may combine with some metals, such as iron, to form a dark colored complex. Some combinations with aluminum produce a bright yellow color. Table 7-3 summarizes the effect of various factors on the color of plant pigments.

The darkening of some pared vegetables, such as potatoes and sweet potatoes, on exposure to air may be attributed to the reaction with oxygen of some phenolic compounds that are present in the plant tissues. Oxidizing enzymes, also present in the plant, bring about the oxidizing reaction when oxygen from the air is available; the eventual result is a brownish color on the exposed surface of the vegetable. These reactions are similar to those occurring in some fruits when they are cut or bruised (see p. 145).

Flavor

Vegetables vary widely in flavor, some being very mild whereas others, such as asparagus and parsnips, have stronger distinctive flavors. Some vegetables, such as carrots, have a high enough sugar content to produce a definite sweet taste. The flavor of some vegetables, such as spinach, includes a slightly bitter component. The natural flavors of vegetables are probably the result of mixtures of many compounds, most of them present in very small amounts. These compounds include aldehydes, alcohols, ketones, organic acids, and sulfur compounds. The flavoring compounds in a number of vegetables and fruits have been and are being studied extensively with the use of modern analytical equipment to find out more about the complex mixtures of substances that contribute to their individual flavors. With a few exceptions, vegetables are relatively bland in flavor. Most of them do not have the tart, fragrant flavor of fruits.

Vegetables of the onion and cabbage families are sulfur-containing vegetables. They are sometimes described as strong flavored but they are not all strong flavored in the raw state. Vegetables of the cabbage (cole) family include cabbage, cauliflower, broccoli, brussels sprouts, kale, kohlrabi, mustard, rutabaga, and turnips. The onion family includes onions, leeks, garlic, and chives. Vegetables of the onion family are usually strong flavored in the raw state but tend to lose some of the strong flavors when they are cooked in water. Vegetables of the cabbage family are relatively mild when raw but may develop strong flavors or odors when improperly cooked, as discussed on p. 121. Onions contain sulfur compounds that are acted upon by enzymes in the tissues when the vegetable is peeled or cut to produce the volatile sulfur compounds that irritate the eyes and give powerful sensations on the tongue.

Some vegetables of the cabbage family contain a sulfur compound called sinigrin. When tissues are damaged by cutting or shredding, an enzyme (myrosinase) breaks down the sinigrin to produce a mustard oil that gives a sharp, pungent flavor. This flavor is typical for shredded raw cabbage. An amino acid, S-methyl-L-cysteine sulfoxide, is also present in raw cabbage and several other members of the cabbage family and appears to be an important precursor of some of the cooked cabbage flavors (see p. 121).

Selection and Storage

Most fresh vegetables, even under ideal conditions of temperature and humidity for storage, retain their top quality for only a few days. All green vegetables of high water content are best when fresh. If allowed to stand long after gathering, the vegetables become wilted and tough through loss of moisture. The flavor is also impaired, mainly because of enzyme actions. Mature vegetables, particularly roots, tubers, and bulbs, deteriorate less in storage than do fresh immature vegetables.

The superior quality of vegetables stored under refrigeration is well known and it is interesting to note that such treatment is usually useful in conserving vitamin potency. However, vegetables vary in the extent of change in ascorbic acid content even when they are kept under refrigeration. In one study [11] fresh broccoli did not lose ascorbic acid when stored up to seven days, whereas green beans lost as much as 88 percent of ascorbic acid when stored for 6 days at a temperature of $2°$ C ($36°$ F) and 95 to 100 percent relative humidity.

Cabbage held in cold storage shows no appreciable loss of ascorbic acid for 1 or 2 months, although some loss occurs by the third month. Cabbages taken out of cold storage at the end of 2 months may be held in the refrigerator for a week without appreciable loss of ascorbic acid, but if they are kept at room temperature distinct loss may occur in 3 days. Decreased ascorbic acid values during 240 days of storage at 7° C (45° F) have been observed for potatoes [1]. Corn that was quick-frozen on the cob showed a significant increase in ascorbic acid immediately after freezing and also after several weeks of frozen storage [32].

One reason for the short storage life of many vegetables is that they are rapidly respiring or metabolizing. A thin coating of a vegetable oil emulsion on snap beans and other fresh vegetables was found to decrease the respiration process [35]. When stored at a temperature of 4° C (40° F) the waxed beans were generally in better condition than the unwaxed beans. This procedure to extend storage life and maintain product quality is commonly used in the marketing of fresh vegetables such as cucumbers and tomatoes. Lettuce may be stored in a controlled atmosphere in order to extend its shelf life [34]. In an atmosphere containing 2.5 percent carbon dioxide and 2.5 percent oxygen, lettuce heads can be stored up to 75 days. The controlled atmosphere combined with polyethylene packaging reduces the rate of respiration in the lettuce tissues (see p. 149 for a discussion of controlled atmosphere storage of fruits).

Most fresh green vegetables, such as lettuce and celery, may be kept fresh and crisp in home storage by being kept in covered containers or plastic bags in the refrigerator. If they are washed before storing they should be drained thoroughly because too much moisture can increase the possibility of spoilage or decay. Seeds, such as peas and limas, remain fresh longer if left in the pods. Tubers and bulbs that are to be held temporarily in the home may be stored in a cool place without refrigeration.

If tomatoes are picked before being fully ripened, the quality and vitamin value will be better if the tomatoes are ripened at room temperature or a little below, that is, 15° to 24° C (59° to 75° F) and are kept in a light place unwrapped. Ripe tomatoes should be stored uncovered in the refrigerator.

Most fresh vegetables are sold on the wholesale market on the basis of U.S. Department of Agriculture grades. These grades specify such characteristics as size, shape, color, texture, uniformity, and freedom from defects. The grades provide a common language for wholesale trading and aid in establishing prices based on quality. Grading is provided on request and a fee charged to the producer or distributor. Grade labeling is not required by law, however, and there is not a large quantity of grade-marked produce available in most retail stores. Generally, potatoes, carrots, and onions are the only fresh vegetables labeled for the consumer with a grade name. Uniform grade terms—U.S. Fancy, U.S. No. 1, U.S. No. 2, and U.S. No. 3—are being phased in gradually by the U.S. Department of Agriculture as existing grades are revised. Because fresh vegetables are perishable, the quality may change between the time of grading and the time of purchase by the consumer. This severely limits the use of consumer grades on fresh fruits and vegetables. The extensive use of prepackaging may help to overcome this problem and makes the use of consumer grades for fresh produce more practical. (See pp. 56–58 for a general discussion of grading.)

Generally, it is good to make your own selection of fresh, perishable vegetables. They should be firm, crisp, and bright in color, with no signs of decay or bruising. They are usually highest in quality and lowest in price when in season in nearby production areas. It is unwise to purchase greater quantities than can be properly stored and utilized without waste. The buyer should distinguish between defects that affect appearance only and those that affect edible quality. Fruits and vegetables should not be handled unnecessarily while selections are being made [21].

In buying head vegetables, a point has been to buy solid heads. In the case of lettuce, however, looser heads may contain more green colored leaves and therefore more vitamin A value. The leaves from less firm heads are often more attractive for salads than the more distinct cups from solid heads.

U.S. Department of Agriculture grades of quality have been established for many canned and frozen vegetables [19]. U.S. Grade A, U.S. Grade B, or U.S. Grade C may appear on the individual cans and packages. Grades are determined on the basis of color, tenderness, and freedom from blemishes. Most canned and frozen vegetables are packed according to grade (whether or not it is indicated on the label) and priced according to their quality. Most products marketed are at least Grade B quality, which is quite good. If a vegetable is packed under continuous USDA inspection, this may appear on the label also. As with fresh produce, use of the U.S. grade standards is voluntary and is paid for by the packer. The specific brand name of a frozen or canned vegetable may be an indication of quality as the packer sets his own standards.

In the use of vegetables, it is good to remember that a liking for vegetables as for other foods is largely a matter of cultivation of habits and attitudes. There are both nutritional safety and variety to be had in a wider selection and use of all foods, including vegetables. For more detailed information on purchasing vegetables and fruits, the reader may consult references 19 to 22 and 40 to 41 at the end of this chapter.

Vegetable Preparation

Emphasis on the important nutritional contributions of vegetables along with the greater availability of vegetables the year around has given impetus to the study of vegetable preparation. The nutrients that vegetables contain should be conserved as completely as possible. Also such factors as flavor, texture, and appearance require careful consideration in order that raw or cooked vegetables may be appetizing.

The vegetables that are generally used raw are those of high water and low starch content. Many such vegetables are tender and crisp and have distinctive pleasant flavors.

Preliminary Preparation

Most vegetables grow near or in the ground. They are contaminated by dirt, sprays, sand, and various kinds of microorganisms, some of which are acquired from the soil and some from the many contacts incident to marketing. Thorough washing in water that is safe for drinking is essential. The use of a stiff vegetable brush is often necessary to aid in the removal of dirt. If vegetables are to be consumed raw, extra care is needed in cleansing them. All spoiled and discolored portions should be trimmed off. If pods, such as lima bean and pea pods, are very dirty, they should be washed before being shelled. Leafy vegetables should have all undesirable leaves and coarse stems removed. The usable leaves require washing through several waters to remove all grit. In washing, the vegetables should be lifted out of the wash water so that the heavier particles of dirt will remain in the water. Alternatively, they may be washed under running water.

Roots and tubers that are covered with skins may or may not have skins removed, depending on the method to be used in cooking them and depending in part on the vegetable itself. Beets, for example, should not be peeled unless they are to be diced or sliced and cooked in a closely covered container with little or no water. The red coloring matter of beets is very soluble in water and is best protected from loss by cooking the beets in the skin with the roots and two or more inches of the tops left on.

If properly scrubbed with a brush, carrots may be cooked without paring or scraping. With some carrots, however, the skins tend to make the vegetable appear darker. Carrots are delicious when they are cooked in their skins and scraped after cooking. If plunged into cold water after boiling, they are easily skinned and they retain their sweetness and nutrients better than when they are scraped before cooking. If the method of preparation requires that carrots have the skin removed before cooking, they should be scraped or pared so as to remove as little tissue as possible with the peel in order to retain more of the vitamins and minerals. Vegetables usually have a valuable layer of nutrients lying directly underneath the skin. Some roots and tubers, such as potatoes, have skins that are too thick to be removed by scraping. These also may be cooked in their skins and peeled after cooking. If they must be pared before

Asparagus may be washed under running water with the use of a small brush to remove soil.

Lower stems may be snapped off with the fingers to leave the tip and tender stem for cooking.

7-6 *Preparation of asparagus for cooking.* (Courtesy of Western Growers Association)

cooking, parings should be as thin as possible. The floating-blade type of peeler removes very thin layers.

In preparing asparagus only the tip and tender stem should be used. The woodiest parts of asparagus may be easily removed if the lower stems are snapped off with the fingers (Figure 7-6). The stems should break where the stalk is tender. If the twigs and leaves of broccoli are tender, they may be used in addition to the flower buds. Woody stems are not easily softened by cooking and are usually inedible. However, large broccoli stems may be peeled and the tender center cores cooked. The outer leaves and heavy stalks of cauliflower and cabbage are usually discarded, although the process of prepackaging fresh vegetables often includes the removal of the outer, less edible portions before the vegetables are placed in the retail market. In cooking heavier stalks with more tender portions of a vegetable it is best to add the more tender parts to the stalks after a few minutes of cooking so that the tender portions will not be overcooked by the time the stalks are tender. Parsnips may have a

7-7 *In preparing globe artichokes, (1) cut off the stem about 1 inch from the base, leaving a stub; (2) cut off about 1 inch of the top, cutting straight across with a knife; (3) pull off any heavy loose leaves around the bottom; (4) with scissors, clip off the thorny tip of each leaf; (5) drop into boiling, salted water. Season by adding a small clove of garlic, a thick slice of lemon, and 1 tablespoon of olive or other salad oil for each artichoke. Cover and boil until a leaf can be pulled easily from the stalk or until the stub can be easily pierced with a fork (20 to 45 minutes). Remove carefully from water. Cutt off the stub.* (Courtesy of Western Growers Association)

woody core, which should be removed. See Figure 7-7 for the preparation of globe artichokes.

Some vegetables that are prepared in advance of being used or cooked discolor unless they are covered with water. As a general precaution against the loss of water-soluble nutrients, the soaking time should be reduced to a minimum. Also, cabbage shredded with a *sharp* knife in advance of being used loses a negligible amount of ascorbic acid when it stands at room temperature for 1 hour in air or 3 hours in water. The sharp knife avoids bruising, which usually causes rapid loss of ascorbic acid. These results with cabbage, however, do not justify indiscriminate and unnecessary cutting, shredding, and exposure of vegetables to air or soaking in water. In some vegetables, certain nutrients may occur in a form that is more stable or better protected against destruction than in other vegetables.

Why Cook Vegetables?

Many vegetables are improved in palatability and are more easily and completely digested when they are cooked. Some valuable vegetables, such as dried legumes, could not be masticated or digested in the raw state. The flavors of cooked vegetables are different from those of raw vegetables and are sometimes more desirable.

The protein of dried legumes is improved in quality by heat, and some of the minerals and vitamins, particularly of soybeans, are rendered more available after the beans are heated [24]. Cooking also gelatinizes starch and increases its digestibility. Microorganisms are destroyed by the heating process. The bulk of leafy vegetables is greatly decreased as they wilt during cooking.

How Cooking Losses Occur

Cooking losses occur in several ways: (1) through the dissolving action of water or dilute salt solutions; (2) by chemical decomposition, which may be influenced by the alkalinity or acidity of the cooking medium; (3) by oxidation of specific molecules such as vitamins; (4) by the mechanical loss of solids into the cooking water; and (5) by volatilization. Mechanical losses of nutrients in vegetable cookery are the result of paring, rapid boiling (agitation), and overcooking. Such loss is represented chiefly by the loss of starch cells from cut surfaces, but other losses can and do occur, especially when parings are too thick and when overcooking results in marked disintegration. The chief volatile loss is water, although other substances that affect flavor also volatilize, which causes marked loss in flavor.

Changes During Cooking

Changes in Fiber Components. Cellulose in vegetables is slightly softened by cooking but appears to be practically indigestible in the human digestive tract. When calculated on a dry weight basis, cellulose content seems to increase somewhat when vegetables are boiled. It has been suggested that this may be the result of cellulose being liberated from the cell walls so that it is more available for analysis [16, 17, 27].

Sodium bicarbonate (baking soda) added to the cooking water tends to cause the hemicelluloses to disintegrate, producing a soft texture in a short cooking period. Acid, on the other hand, prevents softening of the vegetable.

The pectic substances in the intercellular cementing material may be broken down in cooking so that there is some cell separation. Calcium chloride or a saturated solution of calcium hydroxide (lime water) has the effect of making vegetable tissues more firm, probably by forming insoluble calcium salts with pectic substances in the plant tissue. The former is used commercially to help preserve the firmness of tomatoes, and possibly other foods during canning. Its use is approved by the Food and Drug Administration to the extent of 0.07 percent. Calcium chloride may also be used to make melon rinds firm and brittle for preserving or pickling.

Red Delicious.

Golden Delicious.

McIntosh.

Winesap.

Rome Beauty.

Plate I *Eight varieties of apples.* (Courtesy Blue Goose, Inc.)

White Astrachan.

Newtown.

Jonathan.

Irish Cobbler.

Long White.

Russet Burbanks.

Plate II *Eight varieties of potatoes.*
(Courtesy Blue Goose, Inc.)

Cherokee.

Katahdin.

Chippewa.

Kennebec, Washed.

Red Pontiac.

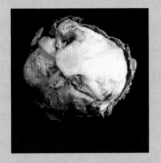
Head lettuce.

Butter leaf lettuce.

Romaine lettuce.

Red leaf lettuce.

French and Italian (flat-leaf) parsley.

Escarole.

Plate III *Several types of salad greens.* (Courtesy Blue Goose, Inc. and Elisabeth Belfer)

Watercress.

Chicory endive.

French endive.

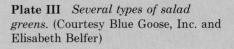

A variety of fruits and vegetables may be attractively served as salads to accompany the main course of a meal or as a separate course. (Courtesy The Betty Crocker Kitchens, General Mills, Inc.)

Upper row, from left to right: Orange-Bermuda Onion Salad, Apple and Grapefruit Salad, Festival Peach Salad (peaches filled with a mixture of cottage cheese, slivered almonds, chopped maraschino cherries, and flaked coconut).

Lower row, from left to right: Tossed Salad, Tomatoes Vinaigrette (tomato slices marinated in a tart dressing), Asparagus Tips with Mayonnaise.

Plate IV *Salads*

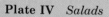

A Chef's Salad containing strips of cold cooked meat, poultry, and cheese along with a variety of fresh, crisp greens and topped with a tangy dressing makes an attractive and nutritious main dish. (Courtesy The Betty Crocker Kitchens, General Mills, Inc.)

Fresh Fruit Combo with Molded Salad Dressing combines a variety of colorful fruits with a bleu cheese flavored gelatine salad dressing mold containing either mayonnaise or sour cream. This tempting plate may be served as a buffet salad or as a dessert. (Courtesy Sunkist Growers, Inc.)

Changes in Water Content. The water content of vegetables is altered during cooking. Water may be absorbed if the vegetable is cooked submerged in water or, to a lesser extent, in steam. Removal of water occurs during baking.

Effect of Cooking on Flavor. Flavor is affected in various ways during cooking. Overcooking often adversely affects flavor, sometimes producing off flavors that are bitter or sulfurous. A covered kettle or steamer tends to increase the intensity of flavor, whereas an open kettle allows some volatile flavor substances to escape. A large amount of cooking water extracts more flavor substances than does a small amount of water. Sugars, acids, and some minerals that contribute to flavor are water soluble. Dimethyl disulfide produced from the amino acid S-methyl-L-cysteine sulfoxide apparently makes a contribution to the characteristic and desirable flavor of cooked cabbage, along with a number of other volatile compounds [26]. However, the flavor of the sulfur-containing vegetables may be marred by extensive decomposition of sulfur compounds during cooking. In overcooked vegetables of the cabbage family, hydrogen sulfide and other volatile sulfur compounds may give a strong, pungent, sulfurous flavor and odor, and vegetable acids may aid in the decomposition. Leaving the lid off for the first part of cooking to allow some volatile acids to escape may help to control these changes. However, it is probably more important to cook sulfur-containing vegetables for the shortest time possible to give tenderness before substantial decomposition of sulfur compounds occurs. Vegetables of the cabbage family have been found to have a milder flavor when they are cooked in an open pan with enough water to cover them than when cooked in a tightly covered pan, a steamer, or a pressure saucepan. A large amount of water dilutes the natural flavors of the vegetables, usually to a very substantial degree. A milder flavor or stronger natural flavor may be a matter of personal preference. The absence of many volatile flavor substances from dehydrated cabbage has been reported [25] and this has been suggested as an explanation for the dehydrated product's being a poor substitute for freshly cooked cabbage in terms of eating quality.

The sharp flavor of onions is reduced on cooking. The flavor of onions may also be very mild if they are cooked in a large amount of water with the lid of the pan loose or off, or the flavor may be sweeter and more concentrated if cooked in a small amount of water with the lid on.

Changes in Plant Pigments. Changes that occur in plant pigments while cooking are among the most important of changes from the standpoint of the appearance of cooked vegetables. Table 7-3 summarizes these changes.

The green pigment, *chlorophyll,* may be so affected by both heat and acid that marked change to the drab olive-green color characteristic of pheophytin production occurs. This change is not dependent upon the addition of acid because the natural acids occurring in plants are sufficient to mar color if heating is continued for too long. Removing the cover from the pan during the first few minutes of boiling should allow some volatile acids to escape, decreasing the likelihood of their affecting the chlorophyll adversely. However, heating is not as even or as complete in an uncovered pan and the total cooking time may be slightly extended. The hues of green vegetables progress from green-yellow toward yellow as cooking time increases beyond the just tender stage [29]. Green beans, broccoli, brussels sprouts, cabbage, and other green vegetables show considerable change in color with 5-minute overcooking in boiling water and with even 1 minute of overcooking in a pressure saucepan. The cooking of frozen broccoli has been reported to produce large losses of total chlorophyll [6]. Green vegetables that are held on a steam table before serving often show pronounced loss of chlorophyll and color. The addition of a mixture of magnesium carbonate and calcium acetate has been shown to decrease the acidity of green beans and maintain a satisfactory green color without affecting palatability or nutritive value [37].

When a small amount of baking soda is added to green vegetables during cooking it changes the chlorophyll to a bright green, more water-soluble pigment called chlorophyllin. However, the use of baking soda when cooking vegetables is *not* generally recommended because it is difficult to avoid adding too much and the flavor, texture, and vitamin content of the vegetables may be adversely affected. The vitamins, thiamin and ascorbic acid, are particularly susceptible to destruction when soda is added during cooking. Texture may be undesirably soft because soda has a disintegrating effect on the hemicelluloses. Some research has shown that *very minute* amounts of baking soda may be used in the cooking of certain green vegetables without a decrease in the vitamin content. The cooking time for green peas was shortened from a period of 10 to 20 minutes to a period of 7 to 9 minutes when $1/16$ teaspoon of baking soda was added to about $1\frac{1}{2}$ pounds of peas. No reduction in total ascorbic acid occurred, probably because the shortened cooking time compensated for the loss of ascorbic acid resulting from increased alkalinity. Similar results have been reported with frozen green lima beans. The addition of about $1/4$ teaspoon of soda per pound of broccoli reduced cooking time from 10 to 5 minutes and had little effect on ascorbic acid retention, but it gave the broccoli an undesirable slippery quality. A word of caution is needed against the indiscriminate use of alkali in vegetable cookery.

The intensified green color of vegetables that occurs at the beginning of cooking is explained in part by the removal of air from the tissues when the vegetable is dropped into boiling water. The removal of air permits greater visibility of the underlying chlorophyll. The bright green color of frozen green vegetables results from brief blanching in boiling water or steam.

The carotenoid pigments are quite stable during ordinary cooking procedures. However, the pigments may be susceptible to some chemical change by a process called *isomerization* in the presence of acid and heat so that the orange color becomes somewhat more yellow.

Not all anthocyanins as they occur in the plant behave in the same way with changes of acidity and alkalinity. This may be the result of the admixture of other pigments or of substances that modify the reactions. Red cabbage is very easily changed in color and it is difficult to retain its typical color while cooking it. The German custom of cooking red cabbage with an apple and of adding a small amount of vinegar when ready to serve it aids in retaining a desirable red color. The anthoxanthin pigments are quite stable to cooking. However, if the cooking water is alkaline the pigments may appear slightly yellow in color.

Changes in Carbohydrates. The gelatinization of starch, described as the swelling of starch granules in the presence of moisture, occurs during the cooking of vegetables. This gelatinization may be partial or complete. Under some circumstances sugars may caramelize. The evaporation of cooking waters in which considerable sugar is dissolved from the plant tissues may result in caramelization, producing a brown color on the vegetable.

Vitamin Losses. There are two ways in which vitamins may be lost during cooking. Some of the vitamins may actually be destroyed by oxidation and some may be dissolved in the cooking water, although the latter applies only to the water-soluble vitamins (the B vitamins and ascorbic acid). Ascorbic acid is easily oxidized, and hence tends to be better retained if conditions favoring oxidation can be eliminated. Some of the undesirable effects of covering the kettle have been mentioned, but a covered kettle hastens cooking, and thus gives less time for either solution losses or inactivation of vitamins. A covered pan does not completely exclude air but reduces the exposure to air. The vitamin A value of vegetables is usually well retained during cooking, so that cooked green leaves and other green and yellow vegetables may be counted upon as good sources of provitamin A in the diet. Thiamin is more unstable to heat than are riboflavin and niacin, and it appears to be less stable if heated in a water medium than when heated in the dry state. The extent of destruction increases with increase in temperature. Riboflavin and niacin are very stable to heat even at temperatures above 100° C (212° F).

The acidity or alkalinity of the cooking water is a factor in the destruction of thiamin, ascorbic acid, and, to a lesser extent, of riboflavin. The more alkaline the solution the faster the rate of destruction, especially as temperatures and the time of heating are increased.

Losses of ascorbic acid during the cooking of broccoli have been studied. Some loss occurs regardless of the cooking method used. The leaching of the vitamin into the cooking water rather than destruction by heat is the chief factor responsible for the loss. Broccoli cooked to satisfactory doneness retains 60 to 85 percent of the original ascorbic acid except when excessive cooking liquid is used [38, 39]. Several cooked vegetables were found to lose significant amounts of ascorbic acid during 1 day of refrigerator storage, with usual losses of approximately 20 to 30 percent more than that lost in the freshly cooked vegetable. Reheating cooked vegetables after 1 day of storage decreased the ascorbic acid content an additional 6 to 12 percent [6]. Holding vegetables at a warm temperature after cooking causes loss of both flavor and nutritive value. It is probably better if the vegetable is cooled and quickly reheated when it is to be served.

Specific Methods of Cooking Vegetables

Baking, frying, stir-frying or panning, steaming, cooking in steam under pressure, and microwave cooking are common methods of cooking vegetables. The desire for variety is one factor that influences the choice of cooking method, as is the suitability of the method for the type of vegetable being cooked. A third and important factor is the influence of the method on the retention of nutrients.

Some loss of food value probably occurs in most methods employed in vegetable cookery. For this reason it is important to serve some vegetables in the raw state. Baking, steaming, panning, and cooking in the skins have been called *conservation methods* of cooking vegetables because they may retain food values more completely than do some other methods.

Baking. Baking may be done by the direct heat of the oven or the vegetable may be pared, sliced, or diced and placed in a covered casserole. In the casserole, however, a moist atmosphere surrounds the vegetable as it cooks. All vegetables that contain a high enough water content to prevent drying out and that have little surface exposed to the heat lend themselves well to baking. This includes potatoes, sweet potatoes, winter squash, and onions. Vegetables are commonly baked in the skin. Figure 7-8 shows several ideas for stuffing and serving baked vegetables.

The overbaking of starchy vegetables and failure to open the skin of the vegetable when baking is finished result in sogginess. Be-

7-8 *Baked stuffed onions, cabbage, artichokes, or tomatoes make delicious and nourishing entrees or meat accompaniments. They may be stuffed with ground beef, diced ham, or seasoned celery and bread crumbs. The photograph on the right shows eggs baked in tomato halves as a luncheon dish.* (Courtesy of Western Growers Association)

cause the time required for baking is greater than for boiling, time and fuel must be considered in using the method. Moderately hot oven temperatures, which form steam quickly within the vegetable, give better texture to starchy vegetables than is obtainable at low temperatures. Prompt serving of baked vegetables as soon as they are done is recommended to maintain quality and lesson vitamin losses.

Frying. Vegetables may be cooked in shallow fat (pan-frying or sautéing) or in deep fat. Certain vegetables, such as potatoes, onions, eggplant, and parsnips, are probably more commonly cooked by this method than are other types of vegetables.

Vegetables such as onion rings and eggplant are often dipped in a batter before being fried in deep fat. Some vegetables, such as carrots, green peppers, parsnips, and mushrooms, should be parboiled before being covered with batter and fried in deep fat. Frying is discussed in Chapter 14, Fats and Emulsions, pp. 335. There appears to be little loss of vitamins and minerals in the frying of vegetables. Table 7-4 give approximate temperatures and time periods for the deep-fat frying of vegetables and vegetable mixtures.

Stir-frying or Panning. Panning or stir-frying may be considered a modification of the frying method because a small amount of fat is used for the pan, but the vegetable is cooked mainly by steam produced from the vegetable's own moisture and held in with a tight-fitting cover. Finely shredded or diced roots, celery, sweet corn,

Table 7-4 *Approximate Temperatures and Times for Frying Vegetables*

Food	Temperature of Fat		Time (min)
	(C)	(F)	
Croquettes (cooked mixtures)	190 to 199	375 to 390	2 to 5
French fried (onions, potatoes, cauliflower)	196 to 202	385 to 395	6 to 8
Fritters	182 to 190	360 to 375	3 to 5

French-cut green beans, and finely shredded cabbage may be cooked by this method. The vegetable is stirred briefly in a small amount of melted fat before the pan is covered. The pieces of vegetable should be thin so that the heat will penetrate rapidly and the cooking time can be short. Panned vegetables should not be overcooked. When done, they may still be slightly firm or crisp. The short cooking time and the small amount of moisture used in cooking aid in conserving the vitamins and minerals present in the vegetable tissue.

Boiling. When vegetables are boiled, they are either partially or fully submerged in water, which means that soluble constituents are likely to be lost in the cooking water. Soluble substances in vegetables include water-soluble vitamins, relatively soluble mineral salts, organic acids, flavor substances, and sugars. Much less loss of soluble material occurs if vegetables are boiled in their skins. For example, pared potatoes may lose up to nine times as many minerals and up to four times as much total dry matter as potatoes cooked in their skins.

Losses of water-soluble constituents vary with the time of cooking and the amount of surface exposed to the water. In general, the more surface exposed and the longer the cooking time the greater is the loss. Losses also appear to be influenced by the amount of cooking water, more losses occurring as the quantity of cooking water increases. However, the length of time of cooking may be a more important factor than either the amount of cooking water or the fineness of division of the vegetable. If the vegetables are such that cooking can be done in little or no water, or if the cooking water is evaporated by the time the vegetable is done, little or no loss of soluble material may occur. Also, the utilization of cooking waters for soups, sauces, and gravies is to be recommended as one way to save valuable nutrients that would otherwise be thrown away.

Several studies [7, 15] have compared the losses of ascorbic acid in cooking vegetables in various amounts of water and by "waterless" methods using only the water that clings to the vegetable after washing. The percentage of retention in the cooked vegetable varies with the vegetable but would seem to be similar when cooking is done either by the "waterless" method or in a small amount of water. The use of a cover while boiling vegetables is a somewhat controversial matter. It is desirable for all vegetables whose flavor and/or color are not impaired by covering. In general, it is the green-colored vegetables and vegetables of the cabbage and onion families in which color and flavor may be most affected by covering, although there are exceptions and different choices of method may be made for various reasons. For example, young, tender peas, which should be cooked quickly enough to avoid the undesirable changes of chlorophyll to an olive-green color, may be sweeter and have more marked flavor when cooked covered. However, if they are compared to a like sample cooked in an open pan, the color is likely to be superior in the latter. Some very tender spinach may retain a good color when it is covered. A cover on the pan hastens cooking, and thus tends to conserve nutrients better and avoids the continuous exposure to air, although it does not wholly exclude air. A cover may also make possible the use of a smaller volume of water in most instances. Some heavy, tightly covered saucepans may develop a small amount of pressure, which also hastens cooking.

From the standpoint of flavor, it is usually conceded that the best time to add salt to vegetables is when they are put on to cook. The loss, if any, of nutrients as a result of the added salt is probably very small. In general terms, putting vegetables into just enough boiling water to prevent scorching, covering with a tight-fitting lid, and cooking just until tender is an appropriate method for boiling most vegetables in order to retain maximum flavor and nutritive value (Figure 7-9).

7-9 *A vegetable platter can be a meal in itself, or it may include meat or meat substitutes, such as shrimp and egg slices.* (Courtesy of United Fresh Fruit and Vegetable Association)

7-10 *A pressure saucepan that can be adjusted for 5, 10, and 15 pounds pressure.* (Courtesy of Aluminum Goods Manufacturing Co.)

Steaming and Pressure Cooking. Steaming consists of cooking in steam with the vegetable suspended in a perforated container over boiling water. Although some tender young vegetables may cook quickly in steam, most vegetables cooked in an ordinary steamer take somewhat longer to cook than those that are boiled. The fact that the vegetable is not actually in water favors the retention of water-soluble constituents, but the longer time required to cook most vegetables tends toward a loss of color in many green vegetables.

Cooking in a pressure saucepan is cooking in steam but the steam is confined in the tightly closed pan and a high pressure is created. The cooking temperature rises as the steam pressure rises. At 15 pounds of pressure the temperature is 121° C (250° F). Experimental use of the pressure saucepan for cooking vegetables has shown that nutrients often tend to be conserved better by that method than by some others because of the short time required at the high temperature obtained and the use of a small amount of cooking liquid. Small, lightweight pressure saucepans may be conveniently used for cooking various types of foods (Figure 7-10). They may be especially desirable for cooking roots, tubers, and legumes. The desirability of the pressure saucepan for all succulent vegetables, particularly those of green color and those of the cabbage and onion families, is somewhat controversial. Most models of pressure saucepans are adjustable for 5, 10, and 15 pounds of pressure and they may have the temperature quickly reduced by being placed in cold water as soon as the cooking period is ended. These features are an aid in obtaining desirable products from various types of vegetables. One disadvantage is the difficulty of testing for doneness during the cooking period if one happens to be using a variety of vegetable that requires a shorter or longer cooking time than the average time periods recommended.

Flavor, color, and ascorbic acid retention in vegetables cooked in a pressure saucepan, in sufficient boiling water to cover, and by "waterless" methods have been compared [15]. In boiling water, the vegetables were generally milder and greener than when cooked by the other methods. The percentage of retention of ascorbic acid was greatest in the pressure saucepan in the majority of vegetables. The retention of ascorbic acid in cabbage, cauliflower, rutabagas, and turnips was somewhat greater in "waterless" cookery than in boiling water but the reverse was true for broccoli and brussels sprouts. It was concluded that if the acceptability of cooking methods was based on a cooked vegetable that is mild, has good color, and high ascorbic acid retention no one method was completely satisfactory for all vegetables.

In Table 7-5, the approximate time is given for the cooking of vegetables by boiling, steaming, baking, and cooking in a pressure saucepan. It should be emphasized that all timetables used in cookery are approximate and are to be used merely as guides. Variations in the maturity of samples of vegetables, the sizes of whole vegetables or cut pieces, the variety, the temperature of the vegetable when placed in the water as well as the temperature of the water itself, and the amount of water are known factors affecting the time required to cook the vegetable tender. Some varieties cook in half the time required by other varieties of the same vegetable.

Microwave Cooking. Both fresh and frozen vegetables generally may be satisfactorily cooked in a microwave oven. Some vegetables may have better color and/or flavor when cooked by microwaves, whereas other vegetables may have higher quality characteristics when boiled in a saucepan or cooked by other conventional methods [2]. Greater retention of ascorbic acid has been reported in broccoli cooked by microwaves than in broccoli cooked by various conventional methods [4,5]. Fresh spinach cooked by microwaves retained 47 percent of its ascorbic acid while spinach boiled in a small amount of water retained 51 percent [23]. In many cases, vegetables may be cooked in a microwave oven without the addition of water. Cooking without water decreases the nutrient loss through leaching. Whole vegetables or pieces of vegetables should be of uniform size so that they will cook evenly. General principles of microwave cookery are discussed in Chapter 25.

Cooking Frozen Vegetables

Essentially, the cooking of frozen vegetables is no different from the cooking of fresh vegetables. With the exception of frozen green soybeans, which require about as long to cook as do fresh ones, the cooking time of frozen vegetables is about half that required for fresh vegetables because they have been blanched before freezing. Vegetables may be defrosted before cooking or may be started by placing the frozen vegetable in boiling water. The vegetable cooks more uniformly and in slightly shorter time if defrosted, at least partially, before starting to cook. It has been suggested that vegetables defrosted prior to cooking may rate higher in texture and flavor because more water is taken up by the tissues as vegetables thaw slowly. Because some vegetables lose ascorbic acid more rapidly after defrosting and because many users of frozen foods are poorly informed regarding the changes that occur in vegetables after defrosting, the producer generally recommends that all vegetables remain frozen until cooking is started.

Corn on the cob requires defrosting before cooking because the time required for cooking the corn is not sufficient to defrost the cob. Corn on the cob requires a longer blanching time to destroy enzymes

Table 7-5 *Approximate Cooking Time for Vegetables*

Vegetable	Approx. Quantity for 4 Serv.	Preparation for Cooking	Approx. Amt. of Water for Boiling	Amt. of Water for Pressure Saucepan	Time in Minutes — Boiling	Steaming	Baking	Pressure Saucepan—15 lb of Pressure
Artichokes								
French	2 lb	Whole.	To cover.	1 c	25 to 40			10
Jerusalem	1 lb	Whole, pared.	Partially cover.	1 c	20 to 30	35	30 to 60	15
Asparagus	About 1 lb	Woody ends broken off, scales removed.	To cover butts.	1/3 c	Tips, 5 to 10 Butts, 10 to 15	10 to 15		Tips, 1 to 1/2 Large tips, 2
Beans, young green or wax	About 3/4 lb	Whole or broken, strings removed.	About half the volume of beans.	1/3 c	20 to 25	25 to 30		1 1/2 to 3
Beans, fresh lima	2 lb in pod (2 c shelled)	Shelled.	About 2 c.	1/3 c	25 to 35	25 to 30		2 to 3
Beets, young	6 med. or 1 1/2 lb	Whole, skin, root, and 2 in. of stem left on.	To cover.	3/4 c	30 to 45	25 to 40 60 to 75		(5 lb pressure) 12, small 18, large
Beet greens	About 1–1 1/2 lb	Whole leaf with tender stem and mid-rib.	Partially cover.	1/2 c	5 to 15			2
Broccoli	1 med. bunch (1 1/2–2 lb)	Woody stems removed, coarse leaves removed, smaller stems pared and split to hasten cooking.	To cover stems.	1/3 c	Flowerets, 5 to 10 Stems, 10 to 15			1 1/2 to 2
Brussels sprouts	3/4 to 1 qt	Whole, outer leaves removed. Larger compact heads may be partially split.	Partially cover.	1/2 c	10 to 15			1 to 2
Cabbage, new green	1 lb	Outer leaves and stalk removed. Shredded.	Partially cover	1/2 c	6 to 9	9 to 10		1 to 1 1/2
Mature, white	1 lb	Outer leaves and stalk removed. Shredded.	Partially cover.	1/2 c	8 to 10	10 to 12		2 to 3
Red	1 lb	Outer leaves and stalk removed. Shredded. Cook with tart apple or add 2–3 T vinegar after cooking.	Partially cover.	1/2 c	15 to 20	25 to 30		3 to 4
Carrots, young	1 lb	Whole, skins on or scraped. Scraped, cut into halves or quarters lengthwise or diced.	Partially cover.	1/3 c	20 to 25 10 to 15	25 to 30	35 to 45	4 2 to 3

		Separated into flowerets.						
		Whole flower.	Partially cover.	½ c	20 to 25	25 to 30		3 to 4
Celery	1 med. bunch	Cut into ½ to ¾ in. pieces.	½-in. depth in pan. Add water if needed.	⅓ c	15 to 20	25 to 30		2 to 3
Corn, young green	4 ears	On cob or cut off.	Cover ears.	½ c on cob	5 to 10	10 to 15		1 to 2
			Partially cover cut corn.	⅓ c off cob	5			2
Okra	1 lb	Sliced or whole.	Partially cover.	⅓ c	10 to 20	20 to 25		3 (sliced)
Onions	1 lb	Two outer layers removed.	Cover or partially cover.	½ c	Whole, 25 to 35		45 to 60	6 to 7
		Whole, cut into halves or quarters or slices.			Quarters, 15 to 20			3
Parsnips	1 lb	Scrape or pare. Cook whole or cut in half lengthwise. Remove woody core.	Partially cover.	½ c	15 to 25	30 to 35		2 (sliced) 7 (whole)
Peas, green	2 lb in pod	Shelled.	½ to 1-in. depth in pan. Add as needed.	⅓ c	10 to 15	15 to 20		2 to 2½ (5 lb pressure)
Potatoes, Irish	1 to 1½ lb	Whole, with or without skins.	Barely cover.	1 c	30 to 35	40	40 to 60	15
		Pared, cut lengthwise into halves or quarters.	Partially cover.	¾ c	20 to 30	30 to 35		8
Potatoes, sweet	1 to 1½ lb	Whole, with or without skins.	Barely cover.	1 c	30 to 35	35 to 40	30 to 50	8 to 10
		Pared, halved.	Partially cover.	½ c	20 to 30	25 to 35		6 to 8
Rutabaga	1¼ lb	Pared and diced.	Partially cover.	½ c	20 to 30			4
Spinach	1 lb	Coarse stems and roots removed.	1 c per lb or none.	½ c	3 to 6	5 to 10		1 to 1½
		Stems not removed.			8 to 10	6 to 12		1 to 1½
Squash, Hubbard	1½ to 2 lb	Pared. Cut into 2 × 3-in. pieces.	½ to 1-in. depth in pan.	¾ c	20 to 25	30 to 35		6 to 8
		Cut into one portion pieces. Rind on.					45 to 60	
Squash, summer	1½ to 2 lb	Pared and sliced.	½ to 1-in. depth in pan.	⅓ c	5 to 15	10 to 20	15 to 20	2
Tomatoes	1 lb	Whole.	Little or none.	¼ c	5 to 10	10	20 to 30 (whole stuffed)	1 to 2
Turnips	1 lb	Pared, sliced or diced.	Partially cover.	½ c	15 to 20	20 to 25		1½ to 4
Turnip greens	1 to 1½ lb		1 to 2 c		15 to 25			1 to 1½

prior to freezing than does cut corn. The longer blanching time tends to overcook the corn kernels and makes necessary a short heating period when the corn is used.

Spinach and other leafy vegetables are better if partially defrosted before cooking to avoid overcooking the outer leaves before the block is defrosted. Using a fork to break solid blocks of frozen vegetables is an aid in shortening cooking time.

Frozen vegetables may be easily defrosted in a microwave oven. This is also a satisfactory method for completing the cooking process. If frozen vegetables are in compact blocks before cooking in a microwave oven, cooking should probably be interrupted midway during the process to separate the unthawed portion in the center and distribute it toward the edges of the container.

Using Canned Vegetables

Canned vegetables are already overcooked in the processing, hence a relatively short reheating time is preferable to avoid further softening of the vegetable. A short heating period is safe for commercially canned foods. However, it is recommended that home-canned vegetables be boiled for at least 10 minutes before tasting them in case botulinum toxin is present. Canned vegetables may be heated in the microwave oven as well as by conventional methods. Vitamin retention was measured when canned vegetables were reheated in two ways: (1) concentrating the drained liquid, then heating the vegetable in the liquid and serving the small amount of concentrated liquid with the vegetable; (2) reheating vegetable and liquid together and discarding the liquid [18]. Ascorbic acid loss varied from 20 to 60 percent in the preparation in which the liquid was concentrated, but the loss was distinctly greater in the method in which the liquid was discarded. No thiamin or riboflavin was lost by oxidation in either method but approximately 30 to 40 percent of these two vitamins was lost when the liquids were discarded. Obviously, other soluble nutrients are also lost when liquids are discarded. The flavor of many canned vegetables may also be improved by concentrating and using the liquid in the can. Canned green vegetables are olive-green in color in usual canning methods and tend to be very soft in texture.

Potatoes

Potatoes are among the most important and economical of vegetables. The white potato is a tuber of American origin, having been grown in northern Chile and Peru before the coming of the white man. There are many varieties of potatoes marketed. In the industry, potatoes are generally classified into five basic types: (1) round white; (2) russet Burbank (long russet group); (3) russet rural or round russet; (4) round red group; and (5) long white group. The skin of russet potatoes has a reddish brown, slightly mottled appearance. Several varieties of potatoes are pictured in Color Plate II. The Cobbler and Cherokee varieties are examples of the round white type; the Pontiac is a round red type; and White Rose is a long white type. A russet Burbank is also shown. Russet Burbank potatoes tend to be mealy and are excellent for baking. A mealy potato separates easily into fluffy particles that feel dry. Many of the other types are generally less mealy and more waxy. A waxy potato is more compact and moist or soggy and does not separate easily into separate fluffy particles. Waxy potatoes are good for boiling and for salads. Some varieties, such as Kennebec and Cherokee, are good all purpose potatoes and function quite well in both boiling and baking. Varieties particularly recommended for boiling include Chippewa, Cobbler, Katahdin, Red Pontiac, and White Rose.

The first U.S. quality standards for potatoes were developed in 1917 for use in wholesale marketing. These standards have been revised a number of times in keeping with changes in production and marketing. The top grade for potatoes is U.S. Extra No. 1 and the second grade is U.S. No. 1. Tolerances are set for defects, such as cuts, bruises, and sprouts, within each grade. Optional size designations may also be used by packers. The wholesale grade, usually U.S. No. 1, often appears on the bags of potatoes that are sold in retail stores.

The reasons why some potatoes are mealy and others waxy have not been completely clarified. The variety is an important influence on these cooking characteristics but the soil in which they are grown, fertilizers, and climate also have an effect. The content of starch in the potato may be related to its mealy or waxy tendencies. The starch granules swell markedly when potatoes are cooked and water tends to be absorbed when they are boiled. It has been suggested that the swelling of starch causes the separation of plant cells that occurs in mealy potatoes.

Even though the basic causes of mealiness and waxiness are not clarified, it has been shown that potatoes with higher starch content are more dense (have a higher specific gravity or weight to volume relationship) and that potatoes with a higher specific gravity, those that are heavier for their size, tend to be more mealy. It is possible to test this characteristic by placing potatoes in a brine solution of 1 cup salt to 11 cups water. If the potato floats, indicating a low solids content, it is probably best for boiling; if it sinks, it is a baker. Mealy potatoes that are high in starch content tend to slough off their outer layers when they are boiled. Storage at temperatures between 10–21° C (50–70° F) seems to decrease the tendency of the potato to slough during cooking. Also, if the cooking water contains enough calcium salt to maintain or slightly increase the calcium content of the potato, sloughing can be partially controlled.

Fresh potatoes are often boiled or baked in the home. Potatoes that are wrapped in aluminum foil before baking compare favorably in mealiness and flavor with those baked unwrapped [8] but baking time is somewhat increased for the foil-wrapped potatoes. Owners of microwave ovens often bake potatoes by microwaves instead of by conventional means. Microwave and conventionally baked Norgold Russet and Viking potatoes were compared by a trained taste panel and also by a group of 120 consumers in a supermarket. Microwave baked potatoes were rated lower in eating quality by the trained panel but the consumers found no significant differences in their acceptability or preference. Microwave baked potatoes had a greater percent cooking loss and were cooked in considerably less time [3].

Some potatoes darken after cooking, the amount of darkening varying with the variety, the locality and/or soil where grown, the season, and differences in chemical composition. It is now generally accepted that discoloration is the result of the formation of a dark-colored complex of ferric iron and a polyphenol, probably chlorogenic acid.

When harvested potatoes are exposed to light a green pigmentation may develop on the surface. This greening has occurred in retail stores where the potatoes are exposed to artificial light. Greening is accompanied by the formation of solanine, a bitter alkaloid, which is toxic if consumed in relatively large amounts. Controlled atmosphere storage of potatoes may help to control greening [14]. When selecting potatoes, avoid green ones. If potatoes start to turn green before they are used, the green-colored portions should be cut away during preliminary preparation.

Large quantities of potatoes are processed in the United States into frozen, dehydrated, and canned potato products that are partially prepared for serving before they are brought into the home. These products are part of the group of convenience foods that are discussed in Chapter 2. Frozen French fried potatoes are a popular convenience item for consumers if they can be baked in the oven rather than finish-fried in the home. A surface-texturizing process that improves the quality of baked French fried potatoes has been developed at USDA's Western Regional Research Laboratory [31]. Fabricated French fried potatoes prepared from mashed potatoes are competing with fries made directly from raw potatoes [30].

Dried Legumes

Legumes include dried beans, peas, and lentils. Many different varieties, varying in color, shape, and size, are used for food. When legumes are cooked, proteins are made more available, starch is at least partially gelatinized [12], the flavor is improved, and some potentially toxic substances are destroyed. The dried legumes offer a special problem in cooking. Water lost in ripening and drying must be replaced by soaking in water and by cooking. Because the legumes are hard and the cellulose or fiber well developed, the legumes must also be softened during the cooking process. The ease of softening depends somewhat upon how readily the legumes absorb water.

Alkali in the form of baking soda has been used to hasten the softening of dried beans during cooking in the home. Alkalies increase water absorption, but there has been some question concerning the use of baking soda because of its destructive effect on the thiamin content of legumes. Another point of objection to the use of baking soda has been the possibility that the bean texture will become too soft. If used, the amount of baking soda needs to be carefully regulated (1/8 teaspoon per pint of water) to prevent deleterious effects insofar as the flavor and appearance of cooked beans are concerned. In these amounts, baking soda can serve as an aid in softening the seed coats if it is necessary to use hard water for cooking the beans. Soft water is preferable for both soaking and cooking dry beans since the calcium and magnesium salts in hard water may form insoluble salts with pectic substances in the cell walls and between cells in the bean tissue and inhibit proper hydration. There is more water absorbed and fewer hard beans remaining at the end of cooking when soft water rather than hard water is used.

The rate of hydration is faster in hot water than at room temperature or by the method of soaking all night in cold water [9]. Dry beans absorb as much water in 1 hour, when soaking is started by first boiling the beans for 2 minutes, as they do in 15 hours of soaking in cold water. If they are hot soaked, as generally recommended, the beans are cooked in the water used for soaking. Additional water is absorbed during the cooking process, making a gain in weight of 150 to 160 percent (about 4 cups of water per cup of dry beans for both soaking and cooking).

The relatively low consumption of dry beans in the United States has been attributed to the long preparation time required. Processes involving vacuum treatment in salt solutions before rinsing and drying beans have been used to produce quick-cooking dry beans [33]. Cooking times for most of the processed beans are between 25 and 35 minutes.

Soybeans are an excellent source of protein and have been used for centuries in various forms as a food staple by millions of people in China and Japan. In the United States their use has been limited by an objectionable flavor and odor, sometimes characterized as "painty" or "beany." Much research has gone into the study of this flavor problem and a number of processes have been developed to control it. The off flavor appears to be caused by the enzyme lipoxidase, and it is now possible to inactivate the enzyme before it can catalyze any off flavor. Many acceptable soybean products are prepared, including canned soybeans with chicken or pork, vegetarian-style soybeans, and soybean soup [28]. A USDA pamphlet [36] gives many suggestions for the use of soybeans in family meals. Soy products are used in the preparation of many convenience foods and meat analogs. The use of soy products as meat extenders decreases costs while adding some protein of reasonably good nutritional quality.

Study Questions

1. What are vegetables? (Define them.)
2. List eight classification groups of vegetables based on the parts of the plant that are used as food and give examples of vegetables in each category.
3. The composition and nutritive value of vegetables differs depending upon the part of the plant used. Indicate which types of vegetables are generally:
   a. High in water content
   b. High in starch
   c. High in protein
   d. High in fiber components (cellulose, hemicelluloses, pectic substances)
   e. Good sources of ascorbic acid and vitamin A
   f. Low in kilocalories
4. The color of fruits and vegetables is due to their content of certain pigments.
   a. List four major groups of plant pigments and describe the colors for each group.
   b. How do the pigments and/or colors change in the presence of acid and of alkali and with prolonged heating?
   c. Explain why it is important to preserve the natural colors of vegetables during cooking.
5. The flavor of vegetables varies from one to another and many substances contribute to the characteristic flavors.
   a. List two different families of vegetables that are considered to be strong flavored and indicate what types of compounds are responsible for these flavors.
   b. Explain how cooking procedures may change these flavors.
6. Describe the usual characteristics of fresh vegetables of good quality.
7. Suggest appropriate methods for the storage of various types of fresh vegetables so that their quality will be retained.
8. Both fresh and processed vegetables may be graded.
   a. What advantages result from the use of grades on fresh vegetables?
   b. What is the factor most limiting the use of consumer grades for fresh vegetables?

    c. List three USDA grades that may be used on canned and frozen vegetables and discuss the value to the consumer of grading these products.

9. Why is it important to thoroughly cleanse fresh vegetables as a first step in their preparation?

10. Describe several ways in which losses may occur during the cooking of vegetables.

11. In the following list, check each of the items that describes what may happen when vegetables are cooked and correct any incorrect statements:

    a. Starch swells and gelatinizes
    b. Cellulose fibers harden
    c. Volatile flavors are trapped inside the cells
    d. Leafy vegetables become limp
    e. Cellulose fibers soften slightly
    f. Intercellular cement is hardened
    g. Vitamins go off in the steam
    h. Some vitamins and minerals dissolve in the cooking water
    i. Texture becomes softer
    j. Some vitamins are lost by oxidation
    k. Some volatile flavors are lost
    l. Chlorophyll may be changed to anthocyanins
    m. Carotenes may become white
    n. Some volatile acids are released
    o. Pheophytin, an olive-green pigment, may be produced from chlorophyll
    p. Proteins are coagulated
    q. Pectic substances are broken down

12. Describe an appropriate procedure for boiling each of the following vegetables and explain why you would use this procedure in each case:

    a. A green vegetable such as broccoli
    b. Cabbage
    c. Onions
    d. Beets

13. Describe five appropriate methods for cooking vegetables in addition to boiling.

14. Describe an appropriate method for preparing the following for service:

    a. Frozen vegetables
    b. Canned vegetables

15. Explain why frozen vegetables require less time for cooking than similar fresh vegetables do.

16. a. Describe characteristics of mealy potatoes and of waxy potatoes.
    b. For what uses is each type of potato best suited and why?
    c. Compare the probable characteristics of potatoes baked after wrapping in foil, those baked unwrapped, and those baked in a microwave oven.

17. Explain why the green pigmentation that sometimes develops on potatoes exposed to light should not be eaten.

18. Describe a satisfactory method for cooking dried beans and explain why this procedure would be appropriate.

References

1. Augustin, J., R. E. McDole, G. M. McMaster, C. G. Painter, and W. C. Sparks. 1975. Ascorbic acid content in russet Burbank potatoes. *Journal of Food Science* **40**, 415.

2. Bowman, F., E. Page, E. E. Remmenga, and D. Trump. 1971. Microwave vs. conventional cooking of vegetables at high altitude. *Journal of the American Dietetic Association* **58**, 427.

3. Brittin, H. C., and J. E. Trevino. 1980. Acceptability of microwave and conventionally baked potatoes. *Journal of Food Science* **45**, 1425.

4. Campbell, C. L., T. Y. Lin, and B. E. Proctor. 1958. Microwave vs. conventional cooking. I. Reduced and total ascorbic acid in vegetables. *Journal of the American Dietetic Association* **34**, 365.

5. Chapman, V. J., J. O. Putz, G. L. Gilpin, J. P. Sweeney, and J. N. Eisen. 1960. Electronic cooking of fresh and frozen broccoli. *Journal of Home Economics* **52**, 161.

6. Charles, V. R., and F. O. van Duyne. 1958. Effect of holding and reheating on the ascorbic acid content of cooked vegetables. *Journal of Home Economics* **50**, 159.

7. Charles, V. R., and F. O. van Duyne. 1954. Palatability and retention of ascorbic acid of vegetables cooked in a tightly covered saucepan and in a "waterless" cooker. *Journal of Home Economics* **46**, 659.

8. Cunningham, H. H., and M. V. Zaehringer. 1972. Quality of baked potatoes as influenced by baking and holding methods. *American Potato Journal* **49**, 271.

9. Dawson, E. H., J. C. Lamb, E. W. Toepfer, and H. W. Warren. *Development of Rapid Methods of Soaking and Cooking Dry Beans.* Technical Bulletin No. 1051. Washington, DC: U.S. Department of Agriculture, 1952.

10. Eheart, M. S. 1970. Effect of storage and other variables on composition of frozen broccoli. *Food Technology* **24**, 1009.

11. Eheart, M. S., and D. Odland. 1972. Storage of fresh broccoli and green beans. *Journal of the American Dietetic Association* **60**, 402.

12. Elbert, E. M., and R. L. Witt. 1968. Gelatinization of starch in the common dry bean, *Phaseolus vulgaris. Journal of Home Economics* **60**, 186.

13. Fordham, J. R., C. E. Wells, and L. H. Chen. 1975. Sprouting of seeds and nutrient composition of seeds and sprouts. *Journal of Food Science* **40**, 552.

14. Forsyth, F. R., and C. A. Eaves. 1968. Greening of potatoes: CA cure. *Food Technology* **22**, 48.

15. Gordon, J., and I. Noble. 1964. "Waterless" vs. boiling water cooking of vegetables. *Journal of the American Dietetic Association* **44**, 378.

16. Herranz, J., C. Vidal-Valverde, and E. Rojas-Hidalgo. 1983. Cellulose, hemicellulose and lignin content of raw and cooked processed vegetables. *Journal of Food Science* **48**, 274.

17. Herranz, J., C. Vidal-Valverde, and E. Rojas-Hidalgo. 1981. Cellulose, hemicellulose and lignin content of raw and cooked Spanish vegetables. *Journal of Food Science* **46**, 1927.

18. Hinman, W. F., M. K. Brush, and E. G. Halliday. 1945. The nutritive value of canned foods. VII. Effect of small-scale preparation on the ascorbic acid, thiamine, and riboflavin content of commercially canned vegetables. *Journal of the American Dietetic Association* **21**, 7.

19. *How to Buy Canned and Frozen Vegetables.* Home and Garden Bulletin No. 167. Washington, DC: Consumer and Marketing Service, U.S. Department of Agriculture, 1977.

20. *How to Buy Dry Beans, Peas, and Lentils.* Home and Garden Bulletin No. 177. Washington, DC: Consumer and Marketing Service, U.S. Department of Agriculture, 1970.

21. *How to Buy Fresh Vegetables.* Home and Garden Bulletin No. 143. Washington, DC: Consumer and Marketing Service, U.S. Department of Agriculture, 1980.

22. *How to Buy Potatoes.* Home and Garden Bulletin No. 198. Washington, DC: Consumer and Marketing Service, U.S. Department of Agriculture, 1972.

23. Klein, B. P., C. H. Y. Kuo, and G. Boyd. 1981. Folacin and ascorbic acid retention in fresh raw, microwave, and conventionally cooked spinach. *Journal of Food Science* **46,** 640.

24. Liener, I. 1979. Significance for humans of biologically active factors in soybeans and other food legumes. *Journal of the American Oil Chemists' Society* **56,** 121.

25. MacLeod, A. J., and G. MacLeod. 1970. The flavor volatiles of dehydrated cabbage. *Journal of Food Science* **35,** 739.

26. MacLeod, A. J., and G. MacLeod. 1970. Effects of variations in cooking methods on the flavor volatiles of cabbage. *Journal of Food Science* **35,** 744.

27. Matthee, V., and H. Appledorf. 1978. Effect of cooking on vegetable fiber. *Journal of Food Science* **43,** 1344.

28. Nelson, A. I., L. S. Wei, and M. P. Steinberg. 1971. Food products from whole soybeans. *Soybean Digest* (January).

29. Noble, I. 1967. Ascorbic acid and color of vegetables. *Journal of the American Dietetic Association* **50,** 304.

30. Nonaka, M., R. N. Sayre, and K. C. Ng. 1978. Surface texturization of extruded and preformed potato products by a three-step, dry-steam-dry process. *Journal of Food Science* **43,** 904.

31. Nonaka, M., and M. L. Weaver. 1973. Texturizing process improves quality of baked French fried potatoes. *Food Technology* **27,** 50 (no. 3).

32. Payne, I. R. 1967. Ascorbic acid retention in frozen corn. *Journal of the American Dietetic Association* **51,** 344.

33. Rockland, L. B., and E. A. Metzler. 1967. Quick-cooking lima and other dry beans. *Food Technology* **21,** 334.

34. Singh, B., C. C. Yang, D. K. Salunkhe, and A. R. Rahman. 1972. Controlled atmosphere storage of lettuce. 1. Effects on quality and the respiration rate of lettuce heads. *Journal of Food Science* **37,** 48.

35. Singh, R. P., R. H. Buelow, and D. B. Lund. 1973. Storage behavior of artificially waxed green snap beans. *Journal of Food Science* **38,** 542.

36. *Soybeans in Family Meals.* Home and Garden Bulletin No. 208. Washington, DC: U.S. Department of Agriculture, 1979.

37. Sweeney, J. P. 1970. Improved chlorophyll retention in green beans held on a steam table. *Food Technology* **24,** 490.

38. Sweeney, J. P., G. L. Gilpin, M. E. Martin, and E. H. Dawson. 1960. Palatability and nutritive value of frozen broccoli. *Journal of the American Dietetic Association* **36,** 122.

39. Sweeney, J. P., G. L. Gilpin, M. G. Staley, and M. E. Martin. 1959. Effect of cooking methods on broccoli. I. Ascorbic acid and carotene. *Journal of the American Dietetic Association* **35,** 354.

40. *The Buying Guide for Fresh Fruits, Vegetables, Herbs, and Nuts,* 7th rev. ed. Hagerstown, MD: Blue Goose, Inc., 1980.

41. *Vegetables in Family Meals.* Home and Garden Bulletin No. 105. Washington, DC: U.S. Department of Agriculture, 1980.

42. Von Elbe, J. H., I. Maing, and C. H. Amundson. 1974. Color stability of betanin. *Journal of Food Science* **39,** 334.

43. Walker, M. A., M. M. Hill, and F. D. Millman. 1973. Fruit and vegetable acceptance by students. *Journal of the American Dietetic Association* **62,** 268.

8

Fruits and Fruit Preparation

Classification

Fruits are produced from a flower or flowers and are the ripened ovary or ovaries of a plant together with adjacent tissues. Botanically, some foods used as vegetables, nuts, or grains are fruits of the plants. However, the foods commonly designated as fruits in food preparation are fleshy or pulpy in character, often juicy, and usually sweet with fragrant, aromatic flavors. The classification according to common usage does not always agree with botanical classifications. Several fleshy botanical fruits, such as tomatoes and squash, are not sweet and are used as vegetables. Cereal grains, nuts, and legumes are dry, not fleshy, fruits and have been classified into separate groups for practical use. Rhubarb, which is not a fruit in the botanical sense, is often used as a fruit in meal preparation.

Fleshy fruits may be classified as simple, aggregate, or multiple, depending upon the number of ovaries and flowers from which the fruit develops. Examples of simple fleshy fruits, which develop from a single ovary in one flower, are the citrus fruits, such as oranges (Figure 8-1), grapefruit, lemons, and limes; drupes, such as apricots, cherries, peaches, and plums, which have a stone or pit enclosing the seed; and pomes, such as apples and pears, which have a core. Examples of aggregate fruits, developing from several ovaries in one flower, are raspberries, strawberries, and blackberries. Pineapple is an example of a multiple fruit that has developed from a cluster of several flowers.

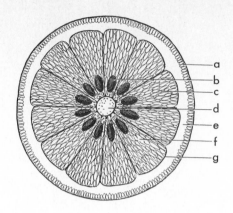

8-1 *Cross section of an orange. a, oil sacs in flavedo; b, seed; c, juice sacs; d, center core; e, albedo; f, segment; g, segment membrane.* (From Chemistry and Technology of Citrus, Citrus Products and By-products, Agricultural Handbook No. 98, USDA)

Composition and Nutritive Value

Most fruits are made up of an edible portion combined with some refuse. Some fruits, such as bananas and pineapple, show as high as 33 to 39 percent refuse or waste. The chief energy constituent present is carbohydrate, which occurs mainly as sugars. Most fruits have only a trace of fat, with a few exceptions such as avocado which has 17 percent. Fruits have only a small amount of protein, and their water content averages about 85 percent. Fruits as a class are valuable chiefly for their vitamin and mineral content and for their dietary fiber or indigestible residue. The caloric value of fruits, as served, is usually higher than that of succulent vegetables because of the higher sugar content of fruits [22].

Some fruits are especially valuable as a source of ascorbic acid (vitamin C), whereas others contain only small amounts of this vitamin (Figure 8-2). Yellow fruits contain carotenoid pigments that are precursors of vitamin A. Pink varieties of grapefruit have higher vitamin A value than white varieties. The B vitamins occur in relatively low concentration in fruits. Fruits may vary widely in their vitamin content. Variety, growing climate and sunlight, and stage of maturity have been shown to be significant factors. In addition, handling practices, methods of processing, storage temperatures, and the length of time of storage of fruits may produce a decrease of as much as 50 percent in some vitamin values. The composition and vitamin content of some selected fruits and fruit juices are given in Appendix C.

The citrus fruits are probably the most dependable all-year source of ascorbic acid. Tomatoes are only about half as rich in vitamin C but, because of their wide use, are also a significant source. In season, dependence may be placed on the strawberry and the cantaloupe as sources of ascorbic acid. A generous serving of strawberries may easily provide the recommended daily allowance of this vitamin for an adult. So long as strawberries are not bruised or hulled, they retain their ascorbic acid well. Wash strawberries before hulling to avoid dissolving some vitamin C from the exposed tissues. When strawberries are prepared for shortcake, less ascorbic acid is lost if they are sliced rather than crushed before being combined with the sugar.

Several varieties of cantaloupe are rich in ascorbic acid. When these fruits are at their optimum ripeness for fine flavor, they have the greatest concentration of ascorbic acid, and the soft center flesh is richer in the vitamin than the harder, firmer flesh near the rind. Honeydew melons rate lower than cantaloupes, and watermelon is a comparatively poor source of ascorbic acid. The guava is not used extensively in the United States although it is extremely rich in ascorbic acid, containing an average of 242 milligrams per 100 grams of edible fruit.

Plants tend to concentrate calcium in leaves and phosphorus in seeds. Iron is found in many green-colored plants, especially in leaves. Fruits are not generally considered to be excellent sources of calcium, phosphorus, or iron (three minerals that require special dietary planning if recommended allowances are to be met). However, blackberries, raspberries, strawberries, and dried apricots, prunes, dates, and figs may contribute appreciable amounts of iron to the diet. Of the fruits available year around, only oranges, grapefruit, and figs are fair sources of calcium.

8-2 *Excellent sources of ascorbic acid include fresh strawberries, citrus fruits, and cantaloupe. Fresh blackberries also contain appreciable amounts of the vitamin. Combined with cottage cheese, fresh fruits make an appetizing fruit salad. (Courtesy of Sunkist Growers, Inc.)*

Cellulose and Pectic Substances

Cellulose contributes to the structure of plant materials by its presence in the cell walls. Hemicelluloses are found along with cellulose. Both of these substances are complex carbohydrates called *polysaccharides,* which furnish indigestible fiber in the diet. The pectic substances constitute another group of polysaccharides which is not digested by humans. They are found in the cell walls and between the cells, where they act as a cementing substance that binds cells together. Pectic substances include protopectin, the insoluble "parent" molecule, pectinic acid or pectin, and pectic acid.

As fruits ripen, protopectin is gradually degraded to pectin and pectin is changed to pectic acid. These changes are at least partially responsible for the softening of fruit tissues during ripening. Heating fruits may also cause pectic substances to be broken down. This is one factor that affects the ease with which cooked plant tissues disintegrate. Acids and alkalies affect the structure of fruits and vegetables when they are boiled. Acids make the structure more firm, whereas alkalies tend to disintegrate the fibrous components, particularly the hemicelluloses.

Flavor Constituents

Fruits owe their characteristic flavors largely to certain aromatic compounds present. Many of these compounds are esters, such as methylbutyrate, which is responsible for the typical odor and flavor of pineapple. Other compounds include aldehydes such as benzaldehyde derivatives and various alcohols which have been found to be responsible for the floral and fruity part of the aroma of apricots [4]. Many different compounds contribute to flavor; for example, at least thirty-two flavor substances have been identified in the aroma of apricots and thirty-seven components in extracted orange essence [17]. Some of the flavor compounds can be synthesized in the laboratory and may form the basis for developing artificial flavorings.

The organic acids of fruits also contribute to flavor. The acid may occur in the free form or combined as salts or esters. Malic and citric are the acids occurring most commonly in fruits, but tartaric acid is a prominent constituent of grapes. Mixtures of acids may occur but one acid usually predominates. Fruits of the plum family and cranberries contain some benzoic acid that cannot be used by the body but is excreted as hippuric acid. Rhubarb contains variable amounts of oxalic acid, depending on the maturity of the plant. Oxalic acid usually combines with calcium in the plant to form insoluble calcium oxalate, which is not absorbed from the digestive tract. Fruits vary in acidity and some of this variation depends upon variety and growing conditions. Scores for flavor have been positively correlated with pH or active acidity in some fruits such as peaches and raspberries [20].

Other substances that affect the flavor of fruits are sugars, some mineral salts, and a group of phenolic compounds formerly called tannins. Fruits cooked in metal containers may form some acid salts with metals. Tin or iron salts may sometimes produce a metallic flavor, but these salts are not harmful. The phenolic compounds impart a bitter taste and produce an astringent or puckery feeling in the mouth. They appear to be present in the largest amount in immature fruits.

Some fruits, as well as other plants, contain essential oils. Oil of lemon and oil of orange, which are well-known examples of such oils, occur in the leathery skin of the fruit and may be expressed and used as flavoring or as the basis of extracts that are made by combining the oil with alcohol. Care must be used in flavoring foods with oils because of their highly concentrated flavor.

The flavor of each fruit is characteristic for that fruit. For example, a raw ripe banana is readily identified by its odor and taste that are the result of a specific combination of flavor components. The flavor of fruits, in general, may be described as tart, fragrant, and

sweet, these characteristics blending together in a pleasant and re-
freshing flavor bouquet.

Color

The pigments in fruits are the same as those in vegetables (see
Chapter 7, Vegetables and Vegetable Preparation, pp. 111–113).
The yellow and orange carotenoid and the red, purple, and blue anthocyanin pigments predominate in fruits. The carotenoids are almost insoluble in water and are not much affected by the presence of
acids or alkalies, although acid may produce a somewhat less intense orange color. The anthocyanins are very soluble and tend to
turn bluish or purplish in an alkaline medium. Certain combinations of fruit juices sometimes show surprising, often unattractive,
color changes. The tin or iron salts that are present in canned fruits
may explain some reactions that occur, the metals combining with
the anthocyanin pigments, producing violet or blue-green colors.
Pineapple juice contains a small amount of iron from equipment
used in its processing and when added to red or purple fruit juices
will change their color to blue or intensify the original blue color.
Usually acid in the form of lemon juice intensifies the red color of
red or blue fruit juice mixtures. Orange juice is best omitted from
combinations of red or blue fruit juices as it often produces a brownish color if present in fairly large quantity. The color of canned
fruits containing anthocyanin pigments tends to deteriorate on storage whether the container is tin or glass. This deterioration is
greater in the presence of light and warm temperatures.

Some raw fruits, such as bananas, apples, and peaches, tend to
turn dark when peeled or cut surfaces are exposed to the air. The
darkening results from the oxidation of phenolic compounds in the
fruit when oxygen from the air is available. The reaction is catalyzed by oxidizing enzymes that are present in the plant tissue (see
p. 74 for a discussion of enzymes). Brown colored pigments are produced.

Lemon juice, which is high in acid and evidently interferes with
enzyme activity, is often used to coat pared fruits to retard discoloration. Pineapple juice accomplishes the same purpose, although its
acidity is less than that of lemon juice. Pineapple juice contains a
sulfhydryl compound that seems to act as an antioxidant in retarding browning. Added ascorbic acid, either alone or as part of several
available commercial products, aids in reducing discoloration because of its ability to act as an antioxidant. Sulfur dioxide may be
used to inhibit enzyme activity before fruits are dehydrated.

Fruit Juices

Fruit juices are a very important means of utilizing fresh fruits. The commercial fruit juice industry in the United States has had a spectacular rise since 1925. During the 1950s the fruit juice consumption in this country surpassed that of fruit processed in all other forms and this trend has continued on into the 1980s. Much of the increase in fruit juice production has been with citrus fruits. Since the commercial introduction of frozen orange concentrate in 1945 and 1946, this product has become the leader among processed fruits in terms of fresh weight equivalent consumed. More than 80 percent of the Florida orange crop is used to produce frozen concentrate [6].

There is a loss of some edible material when citrus juices are squeezed and the juice strained, so that the total nutritive value of the whole fruit is somewhat higher than the juice coming from it. The extraction of juice is a preparatory step and treatment for preservation must follow. Ascorbic acid is easily oxidized and in the making and processing of some fruit juices, such as the pressing of apples where air is incorporated, much of the vitamin may be lost. However, the apple is not a rich source of ascorbic acid even in the raw, fresh form. Fortunately, there is little loss of ascorbic acid during the preparation and canning of citrus juices. The freezing and subsequent storage of orange juice at a temperature of $-18°$ C ($0°$ F) or below does not cause a substantial loss of ascorbic acid, especially if aeration before freezing is avoided. Possibly because of their high acidity citrus juices tend to retain ascorbic acid well. Even after eight days of storage at $3°$ C ($37°$ F), 80 to 85 percent of the original ascorbic acid was reported to be retained in reconstituted frozen orange juice [1]. Apple, cranberry, grape, pineapple, and prune juices and apricot nectar contain little or no ascorbic acid unless enriched. Manufacturers are now adding ascorbic acid to some juices partly to improve the vitamin value and partly to improve their appearance, flavor, and stability during storage. Ascorbic acid added to noncitrus juices may be less stable than the vitamin naturally present in citrus juices. In opened containers stored in a refrigerator, the ascorbic acid in canned orange juice was found to be much more stable up to 16 days than the ascorbic acid in canned apple juice to which the vitamin had been added [18].

In the preparation of orange juice concentrate the fruit is usually graded, washed, and sanitized before it enters the juice extractors. After leaving the extractors the juice may go through a series of finishers to remove the seeds and pulp. It is then concentrated and may also be flash-heated to destroy pectin-degrading enzymes (see p. 148) [5]. Several different processes may be used to remove water from the juice, including evaporation under vacuum, use of osmosis or reverse osmosis through selective membranes, and partial freezing with separation of the resulting ice crystals. Evaporation is the most commonly used procedure [6]. After evaporation the juice is usually mixed with some fresh or single-strength juice to restore much of the fresh flavor and aroma that may have been lost during evaporation. Concentrated orange aroma or essence solutions have been prepared and added back to the concentrated juice instead of or in addition to the fresh single-strength juice [10]. This use of aroma solution appears to be as satisfactory as the addition of fresh juice. The chilled concentrate is then quick-frozen. Frozen concentrated orange juice should be kept stored at a temperature of $-18°$ C $(0°$ F) or below, both in market channels and at home, to retard losses of nutritive value, flavor, and other quality characteristics. Whole fruit citrus purees from oranges or grapefruit have been reported to make excellent bases for beverages and beverage mixes [16].

Noncitrus juices are also sold as concentrates. Problems similar to those encountered with concentrated orange juice in loss of volatile flavor substances have been found with these juices. One of the major advantages in the use of fruit juice concentrates is that the volume is greatly reduced and shipping and handling costs are less. Concentrated juices and fruit purees may be dehydrated by roller- or drum-drying, spray-drying, or foam-mat drying. Although some flavor loss occurs in drying, the final product is acceptable. The ascorbic acid content of dehydrated, reconstituted orange juice is very similar to the canned and frozen products.

A number of synthetic dry beverage mixtures, many of them orange-flavored, have been marketed in recent years. In a preference study with 630 consumers, dry orange drink formulations were found to compare favorably with frozen juices and sweetened canned juices and were rated higher than unsweetened canned juices [7].

The Florida Citrus Commission has established standards for fresh orange juice and permits the word *fresh* to be used in labeling and promoting it. However, as marketed, fresh juice has a shelf life of less than a week. It contains all the active enzymes that cause juices to separate and start deterioration within a few hours. The quality of the juice is, of course, dependent upon the quality of the fruit from which it is made. Fresh juice is limited to delivery in the immediate area in which it is produced.

A stabilized juice has been prepared by a flash pasteurization process or some other method that destroys the enzymes that cause deteriorative changes in the juice. If pasteurized, the juice is very quickly cooled and packaged. As marketed, it has several times the shelf life of fresh untreated juice. This juice is what has become known as *dairy pack* orange juice and is delivered by refrigerated trucks from Florida to the eastern seaboard and as far inland as practicable. Liquid fruit juices are increasingly being transported in bulk. Tanks for this purpose may be installed on trucks, railway cars, or in ships.

To eliminate some of the problems attached to the marketing of fresh or stabilized single-strength fruit juice, a concentrate may be prepared at the point of production. It varies from 42 to 60 percent of its original volume. The concentrate is bulk packaged, quickly frozen at a temperature of $-24°$ C ($-10°$ F), and held until wanted for reconstitution to its original volume. It may be shipped as a concentrate in refrigerated trucks and reconstituted at the point of sales. This is a great saving in the cost of transportation. If facilities permit, the concentrate may be held frozen and reconstituted and packaged as needed.

Orange juice is often sold in food-service establishments from dispensers in which it is kept chilled and aerated. The Florida Citrus Commission has reported that, in a study on eight juice dispensers, the retention of ascorbic acid in the juice was 94 to 97 percent of the original amount after 1 day and 84 to 92 percent after 4 days of holding [2].

Pectic substances in fruit juices are chiefly responsible for a haze or cloudy appearance of the juices. These substances are present in the cell walls and are released into the juice when it is extracted. In citrus juices this cloud is desirable and it is stabilized by flash heating to destroy pectin-degrading enzymes that may destabilize the cloud. However, juices such as apple and grape are preferred when they are clear. Pectinase is added to these juices and allowed to break down the pectic substances so that they do not produce a haze. The treated juice is less viscous and can be easily filtered. This process is called *clarification*. The color and flavor of the clarified juices are also stabilized.

Changes During Ripening

Distinct changes occur in many fruits during ripening. These changes include (1) a decrease in green color and development of yellow-orange or red-blue colors; (2) a softening of the flesh; (3) the development of characteristic pleasant flavors; and (4) changes in soluble solids such as sugars and organic acids. The change in color is associated both with synthesis of new pigments and breakdown of the green pigment, chlorophyll. Chlorophyll may mask yellow carotenoid pigments in the immature fruit. Anthocyanins are probably synthesized as ripening proceeds.

The softening of fruits during ripening involves changes in the pectic substances. The complex insoluble protopectin is degraded to pectinic acid or pectin. Pectin has gel-forming properties that are important in the making of jams and jellies. Pectin is changed to pectic acid, which does not have the same gelling ability. The breakdown of pectic substances found between plant cells may cause separation of cells as part of the softening process. Many fruits soften faster as the temperature of the surrounding air is increased [3].

The development of a characteristic pleasant flavor in ripened fruit involves a decrease in acidity and an increase in sugar along with the production of a complex mixture of volatile substances and essential oils. In some fruits, such as bananas, the increase in sugar is accompanied by a decrease in starch. However, the increase in sugar content occurs even though some fruits, such as peaches, contain no appreciable amount of starch at any time. Some cell wall polysaccharides may decrease as the sugar content increases. The phenolic compounds, with their astringent properties, seem to decrease.

Ethylene gas is usually produced in small amounts in the fruit during maturation and causes some physiological changes associated with the ripening process. Fruits that have been harvested well before ripening has started may be stored in an atmosphere that contains ethylene gas to speed up the ripening process. In general, there is no material difference in the gross composition of fruits that ripen naturally and those ripened by ethylene gas.

Ripeness and the method of ripening may influence the vitamin content of fruits. The ascorbic acid content of bananas is greatest in fully ripe fruit, although the total amount present is relatively small. Vine-ripened tomatoes have a higher ascorbic acid value than tomatoes that were picked green and ripened off the vine.

Storage of Fresh Fruits

Fruits continue to respire after harvesting, that is, they take in oxygen and give off carbon dioxide. Cold temperatures reduce this fruit metabolism. Ripening processes are also retarded by cold storage. Industry may use a process called *controlled atmosphere* for the long-term storage of certain fruits. In this method of storage the oxygen in the atmosphere is reduced below the normal 21 percent level to as low as 2 to 3 percent. This markedly lowers the rate of cell metabolism and aging in the fruit, delaying the changes that would normally occur and prolonging the storage life. For example, changes in pigments, decrease in acid, loss of sugars, and breakdown of pectic substances are retarded in apples stored at 3.5° C (38° F) in an atmosphere containing 5 percent carbon dioxide and 3 percent oxygen [14]. Controlled atmosphere storage of apples has made it possible for the consumer to purchase crisp and juicy apples in late spring and early summer [15].

There is a critical oxygen level for each stored fruit. If a particular fruit is stored below this level, its tissues are injured. Relatively high carbon dioxide levels are sometimes used with the low oxygen atmosphere. However, the atmosphere is carefully monitored and excess carbon dioxide, produced by the fruit during respiration, is removed so that a desirable level of carbon dioxide is constantly maintained. Temperature and humidity are also carefully controlled.

Commercial generators and sensitive monitoring equipment make it possible to control the atmosphere not only in airtight storage warehouses but also in transportation vehicles. This process allows a higher quality to be maintained in fresh fruits and vegetables being shipped over long distances. Not all products respond equally well to controlled atmosphere storage and some may not be at all suited to this kind of treatment.

Most fresh fruits are very perishable and require refrigeration. Soft fruits such as berries keep better if spread out on a flat surface. Citrus fruits, except lemons, which keep best at a temperature of 13° to 15° C (55° to 58° F), should be refrigerated. They can be kept from drying out by being covered so that a more moist atmosphere is provided. The avocado and the banana are so injured by chilling that they discolor and lose the power of ripening if later held at warmer temperatures. Bananas are injured if held at temperatures lower than 13° C (55° F) *before* ripening. If these and other tropical fruits must be held for a while, they should be ripened before being stored at colder temperatures. After ripening, avocados hold best at about 4° C (40° F).

Selection of Some Common Fruits

Apples

Apples are among the most widely used fruits. They may be found locally in most parts of the United States in many varieties that differ in characteristics and seasonal availability. The seasons during which apples are available have been lengthened by controlled atmosphere storage. Of the approximately seven thousand varieties of apples grown in the United States, only about twenty are considered valuable. For good flavor, texture, and storing ability, apples should be mature when picked. Good-quality apples are firm, crisp, and well colored. Many consumer packages may show variety, grade, and size. U.S. grades include U.S. Extra Fancy, U.S. Fancy, U.S. No. 1, and U.S. No. 2. However, the U.S. Department of Agriculture is gradually phasing in the use of four uniform grade terms for all fresh fruits and vegetables. These are U.S. Fancy, U.S. No. 1, U.S. No. 2, and U.S. No. 3 [9]. The qualities of color, maturity, general appearance, and lack of defects determine the grade [13].

Apples have many culinary uses and are relatively inexpensive when grown locally. They may be served fresh in salads or as desserts and cooked in sauces, pies, cobblers, and so on. Table 8-1 lists some of the well-known varieties of apples with suggestions for their use. Color Plate I illustrates several varieties of apples.

Table 8-1 *Desirability of Various Apple Varieties for Different Uses**

Variety	Flavor and Texture	Fresh and Salad	Pie	Sauce	Baking	Freezing (Slices)	Main Season
Cortland	Mild, tender	Excel.	Excel.	V. good	Good	V. good	Oct. to Jan.
Red Delicious	Sweet, mellow	Excel.	Poor	Fair	Poor	Fair	Sept. to May
Golden Delicious	Sweet, semifirm	Excel.	V. good	Good	V. good	V. good	Sept. to Apr.
Gravenstein	Tart, crisp	Good	Good	Good	Good	Good	July to Sept.
R. I. Greening	Slightly tart, firm	Poor	Excel.	Excel.	V. good	Excel.	Oct. to Mar.
Jonathan	Tart, tender	V. good	V. good	V. good	Poor	V. good	Sept. to Jan.
McIntosh	Slightly tart, tender	Excel.	Excel.	Good	Fair	Good	Sept. to Apr.
Rome Beauty	Slightly tart, firm	Good	V. good	V. good	Excel.	V. good	Oct. to Apr.
Stayman	Tart, semifirm	Excel.	Good	Good	Good	Good	Oct. to Mar.
Winesap	Slightly tart, firm	Excel.	Good	Good	Good	V. good	Oct. to June
Yellow Transparent	Tart, soft	Poor	Excel.	Good	Poor	Poor	July to Aug.
York Imperial	Tart, firm	Fair	Good	V. good	Good	Good	Oct. to May

*From [21].

Avocados

The bland flavor and texture of avocados blend well with many other foods. Avocados contain about 17 percent fat. Many varieties of avocados are grown in both California and Florida, and avocados are available all year. They may be purchased slightly underripe and ripened at room temperature, preferably in a dark place. When ready for use they should yield to gentle pressure on the skin. Avocados should be refrigerated only after ripening.

Bananas

Bananas are picked and shipped green; they are stored and ripened as needed. They develop their best eating quality after they are harvested. Since bananas are sensitive to cool temperatures, they should not be kept in the refrigerator. The ideal temperature for ripening bananas is 16° to 21° C (61° to 70° F). When purchased, bananas should be firm, bright, and free from bruises. They are at their best for eating when completely yellow in color with dark flecks on the skin. If bananas are used before they are fully ripened the starch content is high, the sugar low, and certain bitter, astringent properties may be pronounced.

151

Citrus Fruits

Citrus fruits include oranges, lemons, grapefruit, limes, tanger-ines, kumquats, and tangelos, which are a cross between a tanger-ine and a grapefruit. The chief producing areas of these fruits in the United States are Florida, California, Texas, and Arizona. U.S. De-partment of Agriculture grades for oranges and grapefruit are U.S. Fancy, U.S. No. 1, U.S. No. 2, and U.S. No. 3. Grades for lemons are U.S. No. 1, U.S. No. 2, and U.S. No. 3. Grades are based upon color, maturity, firmness, shape, juiciness, quality of the skin, bruises, and blemishes. The consumer may not always know the grade of the fruit.

Citrus fruits are also classified on the basis of size, depending upon the quantity of fruit required to fill certain standard-size con-tainers. Cartons holding 35 to 38 pounds are often used. Large or-anges may be 56 count (56 oranges per carton); medium oranges may be 88 count; and small oranges may be 113 or even 138 count. Large oranges will usually be about $4\frac{3}{8}$ inches in diameter, medium ones about $3\frac{1}{2}$ inches, and small ones about $2\frac{1}{2}$ inches in diameter. The consumer often pays considerable attention to size because cer-tain sizes are profitably purchased for certain uses. Except for juice, large oranges are generally preferred over small ones [11]. The most common criticism of large oranges is that there is too much waste from thick skins or that large oranges are too expensive. Large fruit is often classed as fancy fruit and its price may increase at a faster rate than does the edible portion. For juice extraction, small sizes or ungraded stock may be profitable. Small oranges are often a better buy in quality as well as price for juice extraction. Tests by the U.S. Department of Agriculture on Florida fruit have shown that, gener-ally, the juice from small oranges is higher in total solids, acid, and in ascorbic acid than that of medium-sized fruit and higher still than that of large fruit. In purchasing citrus fruits, it should be noted that relatively thin skinned, firm, and heavy fruits in relation to size usually contain more juice than thicker skinned and lighter weight products. Russeting, which is a tan, brown, or blackish mot-tling or specking on the skin of some Florida and Texas oranges and grapefruit, has no effect on eating quality.

Two principal market varieties of oranges are the Valencia and the navel. For juice extraction the Valencia orange is often prefera-ble, whereas for slicing or sectioning the navel orange may be more satisfactory. The navel orange is distinguished by the navel forma-tion at the apex or blossom end of the fruit. This formation appears to be a tiny orange within a larger one. The navel orange is avail-able from California and Arizona in November until early May and has no seeds; less juice; a thicker, somewhat more pebbled skin than the Valencia; a skin that is easily removed by hand; and segments that separate easily. The western Valencia is available from late April through October. Florida and Texas oranges are marketed from early October until late June and include several varieties, with the Valencias being marketed from late March through June. All Valencias have seeds, but the California Valencia has only a few. Most of the Florida Valencias have yellow skins, much juice, and light-colored juice and pulp. Valencia oranges have a tendency late in the season to turn from a bright orange color to a greenish tinge, particularly around the stem end. This change in color affects only the outer skin. The oranges are matured and fully ripe inside. Some oranges are artificially colored to improve the external appearance.

Some varieties of grapefruit are classed as seedless though they often contain a few seeds, and some are a seeded type. Some grapefruit varieties are white-fleshed while others are pink- or red-fleshed. Although Florida is the main producer of grapefruit, this fruit is also supplied by Texas, California, and Arizona. Grapefruit is available all year but is most abundant from January through May. The citrus fruits, in addition to being one of the most valuable sources of ascorbic acid in the dietary, are noted for their tart flavor and lend appetizing quality to fruit desserts, salads, and cocktails.

Grapes

European types of grapes are firm-fleshed and very sweet and include varieties such as Thompson seedless (an early green grape), Tokay and Cardinal (early bright-red grapes), and Emperor (late deep-red grape). American types of grapes have softer flesh and are very juicy. The blue-black Concord variety is one commonly marketed and is unexcelled for juice or jelly making. Grapes should be plump, well colored, and firmly attached to the stem. Wine grapes are a completely different species of grapes.

Melons

Melons (Figure 8-3) are among the most difficult of fruits to select. No absolute guide for selection is available, but desirability is indicated by such qualities as ripeness; heaviness in relation to size; usually a characteristic aroma; characteristic color; and freedom from abnormal shape, decay, and disease. The ripeness of some melons, such as honeydew, crenshaw, casaba, and cantaloupe, is indicated by color and by a slight yielding to thumb pressure on the bud end or on the surface. If the melon was mature when picked, it usu-

8-3 *A Persian melon half is filled with grapes and is larger than the cantaloupe just behind it. The Casaba, directly to the left of the canta-loupe, has a globular shape with a pointed stem. The gold-with-a-green-flecked rind and oblong shape of the Santa Claus or Christmas melon may be seen directly behind the cantaloupe. Honeydew melon, a sweet, mildly scented fruit, is pictured on the elevated plate, and a crisp quar-ter of watermelon is shown at the back of the group.* (Courtesy of Western Growers Association)

ally shows a round dent where the stem broke away from the melon. Most cantaloupes are firm and not completely ripe when first dis-played in markets. Holding them a few days at room temperature will allow the completion of ripening. The color of uncut watermel-ons is probably the best key to ripeness. A yellowish underside, re-gardless of the green color of the rest of the melon, is a good sign. Other guides in selection might be a relatively smooth surface, a slight dullness to the rind, and ends of the melon that are filled out and rounded. In cut melons, desirable characteristics include firm, juicy flesh with a good red color, dark brown or black seeds, and no white streaks.

Pineapples

Desirable pineapples are often yellow in color but can vary from dark green through brown to gold, are heavy in relation to size, and are well shaped. When ready to eat they have a rich fragrant aroma and feel springy. Once they are ripe, they should be kept in the refrigerator.

Composition and Nutritive Value

When fruits are preserved by drying, the water content is reduced to less than 30 percent. In some fruits, such as dates, figs, raisins, pears, and peaches, the water content may be 15 to 18 percent when fruits come from the drying yards and dehydrators. As marketed, these fruits usually contain 28 percent or more moisture. Therefore, they may be partially rehydrated before being packaged for the consumer. Dried fruits with 28 to 30 percent water are examples of intermediate moisture foods that are generally considered to be plastic, easily chewed, and do not produce a sensation of dryness in the mouth, but are microbiologically stable. In vacuum-drying the water content is reduced to very low levels, about 2.5 to 5 percent. Fruits dried by this method are usually stored in cans or sealed containers to retain the low moisture levels.

The carbohydrate, caloric, and mineral values of dried fruits are higher by weight than those of the corresponding fresh fruits because of the removal of water. Also, the flavor is more concentrated than that of fresh fruit.

The vitamin content of fruits is changed in drying depending upon the methods of drying and sulfuring. Some fruits, such as apricots and peaches, are subjected to the fumes of sulfur dioxide gas or are dipped in a sulfite solution to prevent darkening of color and to act as an insecticide. Sulfuring aids in the preserving of vitamin A and ascorbic acid but adversely affects thiamin (vitamin B_1). A fruit-drying process involving osmotic dehydration has been developed. In this process the fruit is partially dehydrated in the first stages by being placed in a concentrated sugar solution. This protects the color and flavor with little or no use of sulfur dioxide [19]. Peaches and apricots dried by methods involving artificial sources of heat seem to retain vitamin A and ascorbic acid better than do sun-dried fruits. Many of these fruits are sun-dried, however. The riboflavin content is about the same regardless of the method used to dry the fruits.

Dried Fruits

Methods of Drying

The term *dried* is commonly applied to all fruits in which the water content has been reduced to a low level. Sun-drying methods use the sun as a source of heat. Dehydration may be accomplished by artificial heat under well-controlled conditions of humidity, temperature, and circulation of air. The sanitary practices involved in dehydration with artificial heat and the preservation of such physical properties as color, texture, and flavor in cooked dehydrated fruits as compared to cooked sun-dried fruits may represent possible advantages for this method.

Vacuum-drying dries the fruit to very low moisture levels although relatively low temperatures are used in the process. Under vacuum, water evaporates at a lower temperature. These fruits usually have excellent eating quality and they rehydrate quickly and easily. Fruits may also be freeze-dried.

Since dried fruits are greatly reduced in water content, and consequently increased in sugar content, they are resistant to microbial spoilage. Light-colored fruits that have been exposed to sulfur dioxide in order to prevent darkening also become more insect resistant as a result of the sulfur treatment. Dried fruits should be stored in tightly closed plastic, glass, or metal containers to protect them against insect infestation.

Prunes

Prunes are varieties of plums that can be dried without fermenting while still containing the pits. Two main varieties are: (1) the French plum grown chiefly in California and in France; and (2) the Italian plum grown chiefly in Oregon. These fruits are blue or purple on the outside with greenish-yellow to amber colored flesh. They have a high sugar content so that they produce a sweet-flavored prune when dried.

Before drying, plums are dipped in lye to puncture the skin and make it thinner. The lye treatment permits rapid drying and improves the texture of the skin. Careful washing removes the lye before drying. Some packaged prunes have been sterilized and packed hot in a package lined with aluminum foil. The residual heat in the pits seems to be sufficient to sterilize the package and also to tenderize the prune fiber to some extent, thus giving the prune its quick-cooking quality.

Prunes are classified according to size, that is, the approximate number to the pound. It is generally conceded that large prunes of the same variety and quality as small prunes have no better flavor than the small fruit. Large fruit may be preferred for dessert purposes, but it must be remembered that price usually increases with size at a faster rate than does the amount of the edible portion. For the making of pulp, small and medium sizes are more economical to buy.

The laxative value of prunes is the result, in part, of their fiber content and, in part, of a water-soluble extractive that stimulates intestinal activity. This substance is called diphenylisatin. Prune juice also contains the active laxative agent.

The commercial- and home-canning processes make possible an extension of season for many fruits and furnish a readily available supply of fruit all year. Canned fruit is essentially cooked fruit that has been sealed and processed for keeping and, as such, represents a widely used convenience food. Flavors and textures are somewhat altered by cooking or canning and vitamin values may be slightly reduced. Some of the B vitamins may be lost at the temperatures used for canning, although temperatures are lower for processing fruits than for vegetables. More ascorbic acid is destroyed if processes are not controlled to prevent oxidation. The exhausting of the can in the commercial-canning process drives off air and thus may tend to conserve ascorbic acid better than do home processes. High-acid fruits, such as grapefruit and oranges, appear to lose little ascorbic acid in well-controlled canning processes. The vitamins that go into solution are conserved because juices are usually eaten with the fruit.

Canned fruits lose nutrients and flavor less readily when stored at relatively low temperatures. If they are stored for prolonged periods at temperatures above 22° C (72° F), they deteriorate in quality at a relatively rapid rate. (See Chapter 27 for a more comprehensive discussion of canning.)

Many canned fruits and vegetables are graded (Figure 8-4). The U.S. Department of Agriculture has established grade standards that include U.S. Grade A or Fancy; U.S. Grade B or Choice; and U.S. Grade C or Standard. Criteria for grading include color, uniformity of size, shape, degree of ripeness, and lack of blemishes. Availability of graded products allows the consumer to select the quality that will be the most satisfactory for the intended use. Lower grades of fruits are still good and wholesome although they are less perfect than Grade A in color, uniformity, and texture. When a product has been officially graded under continuous inspection by a USDA inspector, it may carry the official grade name and the statement "Packed under continuous inspection of the U.S. Department of Agriculture." The grade name and the statement may also appear within a shield-shaped outline [12].

Canned Fruits

8-4 *USDA graded canned and frozen fruits let the shoppers pick the quality they want.* (Courtesy U.S.D.A.)

Information required by federal regulations to appear on the label of canned fruits includes:

1. The common or usual name of the fruit.
2. The form or style of fruit, such as whole, slices, or halves, unless the fruit is visible through the package.
3. The variety or color for some fruits.
4. A listing of syrups, sugar, or liquid in which the fruit is packed.
5. The total contents (net weight).
6. Additional ingredients, if used.
7. Any special type of treatment.
8. The packer's or distributor's name and place of business.

Labels may also give other useful information such as size and maturity of the fruit, quality or grade, cooking directions, and recipes or serving ideas. If the number of servings in the container is listed, the size of each serving must be given in common measures. Nutrition information in the form specified for nutrition labeling may also be given for canned fruits if the producer chooses to do so.

Frozen Fruits

The fruits that are most commonly frozen are cherries (both sour and sweet), strawberries (both sliced in sugar and whole), boysenberries, loganberries, red and black raspberries, blueberries, and sliced peaches. Frozen mixed fruits, rhubarb, plums, black mission figs, cranberries, pineapple, apple slices, and some varieties of melon are also available in some markets. Most frozen fruits are not heated during processing. Frozen apples, cherries, and some other fruits used for pies should be partially defrosted for ease in using and for draining part of the juice. Otherwise, they are used in the same manner as fresh fruit. If the fruit has been frozen with some sugar or syrup, allowance must be made in adding sugar to prepared products. Rhubarb should be cooked without defrosting. Blueberries or other fruits frozen dry may be used either frozen or thawed if used in cooked dishes.

Many frozen fruits are graded by the U.S. Department of Agriculture. The grade names and the labeling requirements for frozen fruits are the same as those for canned fruits. To maintain their quality, frozen fruits should be stored in a freezer that can maintain a temperature of $-18°$ C ($0°$ F) or lower. Frozen fruits should be moved quickly in market channels with proper precautions for maintaining cold temperatures. They should also be moved quickly from the market to the home freezer in order to avoid partial thawing and consequent loss of quality on refreezing.

All frozen fruits to be used raw should be barely defrosted. If all of the crystals have thawed, the fruit tends to become flabby. This is particularly true in using berries or peaches in shortcake, which is often warm when served. The warm shortcake may complete the defrosting. Some frozen fruits, such as peaches and apples, tend to turn brown during frozen storage and after thawing. The use of ascorbic acid in the syrup aids in the retention of natural color by preventing oxidation. Fruits may be defrosted by leaving them in the refrigerator or at room temperature for shorter periods of time.

Preparation

Most fresh fruits are consumed raw and are considered to be at their best in the raw, ripened state (Figures 8-5, 8-6 and 8-7). Fresh fruits should always be washed to remove dust, soil, some spray residues, and some microorganisms. If fruits that brown easily, such as bananas and apples, are to be peeled and cut they should be dipped in or covered with lemon juice, pineapple juice, or solutions of ascorbic acid mixtures so that discoloration does not readily occur. The acid and/or antioxidants in these solutions retard the enzyme activity that results in the production of brown-colored compounds. Placing the fruit in a sugar syrup or even immersing it in water also retards browning to some degree by excluding air.

Cooking is sometimes desirable or necessary because some fruits are more palatable when they are cooked. Green apples and rhubarb are examples of fruits that are not only more palatable but also more digestible in the cooked state. The cooking of some fruits is one way to add variety to the diet. One may cook overripe fruits to preserve them [8].

Cooking in Syrup or in Water

Simmering in syrup or in water is the principal method employed in cooking fruits. If it is desirable to have fruits retain their shape, they are cooked in syrup. When fruits are cooked in syrup, the cells take up sugar by diffusion; the fruit becomes more transparent and may shrink slightly as water comes out of the fruit to dilute the more concentrated syrup surrounding it. A desirable proportion of water to sugar for most fruits is about two to one by measure. When the shape of the fruit pieces is to be retained, the fruit should not be stirred during cooking.

Fruits that are to be cooked to a smooth pulp are stewed in water until they are of the desired softness, after which sugar is added. These fruits may be stirred during cooking. Some varieties of fruits do not cook to a smooth pulp under any circumstances, and not every variety will hold its shape well when cooked in syrup. The final product obtained is, therefore, partly a matter of choice of variety.

8-5 *Methods of preparing citrus for serving.* (Courtesy of Sunkist Growers, Inc.)

To section citrus fruits, pare deeply enough to remove the membrane that covers the pulp.

Cut toward the center along membrane and remove the section.

Rapid boiling with bumping about is one factor in the breaking of cell walls. Fruits boiled more slowly sometimes tend to hold their form better. Cooking will proceed more evenly and effectively if the pan is covered during cooking. The heat source should be regulated so that the liquid in the pan simmers or boils slowly.

Rhubarb is easily overcooked. The use of a very small amount of water and careful, slow cooking, only until the pieces are tender and partially broken up, give a desirable sauce from rhubarb. Apples sliced for cooking may sometimes include the skin, for added color, flavor, and nutritive value. After cooking, the fruit may be quickly run through a strainer or food mill to increase the smoothness of the pulp if applesauce is being prepared.

Excess sugar in fruit sauces mars the delicate flavor of many

Citrus sections without membranes may be served in many attractive ways.

For a basketball method of peeling, first slice off the stem end of the orange. Without cutting into the meat, score the peel with a knife. Pull the peel away with the fingers, leaving the white inner skin that clings to the fruit.

fruits. The desirable amount is often difficult to determine, especially when fruits are made into pies and other products, where the amount of sugar may not be added gradually until the desired amount is determined. The same variety of apple or other fruits varies in acidity from season to season and at different times during the storage period.

Baking

Some fruits, such as apples and pears, may be baked. Bananas are sometimes baked, although in general they are preferred raw. Rhubarb can also be baked and it will keep its shape. The aim in baking

8-6 *Preparation of avocados.* (Courtesy of Calavo)

Halve the avocado.

Twist the halves apart.

Remove the seed by striking it with a knife.

Peel off the skin and cut balls, crescents, cubes, or slices.

is to have the fruit hold its form but be cooked until tender throughout. Some fruits, such as apples, are baked in their skins (cores removed) in order to hold in the steam that forms within the fruit and that cooks the interior. Pared apple slices or sections may be baked in a covered casserole. An oven temperature of 176° to 205° C (350° to 400° F) is usually satisfactory.

Glazing

A top-of-the-range method known as *glazing* may be satisfactorily used for cooking apples. The apples are cored as for baking and a slit is cut in the skin all around the apple at right angles to or parallel with the core. The apples are then placed in a saucepan with ¼ cup of water and ⅛ cup of sugar for each apple in the pan. They are covered and cooked over low heat. The apples are turned once while cooking and are cooked until tender. The cover is removed for the last minute before the apples are done.

Broiling

Bananas, grapefruit halves, and pineapple slices are some of the fruits that may be satisfactorily broiled. To modify the bland flavor of cooked bananas, lemon juice or broiled bacon may be combined with the fruit.

Sautéing

Apples, bananas, and pineapple slices are the principal fruits prepared by sautéing, which is cooking in a small amount of fat. The fat used is usually a flavorful fat such as butter or bacon fat.

Cooking of Dried Fruits

Some of the water that has been removed from fruit in the drying process is returned by soaking. Cooking after soaking softens the tissues. Soaking in hot water at a temperature of about 80° C (176° F) for no longer than one hour results in good water absorption. After soaking, the fruit is simmered until the desired degree of softness is achieved. Some commercially available dried fruits are tenderized and have a higher moisture content. They require little or no soaking and a short cooking period.

The higher sugar content of dried fruits makes the use of much

8-7 *A sliced orange filled with grapes makes an attractive addition to breakfast. For lunch or supper, various fresh fruit combinations create interest and contribute essential vitamins and minerals to the diet. Slice 'N Serve Bleu Cheese Dressing goes especially well with an attractive platter of fresh fruits.* (Courtesy of Sunkist Growers, Inc.)

sugar for sweetening undesirable. The small amount of sugar that is sometimes used is added at the end of the cooking period. The degree of acidity of the fruit determines the amount of sugar to be used: dried apricots, being much more tart, require more sugar than prunes.

Study Questions

1. What is a fruit? Also define a pome and a drupe. Give examples of each.
2. a. What is the usual percentage of water found in fruits? What is the usual percentage of carbohydrate? What type of carbohydrate usually predominates in ripe fruits?
   b. List and be able to recognize fruits that are good sources of ascorbic acid (vitamin C).
   c. List three plant polysaccharides that are components of indigestible fiber.
   d. Name three pectic substances. What role do these play in plant structure? Which pectic substance is important in making fruit jellies and jams?
3. Describe common characteristics of fruit flavor. List four types of chemical substances that contribute to the flavor of fruits.
4. a. What pigments are often present in fruits?
   b. Explain why content of pigments should be considered when mixing various fruit juices to make a fruit drink.
5. a. Which product is the leader among processed fruits in terms of fresh-weight equivalent consumed?
   b. Describe major steps involved in the production of orange juice concentrate.
   c. What contributes to the stability of the hazy cloud that is characteristic of orange juice? To what treatment may the juice be subjected during processing in order to maintain cloud formation? Explain why this treatment is effective.
6. Describe the major changes that occur during the ripening of fruit.
7. a. Describe the usual characteristics of fruits of good quality and suggest appropriate storage conditions to maintain quality.
   b. What factors are generally controlled during *controlled atmosphere* storage of fruits and vegetables? Why is this type of storage effective for some fruits?
8. Why are some fruits treated with sulfur before drying? Describe some effects of this process on nutritive value.
9. Discuss some advantages to the consumer that may result from the grading of canned and frozen fruits.
10. a. Give several suggestions for effectively controlling the browning of cut surfaces on fruits such as bananas and apples. Explain why each suggested treatment is effective.
    b. Compare the general effects of cooking fruits in water and in sugar syrups. Explain what is happening in each case.
    c. Suggest an appropriate procedure for cooking dried fruits and explain why you would recommend this procedure.

References

1. Andrews, F. E., and P. J. Driscoll. 1977. Stability of ascorbic acid in orange juice exposed to light and air during storage. *Journal of the American Dietetic Association* **71**, 140.
2. Attaway, J. A. 1973. Florida Citrus Commission adds information on vitamin C retention. Letter. *Food Technology* **27**, 14 (no. 4).
3. Bourne, M. C. 1982. Effect of temperature on firmness of raw fruits and vegetables. *Journal of Food Science* **47**, 440.
4. Chairote, G., F. Rodriguez, and J. Crouzet. 1981. Characterization of additional volatile flavor components of apricot. *Journal of Food Science* **46**, 1898.
5. Cook, R. 1983. Quality of citrus juices as related to composition and processing practices. *Food Technology* **37**, 68 (no. 6).
6. Deshpande, S. S., H. R. Bolin, and D. K. Salunkhe. 1982. Freeze concentration of fruit juices. *Food Technology* **36**, 68 (no. 5).
7. Ennis, D. M., L. Keeping, J. Chin-ting, and N. Ross. 1979. Consumer evaluation of the inter-relationships between the sensory components of commercial orange juices and drinks. *Journal of Food Science* **44**, 1011.
8. *Fruits in Family Meals*. Home and Garden Bulletin No. 125. Washington, DC: U.S. Department of Agriculture, 1975.
9. *Grade Names for Fresh Fruits and Vegetables*. AMS-569. Washington, DC: U.S. Department of Agriculture, July 1976.
10. Guadagni, D. G., J. L. Bomben, and H. C. Mannheim. 1970. Storage stability of frozen orange juice concentrate made with aroma solution of cutback juice. *Food Technology* **24**, 1012.
11. *Homemakers Appraise Citrus Products, Avocados, Dates, and Raisins*. Marketing Research Report No. 243. Washington, DC: U.S. Department of Agriculture, June 1958.
12. *How to Buy Canned and Frozen Fruits*. Home and Garden Bulletin No. 191. Washington, DC: Consumer and Marketing Service, U.S. Department of Agriculture, 1976.
13. *How to Buy Fresh Fruits*. Home and Garden Bulletin No. 141. Washington, DC: Consumer and Marketing Service, U.S. Department of Agriculture, 1977.
14. Knee, M. 1971. Ripening of apples during storage. III. Changes in chemical composition of Golden Delicious apples during the climacteric and under conditions simulating commercial storage practice. *Journal of the Science of Food and Agriculture* **22**, 371.
15. Lidster, P. D., H. J. Lightfoot, and K. B. McRae. 1983. Production and regeneration of principal volatiles in apples stored in modified atmospheres and air. *Journal of Food Science* **48**, 400.
16. Lime, B. J., and R. R. Cruse. 1972. Beverages from whole citrus fruit puree. *Journal of Food Science* **37**, 250.
17. Moshonas, M. G., and P. E. Shaw. 1973. Some newly found orange essence components including trans-2-pentenal. *Journal of Food Science* **38**, 360.
18. Noel, G. L., and M. T. Robberstad. 1963. Stability of vitamin C in canned apple juice and orange juice under refrigerated conditions. *Food Technology* **17**, 947.

19. Ponting, J. D., G. G. Watters, R. R. Forrey, R. Jackson, and W. L. Stanley. 1966. Osmotic dehydration of fruits. *Food Technology* **20,** 1365.
20. Sweeney, J. P., V. J. Chapman, and P. A. Hepner, 1970. Sugar, acid, and flavor in fresh fruits. *Journal of the American Dietetic Association* **57,** 432.
21. *The Buying Guide for Fresh Fruits, Vegetables, Herbs, and Nuts,* 7th rev. ed. Hagerstown, MD: Blue Goose, Inc., 1980.
22. White, P. L., and N. Selvey, eds. *Nutritional Qualities of Fresh Fruits and Vegetables.* Mount Kisco, NY: Futura Publishing Co., 1974.

9

Salads and Salad Dressings

At one time the term *salad* may have applied only to green leaves or stalks that were eaten raw. Although today we often refer to green leafy vegetables, such as lettuce, endive, and romaine, as *salad greens,* the term salad has a much broader meaning. It may include mixtures of meat, fish, poultry, cheese, nuts, and eggs, as well as all kinds of vegetables and fruits. It is often composed of raw or uncooked foods but is not limited to these items. It may be made entirely of canned or cooked products or may be a mixture of raw and cooked foods. Set gelatin salads containing a variety of ingredients are popular menu items. A dressing is usually served either mixed with or accompanying the salad. The dressing may be rich and elaborate or it may be as simple as lemon juice.

The salad is not a modern preparation. Green leaves were used by the ancient Romans. Other nationalities from the fifteenth century on favored the use of flavorful herbs and raw vegetables. The introduction of salads into England was apparently made by Catherine of Aragon, one of the wives of Henry VIII and a daughter of Ferdinand and Isabella of Spain. The origin of present-day meat and fish salads was probably the salmagundi of England, used for many years as a supper dish. This meat dish made use of numerous garnishes that are used today, such as hard-cooked eggs, pickles, beets, and anchovy. The influence of southern France is seen in the use of French dressing made of olive oil and seasoned to perfection. Spain has made the pepper a popular salad vegetable and the Mediterranean countries introduced garlic flavor. The original German potato salad has many present-day variations.

The salad is an appetizing form in which to use fresh fruits and vegetables. The element of crispness, which most salads introduce, improves the texture in many menus. Tartness and delicious, fresh flavors are also easily added to the meal in the form of salads.

Uses for Salads

In the United States, the salad has many uses in the meal other than as an accompaniment to the roast or the main course. The salad is often served as a separate course between the main course and the dessert or before the main course. It may be so composed as to serve the purpose of a dessert and is frequently now used as an appetizer. For luncheon or supper the salad may be the main course with the rest of the menu being built around the salad. The type of salad, obviously, will depend upon its use in the meal. The dinner salad is usually a light, crisp, tart accompaniment to the meat. Heavy, high calorie salads, such as macaroni and tuna fish or meat and potato, are not appropriately used in a meal already composed of filling high-protein foods. Meat, poultry, fish, egg, cheese, and potato salads that are combined with some crisp vegetables and relishes are suitable for use as a main course although some small fish salads of high flavor such as crab, shrimp, lobster, and anchovy may serve as an appetizer just as cocktails and canapés made of such kinds of fish may serve as appetizers. Usually the amount of fish used is not large and it is combined with crisp, flavorful foods.

Potato salad may be an accompaniment to cold meats on a supper platter. Used in this way the starchy potato functions as it does in the dinner menu. Potato salad is sometimes served hot as was the original German potato salad.

The fruit salad is particularly suitable as an appetizer or dessert salad, but if kept tart and not too large it may be used suitably in the dinner menu. The fruit salad is a delightful salad to use as refreshments for an afternoon or evening party. A fruit salad used as dessert may have served with it a cheese plate and crisp crackers, although it may be eaten with no breadstuff.

Salad Plants

*Salad Ingredients and
Their Preparation*

The best known salad plant is lettuce, either of the crisphead type or the Boston (butter leaf) variety. Romaine is regarded by many who relish its sharp flavor as the salad plant without equal. Endive, escarole, and chicory are also much used as salad greens. However, there is some confusion concerning the use of these three terms in various parts of the country. Curly endive grows in a head with narrow, ragged-edged leaves that curl at the ends. A broader leaf variety of endive that does not curl at the tips is usually marketed as escarole. Witloof chicory, commonly known as French endive, is a tightly folded plant that grows upright in a thin, elongated stalk. It is usually white. Watercress and Chinese cabbage or celery cabbage are also highly acceptable as salad plants. Color Plate III shows some of these common salad greens.

Any crisp, tender, young leaves, such as spinach, sorrel, mustard, and dandelion, may be used. Shredded cabbage may constitute the entire salad, may serve as a foundation for other ingredients, or may be part of a vegetable salad mixture. Parsley is an attractive garnish for some types of salads, and celery, green or red pepper, tomato, and cucumber are among the most flavorful of salad plants. They are the ones most likely to be used for crispness and flavor in salad mixtures. Cooked beets have a desirable texture and flavor for some types of salads but because of the soluble anthocyanin pigment present, they may mar the color of other salad ingredients. If used carefully and kept separate from other ingredients, beets are valuable additions to some salads. Raw turnip is another interesting addition to salad plants. It may be used in thin slices (often allowed to curl in cold water), sticks, or fine shreds. Raw carrots may be used similarly. Small pieces of raw cauliflower and broccoli flowerets may also be added.

Preparation of Salad Ingredients

Crispness is one of the most desirable characteristics of salad plants. If green leaves and celery are washed, placed in a tightly closed container, and chilled in the refrigerator for several hours, they will be crisp and fresh. Most salad ingredients should be prepared immediately before the salad is served for maximum retention of nutrients and fresh, flavorful appeal. It is also good to remember that green leaves contain more vitamins and iron than do lighter colored leaves.

In preparing salad plants, all inedible portions should be removed and thorough cleansing is essential because the plants are used raw. Although some soluble minerals and vitamins are dissolved out if the vegetables are allowed to stand too long in water, it is necessary that the vegetables take up some water through cut stems or cores in order to become crisp. Ice added to the water aids in chilling the vegetables. The water that clings to leaves and stems after washing will help accomplish the purpose of developing crispness, provided that enough time is allowed for chilling, as in the storing of washed vegetables for several hours in a refrigerator. The salad plants may be wrapped in plastic material, in a wet cloth, or stored in a hydrator (Figure 9-1). All excess water should be removed from the vegetables before they are used in order to prevent a watery salad. The Boston variety of lettuce does not become crisp, but its tender leaves and delicate flavor make it a desirable salad plant. The softness of Boston lettuce combines attractively with crisp salad plants.

Cutting out the stems of heads of lettuce not only speeds up the absorption of water but also simplifies the separation of the leaves from the head. Firmly striking the core of a head of lettuce on a hard surface loosens the core for easy removal.

If carefully prepared salad materials are kept ready in the refrigerator, salad preparation becomes a simple, easy procedure. Sections of citrus fruits are usually left whole, but many fruits are cut into pieces of convenient size for eating. Canned pineapple, peach, and pear can be cut easily with a fork and may be left whole if desired.

Vegetables are left whole or are diced, shredded, sliced, or sectioned, depending on the type of vegetable (Figure 9-2). Potatoes

9-1 *Storing salad greens. A head of lettuce that is not to be used for 3 or 4 days may be washed in cool water, drained thoroughly, and wrapped in film or put in a plastic bag before refrigerating. Lettuce to be used the next day may be trimmed and the core removed, cold water run into the center to loosen the leaves, and the head then turned upside down and drained thoroughly before storing in a plastic bag or film wrap. Lettuce to be used the same day as purchased may have the washed leaves separated, rolled in a clean tea towel, and stored in the refrigerator until ready for use. (Courtesy of Western Growers Association)*

9-2 *Fresh vegetables, cut in various forms and served with cheeses or tangy dips, may comprise the salad dish itself. They may also be used as accompaniments to a tossed green salad. Vegetables include radish roses, rings of green pepper, celery curls or sticks, carrot curls, thin cucumber slices, cherry tomatoes, cauliflower sections, slices of mushroom, jade trees from green onion stems, marinated artichokes, red onion rings, and water chestnuts. (Courtesy of Western Growers Association)*

used for salad should be of a variety that holds its form when diced. Starchy, mealy potatoes tend to form a mushy mass when made into salad. Tiny beets may be left whole, and cooked cauliflower may be used in separate flowerets. Tomatoes are often peeled and left whole or cut into wedges or slices. Cucumbers are sliced or diced depending on the type of salad. Celery is usually diced but may be cut into sections that are prepared to form celery curls or cut into shreds. Green beans and asparagus tips are usually left whole, although in a combination salad beans may be cut into shreds or short lengths. Carrots may be finely diced or cut into tiny sticks, or thin slices, which can be made into curls by being soaked in ice water. For some uses carrots may be grated. Peppers are often cut into rings but may be cut into fine shreds or coarsely chopped for some purposes. Precaution should be taken to not mince salad materials since softer foods that are cut too fine form almost a paste when they are mixed with salad dressings.

For molded gelatin salads, vegetables are often cut finer than for salads that are not molded. Cabbage, regardless of how used, is more attractive and becomes better seasoned if it is finely shredded. Coarse shreds of cabbage are difficult to chew, particularly if the variety of cabbage is one that does not become crisp easily.

Meats and chicken used in salads are usually diced, but fish is more often coarsely flaked with a fork. Small shellfish, such as shrimp, may be left whole or diced if preferred. Canned salmon and tuna fish are difficult to prepare in a way that retains the form of pieces, although tuna is firmer than salmon. Canned fish that has considerable oil in the can may have the oil washed off with boiling water before the fish is chilled. Alternately, the oil may become part of the dressing.

Marinating

Meats, fish, and some vegetables are marinated for an hour or more before being made into salad. Marinating consists of coating foods lightly with dressing (in this case called a *marinade*) to improve the flavor. Leafy vegetables cannot be so treated, as they wilt. Starchy vegetables and whole firm pieces of more succulent vegetables are greatly improved by marinating. Any excess dressing is drained off when the salad is prepared.

Arrangement

Preparing the Salad

Salads should be artistically and attractively arranged although these arrangements may be very simple. Whole tomatoes or fruits, halves of peaches or pears, slices of pineapple, and gelatin molds necessarily take on a more fixed appearance than do combination salads made from cut pieces (Figures 9-3 and 9-4).

Color may be added by mixing a colorful ingredient in the main body of the salad or it may be placed in a fixed form on top. Garnishes are not used solely as garnish but are edible constituents that form part of the salad. Ripe or stuffed green olives, radishes, and small cheese-stuffed celery stalks may often have the effect of garnishings when placed on the lettuce beside the salad proper. Sprigs of watercress, which introduce a darker value of green color and an interesting leaf design, do more for many vegetable salads than strips of pimiento. A bit of paprika is often the only touch of color needed, but too much paprika may be detract from the appearance of the salad. Overgarnishing should be avoided.

Color Plate IV illustrates some different kinds of salads and their arrangements.

Dressing the Salad

9-3 Heads of lettuce cut into wedges make simple, yet attractive salads. (Courtesy of Western Growers Association)

Only certain types of salads, such as potato, macaroni, meat, chicken, or fish, are improved by standing for a time with the dressing. These are often mixed with the dressing a few hours before

9-4 Gelatin molds take on a more fixed, formal appearance than many other salads. (Courtesy of United Fresh Fruit and Vegetable Association and Western Growers Association)

A shimmering gelatin mold containing green peppers, celery, radishes, and cucumber slices.

An elegant gelatin salad ring including carrots, pimiento cheese, and minted pineapple is garnished with deep red grapes.

174

serving. Shredded cabbage may be improved by brief contact with the dressing.

Usually the texture, appearance, and flavor of the salad are better if the dressing is added when the salad is served. The dressing may coat all the salad ingredients as when the dressing is applied to a large amount of salad in a bowl either at the table or immediately before serving. The ingredients are tossed with a spoon and fork until they are well coated with dressing. Alternatively, a small amount of dressing may be applied to individual servings before the salad is placed on the table or the dressing may be passed for individuals to serve themselves.

Summary of Essentials in the Making of Salads

1. Unless salads are purposely served hot, as are German potato salad and wilted lettuce, all materials should be cold. If materials are such that they may be made crisp, they should be treated for the development of crispness some time before they are used. Obviously, because many plants used for salads are used raw, a thorough cleansing in water safe for drinking is an important sanitary measure.

2. All materials that have stood in water should be dried or a watery salad results. Careful drying prevents the bruising of leaves.

3. Most salads are last-minute preparations insofar as the actual mixing and dressing of the salad are concerned, but some materials that are to go into the salad, such as sections of citrus fruits, may be prepared in advance.

4. Light mixing with forks or fork and spoon is necessary to retain the characteristic form of each of the salad plants in the mixture.

5. The salad dressing should be suitable for the salad both in its flavor and in its consistency. The amount of dressing used should flavor the whole salad well but should not be used in excess to cover up the flavor of the salad ingredients. Cooked dressings to be thinned for combining with shredded cabbage or other vegetables should be tart and fairly highly seasoned in order to stand dilution and yet retain good flavor.

6. It is well to consider flavor and color combinations from the standpoint of attractive appearance as well as palatability (Figure 9-5 and Color Plate IV). For example, the clear red lycopene pigment of tomato does not always combine attractively with the purplish red pigment of beets.

7. Foods with very pronounced flavor may be used sparingly in mixtures to avoid masking more delicate flavors.

9-5 *Salads contribute valuable nutrients to the diet and may also provide the main attraction for a luncheon or supper menu. A chef salad with marinated cooked vegetables and hard-cooked eggs is an example of a salad dish contributing valuable protein. (Also see Color Plate IV.) Bright green cabbage, a good source of ascorbic acid, may be attractively combined with red cabbage, coconut, and pineapple in a slaw. Individual salads, displayed all on one platter, combine orange, banana, and pineapple slices with whole apricots on a bed of lettuce for ascorbic acid and vitamin A value. Whole blueberry-sour cream dressing adds zest and color. (Courtesy Western Growers Association; individual salads courtesy of Sunkist Growers, Inc.)*

Definitions and standards of identity for mayonnaise, French dressing, and salad dressing have been published by the Food and Drug Administration. If products are labeled and sold under these names they must meet the standards of identity. Mayonnaise must contain not less than 65 percent by weight of edible vegetable oil and an egg yolk-containing ingredient. French dressing must contain not less than 35 percent by weight of edible vegetable oil. Salad dressing must contain not less than 30 percent by weight of edible vegetable oil and also may contain a cooked starchy paste as well as an egg yolk-containing ingredient. All three of the dressings contain an acidifying ingredient. Many variations of these three basic dressings are possible by use of different optional ingredients. Thus, a wide variety of dressings is available commercially. Reduced-calorie dressings, containing less oil, are available commercially but are prominently labeled as "reduced-calorie" dressings [4]. Some dressings that contain no oil are also available.

When dressings for salads are made at home these are not, of course, governed by "standards of identity." Many of these dressings are very simple combinations of ingredients and are difficult to classify. In fruit dressings, fruit juices replace vinegar and other liquids. Sour cream, sometimes with added ingredients such as crumbled cheese, may be added to vegetable or fruit salads. Mixtures of vinegar or lemon juice and seasonings, with or without small amounts of fat-containing ingredients, are sometimes used as low or reduced-calorie dressings.

In addition to the many different prepared dressings that are available, dry seasoning mixes are sold, usually to be mixed with oil and vinegar for preparation of the finished dressings. Dry salad seasoning mixes may also be prepared at home. Cost as well as flavor comparisons might be made among commercially prepared dressings, homemade dressings, and dressings made at home with dry seasoned mixes.

Mayonnaise

According to the standard of identity under the Federal Food, Drug, and Cosmetic Act, mayonnaise or mayonnaise dressing is the emulsified semisolid food prepared from edible vegetable oil, vinegar and/or lemon juice or citric acid, egg yolk or whole egg, and one or more optional ingredients, such as salt, mustard, paprika, a sweetening agent, and monosodium glutamate. As mentioned previously, the edible oil content of mayonnaise must be not less than 65 percent by weight and is emulsified or finely divided in the vinegar or lemon juice. Mayonnaise, therefore, is an emulsion, with one liquid (oil) dispersed in a second liquid (vinegar or lemon juice). These liquids do not usually mix well and it is a third agent, an emulsifier, that makes possible the mixing on a relatively permanent basis [1]. Certain components of egg or egg yolk (probably lipoproteins) act as the emulsifying agent, coating the dispersed particles of oil to keep them dispersed. (See p. 349 for a discussion of emulsions.)

Mayonnaise may be made at home. The factors that affect the formation of mayonnaise, its stability, and the ease of preparation are similar whether the product is made commercially or at home. A brief discussion of some of these factors follows.

Temperature Cold oil is more difficult to break up into small globules than is warm, less viscous oil. Thus, the start of emulsification is delayed by chilling, but after the emulsion is formed chilling thickens and stabilizes the product.

Ingredients and Proportions Used Egg yolk is the chief emulsifying ingredient in mayonnaise. It is a more efficient emulsifier than either whole egg or egg white. Egg yolk is itself an emulsion containing about 30 percent fat. Fresh yolks are superior to those of aged eggs for making both a stiff and a stable emulsion. Freezing egg yolks, particularly without additives such as salt or sugar, changes their physical properties so that on being thawed they are very viscous. A larger quantity of frozen yolk than of fresh yolk is required for making mayonnaise. Salt, mustard, paprika, and pepper are used mainly for flavor but both the salt and the powdery seasoning ingredients help to stabilize the emulsion as well [3]. Any edible oil may be used for mayonnaise.

The usual homemade mayonnaise contains 65 to 75 percent of oil or about ¾ to 1 cup of oil per egg yolk and 2 tablespoons of acid ingredient. Adding more oil than is needed for optimum dispersion and thickening may result in the breaking of the emulsion.

Equipment Used Commercial firms generally use a homogenizing apparatus to disperse the oil because it produces finer globules than any other device. In home preparation of mayonnaise, hand or mechanical beaters or electric blenders may be used. Of hand-operated beaters the rotary type is more efficient than the whisk type. The size and shape of the bowl is important. A bowl with sloping sides and a rounded bottom of narrow diameter permits the beater to pick up the mass to be beaten. The bowl should not be too large in relation to the amount of mixture.

Method of Mixing Stable mayonnaise may be mixed by various methods:

1. All of the acid and seasonings may be added to the egg yolk before any additions of oil.
2. Acid may be added at various intervals during the mixing.
3. Acid may be added alternately with the oil.

4. Acid may be added after a large percentage of the oil is added to the egg yolk.

By the use of method 1, emulsification occurs more rapidly and larger quantities of oil may be added for the first and second additions, although the first dispersed oil particles are larger than when the oil is added to the egg yolk before the addition of the acid. The acid tends to thin the emulsion at whatever stage it is added.

The first additions of oil must be small in order to allow a stable emulsion to form. After the first two or three additions of oil, the volume of oil that is added at one time may be increased to a variable extent, depending on the temperature of the ingredients, the rate of beating, and other factors, but in any case should be less than the volume of emulsion that is already formed.

Rapid and thorough beating after each of the first additions of oil is one of the most important points in connection with the mixing of mayonnaise. When this is done, separation of the emulsion is less likely to occur and the final product is more viscous than when beating is inadequate.

Stable emulsions may be made by either continuous or intermittent beating. It has been suggested that rest periods facilitate emulsification by giving time for the films of the emulsifier to be adsorbed by the oil droplets.

Effect of Adding Emulsified Mayonnaise. The addition of a small amount of previously made mayonnaise to the egg yolk-acid mixture greatly facilitates emulsification. This method also makes possible a dressing of high viscosity with a low egg yolk content.

Separation or Demulsification of Mayonnaise If oil particles coalesce, separation or breaking of the mayonnaise occurs. If separation occurs while the emulsion is forming, it is caused by incomplete preliminary emulsification, too rapid addition of oil, too high a ratio of oil to emulsifier (or other wrong proportion), or an inefficient method of agitation. Emuslified mayonnaise may separate during storage.

Freezing of mayonnaise, which damages or ruptures the film of emulsifying agent, allows the dispersed oil to reunite and separation occurs [2]. Mayonnaise stored at too high a temperature may separate because of differences in the rate of expansion of warm water and oil. Mayonnaise stored in an open container may lose sufficient moisture from the surface by evaporation to damage the emulsion.

The agitation or jarring of an emulsion may result in separation. This cause of separation is doubtless of more concern to the commercial maker of mayonnaise than to the homemaker, because of the jarring that is incident to shipping.

A broken mayonnaise emulsion may be reformed by starting with a new egg yolk, or with a tablespoon of water or vinegar, and adding the separated mayonnaise to it gradually. A thorough beating after each addition of separated mayonnaise is important. If separation occurs in the preparation of mayonnaise before all of the oil is added, the remainder of the original oil may be added only after reemulsification has been achieved as described.

Proportions for Mayonnaise

1 egg yolk	½ t (4 g) sugar
2 T (30 ml) vinegar or lemon juice or a combination of the two	¼ t mustard
	¼ t paprika
½ t (3 g) salt	½ to 1 c (105 to 210 g) salad oil

Mix seasonings with acid and add to egg yolk, stirring until well blended. Add 1 tablespoon of oil and beat rapidly and thoroughly until a good emulsion is started. Add another tablespoon of oil and continue beating. Later additions of oil may be somewhat larger but should always be less than the volume of the formed mayonnaise, and should be followed by thorough beating. Too rapid additions of oil may produce a less stable mayonnaise and a less viscous one.

Variations of Mayonnaise

Additions may be made to mayonnaise to vary the flavor and consistency. Chopped foods, such as vegetables, olives, pickles, hard-cooked eggs, and nuts, may be added with discretion. Chili sauce, sour cream, and whipped cream may also enhance flavor and consistency for certain uses.

French Dressing

According to the standard of identity under the Federal Food, Drug, and Cosmetic Act, French dressing is the separable liquid food or the emulsified viscous fluid food prepared from edible vegetable oil (oil content not less than 35 percent by weight), specified acidifying agents, and optional seasonings. It may be emulsified, in which case certain gums, pectin, or other emulsifier, including egg or egg yolk, may be used to the extent of 0.75 percent by weight of the finished dressing. Large amounts of paprika and other powdered seasonings also help to keep the oil and acid emulsified. In unemulsified French dressing a temporary emulsion is formed as the dressing is shaken or beaten. Oil and acid ingredients separate soon after mixing but may be shaken or mixed each time the dressing is used.

Proportions for French Dressing

¾ c (158 g) salad oil
¼ c (60 ml) vinegar or lemon juice
  or a combination of the two
¼ t mustard

½ t (3 g) salt
½ t (4 g) sugar
¼ t paprika

Variations of French Dressing

1. Add a slice or two of onion to the jar of dressing to enhance the flavor.
2. To 1 c dressing add ¼ c tomato ketchup or chili sauce.
3. To 1 c dressing add 2 T horseradish.
4. To 1 c dressing add 2 T capers, 2 T chopped stuffed olives, and 1 t chopped parsley.
5. To 1 c dressing add 1 T chopped parsley, ½ T chopped red pepper, ½ T chopped green pepper, 1 T chopped celery, 1 T chopped onion, 2 T finely chopped hard-cooked egg, 1 T chopped sweet pickles. This dressing is commonly known as *chiffonade*. The chopped ingredients may vary.
6. To 1 c dressing add ¼ c crumbled Roquefort cheese.
7. A modification of this type of emulsion makes use of cream instead of oil and is particularly desirable for cole slaw. The proportions are: ¾ c light cream, ¼ c vinegar, 2 T sugar, 1 t salt, and ¼ t paprika. Beat with a spoon until well blended.

Salad Dressing

According to the standard of identity under the Federal Food, Drug, and Cosmetic Act, salad dressing is the emulsified semisolid food prepared from edible vegetable oil, an acidifying ingredient, egg yolk or whole egg, and a cooked or partly cooked starchy paste prepared with a food starch or flour. Water may be added in the preparation of the starchy paste. Optional seasonings and emulsifying agents may also be used. Salad dressing must contain not less than 30 percent by weight of edible vegetable oil and not less than 4 percent by weight of liquid egg yolks or their equivalent.

Many different dressings for salads may be made at home. Some of these are cooked dressings and may be of the custard type, in which all thickening is accomplished with egg yolk or whole egg, but more frequently some starchy agent aids in thickening because there is less tendency for curdling to occur when cream or milk is used as the liquid. Some cooked dressings made with milk or cream are of a consistency suitable for immediate use but, if preferred, the dressing may be made thicker than is desirable and may be highly seasoned to permit dilution without impairment of flavor.

Plain Cooked Dressing

2 eggs	4 T (29 g) flour
1 t (6 g) salt	2 t (25 g) sugar
¾ t mustard	1¼ c (296 ml) water
⅛ t paprika	¼ c (60 ml) vinegar

Mix dry ingredients. Add water to form a smooth paste. Beat eggs slightly in the top of double boiler. Add water mixture, then vinegar. Cook over hot water until thickened. This dressing is thick and is to be thinned when used with ½ c whipped cream, light cream, or buttermilk. The latter is a good and inexpensive diluting agent for such salads as potato or mixed vegetable.

Nutritive Significance of Salads

The nutritive value of salads (both the caloric value and the types of nutrients supplied) varies with the salad. Starchy salads, such as potato, are higher in kilocalories than are salads made from many fruits and from succulent vegetables. Meat, fish, egg, and cheese salads furnish chiefly protein, although some crisp vegetables usually form a part of such mixtures.

The majority of salads prepared from fresh fruits and vegetables are comparatively low in kilocalories (not including the dressing) but are important sources of minerals, vitamins, and fiber. The green-leaf vegetable salads are especially valuable for iron, vitamin A, and ascorbic acid. If the whole salad is made from green leaves, it is sufficient to constitute a serving of green leafy vegetable, but the usual amount of green leaf used as a base for a salad cannot serve that purpose. The greener the leaf the greater is its nutritive contribution.

The caloric value of all salads, as consumed, will vary considerably with the type and quantity of dressing used. The amount of fat, in the form of salad oil or cream, is the chief factor influencing the quantity of kilocalories in the dressing. Cooked dressings, particularly those made from water or milk, have a lower caloric value than do mayonnaise and French dressings. The energy value of French and salad dressings averages about 65 kilocalories per tablespoon and of mayonnaise about 100 kilocalories per tablespoon. Special low calorie dressings may furnish as low as 4 to 6 kilocalories per tablespoon.

Study Questions

1. a. Describe four or five ways in which salads may be used in a meal.
   b. Describe ten or twelve different salads and suggest appropriate uses in a menu.

2. a. Describe and be able to identify several leafy plants that may be appropriately used as salad greens.
   b. Suggest a satisfactory way to prepare these greens for use in salads and explain why this procedure is effective.
3. Marinating may be appropriate for what types of salads? Explain why.
4. Give several appropriate suggestions for the arranging of salads as they are served.
5. a. When should the dressing usually be added to a salad and why?
   b. Suggest several salads that are exceptions to the general rule discussed in question a.
6. a. Standards of identity have been published for which three types of dressings for salads?
   b. What percentage of oil is specified for each type?
   c. Which governmental agency is responsible for these standards?
7. a. Describe mayonnaise and list the major ingredients it contains.
   b. Suggest an appropriate procedure for making mayonnaise at home.
   c. Explain what precautions must be taken to assure that a stable emulsion will be formed.
   d. If the emulsion breaks during the preparation or storage of mayonnaise, how may it be reformed?
8. a. Describe French dressing and list the major ingredients it contains.
   b. Suggest an appropriate method for its preparation.
9. Explain how salad dressing generally differs from mayonnaise.

References

1. Becher, P. *Principles of Emulsion Technology*. New York: Reinhold Publishing Corp., 1955.
2. Hanson, H. L. 1964. Recent research on prepared frozen foods. *Journal of the American Dietetic Association* **45,** 523.
3. Jordan, R. 1962. Salt as a factor in the stability of emulsions. *Journal of Home Economics* **54,** 394.
4. Sharma, S. C. 1981. Gums and hydrocolloids in oil-water emulsions. *Food Technology* **35,** 59 (no. 1.).

10

Meat and Meat Cookery

The term *meat,* as commonly used, includes the edible portion of mammals, the chief ones in the United States being cattle, swine, and sheep. Rabbits are also used to some degree as sources of meat. Meat, poultry, and fish play similar roles in meal planning and nutrition.

Structure of Meat

Muscle Tissue

The muscle or lean part of meat is composed of cylindrical microscopic cells that are shaped like fibers (Figure 10-1). The fibers vary in size but average about $\frac{1}{500}$ inch in diameter and 1 to 2 inches in length. Inside these muscle fibers or cells are many smaller fibers, called myofibrils, that are made up of long, thin protein molecules. These protein molecules are chiefly responsible for the ability of the muscle to contract and relax as some of the molecules slide past other molecules somewhat like a telescope (Figure 10-2).

The muscle cells or fibers are surrounded by very thin sheaths of connective tissue. Small bundles of the fibers, surrounded by additional thin sheaths of connective tissue, make up the larger macroscopic fiber bundles that can be seen in a cut of meat without the use of a microscope and are referred to as the *grain* of meat. A coarse-

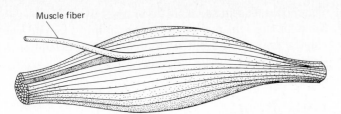

textured piece of muscle meat has a larger grain and a fine-textured piece has smaller fiber bundles producing the grain.

Individual muscles of an animal, such as the tenderloin muscle, are composed of secondary bundles of the small primary bundles of muscle fibers and are enclosed in a sheath of connective tissue that extends beyond the end of the muscle to form tendons. Tendons attach muscles to bones. Blood vessels, fat cells, and nerves are found within the muscle tissue. (See Color Plate VIII.)

Connective Tissue

Muscle tissue does not occur without connective tissue. The connective tissue binds muscle cells together in various size bundles and makes up the tendons and ligaments of an animal. Connective tissue contains the proteins collagen and elastin. These form long, strong fibrils that are embedded in a background matrix called ground substance. Although collagen fibers are flexible, they do not stretch as much as elastin fibers. Collagen-containing connective tissue is white while connective tissue in which elastin predominates is yellow. In muscles that are used for locomotion by an animal, such as those in the legs and neck, connective tissue tends to develop more extensively. Less tender cuts of meat usually contain more connective tissue than tender cuts, although this is not the only factor affecting meat tenderness. Some collagen is broken down or hydrolyzed to produce gelatin when meat is heated and tenderness thus increases. Heating causes only slight softening of elastin.

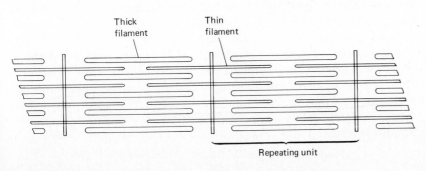

Thick filament   Thin filament

Repeating unit

10-2 *Thick and thin rod-like components or filaments inside the muscle cell or fiber are composed of protein molecules. Myosin is the protein found in the thick filaments while actin makes up the thin filaments. They are systematically arranged in a cylindrical shape. When muscle contracts, the thin filaments in each repeating unit push together, thus shortening the length of the muscle.*

185

Very little elastin seems to be present in most muscles, particularly those of the loin and round regions, but a considerable amount of elastin may be present in the connective tissue of a few muscles, including some in the shoulder area.

Fatty Tissue

Special cells contain large amounts of fat for storage in the body. These cells are embedded in a network of connective tissue to form adipose or fatty tissue. Some hard fats, such as beef suet, have visible sheets of connective tissue separating layers or masses of fat cells. Fatty tissue is also supplied with blood vessels. Fatty deposits are found under the skin and around glandular organs. As an animal is fattened, fat cells are deposited between muscles, and finally there is intramuscular distribution to produce the marbling of muscle tissue.

Bone

Long shafts of bone are composed chiefly of compact bony tissue. A center canal is filled with yellow marrow. Other bones may be spongy in character and may contain red marrow, which has many blood vessels. Bones or pieces of bone that appear in retail cuts of meat may aid in the identification of the cut in regard to its location on the carcass.

Composition of Meat

Meat is composed chiefly of water, protein, fat, and mineral matter. Some tissue, chiefly liver, has an appreciable carbohydrate content in the form of glycogen. The percentage of carbohydrate in liver is extremely variable, but usually ranges from 1 to 5 percent. The percentage of fat in meats shows wide variation, depending on the kind of animal, the state of nutrition, and the part of the carcass from which the cut is taken. An external fat layer on meat is often not eaten and thus must be considered waste in calculating percentages.

Lean uncooked muscle contains about 75 percent water and about 20 percent protein. In the muscle cells, much of the water is held by the proteins in a gel-type structure. The chief intracellular proteins that take part in the contraction process are myosin and actin. Other proteins, many of which are soluble in water, are present in small amounts.

The term *extractives* is applied to certain nonnitrogenous substances, mainly lactic acid, and nitrogenous constituents that are nonprotein. The principal nitrogenous extractives are creatine and creatinine but there are small amounts of urea, uric acid, and others. Extractives are more prominent in older animals and in more exercised muscles and have been considered to be of some importance in the development of meat flavor.

The color of meat is chiefly the result of the quantity of the muscle pigment myoglobin that is present. In a well-bled animal most of the red hemoglobin pigment of the blood is removed. Myoglobin and hemoglobin are similar in chemical structure, both being made up of the protein globin and the iron-containing pigment heme, but myoglobin is smaller in size. The quantity of myoglobin increases with age. Beef has a darker color than veal. The color of meat also varies with the species of animal from which it is obtained. Pork muscle generally contains less myoglobin than beef muscle and appears lighter in color. Different muscles of the same animal also may differ in color.

When meat is first cut, the myoglobin is in a chemically reduced form and appears purplish-red in color. As it combines with oxygen, or is oxygenated, the myoglobin changes to a bright red pigment called *oxymyoglobin,* which is characteristic of fresh cuts of meat seen in the meat market. After a certain period of storage, when reducing substances are no longer produced in the tissues, the appearance of the meat may be brownish because of the change of myoglobin or oxymyoglobin to an oxidized form, metmyoglobin.

Fats from different species and from different parts of the same animal differ to some extent in composition. The more brittle, hard fats of beef and mutton contain higher percentages of saturated fatty acids. Softer fats contain more unsaturated fatty acids. The high melting point of lamb fat causes it to congeal when it is served unless the meat is very hot. Lard extracted from the fatty tissue around the glandular organs has a somewhat higher melting point than the lard produced from back fat.

Nutritive Value

Since nutritive value is dependent upon composition, it is evident from the foregoing discussion that meats are valuable chiefly for their protein or tissue-building constituent. The cell proteins are of excellent quality in nutrition but the gelatin formed from white connective tissue by cooking has a lower biological value.

Leverton and Odel [34] reported that when the lean and lean-marbled-with-fat portions of cooked meat were analyzed together they were found to contain 10 to 21 percent fat and 23 to 32 percent protein. The lean portion or the lean-plus-marble portions of cooked pork contained no more fat than similar portions of beef, veal, or lamb.

Meat is a good source of iron and of phosphorus. Some copper is found in muscle meats but liver is richer than muscle in both iron and copper. Meat is among the poorest sources of calcium because the calcium is chiefly in the bones, which are not eaten.

Meat furnishes valuable amounts of certain vitamins. Lean meats are a good source of thiamin, riboflavin, and niacin as well as other members of the B complex. Lean pork is a rich dietary source of thiamin, whereas other lean meats (beef, veal, and lamb) furnish a somewhat lower concentration of this vitamin. Liver and kidney are good dietary sources of riboflavin and are richer in niacin than most other tissues. All meats furnish tryptophan, the amino acid that serves as a precursor of niacin for the body. Liver is a variable but excellent source of vitamin A; the animal source of liver is not of practical significance in the variance of vitamin A content.

Normal cooking procedures appear to have little effect on protein quality. Severe heating, however, could decrease the biological value of meat proteins. Minerals dissolved in the juices or cooking water may be consumed in gravies. The loss of thiamin in cooking or processing meats appears to be related to the severity of heat treatment. Canned meats usually contain less thiamin than do other cooked or processed meats because of the high temperatures required for sterilization. The average retention of thiamin in cooked meats is about 65 percent. Riboflavin and niacin are more resistant to destruction in cooking than is thiamin and seem to be well retained (see Appendix C for nutritive value of selected meats).

Classification

Beef

Beef carcasses are classified on the basis of age and sex. A *steer* is a male castrated when young; a *heifer* is a young female that has not yet borne a calf; a *cow* is a female that has borne a calf; a *stag* is a male castrated after maturity; and a *bull* is a mature male, not castrated.

Steer carcasses are preferred by the retailer because of their heavier weight and the higher proportion of meat to bone, but steer and heifer carcasses of the same grade are of equal value to the consumer insofar as quality of meat is concerned. The meat from cows is variable, depending upon maturity, but is usually inferior to both steer and heifer. Very little stag meat is found on the market. Meat from bull carcasses usually goes into processed meats.

Veal

Veal is meat from immature bovines. In the wholesale market, veal carcasses are usually from animals of either sex that are at least 3 weeks but less than 3 months of age. They are largely fed on milk or milk products. The term *calf* is applied to animals slaughtered between 3 months and about 8 months of age. The older animals have passed the good veal stage but do not yet possess the properties of good beef. In practice, however, the term *veal* may be applied to animals somewhat older than 3 months. The term *baby beef* is sometimes used to refer to animals 8 to 12 months of age.

Lamb and Mutton

Sheep carcasses are classified as lamb and mutton according to the age of the animal. Lamb is obtained from young animals of either sex that are less than 14 months of age, although the exact age at which lamb changes to mutton is somewhat indefinite. Mutton carcasses are those that have passed the lamb stage. The usual test for a lamb carcass is the "break joint." The feet of a lamb when broken off sharply will separate from the leg *above* the regular joint. The break shows four distinct ridges that appear smooth, moist, and red with blood. In mutton, the break comes *in* the true joint, which is below the break joint.

Most of the meat from sheep is marketed as lamb. Relatively little older mutton is sold. The flesh of all carcasses in the mutton class is darker in color than lamb. It is also less tender and has a stronger flavor if it is from animals beyond 2 years of age.

Pork

Pork is the meat of swine. Good quality pork is obtained from young animals usually 7 to 12 months of age. In young animals there is no distinction in quality or grade because of sex. In older animals, sex differences are pronounced.

Postmortem Changes and Aging

Just before an animal is slaughtered the muscles are soft and pliable, but upon death, as metabolism in the cells is interrupted, processes begin that lead to a stiffening of the carcass known as *rigor mortis*. Lactic acid accumulates in the muscle and the *p*H decreases as an indication of the increased acidity. The high energy compound produced in metabolism in the living animal, adenosine triphosphate (ATP), gradually disappears and the muscle contracts. Then rigor mortis sets in as the muscle proteins, actin and myosin, bond together and the muscle is no longer extensible. Various factors affect the time required for the changes to occur after the death of the animal. Rigor mortis begins and is completed relatively slowly when the carcass is held under the usual refrigeration conditions. Both colder and warmer temperatures than this speed up the development of rigor [15]. The species of animal, age, and activity just before slaughter may affect the time of onset of rigor. Rigor mortis begins more slowly in large animals, such as beef, and lasts longer. It is usually complete in 24 to 48 hours in beef. If meat is separated from the carcass immediately after slaughter and cooked rapidly before rigor has a chance to develop, it will be tender. However, if the cooking process is slow, rigor may develop during heating and increase toughness in the cooked meat [15,25].

If the supply of glycogen in the muscle is low at the time of death, as is the case when much activity occurs just before slaughter, less lactic acid is produced from glycogen and the pH of the muscle remains relatively high. The muscle tissue is only slightly acid. This results, in beef, in a dark color that is less acceptable in market channels. The muscle tissue is also relatively dry. The average incidence of dark-cutting beef at a large Canadian packing plant was estimated to be 8 percent [46].

If meat is allowed to hang under refrigeration for 1 or 2 days after slaughter it will gradually begin to soften as rigor mortis passes. As it is held for a still longer time a process of ripening or aging occurs, resulting in some increase in tenderness, improvement of flavor and juiciness, better browning in cooking of both lean and fat, and a loss of red interior color at a lower cooking temperature [26]. Too long aging may result in a strong flavor or an off-flavor and odor. The increase in tenderness may come from an increased water-binding capacity of muscle proteins or possibly from some enzymatic breakdown of proteins. The effect of enzymes is more marked when the meat is held at temperatures higher than 4° C (39° F). Postmortem aging of beef produces some breakdown of mucoprotein, which is a component of connective tissue [40]. Fragmentation of the myofibrils in the muscle also appears to be related to the tenderizing effect of aging [49].

Meat is commonly aged at a temperature of approximately 2° C (36° F). It has been reported, however, that aging sides of beef at a temperature of 16° C (61° F) produces changes in tenderness more rapidly than aging at 2° C (36° F). The higher temperature of aging may sometimes be used [49] but some means of retarding microbial growth at the higher temperature is necessary. Aging of meat is a commercial process and is not accomplished in the home.

Some cuts of meat are packaged under vacuum in order to reduce the shrinkage and to improve sanitation during the holding period. It was shown that vacuum packaging of beef loins and ribs during aging for either 7 or 15 days had no significant influence on tenderness, flavor, and juiciness, but it produced a significant reduction in weight loss during aging. Bacterial counts on the surface of the meat were also significantly lower with vacuum packaging [42].

Aging does not improve veal. The lack of fat on the carcass results in excessive surface drying. Pork is usually obtained from a young tender animal and toughness is not a problem. Aging also may be complicated in pork by the relatively rapid development of rancidity from the fat on holding. Pork is not generally aged although it has been suggested that the tenderness of pork loin may be increased by aging [13, 16, 52].

Beef is the only type of meat that is commonly aged, although some consumers also prefer lamb when it is aged. Beef will usually be in market channels for a week to 10 days before the consumer purchases it. This time seems to be sufficient for aging.

Tenderness

One of the most important attributes in rating meat is that of tenderness. The grading of meat does not directly measure tenderness although the probability of a beef carcass's being tender is greater in a higher grade than it is in a lower grade of beef. Pork and lamb, because they are usually marketed young, are tender. Much more variation exists in beef, and much of the research on tenderness has been concerned with beef cuts.

In studying the tenderness of meat with the use of taste panels, several components of tenderness that are apparent during the biting and chewing of meat have been described. These include (1) the ease with which teeth sink into the meat, or softness; (2) the crumbliness of the muscle fibers; and (3) the amount of connective tissue or the amount of residue remaining after the meat is chewed for a certain time. Each of these components of tenderness may be influenced by various factors in the production and preparation of beef.

It is generally agreed that larger amounts of connective tissue in a cut of meat cause decreased tenderness. More connective tissue is usually found in older than younger animals and the meat from younger animals is generally more tender. However, in immature animals such as veal the lack of muscular development contributes to a higher percentage of connective tissue. The least used muscles of an animal, particularly in the rib and loin sections, generally contain less connective tissue and are more tender than the muscles used in locomotion.

The fattening of animals has long been thought to improve the tenderness of meat. It has been suggested that a layer of subcutaneous fat on a carcass delays chilling of the meat, thereby allowing postmortem metabolic changes to occur which result in greater tenderness [8]. The method of cooking meat as discussed later in this chapter affects its tenderness. Aging increases tenderness in beef. Carcasses of beef may be subjected to electrical stimulation immediately after slaughter to increase tenderness [55]. The beneficial effects may be due to an increase in the postmortem metabolic processes and a disruption of the myofibrils [4, 57]. The hereditary background of the animal, the management of its feeding, and size of muscle fibers are other factors that may affect meat tenderness. Many of these factors are undoubtedly interrelated, and more research is needed to clarify the whole picture of tenderness in meat.

Because of the lower cost of certain less tender cuts of meat in comparison with more tender pieces, attempts have been made to tenderize the less tender cuts. Grinding and cubing break up the connective tissue and make meat more tender. Tenderizing compounds containing papain, a protein-digesting enzyme taken from the papaya plant, or bromelin, a similar enzyme obtained from pineapples, may be applied to the surface of meats prior to cooking. A fork may be used to pierce the meat and to allow the compound to penetrate. Papain acts upon the muscle cell proteins as well as on the connective tissue, and care must be used to control excessive action on the meat fibers, which will result in a mealy texture. The optimum temperature for papain activity is 60° to 71° C (140° to 160° F); this temperature is achieved during cooking.

A papain or other enzyme mixture may be injected into the bloodstream of the animal just before slaughter. Theoretically the enzyme is carried to all parts of the body and is evenly distributed throughout the various retail cuts. The enzyme remains inactive until the meat is heated in cooking. Cuts of meat that are usually classified as less tender may be cooked as tender cuts in beef animals that have been treated by enzyme injection. This type of meat usually sells for slightly more per pound than untreated cuts.

Buying of Meats

American families tend to spend a substantial percentage of food money on meats. If as much as 38 to 40 percent of food money goes for meats, it is quite possible that other important items of the diet, such as milk, fruits, and vegetables, are being neglected. Meats are among the most expensive items of the diet; they are well liked; and many families place undue emphasis on the need for meat in every meal. There is also a lack of information on the part of many consumers as to what determines the price and quality of meats.

A number of laws have been passed and regulations have been published, at both the national and local levels, to protect and inform the consumer in connection with the purchasing of meat and poultry products. The U.S. Department of Agriculture has the responsibility at the federal level for the inspection, grading, and setting of standards for meat and poultry products. The kinds and amounts of additives that can be used in meat products are approved by the U.S. Department of Agriculture, using Food and Drug Administration guidelines. During the 1950s the practice of administering compounds with estrogenic activity to beef cattle developed and became widespread. The use of these compounds in livestock raising is for the purpose of increasing weight gain with less feed, thus allowing earlier marketing. Diethylstilbestrol (DES) has been the most commonly used compound for this purpose. Considerable controversy over the safety of this product was generated and its use has been prohibited by federal regulating agencies.

Standards of identity have been published by the U.S. Department of Agriculture for some meat products, including corned beef hash. However, for most meat and poultry products, standards of composition have been set. These standards identify the minimum amount of meat or poultry required in a product's recipe. For example, meat pie must contain at least 25 percent meat, beef with gravy or beef with barbecue sauce must contain at least 50 percent beef, and chili con carne must have at least 40 percent meat. Frankfurters and similar cooked sausages must contain no more than 30 percent fat, 10 percent added water, and 2 percent corn syrup. Their labels must clearly indicate the products used in their formulation.

The consumer should be aware of standards and inspection procedures required for meat and meat products. Since enforcement of regulations at all levels is extremely difficult, the consumer has a responsibility to report any infractions that he observes. Information on buying and use of meats is found in the U.S. Department of Agriculture bulletins listed as references 2, 20, 21, 22, 23, 32, and 51.

Inspection stamp used on meat carcasses.

Seal used on prepared meat products.

10-3 *Federal meat inspection stamps.* (Courtesy of the U.S. Department of Agriculture)

Government Inspection

All meats entering interstate commerce must be inspected by qualified agents from the U.S. Department of Agriculture, Food Safety and Inspection Service. Animals are inspected alive and at various stages of the slaughtering process. The cleanliness and operating procedures of meat packing plants are also supervised to ensure that meat and meat products are not contaminated or adulterated and that labeling is proper and truthful. If meat carcasses are sound and wholesome, the inspector's stamp (Figure 10-3) is placed on each wholesale cut of the carcass. This stamp carries numbers that indicate the packer and identify the carcass. If the meat is unsound, it is not permitted to enter retail trade. The Federal Meat Inspection Act also requires that all meat imported into the United States comes under the same standards of inspection that are applied to meat produced in the United States.

The Wholesome Meat Act of 1967 requires that state governments have, for meat that is sold within state boundaries, local programs of meat inspection equal to those of the federal government. Otherwise, the federal government will assume the responsibility for inspection. State programs are periodically reviewed to see that satisfactory standards are maintained. This protects the meat-buying public against diseased animals.

There is no practical means of inspecting for the presence of the small parasite, *Trichinella spiralis,* which may be found in the muscle of approximately one in 1,000 pork carcasses. If consumed, this organism causes *trichinosis.* Regulations for inspection of meat products containing pork that are usually eaten without cooking require treatment of such products in a way that destroys any live trichinae that may have been in the pork muscle tissue. This may be accomplished in one of three ways: (1) heating uniformly to a temperature of 58.5° C (137° F); (2) freezing for not less than 20 days at a maximum temperature of −15° C (5° F); (3) curing under special methods prescribed by the USDA. Products such as dried and summer sausage, bologna, frankfurter-style sausage, cooked hams, and cooked pork in casings are among those requiring this treatment.

Much of the meat and poultry slaughtered goes into processed items like sausages, ham, pizza, frozen dinners, soups, etc. The federal inspection program is responsible for the safety of these products also.

Grades and Grading

The U.S. Department of Agriculture has established a system of grading for meat (Figure 10-4) that is a separate program from the inspection service. Whereas inspection of meat for wholesomeness is mandatory for all meat as it is slaughtered, grading is voluntary. It is not required that meat be graded in order to be marketed. However, grading provides a national uniform language for use in the buying and selling of meat. Grades are also useful to the consumer in knowing what quality to expect from purchased meats. The grading program is administered by the Department of Agriculture but the cost of the service is borne by those meat packers who use it.

Quality grades have been established for beef, veal, lamb, and mutton. Several factors are considered in designating quality.

10-4 *U.S. federal meat quality grade stamps.* (Courtesy of the U.S. Department of Agriculture)

Grades for pork are not intended to identify differences in quality to consumers since much of the pork is processed before it reaches the retail market. The grades for pork are more concerned with yield than with quality. Pork carcasses and cuts are graded for wholesale trade and for price control on a weight basis, heavier weights grading lower than lighter weights. Pork, as marketed, is less variable in age and quality than carcasses from other animals.

For beef and lamb, *yield grades* have been established for use along with quality grades. Yield grades are based on cutability, which indicates the proportionate amount of salable retail cuts that can be obtained from a carcass. Number 1 indicates the highest yield and number 5 indicates the lowest. A large proportion of edible meat is indicated by a relatively large rib eye area, a thin layer of external fat, and a small amount of fat around the internal organs. The dual system of grading, for both quality and yield, attempts to offer the consumer high-quality meat without excess fat. Both quality and yield grades must be used when beef and lamb are federally graded.

The major factors considered in the quality grades all have to do with palatability or eating quality. Conformation, or shape and build of the animal, is reflected to some degree in the yield grade. A stocky, muscular build will usually represent a relatively high proportion of salable meat and will receive a high yield grade.

Marbling and maturity are the two major factors used to evaluate the quality of beef. Marbling refers to the flecks of fat within the lean muscle. The standards for grading beef have been adjusted so that marbling requirements for prime and choice grades are not as high as they were under the previous standards. Marbling apparently contributes to juiciness and tenderness of meat. An optimum thickness of surface fat layer also appears to contribute to palatability [8, 58, 59].

The maturity of an animal affects the lean meat texture, the grain generally becoming more coarse with increasing maturity. Fine-textured lean is usually slightly more tender than lean with a very coarse texture. A very mature animal usually develops changes in connective tissue that contribute to decreased tenderness. Very young veal animals, however, may actually increase in apparent tenderness of the meat as they mature to an optimum stage. The muscle is not well developed and the connective tissue is proportionately greater than when additional muscular development has occurred.

In a good quality of beef the lean has a bright red color after the cut surface is exposed to air for a few minutes. It is fine-grained and smooth to the touch, and the fat is firm. The chine or backbone is soft, red, and spongy, and shows considerable cartilage. The lean of a poor carcass is darker red in color, is coarse grained, and lacks the smooth, "satiny" surfaces when cut. The fat of a poor quality carcass is oily or soft in texture. The bones of a poor quality of carcass are white, hard, and brittle and show little or no cartilage.

Good quality in veal is shown by the grayish-pink color of flesh and a texture that is fine grained and smooth to the touch. The interior fat of good quality veal is firm and brittle. The bones are red, spongy, and soft and have an abundance of cartilage. Poor quality in veal is characterized either by a very pale or a dark color of the lean and little or no fat distributed throughout the carcass.

Good quality in lamb is shown by the pinkish-red color of the flesh, the fine grain of the flesh, and smooth cut surfaces. The fat of good lamb is firm, flaky, and brittle. The bones are soft, red, and spongy and show cartilage. Poor quality in lamb is characterized by darker color of the lean, heavier fat layers, and a stronger flavor.

The flesh of good quality pork is grayish-pink in color, and is fine grained. The fat of pork should be very firm but it is not brittle as in other types of meats. The bones are soft, red, and spongy. Pork of poor quality has an excess of fat distributed in the lean tissues as well as on the exterior. The color of the lean is darker, the grain coarser, and the bones may tend to appear less red and spongy, particularly if the meat is from an animal beyond the optimal age limit.

Grading does not directly measure tenderness, and many factors may influence the tenderness of meat. Various studies have given inconsistent results in relating the U.S. Department of Agriculture carcass grades to tenderness. Some researchers have reported that higher grades of beef showed significantly more tenderness than did lower grades [38, 44]. Other studies, however, have not found significant tenderness differences among grades of beef, particularly between choice and good grades [58]. The variation in tenderness from one carcass to another within a grade would appear to be great.

Table 10-1 shows USDA quality grades for beef, veal, lamb, and mutton. Utility and lower grades of meat are rarely, if ever, sold as cuts in retail stores. They are used in processed meat products. The appropriate USDA quality grade mark is applied to meat with a roller stamp that leaves its mark the full length of the carcass.

Because beef can vary so much in quality, there are eight designated grades for this product, with USDA prime beef being the highest quality. Only about 6.5 percent of marketed beef is likely to be graded prime. Most of the prime beef is purchased for use in commercial food service, and the consumer does not generally find this grade on the retail market. USDA choice grade beef has slightly less marbling than prime but is still of very high quality. USDA good grade beef lacks some of the juiciness and quality of the higher grades, but is usually relatively tender and palatable. USDA standard beef has a high proportion of lean meat and little fat. It comes from young animals, since the top four grades are all restricted to

Table 10-1 *USDA Quality Grades for Meat*

Beef	Veal	Lamb	Mutton
Prime	Prime	Prime	Choice
Choice	Choice	Choice	Good
Good	Good	Good	Utility
Standard	Standard	Utility	Cull
Commercial	Utility	Cull	
Utility	Cull		
Cutter			
Canner			

beef from young animals, and is, therefore, usually fairly tender. USDA commercial grade beef comes from mature animals and generally requires long cooking with moist heat to tenderize it. It has the full flavor of mature beef.

Cuts of Meat and Identification

An important aspect of the buying of fresh meat is a knowledge of the various retail cuts into which the carcasses are divided and an understanding of the relative quality characteristics of these cuts. Meat carcasses are commonly divided into relatively large wholesale or primal cuts, such as the square cut chuck section of beef. Wholesale cuts are further divided into smaller retail cuts. The wholesale and retail cuts for beef, pork, veal, and lamb are shown in Figures 10-5, 10-6, 10-7, and 10-8, respectively. Division into cuts is made in relation to bone and muscle structure. Muscles that are found together in any one retail cut generally have similar characteristics of tenderness and texture. The shapes and sizes of bones and muscles in retail cuts are guides to identification. The seven basic retail meat cuts that can be identified by their characteristic bone structures are shown in Figure 10-9 and the basic bone shapes are presented in Figure 10-10. Since the skeletal structure is similar for all of the meat animals, the basic cuts are similar for beef, pork, veal, and lamb. However, each type of meat carcass is divided in a slightly different manner.

Some meat cuts have been known by different common names in various parts of the country. For example, beef rib eye steaks are sometimes called Delmonico or Spencer steaks, and flank steak may also be called London broil or minute steak. Because of the confusion created in merchandising by the wide variety of names for retail meat cuts, an industry-wide Cooperative Meat Identification Standards Committee was organized by the meat industry. This committee developed standards for the retail meat trade and provided a master list of *recommended* names for retail cuts of beef,

BEEF CHART

RETAIL CUTS OF BEEF — WHERE THEY COME FROM AND HOW TO COOK THEM

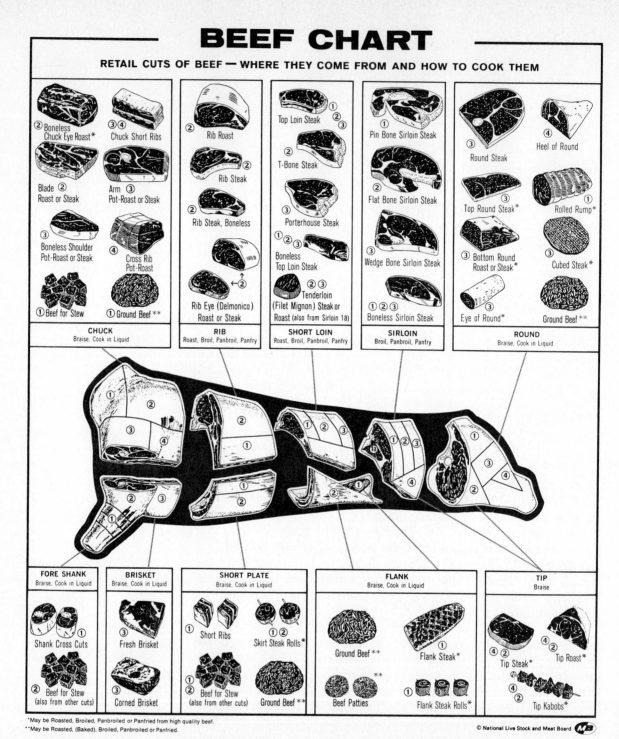

② Boneless Chuck Eye Roast*
③④ Chuck Short Ribs
② Blade Roast or Steak
③ Arm Pot-Roast or Steak
③ Boneless Shoulder Pot-Roast or Steak
④ Cross Rib Pot-Roast
① Beef for Stew
① Ground Beef**

CHUCK
Braise, Cook in Liquid

② Rib Roast
② Rib Steak
② Rib Steak, Boneless
←②
Rib Eye (Delmonico) Roast or Steak

RIB
Roast, Broil, Panbroil, Panfry

② ③ Top Loin Steak
② T-Bone Steak
Porterhouse Steak
① ② ③ Boneless Top Loin Steak
② ③ Tenderloin (Filet Mignon) Steak or Roast (also from Sirloin 1a)

SHORT LOIN
Roast, Broil, Panbroil, Panfry

① Pin Bone Sirloin Steak
Flat Bone Sirloin Steak
Wedge Bone Sirloin Steak
① ② ③ Boneless Sirloin Steak

SIRLOIN
Broil, Panbroil, Panfry

③ Round Steak
④ Heel of Round
③ Top Round Steak*
① Rolled Rump*
③ Bottom Round Roast or Steak*
③ Cubed Steak*
③ Eye of Round*
Ground Beef**

ROUND
Braise, Cook in Liquid

FORE SHANK
Braise, Cook in Liquid
① Shank Cross Cuts
② Beef for Stew (also from other cuts)

BRISKET
Braise, Cook in Liquid
③ Fresh Brisket
③ Corned Brisket

SHORT PLATE
Braise, Cook in Liquid
① Short Ribs
① ② Skirt Steak Rolls*
① ② Beef for Stew (also from other cuts)
Ground Beef**

FLANK
Braise, Cook in Liquid
Ground Beef**
① Flank Steak*
Beef Patties**
① Flank Steak Rolls*

TIP
Braise
④ ② Tip Steak*
④ ② Tip Roast*
④ ② Tip Kabobs*

*May be Roasted, Broiled, Panbroiled or Panfried from high quality beef.
**May be Roasted, (Baked), Broiled, Panbroiled or Panfried.

© National Live Stock and Meat Board

10-5 *Wholesale and retail cuts of beef.* (Courtesy of National Live Stock and Meat Board)

198

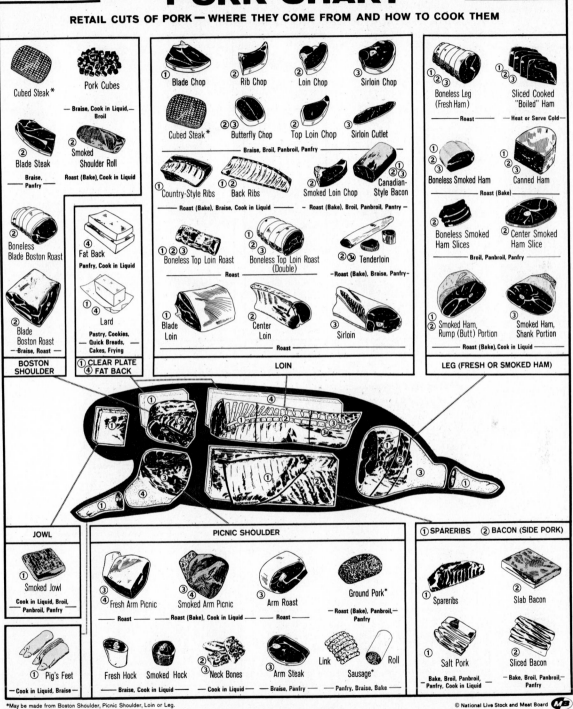

PORK CHART
RETAIL CUTS OF PORK — WHERE THEY COME FROM AND HOW TO COOK THEM

BOSTON SHOULDER

Cubed Steak*

Pork Cubes
— Braise, Cook in Liquid, —
Broil

② Blade Steak
Braise, Panfry

② Smoked Shoulder Roll
Roast (Bake), Cook in Liquid

Boneless Blade Boston Roast

② Blade Boston Roast
— Braise, Roast —

① CLEAR PLATE
④ FAT BACK

④ Fat Back
Panfry, Cook in Liquid

① ④ Lard
Pastry, Cookies, Quick Breads, Cakes, Frying

LOIN

① Blade Chop
② Rib Chop
② Loin Chop
③ Sirloin Chop

② ③ Cubed Steak*
② ③ Butterfly Chop
② Top Loin Chop
③ Sirloin Cutlet
— Braise, Broil, Panbroil, Panfry —

① Country-Style Ribs
① ② Back Ribs
② Smoked Loin Chop
② ③ Canadian-Style Bacon
— Roast (Bake), Braise, Cook in Liquid —   — Roast (Bake), Broil, Panbroil, Pantry —

① ② ③ Boneless Top Loin Roast
② ③ Boneless Top Loin Roast (Double)
② ③ Tenderloin
— Roast —   — Roast (Bake), Braise, Panfry —

① Blade Loin
② Center Loin
③ Sirloin
— Roast —

LEG (FRESH OR SMOKED HAM)

① ② ③ Boneless Leg (Fresh Ham)
① ② ③ Sliced Cooked "Boiled" Ham
— Roast —   — Heat or Serve Cold —

① ② ③ Boneless Smoked Ham
① ③ Canned Ham
— Roast (Bake) —

② Boneless Smoked Ham Slices
② Center Smoked Ham Slice
— Broil, Panbroil, Panfry —

② Smoked Ham, Rump (Butt) Portion
② Smoked Ham, Shank Portion
— Roast (Bake), Cook in Liquid —

JOWL

① Smoked Jowl
Cook in Liquid, Broil, Panbroil, Panfry

① Pig's Feet
— Cook in Liquid, Braise —

PICNIC SHOULDER

③ ④ Fresh Arm Picnic
— Roast —

③ ④ Smoked Arm Picnic
— Roast (Bake), Cook in Liquid —

③ Arm Roast
— Roast —

Ground Pork*
— Roast (Bake), Panbroil, — Panfry

Fresh Hock
Smoked Hock
— Braise, Cook in Liquid —   — Cook in Liquid —

② Neck Bones
— Cook in Liquid —

③ Arm Steak
— Braise, Panfry —

Link
Roll
Sausage*
— Panfry, Braise, Bake —

① SPARERIBS   ② BACON (SIDE PORK)

① Spareribs
② Slab Bacon

① Salt Pork
② Sliced Bacon
— Bake, Broil, Panbroil, Panfry, Cook in Liquid —   — Bake, Broil, Panbroil, — Panfry

*May be made from Boston Shoulder, Picnic Shoulder, Loin or Leg.

© National Live Stock and Meat Board

10-6 *Wholesale and retail cuts of pork.* (Courtesy of National Live Stock and Meat Board)

199

VEAL CHART

RETAIL CUTS OF VEAL — WHERE THEY COME FROM AND HOW TO COOK THEM

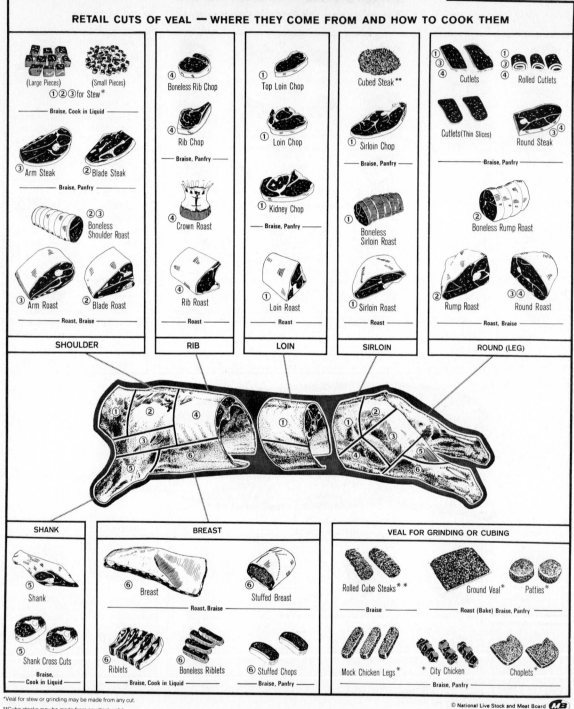

SHOULDER

(Large Pieces)   (Small Pieces)
①②③ for Stew*
— Braise, Cook in Liquid —
③ Arm Steak   ② Blade Steak
— Braise, Panfry —
②③ Boneless Shoulder Roast
③ Arm Roast   ② Blade Roast
— Roast, Braise —

RIB

④ Boneless Rib Chop
④ Rib Chop
— Braise, Panfry —
④ Crown Roast
④ Rib Roast
— Roast —

LOIN

① Top Loin Chop
① Loin Chop
① Kidney Chop
— Braise, Panfry —
① Loin Roast
— Roast —

SIRLOIN

Cubed Steak**
① Sirloin Chop
— Braise, Panfry —
① Boneless Sirloin Roast
① Sirloin Roast
— Roast —

ROUND (LEG)

①③④ Cutlets   ①③④ Rolled Cutlets
Cutlets (Thin Slices)   ③④ Round Steak
— Braise, Panfry —
② Boneless Rump Roast
② Rump Roast   ③④ Round Roast
— Roast, Braise —

SHANK

⑤ Shank
⑤ Shank Cross Cuts
— Braise, Cook in Liquid —

BREAST

⑥ Breast   ⑥ Stuffed Breast
— Roast, Braise —
⑥ Riblets   ⑥ Boneless Riblets   ⑥ Stuffed Chops
— Braise, Cook in Liquid —   — Braise, Panfry —

VEAL FOR GRINDING OR CUBING

Rolled Cube Steaks**   Ground Veal*   Patties*
— Braise —   — Roast (Bake) Braise, Panfry —
Mock Chicken Legs*   * City Chicken   Choplets*
— Braise, Panfry —

*Veal for stew or grinding may be made from any cut.

**Cube steaks may be made from any thick solid piece of boneless veal.

© National Live Stock and Meat Board

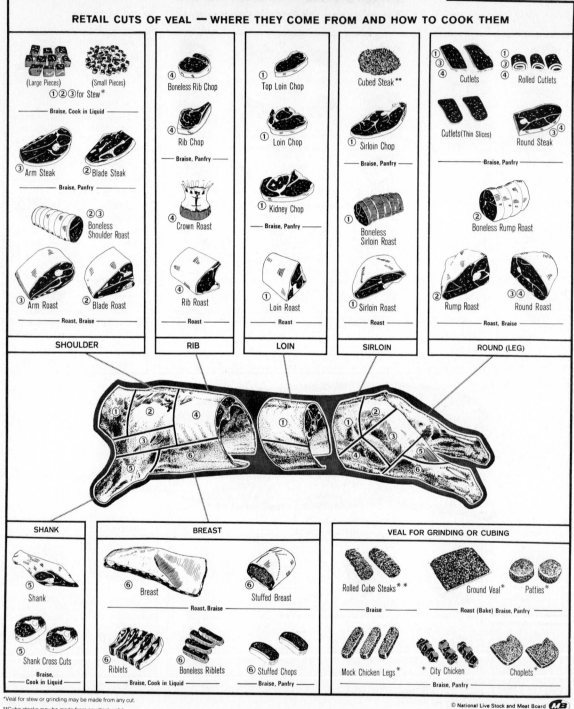

10-7 *Wholesale and retail cuts of veal.* (Courtesy of National Live Stock and Meat Board)

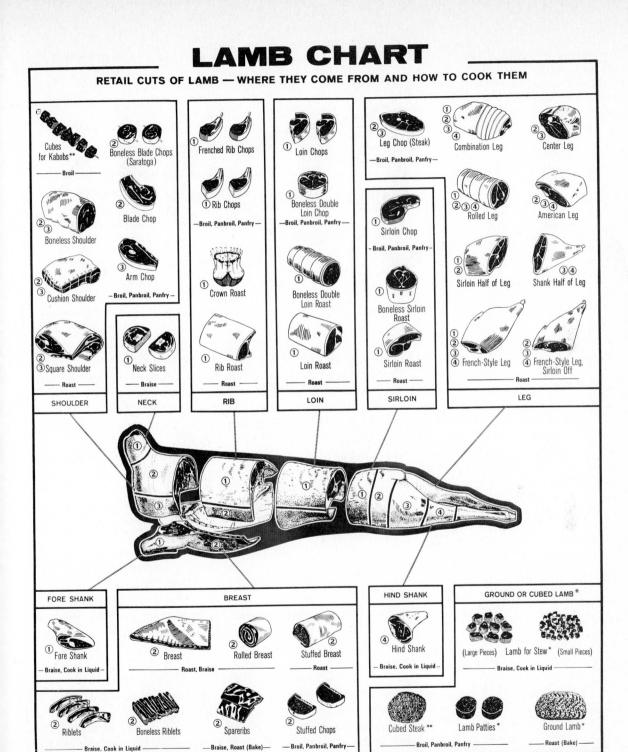

10-8 *Wholesale and retail cuts of lamb.* (Courtesy of National Live Stock and Meat Board)

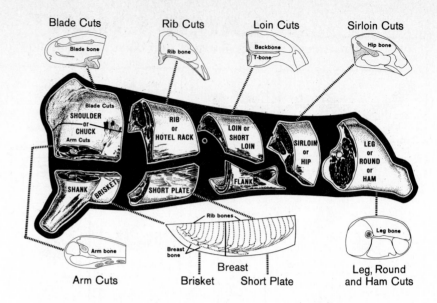

10-9 *The seven basic retail cuts of meat.* (From Uniform Retail Meat Identity Standards, Industrywide Cooperative Meat Identification Standards Committee, National Live Stock and Meat Board, 1973.)

pork, veal, and lamb. The list serves all regions of the United States. The recommended retail package label information includes the species or kind of meat, the wholesale cut name, and the specific retail name from the master list. A typical label reads: BEEF CHUCK—BLADE ROAST. Photographs of beef and pork retail cuts are shown in Color Plates V, VI, VII, and VIII.

Beef. Cuts of beef are sometimes classified into the most tender, medium tender, and the least tender cuts, as follows:

Most Tender Cuts	*Medium Tender Cuts*	*Least Tender Cuts*
Rib	Chuck	Flank
Short loin	Rump	Plate
Sirloin	Round	Brisket
		Neck
		Shanks

The rib and loin sections lie along the center of the back. Because that part of the body is affected little by the exercise of the animal, the meat is tender. The rib section yields the choicest roasts in the carcass.

The short loin and sirloin are cut into steaks as follows: top loin, sometimes called club, nearest the rib, then T-bone, porterhouse, and sirloin. The tenderloin muscle, which lies on the underside of the backbone (between the backbone and kidney fat), forms one eye of meat in the loin steaks. It is very small or even nonexistent in the top loin steak area, but increases in size further back, having maximum size in the porterhouse steaks. The tenderloin may be bought

BONES IDENTIFY SEVEN GROUPS OF RETAIL CUTS

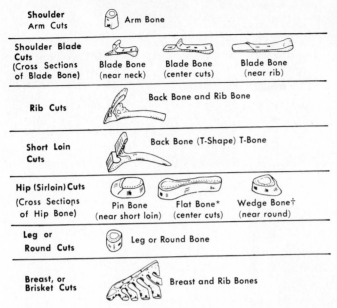

Shoulder Arm Cuts	Arm Bone		
Shoulder Blade Cuts (Cross Sections of Blade Bone)	Blade Bone (near neck)	Blade Bone (center cuts)	Blade Bone (near rib)
Rib Cuts	Back Bone and Rib Bone		
Short Loin Cuts	Back Bone (T-Shape) T-Bone		
Hip (Sirloin) Cuts (Cross Sections of Hip Bone)	Pin Bone (near short loin)	Flat Bone* (center cuts)	Wedge Bone† (near round)
Leg or Round Cuts	Leg or Round Bone		
Breast, or Brisket Cuts	Breast and Rib Bones		

*Formerly part of "double bone" but today the back bone is usually removed leaving only the "flat bone" (sometimes called "pin bone") in the sirloin steak.

†On one side of sirloin steak, this bone may be wedge shaped while on the other side the same bone may be round.

10-10 *Basic bone shapes aid in meat cut identification.* (From Uniform Retail Meat Identity Standards, Industrywide Cooperative Meat Identification Standards Committee, National Live Stock and Meat Board, 1973.)

as a boneless cut suitable for roasting or cutting into steaks. It is not removed from high-grade but from lower-grade carcasses. Because of its tenderness tenderloin commands a high price.

The medium-tender cuts listed are more easily made tender by moist heat cookery than are the least tender cuts. In the latter the connective tissue is more developed.

Veal, Lamb, and Pork. These carcasses, being smaller than beef, are divided into fewer wholesale and retail cuts. The loin of pork is a long cut including both rib and loin sections. The rib and loin sections of veal, lamb, and pork are cut into chops or roasts. The hind legs are also tender enough for roasts. The individual cuts are identical in general shape and characteristics with similar cuts from beef, but there is less variation in the tenderness of cuts from different sections of the animal. All cuts of young pork of good quality, both fresh and cured, are tender.

Lamb and veal are similar to beef in that neck, shoulder or chuck, breast, and shanks may require some moist heat for the best results. Some cuts of lamb are shown in Figures 10-11 and 10-12. Even the

Lamb rib chops

Lamb loin chops

Lamb sirloin chops

10-11 *Lamb chops.* (Courtesy of National Live Stock and Meat Board)

10-12 *Leg of lamb.* (Courtesy of National Live Stock and Meat Board)

Lamb leg, American style roast

Lamb leg, Frenched style roast

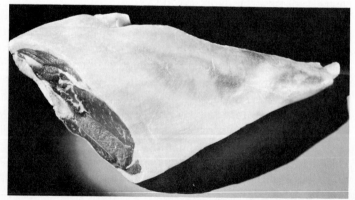

204

most tender cuts of veal may be improved by some application of moist heat to hydrolyze the collagen in connective tissue. The lack of fat marbling in veal may also affect its tenderness. Larding, which involves inserting strips of fat into lean meat, supplies fat and enhances the flavor. The leg, loin, and rib sections of good quality veal may be satisfactorily roasted.

Considerations in Buying Meat

Retail cuts may vary greatly in the percentage of bone, muscle meat, and visible fat. Table 10-2 gives the yield of boneless cooked meat from retail cuts of beef and veal. Ground beef gives the largest number of 3-ounce servings per pound of beef; short ribs, bone-in, yield the smallest number of servings. In general, the cost per pound of an edible portion is greatest in those cuts that command the highest prices, and vice versa. However, a number of exceptions will occur because of differences in the percentage of bone and fat in the cuts. For example, at the same price per pound the rump (bone-in) may cost almost double the price of round per pound of edible portions because only about 43 percent of the rump is edible as compared with about 76 percent for round. Also, the price per pound of short ribs would need to be quite low for this cut to be a very economical buy in terms of cooked lean meat yield. Therefore, it is important to recognize that cost per pound of meat as purchased is not the sole consideration. Waste is also a factor.

The usual amount to buy per serving is 4 ounces of meat with little or no bone, and ¾ to 1 pound for meat with a high refuse content. One average pork chop is a serving; and one to two lamb chops, depending on the size and thickness of the chops.

Most of the less expensive cuts of meat are a more economical source of lean than are expensive cuts. Retail prices are largely determined by such factors as tenderness, general appearance, and ease or convenience in cooking. The consumer tends to buy on the basis of these qualities to so great an extent that the loins and ribs, which comprise about one fourth of the beef carcass, represent about one half of the retail cost. A great saving to the consumer would result from an increased utilization of the less tender cuts. Neither palatability nor food value correspond directly to market price. Many of the less expensive, less tender cuts of meat have more flavor than tender cuts and, if properly cooked, are among the most palatable of meats. The food value is similar in both tender and less tender lean meat cuts.

A maximum fat content of 30 percent by weight for ground beef has been set for beef ground in federally inspected plants. However, most ground beef is prepared in local supermarkets to maintain

Table 10-2 *Yield of Boneless Cooked Meat from 1-Pound Retail Cuts of Beef and Veal**†

Kind and Cut of Meat	Number of 3-Ounce Servings	Volume, Chopped or Diced (cups)
Beef		
Brisket		
Bone-in	2	1 to $1\frac{1}{2}$
Boneless, fresh or corned	3	$1\frac{1}{2}$ to 2
Chuck roast		
Arm		
Bone-in	$2\frac{1}{2}$ to 3	$1\frac{1}{2}$ to 2
Boneless	$3\frac{1}{2}$	2
Blade		
Bone-in	$2\frac{1}{2}$	$1\frac{1}{2}$
Boneless	3 to $3\frac{1}{2}$	2
Club or T-bone steak, bone-in	2	—
Flank steak, boneless	$3\frac{1}{2}$	—
Ground beef	4	—
Porterhouse steak, bone-in	2 to $2\frac{1}{2}$	—
Rib roast		
Bone-in	$2\frac{1}{2}$	$1\frac{1}{2}$
Boneless	3	$1\frac{1}{2}$ to 2
Round steak		
Bone-in	3 to $3\frac{1}{2}$	—
Boneless	$3\frac{1}{2}$ to 4	—
Rump roast		
Bone-in	$2\frac{1}{2}$	$1\frac{1}{2}$
Boneless	$3\frac{1}{2}$	2
Short ribs, bone-in	$1\frac{1}{2}$	1
Sirloin steak		
Bone-in	2 to $2\frac{1}{2}$	—
Boneless	$2\frac{1}{2}$ to 3	—
Veal		
Breast		
Bone-in	2	1 to $1\frac{1}{2}$
Boneless	3	$1\frac{1}{2}$ to 2
Cutlet		
Bone-in	$3\frac{1}{2}$	—
Boneless	4	—
Leg roast		
Bone-in	$2\frac{1}{2}$	$1\frac{1}{2}$
Boneless	$3\frac{1}{2}$	2
Loin chops, bone-in	$2\frac{1}{2}$ to 3	—
Loin roast		
Bone-in	$2\frac{1}{2}$	$1\frac{1}{2}$
Boneless	$3\frac{1}{2}$	2
Rib chops, bone-in	$2\frac{1}{2}$	—
Rib roast		
Bone-in	2 to $2\frac{1}{2}$	1 to $1\frac{1}{2}$
Boneless	$3\frac{1}{2}$	2
Shoulder roast		
Bone-in	$2\frac{1}{2}$	$1\frac{1}{2}$
Boneless	$3\frac{1}{2}$	2

*Used by permission of the U.S. Department of Agriculture.
†These figures allow no more than 10 percent fat on a cooked bone-in cut and no more than 15 percent fat on a cooked boneless cut.

freshness. Here it is generally labeled to show the proportion of lean muscle tissue and fatty tissue that has been included. Although the term *hamburger* is usually not used in the retail meat market, federal inspectors make a distinction between ground beef and hamburger. Ground beef has nothing added to it during grinding, whereas hamburger may have a limited amount of loose beef fat and seasonings added during grinding. Ground chuck must come specifically from the chuck area of the carcass, and ground round must come only from the round. Because of marked differences in cost per pound for ground beef, ground chuck, and ground round, ground beef is often the best buy per pound of protein and per pound edible yield even though the fat content may be highest in ground beef, intermediate in ground chuck, and lowest in ground round. Much of the fat in the ground beef is rendered out during cooking. A general increase in tenderness and juiciness of cooked ground beef patties with increases in raw fat content from 16 to 28 percent has been reported [7].

From the standpoint of economy as well as nutritive value, the consumer would do well to make greater use of variety meats or sundry edible parts (Figure 10-13). These include sweetbreads, brains, heart, tongue, tripe, liver, kidney, and oxtail. Sweetbreads are the thymus gland of the calf or young beef. This gland disappears as the animal matures. The thymus gland of lamb is sometimes used for sweetbreads but is too small to be of practical value.

The thymus gland has two parts—the heart sweetbread and the throat, or neck, sweetbread. It is white and soft. The brains are also soft and delicate in flavor, and are very tender. Tripe is the smooth lining from the first beef stomach, the honeycombed lining from the second stomach, and the pocket-shaped part from the end of the second stomach. Heart and tongue are much exercised muscles and are among the least tender of variety meats. They, as well as tripe, require relatively long, slow cooking for tenderization. Liver is a fine-textured variety meat. Veal or calf liver, because of its tenderness and mild flavor, is usually preferred to other kinds of liver and for that reason is more expensive. However, livers from all meat animals are high in nutritive value. Kidneys from beef and veal are made up of irregular lobes and deep clefts. Kidneys from veal are more tender and delicate in flavor than those from beef.

Cured Meats

Curing has been used for centuries as a means of preserving meat. Historically, salt (sodium chloride) in comparatively large amounts was the substance used in curing meat. Curing ingredients today include sodium nitrite, sugar, and seasonings, in addition to salt. Nitrite reacts with the red pigment of meat, myoglobin, producing

Beef, veal, pork, and lamb hearts, in order of size.

nitrosylmyoglobin which later changes to the characteristic pink color of cured meats during the heating portion of the curing process. There has been controversy about safe levels of nitrite for use in curing meats [14, 61]. Nitrite is toxic if consumed in excessive amounts, and certain cancer-producing substances, called *nitrosamines,* can be formed in food products by reactions between nitrite and other chemical substances called *secondary amines.* The U.S. Food and Drug Administration has, therefore, limited the amount of nitrite that can be present in a finished cured product. Nitrite, in addition to fixing color in cured meats, also contributes to the development of characteristic flavor and inhibits the growth of the bacterium *Clostridium botulinum.* This organism has the ability, under suitable conditions, to produce a deadly toxin. The salt in the curing mixture inhibits the growth of undesirable microorganisms during curing and adds flavor. Sugar flavors and reduces the harshness of the salt. Phosphates may also be used in curing solutions to decrease shrinkage in meat by retaining moisture.

Ham, bacon, smoked pork-shoulder picnic, and Canadian bacon are commonly cured pork cuts. Corned beef is the cured brisket of beef. Frankfurters and a variety of sausages are also cured products.

The curing mixture may be rubbed dry on the outside of a cut of meat or the meat may be submerged in a solution of the curing ingredients. The rate of diffusion of the ingredients into the meat is, however, slow. The curing ingredients may be much more rapidly and uniformly distributed throughout the meat by injecting them internally. In cuts where the vascular system is still intact, as in hams, briskets, and tongues, the curing solution may be pumped into the arteries. Brine may be injected with needles into other cuts such as bacon. Pumping curing solution into meat increases the weight of the meat. Federal regulations require that a ham must be

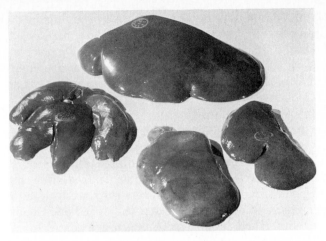

Beef, pork, veal, and lamb livers, in order of size.

Top left in picture is beef kidney; top right, veal; lower left, pork; and lower right, lamb.

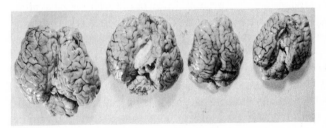

Beef, veal, pork, and lamb brains (left to right).

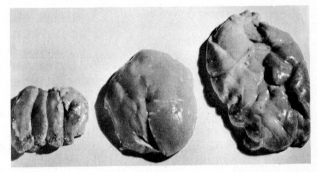

Lamb, veal, and beef sweetbreads (left to right).

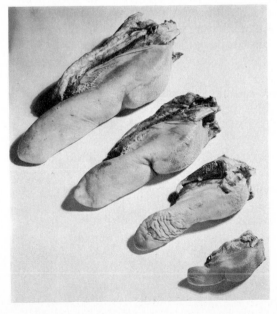

Tripe.

Beef, veal, pork, and lamb tongues (top to bottom).

209

"shrunk" back to at least its original fresh weight by the time heating and/or smoking is completed. If not, the ham must be labeled "Ham, Water Added" if it contains up to 10 percent added moisture. Hams labeled as *country-style* are processed by using a dry cure, slow smoking, and a long drying process. They are firm textured, relatively low in moisture (about 85 percent of the original weight), and always require cooking before eating.

Modern processing techniques are used for most of the ham now on the market. It is not necessary to cure ham primarily for preservative purposes since refrigeration is readily available. There is more interest in flavor and color. Hams are heated or smoked after the injection of curing solution. During this process they are heated to an internal temperature of 60° C (140° F) but they need additional cooking before serving. Hams labeled *fully cooked* are heated to an internal temperature of about 66° C (151° F). No additional cooking is required but they may be cooked further, if desired. Canned hams which have been processed at sterilizing temperatures are also sold. All processed products containing pork must be treated so that any trichinae present are destroyed since this organism causes trichinosis in man.

More than two hundred varieties of sausages and luncheon meats are marketed in the United States. These are made with chopped or ground meat with various seasonings and often contain curing ingredients. Sausages are usually molded in casings, either natural or manufactured, or in metal molds. If starchy extenders or dry milk are used in these products, federal regulations require that these be declared on the label and must not exceed 3.5 percent. Frankfurters may contain up to 15 percent chicken without special labeling; the maximum fat content in frankfurters is limited to 30 percent. Some sausages are listed as follows:

1. Uncooked.
   a. Fresh pork sausage in bulk or encased as links.
   b. Fresh bratwurst.
   c. Bockwurst.
2. Cooked.
   a. Bologna (small, medium, and large). Bologna often contains two-thirds beef and one-third pork.
   b. Frankfurters (weiners).
   c. Knockwurst.
   d. Liver sausage or Braunschweiger.
   e. Miscellaneous loaves.
3. Semidry or dry.
   a. Salami.
   b. Cervelat.
   c. Pepperoni.

Cured meat pigments tend to become oxidized and discolor when exposed to the lighting of display cases in supermarkets. Vacuum packaging, which eliminates oxygen from contact with the meat, has increased the shelf life of processed products such as bacon and luncheon meats by controlling the oxidation of pigments and the development of oxidized off-flavors.

Storage of Meat in the Home

Fresh meats require as cold a storage temperature as other highly perishable foods, such as milk, ideally below 7° C (45° F). Many meats on the retail market are prepackaged for self-service. The films used for covering the packages of fresh meats are usually permeable to oxygen so that the color of the meat will remain bright red. When brought into the home, prepackaged meats may be placed in the refrigerator in the original wrapper if the meat is to be used in 1 to 2 days. If it is to be kept longer than this, the ends of the packages should be loosened. Fresh meat that has not been prepackaged should be removed from the market wrapping and stored loosely wrapped in waxed paper, plastic wrap, or aluminum foil.

Moist meat surfaces are conducive to bacterial growth. Slight drying of the surface is preferable to bacterial action. Ground meats and variety meats are particularly perishable and should be cooked within 1 to 2 days if not frozen. Suggested home storage times for some meats are given in Table 10-3. For freezing, meat should be wrapped tightly in moisture-vapor-proof material. The meat may be divided into serving-size portions before freezing. It should be kept frozen at a temperature of −18° C (0° F) until it is used.

Table 10-3 *Suggested Home Storage Periods to Maintain High Quality in Beef and Veal**

Product	Storage Period	
	Refrigerator (35° to 40° F) (2° to 4° C)	**Freezer** (0° F) (−18° C)
Fresh meat		
Chops and cutlets	3 to 5 days	3 to 4 months
Ground beef or veal	1 to 2 days	2 to 3 months
Roasts		
Beef	3 to 5 days	8 to 12 months
Veal	3 to 5 days	4 to 8 months
Steaks	3 to 5 days	8 to 12 months
Stew meat	1 to 2 days	2 to 3 months
Variety meats	1 to 2 days	3 to 4 months
Cooked meat and meat dishes	1 to 2 days	2 to 3 months

*Used by permission of the U.S. Department of Agriculture.

When meat is being prepared for cooking, the outer surfaces may require some cleansing but, because of the soluble constituents, cut meats should not be dipped into water. Sponging cut meats with a clean damp cloth or paper towel will be sufficient. Any dried and other undesirable portions should be trimmed off: it is not necessary to trim off government stamps. Splinters of bone should be removed, if present.

Meats present a better appearance and are more palatable for most individuals when they are cooked. Cooked meats are also safer, because flesh foods may contain parasites or the larvae of tapeworm when in the raw state. All raw meats are more or less contaminated with bacteria of various types.

In meat cookery it is very important to know the nature of the cut to be cooked and then choose the proper method for cooking it. As previously stated, the meat from most young animals and from the least exercised muscles of more mature animals is tender. It has a small amount of connective tissue and should be kept tender during cooking. Less tender meats often have a coarser grain than do tender cuts and a larger amount of connective tissue so that they require tenderization during cooking to make them palatable. Nutrients and flavor should be conserved as completely as possible. Flavor may be developed by some methods of cooking.

General Methods of Meat Cookery

Conventional meat cookery methods are divided into dry-heat and moist-heat methods. Traditional methods of dry-heat cookery include roasting or baking, broiling, and pan-broiling. Frying is often included in this classification also because fat, and not moisture, comes in contact with the surface of the meat during cooking. Cooking by microwaves is a more recent method that is suitable for tender cuts of meat. Moist-heat methods are braising, stewing or cooking in water, and pressure cooking. Simmering temperatures for stewing have previously been specified on the assumption that the boiling temperature would toughen meat. However, there is apparently little difference in the final tenderness of meats cooked in water at simmering or boiling temperatures. The term *fricassee* may be applied to braised meats cut into small pieces before cooking. The braising of large pieces of meat is sometimes called pot-roasting. When meats are braised, dry heat may be first applied by pan-broiling, frying, or baking in order to produce browning.

The traditional practice of using dry-heat methods of cookery for only tender cuts of meat is based on assumed differences in the effect of these methods as well as on differences in the composition of the raw cuts. Dry-roasting has been applied to less tender beef cuts, using very low oven temperatures and long periods of time, with satisfactory results [31]. The flavors developed in beef during roasting and broiling seem to be favored by most people over those developed in braising or pot-roasting. It has been suggested that many variations of traditional cooking procedures may be adaptable to the cuts and grades of meat ordinarily prepared by moist-heat methods.

Beef loin, generally considered a tender cut, and bottom round, generally considered less tender, do not respond alike to moist- and dry-heat methods of cooking. Cover and Hostetler [6] found that loin steaks became tougher as they were cooked thoroughly and that moist heat did not seem to tenderize them. Bottom round steaks braised very well done were much more tender than loin steaks cooked in the same way. Although moist-heat methods seem to be unsuitable for tender cuts of meat, dry-heat methods seem to be suitable for both tender and less tender cuts if the time of cooking is adapted. Apparently there is enough water in the meat itself to provide for the hydrolysis of connective tissue during cooking. Additional water, as in braising or stewing, is not necessary for this purpose.

Effect of Heat on Meat

Heat produces many changes in meat. Studies with small pieces of meat that are heated more quickly and uniformly than large roasts have shown that a decrease in tenderness occurs when the meat reaches temperatures from 40° to 60° C (104° to 140° F). This is followed by a gradual increase in tenderness at temperatures above 60° C (140° F) or even above 50° C (122° F) in young animals. The original toughening appears to be the result of a shortening of the fibers accompanied by hardening as the proteins denature and coagulate. The later tenderizing evidently comes as a result of the softening of connective tissue and the hydrolysis to gelatin of some collagen in this tissue [3, 18, 33, 39]. The response of an individual muscle to heating apparently depends to some degree on the amount of connective tissue. The muscle fibers from different muscles may also react differently toward heat. Sanderson and Vail [54] heated a tender muscle *(longissimus dorsi)* and less tender muscles *(semitendinosus* and *semimembranosus)* of beef to internal temperatures of 60°, 70°, and 77° C (140°, 158°, and 170° F). Increasing the temperature did not change the tenderness of the tender muscle, but the two less tender muscles increased in tenderness with higher internal temperatures. The less tender muscles contained more connective tissue, which was evidently softened with increased temperatures, and a different balance between the hardening of muscle fibers and the softening of connective tissue was achieved in these muscles than in the tender muscle.

Fat melts when meat is heated, and the capacity of the muscle proteins to hold water is lessened, thus causing reduced juiciness and tenderness and increased weight loss. The volume of the meat decreases on cooking.

Cooking Losses

Cooking losses include loss of weight and loss of nutrients. Loss of weight results from the formation of drippings, evaporation of water, and evaporation of other volatile substances. When meat is roasted in an open pan, considerable evaporation of water from the meat surface occurs. However, nutrients and flavor substances are better retained in the meat than when the meat is cooked in water or steam. As water evaporates, minerals and extractives are deposited on the surface of the meat. This probably accounts in part for the pronounced flavor of the outer brown layer in roasted meat.

Fat losses are less consistent than those of other constituents. This is probably because of the unequal distribution of fat throughout most pieces of meat. Fat on or near the surface will be lost to a greater extent than fat in the interior because of the slowness of heat penetration. Not all fat that liquefies is lost because some of it can and does penetrate to the interior. The fat layer on the outside of meat aids in decreasing water loss by preventing evaporation.

The method of cooking meat has been shown to affect the retention of thiamin, riboflavin, and niacin (Figure 10-14). Thiamin is lost to the greatest extent but cooked meats are still good sources of all three of these vitamins. The greatest losses of vitamins occur in braising and stewing, although much of the loss is accounted for in the drippings. Therefore, if drippings are used with the cooked meat, the differences in B vitamin retention among methods of cooking are not so marked. Vitamin retention in meats during cooking in water is dependent upon the length of cooking time with greater losses occurring as cooking continues. In addition to the loss of vitamins by their dissolving in the cooking water, some oxidation may occur. Riboflavin and niacin are more resistant to destruction by heat than is thiamin.

Funk and Boyle [12] compared cooking losses of fabricated ground beef cylinders containing three different levels of fat when roasted at temperatures of 250° F, 300° F, or 350° F. They found that both total and volatile cooking losses increased as the oven temperature decreased. Longer times were required to cook to the same internal temperature of the meat at the lower oven temperatures and more

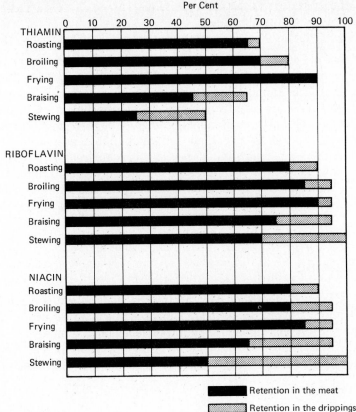
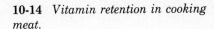

Per Cent

10-14 *Vitamin retention in cooking meat.*

Retention in the meat
Retention in the drippings

moisture was evidently evaporated from the surface of the meat during these long periods than when shorter roasting times were used. Total drippings loss increased with increased fat content of the meat but was not different for the various oven temperatures.

The final internal temperature to which meat is cooked influences total weight losses. Weight loss increases with increasing internal temperature. Total weight loss is usually greater in moist-heat than in dry-heat methods of cooking meat. Total losses from roasting meat have been found to be about 6 to 8 percent less than losses from meat cooked by moist heat in a pressure saucepan [5]. Top round steaks showed total cooking losses of 27.5 percent when cooked by moist heat as compared to 20.6 percent when cooked by dry heat methods [45]. Roasts cooked in the pressure saucepan retain more thiamin but less riboflavin than similar cuts cooked in the oven. Both vitamins are better retained in pan-broiling than in oven-broiling.

Shrinkage of Meat During Cooking

Shrinkage in cooked meats begins at a temperature of 50° to 60° C (122° to 140° F) because of the shortening of muscle fibers and coagulation of proteins with loss of water and melting of fat. The higher the interior temperature of the meat, the greater is the shrinkage. Less shrinkage usually occurs in meats roasted at a temperature of 300° to 350° F than in meats roasted at higher oven temperatures. Meats roasted for the whole time at a high oven temperature may shrink as much as 40 to 60 percent as compared to 15 or 20 percent at low temperatures. Excess shrinkage may be considered partly an economic matter, in that fewer servings can be had from meats that have been allowed to shrink excessively while cooking.

Basting

Basting consists of pouring liquids such as a marinade or meat drippings over the surface of meat while it is roasting. The chief purpose of basting is to keep the surface moist. If meats are placed in the roasting pan with the fat layer on top, the melted fat flows down over the surface of the roast as it cooks and self-basting occurs.

Salting

When shall meat be salted? If the piece of meat is large, it is not possible to salt the interior, because salt does not penetrate a roast to a greater depth than ½ inch. Putting much salt on the outer surface may result in too salty an outer layer or salty drippings. The outer layer also becomes crusty. It is, therefore, unnecessary to salt a roast before cooking. Salt retards the browning of meat and for that reason, if for no other, it is best applied to steaks and chops when they are ready for the platter or after they are cooked and browned on one side.

Meat loaves cannot be well seasoned unless salt is mixed with the meat before the loaf is shaped. To season small pieces of meat, as in stew, salt may be added to the cooking water. Total losses from the meat seem to be no greater than in unsalted stews.

Although salting a raw or slightly cooked surface of meat draws juice to the surface, it has not been proven that salting meats before or during cooking results in any greater total losses from the meat than would occur if meats were not salted. More information is needed on the effect of salting on cooking losses.

Beef rib steak.

Beef loin, top loin steak.

Beef loin, T-bone steak. Tenderloin muscle is fairly prominent.

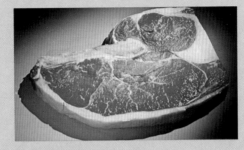

Beef loin, flat bone sirloin steak.

Plate V *Cuts of beef steak.* (Courtesy National Live Stock and Meat Board)

Beef loin, Porterhouse steak. Tenderloin muscle is largest in this cut.

Beef round steak.

Beef chuck, blade steak. Note the shoulder blade bone.

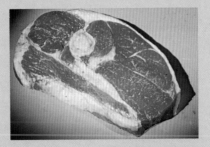

Beef chuck, arm steak. The round bone and rib ends are identifying characteristics.

Beef rib eye steak.

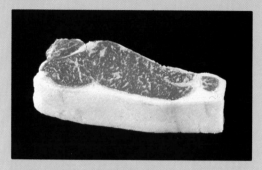

Beef loin, top sirloin steak boneless.

Beef loin, Tenderloin steak (Filet Mignon).

Beef round, top round steak.

Beef round, rump roast boneless.

Beef round, eye round steaks.

Plate VI *Cuts of beef.* (Courtesy National Live Stock and Meat Board)

Beef for stew.

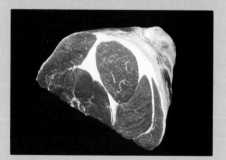

Beef round, heel of round.

Beef flank steak.

Beef rib roast.

Beef short ribs.

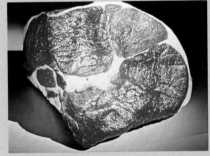

Beef round rump, bone in.

Plate VII *Cuts of beef.* (Courtesy National Live Stock and Meat Board)

Beef shank cross cuts.

Beef round, tip roast.

Beef brisket (corned).

Beef chuck, cross rib pot-roast.

Pork loin rib chops.

Pork loin chops.

Pork shoulder, blade steak.

Smoked ham, rump portion.

Smoked ham, shank half.

Plate VIII *Cuts of pork.*
(Courtesy National Live Stock and Meat Board)

Pork shoulder, arm picnic.

Large heavy muscles contribute to lack of waste in a pork carcass.
(Courtesy R. E. Hunsley, Purdue University)

Smoked pork shoulder, picnic.

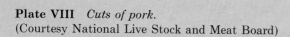

Juiciness

Juiciness is a desirable quality in cooked meats. Meats differ in their juiciness, depending on such factors as the quality of the meat, the presence of fat marbling, and aging of the carcass. The meat from younger animals is often more juicy than that from older animals. The presence of fat around and within the muscle fibers may increase the apparent juiciness of meat as it is eaten. Aged meats are usually more juicy than meats that are not aged.

The interior temperature to which meats are cooked affects juiciness. Meats cooked to the rare and medium-done stages are more juicy than well-done meats. In fact, it is difficult to cook meats to a brown interior color without a substantial loss of juiciness.

Meats that are cooked for a long time in moist heat to develop tenderness reach so high an interior temperature that they cannot fail to be dry. If meats are cooked in moisture and are served in the cooking liquid, as Swiss steak is, they may appear moist, but that moistness is not juiciness within the meat itself.

Tenderization

Tenderness is one of the most highly valued palatability characteristics for meat. Proper cooking may contribute to the development of this desirable trait in less tender meat and to its preservation in already tender cuts. The tender cuts do not contain large amounts of connective tissue, which may need to be softened by long cooking. Therefore, overcooking of these cuts should be avoided and, in fact, long cooking will toughen thin cuts.

Adequate tenderization of connective tissue generally occurs with either application of moist heat or use of dry heat for extremely long cooking periods at low temperatures. In either case, tenderization is the result of hydrolysis of the collagen in connective tissue to produce gelatin. A firming effect that may take place in the muscle fibers subjected to long cooking is more than counterbalanced by the softening of connective tissue. However, if the meat is not carved across the grain, producing short muscle fiber segments, the long intact muscle fibers that are separated because of connective tissue disintegration may contribute to apparent toughness as the meat is eaten. Proper carving of meat thus contributes to tenderness as the meat is served.

Less tender cuts of beef may be tenderized to some degree by soaking the meat in an acid-containing marinade for 24 to 48 hours before cooking [24, 35]. Water is absorbed during the soaking period and the moisture content of the cooked marinated meat remains higher than a similar sample that is not marinated. Tenderization may result from the action of acid on meat components. Losses of iron, zinc, and magnesium may be higher in marinated than non-marinated meats.

The use of meat tenderizers produces an increase in the tenderness of meat by hydrolyzing or breaking down proteins in the tissue as the meat is heated in the cooking process [11, 41]. The enzymes commonly used include papain from the papaya plant, bromelin from pineapple, and ficin from figs. These enzymes are not specific for the proteins of connective tissue but break down muscle fiber proteins as well. This may produce some mushiness in the meat. A major problem in the satisfactory use of enzyme tenderizers is the difficulty of dispersing the enzyme mixture so that it penetrates the tissue. Injection of the enzyme mixture into the bloodstream of the animal immediately prior to slaughter helps to solve this problem.

Specific Cooking Methods

Roasting or Baking. The term *roasting* was formerly applied to the method of cooking large cuts of meats before an open fire. Today

10-15 *These four photographs show a comparison of shrinkage and drippings when roasting is done to the same internal temperature by a constant low oven temperature or a constant high oven temperature.* (Courtesy of National Live Stock and Meat Board)

Beef standing rib roast to be cooked at a temperature of 300°F. Weight 9 lb 10 oz.

Same roast after cooking. Weight after cooking 7 lb 8 oz. Shrinkage 2 lb 2 oz (22 percent). Drippings (good) 1 lb 4 oz.

the terms *roasting* and *baking* are used synonymously and apply to the method of placing meat on a rack in an open pan and cooking by the dry heat of an oven. Previously, roasted meats were practically always *seared* in a hot oven of about 500° F for 20 to 30 minutes, after which the temperature of the oven was reduced to about 300° F for the remainder of the cooking period. *Searing* produces coagulation of the surface proteins and was formerly believed to prevent the loss of juices and nutrients. It is now fairly certain that searing does not form a pellicle and does not prevent the loss of interior juices. It may increase total cooking losses because of the high temperature used, although the losses may be chiefly surface losses. An oven temperature of 325° F is commonly recommended for roasting tender cuts of meat. As the oven temperature is increased from 300° F to 450° F the cooking time for meats cooked to the same internal temperature is usually decreased, total cooking losses are increased, and there is decreasing uniformity of doneness throughout the meat (Figure 10-15).

Adequate browning for good flavor and good appearance occurs at low constant oven temperatures, particularly if temperatures of

Beef standing rib roast to be cooked at a temperature of 450°F. Weight 9 lb 10 oz.

Same roast after cooking. Weight after cooking 6 lb 2 oz. Shrinkage 3 lb 8 oz (36 percent). Drippings (burned) 2 lb 3 oz.

325° F or 350° F are used. It is possible to use a higher temperature at the end of the roasting period merely for browning purposes, if desired.

Meat may also be roasted in a convection oven in which the heated air is constantly being recirculated by means of a fan. The cooking process is speeded up in convection ovens and the roasting time, therefore, is somewhat less than with a conventional oven.

Previously, roasting has been recommended only for cuts of meat that are expected to be tender, and moist-heat methods of cooking have been suggested for less tender cuts. However, studies have shown that less tender cuts of beef are tender and acceptable when roasted at oven temperatures of 225° to 250° F [47]. They are more moist and juicy than similar cuts that are braised. The cooking time at the low temperature is considerably extended.

Roasts of meat may be cooked to various stages of doneness, from rare to very well done. The color of the interior of the meat changes as the internal temperature increases and the muscle pigments are denatured and coagulated. Rare beef is bright red or pink in color and there is a gradual change to grayish-pink and finally to grayish-brown as the beef is cooked to a well-done stage. Juiciness also decreases as the degree of doneness is increased. A pink juice usually comes from the cut surfaces of rare beef, but no juice is apparent from well-done beef. Tenderness of the muscle fibers decreases with increasing degree of doneness to the well-done stage.

If a meat thermometer is used to determine the stage of doneness, the bulb of the thermometer is inserted in the thickest portion of the meat (Figure 10-16). The use of the thermometer is at present the only accurate way to know the interior temperature or stage of doneness of the meat.

If no thermometer is available, an alternative is to cook by minutes per pound (Table 10-4). This is much less accurate, because pieces of meat of the same weight may vary so much in shape, thickness, and in the proportion of meat to bone as to cause a difference in roasting time. For example, a rolled roast weighing 5 pounds that is of wide diameter and shallow depth will require much less time than a roast of the same weight that is narrow in diameter but deep. A standing rib roast will cook in less time than a rolled rib roast because the latter is made more compact by boning and rolling. Large roasts of the same general shape as small roasts will require fewer minutes per pound.

The usual interior temperatures for beef cooked to various stages of doneness are as follows:

Rare	58° to 60° C or 136° to 140° F
Medium	71° to 75° C or 160° to 167° F
Well done	78° to 82° C or 172° to 180° F

10-16 *A beef standing rib roast prepared for roasting. The meat thermometer is inserted so that the bulb rests in the center of the largest muscle.* (Courtesy of National Live Stock and Meat Board)

The appearance of meats will vary at a specific internal temperature depending on the cooking procedure and the particular cut of meat being cooked. The length of time required to reach the final internal temperature, particularly, will influence the appearance. A beef roast may appear less well done if cooked to the same internal temperature at a high oven temperature than at a low oven temperature because of the shorter time required at the high temperature to reach that internal endpoint. Some unaged beef may still have considerable pink color at a temperature of 75° C (165° F) and may require cooking to a temperature of 77° C (170° F) or higher to reach a gray stage. Other aged meat that loses the red color at lower temperatures may appear overdone if cooked to a temperature of 77° C (170° F).

A final internal temperature of 80° to 85° C (176° to 185° F) has been recommended for fresh pork since the 1940s. The parasite, *Trichinella spiralis,* may occur in some pork carcasses and must be destroyed in cooking if it is present. However, on the basis of more recent studies [30], it is recommended that pork may be safely cooked to an internal temperature of 77° C (170° F) as long as the cooking methods are relatively slow ones such as conventional or convectional ovens, flat grills, and broilers. Rapid microwave cooking of pork chops does not allow the uniform heating that is necessary to assure destruction of all trichinae when the chop has an

Table 10-4 *Approximate Roasting Time for Some Typical Meat Cuts**

Cut	Weight (lbs)	Constant Oven Temp. (° F)	Interior Temp. on Removal from Oven (° C)	(° F)	Approximate Time per Pound (min)
Beef					
Standing rib	6 to 8	300 to 325	60	140	23 to 25
			65.5 to 71	150 to 160	25 to 30
			74 to 76.5	165 to 170	27 to 34
Rolled rib	5 to 8	300 to 325	60	140	30 to 32
			65.5 to 71	150 to 160	35 to 38
			74 to 76.5	165 to 170	45 to 48
Rolled rump	4 to 6	300 to 325	65.5 to 76.5	150 to 170	25 to 30
Pork (fresh)					
Loin	3 to 5	325 to 350	76.5 to 85	170 to 185	30 to 45
Shoulder (cushion)	3 to 5	325 to 350	76.5 to 85	170 to 185	30 to 40
Ham (whole)	10 to 14	325 to 350	76.5 to 85	179 to 185	20 to 35
Pork (cured)					
Ham (whole)	10 to 14	300 to 325	71	160	18 to 20
Ham (half)	5 to 7	300 to 325	71	160	22 to 25
Picnic shoulder	5 to 8	300 to 325	76.5	170	35
Lamb					
Leg	5 to 8	300 to 325	79.5 to 82	175 to 180	30 to 35
Shoulder (cushion)	3 to 5	300 to 325	79.5 to 82	175 to 180	30 to 35
Shoulder (rolled)	3 to 5	300 to 325	79.5 to 82	175 to 180	40 to 45
Veal					
Leg	5 to 8	300 to 325	74 to 76.5	165 to 170	25 to 35
Loin	4 to 6	300 to 325	74 to 76.5	165 to 170	30 to 35
Rib (rack)	3 to 5	300 to 325	74 to 76.5	165 to 170	35 to 40

*If higher or lower temperatures are used for roasting, the times will obviously be somewhat shorter or longer respectively.

internal temperature in the center of 77° C (170° F). Generally, fresh pork roasted to an internal temperature of 77° C (170° F) is juicier and has greater cooked meat yields than similar cuts roasted to a temperature of 85° C (185° F). Flavor and tenderness are comparable in roasts cooked to either of these two internal temperatures.

Veal, lamb, and cured pork are usually cooked to the following internal temperatures:

Veal, well done	74° to 77° C (165° to 170° F)
Lamb, medium	70° to 71° C (158° to 160° F)
Lamb, well done	80° to 82° C (175° to 180° F)
Cured pork, well done	71° to 77° C (160° to 170° F)

Veal, which has a tendency to become very dry during cooking, may be successfully roasted in an open pan if low oven temperatures are used. Larding the roast will improve both flavor and juiciness because of the addition of fat.

The following cuts of meats are suitable for roasting:

Veal	*Lamb*	*Pork*
Leg	Leg	Leg or fresh ham
Rib	Crown roast	Loin
Loin	Boned shoulder	Boston butt
Shoulder	Saddle or loin	Boned shoulder
		Cured ham
		Spare ribs
		Thick pork chops

When meat is wrapped in aluminum foil before roasting, it cooks in a moist- rather than a dry-heat atmosphere. The foil is thought to have an insulating effect on the meat and, for this reason, higher oven temperatures are sometimes recommended for foil-wrapped roasts in comparison with unwrapped roasts. However, this insulating effect may not be present at oven temperatures as low as 200° F [1]. In a comparison of unwrapped and tightly foil-wrapped beef roasts cooked at an oven temperature of 300° F to an internal temperature of 77° C (170° F), the foil-wrapped roasts were found to be less juicy, less tender, and received lower flavor scores than the unwrapped roasts [19].

Rise in Temperature After Removal from the Oven. After a relatively large roast is removed from the oven, it will continue to cook unless it is cut at once. The heat continues to penetrate to the center. The rise in temperature will continue for a period of 15 to 45 minutes or longer depending on the oven temperature at which the meat is roasted, the internal temperature at which the roast is removed from the oven, the size of the roast, and the composition of the meat. The higher the oven temperature at which the roast is cooked, the greater is the increase in internal temperature of the roast after removal from the oven. The lower the internal temperature of the roast when it is removed from the oven, the greater is the rise in temperature after removal from the oven. Small, thin roasts may show little or no rise in temperature because of the rapid cooling from the surface. Meat containing much fat and meat having a thick external layer of fat will take longer to reach the maximum internal temperature after removal from the oven than does very lean meat.

Broiling and Pan-broiling. Broiling consists of cooking meats with a direct heat source, such as a gas flame, live coals, or an electric element. Broiling is applied to cuts such as steaks or chops that are thinner than roasts. Broiling is usually done using the broil setting on a range, with the door closed for a gas range and open for an electric range. Steam may accumulate in an electric oven with the door closed and steam retards browning. A rack for holding the meat out of the drippings is essential, both to keep the meat from stewing in its juices and to prevent burning of the fat. Since the source of heat used for broiling is usually constant, some variation in temperature is achieved in the regulation of the distance of the surface of the meat from the source of radiant heat. The distance should be further if the meat is thicker to allow more uniform cooking throughout the meat. The relatively high temperatures that are usually used in broiling do not seem to toughen the meat, possibly because cooking times are relatively short or because tender cuts of meat are used. Broiling may be used for relatively thin, less tender cuts of meat if they have been treated with meat tenderizers.

If steaks are very thick they may be broiled using a thermometer that registers interior temperature, or tested by pulling the fibers in the thickest portion apart to see the color of the juice. A cut is sometimes made next to the bone for the purpose of determining the interior color. Table 10-5 gives the approximate broiling time for some typical cuts, but like the timetable for roasting, it is meant as a guide rather than as a precise statement of time.

Pan-broiling is a variation of broiling. Heat is applied by means of contact with a hot surface. The pans used should be of heavy material. The surface of the pan is lightly oiled with a piece of fat meat. Fat should be dipped or poured from the pan as it accumulates to avoid frying the meat in its own fat.

Veal, because of its lack of fat, yields a poor product when it is broiled or pan-broiled. Pork chops are tender enough for dry-heat methods of cooking but should be thoroughly cooked. Broiling or pan-broiling, as usually practiced, may not ensure the reaching of a well-done stage in the center of pork chops, especially if they are very thick.

The pan-broiling of bacon is best accomplished by placing the slices of bacon in a cold pan and heating them slowly with frequent turning until they are crisp. Much of the fat should be drained off, but the bacon will brown more evenly if a small amount of fat is left in the pan.

Cuts of beef, lamb, and pork suitable for broiling or pan-broiling are as follows:

Beef	*Lamb*	*Pork*
Top loin, T-bone, porterhouse, and sirloin steaks	Rib chops	Cured bacon
	Loin chops	Cured ham
Tenderloin	Shoulder chops†	
Ground beef*		

*Ground beef, although prepared from less tender meat, is made tender by grinding. Some fat intermingled with the lean also increases flavor and juiciness.
†If from a good grade of lamb: shoulder cuts from a poor grade are best braised.

Table 10-5 *Approximate Broiling Time for Some Typical Meat Cuts*

Cut	Average Weight (lbs)	Time (min)		
		Rare	Medium	Well-done
Beef				
Club steak (top loin)				
1 in.	1	14 to 17	18 to 20	22 to 25
1½ in.	1¼	25 to 27	30 to 35	35 to 40
Porterhouse				
1 in.	2	19 to 21	22 to 25	26 to 30
1½ in.	2½	30 to 32	35 to 38	40 to 45
Sirloin				
1 in.	3	20 to 22	23 to 25	26 to 30
1½ in.	4½	30 to 32	33 to 35	36 to 40
Ground beef patty, 1 in. thick by 3½ in. diameter	¼	12 to 15	18 to 22	24 to 28
Lamb				
Loin chops				
1 in.	3/16		10 to 15	16 to 18
1½ in.	5/16		16 to 18	19 to 22
Rib chops				
1 in.	⅛		10 to 15	16 to 18
1½ in.	¼		16 to 18	19 to 22
Ground lamb patty 1 in. thick by 3½ in. diameter	¼		18 to 20	22 to 24

Frying. Frying has been largely displaced by pan-broiling or broiling as a commonly used method for cooking tender cuts of meat.

Frying may be pan-frying, in which only a small amount of fat (enough to form a layer of melted fat ¼ to ½ inch deep) is used, or deep-fat frying, in which the melted fat is deep enough to cover the food. Fried food requires draining on absorbent paper so that excess fat may be removed. Meats may be dipped in flour or in egg and crumbs before frying. This produces a brown crust on the meat. Frying may be one method of browning meats that are to be braised.

Microwave Cooking. The use of microwave ovens has increased in recent years and more meat is being cooked by microwaves. Cooking meat in a microwave oven has an important advantage of using substantially less energy for the same degree of doneness than conventional methods [29]. Use of the convection oven also conserves energy because lower cooking temperatures and shorter cooking and preheat times can be used. Microwave appliances that are available to the consumer are constantly being improved in terms of their cooking performance. Earlier studies involving comparisons of meat cookery using microwave and conventional ovens often found greater cooking losses and somewhat less palatable products with microwave cooking. This was particularly true when less tender cuts of meat were prepared [28, 37, 53]. However, microwave ovens with a variable power feature now allow cooking at different energy levels. Cooking top round roasts of beef, particularly from the frozen state, at "simmer" power levels produces more palatable products than cooking similar roasts at "high" power levels. Roasts cooked at the lower power level are often similar in palatability to roasts cooked in conventional ovens [10, 60]. A low microwave setting was also reported to give more palatable pork chops than did a high setting [17]. If pork chops are cooked by microwaves, however, it must be made certain that the temperature is at least 77° C (170° F) throughout the meat in order to destroy trichinae organisms that might be present.

Roasts that are about twice as long as they are wide cook well in a microwave oven. Boned and rolled roasts, such as rolled rib roasts, are excellent. Frequent turning and basting with a sauce assure full flavor and color development of the surface. A rapid reading thermometer may be inserted in the roast *after it is removed from the oven* to check the degree of doneness. Some special thermometers are available for use inside the microwave oven.

Small pieces of meat, particularly, do not brown when cooked in a microwave oven. Various browning elements and special browning grills have been developed by the manufacturers of microwave equipment to solve this problem. Use of browning devices increases fuel consumption by 50 percent or more over cooking by microwaves alone. Total cooking time is also increased [9].

After they come from the microwave oven, roasts of meat need to be set aside before carving. Heat is stored inside the product during cooking and the standby time allows this heat to distribute itself throughout the meat so that proper doneness is achieved. Most roasts require a standby time of 30 to 50 minutes.

The microwave oven is particularly useful for reheating cooked meats. It generally gives less "warmed-over" aroma and flavor than reheating by conventional means [27].

Braising. Braising is a moist-heat method of cooking and is usually applied to less tender cuts of meat. The meat may be browned by frying, pan-broiling, or broiling before it is braised. A small amount of water is usually added, although braising may be done without added water because steam from the water in the meat itself can provide the moisture needed to hydrolyze the collagen in connective tissue. The pan or kettle is closely covered and cooking is continued until the meat becomes tender. The water, if added, should be simmering or slowly boiling. Using small quantities of water added frequently, rather than adding a somewhat larger amount of water at one time, will help to retain the brown surface in meats that were browned before braising began.

Braising may be done either on the top of the range or in the oven.

Braising time is usually longer in the oven than on a surface unit and more energy is expended. Since the pan is tightly covered, the meat is cooked in a moist atmosphere even though it is cooked in the oven. The time of cooking will depend on the character of the meat and the size of the cut. Braised meat is always cooked well done. Braising large cuts of meat, such as beef chuck roasts, is often called pot-roasting. Swiss steaks are braised beef steaks.

Cuts from the chuck and round of beef are commonly braised. Braising is recommended for veal and pork chops, although pork chops are also effectively cooked by roasting or baking.

Stewing. Stewing consists of cooking meats in liquid at simmering or slow boiling temperatures. For brown stew, part or all of the meat may be browned preliminary to stewing. This may develop flavor as well as color in the stew. If vegetables are used in the stew, they should be added just long enough before the stew is to be served so that they will not be overcooked.

Pressure Cooking. Cooking meat in a pressure saucepan is a moist-heat method and may be used for less tender cuts. A relatively short cooking time is required because cooking is done at a temperature higher than that of the boiling point of water, which is the temperature used for braising and stewing. Meats prepared in a pressure saucepan are commonly cooked to a well-done stage. A distinctive steamed flavor is usually produced in pressure-cooked meats.

Crockery Slow Cooking. Various types of crockery slow cooking pots have become available in recent years and are often used for meat cookery. These electric appliances have a low-temperature setting that allows meat and other foods to be cooked for long periods of time without constant watching. For example, a beef roast may be placed in the cooker with no added liquid, covered, and cooked on the lowest setting for 10 to 12 hours. Meat dishes with added liquid, such as beef stew or Swiss steak, are also satisfactorily cooked in the crockery slow cookers. The low setting usually represents a temperature of about 200° F.

Cooking in the covered pots is by moist heat. The long cooking period allows the breakdown of the connective tissue to gelatin in less tender meats, thus increasing tenderness.

Cooking Variety Meats

The choice of a cooking method for variety meats is influenced by the tenderness of the various parts. Heart, kidney, tongue, and tripe all require cooking for tenderness and are braised or simmered. Older beef liver may also require tenderizing by braising. Brains, sweetbreads, and veal or calf liver are tender. They may be cooked

Table 10-6 *Variety Meats*

Name	Preliminary Preparation	Cooking Methods
Liver	Liver from young animals should be sliced ½ in. thick for best results in retaining juiciness. Remove outside membrane, blood vessels, and excess connective tissue. Wash large pieces before removing membrane.	Broil or pan-broil young liver. Fry or bread young liver. Braise whole piece of older beef liver. Grind and make into liver loaf. (Liver is easier to grind if first coagulated in hot water.)
Kidney	Wash kidneys and remove outer membrane. Lamb kidneys may be split in half and veal kidneys cut into slices. Cook beef kidneys in water for tenderness, changing the water several times.	Young kidneys may be broiled, pan-broiled, made into stew or kidney pie, or ground and made into loaf. Beef kidneys, after being cooked for tenderness, may be cooked in the same way, except that they should not be broiled or pan-broiled.
Sweetbreads and brains	Soak in cold water to remove blood. Remove blood vessels and excess connective tissue. Parboil in salted, acidulated water to make firm and white using 1 t salt and 1 T vinegar per quart of water.	Sweetbreads may be creamed, dipped in egg and crumbs and fried in fat, combined with cooked chicken and creamed or scalloped, or dipped in melted fat and broiled. Brains may be breaded or broiled as suggested for sweetbreads or cut into small pieces and scrambled with eggs.
Heart	Heart is a muscular organ that is usually cooked by moist-heat methods for tenderness. Wash in warm water and remove large blood vessels.	Stuff with bread dressing and braise until tender. May be cooked in water seasoned with salt, onion, bay leaf, celery, and tomato and served hot or cold.
Tongue	Tongue is a muscular tissue that requires precooking in water for tenderness. After cooking, the skin is removed and the roots are cut out. Smoked or pickled tongue is usually soaked for several hours before cooking.	May be cooked in water, seasoned with salt, onion, bay leaf, and celery. If to be served cold, it is more moist if allowed to cool in the water. After cooking in water, the tongue may be covered with brown or tomato sauce and braised in the oven. The cooked tongue may be reheated in a sweet pickling solution. For this method, the tongue is best precooked in plain salted water.
Tripe	Fresh tripe is cooked before selling but requires further cooking in water until tender (1 or more hours).	Serve precooked tripe with well-seasoned tomato sauce. Dip in batter and fry in deep fat. Brush with flavorful fat and broil.

by dry heat methods such as broiling or frying. For variety, they may also be cooked by moist-heat methods. Brains and sweetbreads are delicate tissues that are made more firm and white if they are precooked for about 20 minutes at simmering temperature in salted, acidulated water. After this preliminary treatment they may be prepared in various ways. Table 10-6 gives pertinent points that are applicable to the preparation of variety meats.

Cooking Frozen Meats

Meats may be cooked either thawed or frozen. Temperatures must be lower and the time of cooking increased if the meat is frozen when cooked. If pieces of frozen meat are large, the cooking time may be considerably longer than in similar thawed or fresh cuts.

Frozen roasts may take one and one-half times as long to cook as unfrozen roasts of the same size. If frozen meats are braised, they may be browned at the end of the braising period rather than at the beginning.

There are no appreciable differences in palatability or nutritive value in meats cooked from the thawed or frozen state. Thawed meats are cooked in the same way as fresh meats. Thawing of frozen meat in the refrigerator is recommended for microbiological safety. This is particularly true for large pieces of meat.

Meat Flavor

Flavor is one of the most important quality characteristics of meat. USDA quality grades for meat are concerned with palatability and, in the evaluation of grade, consider such characteristics as marbling and firmness of the lean cut surface in relation to evidences of carcass maturity or age. It is quite likely that USDA quality grades are related to flavor of the meat because grade indirectly assesses the extent to which flavor compounds are likely to be present in high or low concentrations [56]. For example, carcasses from older and leaner animals and from animals not fed large amounts of grain are assigned low USDA quality grades and these animals are likely to yield meat of less desirable flavor than young, fatter animals fed large quantities of grain and graded higher.

The flavor of meat involves responses from taste and smell or aroma and also sensations from pressure-sensitive and heat-sensitive areas of the mouth. Flavor of meat is developed primarily by cooking; raw meat has little aroma and only a bloodlike taste. The flavor of boiled meats differs from that of roasted meats. The chemistry of meat flavor is very complex. The flavor of cooked meat is due to a mixture of many compounds. Some of these are volatile and give rise to odor. One study of the volatile flavor components of fresh beef stew resulted in the identification of 132 different compounds [50]. Volatile components are probably the most important part of meat flavor. Nonvolatile compounds, however, stimulate taste buds and contribute to overall meat flavor. The most important taste compounds are inorganic salts, giving a salty taste, sugars, producing a sweet taste, hypoxanthine, contributing some bitterness, organic acids, giving a sour taste, and some nitrogen-containing compounds including nucleotides, amino acids, and peptides. In addition to volatile and nonvolatile components of meat flavor, there are other substances called flavor potentiators and synergists that enhance the flavor contributions of other substances although they have no flavor by themselves. Flavor potentiators in meat include some amino acids, such as glutamic acid, and certain 5'-nucleotides such as inosinic acid [43].

The serving temperature may influence perceived meat flavor. Beef steaks tasted at 50° C (122° F) were more flavorful and juicy than similar samples tasted at 22° C (72° F) [48].

The study of meat flavor, both boiled and roasted, is important in order to learn more about how to duplicate these flavors in the laboratory. Simulated meat flavors are needed for flavoring meat analogues made from plant proteins. They are also useful in the preparation of various convenience foods. Although a number of simulated meat flavors are available, they cannot completely duplicate the natural flavors. They have been found to be different both chemically and organoleptically and are less desirable than natural meat flavors when compared by both trained and consumer panels [36].

Soup Stock

A stock is a flavored liquid used chiefly in the making of soups. Beef is the most commonly used meat for stock. Veal has too little flavor to be used alone but may be combined with other meats. Lamb or mutton gives excellent broth but should be used only when lamb or mutton flavor is desired. The bones and meat from poultry also make desirable additions to the kettle. Stock for fish soups is made from fish.

In preparing meat for making stock, the more surface of the meat that is exposed to the water, the more flavor will be extracted. This means cutting the meat into small cubes or grinding it through a coarse grinder rather than cooking it in one piece. The meat may be soaked for ½ to 1 hour in cold water. The cooking is started in cold water and the water is allowed to simmer for 3 to 4 hours. Some bone and some fat cooked with the lean meat are thought to improve the flavor.

Vegetables and seasonings should be added during the last hour of cooking to avoid the development of undesirable flavors from overcooking some of the vegetables. When cooking is finished, the stock is poured through a colander to remove meat, bone, and seasonings. After the stock is cool, the hard fat layer may be removed from the top.

The only difference between brown and white soup stock is that in the making of brown stock about one-third of the meat cubes are first browned in a skillet. Water may be added to dissolve brown matter from the pan. The browned meat and water are then added to the soup kettle in which the remaining cubes have been placed in cold water.

The meat left from making soup stock retains many of its nutrients. The flavor is lacking, but other flavors from vegetables and condiments may be added in order that the meat may be utilized. The meat may be cut into small pieces and served in the soup.

Bouillon is prepared by seasoning a soup stock. *Consommé* is an enriched or double-strength bouillon that has been clarified. It may be made from any kind of stock although beef is most commonly used. One egg white and one crushed shell per quart of broth accomplish clarification. The broth is heated to the boiling point and boiled for a few minutes, after which it is poured through several thicknesses of cheesecloth to strain out the coagulated egg with its adhering particles. The material that is removed from the soup stock by clarifying is chiefly coagulated protein.

Gravy

Gravies or sauces are commonly used as meat accompaniments to enhance the flavor of meat. The drippings from fried, pan-broiled, or roasted meat and the cooking liquid from stewed or braised meats or poultry may be used to make gravy. Low temperatures for meat cookery usually produce a minimum of brown material. Particularly for the making of gravy, there should be no burned drippings.

Gravies and some sauces may be thickened or unthickened. *Au jus* gravy goes naturally with roast beef and is unthickened. To thicken gravy, flour or other starch thickener may be added (1½ to 2 tablespoons per cup of liquid) in one of two ways: (1) as a smooth flour and water paste or slurry; or (2) as dry flour stirred into the fat. The latter method is usually preferable where the drippings contain little or no water. Excess fat in the pan should be removed before the flour is added. It is well to determine the approximate quantity of gravy desired and on that basis retain about 2 tablespoons of fat for each cup of gravy. When dry flour and fat in the drippings are blended together and cooked for a few minutes they form a *roux*. Cold liquid can then be mixed gradually with the hot roux until a smooth gravy is formed. Heating is continued, with stirring, until the starch gelatinizes (granules take up water and swell) and the mixture thickens. Seasonings may then be added.

In the alternate method of making gravy, a cold slurry of liquid and a thickener, such as flour, is mixed with hot liquid that has been added to the drippings, with constant stirring until the gravy thickens. The liquid used in gravies is usually water, but milk, meat stock, tomato juice, wine, vegetable juice, or any other liquid may be used. The richer and more flavorful the drippings, the better is the gravy. Gravies should be tasted before serving to make certain that the proper blending of flavors has been achieved.

A great variety of sauces may be served with meats. Sauces may be made from drippings but are often made without any meat components. White sauce may be the basis for some sauces served with meats. White sauces are discussed on pp. 413–414. Tomato sauces go with meatballs and spaghetti, mushroom sauce is often served with Swiss steak, and brushing broiled lamb chops with melted butter produces a sauce called *maître d'hôtel* butter.

Carving Meat

Successful carving of meat is partly dependent upon some knowledge of the anatomy of the cut to be carved. It is important to know something of the location of the joints and the direction in which the muscle fibers run. Insofar as possible, meats should be carved across the grain. Knives for carving should be well sharpened and of good quality steel which will hold an edge well.

Carving should be done rapidly in order that the meat may not become cold. Neatness and economy of cutting are also important. If some parts of the meat are better than others, such parts should be divided among those at the table rather than given to the first ones served.

Enough meat to serve all at the table should be carved before the host starts to serve the plates. The slices are arranged neatly on the platter. Before inviting guests to be served a second time, the host should be sure that some meat is carved and ready.

Carving Specific Cuts

Diagrams showing techniques for carving specific cuts of meat are shown in Figure 10-17.

Beef Steak. Steak is one of the easiest of meats to carve. With the steak lying flat upon the platter the fork is inserted in a suitable position for holding the steak firmly. Steaks from the loin (top loin, T-bone, porterhouse, and sirloin) have the bone separated from the meat before the meat is carved. The knife is allowed to follow the bone closely until the meat is completely separated. The meat is then cut into pieces of a suitable size for serving. Porterhouse and T-bone steaks are usually carved so that each person receives some tenderloin and some outer muscle. Steaks are cut with, rather than across, the fiber.

Standing Rib Roast. The standing rib roast is one of the more difficult cuts to carve. The roast is placed before the carver with the rib side to his left. The carver inserts a fork between two ribs. The knife passes from the outer edge toward the ribs in removing a slice of meat. Slices may vary in thickness but a slice of desirable thickness is about ¼ to ⅜ of an inch. After several slices have been

Beef porterhouse steak.

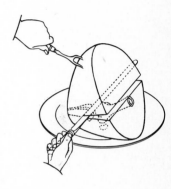

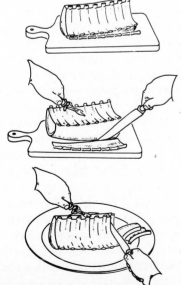

Standing rib roast of beef.

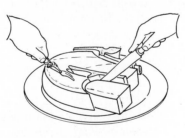

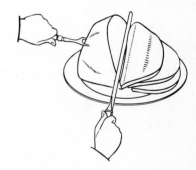

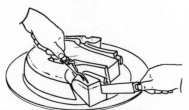

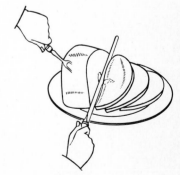

Loin roast of pork.

Blade pot roast of beef.

Ham, butt end.

carved the knife is used to separate the slices from the bone. Each slice is then transferred to the platter.

Rolled Rib Roast.   Horizontal slices are cut from the top of the roast.

Pot Roasts.   Insofar as possible, slices should be cut across the grain. Some cuts used for pot roasts may have fibers running in several directions, in which case it is difficult to carve across the fibers. If the muscles are separated first, cutting across the grain is easier.

Ham.   The shank bone is placed toward the carver's right. The larger muscles of the ham are sliced by cutting straight down from the outer edge to the leg bone. After several slices have been carved, the knife is inserted in the last opening and is allowed to follow the bone, thus separating slices from the bone. Slices may then be lifted out.

Loin Roast.   A loin roast of pork is carved by cutting slices from the end of the roast. The roast is prepared at the market to make carving easy. The rib section has the backbone sawed loose from the ribs. The backbone is removed in the kitchen before the roast is placed on the platter. Cutting is done close along each side of the rib bone. One slice will contain the rib, the next will be boneless, and so on.

Leg of Lamb.   The cushion of the leg, which is the most meaty portion, lies below the tail. The carver inserts a fork to bring the cushion into an upright position. Slices are then carved as from ham.

Plant Proteins in Meat Processing

Plant proteins, particularly soy protein and wheat gluten, are used in various ways in the processing of meats and for the production of main course entrees that have the flavor and appearance of beef, chicken, ham, bacon, fish, or shellfish. These protein substances may also be used to produce an entirely new line of foods unlike any that are in use today.

Soybean protein products are available in various forms. Soy flour may be made from dehulled soybeans that contain the oil normally present in this product (about 18 percent). However, soy flour is more commonly prepared by grinding soy flakes from which soybean oil has been pressed. Soy protein concentrate is made by extracting soluble carbohydrates from defatted soy flour. Soy protein concentrates contain 70 percent or more protein. Isolated soy proteins are produced by further removal of nonprotein substances, and isolated soy protein mixtures contain 90 percent or more protein.

Texture is given to soy and other high protein products by additional treatment. In one method, the protein isolate is spun into long fibers by a process that is similar to the spinning of textile fibers. The wet protein mixture is forced through spinnerettes into a coagulating bath. The resulting fibers are gathered into bundles. These meatlike fibers are shown in Figure 10-18. A second method of producing textured vegetable protein involves a process called *extrusion*. In this process, soy flour or protein concentrate is blended with water, flavors, colors, and possibly other additives. The mixture is then fed into a cooking extruder that works the material into a dough and extrudes it through small openings. The release of pressure as the protein mixture is extruded causes expansion with tiny air pockets uniformly dispersed throughout the mass. This creates texture in the extruded product.

Spun protein fibrils may be blended with other ingredients, often using egg albumen as a binding agent, and fabricated into many different food products, some of which can simulate slices of beef or bacon. Textured soy protein is available to the consumer and can be combined with other foods such as ground meats or various casserole mixtures as a meat extender. Extruded soy protein has been used in such products as tacos, chili, pizza, lasagne, stews, omelets, and stuffed peppers. Textured soy products are generally hydrated before being combined with ground meat. They are available in both seasoned and unseasoned forms. The U.S. Department of Agriculture has written specifications for textured vegetable protein products that permit their use in school food service and other child-feeding programs. The use of these products is on a voluntary basis. The vegetable protein products are blended in specified amounts with ground or diced meats in various menu items.

Formed ground beef patties containing soy protein products in various proportions are also sold on the retail market. Use of soy

10-18 Many convenience foods are created from vegetable protein sources. (Courtesy of Worthington Foods)

Meatlike fiber is spun from soybean protein.

A baconlike product made from soybeans.

protein in appropriate amounts, up to 30 percent by weight, reduces cooking losses and thus increases cooking yields while generally maintaining acceptable sensory quality. Soy flavor may be detected at high substitution levels. The use of strong flavored ingredients such as onions, tomatoes, and chili powder masks the flavor of textured soy products.

The soybean is a source of good quality protein, particularly in combination with some animal protein. Convenience foods produced from these vegetable protein products are marketed frozen, dehydrated, freeze-dried, or canned. An example of one of these foods is hickory-smoked strips, which can be used in place of bacon (Figure 10-18). Bacon-flavored bits for use in salads or combined with eggs and other foods are made from soy protein.

Sectioning muscles from carcasses into small pieces and then reforming these pieces into a continuous body of meat has become an important process in the meat industry today. Such meats are called restructured meats. Sectioned and formed hams are produced in this manner and make up a significant amount of all the ham sold in the United States. Restructuring of carcass meats can convert less desirable fresh meat cuts into more palatable steaktype products. Soy protein or wheat gluten products may be used in the preparation of restructured meats to improve binding properties and to increase the cooking yield due to a higher retention of water.

Study Questions

1. Meat is basically muscle tissue containing some fat and bone. Briefly describe what meat is like in structure, including each of the following components in your explanation.
   a. Muscle proteins—myosin and actin
   b. Myofibrils
   c. Muscle fibers
   d. Bundles of muscle fibers (making the grain of the meat)
   e. Muscles (such as tenderloin and rib-eye)
   f. Connective tissue
   g. Connective tissue proteins—collagen and elastin
   h. Fat cells, fatty tissues, and marbling
   i. Bone
2. a. The protein content of meat varies with the amount of fat. How much protein is usually present in relatively lean meat?
   b. What vitamins and minerals does meat provide in significant amounts?
3. Explain why the color of meat may change from a purplish red to a bright red when exposed to air. Explain why meat may turn a brownish color when held too long. What is responsible for the typical cured meat color?
4. a. What is rigor mortis and why is it important in a study of meat?

b. Why is beef aged? What changes occur during aging or ripening of meat?

5. List several factors that may affect tenderness of meat and discuss what effect each factor has on tenderness.

6. Explain what the round inspection stamp on meat carcasses implies.

7. a. Why are meats graded and by whom are they graded? Is this a mandatory or voluntary program?

   b. Explain the difference between quality grades and yield grades for meat. What factors are considered in each?

   c. From the following list of quality grade names, indicate which apply to beef, which to veal, and which to lamb.
      (1) Prime
      (2) Choice
      (3) Good
      (4) Standard
      (5) Commercial
      (6) Utility
      (7) Cutter
      (8) Canner
      (9) Cull

8. a. Name the wholesale cuts of beef and pork.

   b. Name several retail cuts that may come from each wholesale cut listed in question a.

   c. Which wholesale cuts of beef are usually tender? Which are less tender?

   d. Be able to identify pictures of each of the following retail cuts of meat.

Beef
Rib steak and roast
Top loin steak
T-bone steak
Porterhouse steak
Sirloin steak
Round steak or roast
Blade steak or roast
Arm steak or roast
Flank steak
Brisket
Short ribs

Pork
Rib chops
Loin chops
Blade steak
Ham

9. Name seven variety meats and discuss several advantages for their use in meal planning.

10. a. Name several cuts of meat that are commonly cured.

    b. What ingredients are usually used in the curing process? Discuss advantages and disadvantages to the use of nitrite as a curing ingredient.

11. Describe appropriate storage conditions for meat in the home.

12. How does heat generally affect muscle fibers? Connective tissue? Explain why this information is important in deciding how to cook tender and less tender cuts of meat.

13. When meat is cooked by any method it usually loses weight. Account for this weight or cooking loss.

14. Describe the usual procedures used in cooking meat by each of the following methods. Indicate whether each is a dry heat or a moist heat method. Also suggest several cuts of meat that may appropriately be cooked by each of the methods listed.
    a. Roasting
    b Broiling
    c. Pan-broiling
    d. Frying
    e. Microwave cooking
    f. Braising
    g. Stewing
    h. Pressure cooking

15. In roasting, broiling, and pan-broiling, when should meats be salted and why?

16. Describe how frozen meats may be appropriately handled in preparation for cooking.

17. a. What oven temperatures are most satisfactory when roasting tender cuts of beef? Less tender cuts? Explain why these temperatures are appropriate.
    b. Why should a meat thermometer be used when roasting meat?

18. What types of compounds appear to be important components of meat flavor?

19. Describe appropriate procedures for the preparation of:
    a. Soup stock
    b. Gravy

References

1. Baity, M. R., A. E. Ellington, and M. Woodburn. 1969. Foil wrap in oven cooking. *Journal of Home Economics* **61,** 174.

2. *Beef and Veal in Family Meals.* Home and Garden Bulletin No. 118. Washington, DC: U.S. Department of Agriculture, 1975.

3. Bouton, P. E., P. V. Harris, and D. Ratcliff. 1981. Effect of cooking temperature and time on the shear properties of meat. *Journal of Food Science* **46,** 1082.

4. Calkins, C. R., L. J. Branecky, T. R. Dutson, G. C. Smith, and Z. L. Carpenter. 1983. Postmortem muscle metabolism and meat tenderness. *Journal of Food Science* **48,** 23.

5. Clark, R. K., and F. O. van Duyne. 1949. Cooking losses, tenderness, palatability, and thiamine and riboflavin content of beef as affected by roasting, pressure saucepan cooking, and broiling. *Food Research* **14,** 221.

6. Cover, S., and R. L. Hostetler. *Beef Tenderness*. Texas Agricultural Experiment Station Bulletin No. 947. College Station, TX: Texas Agricultural Experiment Station, 1960.

7. Cross, H. R., B. W. Berry, and L. H. Wells. 1980. Effects of fat level and source on the chemical, sensory, and cooking properties of ground beef patties. *Journal of Food Science* **45,** 791.

8. Dolezal, H. G., G. C. Smith, J. W. Savell, and Z. L. Carpenter. 1982. Comparison of subcutaneous fat thickness, marbling and quality grade for predicting palatability of beef. *Journal of Food Science* **47,** 397.

9. Drew, F., and K. S. Rhee, 1979. Microwave cookery of beef patties: Browning methods. *Journal of the American Dietetic Association* **74,** 652.

10. Drew, F., K. S. Rhee, and Z. L. Carpenter. 1980. Cooking at variable microwave power levels. *Journal of the American Dietetic Association* **77,** 455.

11. Fogle, D. R., R. F. Plimpton, H. W. Ockerman, L. Jarenback, and T. Persson. 1982. Tenderization of beef: Effect of enzyme, enzyme level, and cooking method. *Journal of Food Science* **47,** 1113.

12. Funk, K., and M. A. Boyle. 1972. Beef cooking rates and losses. *Journal of the American Dietetic Association* **61,** 404.

13. Gould, P. F., L. J. Bratzler, and W. T. Magee. 1965. Effect of aging on tenderness of pork loin chops. *Food Technology* **19,** 248.

14. Gray, J. I., S. K. Reddy, J. F. Price, A. Mandagere, and W. F. Wilkens. 1982. Inhibition of N-nitrosamines in bacon. *Food Technology* **36,** 39 (no. 6).

15. Hamm, R. 1982. Postmortem changes in muscle with regard to processing of hot-boned beef. *Food Technology* **36,** 105 (no. 11).

16. Harrison, D. L., J. A. Bowers, L. L. Anderson, H. J. Tuma, and D. H. Kropf. 1970. Effect of aging on palatability and selected related characteristics of pork loin. *Journal of Food Science* **35,** 292.

17. Hines, R. C., C. B. Ramsey, and T. L. Hoes. 1980. Effects of microwave cooking rate on palatability of pork loin chops. *Journal of Animal Science* **50,** 446.

18. Holmes, Z. A. 1978. Factors affecting the acceptability of beef: Clues from bibliographic research. *Journal of the American Dietetic Association* **72,** 622.

19. Hood, M. P. 1960. Effect of cooking method and grade on beef roasts. *Journal of the American Dietetic Association* **37,** 363.

20. *How to Buy Beef Roasts*. Home and Garden Bulletin No. 146. Washington, DC: U.S. Department of Agriculture, 1977.

21. *How to Buy Beef Steaks*. Home and Garden Bulletin No. 145. Washington, DC: U.S. Department of Agriculture, 1977.

22. *How to Buy Lamb*. Home and Garden Bulletin No. 195. Washington, DC: U.S. Department of Agriculture, 1971.

23. *How to Buy Meat for Your Freezer*. Home and Garden Bulletin No. 166. Washington, DC: U.S. Department of Agriculture, 1980.

24. Howat, P. M., L. M. Sievert, P. J. Myers, K. L. Koonce, and T. D. Bidner. 1983. Effect of marination upon mineral content and tenderness of beef. *Journal of Food Science* **48,** 662.

25. Jacobs, D. K., and J. G. Sebranek. 1980. Use of prerigor beef for frozen ground beef patties. *Journal of Food Science* **45,** 648.

26. Jennings, T. G., B. W. Berry, and A. L. Joseph. 1978. Influence of fat thickness, marbling, and length of aging on beef palatability and shelf-life characteristics. *Journal of Animal Science* **46,** 658.

27. Johnston, M. B., and R. E. Baldwin. 1980. Influence of microwave reheating on selected quality factors of roast beef. *Journal of Food Science* **45,** 1460.

28. Korschgen, B. M., R. E. Baldwin, and S. Snider. 1976. Quality factors in beef, pork, and lamb cooked by microwaves. *Journal of the American Dietetic Association* **69,** 635.

29. Korschgen, B. M., J. M. Berneking, and R. E. Baldwin. 1980. Energy requirements for cooking beef rib roasts. *Journal of Food Science* **45,** 1054.

30. Kotula, A. W., K. D. Murrell, L. Acosta-Stein, L. Lamb, and L. Douglass. 1983. Destruction of *Trichinella spiralis* during cooking. *Journal of Food Science* **48,** 765.

31. Laakkonen, E., G. H. Wellington, and J. W. Sherbon. 1970. Low-temperature, long-time heating of bovine muscle. 1. Changes in tenderness, water-binding capacity, pH and amount of water-soluble components. *Journal of Food Science* **35,** 175.

32. *Lamb in Family Meals.* Home and Garden Bulletin No. 124. Washington, DC: U.S. Department of Agriculture, 1980.

33. Leander, R. C., H. B. Hedrick, M. F. Brown, and J. A. White. 1980. Comparison of structural changes in bovine longissimus and semitendinosus muscles during cooking. *Journal of Food Science* **45,** 1.

34. Leverton, R. M., and G. V. Odell. *The Nutritive Value of Cooked Meat.* Oklahoma Agricultural Experiment Station Miscellaneous Publication No. MP-49. Stillwater, OK: Oklahoma Agricultural Experiment Station, 1958.

35. Lind, J. M., R. M. Griswold, and V. D. Bramblett. 1971. Tenderizing effect of wine vinegar marinade on beef round. *Journal of the American Dietetic Association* **58,** 133.

36. MacLeod, G., and M. Seyyedain-Ardebeli. 1980. Sensory comparisons of the aroma of natural and some simulated beef flavors. *Journal of Food Science* **45,** 431.

37. Marshall, N. 1960. Electronic cookery of top round of beef. *Journal of Home Economics* **52,** 31.

38. McBee, J. L., Jr., and J. A. Wiles. 1967. Influence of marbling and carcass grade on the physical and chemical characteristics of beef. *Journal of Animal Science* **26,** 701.

39. McDowell, M. D., D. L. Harrison, C. Pacey, and M. B. Stone. 1982. Differences between conventionally cooked top round roasts and semimembranous muscle strips cooked in a model system. *Journal of Food Science* **47,** 1603.

40. McIntosh, E. N. 1967. Effect of postmortem aging and enzyme tenderizers on mucoprotein of bovine skeletal muscle. *Journal of Food Science* **32,** 210.

41. Mier, G., V. J. Rhodes, L. G. Mahard, N. S. Webb, C. Rodgers, M. Mangel, and R. Baldwin. 1962. Beef tenderization by proteolytic enzymes:

The effects of two methods of application. *Food Technology* **16**, 111 (April).

42. Minks, D., and W. C. Stringer. 1972. The influence of aging beef in vacuum. *Journal of Food Science* **37**, 736.

43. Moody, W. G. 1983. Beef flavor—A review. *Food Technology* **37**, 227 (no. 5).

44. Moore, A. J. 1966. The differential response of choice, good, and commercial grades of the *Longissimus dorsi* of beef to controlled aging. *Journal of Home Economics* **58**, 171.

45. Moore, L. J., D. L. Harrison, and A. D. Dayton. 1980. Differences among top round steaks cooked by dry or moist heat in a conventional or a microwave oven. *Journal of Food Science* **45**, 777.

46. Munns, W. O., and D. E. Burrell. 1966. The incidence of dark-cutting beef. *Food Technology* **20**, 1601.

47. Nielsen, M. M., and F. T. Hall. 1965. Dry-roasting of less tender beef cuts. *Journal of Home Economics* **57**, 353.

48. Olson, D. G., F. Caporaso, and R. W. Mandigo. 1980. Effects of serving temperature on sensory evaluation of beef steaks from different muscles and carcass maturities. *Journal of Food Science* **45**, 627.

49. Parrish, F. C., Jr., R. B. Young, B. E. Miner, and L. D. Andersen. 1973. Effect of postmortem conditions on certain chemical, morphological and organoleptic properties of bovine muscle. *Journal of Food Science* **38**, 690.

50. Peterson, R. J., and S. S. Chang. 1982. Identification of volatile flavor compounds of fresh, frozen beef stew and a comparison of these with those of canned beef stew. *Journal of Food Science* **47**, 1444.

51. *Pork in Family Meals.* Home and Garden Bulletin No. 160. Washington, DC: U.S. Department of Agriculture, 1977.

52. Ramsey, C. B., K. D. Lind, L. F. Tribble, and C. T. Gaskins, Jr. 1973. Diet, sex and vacuum packaging effects on pork aging. *Journal of Animal Science* **37**, 40.

53. Ream, E. E., E. B. Wilcox, F. G. Taylor, and J. A. Bennett. 1974. Tenderness of beef roasts. *Journal of the American Dietetic Association* **65**, 155.

54. Sanderson, M., and G. E. Vail. 1963. Fluid content and tenderness of three muscles of beef cooked to three internal temperatures. *Journal of Food Science* **28**, 590.

55. Savell, J. W., F. K. McKeith, and G. C. Smith. 1981. Reducing postmortem aging time of beef with electrical stimulation. *Journal of Food Science* **46**, 1777.

56. Smith, G. C., J. W. Savell, H. R. Cross, and Z. L. Carpenter. 1983. The relationship of USDA quality grade to beef flavor. *Food Technology* **37**, 233 (no. 5).

57. Sonaiya, E. B., J. R. Stouffer, and D. H. Beermann. 1982. Electrical stimulation of mature cow carcasses and its effect on tenderness, myofibril protein degradation and fragmentation. *Journal of Food Science* **47**, 889.

58. Tatum, J. D., G. C. Smith, B. W. Berry, C. E. Murphey, F. L. Williams, and Z. L. Carpenter. 1980. Carcass characteristics, time on feed and cooked beef palatability attributes. *Journal of Animal Science* **50**, 833.

59. Tatum, J. D., G. C. Smith, and Z. L. Carpenter. 1982. Interrelationships

between marbling, subcutaneous fat thickness and cooked beef palatability. *Journal of Animal Science* **54,** 777.

60. Voris, H. H., and F. O. van Duyne. 1979. Low wattage microwave cooking of top round roasts: Energy consumption, thiamin content and palatability. *Journal of Food Science* **44,** 1447.

61. Wasserman, A. E., J. W. Pensabene, and E. G. Piotrowski. 1978. Nitrosamine formation in home-cooked bacon. *Journal of Food Science* **43,** 276.

11

Poultry and Fish

The term *poultry* is applied to all domesticated birds used as food and includes chickens, ducks, geese, turkeys, guinea fowl, squab (young pigeons), and pigeons. The types of poultry most commonly used in the United States are the first four mentioned. Poultry is now available in this country in many convenient forms and sizes throughout the year. The production of poultry may be adapted to most areas of the world.

In the United States much of the poultry is produced using modern management practices with thousands of birds being raised in one large building (Figure 11-1).

Classification and Market Forms

Each kind of poultry may be divided into several groups or classes as follows:

1. *Chickens*—classified chiefly on the basis of age and tenderness.
   a. Young, tender birds.
      (1) *Broiler-fryer:* 9 to 12 weeks old; 2 to 2½ lbs; of either sex.
      (2) *Roaster:* 3 to 5 months old; 3 to 5 lbs; of either sex; breast-bone cartilage somewhat less flexible than that of broiler-fryer.
      (3) *Capon:* castrated male; usually less than 8 months old.
      (4) *Rock Cornish game hen* or *Cornish game hen:* young immature bird bred from Cornish chicken crossed with an-

11-1 *In this modern poultry house, 19,000 broilers live under one roof. These broilers are all 56 days old and ready for market.* (Courtesy of the U.S. Department of Agriculture)

other breed of chicken; usually 5 to 7 weeks old and up to 2 lbs in weight.
b. Older, less tender birds.
   (1) *Fowl* or *stewing hen:* mature female; usually more than 10 months old.
   (2) *Cock:* mature male.

Ready-to-cook chickens are sold whole, halved, quartered, and in serving-sized pieces. They may be chilled or frozen. Boned, canned chicken is also commonly available. A number of precooked frozen convenience items including chicken rolls, barbecued chicken, fried chicken parts, chicken dinners, and many main dishes that include chicken as an ingredient are also sold.

2. *Turkeys.*
   a. *Fryer-roaster:* usually less than 16 weeks old; 4 to 8 lbs; of either sex; flexible breastbone cartilage.
   b. *Young hen:* usually 5 to 7 months old; 8 to 14 lbs; female; breastbone cartilage somewhat less flexible than fryer-roaster.

c. *Young tom:* usually 5 to 7 months old; over 12 lbs; male; similar characteristics as young hen.

d. *Yearling hen:* under 15 months of age; fully matured female.

e. *Yearling tom:* under 15 months of age; fully matured male.

f. *Mature or old turkey:* more than 15 months old.

Turkeys are usually marketed as frozen whole birds, which are essentially oven-ready. Boneless turkey roasts and boneless turkey rolls are available in all white meat, all dark meat, or a combination of both. Canned boned turkey and many frozen turkey products, such as turkey pies, main-dish items, and turkey dinners, are available.

3. *Ducks*—Most ducks are marketed as ducklings or young ducks weighing 3 to 7 lbs.

4. *Geese*—Most geese are marketed young and usually weigh 6 to 12 lbs.

Processing Poultry

In modern times, many improvements in technology have occurred in poultry processing plants. Automatic picking machines, which remove feathers from the slaughtered and scalded birds, have been developed and perfected, eliminating much hand labor. Processors eviscerate birds at the processing plant, rather than at the retail market, and then freeze them. Availability of new equipment has continued to mechanize the processing of poultry. For example, a cutting machine that makes possible the cutting up of broilers in the processing plant has greatly decreased labor requirements. Slaughtered, eviscerated poultry are chilled immediately to control the growth of microorganisms. This is often done by immersing the carcasses in chilled water on a continuous basis [13].

Composition and Nutritive Value

The composition and nutritive value of poultry do not differ substantially from that of other meats except that chicken and turkey breast, particularly, are lower in fat and cholesterol and higher in niacin than other lean meats with separable fat removed [17]. Dark meat is superior to white meat as a source of riboflavin and thiamin. The light meat of poultry, such as the breast, has shorter, more tender fibers that are less firmly bound together with connective tissue than those of dark meat. As in mammals the amount of connective tissue in poultry varies with age; it is more abundant in old birds, especially in male birds.

The fat of poultry is deposited in the muscle tissue, in thick layers under the skin, and in the abdominal cavity. In capons there is more fat and a more uniform distribution of fat in the flesh than in chickens that have not been castrated. The fat of all types of poultry is of a softer consistency than that of other meats. It also has a lower melting point. The fat of mature birds has a pronounced flavor, that of geese, particularly, having a distinctive flavor that may be objectionable in old birds. The fat content of goose and duck is higher than that of chicken. The composition of chicken and turkey is given in Appendix C.

Buying of Poultry

In poultry there is a relatively high proportion of waste from live weight to the ready-to-cook bird. Poultry loses about one third of the live weight in dressing and drawing and another 12 percent in bone and other inedible parts. The edible portion, therefore, is only about 55 percent of the live weight. Further losses result from cooking, as in all meats, and will vary with the temperature and method of cooking and with the degree of fatness. The high fat content of ducks and geese results in a particularly high cooking loss. However, changes in the efficiency of production and the processing of poultry have greatly increased the supply of poultry meat on a year-round basis. Prices of poultry have become competitive with other meat products, and poultry is a popular item with the American consumer, more and more often being chosen in preference to red meats.

11-2 *A USDA poultry inspector examines birds in a modern broiler processing plant to insure that they are free from disease.* (Courtesy of the U.S. Department of Agriculture)

Inspection and Grading. The Wholesome Poultry Products Act of 1968 requires that all poultry marketed in the United States be inspected either by agents of the federal government or by adequate state systems. The inspection process in a production plant is shown in Figure 11-2 and the U.S. Department of Agriculture inspection mark appears in Figure 11-3. Poultry bearing the official mark must be from a healthy flock, processed under specified sanitary conditions, contain only approved additives, and be properly packaged and truthfully labeled. Poultry and meat inspection are both handled at the federal level by the Food Safety and Inspection Service. Prepared poultry products, such as canned, boned poultry, frozen dinners and pies, and specialty items, also must be prepared under U.S. Department of Agriculture inspection. The label on these prepared products must bear the common name of the product, the net weight, the name and address of the packer or distributor, the official plant number and inspection mark, and a list of ingredients in the order of their proportion in the product. The ingredient present in largest amount is listed first. After the product leaves the processing plant it comes under the jurisdiction of the Food and Drug Administration, which is responsible for preventing the sale of adulterated food, including poultry.

In addition to inspection for wholesomeness the U.S. Department of Agriculture has also developed standards for quality grades—Grades A, B, and C (Figures 11-4 and 11-5). The qualities considered in grading are conformation, fleshing, fat, and freedom from pinfeathers, skin and flesh blemishes, cuts, and bruises.

Many states participate in a grading program, and in such states the official stamp reads "Federal-State Graded." In other states the stamp reads "U.S. Grade." Grading of poultry is not mandatory but the consumer profits by its use, as it provides the consumer with an assurance of quality and class as stated, permits selection of the desired quality for the intended use, and helps in evaluating variable prices. Figure 11-6 illustrates the difference between Grades A and B.

Characteristics That Aid in Selection of Poultry. In a young bird, the end of the breastbone is pliable and the wing offers little resistance when bent into an upright position. A slight twist of the wing may sever the shoulder joint readily. The skin of a young bird is pliable and soft and tears easily. An older bird will have a hard, calcified breastbone and may show an abundance of long hairs. Greater weight is not necessarily an indication of age of a bird as some breeds grow very large. In young birds, sex differences are not significant but with increase in age, male birds are inferior in flavor to female birds. They are also more tough and stringy and less juicy.

Most poultry in retail markets are young birds. However, poultry should be purchased specifically for the intended use. The class

11-3 *U.S. Department of Agriculture inspection mark for poultry.* (Courtesy of the U.S. Department of Agriculture)

11-4 *The U.S. Department of Agriculture grade shield denotes that poultry has been graded for quality. Poultry must first be inspected for wholesomeness, however.* (Courtesy of the U.S. Department of Agriculture)

11-5 *The wing tag may include the class name—in this case, "Frying Chicken"—in addition to the inspection mark and the grade mark. (Courtesy of the U.S. Department of Agriculture)*

name on poultry suggests one cooking method and helps the consumer to make a correct choice.

Amount to Buy. Table 11-1 gives the estimated number of servings from a pound of ready-to-cook poultry. Whole chickens often cost less per pound than those already cut into individual pieces. Figure 11-7 shows a procedure to follow in disjointing whole chickens. Pieces of all one kind, such as chicken breasts or legs, are also sold so that individual preferences for various parts may be satisfied. As Table 11-1 indicates, one would need to buy more poultry per serving if purchasing pieces such as wings or thighs than if buying breasts which contain less bone. The costs per serving should be compared, in these cases, rather than the cost per pound.

Storage in the Home

Chilled, raw poultry is a very perishable product but may be kept 2 or 3 days in the coldest part of the refrigerator. When the poultry is stored at home, it may be left in the polyethylene bags or transparent wrap that were applied in the retail market. Repackaging chicken for short term storage in the refrigerator may actually increase the bacterial count due to the additional handling [7].

Cooked poultry should be cooled quickly, loosely wrapped, and stored in the coldest part of the refrigerator. Stuffing should be removed from cooked poultry and stored separately in a covered container. Cooked poultry, stuffing, broth, or gravy should be used within 2 or 3 days. Poultry products are ideal for the growth and toxin production of food-poisoning organisms. They should be handled carefully, always refrigerated, and used promptly to minimize

11-6 *Grading for quality is not required by law but many firms choose to have their poultry graded. U.S. Grade A (left) and U.S. Grade B (right) young turkeys. (Courtesy of the U.S. Department of Agriculture)*

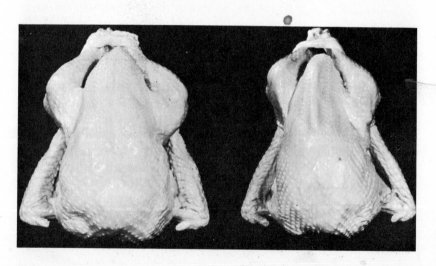

Table 11-1 *Number of servings from a pound of ready-to-cook poultry[a]*

Kind and Class	Approximate Servings of Cooked Meat		Approximate Yield of Cooked, Diced Meat (Cups)
	Size of Serving	Number of Servings	
Chicken:			
Whole:			
Broiler-fryer	3 ounces without bone	2	1¼
Roaster	3 ounces without bone	2¼	1½
Stewing hen	3 ounces without bone	2	1¼
Pieces:			
Breast halves (about 5¾ ounces each)	1, about 2¾ ounces without bone	2¾	
Drumsticks (about 3 ounces each)	2, about 2½ ounces without bone	2½	
Thighs (about 3¾ ounces each)	2, about 3 ounces without bone	2¼	
Wings (about 2¾ ounces each)	4, about 2¾ ounces without bone	1½	
Breast quarter (about 11 ounces each)	1, about 4½ ounces without bone	1½	
Leg quarter (about 10¾ ounces each)	1, about 4¼ ounces without bone	1½	
Turkey:			
Whole	3 ounces without bone	2¼	1¼
Pieces:			
Breast	3 ounces without bone	2¾	1¾
Thigh	3 ounces without bone	2¾	
Drumstick	3 ounces without bone	2½	
Wing	3 ounces without bone	1¾	
Ground	3 ounces	3¾	
Boneless turkey roast	3 ounces	3¼	
Duckling	3 ounces without bone	1	
Goose	3 ounces without bone	1¾	

[a]From [15].

possible food-poisoning problems. Any surfaces, such as kitchen counters and cutting boards, that have come in contact with raw poultry during its preparation for cooking, should be thoroughly cleaned before other foods are placed on them. This precaution will help to avoid cross-contamination of salmonellae microorganisms if poultry are infected with them.

Both uncooked and cooked poultry may be frozen for longer storage periods. Better flavor and texture are maintained in the uncooked than in the cooked frozen product. In the home it is wise not to freeze or even refrigerate uncooked, stuffed poultry. Stuffed poultry should be cooked immediately upon stuffing. The time required for total cooling and freezing are too long, and undesirable microorganisms may grow. Stuffings are an excellent medium for bacterial growth.

11-7 *Disjointing a chicken.* (Courtesy of the U.S. Department of Agriculture)

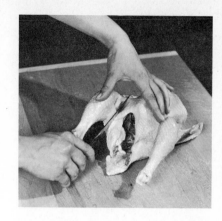 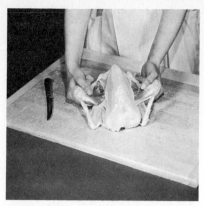

Cut the skin between the thighs and body of the bird.

Grasp a leg of the bird in each hand and lift the bird from the table, bending its legs back as you lift. Bend the legs until the hip joints are free.

Remove the leg-and-thigh piece from one side of the body by cutting from back to front as close as possible to the bones in the back of the bird.

Locate the knee joint by squeezing the thigh and leg together. Cut through this joint to separate the thigh and leg.

Remove the wing from the body. Start cutting on the inside of the wing just over the joint. Cut down and around the joint. To make the wing lie flat, either cut off the wing tip or make a cut on the inside of the wing at the large wing joint; cut just deep enough to expose the bones.

Turn the body of the bird over and remove the other leg-and-thigh piece and the other wing in the same way. Separate the thigh and leg at the knee joint.

Divide the body by placing the bird on its neck end and cutting through the meat from the back to the tail along the end of the ribs. Then cut along each side of the backbone through the rib joints, then between the backbone and flat bone at the side of the back. Cut the skin that attaches the neck-and-back strip to the breast.

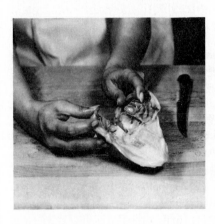 

Place the neck-and-back strip, skin side up, on a cutting board. Cut the strip in two just above the spoon-shaped bones in the back. Place the breast, skin side down, on the cutting board. Cut through the white cartilage at the V of the neck as shown.

Grasp the breast piece firmly in both hands. Bend each side of the breast back and push up with the fingers to snap out the breastbone. Cut the breast in half lengthwise.

The disjointed chicken. Meaty pieces at left—legs, thighs, wings, breast halves. Bony pieces at right—wing tips, back strip, back, and neck.

Cooking of Poultry

The fundamental principles of cooking poultry do not differ from those applied to other meats. Dry-heat methods (broiling, frying, baking, or roasting) are applicable to young, tender birds. Moist-heat methods should be applied to older, less tender birds in order to make them tender and palatable. Most of the poultry sold on the market today is young and tender and may be cooked by dry-heat methods.

Roasting. All kinds of young, tender poultry may be roasted [1]. Poultry roasted whole may be stuffed (Figure 11-8) or unstuffed. If unstuffed, it will cook more rapidly. One of the problems concerned with roasting poultry arises from the usual necessity of cooking the whole bird in one cooking operation when some parts are more tender than others. The breast may be overcooked and dry in the time required to cook the legs and thighs to the desired degree of doneness.

To determine the stage of doneness of large-sized poultry, particularly turkeys, a thermometer may be inserted in the thickest part of the thigh muscle or in the breast muscle. Internal thigh temperatures of 82° to 85° C (180° to 185° F) appear to produce a desired degree of doneness without an objectionable decrease in juiciness [2, 10]. Pop-up timers, which are internal temperature-indicating devices, are sometimes placed in the breasts of turkeys during processing and are usually set for 85° C (185° F). However, cooking frozen turkeys to an internal temperature, measured in the breast and thigh, of at least 71° ± 2° C (160° ± 4° F), by both high and low oven temperatures, has also been reported to be satisfactory. This internal temperature was high enough to essentially sterilize the poultry so that no food poisoning problems would be likely to occur [3].

Variable oven temperatures have been employed for roasting turkeys. Palatability scores for the tenderness and juiciness of both light and dark meat have been reported to be similar for turkeys roasted at three oven temperatures—300°, 325°, and 350° F [8]. Total cooking and dripping losses were also similar at the three temperatures.

An aluminum foil tent is sometimes used to cover the breast of turkeys during roasting to prevent overbrowning. Alternatively, the whole bird may be wrapped in foil, although lower palatability for foil wrapped turkeys versus open pan roasted birds has been reported [6]. General recommendations for roasting turkey might be an oven temperature of 325° F and an internal temperature in the thigh muscle of 82° to 85° C (180° to 185° F). A roasting guide for poultry is given in Table 11-2. Palatability is probably similar for birds roasted with the breast up or with the breast down in the roasting rack.

11-8 *Preparing a turkey for roasting.* (Courtesy of National Turkey Federation)

Lightly salt body cavity, if desired.

Fill the body and neck cavities lightly with prepared stuffing; allow about ½ cup stuffing for each pound of ready-to-cook poultry.

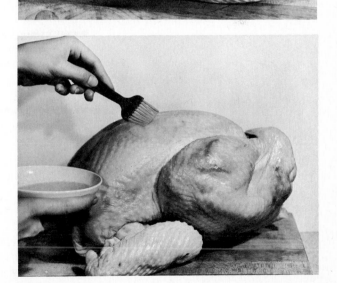

Fold the neck skin over to the back and fasten with a skewer. Turn the wing tips back to rest against the folded neck skin. Tuck the ends of the legs under the band of skin at the tail.

Poultry may be lightly brushed with melted fat before placing with breast side up on a rack in an open roasting pan. If poultry browns early in the roasting period, the breast and drumsticks may be lightly covered with aluminum foil or with a thin cloth moistened with fat.

253

Table 11-2 *Timetable for roasting poultry[a]*

Kind	Purchased Weight (pounds)[b]	Approximate Total Roasting Time at 325° F (hours)[c]	
		Fresh or thawed poultry (32° to 40° F)	Frozen poultry (0° F or below)[d]
Chickens:			
Whole:			
Broiler-fryer	2¼ to 3¼	1¾ to 2½[e]	2 to 3
Roaster	3¼ to 4½	2 to 3[e]	2½ to 3½
Capon	5 to 8½	3 to 4[e]	
Rock Cornish game hen	1 to 2	1½ to 2[e]	
Pieces	¼ to ¾	1 to 2½	1 to 2¾
Ducks	4 to 6	2½ to 4[e]	3½ to 4½
Geese	6 to 8	3 to 3½	
Turkeys:			
Whole	6 to 8	3 to 3½[e]	
	8 to 12	3½ to 4½[e]	
	12 to 16	4½ to 5½[e]	5½ to 6½
	16 to 20	5½ to 6½[e]	
	20 to 24	6½ to 7[e]	7 to 8½
Halves, whole breasts	5 to 11	3 to 5½	4¼ to 6¼
Quarters, thighs, drumsticks	1 to 3	2 to 3½	2 to 3¾
Boneless turkey roasts	3 to 10	3 to 4	

[a]From [15].
[b]Weight of giblets and neck included for whole poultry.
[c]Cooking time is only approximate; a meat thermometer can be used to help determine doneness of whole turkeys, large turkey pieces, and boneless turkey roasts. The temperature in the inner thigh of whole turkeys and in the center of the thickest part of turkey pieces should reach 180° to 185° F. Turkey roasts are done when the temperature reaches 170° to 175° F in the center. Stuffing temperature should reach at least 165° F.
[d]Unstuffed poultry; do not use for frozen commercially stuffed turkeys; follow package directions.
[e]Cooking time suggested is for stuffed poultry; unstuffed poultry may take slightly less time to cook.

Oil is sometimes injected into the breast just below the skin during the processing of turkeys to produce a self-basting effect during cooking. According to one study [14], moisture in the breast meat was not affected by self-basting but a higher proportion of fat appeared in the drippings. However, in another study [3] oil-basted turkeys were considered to be significantly more juicy and tender than unbasted birds.

The yields of cooked meat, fat, and skin from roasted or braised turkeys have been reported [5] to be about 55 percent of the ready-to-cook weight. The meat, fat, and skin of roasted or stewed chickens made up 50 to 52 percent of the ready-to-cook weight of chickens weighing 2 to 3 pounds. The similar yield for ducklings was 39 percent. The yield of cooked lean meat without fat and skin was 46 percent for turkeys and 41 percent for chickens.

Light and dark meat turkey roasts, available on the market, may be satisfactorily cooked at a range of oven temperatures from 250° to

400° F. The internal temperature would appear to be a good guide in cooking these roasts, the yields and juiciness of cooked meat decreasing at internal temperatures of 40° to 90° C (104° to 194° F), but with increasing scores for odor, flavor, and mealiness [11].

Broiling and Frying. Although very young chickens are usually described as broilers, they are now less frequently cooked by broiling than by frying and baking. For any method of preparation broilers are split down the back and the center front.

Poultry is generally preferred well done. With the broiler rack placed about 6 inches from the flame or heating element, chicken pieces may be broiled for 20 to 25 minutes on each side to ensure thorough cooking and avoid stringiness. Because of the low fat content of very young birds, both color and flavor will be improved if the outside is greased well and if the pieces are basted with melted fat during the broiling process. Juiciness may be increased by starting the pieces with the skin side down. The halves of broilers, as well as cut-up fryers, are frequently fried. They may first be rolled in flour, batter, or in egg and crumbs [4, 18]. Slow, careful cooking is necessary to prevent overbrowning before the birds are done. Usually 30 to 60 minutes will be required to cook the flesh thoroughly (depending on the thickness of the muscles). If deep-fat fried, the pieces may be steamed almost done before being dipped in flour, batter, or in egg and crumbs and being browned in the fat, or they may be baked in a slow oven after frying. The time required for browning in deep fat sometimes is too short to permit thorough cooking of the flesh.

Broilers and fryers may also be oven "fried" at about 400° F. The pieces are first dipped in egg and then coated with a breading mixture containing fat, or a small amount of oil may be placed in the baking pan. The chicken is turned mid-way in the baking process.

Braising. The term *fricassee* may be applied to cut pieces of chicken that are braised. Usually the browning is accomplished by frying, after which moisture is added and the bird is simmered until it is tender. If preferred, the pieces of chicken may be stewed until they are tender, after which the meat may be fried until brown. A sauce or gravy made from the pan liquor may be served over the chicken.

Stewing. For stewing, birds are usually cut into pieces, although whole birds may be cooked in water seasoned with spices and herbs and vegetables. The poultry should be simmered until tender.

Microwave Cooking. Poultry may be satisfactorily cooked in microwave ovens. Problems encountered with poultry are similar to those occurring with meat cookery as discussed in Chapter 10. Turning of the product is necessary for more uniform cooking. Dressing is best cooked separately rather than stuffed in the bird.

Discoloration of Poultry Bones. The bones of frozen young birds often show considerable dark color after the birds are cooked. Freezing and thawing break down the blood cells of bone marrow and cause a deep red color to show. During cooking, this red color changes to brown, although this color change does not affect flavor. Cooking directly from the frozen state has been shown to give less darkening than rapid or slow thawing, and birds cooked rapidly with microwaves exhibit less darkening than those that are deep-fat fried [9].

Fish

Each year several billion pounds of fish and shellfish are caught commercially for food in the United States. This amount includes about two hundred different species of fish and about forty kinds of shellfish and miscellaneous items. However, only a few species are well known as edible fish and shellfish in this country. Compared with many other countries in the world, the United States is a relatively small consumer of fish and fish products. The sea offers an excellent source of protein food.

Classification and Market Forms

Fish may be classified into two major categories: vertebrate fish with fins and shellfish (invertebrate). The former are covered with scales and the latter with some type of shell. Fish with vertebrae may be further classified on the basis of their fat content as lean or fat. Lean fish have less than 5 percent fat in their edible flesh. Examples include sole, cod, haddock, halibut, and perch. Fish with more than 5 percent fat in the edible flesh include such varieties as mackerel, shad, lake trout, butterfish, and some salmon. The higher fat content of some fish is a factor in the choice of cooking method. A method, such as broiling or baking, that does not add fat may result in a more palatable cooked product for many consumers.

Shellfish are also of two types—the mollusks and the crustaceans. The mollusks are of soft structure and are either partially or wholly enclosed in a hard shell that is largely of mineral composition. Examples of mollusks are oysters, clams, abalone, scallops, and mussels. The crustaceans are covered with a crustlike shell and have segmented bodies. Common examples are lobster, crab, shrimp, and crayfish.

The kinds of fish available for food vary widely in different localities. They include both saltwater and freshwater varieties and differ in flavor and quality depending partly on the water in which they are grown. Fish from cold, clear, deep waters are superior in quality and in flavor to fish from warm, muddy, shallow waters. Saltwater fish usually have a more distinctive flavor than freshwater fish, and oily fish have more flavor than the lean varieties.

Fish, fresh or frozen, may be marketed in various forms, some of which are shown in Figure 11-9. Whole or round fish are marketed just as they come from the water. Drawn fish have had only the entrails removed and dressed fish are scaled and eviscerated and usually have the head, tail, and fins removed. Steaks are crosscut sections of the larger sizes of dressed fish. Fillets are sides of the fish cut lengthwise away from the backbone. A butterfly fillet is the two sides of a fillet. Sticks are uniform pieces of fish cut lengthwise or crosswise from fillets or steaks. However, some breaded, frozen fish sticks may be made by reforming small pieces of fish. Shellfish may be marketed (1) in the shell; (2) shucked (removed from the shell); (3) headless (shrimp and some lobster); or (4) as cooked meat.

About half the fish marketed in the United States is fresh or frozen and about half is canned. A small amount of fish is cured. Because fish is highly perishable it cannot be held in the fresh form very long.

Many convenience items containing frozen fish are now available. These include frozen, breaded, precooked fish fillets and sticks; frozen, creamed fish dishes; fish soups; fish pies; and fish dinners.

Composition and Nutritive Value

The gross composition of seafood is similar to that of meat. (See Appendix C) The amount of connective tissue in fish, however, is less than that usually found in tender beef. Practical experience in the cookery of fish confirms that fish have little connective tissue and a kind of connective tissue that is very easily hydrolyzed. The structure of fish is very delicate and tender even in the raw state. Shellfish, which appear to differ from other fish in structure, are much firmer and are easily toughened by high temperatures. Whether it is a matter of the amount and kind of connective tissue is not certain.

11-9 *Market forms of fish.* (Courtesy of National Marine Fisheries Service, U.S. Department of Commerce)

Whole or round fish.

Drawn fish.

Dressed or pan-dressed fish.

Steaks.

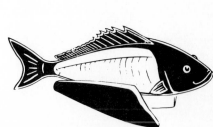

Single fillet.

Sticks.

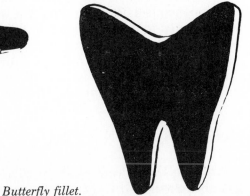

Butterfly fillet.

Seafood is valuable as a source of good quality protein. Fish protein is interchangeable with meat protein in nutritive value. Many fish are lower in fat than moderately fat beef. Some of the fat fish, which range in fat content from 11 to 20 percent, resemble beef in total fat content. The fat in most fish is very unsaturated. Shellfish are notably low in fat.

All shellfish have some carbohydrate in the form of glycogen. Lobster has less than 1 percent, but abalone, clams, mussels, oysters, and scallops have from 3 to 5 percent. The sweet taste of various shellfish is due to the glucose formed by enzyme action from the glycogen.

The edible flesh of all fish has a slightly higher percentage of mineral matter than meat. Shellfish has almost twice as much mineral as other kinds of fish. Oysters are rich in iron, zinc, and copper, and oysters, clams, and shrimp contain a somewhat higher percentage of calcium than other fish and meats, which are notably low in calcium. Marine fish are a dependable source of iodine. Oysters, clams, and lobster are the highest in iodine of all sea food. Shrimp ranks next, with crab and other ocean fish last in order.

Fat fish contain more vitamin A than lean varieties. Canned salmon is a fair source of vitamin A and a good source of riboflavin and niacin. The presence in raw fish of an enzyme, thiaminase, which destroys thiamin, may make the vitamin unavailable if fish is held in the raw state or consumed raw as some shellfish may be. Several fish-liver oils are rich sources of vitamins A and D. The body oils of salmon, herring, and sardine are good but variable sources of vitamin D.

Fish Protein Concentrate. Fish protein concentrate or fish flour may be produced from dehydrated and defatted whole fish. It appears to be an excellent, concentrated source of high-quality protein which may be used to supplement the breads and cereal products consumed by humans in many parts of the world. The Food and Drug Administration has approved the use of fish protein concentrate made from whole fish as a food additive under prescribed conditions. When fish protein concentrate was added to biscuits, 7 percent appeared to be in the upper level of acceptability as shown by taste panel scores [12]. The making of acceptable crackers containing up to 12 percent fish protein concentrate has been reported [16]. Fish protein concentrate has also been used to enrich noodles that are acceptable to Orientals, especially children [19].

Care of Fish

Because of the delicate structure of fish, it is extremely perishable and spoils rapidly. If it is necessary to keep fish for a short time it must be packed in ice or frozen. Even when packed in ice, fish remains in prime condition for only a few hours although it may remain edible for a few days.

In addition to the delicate structure of fish, which makes bacterial invasion easy, it has been shown that rapid spoilage is partly the result of the high degree of activity of the enzymes present in fish. The low temperatures of the natural environment of fish are thought to account for the unusual activity of the body enzymes.

Fish must be kept as cold as other highly perishable foods. Because of the odor, however, fish must be tightly covered when being held in the refrigerator to prevent contamination of other foods.

Selection of Fish

Freshness. Fresh fish has firm flesh, a stiff body, and tight scales. The gills are red and the eyes are bright and unsunken. Pressure on the body does not leave an indentation in the flesh except in the case of fish that has been frozen and thawed. The exterior of fresh fish has little or no slime and the odor is fresh but characteristic. Stale fish, on the other hand, is flabby and the eyes are dull and sunken. The scales are easily brushed off, the gills are no longer bright red, and the odor is stale or sour.

Frozen fish should be solidly frozen when purchased, and there should be no discoloration or brownish tinge in the flesh. Frozen fish should have little or no odor, and it should be wrapped in a moisture-vapor-proof material.

Inspection and Grading. Standards for the inspection and grading of some fish products have been established and are administered by the National Marine Fisheries Service in the U.S. Department of Commerce. A fee for the voluntary inspection and grading of the product is paid by the buyer or seller who requests the service. Fishery products meeting the official standards may carry U.S. inspection and grade labels.

Quality grades are determined largely on the basis of appearance, uniformity, absence of defects, character (mainly texture), and flavor and odor of the product. Grades for breaded items also consider the amount of edible fish as compared to the amount of breading and the presence of bone in fish sticks. For most items specific grades are U.S. Grade A, U.S. Grade B, and Substandard.

Shellfish

The shellfish to be found in most city markets include clams, crabs, lobsters, oysters, scallops, and shrimp. From the standpoint of the quantity consumed, shrimp and oysters are the most important.

The various kinds of shrimp marketed in the United States include the common or white shrimp, which is greenish-gray when caught; the brown or Brazilian shrimp, which is brownish-red when raw; the pink or coral-colored shrimp; and the Alaska and California varieties, which vary in color and are relatively small. Despite the differences in color in the raw state, cooked shrimp differ little in appearance and flavor. Raw shrimp in the shell are often called *green shrimp.* Shrimp are usually sold with the head and thorax removed.

Shrimp are designated, according to the number required to weigh a pound, as Jumbo, Large, Large Medium, Medium, and Small. The largest size runs fifteen or fewer shrimp to the pound; the smallest size runs sixty or more to the pound. Breaded shrimp, which have been peeled, cleaned, and breaded ready for frying, are available. Prawns are shrimplike crustaceans, which are usually relatively large in size.

Oysters may be purchased live in the shell, fresh or frozen shucked (removed from the shell), or canned. When alive, they have a tightly closed shell. Gaping shells indicate that they are dead and therefore no longer usable. Shucked oysters should be plump and have a natural creamy color, with clear liquor. Eastern shucked oysters are usually packed in the following commercial sizes: Counts or Extra Large, Extra Selects or Large, Selects or Medium, Standards or Small, and Standards or Very Small. For the Pacific

11-10 *Two types of lobster.* (Courtesy of Bureau of Commercial Fisheries, U.S. Department of the Interior)

Northern lobster.

Spiny or rock lobster.

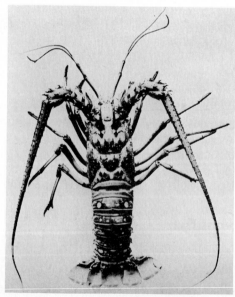

Blue crab.

Dungeness crab.

11-11 *The most common types of crabs available in this country.* (Courtesy of the U.S. Department of Commerce)

area the designations vary somewhat: size 1 is extra large; size 2, large; size 3, medium; and size 4, small.

The true lobster, or Northern lobster, is found near the shores of Europe and north America in the cold waters of the north Atlantic Ocean. The spiny or rock lobster is nearly worldwide in its distribution. The spiny lobster may be distinguished by the absence of large, heavy claws and the presence of many prominent spines on its body and legs. Figure 11-10 shows both of these lobsters.

The lobster is a dark bluish-green color when taken from the water but changes to a "lobster-red" during cooking. Lobsters and crabs must be alive at the time of cooking to ensure freshness. The tail should curl under the body when the live lobster is picked up. Whole lobsters and crabs cooked in the shell are available. They should be bright red in color and have a fresh odor. Frozen lobster tails may be purchased in some markets. The cooked meat, picked from the shells of lobsters and crabs, may be marketed fresh, frozen, and canned.

Blue crabs, composing about three fourths of all the crabs marketed in this country, come from the Atlantic and Gulf coasts. Dungeness crabs are found on the Pacific coast from Alaska to Mexico. Both of these types of crabs are shown in Figure 11-11. Fresh cooked meat from blue crabs may be packed in several grades: lump meat, or solid lumps of white meat from the body of the crab; flake meat, or small pieces of white meat from the rest of the body; lump and flake meat combined; and claw meat, which has a brownish tinge. Fresh cooked meat from both body and claws of Dungeness crabs has a pinkish tinge and is packed as one grade.

Scallops are mollusks similar to oysters or clams except that they swim freely through the water by snapping their shells together. The oversize adductor muscle that closes the shell is the only part of the scallop eaten by Americans. Europeans eat the entire scallop.

Several species of clams are used for food. They may be marketed live in the shell, fresh or frozen shucked, or canned. A tightly closed shell indicates that they are alive and therefore usable. Shucked clams should be plump, with clear liquor, and free from shell particles.

Fish Roe

Although of minor importance in the marketing of fish and available only during spawning season, fresh fish roe are much liked by some persons. Roe is the mass of eggs of fish and consists of sacs of connective tissue enclosing thousands of small eggs. It is important that the sacs remain intact as the eggs cannot otherwise be held together. Shad roe is the most highly prized for flavor although in the Great Lakes area whitefish roe is regarded as among the best.

Some method of cooking that intensifies flavor is preferable for fish roe. It is usually parboiled for 2 to 5 minutes, after which it is dipped in corn meal or in egg and crumbs and fried. Parboiling aids in thorough cooking without the danger of hardening the roe by frying it for too long.

Caviar, or sturgeon roe preserved in brine, is becoming increasingly scarce because of the lower water level of the Caspian sea, where most sturgeon have been produced. Caviar is expensive and is used mainly for making appetizers.

Cured Fish

Fish may be cured to preserve it, but the cure often imparts a distinctive flavor that is greatly appreciated for variety. Some hardening and toughening of the outer surface occurs when fish is salted, dried, or smoked. Common examples of cured fish are salt cod, mackerel, finnan haddie, and kippered herring. Finnan haddie is haddock that has been cured in brine to which carotene pigment has been added and which is later smoked. It is preferred lightly cured but does not keep long with a light cure. If finnan haddie is to be kept for some time or shipped long distances, the cure must be stronger. Kippered herring is also lightly brined and smoked. It is often canned to preserve its typical flavor rather than being cured in a heavier brine.

Most cured fish may be cooked without soaking out part of the brine. Dry salt cod, however, requires the removal of some salt by soaking in order to be palatable.

Canned Fish

The principal kinds of canned fish are salmon, tuna, sardines, shrimp, crab, lobster, and clams.

Salmon packing is one of the big industries of the Pacific Northwest. Five principal varieties of salmon are packed, depending on the locality. The five varieties in order of consumer preference are (1) red salmon or sockeye; (2) chinook; (3) coho, medium red or silverside; (4) pink; and (5) chum. The fish with red flesh and high oil content are preferred by consumers although they are the most expensive. The red-fleshed varieties are somewhat higher in vitamin A content.

In the United States only six species of tuna may be labeled *tuna* when canned. These are yellowfin, skipjack, albacore, bluefin, Oriental tuna, and little tuna. The related species of bonito and Pacific yellowtail cannot legally be marketed as tuna. Albacore may be labeled *white meat;* the other species are labeled *light meat* tuna. There are three different styles of packing for canned tuna: fancy or solid pack, chunk style, and flake or grated style. Each style may be packed either in oil or water. The normal color of precooked or canned tuna is pinkish. Some fish do not develop the pink color but take on a tan or tannish-green color and are rejected. These fish are referred to in the industry as *green* tuna.

Economy in the Use of Fish

The relative economy of different types of flesh foods varies with location and season. Even in some areas of high production, certain fish that rank high in quality and palatability may cost about as much per pound as some of the higher priced meats. In other areas of high production, where marketing facilities are poor, fish may be very inexpensive. During seasons of surplus, fish costs are lower although, as in the case of poultry, efforts are made to equalize the supply and price by the use of cold storage and freezing.

The refuse of fish is high, being rather commonly around 50 percent by weight. The smaller the fish the higher, in general, is the percentage of refuse. The waste is composed chiefly of scales, head, and bones, although in some cases the skin, being tough, is also waste. In shellfish, the shell constitutes the chief waste and in some instances runs as high as 60–80 percent of the total weight. For example, a lobster weighing 1¼ pounds will yield only about ¼ pound of edible flesh. The percentage of waste in large lobsters is somewhat less but is still very high. In addition to the shell, clams have a tough portion that must be discarded. The scallop, as it is eaten in the United States, is only the muscle that operates the opening and closing of the shell.

Preparation

Fish may be cooked by either dry- or moist-heat methods. Because extractives are low in fish, some method, such as frying, broiling, or baking, that develops flavor is usually preferred. Moist-heat methods are not used to make fish tender but simply for variety. Fish, except for some shellfish, are already tender. The chief problem in fish cookery is to retain the form of the fish, which must be carefully handled and not overcooked. If fish is cooked in water, it is usually necessary to tie the piece of fish in cheesecloth or wrap it in parchment to prevent the fish from falling apart.

Although overcooking is to be avoided, fish must be cooked until it is thoroughly done. Fish is unpalatable to many people when it is rare and may also be unsafe. For example, fish from some localities may be a source of tapeworm. Fish is fully cooked when the flakes separate easily. It should be tested with a fork in a thick portion, as the outer, thin edges will cook more readily than the thicker muscles.

Fish for broiling may be fillets, steaks, or boned or unboned whole fish (head removed) that, if unboned, has been cut through the ribs along the backbone to permit the fish to lie flat. If the skin has been left on, the fish is placed skin side down on the broiler rack. It may later be turned, but turning large pieces of fish is difficult and tends to break the fish apart. With the use of a relatively low broiling temperature to prevent overbrowning, and basting the top surface with fat to keep it moist, it is usually possible to broil the fish until done without turning.

Fish for baking may be fillets but is often whole fish, stuffed and sewed or skewered to prevent loss of stuffing. It is usually placed in a shallow, open pan and is basted to keep the skin from becoming hard and dry. A moderate oven gives the most satisfactory results, especially if the fish is stuffed. Figures 11-12 and 11-13 illustrate methods of baking fish.

Small whole fish, fillets, or steaks may be fried. Pieces of a suitable size for serving are usually dipped in water, milk, or egg mixed with milk, then in a dry ingredient, such as cornmeal, flour, or fine crumbs. If the fish is to be deep-fat fried, the temperature of the fat should not exceed 196° to 202° C (385° to 395° F) in order that the fish may be cooked done by the time it is browned.

11-12 *Preparing baked stuffed halibut steaks.* (Courtesy of Bureau of Commercial Fisheries, U.S. Department of the Interior)

Place steak in a baking dish.

Arrange stuffing on the steak.

Place a second steak on top of the stuffing and brush with melted fat.

Serve baked stuffed halibut steaks with garnishes of parsley sprigs and radishes.

Fish may be cooked by steaming or simmering. These are closely related methods of cookery, varying in the amount of the cooking liquid used. When steaming fish, the fish may be placed on a rack over a boiling liquid with a tight cover on the pan, and cooked until done. Steaming may also be done in the oven in a covered pan or the fish may be wrapped tightly in aluminum foil. The foil retains mois-

11-13 *Preparing oven-fried haddock fillets.* (Courtesy of the U.S. Department of Commerce)

Dip the fish in milk and roll in bread crumbs.

Pour melted fat over the fillets.

Bake the fillets in a shallow baking pan.

Serve the fillets with appropriate garnishes.

ture and the fish cooks in an atmosphere of steam. Finnan haddie, which is a cured fish, retains its characteristic flavor particularly well when it is steamed and served with melted butter. In simmering, the fish is covered with a liquid. A simmering rather than a boiling temperature should be used and the fish will hold its form better if, as mentioned, it is tied in cheesecloth, wrapped in parchment paper, or placed in a wire basket in the water. Large, firm-fleshed fish are better used for this method as they do not cook apart so readily as less firm or fatty fish. The addition of 3 tablespoons of vinegar or lemon juice and 1½ tablespoons of salt per quart of water, will season fish well. Fish cooked in moist heat is usually served with a sauce.

If two or more fish fillets have been frozen in a package, it is necessary to partially defrost them in order to separate them for cooking. Individual steaks or fillets may be cooked either thawed or frozen. If thawed, they may be cooked as fresh fish. If the fish is partially or wholly frozen, the cooking temperature must be lower and the time of cooking longer than for defrosted fish in order to permit thawing as the fish cooks. Otherwise, ice may remain in the center of the cut even when the outside is thoroughly cooked.

In the cooking of most shellfish, high temperatures and long cooking are to be avoided because of the toughening effect. Moist heat cooking methods are generally best. If the shellfish is cooked in a liquid medium, as in the making of oyster stew, a simmering temperature (82° to 85° C or 181° to 185° F) should be used. Overcooking and boiling temperatures toughen and shrink shellfish.

Live lobster and green shrimp are parboiled in salted water (2 teaspoons salt per quart of water). The water should be boiling when the fish is added but kept at a simmering temperature once the fish has been added. Overcooking toughens the flesh. After parboiling, the flesh is removed from the shell and prepared in any desired manner. The pink coral on the outside adds attractiveness to the lobster meat, and should not be discarded. The edible meat is in the claws, which must be cracked to remove the meat, and in the tail. The whole tail may be separated from the body and the segmented shell removed.

Large shrimp are often deep-fat fried. The head is removed and the segmented shell is peeled off the tail. In northern and inland markets more shrimp is purchased in cooked, canned, or frozen forms than in the raw state.

In both canned and bulk cooked shrimp the fine dark streak or sand vein, which is the intestinal tract, located just under the outer curved surface must be removed. In the use of canned fish such as salmon, the skin and bones are removed.

Study Questions

1. Poultry may be divided into several groups which consider type, age, and sex.
   a. Describe each of the following classes of chickens and turkeys:

Chickens	*Turkeys*
Broiler-fryer	Fryer-roaster
Roaster	Young hen
Capon	Young tom
Cornish game hen	
Fowl or stewing hen	

    b. Suggest satisfactory methods of cooking each type of poultry listed in question a and explain why each method is appropriate.

2. a. What does the round USDA inspection mark mean when placed on poultry?
    b. List the USDA grades that may be used on poultry and describe the qualities that are considered in grading.

3. Explain why it is so important to handle poultry properly, both in the raw and cooked state.

4. Describe an appropriate method for roasting stuffed and unstuffed turkeys and explain why you would suggest this procedure.

5. Describe general procedures for broiling, frying, braising, and stewing poultry.

6. How do fish and shellfish differ? Give several examples of each.

7. Describe five forms in which fish may be sold (market forms).

8. Suggest appropriate procedures for handling and storing fish in the home and explain why these procedures are necessary.

9. Describe typical characteristics of fresh fish.

10. Describe or identify:
    a. Green shrimp
    b. Northern lobster
    c. Spiny or rock lobster
    d. Scallops
    e. Fish roe
    f. Finnan haddie
    g. Tuna

11. List five principal varieties of salmon.

12. Explain why it is appropriate to cook fish by either dry or moist heat methods.

13. Describe satisfactory procedures for cooking fish by:
    a. Broiling
    b. Baking
    c. Frying
    d. Steaming

14. What chief precaution should be taken when cooking shellfish and why?

References

1. Baker, R. C., and J. M. Darfler. 1981. A comparison of fresh and frozen poultry. *Journal of the American Dietetic Association* **78,** 348.
2. Bramblett, V. D., and K. W. Fugate. 1967. Choice of cooking temperature for stuffed turkeys. Part I, Palatability factors. *Journal of Home Economics* **59,** 180.

3. Cornforth, D. P., C. P. Brennand, R. J. Brown, and D. Godfrey. 1982. Evaluation of various methods for roasting frozen turkeys. *Journal of Food Science* **47,** 1108.

4. Cunningham, F. E., and L. M. Tiede. 1981. Influence of batter viscosity on breading of chicken drumsticks. *Journal of Food Science* **46,** 1950.

5. Dawson, E. H., G. L. Gilpin, and A. M. Harkin. 1960. Yield of cooked meat from different types of poultry. *Journal of Home Economics* **52,** 445.

6. Deethardt, D., L. M. Burrill, K. Schneider, and C. W. Carlson. 1971. Foil-covered versus open-pan procedure for roasting turkey. *Journal of Food Science* **36,** 624.

7. Gardner, F. A., W. Hopkins, and J. H. Denton. 1980. A comparison of consumer methods of storing chicken broilers at home. *Poultry Science* **59,** 743.

8. Goertz, G. E., and S. Stacy. 1960. Roasting half and whole turkey hens. *Journal of the American Dietetic Association* **37,** 458.

9. Hatch, V., and W. J. Stadelman. 1972. Bone darkening in frozen chicken broilers and ducklings. *Journal of Food Science* **37,** 850.

10. Hoke, I. M., and M. K. Kleve. 1966. Heat penetration, quality, and yield of turkeys roasted to different internal thigh temperatures. *Journal of Home Economics* **58,** 381.

11. Hoke, I. M., B. K. McGeary, and M. K. Kleve. 1967. Effect of internal and oven temperatures on eating quality of light and dark meat turkey roasts. *Food Technology* **21,** 773.

12. Jezorek, S. M., and E. J. McCreary. 1968. The effect of fish protein concentrate on biscuits. *Journal of Home Economics* **60,** 287.

13. Lillard, H. S. 1982. Improved chilling systems for poultry. *Food Technology* **36,** 58 (no. 2).

14. Moran, E. T., Jr., and E. Larmond. 1981. Carcass finish and breast internal oil basting effects on oven and microwave prepared small toms: Cooking characteristics, yields, and compositional changes. *Poultry Science* **60,** 1229.

15. *Poultry in Family Meals.* Home and Garden Bulletin No. 110. Washington, DC: U.S. Department of Agriculture, 1979.

16. Sidwell, V. D., and B. R. Stillings. 1972. Crackers fortified with fish protein concentrate (FPC). *Journal of the American Dietetic Association* **61,** 276.

17. Stadelman, W. J. 1978. Tenderness, flavor, and nutritive value of chickens. *Food Technology* **32,** 80 (no. 5).

18. Suderman, D. R., and F. E. Cunningham. 1980. Factors affecting adhesion of coating to poultry skin, effect of age, method of chilling, and scald temperature on poultry skin ultrastructure. *Journal of Food Science* **45,** 444.

19. Woo, H. C., and A. M. Erdman. 1971. Fish protein concentrate enrichment of noodles. *Journal of Home Economics* **63,** 263.

12

Milk and Milk Products*

Although milk from various species of animals, including cows, goats, buffalo, and camels, is used as food in different parts of the world, only cow's milk is of commercial importance in the United States. Milk is the one food for which there seems to be no adequate substitute. It constitutes almost the entire diet for the young of all mammals. Each species produces milk that is especially adapted to the growth of its own young but milk from one species may be used as food for others.

Composition and Properties of Milk

The average percentage composition of whole cow's milk is water, 88; protein, 3.3; fat, 3.3; carbohydrate, 4.7; and ash, 0.7. The fat content of milk may vary, being adjusted to a desired level by the dairy processor. Standards for minimum fat content differ somewhat in various states.

The quantitative composition of milk varies chiefly with breed and individual characteristics of the cow but other factors, such as season, stage of lactation, and rations, may alter the proportion of constituents to some extent. Fat is the most variable constituent, with protein next. Carbohydrate and ash vary only slightly. Jersey

*Other than butter and ice cream.

and Guernsey cattle produce milk with about 5.0 percent fat as compared with about 3.5 percent fat in Holstein milk. The composition of some common milk products is given in Appendix C.

Protein

The principal protein of milk is casein and most of the remainder is lactalbumin and lactoglobulin [12]. Small amounts of other proteins are also present. The proteins are in colloidal form, that is, they are dispersed in particles of intermediate size between the small sugar molecules in true solution and the larger fat particles in suspension. Casein is a phosphoprotein, containing phosphoric acid in its molecular structure. At the normal acidity of fresh milk (about pH 6.6) the casein is largely combined with calcium as calcium caseinate. Casein is easily coagulated by the addition of acid or the enzyme rennin, used in the manufacture of cheese. Lactalbumin and lactoglobulin are the chief whey proteins, not being precipitated by acid or rennin. They can be coagulated by heat and are probably chiefly responsible for the precipitate that usually forms on the bottom and sides of a container in which milk is heated.

Fat

The fat of milk (butterfat) is characterized by the presence of short chain, saturated fatty acids, such as butyric and caproic acids. The disagreeable odor and flavor of spoiled or deteriorated butter are chiefly the result of the release of free butyric and caproic acids from the fat molecules. The comparatively large proportion of short chain fatty acids in butter is also an important factor influencing the soft solid consistency or relatively low melting point.

The fat exists as small droplets dispersed in the milk serum, making milk an emulsion. The fat globules vary in size; all are very minute yet easily visible under the microscope (see Figure 12-1). To keep the fat globules dispersed in an emulsified form, small amounts of protein and phospholipids surround the fat globules in thin films. These proteins and phospholipids act as emulsifying agents. Some of the fat globules are loosely grouped together in clusters. As whole, nonhomogenized milk stands, the fat globules tend to cluster into larger groups and rise to the surface of the milk as cream. The size of the dispersed fat globules in milk is decreased by the process of homogenization and they no longer rise to the surface on standing. Homogenization is discussed later in the chapter.

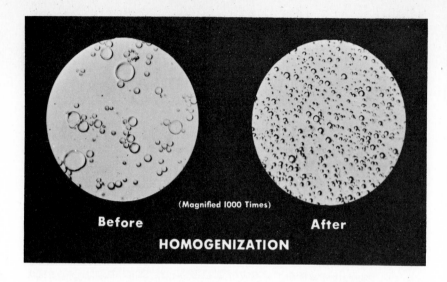

12-1 *Homogenization of milk decreases the size of the dispersed fat particles as shown in this photomicrograph of evaporated milk.* (Courtesy of Evaporated Milk Association)

(Magnified 1000 Times)

Before   After

HOMOGENIZATION

Carbohydrate

The chief carbohydrate of milk, lactose, is a disaccharide, yielding glucose and galactose on hydrolysis. Lactose is the least soluble of the common sugars. The enzyme lactase is normally produced in the small intestine and breaks down lactose into its two component simple sugars. In some individuals, however, this enzyme is present in insufficient amount for them to handle more than a very small amount of milk sugar without discomfort. Since lactose is not digested when there is an enzyme deficiency, it remains in the intestine and is broken down by microorganisms, producing gas, cramping, and diarrhea. A deficiency of lactase, producing a lactose intolerance, seems to develop quite frequently, even in early childhood, among certain populations, particularly non-Caucasian peoples. Individuals with lactose intolerance may be able to tolerate some fermented milk products, such as yogurt, buttermilk, or aged cheese, if the lactose in these products has been broken down to glucose and galactose.

Color

The white appearance of milk is due to the reflection of light by the colloidally dispersed protein, casein, and by the calcium phosphate. The color of milk is the result of two yellowish pigments: carotenes and riboflavin. The carotene is fat soluble and is, therefore, found in the fat of milk. The intensity of color is variable, depending on the concentration of carotene present, which in turn depends on the amount of carotene in the feed of the cow and on her ability to change it to the colorless vitamin A. Riboflavin, a water-soluble B vitamin, imparts a greenish-yellow fluorescent color plainly visible in the whey of milk.

Flavor

The flavor of milk is bland. It is slightly sweet because of its lactose content. A major flavor sensation of milk has been ascribed to its mouth-feel because of the emulsion of milk fat and the colloidal structure of the proteins and some calcium phosphate. The slight aroma of fresh milk is produced by a number of low molecular weight compounds such as acetone, acetaldehyde, dimethyl sulfide, methyl ketones, short-chain fatty acids, and lactones. Some of the volatile compounds contributing to the flavor of milk are unique to the fatty portion of milk.

Heat processing may affect the flavor of milk, the change in flavor being dependent on the time and temperature of heating. The effect on flavor of heating to pasteurize milk, including the use of ultra-high temperatures for very short periods of time, is minimal and tends to disappear during storage. Ultra-high-temperature sterilized milk tastes very much like conventionally pasteurized milk, although some individuals may notice a slightly cooked flavor [12].

Off flavors that may occur in milk may be influenced by the feed that is consumed by the cow, the action of bacteria, chemical changes in the milk, or the absorption of foreign flavors after the milk is drawn. One chemical off flavor is called *oxidized* flavor [16]. This flavor may result from oxidation of phospholipids in the milk. Since traces of copper accelerate the development of oxidized flavor in milk, copper-containing equipment has been eliminated from dairies. An off flavor may be produced when milk is exposed to light. This off flavor, which develops rapidly, involves both milk protein and riboflavin. The amount of riboflavin in milk is decreased as the off flavor develops. Waxed cartons and opaque plastic containers help to protect milk from light.

Acidity

Fresh milk has a pH of about 6.6, which is close to the neutral pH of 7. As milk stands exposed to air the acidity of milk decreases slightly because of the loss of carbon dioxide from the milk. Raw milk, which normally contains some lactic acid producing bacteria, will gradually increase in acidity on storage, eventually resulting in "sour" milk when enough lactic acid has been produced from lactose.

However, pasteurized milk does not generally become sour because the lactic acid bacteria are destroyed during the heating process. When pasteurized milk spoils, it is usually due to the action of putrefactive bacteria that break down proteins in the milk.

Nutritive Contributions of Milk

Milk is much more than a beverage. Its caloric value is significant and it is a source of high quality protein [3]. In the quantities normally recommended for consumption, it can make a significant contribution to the protein needs of adults as well as children.

Milk is a rich source of minerals, particularly calcium. Most other foods commonly used in the United States cannot be favorably compared with milk and milk products as good dietary sources of calcium. Without milk or milk products in the diet, very careful planning must be done to meet the recommended dietary allowance of calcium. Milk is also a good source of phosphorus as well as several other minerals. Milk is a poor source of iron. Young children may become anemic if they remain on an unsupplemented milk diet too long.

All vitamins known to be essential in human nutrition are present in milk to some extent. The vitamin A value varies with the diet of the cow, usually being more abundant in milk from cows on green pasture than in milk produced on dry feed. The removal of fat in making skim milk takes the fat-soluble vitamins dissolved in the cream. However, both vitamins A and D are commonly added to skim and low-fat milks.

Thiamin occurs in only fair concentration in milk but is relatively constant in amount. Riboflavin is present in a higher concentration in milk than the other B vitamins and its stability to heat makes milk a dependable source of the vitamin. Riboflavin is very unstable to light, which means that milk exposed to light may lose large amounts of the vitamin. Milk is a good source of the amino acid tryptophan, which is a precursor or provitamin for niacin. Thus, the niacin value of milk is high. Only a small amount of ascorbic acid is present in raw milk and approximately 25 percent of this is destroyed during pasteurization [15]. Milk is, therefore, not a dependable source of ascorbic acid.

Sanitation and Milk Quality

Milk is among the most perishable of all foods because it is an excellent medium for the growth of bacteria, some of which are harmless but some of which may be pathogenic to man. Quality milk is milk that has been produced, processed, and distributed under rigid sanitary conditions so that it has a relatively low bacterial count, is free from disease producing organisms, has good flavor and appearance, high nutritive value, and satisfactory keeping quality. Various controls and treatments for milk have been instituted to ensure quality in this product. The responsibility for a safe milk supply does not rest solely with the dairy industry but must be shared by public health officials and the consumer.

The Grade A Pasteurized Milk Ordinance is a set of recommendations by the U.S. Public Health Service-Food and Drug Administration; this ordinance describes the steps necessary to protect the milk supply. It includes recommendations concerning sanitary practices at farms and milk processing plants, proper pasteurization, and laboratory examination of milk, and it is revised periodically. This ordinance was formulated as a guide to states and other jurisdictions responsible for milk quality and has been voluntarily adopted by many state and local governments. The majority of people in the United States live in areas where the guidelines of this ordinance are in effect.

Sanitary codes generally determine the grading of milk. Grades and their meanings may vary according to local regulations unless the pasteurized milk ordinance has been adopted, in which case standards are uniform. Most rigid control is placed on the production and processing of Grade A market milk, the grade supplied to consumers as fluid milk.

The U.S. Department of Agriculture has set quality grade standards for nonfat dry milk and also for butter and some cheeses. In addition, it gives a "Quality Approved" rating for certain products (Figure 12-2). If a manufacturer uses the USDA grade or the "Quality Approved" shield on product labels, the plant must operate under the continuous inspection of USDA agents. The grades for nonfat dry milk are U.S. Extra and U.S. Standard for regular dry milk and U.S. Extra for the instantized product. Grading is a voluntary, fee-for-service program.

Pasteurization

Low bacterial count and high standards of production do not always ensure a milk supply that is free from pathogenic organisms. Even under the best sanitary practices disease-producing organisms may enter raw milk accidentally from environmental and human sources. Therefore, milk is pasteurized as an additional safeguard for the consumer. Pasteurization is required by law for all Grade A fluid milk and milk products that enter interstate commerce for

12-2 *The use of USDA shields indicates quality in dairy products. (Courtesy of the U.S. Department of Agriculture)*

U.S. Extra Grade is the grade name for instant nonfat dry milk of high quality.

The "Quality Approved" shield may be used on cottage cheese, or other cheeses for which no official U.S. grade standards exist, if the products have been inspected for quality under USDA's grading and inspection program.

275

retail sale [12]. Pasteurization consists of heating raw milk at a sufficiently high temperature for a specified length of time to destroy pathogenic bacteria. It generally destroys 95 to 99 percent of all other nonpathogenic bacteria as well but does not completely sterilize the milk. Its keeping quality is greatly increased over that of raw milk.

Various time and temperature relationships may be used in pasteurization. Milk may be heated to a temperature of at least 63° C (145° F) and held at this temperature for 30 minutes. This is called the *holding* process. A high-temperature, short-time process which consists of heating milk to a temperature of at least 71° C (160° F) for about 15 seconds is, however, more commonly used. Additional higher heat, shorter time combinations may also be used. An ultra-pasteurization process involves heating milk to a temperature of 138° C (280° F) for 2 seconds or more. This product has a longer shelf life than milk pasteurized by the other methods. Following pasteurization, the milk is cooled rapidly to a temperature of 7° C (45° F) or lower.

Various tests may be applied to ascertain the thoroughness of pasteurization of milk supplies. It is also imperative that no raw milk be mixed accidentally with properly pasteurized milk.

The temperatures and times for pasteurization are not sufficient to alter the milk constituents or properties to a significant extent. The whey proteins are denatured to only a slight extent, minerals are not appreciably precipitated, and vitamin destruction is generally slight. If any changes in curd characteristics occur as a result of pasteurization, they tend toward the production of a finer curd during the digestion of milk.

Care of Milk in the Home

Fundamentals to the care of milk, whether by producer or consumer, are cleanliness, cold temperature, and the prevention of contamination by keeping the milk covered. So perishable a food as milk should be placed in the coldest part of the refrigerator. Exposing milk to light destroys riboflavin rapidly and may produce an oxidized off flavor which apparently involves both milk protein and riboflavin. Proper containers should be used to protect the milk. The containers should be closed to prevent the absorption of other food odors. The container of milk should be returned to the refrigerator immediately after use to prevent warming of the milk which encourages bacterial growth. Milk that has been poured out but not used should never be returned to the original container where it may contaminate the rest of the milk.

The differences in specific gravity of the milk fat and milk serum result in the tendency of the fat to rise to the top surface, producing a cream line. Large fat globules and clusters of globules rise more rapidly and more completely than small, single globules. Rapid cooling of fresh milk aids in the clumping of fat globules. Homogenization divides the fat globules of milk into very small particles that are dispersed permanently in a fine emulsion throughout the milk. They do not clump and rise to the surface (Figure 12-1). Most of the market milk in the United States is now homogenized and cream-line milk is generally not available.

Homogenization consists of pumping milk or cream under pressures of 2000 to 2500 pounds per square inch through very small openings in a machine called a *homogenizer* in order to break up the fat globules into much smaller globules [12]. A film of adsorbed protein immediately surrounds each of the new globules and prevents them from reuniting. It is estimated that about one fourth of the protein of milk is adsorbed on the finely dispersed fat particles of homogenized milk. The increased dispersion of fat imparts richer flavor and increased viscosity to the milk. Homogenization causes the milk proteins to be somewhat more readily coagulated by heat or acid than the nonhomogenized product so that care must be taken to avoid curdling when homogenized milk is used in food preparation.

The greatly increased surface exposed in the highly dispersed fat of homogenized milk increases the tendency toward the development of rancidity. Pasteurization before homogenization retards the development of rancidity because it destroys the enzymes that could otherwise attack the more highly dispersed fat.

Fortification consists of the addition of certain nutrients to milk as a means of improving the nutritional value. The principal form of fortification is the addition of vitamin D to the extent of about 400 International Units per quart. Milk is generally regarded as a logical food to fortify with vitamin D in view of the relationship of vitamin D to calcium and phosphorus utilization and because of the fact that milk is an outstanding source of those two minerals. The fortification of skim and low-fat milks with both vitamins A and D is common. Fortification of nonfat dry milk with vitamin A is particularly important when this product is sent to developing countries and used in feeding infants and young children since these children may not be receiving adequate amounts of vitamin A from other sources.

Kinds of Milk

Milk appears on the market in different forms that appeal to the varied tastes and desires of consumers [7, 10]. Many milk products have been developed to improve keeping quality, facilitate distribution and storage, make maximum use of by-products, and preserve surpluses [12].

The cost of the different forms of milk varies, depending upon such factors as supply and demand, production and processing costs, and governmental policies. Fresh milk and cultured milks generally cost more than dried and evaporated milks. Nonfat dry milk is often the most economical form of milk for the consumer.

Federal standards of identity have been set for a number of milk products that enter interstate commerce. These standards define the composition, the kind and quantity of optional ingredients permitted, and the labeling requirements. State and local agencies are encouraged to adopt the federal standards to enhance uniformity.

Fluid Milk

Depending upon the milkfat content, fresh fluid milk is classified as *milk, low-fat milk,* or *skim milk* and is labeled accordingly.

Whole Milk. The term *milk* usually refers to whole milk. According to the federal standards, whole milk packaged for beverage use must contain not less than 3.25 percent milkfat and not less than 8.25 percent milk-solids-not-fat. Milk-solids-not-fat are mostly protein and lactose. Other standards, however, allow milkfat minimums in whole milk to vary from 3.0 to 3.8 percent. At the milk processing plants, the milk from different suppliers is standardized to one fat level by removing or adding milkfat as necessary.

Whole milk may be canned and is available chiefly for use on ships or for export. It is heated sufficiently to sterilize it and then is put into sterilized cans. It can be stored at room temperature until opened.

Low-fat and Skim Milks. *Low-fat milks* may contain 0.5, 1.0, 1.5, or 2.0 percent milkfat and are labeled with the appropriate fat level. *Skim* or *nonfat milk* is milk from which as much fat has been removed as is technologically possible. The fat content is less than 0.5 percent. All of these milks contain at least 8.25 percent milk-solids-not-fat. Additional milk-derived ingredients, such as nonfat milk solids, may be added to low-fat milk to increase the viscosity and opacity of the milk and improve the palatability and nutritive value. If enough nonfat milk solids are added to reach the "10 percent solids not fat" level, the product must be labeled *protein-fortified* or *fortified with protein.* The addition of vitamin A to low-fat and skim milk is required for milk shipped in interstate commerce. The addition of vitamin D is optional.

Ultra-High-Temperature Processed Milk. Ultra-high-temperature processed (UHT) milk is heated at temperatures higher than those used for pasteurization. It is then, under sterile conditions, packaged into presterilized containers and aseptically sealed so that spoilage organisms cannot enter. Hydrogen peroxide may be used to sterilize the milk packaging materials. UHT milk can be stored unrefrigerated for at least 3 months, thus representing a considerable savings of energy usually expended for the refrigeration process. After the milk is opened it must be refrigerated, however.

Flavored Milk and Milk Drinks. A flavored milk is whole milk with a flavored syrup or powder and sugar added. A flavored milk drink is skim or partially skimmed milk that is similarly flavored and sweetened. Flavored milk and flavored milk drinks are pasteurized and homogenized. Chocolate milk usually contains 1 percent cocoa with 5 percent sugar and less than 1 percent stabilizers.

Evaporated and Condensed Milk

Evaporated milk has had about 60 percent of the water removed from milk in a vacuum pan at 50° to 55° C (122° to 131° F). A forewarming period of 10 to 20 minutes at a temperature of 95° C (203° F) is usually effective in preventing coagulation of the casein during the sterilization period after the product is homogenized and canned. In a newer process the concentrated milk may be heated in a continuous system by ultra-high temperatures and then canned aseptically. This product has a lower viscosity, is whiter in color, and has a flavor more like that of pasteurized milk than does evaporated milk processed by the traditional method. Evaporated milk is fortified with 400 International Units of vitamin D per quart. Federal standards require that evaporated milk contain not less than 7.5 percent milkfat and not less than 25 percent total milk solids. Evaporated skimmed milk is also made and must contain not less than 20 percent milk solids. Vitamins A and D must be added to this product.

Theoretically, sterilized evaporated milk keeps indefinitely until opened but on long standing the homogenized fat particles tend to separate, thus breaking the emulsion. Stored cans of evaporated milk and condensed milk should be turned every few weeks because the solids tend to settle or the product thickens and clots. The vegetable gum, carrageenan, is often added to evaporated milk as a stabilizer.

Sweetened condensed milk has about 15 percent sugar added to the milk, after which the product is concentrated to about one-third its former volume. Because the 42 percent sucrose content of the finished product acts as a preservative, the milk is not sterilized after canning. Federal standards require 28 percent total milk solids and 8 percent milk fat.

The browning of evaporated milk and condensed milk is probably of the Maillard reaction type (sugar-protein interaction) and occurs during both sterilization and storage. The rate of browning is greater at room temperature and with longer time of storage.

Dry Milk

Nonfat dry milk powder is usually made from fresh pasteurized skim milk by removing about two-thirds of the water under vacuum and then spraying this concentrated milk into a chamber of hot filtered air. This process produces a fine powder of very low moisture content, about 3 percent. Nonfat dry milk may also be produced by spraying a jet of hot air into concentrated skim milk (foam spray drying). Regular nonfat dry milk reconstitutes in warm water with agitation. Instant nonfat dry milk disperses readily in cold water. To make the instant product, regular nonfat dry milk is remoistened with steam to cause an agglomeration of small particles into larger, porous particles that are creamy white and free flowing. The lactose may be in a more soluble form, particularly on the outside of the particles. Vitamins A and D may be added to nonfat dry milk.

Whole milk or low-fat milk may also be dried. The major form of deterioration in these products is oxidative changes in the fat.

Another dried dairy product is buttermilk, which has a rather wide use in commercial flour mixes. It is also available in the retail market for the consumer. Dried churned buttermilk contains phospholipids that function as emulsifiers in baked products. Dried whey solids are available and are used in some commercial baked products.

When dried milk is reconstituted, the powder is added to water and is shaken or stirred. If used in flour mixtures and some other products, the dry milk may be mixed with dry ingredients or with melted fat. The quantity of instant milk powder to use for 1 quart of fluid milk is usually $1\frac{1}{3}$ cups.

Cultured Milk Products

Cultured milks have had appropriate bacterial cultures added to the fluid product. The bacteria produce lactic acid from lactose and also coagulate the protein, casein. The acidity of cultured milk products is often between pH 4.1 and 4.9. Certain cultures produce flavor components that are characteristic of a particular product.

Fluid buttermilk is generally a cultured product rather than the by-product of churning cream into butter. It is usually made from pasteurized low-fat or skim milk with nonfat dry milk solids added. However, it can also be made from fluid whole milk or reconstituted nonfat dry milk. A culture of *Streptococcus lactis* is added for acid production and flavor and the milk is incubated at 20° to 22° C (68° to 72° F) until the acidity is 0.8 to 0.9 percent (pH 4.6), expressed as lactic acid [12]. Butter granules or flakes, salt, and a small amount of citric acid may be added to enhance the flavor.

Yogurt may be made from whole, low-fat, or skim milk, often with nonfat milk solids added. A mixed culture of *Lactobacillus bulgaricus* and *Streptococcus thermophilus* is generally added and the product incubated at 42° to 46° C (108° to 115° F) until the desired degree of acidity and flavor is achieved. Yogurt has a sharp, tangy flavor. It is often sold with sweetened fruit added and may be served as a dessert. Frozen yogurt is a popular dessert similar to ice cream.

Low-fat or skim milk may be cultured with *Lactobacillus acidophilus* and incubated at 38° C (100° F) until a soft curd forms. It is called *acidophilus-cultured milk* and has an acid flavor. In another process, a concentrated culture of *L. acidophilus* is grown and then added to pasteurized milk. This product is not acid in taste and its consistency is similar to that of fluid milk. This milk introduces acidophilus bacteria into the intestine where they are thought to help maintain a proper balance of microorganisms.

Filled and Imitation Milks

Filled milk is made by combining fats or oils other than milk fat with milk solids. The resulting product appears very much like milk [4]. Coconut oil was previously the main source of fat in filled milk. However, partially hydrogenated soybean, corn, and cottonseed oils containing approximately 30 percent linoleic acid have been developed for use in filled milk. The Federal Filled Milk Act of 1923 specifies the type of milk solids as any milk, cream, or skimmed milk, which may be condensed, evaporated, concentrated, or dried, if desired. *Imitation milk* resembles milk in appearance but usually contains no milk products as does filled milk. Such ingredients as water, corn syrup solids, sugar, vegetable fat, and a source of protein such as sodium caseinate or soy protein are often used in imitation milk. Some imitation milk contains whey products. Coconut oil is commonly used as the vegetable fat. Both filled and imitation milks are subject to variable state regulations but are not as yet governed by the same rigid sanitation and composition requirements as pasteurized Grade A milk or milk products. The Food and Drug Administration has defined an *imitation* product as one that looks like, tastes like, and is intended to replace the traditional counterpart but is nutritionally inferior to it.

Heating milk to temperature and time combinations more extensive than those used in pasteurization brings about some changes, the changes increasing in number and degree with increasing temperature and time of heating. The tendency for milk to curdle is diminished by the use of low or moderate temperatures. It may be observed that scalloped potatoes cooked in a low or moderate oven show less curdling of the milk than when the milk is allowed to boil. The use of evaporated milk, which because of its previous heating appears to be more resistant to coagulation, may prevent or diminish the extent of curdling. The general effect of heat on milk, as it relates to its use in food preparation, is considered in this section. The preparation of white sauces and cream soups, using heated milk, is discussed in Chapter 17. The preparation of hot chocolate, containing milk, is discussed in Chapter 24.

Effects of Heat

Protein Coagulation. The whey proteins, lactalbumin and lactoglobulin, may be precipitated or become insoluble on heating. Lactalbumin begins to precipitate or coagulate at a temperature of 66° C (150° F). The amount of coagulum increases with an increase in temperature and time of heating. The coagulum formed appears as small particles rather than a firm mass. It collects on the bottom of the pan in which the milk is heated and contributes to the scorching that is characteristic of heated milk. Stirring the milk while it heats aids in lessening the amount of precipitate on the bottom but may not prevent scorching, particularly if a large quantity of milk is being heated. Heating milk over hot water rather than over direct heat will retard or completely prevent scorching.

Casein, the protein found in largest amount in milk, is not precipitated or coagulated at the usual temperatures and time periods used in food preparation. It may be changed somewhat in properties but coagulates only when heated to very high temperatures or for a long period of time at boiling temperature. It may require as long as 12 hours for casein to coagulate when heated at a temperature of 100° C (212° F).

Heating periods that will produce casein coagulation are shorter when the concentration of casein is increased above that in regular fluid milk. In the sterilizing of evaporated milk, which contains double the amount of casein found in ordinary milk, measures are necessary to prevent coagulation of the casein. Forewarming prior to sterilizing is usually effective.

The coagulation of milk protein by heat is accelerated by an increase in acidity. The addition of acid foods, such as tomato juice or fruits, to heated milk may result in coagulation.

Heat coagulation of milk is influenced by the kinds and concentration of the salts present. The salts present in some foods, such as ham hocks and vegetables, that are cooked in milk are partly responsible for coagulation of the casein.

Effect of Heating Sugar-Protein Mixtures. The Maillard reaction, sometimes called *nonenzymatic browning,* occurs when sugars and proteins are heated together. Concentrated milk products contain substantial amounts of both protein and lactose and develop some brown color on heating. The prolonged heating of sweetened condensed milk in the can results in a product of brown color, caramel flavor, and thickened consistency, which is sometimes used as a dessert. The extent of change varies with the length of time of heating, being more intense with long heating.

Effect of Heating on Minerals. The dispersion of calcium phosphate in milk is decreased by heating and a small part of it is precipitated. Some of the calcium phosphate collects on the bottom of the pan with coagulated whey proteins and some is probably entangled in the scum on the top surface of the milk.

Film Formation on Heated Milk. Film or scum formation is one of the most troublesome of reactions that occurs during the heating of milk. The formation of the scum is the principal reason for the usual behavior of milk in boiling over. A certain amount of pressure develops under the film, which later forces the film upward and the milk flows over the sides of the pan. A slight film may form at relatively low temperatures and may be prevented by covering the pan, by diluting the milk, or by the presence of fat floating on the surface. As the temperature is increased, a tough scum forms, which is insoluble and can be removed from the surface. As soon as it is removed, however, another film forms. A method that is sometimes used for breaking up the film or scum consists of beating the cooked milk with a rotary type of egg beater. This procedure has limited usefulness because of the continuous formation of fresh film, although the film may be broken by beating and foam formation at the surface appears to aid in preventing so tenacious a scum. The composition of this film is variable, and may contain such products as coagulated protein with some precipitated salts and fat globules entangled with the coagulated matter.

Coalescence of Fat Globules on Heating. The layer of fat that may form on milk that has been boiled is the result of the breaking of the films of protein that surround the fat globules in the unheated milk. The breaking of films of emulsifying agent permits the coalescence of fat globules.

Acid Coagulation of Milk

Acid, either that which forms by bacterial action in milk or added acid, precipitates casein as a curd. The acid curdling of milk is a desired reaction in the making of some products such as buttermilk, yogurt, sour cream, and some cheeses, but is undesirable when it occurs in other food products. Cream of tomato soup is a product in which the prevention of casein coagulation or curdling is fundamental to the success of the product. Fruit-milk mixtures may also curdle, as may be observed in the use of cream on fruits and in the making of fruit-milk beverages or sherbets. The acid in the fruit lowers the pH (increases the acidity) of the milk or cream and causes casein to become unstable and to precipitate.

Enzyme Coagulation of Milk

A number of enzymes from plant, animal, and microbial sources are capable of clotting milk. Rennin is such an enzyme that occurs in the stomach of young animals with the function of clotting milk prior to the action of other protein-digesting enzymes. As a crude product it is called rennet. Rennet has been used for many years in the preparation of most varieties of cheeses. Today, however, the sources of rennet are limited and a number of other nonrennin milk clotting enzymes are being used as rennet substitutes [5]. Rennet may also be used in the making of some ice creams.

Since rennet is an enzyme, it requires specific conditions of temperature and acidity for its action. The optimum temperature is 40° to 42° C (104° to 108° F). Refrigerator temperatures retard the action. No action occurs below 10° C (50° F) or above 65° C (149° F). Rennet acts best in a faintly acid medium. Action does not occur in an alkaline medium.

The action of the enzyme bromelin from raw or frozen pineapple in preventing the gelation of gelatin is well known. The enzyme digests proteins, hence changes the gelatin to smaller compounds that do not form a gel. The enzyme bromelin also clots milk but later digests the clot. Other enzymes in fruits are probably responsible for some of the curdling action that occurs when milk or cream and certain fruits are combined. All fruits contain some organic acids but not always in sufficient concentration to cause the curdling of milk. Destroying the enzymes before combining fruit with milk will, of course, prevent curdling caused by enzyme action.

Coagulation of Milk by Phenolic Compounds

Fruits and vegetables contain some phenolic-type compounds. In fruits, these compounds are found chiefly in the green stages and are present in a greater amount in some varieties than in others. Seeds and stems may contain significant amounts of phenolic substances. Among vegetables, roots, pods, some seeds, and woody stems are likely to contain more phenolic compounds than other parts of the plant although distribution is general throughout the plant. Curdling of milk may occur if phenolic-containing foods, such as potatoes, are cooked in the milk. Phenolic compounds are also present in brown sugar and in cacao products. Organic acid present in vegetables may be a factor in curdling although the acidity of most vegetables is low as compared with that of many fruits.

Coagulation of Milk by Salts

The cause of curdling when foods are cooked in milk is likely to be a combination of factors. The salts present in the milk, in the food combined with the milk, or added sodium chloride may also influence coagulation of the casein. Of the meats commonly cooked in milk, ham usually causes more coagulation than chicken, veal, or pork although the latter may vary in their action probably partly because of differences in the acidity or in the salts of the meat. The high sodium chloride content of ham may be responsible for the excessive curdling that occurs when ham is cooked in milk.

Freezing of Milk

The freezing of milk or cream at a relatively slow rate weakens or ruptures the film of protein that acts as an emulsifying agent on the fat globules. As a result, fat globules tend to coalesce. The oily masses that float on top of hot coffee, when cream that has been frozen is added to coffee, show the cohesion of fat particles that results from freezing. The dispersion of protein and of calcium phosphate is also disturbed by freezing. Both constituents tend to settle out on thawing and standing, thus reducing the whiteness of milk. The effects of freezing are not harmful and do not affect food value.

Cream

Cream is the fat of milk which is removed by the use of a separator from the other constituents of milk. According to the federal standard of identity, light or coffee cream may contain a range of 18 to 30 percent milkfat, light whipping cream contains 30 to 36 percent fat, and heavy whipping cream must have at least 36 percent fat [12]. Half-and-half is a mixture of milk and light cream and contains not less than 10.5 percent fat. Very little light or coffee cream is now available as such, half-and-half being commonly used in its place. Commercial sour cream may be a cultured or an acidified light cream. It may also have added nonfat milk solids and stabilizing vegetable gums such as carrageenan. Half-and-half sour cream is also available.

The thickness of cream is related to its fat content. However, factors other than fat content also affect the thickness of cream. The temperature of cream markedly affects its body. Cream at room temperature is thinner than cream at refrigerator temperature because chilling makes the fat globules firmer, thereby increasing the thickness of the cream. When chilled to a temperature of 5° C (41° F) and held at that temperature for 24 to 48 hours, cream gradually increases in thickness.

Dried cream, to be used reconstituted to liquid form, has been produced. An instant dry creamed milk made from modified skim milk (calcium reduced), light cream, and lactose has also been manufactured. When sprinkled on the surface of a beverage, it disperses quickly. A number of nondairy cream products are available and widely used in hot beverages. They usually contain corn syrup solids, vegetable fat, a source of protein such as sodium caseinate or soy protein, emulsifiers, and salts. Nondairy products for whipped toppings are also widely used. They often contain sugar, hydrogenated vegetable oil, sodium caseinate, and emulsifiers. They are available in a dry form added to cold milk before whipping and also in whipped form as a frozen product. The foam is stable and requires only defrosting before use.

Cream containing sugar, stabilizers, and flavoring is sold in pressurized containers. When a valve is pressed, a whipped-cream product comes out, as a result of the action of propellant gases. Nondairy products containing water, vegetable fat, sugar, sodium caseinate, emulsifiers, and vegetable gums, and resembling whipped cream, are also available in pressurized cans. These products must be refrigerated. Many nondairy products for whipped toppings, coffee whiteners, sour cream-type mixtures, and snack dip bases have been developed and marketed. Initially these were promoted as low-cost substitutes for the more expensive natural dairy products. Gradually many of them, particularly whipped toppings and coffee whiteners, have been accepted on their own merits rather than as substitutes and have taken over the market.

The Whipping of Cream

Whipped cream is a product that results from the agitation of cream. During whipping, air is incorporated thus forming a foam, and fat particles are clumped together producing the characteristic rigidity or stiffness of whipped cream. Because whipping is the first stage of churning, the emulsion breaks and butter is formed if whipping is continued too long. The air bubbles formed in whipped cream are surrounded by protein films in which the clumps of fat particles lie. The clumps of fat globules offer structural support, which increases the rigidity of the foam and permits the formation of more air bubbles and the extension of the protein film to surround them.

Because air bubbles must be surrounded by protein films and because so much of the protein of homogenized cream is used to surround the increased number of fat globules, little protein remains to surround the air bubbles formed in whipping. Therefore, whipping cream is usually not homogenized. Several factors affect the whipping properties of cream.

Temperature. Cream held at a cold temperature (7° C or 45° F or below) whips better than cream at warmer temperatures. At temperatures above 10° C (50° F) agitation of cream increases the dispersion of the fat instead of decreasing it. In the whipping of cream the aim is to increase *clumping* of fat particles and at low temperatures agitation results in clumping. Lower temperatures also increase viscosity, which increases the whipping properties of cream. The beater and bowl used as well as the cream, should be chilled.

Viscosity. Any condition that increases viscosity increases the whipping property of cream. The effect of temperature on viscosity has already been noted. Higher fat content also increases viscosity and furnishes more fat globules for clumping. Because viscosity increases with aging, the whipping property improves with the aging of cream (Figure 12-3).

Amount of Fat. In cream 30 percent fat is about the minimum that will whip with ease and give a stiff product. Increased fat up to 40 per cent improves the whipping quality of cream (Figure 12-3).

Amount of Cream Whipped. It is better in whipping large amounts of cream to do successive whippings of amounts regulated

35%   30%   25%   20%   20%   25%   30%   35%

12-3 *Effect of percentage of fat and of aging on whipping property of cream: Left: cream whipped immediately after separating; Right: cream whipped after aging for 24 hours. Note the greater permanence of the whipped cream at the right as shown by the smaller amount of leakage after standing for 18 hours at a temperature of 4°C (40°F). Foam stability also increases with increasing fat content of the cream between 20 and 35 percent. (Courtesy of J. C. Hening)* to the size of the whipper used rather than to attempt to whip a large amount in one lot.

Effect of Other Substances. Increased acidity up to the concentration required to give a sour taste (0.3 percent) has no effect on whipping quality. The addition of sugar decreases both volume and stiffness and increases the time required to whip cream if it is added before whipping. If sugar is to be added it is best added after the cream is stiff or just prior to serving.

Compounds on the market that are said to improve the whipping quality of thin cream have as a common constituent sucrate of lime, which is a compound formed from sucrose and calcium hydroxide. Used in small amounts this compound increases viscosity.

The stand-up quality of whipped cream is improved if the cream is whipped as stiff as possible without forming butter, if cream of optimum fat content (about 40 percent) is used, and if the whipped cream is held at a cold temperature (below 10° C or 50° F).

The Whipping of Other Milk Products

When evaporated milk is chilled to the ice crystal stage it will whip to about three times its original volume. This ability to whip is evidently the result of the larger concentration of milk solids in evaporated than in fresh whole milk. The protein in the milk acts as a foaming agent, although this foam is not stable on standing. The addition of acid, such as a small amount of lemon juice (about 1 tablespoon per cup of undiluted milk), helps to stabilize the protein and makes a more lasting foam.

A light and airy whipped product may be produced by the whipping of nonfat dry milk. Equal measures of dry milk and very cold water are usually used, with the dry milk being sprinkled over the surface of the water before whipping. This foam is very unstable but its stability may be increased somewhat by adding small amounts of an acid substance such as lemon juice before whipping.

Cheese

The Food and Drug Administration defines cheese as "a product made from curd obtained from the whole, partly skimmed, or skimmed milk of cows, or from milk of other animals, with or without added cream, by coagulating with rennet, lactic acid, or other suitable enzyme or acid, and with or without further treatment of the separated curd by heat or pressure, or by means of ripening ferments, special molds, or seasoning." Cheese is usually ripened, but cottage and cream cheeses are examples of unripened cheese [1, 2].

Most of the cheese consumed in the United States is made commercially. However, some consumers may make cottage cheese at home and the U.S. Department of Agriculture has published a bulletin giving instructions on how to do this [9]. Similar steps are followed in the manufacture of most cheeses. These include (1) formation of curd by milk-clotting enzymes such as rennin or acid; (2) cutting the curd into small pieces to allow the whey to escape; (3) heating the curd; (4) draining, salting, and pressing the curd; and (5) ripening or curing [11].

USDA grade standards U.S. Grade AA and U.S. Grade A have been developed for Swiss, Cheddar, Colby, and Monterey cheese. Cheese bearing these grades must be produced in a USDA inspected and approved plant under sanitary conditions. Graders evaluate the flavor and the texture of the cheese. Some cheese and cheese products not covered by a U.S. grade standard may be inspected and bear a USDA "Quality approved" inspection shield on the label. This shield indicates that the cheese has been manufactured in a plant meeting USDA sanitary specifications and is a cheese of good quality.

Nutritive Value

Cheese is one of the most concentrated of foods, a pound of cheese containing the protein and fat of approximately a gallon of milk. Cheese that contains milk fat is also an excellent source of vitamin A. Cheese made with rennet coagulation is an excellent source of calcium and phosphorus. Some soluble constituents, such as lactose, much of the ash, and the water-soluble vitamins thiamin, ascorbic acid, and riboflavin, tend to be lost in the whey. Whey cheeses and concentrated whey added to cheese spreads or cheese foods save the valuable nutrients of whey.

Composition and Characteristics

The chief constituents of cheese are protein, fat, and water. The composition varies widely with the fractions of milk used and the amount of moisture retained. In cheese made from whole milk the fat remains with the curd when the whey is drained off. Much of the milk sugar, the soluble salts, and the water-soluble vitamins are drained off in the whey, although even in hard cheeses the whey is never entirely removed. There is a greater loss of calcium in cheeses made by acid than by rennet coagulation. This is because of the effect of a more acid pH on the release of calcium ions (Ca^{++}) from the phosphate groups on the casein molecules. Under more acid conditions, a larger amount of the calcium goes into the whey and is not retained in the curd. Cheeses of the Cheddar type, made chiefly by rennet coagulation of the milk, may retain up to 80 percent of the original calcium. Soft cheeses made by acid precipitation, such as cottage cheese, may retain not more than one fourth to one half of that amount. The amount of sodium chloride added to cheese for flavor varies but is usually fairly high.

American Cheddar cheese averages, roughly, one-third water, one-third fat, and one-fourth protein. It also contains about 4 percent ash and less than 1 percent carbohydrate, including lactic acid. Low-fat cheeses that are acceptable in flavor, body, and texture are now available [8, 13]. These are made from part-skim milk. Cheese containing vegetable oil instead of butterfat is also available for those who want to decrease their intake of animal fat.

The moisture content of soft cheese varies from 40 to 75 percent, whereas hard cheeses tend to contain a more nearly uniform

12-4 Many kinds of cheese are available. To identify the cheeses shown here, see the labeled drawing. (Courtesy of American Dairy Association)

amount of water—from 30 to 40 percent. High moisture content is a factor in the perishability of cheese, those with a large amount of moisture being more perishable.

The groupings of cheeses may be determined by two factors: (1) the amount of moisture in the finished cheese, and (2) the kind and extent of ripening. Based on moisture content, cheese may be classified as soft, semihard, and hard. Based on the kind and extent of ripening, cheese may be classified as strong or sharp and mild, and as mold ripened or bacteria ripened.

More than two thousand names have been given to cheeses with somewhat different characteristics, but there are only about ten distinct types of natural cheese. Table 12-1 describes the characteristics of some popular varieties of natural cheeses.

Ripening. Ripening refers to the changes in physical and chemical properties, such as aroma, flavor, texture, and composition, that

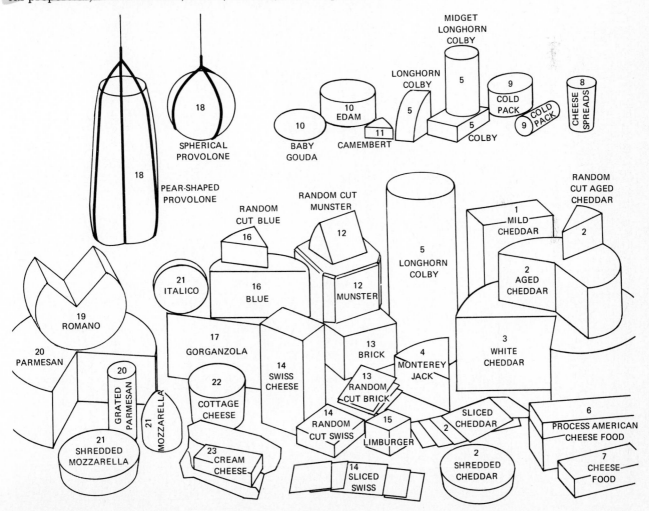

Table 12-1 *Characteristics of Some Popular Varieties of Natural Cheeses*

Kind or Name Place of Origin	Kind of Milk Used in Manufacture	Ripening or Curing Time	Flavor	Body and Texture	Color	Retail Packaging	Uses
Soft, Unripened Varieties							
Cottage, plain or creamed (Unknown)	Cow's milk skimmed; plain curd, or plain curd with cream added	Unripened	Mild, acid	Soft, curd particles of varying size	White to creamy white	Cup-shaped containers, tumblers, dishes	Salads, with fruits, vegetables, sandwiches, dips, cheese cake
Cream, plain (United States)	Cream from cow's milk	Unripened	Mild, acid	Soft and smooth	White	3- to 8-oz packages	Salads, dips, sandwiches, snacks, cheese cake, desserts
Neufchatel (Nú-shä-tĕl´) (France)	Cow's milk	Unripened	Mild, acid	Soft, smooth similar to cream cheese but lower in milkfat	White	4- to 8-oz packages	Salads, dips, sandwiches, snacks, cheese cake, desserts
Ricotta (Rĭ-cŏ´-ta) (Italy)	Cow's milk, whole or partly skimmed, or whey from cow's milk with whole or skim milk added; in Italy, whey from sheep's milk	Unripened	Sweet, nutlike	Soft, moist or dry	White	Pint and quart paper and plastic containers, 3 lb metal cans	Appetizers, salads, snacks, lasagne, ravioli, noodles and other cooked dishes, grating, desserts
Firm, Unripened Varieties							
Gjetost,** (Yĕt´ŏst). (Norway)	Whey from goat's milk or a mixture of whey from goat's and cow's milk	Unripened	Sweetish, caramel	Firm, buttery consistency	Golden brown	Cubical and rectangular	Snacks, desserts, served with dark breads, crackers, biscuits or muffins

Name	Kind of Milk	Ripening or Curing Time	Flavor	Body and Texture	Color	Retail Packaging	Uses
Mysost (Müs-ôst) also called Primost (Prēm´-ôst) (Norway)	Whey from cow's milk	Unripened	Sweetish, caramel	Firm, buttery consistency	Light brown	Cubical, cylindrical, pie-shaped wedges	Snacks, desserts, served with dark breads
Mozzarella (Mŏ-tsa-rel´la) (Italy)	Whole or partly skimmed cow's milk; in Italy, originally made from buffalo's milk	Unripened	Delicate, mild	Slightly firm, plastic	Creamy white	Small round or braided form, shredded, sliced	Snacks, toasted sandwiches, cheeseburgers, cooking, as in meat loaf, or topping for lasagne, pizza, and casseroles

Soft, Ripened Varieties

Name	Kind of Milk	Ripening or Curing Time	Flavor	Body and Texture	Color	Retail Packaging	Uses
Brie (Brē) (France)	Cow's milk	4 to 8 weeks	Mild to pungent	Soft, smooth when ripened	Creamy yellow interior; edible thin brown and white crust	Circular, pie-shaped wedges	Appetizers, sandwiches, snacks, good with crackers and fruit, dessert
Camembert (Kăm´ĕm-bâr) (France)	Cow's milk	4 to 8 weeks	Mild to pungent	Soft, smooth; very soft when fully ripened	Creamy yellow interior; edible thin white, or gray-white crust	Small circular cakes and pie-shaped portions	Appetizers, sandwiches, snacks, good with crackers, and fruit such as pears and apples, dessert
Limburger (Belgium)	Cow's milk	4 to 8 weeks	Highly pungent, very strong	Soft, smooth when ripened; usually contains small irregular openings	Creamy white interior; reddish yellow surface	Cubical, rectangular	Appetizers, snacks, good with crackers, rye or other dark breads, dessert

*From [6].
**Imported only.

Table 12-1 *Characteristics of Some Popular Varieties of Natural Cheeses (continued)*

Kind or Name Place of Origin	Kind of Milk Used in Manufacture	Ripening or Curing Time	Flavor	Body and Texture	Color	Retail Packaging	Uses
Semisoft, Ripened Varieties							
Bel Paese† (Běl Pä-ā´-zě). (Italy)	Cow's milk	6 to 8 weeks	Mild to moderately robust	Soft to medium firm, creamy	Creamy yellow interior; slightly gray or brownish surface sometimes covered with yellow wax coating	Small wheels, wedges, segments	Appetizers, good with crackers, snacks, sandwiches, dessert
Brick (United States)	Cow's milk	2 to 4 months	Mild to moderately sharp	Semisoft to medium firm, elastic, numerous small mechanical openings	Creamy yellow	Loaf, brick, slices, cut portions	Appetizers, sandwiches, snacks, dessert
Muenster (Mŭn´stẽr). (Germany)	Cow's milk	1 to 8 weeks	Mild to mellow	Semisoft, numerous small mechanical openings. Contains more moisture than brick	Creamy white interior; yellow tan surface	Circular cake, blocks, wedges, segments, slices	Appetizers, snacks, served with raw fruit, dessert
Port du Salut (Por dŭ Să-lü´´). (France)	Cow's milk	6 to 8 weeks	Mellow to robust	Semisoft, smooth, buttery, small openings	Creamy yellow	Wheels and wedges	Appetizers, snacks, served with raw fruit, dessert
Firm Ripened Varieties							
Cheddar (England)	Cow's milk	1 to 12 months or more	Mild to very sharp	Firm, smooth, some mechanical openings	White to medium-yellow-orange	Circular, cylindrical loaf, pie-shaped wedges, oblongs, slices, cubes, shredded, grated	Appetizers, sandwiches, sauces, on vegetables, in hot dishes, toasted sandwiches, grating, cheeseburgers, dessert

Name (origin)	Kind of milk	Ripening time	Flavor	Body and texture	Color	Shape and style	Uses
Colby (United States)	Cow's milk	1 to 3 months	Mild to mellow	Softer and more open than Cheddar	White to medium-yellow-orange	Cylindrical, pie-shaped wedges	Sandwiches, snacks, cheeseburgers
Caciocavallo (Kä'chô-kä-väl'lô) (Italy)	Cow's milk; in Italy, cow's milk or mixtures of sheep's, goat's, and cow's milk	3 to 12 months	Piquant, similar to Provolone but not smoked	Firm, lower in milkfat and moisture than Provolone	Light or white interior; clay or tan colored surface	Spindle or ten-pin shaped, bound with cord, cut pieces	Snacks, sandwiches, cooking, dessert; suitable for grating after prolonged curing
Edam (Ē'dăm) (Netherlands)	Cow's milk, partly skimmed	2 to 3 months	Mellow, nutlike	Semisoft to firm, smooth; small irregularly shaped or round holes; lower milkfat than Gouda	Creamy yellow or medium yellow-orange interior; surface coated with red wax	Cannon ball shaped loaf, cut pieces, oblongs	Appetizers, snacks, salads, sandwiches, seafood sauces, dessert
Gouda (Gou'dä) (Netherlands)	Cow's milk, whole or partly skimmed	2 to 6 months	Mellow, nutlike	Semisoft to firm, smooth; small irregularly shaped or round holes; higher milkfat than Edam	Creamy yellow or medium yellow-orange interior; may or may not have red wax coating	Ball shaped with flattened top and bottom	Appetizers, snacks, salads, sandwiches, seafood sauces, dessert
Provolone (Prô-vô-lô'-nĕ) also smaller sizes and shapes called Provolette, Provoloncini. (Italy)	Cow's milk	2 to 12 months or more	Mellow to sharp, smoky, salty	Firm, smooth	Light creamy interior; light brown or golden yellow surface	Pear shaped, sausage and salami shaped, wedges, slices	Appetizers, sandwiches, snacks, souffle, macaroni and spaghetti dishes, pizza, suitable for grating when fully cured and dried
Swiss, also called Emmentaler (Switzerland)	Cow's milk	3 to 9 months	Sweet, nutlike	Firm, smooth with large round eyes	Light yellow	Segments, pieces, slices	Sandwiches, snacks, sauces, fondue, cheeseburgers

†Italian trademark—licensed for manufacture in U.S.A.; also imported.

Table 12-1 *Characteristics of Some Popular Varieties of Natural Cheeses (continued)*

Kind or Name Place of Origin	Kind of Milk Used in Manufacture	Ripening or Curing Time	Flavor	Body and Texture	Color	Retail Packaging	Uses
Very Hard Ripened Varieties							
Parmesan (Pär´ mĕ-zăn´) also called Reggiano (Italy)	Partly skimmed cow's milk	14 months to 2 years	Sharp, piquant	Very hard, granular, lower moisture and milkfat than Romano	Creamy white	Cylindrical, wedges, shredded, grated	Grated for seasoning in soups, or vegetables, spaghetti, ravioli, breads, popcorn, used extensively in pizza and lasagne
Romano (Rô-mä´-nō) also called Sardo Romano Pecorino Romano (Italy)	Cow's milk; in Italy, sheep's milk (Italian law)	5 to 12 months	Sharp, piquant	Very hard granular	Yellowish-white interior, greenish-black surface	Round with flat ends, wedges, shredded, grated	Seasoning in soups, casserole dishes, ravioli, sauces, breads, suitable for grating when cured for about one year
Sap Sago** (Săp´-sä-gō) (Switzerland)	Skimmed cow's milk	5 months or more	Sharp, pungent clover-like	Very hard	Light green by addition of dried, powdered clover leaves	Conical, shakers	Grated to flavor soups, meats, macaroni, spaghetti, hot vegetables; mixed with butter makes a good spread on crackers or bread
Blue-vein Mold Ripened Varieties							
Blue, spelled Bleu on imported cheese (France)	Cow's milk	2 to 6 months	Tangy, peppery	Semisoft, pasty, sometimes crumbly	White interior, marbled or streaked with blue veins of mold	Cylindrical, wedges, oblongs, squares, cut portions	Appetizers, salads, dips, salad dressing, sandwich spreads, good with crackers, dessert

Name	Kind of milk used in manufacture	Ripening or curing time	Flavor	Body and texture	Color	Retail packaging	Uses
Gorgonzola (Gôr-gŏn-zō′-là) (Italy)	Cow's milk; in Italy, cow's milk or goat's milk or mixtures of these	3 to 12 months	Tangy, peppery	Semisoft, pasty, sometimes crumbly, lower moisture than Blue	Creamy white interior, mottled or streaked with blue-green veins of mold; clay colored surface	Cylindrical, wedges, oblongs	Appetizers, snacks, salads, dips, sandwich spread, good with crackers, dessert
Roquefort** (Rŏk′-fêrt or (Rôk-fôr′) (France)	Sheep's milk	2 to 5 months or more	Sharp, slightly peppery	Semisoft, pasty, sometimes crumbly	White or creamy white interior, marbled or streaked with blue veins of mold	Cylindrical, wedges	Appetizers, snacks, salads, dips, sandwich spreads, good with crackers, dessert
Stilton** (England)	Cow's milk	2 to 6 months	Piquant, milder than Gorgonzola or Roquefort	Semisoft, flaky; slightly more crumbly than Blue	Creamy white interior, marbled or streaked with blue-green veins of mold	Circular, wedges, oblongs	Appetizers, snacks, salads, dessert

**Imported only.

take place between the time of precipitation of the curd and the time when the cheese develops the desired characteristics for its type. Changes that occur include the formation, by bacteria, of lactic acid from the lactose; digestion of the protein by enzymes into end products that include peptides and amino acids; the development and penetration of molds; gas formation from certain types of microorganisms used; and the development of characteristic flavor and aroma substances, including those developed from the decomposition by enzymes of fat. The flavor of cheese results from a blend of decomposition and hydrolysis products formed from the milk components during ripening. Flavor substances come from protein, lactose, and milk fat. Typical Cheddar cheese flavor has been found to be related to a balance of various free fatty acids and acetate [14]. The texture of cheese is changed during ripening from a tough, rubbery character to a soft, sometimes crumbly, state. The fat in cheese, although not so well emulsified as in milk, is still finely divided and uniformly distributed. The changes that occur in cheese during ripening not only affect flavor and texture but also improve the cooking quality. The increased dispersibility of the protein of ripened cheese is a factor in the ease of blending cheese with other food ingredients.

Various types of organisms produce distinctive flavor, aroma, and texture in cheeses. The *Penicillium roqueforti* or *Penicillium glaucum* types of molds are responsible for the mottled blue-green appearance of such cheese as blue, Roquefort, Gorgonzola, and Stilton. The curd is inoculated with pure cultures of the mold, which penetrate during the curing process. Camembert cheese is inoculated with two molds: *Oidium lactis,* which covers the cheese in the first stages of ripening, and *Penicillium camemberti,* which grows later. The enzymes produced by the molds penetrate and soften the cheese. Organic acids used as food by the molds gradually disappear, providing a more favorable medium for putrefactive bacteria. Swiss cheese owes its large holes to gas-forming organisms, which grow and produce carbon dioxide gas during the early stage of ripening while the cheese is soft and elastic. Limburger cheese owes its characteristic odor to the development of putrefactive bacteria, which are allowed to act over a considerable period of time. Ordinary Cheddar cheese varies widely in flavor and texture depending on the organisms that predominate and the length of time of ripening. The better examples of Cheddar have *Lactobacilli* and *Streptococcus lactis* predominating. Some species present in this type of cheese produce off flavors and gas, which are not formed by the desirable types producing clean lactic acid fermentation. Mild cheeses, such as brick and Monterey jack, are allowed to ripen for a shorter period of time than are strong cheeses, such as Parmesan. Blue cheese is usually aged 3 to 4 months but may be aged up to 9 months for more pronounced flavor. Strong cheeses are usually in small molds although longer ripening periods will increase the development of flavor in large molds. In hard cheeses the ripening agents are distributed throughout the mass at the beginning of ripening and act in a more or less uniform way, whereas in soft cheeses the curing agents are on the outside surfaces and gradually penetrate the mass. It is necessary that cheeses of the latter type, such as Camembert, be molded in small sizes. Damp caves are used for ripening some types of cheese that depend on mold action for the development of flavor. The presence of salt delays bacterial growth, and hence alters the rate of ripening.

Cold-pack Cheese. Cold-pack or club cheese is made by grinding and mixing together one or more varieties of cheese without the aid of heat. Acid, water, salt, coloring, and spices may be added, but the final moisture content must not exceed that permitted for the variety of natural cheese from which it was prepared. The cheese is packaged in jars or in moisture-proof packages in retail-size units. Cold-pack cheese food is prepared in the same manner as cold-pack cheese but it may have other ingredients such as cream, milk, skim milk, nonfat dry milk, or whey. It may also contain pimientos, fruits, vegetables, or meats, and sweetening agents such as sugar and corn syrup.

Process Cheese. A large proportion of the cheese produced in the United States today is made into pasteurized process cheese and related products. Process cheese is made by grinding and mixing together different samples of natural cheese with the aid of heat and an emulsifying agent. A selected blend of cheese is used or portions of the same variety selected at different stages of ripeness, and the product is pasteurized before packaging. The cheese is ground and heated with sufficient water added to replace that lost by evaporation. To aid in producing a uniform blend that melts without separation of fat, an emulsifying agent, such as disodium phosphate or sodium citrate, is added to the ground cheese before heating. When the cheese is melted it is run into molds, which are sometimes jars or glasses but are often cardboard boxes lined with metal foil, or the wrapper may be of a transparent plastic material. As the cheese hardens it clings closely to the jar or foil, thus preventing molds from attacking the surface. Pasteurization of the cheese destroys bacteria and enzymes, thus stopping all ripening. Process cheese is also sold in individual slices and can be purchased with individual slices separately wrapped. This extends the shelf life of the cheese.

The quality and flavor of process cheese depend on the quality and flavor of the cheese used to make it. Several varieties of cheese are made into pasteurized process cheeses including Cheddar, Swiss, and brick cheese. Its convenience, ease of blending in cooked dishes, and the protection offered by the package against spoilage are factors influencing the consumer's choice to use process cheese. The blend of cheeses is such as to retain insofar as possible the characteristic flavor of the type of cheese used, but the flavor of the process cheese is seldom, if ever, the equal of the original product. The characteristic differences in texture of the original cheeses tend to be lost, as the texture of processed cheese is more or less uniform and soft. The moisture content of process cheese may not exceed 40 percent.

Low-fat (about 8 percent) pasteurized process cheese products in individual slices are also available on the market. These products contain skim milk cheese, water, emulsifier salts, flavorings, and a preservative (sorbic acid).

Process Cheese Foods and Spreads. Pasteurized process cheese food is produced similarly to process cheese except that it contains less cheese and cream, milk, skim milk, nonfat milk solids or whey, and sometimes other foods, such as pimientos, may be added to it. Cheese food is more mild in flavor, melts more quickly, and has a softer texture than process cheese because of its higher moisture content.

Pasteurized process cheese spread generally has a higher moisture and lower milk fat content than process cheese food. A stabilizer is added to prevent separation of ingredients. It is also generally more spreadable than process cheese food.

Cheese Storage

Soft and unripened cheeses have limited keeping quality and require refrigeration. All cheese is best kept cold and dry, and—to prevent drying—should be wrapped in waxed paper, plastic wrapping material, or metal foil, or be kept in the original container if it is one that protects the cheese. Miscellaneous molds growing on the surface of cheese are undesirable and should be trimmed off. In the refrigerator, strong cheeses that are not tightly wrapped may easily contaminate other foods that readily absorb odors. Freezing is not recommended for most cheeses because, on thawing, they tend to be mealy and crumbly. However, some varieties of cheese can be frozen satisfactorily in small pieces (1 pound or less, not more than 1 inch thick). These varieties include brick, Cheddar, Edam, Gouda, Muenster, Port du Salut, Swiss, Provolone, mozzarella, and Camembert. When frozen cheese is to be thawed, it may be taken from the freezer and placed in the refrigerator for a minimum of 10 days before using it to accomplish what is called "slow thawing." This helps to avoid the detrimental effects of freezing and aids in preserving the original flavor, body, and texture.

Cheese soufflé.

Hot blue cheese and chicken sandwich topped with grated Parmesan cheese.

Pineapple refrigerator cheesecake containing cottage cheese.

12-5 *Cheese is used in prepared dishes in a variety of ways which include Welsh rabbit, macaroni and cheese, and cheese omelets. Some unusual and interesting uses of cheese in cooking are shown here. (Courtesy of American Dairy Association; soufflé, courtesy of Kraft Foods)*

Cheese in Cooked Foods

A hard cheese, such as Cheddar, softens and then melts when heated at low to moderate temperatures. Further heating results in the separation of fat and the development of a tough, rubbery curd, which will form long strings when manipulated with a spoon. If the cheese has been heated to the latter stage, it will tend to harden on cooling. Finely dividing the cheese by grating or grinding before combining it with other ingredients facilitates melting without overheating. Cheese sauces should be cooked in a double boiler or cooked over low heat with continuous stirring. Well-ripened cheese and process cheese blend better in mixtures than mild (less-aged) natural cheese and are less likely to produce stringiness. Welsh rabbit is a thickened cheese sauce with seasonings and may contain egg. It is served over toast.

Cheese soufflé is a combination of eggs, white sauce, and cheese for flavor. The white sauce used as a basis may vary in consistency or in amount, but soufflés made with a thick sauce base are usually easier for the inexperienced person to make and possibly tend to shrink less after baking. Shrinkage, however, is principally a matter of the temperature and time of cooking. The baking dish containing the soufflé should be placed in a pan of water during baking to avoid overcooking.

Figure 12-5 gives several examples of the use of cheese in cooked foods.

Study Questions

1. What is the average percentage composition of whole cow's milk?
2. Name:
   a. The protein found in milk in largest amount
   b. Two major whey proteins
   c. The major carbohydrate of milk
   d. Two minerals for which milk is considered to be a particularly good source
   e. The vitamin, for which milk is a good source, that is easily destroyed when milk is exposed to sunlight
3. Explain why milk is classified as an emulsion. Describe how the fat in milk is dispersed.
4. How do opaque containers help to protect milk against the development of off flavor? Explain.
5. Describe the purpose, process, and resulting product when milk is:
   a. Pasteurized
   b. Homogenized
   c. Fortified
6. Briefly describe the major characteristics of each of the following processed milk products:
   a. Whole fluid milk
   b. Skim milk
   c. Low-fat milks
   d. Ultra-high-temperature processed milk
   e. Evaporated milk
   f. Sweetened condensed milk
   g. Nonfat dry milk, regular and instantized
   h. Dried buttermilk (churned)
   i. Buttermilk (cultured)

    j. Acidophilus milk, acid and sweet
    k. Yogurt
    l. Flavored milk
    m. Flavored milk drinks
    n. Filled milk
    o. Imitation milks
    p. Whipping cream
    q. Half-and-half
    r. Sour cream

7. a. Explain why it is so important that milk be handled properly, both in processing and in the home.
   b. What does the USDA Quality Approved shield mean when placed on certain dairy products?
8. a. What causes milk to scorch when it is heated over direct heat?
   b. Which milk proteins coagulate quite easily with heating? Which does not?
9. Suggest ways to prevent or control the formation of a film or scum on the surface of heated milk.
10. a. Which milk protein coagulates easily with the addition of acid?
    b. Give examples illustrating when the acid coagulation of milk is desirable and when it is undesirable.
11. a. What is rennin and what does it do to milk?
    b. What role does rennin play in cheese making?
12. a. Describe what happens when cream is whipped.
    b. What conditions should be controlled, and why, if cream is to whip properly?
    c. Suggest effective procedures for whipping evaporated milk and non-fat dry milk.
13. Describe the general steps usually followed in the manufacture of cheese.
14. a. What is meant by ripening cheese?
    b. Describe general changes that may occur during the ripening process.
15. Give examples of each of the following types of cheese:
    a. Soft, unripened
    b. Firm, unripened
    c. Soft, ripened
    d. Semisoft, ripened
    e. Firm, ripened
    f. Very hard, ripened
    g. Blue-vein mold ripened
16. Describe the major characteristics of:
    a. Cold-pack cheese
    b. Process cheese
    c. Process cheese food
    d. Process cheese spread
17. a. Describe what happens when cheese is heated too long or at too high a temperature.
    b. Suggest an appropriate way for preparing a cheese sauce and explain why this method should be effective.

References

1. *Cheese in Family Meals.* Home and Garden Bulletin No. 112. Washington, DC: U.S. Department of Agriculture, 1977.
2. *Cheese Varieties and Descriptions.* Agriculture Handbook No. 54. Washington, DC: U.S. Department of Agriculture, 1969.
3. Composition and nutritive value of dairy foods. 1971. *Dairy Council Digest* **42,** 1 (no. 1).
4. Council on Foods and Nutrition. 1969. Substitutes for whole milk. *Journal of the American Medical Association* **208,** 58.
5. Gupta, C. B., and N. A. M. Eskin. 1977. Potential use of vegetable rennet in the production of cheese. *Food Technology* **31,** 62 (no. 5).
6. *How to Buy Cheese.* Home and Garden Bulletin No. 193. Washington, DC: U.S. Department of Agriculture, 1974.
7. *How to Buy Dairy Products.* Home and Garden Bulletin No. 201. Washington, DC: U.S. Department of Agriculture, 1979.
8. Madsen, F. M., W. S. Clark, and G. W. Reinbold. 1970. Effect of fat content in Cheddar, Colby, and Swiss cheeses on consumer preference. *Food Technology* **24,** 85 (no. 9).
9. *Making Cottage Cheese at Home.* Home and Garden Bulletin No. 129. Washington, DC: U.S. Department of Agriculture, 1975.
10. *Milk in Family Meals.* Home and Garden Bulletin No. 127. Washington, DC: U.S. Department of Agriculture, 1974.
11. *Newer Knowledge of Cheese.* Rosemont, IL: National Dairy Council, 1983.
12. *Newer Knowledge of Milk.* Rosemont, IL: National Dairy Council, 1983.
13. Nystrom, P. J., J. G. Ostrander, and C. S. Martinsen. 1974. Cheese products: Protein, moisture, fat, and acceptance. *Journal of the American Dietetic Association* **65,** 40.
14. Ohren, J. A., and S. L. Tuckey. 1969. Relation of flavor development in Cheddar cheese to chemical changes in the fat of the cheese. *Journal of Dairy Science* **52,** 598.
15. Rolls, B. A., and J. W. G. Porter. 1973. Some effects of processing and storage on the nutritive value of milk and milk products. *Proceedings of the Nutrition Society* **32,** 9.
16. Shipe, W. F., R. Bassette, D. D. Deane, W. L. Dunkley, E. G. Hammond, W. J. Harper, D. H. Kleyn, M. E. Morgan, J. H. Nelson, and R. A. Scanlan. 1978. Off flavors of milk: Nomenclature, standards, and bibliography. *Journal of Dairy Science* **61,** 855.

13

Eggs and Egg Cookery

The eggs of all birds may be eaten, but because the egg of the hen is more often used than any other, this discussion concerns, unless otherwise specified, hen's eggs. The natural function of the egg is to provide for the development of the chick. Much symbolism has been attached to the egg in various cultures over the centuries.

In food preparation, eggs are used to make emulsions, such as mayonnaise; to make foams, such as meringues and angel food cakes; to make gels, such as baked custards; to coat certain foods, such as breaded pork chops; and to clarify some liquids, such as broth and coffee.

Composition and Nutritive Value

Whole egg is about three-fourths water, 12 percent protein, 11 percent fat, 1 percent carbohydrate, and 1 percent mineral matter or ash. The white and the yolk of the egg are very different in composition as shown in Table 13-1. The yolk contains less water and essentially all of the fat of the egg. The shell makes up about 11 percent of the total weight of the egg [18].

Although the ratio of white to yolk varies in individual eggs, the white is usually about two-thirds by weight of the total edible portion and the yolk is approximately one-third. A small egg does not always have a correspondingly small yolk and vice versa. The yolk of the egg has higher nutritive density than does the white, generally containing more minerals and vitamins in relation to the caloric content (see Table 13-1).

Table 13-1 *Chemical Composition of Egg, Without Shell**

	Amount	Weight (g)	Water (%)	Energy (kcal)	Protein (g)	Fat (g)	Iron (mg)	Vit. A (IU)	Thiamin (mg)	Riboflavin (mg)
Whole egg, large	1	50	75	80	6	6	1.0	260	0.04	0.15
Egg white	1	33	88	15	3	trace	trace	0	trace	0.09
Egg yolk	1	17	49	65	3	6	0.9	310	0.04	0.07

**Nutritive Value of Foods*. Home and Garden Bulletin No. 72. Washington, DC: U.S. Department of Agriculture, 1981.

Because certain yellow carotenoid pigments can be converted into vitamin A in the body, the question has been raised as to whether more highly colored egg yolks are a better source of vitamin A than pale-colored yolks. The predominant yellow pigment of egg yolk is a xanthophyll which is not changed to vitamin A in the body. Usually, however, deep-colored yolks are high in vitamin A content because the same rations that produce color in the yolks also contain more provitamin A, which the hen is able to convert into vitamin A and deposit in the yolk. Hens that do not have access to green or yellow feed and that produce pale yolks may be given vitamin A-supplemented rations. When this is done the pale yolks will be high in vitamin A content. The vitamin A content of egg yolk, therefore, cannot be predicted solely on the basis of the depth of the yellow color. In practice, egg producers usually feed sufficient green vegetation to give a yolk of medium color intensity.

The proteins of egg are of excellent nutritional quality. Because of the quality and the quantity of protein present, the egg is an important protein food in the diet of many people. The major protein in egg white is ovalbumin. The major proteins in the yolk are lipoproteins (proteins combined with lipid or fatty material). Cooked egg white is somewhat more completely digested and utilized than raw white, especially if raw whites are ingested clear or unbeaten. Raw egg yolk is probably as well utilized by the body as is cooked yolk. It is generally recommended that eggs be cooked before eating because they have been found to be infected sometimes with salmonella organisms that may produce illness in humans. These microorganisms, if present, can be destroyed by cooking.

Structure and Quality

The contents of an egg are held in a porous shell composed of approximately 95 percent calcium carbonate in crystal form. The shell allows an exchange of gases and loss of moisture from the egg. The shell of an egg is usually brown or white, depending on the breed of the hen, but the color of the shell has no effect on the flavor or quality of the contents. An air cell formed at the large end of the egg is produced on cooling by the separation of two thin fibrous protein membranes that are present between the shell and the egg white (Figure 13-1).

It has previously been suggested that the protective dull waxy coat, referred to as the *cuticle* or the *bloom* on the outside of the egg should not be washed off, as the porous shell may then permit odors, flavors, bacteria, and molds to enter the egg and may permit greater evaporation of moisture from the egg unless preventive measures are taken. However, dirt or soil on shells is probably the most prominent cause of the bacterial invasion of eggs. In commercial practice, therefore, dirty eggs are washed. The eggs are usually washed in automatic washers using alkaline cleaning compounds. Following washing, the eggs may be rinsed with a sanitizing agent. If eggs are washed properly, the undesirable effects of washing are kept at a minimum [13].

Egg white is composed of a thin and a thick portion. The proportion of thin and thick white may vary widely in different eggs and changes during storage under varying conditions. It has been estimated that about 20 to 25 percent of the total white of fresh eggs (1 to 5 days old) is thin white.

Surrounding the yolk is a thin membrane called the *vitelline membrane*. Extending from the vitelline membrane on opposite sides are two *chalazae* (singular, *chalaza*) that appear as small bits of thickened white and anchor the yolk in the center of the egg. The yolk is actually composed of layers of light and dark material. Marketed eggs are usually infertile and the germ will not develop. There is no difference in nutritive value between infertile and fertilized eggs but fertile eggs may tend to deteriorate more rapidly.

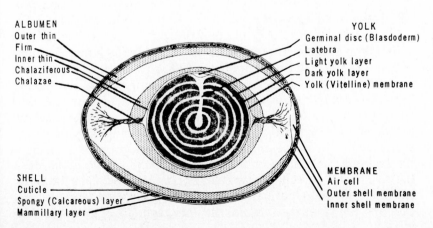

ALBUMEN
Outer thin
Firm
Inner thin
Chalaziferous
Chalazae

YOLK
Germinal disc (Blasdoderm)
Latebra
Light yolk layer
Dark yolk layer
Yolk (Vitelline) membrane

SHELL
Cuticle
Spongy (Calcareous) layer
Mammillary layer

MEMBRANE
Air cell
Outer shell membrane
Inner shell membrane

13-1 *The parts of an egg.* (Courtesy of the U.S. Department of Agriculture)

Characteristics of Fresh and Deteriorated Eggs

A very fresh egg, when broken onto a plate, stands up in rounded form, partly because of the viscosity of the thick portion of the egg white that surrounds the yolk. As eggs deteriorate, the percentage of thin white increases although the exact cause of this thinning of the thick white is not known. The yolk takes up water from the white and the yolk membrane stretches. When broken onto a plate, the deteriorated egg flattens and tends to spread over the plate. If stretched excessively by movement of water into the yolk, the yolk membrane is weakened and may break when the egg is removed from the shell. Separation of the yolk from the white is thus rendered difficult or impossible. The chalazae start to disintegrate and no longer hold the yolk in the center of the egg, and the yolk moves freely. As an egg ages, especially in a warm, dry atmosphere, there is loss of moisture through the shell and the air cell, which is very small in a fresh egg, increases in size.

The yolks of fresh eggs are slightly acid (usual pH 6.0 to 6.2), whereas the whites are alkaline in reaction (usual pH 7.6 to 7.9). A loss of carbon dioxide from the egg on storage results in increased alkalinity of both white and yolk. The whites may eventually reach a pH of 9.0 to 9.7. The pH of eggs may be kept lower or less alkaline during storage if the egg shells are coated with a thin layer of oil on the day the eggs are laid. It has been suggested that damage to some egg white proteins by a very alkaline pH results in a decreased volume of angel food cakes from these whites [17].

The flavor and odor of fresh eggs is affected by the feed of the hen and by her individuality. During storage, off flavors may be produced in eggs by the invasion of microorganisms or by the absorption of flavors from the environment. See pp. 313-314 for a discussion of egg storage.

Measures of Quality

Candling is the method used for determining the interior quality of eggs that go into trade channels (Figure 13-2). Hand candling is used very little in present commercial grading operations, having been replaced by automated equipment and mass scanning devices. However, it is still used for spot checking and is useful for teaching and demonstrating quality determination. In candling by hand, the egg is held up to an opening behind which is a source of strong light. As the light passes through the egg it shows the quality of the shell, the size of the air cell, the position and mobility of the yolk, blood spots, molds, and a developing embryo, if present. As eggs deteriorate and the chalazae weaken, the yolk tends to settle toward the

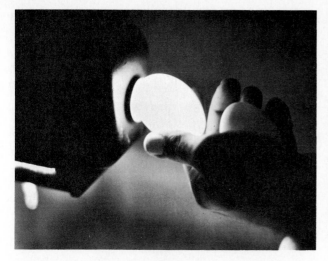

Eggs are held to a bright light during hand candling.

Mass scanning devices speed up the candling process.

shell rather than remain suspended in the firm white. Under such circumstances the yolk is more fully visible when the egg is candled. Dark yolks also cast a more distinct shadow than light-colored yolks. USDA grades for eggs are based on candled appearance.

Although candling is the best available method for rating unbroken eggs, it may not always be reliable in indicating the quality of the egg when it is opened. Some tests done on the broken-out egg include a measurement of the height of the thick white in relation to the weight of the egg (Haugh unit) and the measurement of the height of the yolk in relation to the width of the yolk (yolk index). Figure 13-3 shows the operation of an instrument for measuring Haugh units in a broken-out egg.

Grading and Sizing Eggs

The grading for quality of shell eggs is the classifying of the individual eggs according to established standards. The U.S. Department of Agriculture has formulated egg grade standards that are widely used throughout the country. These standards are summarized in Table 13-2 on p. 312. Egg grades are determined on the basis of the candled appearance of the shell, air cell, egg white, and yolk. The three consumer grades are U.S. Grade AA, U.S. Grade A, and U.S. Grade B, illustrated in Figures 13-4 and 13-5. U.S. Grade B eggs are less frequently found in retail stores. Grades AA and A have a large proportion of thick white that stands up around a firm high yolk. These eggs are especially good for frying and poaching, when appearance is important. Grade B eggs, which have thinner

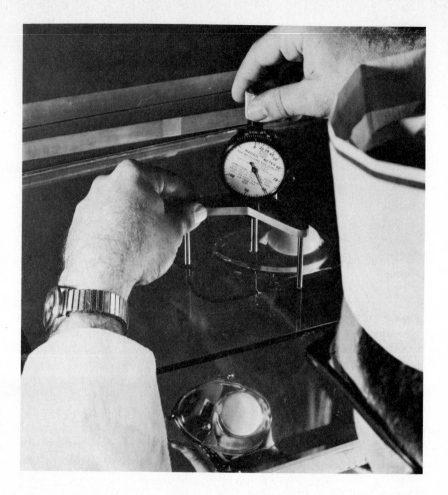

AA

A

B

whites and spread out more, are good for general baking and cooking. The nutritional value is similar in all grades. Eggs are divided
into grade groups on the basis of internal quality as illustrated in
Figure 13-6.

After eggs have been graded they must be handled properly since
egg quality is relatively unstable, even under favorable conditions.
The interior quality of the egg deteriorates from the time it is laid
until it is consumed. The decline in quality can be minimized, however, by proper care.

USDA grading services are available for individuals, firms, or
agencies that request them on a fee for service basis. Cooperative
agreements may be made between USDA and parties within each
state to supply official graders and services. The Egg Products Inspection Act of 1970 assures the consumer that only wholesome,
unadulterated, and truthfully labeled egg products will be
marketed.

13-5 *Know the eggs you buy. Both size (an indication of quantity) and grade (an indication of quality) should be considered in deciding which eggs to purchase.* (Courtesy of the U.S. Department of Agriculture)

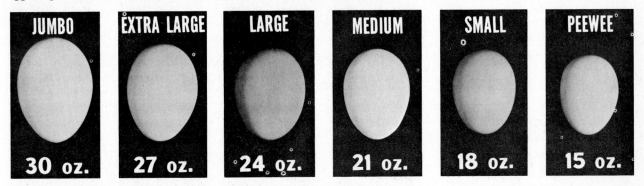

Six sizes for eggs are shown. Sizing is separate from grading. The weights shown in the illustration represent ounces per dozen eggs.

Characteristics of egg quality, with the yolk standing highest on the thick white of the U.S. Grade AA eggs, are evident in broken-out eggs and in poached eggs.

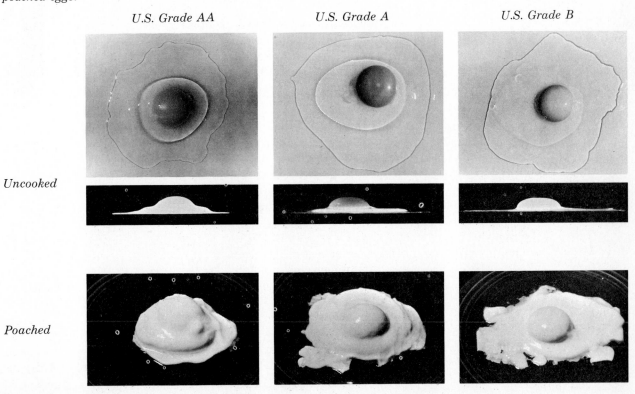

Table 13-2 *Summary of United States Standards for Quality of Individual Shell Eggs**

Quality Factor	Specifications for Each Quality Factor		
	AA Quality	A Quality	B Quality
Shell	Clean. Unbroken. Practically normal.	Clean. Unbroken. Practically normal.	Clean to slightly stained. Unbroken. Somewhat abnormal.
Air Cell	⅛ inch or less in depth. Unlimited movement and free or bubbly.	3⁄16 inch or less in depth. Unlimited movement and free or bubbly.	Over 3⁄16 inch in depth. Unlimited movement and free or bubbly.
White	Clear. Firm.	Clear. Reasonably firm.	Clear. Somewhat watery. Small blood and meat spots may be present.
Yolk	Outline slightly defined. Practically free from defects.	Outline fairly well defined. Practically free from defects.	Outline plainly visible. Enlarged and flattened. Clearly visible germ development but no blood.

*From [3].

Along with being graded for quality, eggs are also sorted out for size into six weight classes, which are shown in Figure 13-5. The commercial weighing and packaging of eggs may be automated as illustrated in Figure 13-7. Several sizes will usually be available to the consumer within each grade. Size in relation to cost per dozen is

13-6 *The graded quality of eggs declines with the time of holding.* (Courtesy of the U.S. Department of Agriculture)

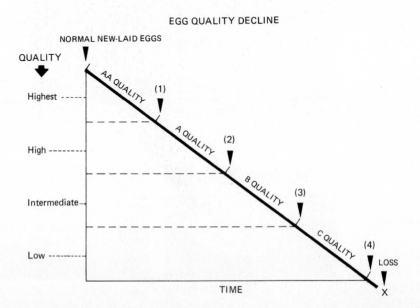

Automatic egg packaging equipment.

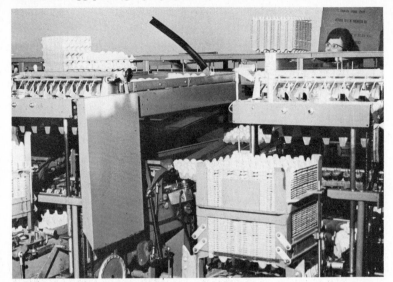

In-line scales. Eggs of different sizes are weighed and ejected at different points on the line.

13-7 *Eggs are handled and processed by automatic equipment.* (Courtesy of the U.S. Department of Agriculture)

an important factor in egg buying [11]. Eggs marketed in cartons will usually list on the carton the minimum weight per dozen in ounces. A shopper may easily divide this weight into the price per dozen to determine the cost per ounce of egg. The cost per ounce of the various sizes of eggs may then be compared to determine which is the best buy.

Another point to consider in buying eggs is the use for which they are purchased. There is no one best size to buy. Large eggs may be preferred for table use but for cooking purposes price in relation to size may be a more important consideration.

Recipes calling for a specific number of eggs are usually formulated on the basis of the large size. Actually, *measuring* or *weighing* eggs in recipes will give much more uniform results. If jumbo and extra large or small and peewee-sized eggs are used in a recipe, some adjustment should be made, reducing or increasing the number of eggs by one fourth to one third for the jumbo and extra large or for the small and peewee sizes, respectively. If a large number of eggs is used in a recipe, the potential for error becomes very great.

Commercial Cold Storage

Preservation

To equalize both egg prices and supplies, some of the eggs produced in the United States may be placed in commercial cold storage during periods of higher production. Eggs are usually stored at a temperature of −1.5° to 0° C (29° to 32° F), which is just above their freezing point. To keep well and to retain their quality, only eggs of original high quality should be stored. They will remain in desirable condition only if the storage room is well controlled as to humidity (85 to 90 percent), circulation of air, and freedom from objectionable odors. A controlled atmosphere of carbon dioxide or ozone is advantageous in maintaining quality. Eggs may retain Grade A quality for as long as 6 months in cold storage. If eggs were of good quality when they went into storage and if they have been successfully kept under controlled conditions, storage eggs may be of higher quality than many so-called fresh eggs on the market. Some changes occur in eggs as in any other food during storage. Enzyme action continued over a period of months may result in changes in flavor. These changes need not be objectionable over a period of 6 months or more. As previously stated, egg whites become thinner during storage and egg yolks absorb water from the white, but for essentially all cooking purposes storage eggs of good quality are entirely satisfactory.

Before being placed in cold storage, eggs may be dipped in light mineral oil [9]. The thin film of oil left on the eggs partially closes the pores in the shell, reducing the loss of moisture and carbon dioxide. If the oiling process is done at the proper time after laying, usually up to 12 hours, the pH of the egg will not rise appreciably on storage. It has been suggested [5] that this control of pH minimizes changes in the egg white proteins ovomucin and ovalbumin and retards the increase in permeability of the vitelline membrane around the yolk.

Home Storage

Deterioration of egg quality is more rapid when eggs are kept in a household refrigerator than when they are kept under carefully controlled commercial cold storage conditions. However, eggs may be satisfactorily kept under household refrigeration for several weeks. These eggs should be stored in a closed container to retard moisture loss. Uncovered egg storage areas that are now built into many refrigerators are not satisfactory for egg storage. The eggs tend to lose moisture fairly rapidly, resulting in greatly enlarged air cells in the eggs.

The method of home preservation of eggs using water glass (sodium silicate) to close the pores in the shell is rarely practiced today. Eggs broken out of the shell may be frozen for longer storage.

Freezing and Drying

Both freezing and drying are common methods of egg preservation, but eggs so preserved are more often used in commercial establishments than in home preparation.

The safe use of the freezing and drying methods of egg preservation is largely dependent upon the sterilization of equipment, scrupulous cleanliness, and the avoidance of contamination of the egg mass by the introduction of any unwholesome eggs. Bacteria of the salmonellae species are sometimes found in eggs [2]. It seems virtually impossible to completely prevent the occurrence of salmonellae organisms in liquid egg products unless pasteurization is used. The pasteurization of eggs must be done in such a way that it destroys bacteria while, at the same time, the functional properties (whipping and baking performances) are not damaged [14]. Usual pasteurization practice for liquid whole egg involves heat treatment at a temperature of 60° to 61.5° C (140° to 143° F) for not less than 3½ minutes. However, egg white proteins cannot tolerate the temperatures usually used to pasteurize whole eggs without becoming denatured, with consequent decreases in foaming power. Increasing the acidity of the egg whites before pasteurization seems to protect the proteins from damage by heat. The addition of a very small amount of sodium polyphosphate to egg whites and pasteurization at a temperature of 52° to 55° C (126° to 131° F) for 3½ minutes has also been recommended [15].

The functional properties of egg whites are not altered by freezing and thawing. However, frozen egg yolks become viscous and gummy on thawing unless they are mixed with sugar, salt, or syrup before freezing (see pp. 568–569 for directions on freezing eggs at home). It has been suggested that the freezing process destabilizes the surface of the tiny lipid-protein particles, called lipoproteins, in egg yolk and the fragments that are liberated then aggregate together on thawing to form a mesh-type structure or gel [16]. Although whole mixed eggs are often frozen without added salt or sugar, because of the presence of the yolk they probably retain their culinary qualities better if a stabilizer is added.

Drying is a satisfactory method for preserving eggs either as whole eggs or as separated yolks or whites. To retain their functional properties, as well as good color and flavor, whites require treatment to remove the last traces of glucose. This helps to control the Maillard or browning reaction during storage. Dried eggs keep best if the initial moisture content is low and if they are kept in a tightly sealed container. Low storage temperatures are also important in maintaining the quality of the dried products. Dried eggs may be reconstituted before use, or they may be sifted with dry ingredients and extra liquid may be used in a recipe. The latter method applies to the flour mixes on the market that contain dried egg.

General directions for use are to sift prior to measuring and to place lightly in a measuring cup or spoon before leveling off the top with a spatula or straight edge. For reconstitution, dried egg should be sprinkled over the surface of lukewarm water, stirred to moisten, and then beaten until smooth. Reconstituted dried whites are beaten very stiff for most if not all uses.

Eggs in Food Preparation

Eggs have numerous uses in food preparation [4]. Used alone or in combination with other foods they may constitute the protein dish of a meal. Certain properties, such as color, flavor, viscosity, emulsifying ability, and coagulability, make eggs valuable in many different cookery processes. (See Figure 13-8.)

The proteins of egg coagulate when heated, which makes possible the use of egg as a thickening agent in such dishes as custards, sauces, and puddings. The coagulation of egg protein, along with the viscosity of the uncooked egg, is the basis for the use of egg as a binding agent and as a coating to hold crumbs together for crust formation on breaded foods. The coagulation of egg increases the rigidity of cell walls and of crusts in numerous doughs and batters. The use of eggs for clarifying purposes is also dependent upon the coagulating property of the proteins of egg. The presence in the yolk of lipoproteins (lipid materials such as phospholipids in combination with protein) make the egg yolk valuable as an emulsifying agent. The surface activity of the proteins of egg also makes the egg useful in the production of films that hold air, thus creating a foam. This characteristic aids in the leavening of various food mixtures. Most

13-8 *The yolk of an egg may be separated from the white by pouring the yolk back and forth from one half of the broken shell to the other. Each egg should be broken separately into a small dish before combining with other eggs or ingredients.* (Courtesy of Black Star)

foods to which eggs are added are improved in color and in flavor by the inclusion of egg in the mixture.

Heat Coagulation of Egg Proteins

Both egg white and egg yolk proteins coagulate when heated and, as previously stated, can therefore be used for thickening. Egg functions better as a thickener if beaten only enough to blend the egg mass smoothly. Beating to the extent of incorporating a considerable amount of air results in the floating of egg foam on the surface of the mixture to be thickened. The following factors affect the heat coagulation of egg proteins.

Concentration and Part of Egg Used. The temperature at which egg proteins coagulate and the time required for coagulation depend in part on the proportion of egg in any mixture. At a moderate rate of heating, undiluted egg white begins to coagulate and change from a clear mass to an opaque substance at a temperature of about 60° C (140° F). The egg white gradually becomes completely opaque and more firm as the temperature is increased above 60° C (140° F). Coagulation is probably complete at a temperature of 65° C (149° F).

Egg yolk proteins require a slightly higher temperature for coagulation than do those of egg white. Because little color change occurs in egg yolk at the beginning of coagulation, the exact temperature at which thickening starts is more difficult to judge than is the case with egg white, which loses its transparency and becomes opaque white on coagulation. The beginning of coagulation and the thickening of undiluted egg yolk probably occurs at a temperature of about 65° C (149° F). At a temperature of approximately 70° C (158° F) the yolk is fully coagulated and will not flow. Coagulated egg yolk is solid but has a mealy texture. To achieve complete coagulation, whole egg must be heated to the temperature required for yolk protein coagulation since whole egg includes the yolk.

Dilution of egg increases the temperature at which coagulation occurs. If an egg is diluted with 1 cup of milk the coagulation temperature of the mixture is around 80° C (176° F), although the exact temperature varies with the rate of heating and the presence or absence of other substances in the dispersion.

Time and Temperature. The rate of coagulation and the amount of coagulum formed in a definite time increase with increasing temperature. The character of the coagulum formed when egg white is heated at high temperature is firm, even tough, as compared with the soft, tender, more evenly coagulated product obtained when coagulation takes place at lower temperatures.

The toughness and greater shrinkage of the protein coagulated at a high temperature is the basis for the recommended use of low or moderate temperatures for egg cookery. Temperatures used for egg cookery need not be so low as 70° C (158° F), although that temperature, maintained for a sufficient length of time, will eventually bring about complete coagulation of egg proteins. If eggs are cooked in water, the water should not boil. Water at a temperature of about 85° C (185° F) will produce a texture that is tender, yet firm, and coagulation will take place in a noticeably shorter time than is required at a temperature of 70° to 75° C (158° to 167° F). In cooking an omelet in a skillet over direct heat, the heat should be kept low so that the mass cooks slowly and can be heated uniformly throughout without toughening the bottom layers. The coagulation of a puffy omelet may be finished in a moderate oven. Oven temperatures from 300° to 350° F have been found to be satisfactory for cooking eggs and egg dishes although there are indications that somewhat higher temperatures are also satisfactory if time is carefully controlled. Placing egg dishes in a pan of water when baking them in the oven helps to protect the egg product from becoming overcooked.

Effect of Rate of Heating. Rapidly heated egg mixtures, such as custards, coagulate at a higher temperature than similar mixtures that are slowly heated. The fact that the coagulation temperature with rapid heating is very close to the curdling temperature means that a rapidly cooked custard is more likely to curdle than one that is slowly heated. A slowly heated custard can, nevertheless, curdle if it is heated to too high a temperature.

Effect of Added Substances. Egg mixtures containing sugar require a higher temperature for coagulation than do mixtures containing no sugar. Slightly acid egg mixtures, such as those with added dates or raisins, omelets made with tomato or orange juice, and Hollandaise sauce containing lemon juice, coagulate more rapidly and the coagulum formed is more firm than that of mixtures that are not slightly acidified. Great care, however, must be exercised to avoid too great acidity, which results in curdling. Certain salts, such as chlorides, phosphates, sulfates, and lactates, aid in gel formation in cooked egg mixtures.

Beating as a Mechanical Method of Coagulation

As egg whites are beaten, they first become foamy and then form soft peaks. With additional beating more stiff peaks are formed but overbeating produces dryness (Figure 13-9). Part of the protein in the films surrounding the air cells of beaten egg white foams is coagulated in the beating process. If overcoagulated, the beaten white becomes very rigid and takes on a dry, lumpy appearance because of the breaking of many air cells. Undesirable effects on

13-9 *Stages of beating egg white foams.*

Egg whites beaten to a foamy stage.

Soft peaks.

foam volume and stability may be expected when whites are over-beaten. The foam is brittle and inelastic and large amounts of liquid will drain from it on standing. This type of foam is undesirable for use in food preparation.

For most uses in food preparation, including the making of souf-flés, soft meringues, and puffy omelets and the beating of egg whites with sugar for angel cakes, egg whites should be beaten to form moderately stiff peaks while the tips should fall over when the beater is withdrawn from the beaten whites. The foam should retain a shiny, smooth surface and the mass should flow very slowly if the bowl is partially inverted. Air cells should be quite fine and of even size. Reconstituted dried egg whites, such as those in angel cake mixes using a two-stage mixing method, are beaten to a very stiff stage, as indicated in package directions.

Moderately stiff peaks but still moist and glossy.

Whole eggs can be beaten much stiffer than might be expected if beating is continued for a long enough time. As a result of the presence of the fat from the yolk there is little danger of overbeating the whole egg.

Egg yolks increase slightly in volume when beaten. They change to a pale lemon color as air is incorporated and the mass may become thick and full of fine cells. It is difficult if not impossible to beat a small quantity of egg yolk thoroughly unless a small dish of narrow diameter and a small egg beater are used.

Because beaten eggs, particularly beaten egg whites, are used in so many cooked dishes, they require favorable handling in order to accomplish their purpose. A number of factors have been found to affect the whipping quality of eggs.

Thin and Thick Whites. The character of the foam produced from beating thin egg whites is different from that produced by beating thick, viscous whites. The foam from thin whites is more fluffy and

Stiff, dry peaks of overbeaten egg whites.

319

has less body than the foam from thick whites. The volume of cooked products, such as angel food cake and meringues, is greater when thick whites are used rather than thin whites. Thick whites seem to give a more stable foam even though thin whites may initially beat to a larger volume than thick, viscous whites.

Temperature. Eggs at room temperature whip more easily, quickly, and to a larger volume than do eggs at refrigerator temperature.

Type of Beater Used. The type of beater used as well as the fineness of the wires or blades of the beater can affect the size of the air cells that are obtained and the ease with which the eggs are beaten. Thick blades or wires do not divide egg whites as easily as fine wires, and the resulting air cells are therefore larger. All cells will become smaller with longer beating regardless of the type of beater used. Egg whisks sometimes give a larger volume of beaten egg mass than do rotary types of beaters but the cells are also larger.

Types of Container in Which Eggs Are Beaten. Bowls with small rounded bottoms and sloping sides are preferable in shape to bowls with large flat bottoms because, in the former, the beater can more easily pick up the egg mass. The size of bowl must obviously be adapted to the amount of egg to be beaten. If whisks are used for beating egg whites a large plate or platter is preferable to a bowl for holding the whites because of the over-and-over strokes that are used.

Effect of Added Substances.

Fat. Fat in the form of refined cottonseed oil has been shown to interfere with whipping if present to the extent of 0.5 percent or more. The presence of small amounts of yolk in egg white greatly retards foam formation. This effect of retarding or preventing the development of a foam is thought to be the result of the fat, probably the lipoproteins, in the egg yolk. The directions on packages of angel cake mix indicate that plastic bowls should not be used for mixing because of the difficulty in removing all fat from the surface of the plastic.

Salt. A small amount of salt added to egg whites (1 gram to 40 grams egg white) has been reported to decrease the volume and stability of the foam and to increase the whipping time [8]. Egg white foams are less elastic when beaten with salt as compared to being beaten without salt.

Acid. The addition of acid or acid salts to egg white decreases the alkalinity of the white and increases the stability of the egg white foam. The whipping time is increased. A stiff foam and a large foam volume result from adding acid before or shortly after foaming has started.

Sugar. Sugar retards the denaturation and coagulation of egg proteins and increases the beating time required to attain maximum volume. It is, therefore, important not to add sugar before beating is started and to add the sugar very gradually after foaming has occurred. When sugar is present in an egg white foam, the possibility of overbeating is greatly decreased and the foam is stabilized. In the preparation of any sugar-containing egg white foam it is probably best to beat the egg white to soft peaks before sugar is added. Otherwise the beating time is greatly prolonged. The sugar should be added gradually, possibly 1 tablespoon at a time, with beating in between additions.

Specific Methods of Egg Preparation

Poached Eggs. Poaching consists of cooking the edible portion of an egg in hot water, milk, cream, or other liquids. To guard against scorching, eggs poached in milk or cream should have the dish suspended over hot water. For adequate coagulation of egg proteins to occur, the liquid in which the eggs are poached need not approach the boiling point. However, as previously stated, a temperature of about 85° C (185° F) will still maintain the desirable tender quality of the coagulated egg while requiring less time than when the egg is poached at a temperature of 70° to 75° C (158° to 167° F). Because the addition of cold eggs to hot liquid will immediately lower the temperature of the liquid, it is possible to have the temperature of the liquid at the boiling point when the eggs are added. The heat can then be regulated to keep the liquid at a simmering temperature of about 85° C (185° F). If the water is not hot enough when the egg is added, the egg white will spread throughout the liquid rather than set quickly and hold its original shape.

The liquid in the pan used for poaching should be deep enough to cover the eggs in order that a film of coagulated white may form over the yolk. Salt and acid added to the cooking water are both aids in coagulation but are not necessary. If used, 2 teaspoons of vinegar and ½ to 1 teaspoon of salt per pint of water are effective. Eggs poached in salted water are more opaque white and less shiny than eggs poached in unsalted water. They may also appear puckered or ruffled as they do when poached in boiling water. The time required for coagulation will depend on the temperature of water but at a water temperature of 85° C (185° F) the time required is about 4 to 6 minutes.

Most people enjoy a poached egg that is rounded with a film of coagulated white covering the yolk. The yolk is liquid or semiliquid and the white completely coagulated but jellylike and tender (Figure 13-5). However, there is a wide range of individual preference in the preparation of poached eggs and other types of egg cookery as well.

The freshness of eggs and thickness of whites are factors in successfully attaining the suggested standard. For example, eggs with thin whites will tend to spread out in a flat layer on the bottom of the pan. The technique of adding the egg to the water is also important to the quality in the cooked egg. It is usually desirable to remove the egg from the shell and place in a small flat dish from which the egg can easily and quickly be slipped into the poaching water.

Soft-cooked Eggs (in the Shell).   Several methods are possible for cooking eggs in the shell. The objectives are to attain a tender coagulated white and a yolk that is either liquid or semiliquid, according to personal preference. Water maintained at boiling temperature for the whole cooking period has a definite toughening effect on that part of the white lying near the shell, but the time required for coagulation is shorter than when water below boiling is used to cook the eggs. Either of the following two methods may be used to ensure satisfactory tenderness of the coagulated white:

Method I.   Allow 1 pint of boiling water for each egg. Add eggs to the water (the temperature of the water will immediately be lowered). Turn off the heat, cover the pan, and allow the eggs to remain in the water for 4 to 6 minutes depending on the degree of coagulation desired.

Method II.   Add eggs to water at a simmering but not boiling temperature of about 85° C (185° F). Maintain this temperature for 4 to 6 minutes.

Hard-cooked Eggs (in the Shell).   The white of hard-cooked eggs should be firmly coagulated, yet tender. The yolk should be dry and mealy. If the yolk is waxy, it is not sufficiently cooked. The surface of the yolk should be yellow, with no dark green deposit. Hard-cooked eggs may be prepared by either of the methods previously outlined for soft-cooked eggs but with an extension of the time that the eggs remain in water. The eggs may need to stay in the water for 30 to 40 minutes in Method I and 20 to 25 minutes in Method II. One group of researchers [12] prepared hard-cooked eggs by two methods:

1. Place the eggs in cold water in a covered pan, bring the water to boiling, remove the pan from the heat, and hold for 25 minutes.
2. Carefully place the eggs in boiling water, reduce the heat, and simmer (at a temperature of 85° C or 185° F) eggs for 18 minutes.

In both methods the eggs were submerged in cold running water for 5 minutes at the end of the cooking period. They reported that method 2 produced eggs that were easier to peel and rated higher in all criteria than those prepared by starting with cold water.

Cooling hard-cooked eggs in cold water immediately after cooking facilitates the removal of the shell. However, very fresh eggs (less than 48 hours old) are difficult to peel without considerable white adhering to the shell. The rapid cooling of cooked eggs also aids in the prevention of a dark green deposit, ferrous sulfide (FeS), which tends to form on the outside of the coagulated yolk and detracts from its appearance. Most of the iron in an egg is present in the yolk. Sulfur occurs in about equal amounts in yolk and white, but the sulfur compounds in the white are more labile to heat than those in the yolk. Hydrogen sulfide (H_2S) is therefore easily formed from the sulfur compounds in the white during prolonged heating. Reaction of the iron in the yolk with hydrogen sulfide from the white produces the greenish ferrous sulfide deposit. Hydrogen sulfide forms more readily when the pH of the egg is markedly alkaline, as in an aged egg. Ferrous sulfide forms very slowly until the yolk reaches a temperature of about 70° C (158° F) and seldom occurs in fresh eggs cooked 30 minutes at a temperature of 85° C (185° F). The green color tends to form less in eggs that are cooled rapidly because the hydrogen sulfide gas is drawn to the lowered pressure at the surface of the cooling egg and thus combines less readily with iron at the surface of the yolk. However, if an egg is cooked 30 minutes in boiling water, the ferrous sulfide will probably form regardless of cooling. Also, in older eggs that are very alkaline, the green color may be produced in spite of precautions taken during cooking [1].

In summary, fresh eggs of high quality should be selected for the preparation of hard-cooked eggs. The temperature of the water in which the eggs are cooked should be maintained below the boiling point and the time of cooking should be no longer than is required to coagulate both the white and the yolk. The eggs should be cooled as quickly as possible after cooking.

Fried Eggs. Because of the difficulty in controlling the temperature of the fat and of the pan, fried eggs may often be somewhat tough and for this reason are among the preparations requiring the greatest skill. If excess fat is used during the frying of eggs or if the hot fat is dipped with a spoon and poured over the top surface of the eggs as they cook, the eggs may be too greasy for many preferences. A suggested method of preparation is to use only enough fat to prevent the eggs from sticking to the pan and to provide the desired flavor. The pan should be sufficiently hot to coagulate the egg white, but not hot enough to toughen it or to decompose the fat. A cover on the pan provides steam, which cooks the top surface of the egg. A small amount of water may be added to the pan just before covering. The water not only furnishes more steam but tends to prevent toughening or hardening of the edges of the eggs. If the underside of a fried egg is brown and the edges crisp and frilled, the pan and fat were probably too hot unless there is a definite preference for crispness in a fried egg (Figure 13-10).

Omelets. Omelets are of two types: plain or French, and foamy or

puffy. The puffy omelet has a more spongy texture than the French omelet because of the greater incorporation of air. The French omelet may be made with or without small amounts of liquid. The liquid used in omelets may be water, milk, cream, or acid juices such as tomato and orange.

Proportions for French Omelet

4 eggs	½ t (3 g) salt
4 T (59 ml) liquid	f g pepper

Whole eggs are beaten enough to blend white and yolk, then diluted slightly with liquid and seasoned.

The mixture is cooked in a greased pan until it is coagulated, after which the omelet is folded (Figure 13-11). To aid in more rapid coagulation, a spatula may be used to carefully lift the edges of the egg mass as it coagulates, thus allowing the liquid portion on top to flow underneath where it may come in contact with the pan. Another aid consists of covering the pan to furnish steam to cook the top surface of the omelet. The omelet should be cooked slowly, keeping the heat low to avoid toughening the coagulated eggs. It may be considered done when the liquid is thickened but not totally set.

Proportions for Puffy Omelet

4 eggs	½ t (3 g) salt
2 to 4 T (30 to 59 ml) liquid	f g pepper
⅛ t cream of tartar	

13-11 *Folding and serving a plain omelet.* (Courtesy of the Poultry and Egg National Board)

The cream of tartar is added to the egg whites and they are beaten until moderately stiff. The liquid, salt, and pepper are added to the egg yolks and the mixture beaten until it is so thick and lemon-colored that it will pile. The beaten yolk mixture is folded into the beaten whites, care being taken to blend the mass evenly and yet avoid too much loss of air.

The greased pan in which the omelet is cooked should be hot enough to start coagulation but not hot enough to toughen the coagulated layer in contact with the pan, or to brown it excessively. The omelet is cooked slowly until light brown underneath.

Several methods may be used to coagulate the top of the foamy omelet:

1. A cover on the pan during part of the cooking period forms steam, which cooks the top layer of egg. The cover must not stick to the omelet, as the omelet is likely to collapse when the cover is removed. There is some risk in this method as a covered pan is hotter than an open pan and overheating may cause the omelet to collapse. If the cover is lifted occasionally and the omelet is cooked successfully by this method, the omelet is usually very tender and moist, partly because it cooks in less time and partly because less evaporation occurs.

2. When the mass is coagulated to within ¼ to ⅓ inch of the top, the omelet pan may be placed in a moderate oven to dry the top (Figure 13-12).

3. Following method 1, the pan may be held in a broiler to dry the top. This method must be used with caution as a broiler flame may very easily overheat the mass and cause collapse.

4. The omelet may be cooked in an oven at a temperature of 300° to 350° F for the entire time.

Soufflés. Soufflés are similar to foamy omelets except that they have a thick white sauce base and contain additional ingredients such as grated cheese, vegetable pulp, or ground meats. Dessert soufflés are sweet and may contain such ingredients as lemon, strawberry, and chocolate. Because the proportion of egg is slightly lower in soufflés than in omelets, or because of the protection to the egg furnished by the starchy white sauce and some of the additional ingredients used, somewhat less skill is required in making a soufflé than in making a foamy omelet. The percentage of egg present is sufficient, however, to require moderate temperatures and the application of other principles of egg cookery. Soufflés are usually baked, although they may be steamed. If they are baked, the dish containing the mixture is often placed in a pan of hot water for protection against excessive heating.

Custards. A true custard consists only of eggs, milk, sugar, and flavoring. No starchy agent is added. Custards are of two types: (1) the stirred or soft custard, which is given a creamy consistency by being stirred while it is cooking, and (2) the baked custard, which is allowed to coagulate without stirring. The baked custard must contain sufficient egg to produce a firm mass, particularly if it is to be turned from the mold in serving. The proportion of egg to milk may be the same for baked and stirred custards. However, less egg may be used in stirred custard if a thin consistency is desired.

Proportions for Custards

1 c (237 ml) milk	2 T (25 g) sugar
1 to 1½ eggs or 2 to 3 yolks	¼ t vanilla or ¹⁄₁₆ t nutmeg

13-12 *Preparation of a puffy omelet.* (Courtesy of the Poultry and Egg National Board)

Cook the omelet slowly until it is lightly browned on the bottom.

After drying the top of the omelet in a moderate oven, test it for doneness with a spatula inserted in the center. The spatula should come out clean.

Make a shallow crease across the middle of the omelet.

Fold the omelet over and carefully transfer it to a serving platter.

(To measure ½ egg, mix together white and yolk of whole egg; then divide into two equal portions by measuring 1 tablespoon at a time.)

Baked Custard

Because the egg is used for thickening, it is beaten only enough to blend the white and yolk well. Sugar may be added to the egg or dissolved in the milk. Milk is usually scalded before being added to the egg mixture. Scalding hastens the cooking and helps retain a mild, sweet flavor, but does not give a smoother custard. Flavoring must be added when the mixture is prepared for cooking.

It is desirable to place the custard cups in a pan of hot water as a protection against overheating, even though a moderate oven temperature may be used (about 350° F). Custards, placed in a pan of very hot water, may be baked at a 400° F oven temperature for a much shorter time than when a 350° F oven temperature is used. However, care must be exercised in removing the custard from the oven as soon as it is coagulated in order to avoid undesirable overcooking.

The baked custard is done when the tip of a knife inserted half way between the center and outside comes out clean (Figure 13-13). An overcooked custard separates sufficiently to appear watery. The separation of water from the gel is called *syneresis*. The custard may also appear porous and contain holes, especially on the outer surfaces, when the custard is unmolded. The top surface may be concave and browned. In an overcooked custard the egg proteins that form the mesh-like gel structure apparently shrink and squeeze out some of the liquid that was held in the meshes.

Soft Custard

The mixture of egg, milk, and sugar is prepared in the same manner as for baked custard. The vanilla, because of its volatility, is added after the other ingredients are cooked. As previously mentioned, custards that are cooked more slowly coagulate more completely at a lower temperature than custards which are cooked rapidly. There is less danger of curdling and both consistency and flavor are better in stirred custards cooked relatively slowly. The total cooking time should probably be 12 to 15 minutes. The mixture should be heated more rapidly at first and then more slowly, stirring thoroughly and rapidly during the entire process.

It is desirable to keep water in the lower part of the double boiler under the boiling point, particularly after the custard becomes hot (70° to 75° C or 158° to 167° F).

Constant stirring is necessary to prevent lumping. Stirring separates the coagulated particles, giving a creamy consistency regardless

13-13 *Custards make attractive and nutritious desserts.*

A baked custard is done when the tip of a knife comes out clean after being inserted into the custard about halfway between the center and the outside.

A baked custard that is overcooked has a porous surface when it is unmolded. Liquid seeps from the gel structure in a process called syneresis.

Unmolded baked custards may be served with fruit sauce. (Courtesy of the Poultry and Egg National Board)

A stirred custard does not coat the spoon during the beginning stages of cooking.

A stirred custard coats the spoon when it is done and should be cooled quickly to prevent curdling.

of the amount of egg used. The tendency is to cook a soft custard until it appears as thick as is desired but caution should be exercised. The custard will be thicker when it is cold. When the custard coats the spoon well (Figure 13-13) it should be removed from the heat and be either poured into a cold dish or suspended in cold water in the pan used for cooking.

Overheating a stirred custard results in curdling. A very slightly curdled custard may be improved if it is beaten with a rotary beater but such treatment is valueless for excessively curdled custards. In an overcooked custard the coagulated proteins shrink and separate out from the more liquid portion of the mixture, giving an appearance of curds. Also, the flavor of an overcooked custard tends to be strong and sulfury.

A stirred custard may be used in creating some interesting and delicious desserts. For example, hard meringue shells may be filled with crushed or whole sweetened strawberries or other fruit and the custard poured over the fruit. This may then be topped with whipped cream. Or, the custard may be flavored with caramelized sugar and then poured into individual serving dishes. Small soft meringues that have been previously baked may be placed on top of the custard.

Meringues. Meringues are of two types: the soft meringue used for pies and puddings, and the hard meringue generally used as a crisp dessert base or as a cookie.

Proportions for Soft Meringues

1 egg white	f g salt
2 T (25 g) sugar	1/8 t flavoring (if desired)
1/16 t cream of tartar (optional)	

The following factors are of importance in obtaining a soft, fine-textured meringue that is tender, cuts easily without tearing, and does not show leakage (syneresis) or beading on top of the baked meringue:

1. When the egg whites are partially beaten (possibly to a soft foam), sugar is gradually added, 1/2 to 1 tablespoon at a time, and the beating is continued until the mixture is stiff but with soft peaks that still tip over.
2. The meringue should be placed on a *hot* filling.
3. The meringue should be baked at a temperature of 375° F for 12 to 18 minutes, depending upon the depth of the meringue.

Heating must be sufficient throughout the soft meringue to destroy any salmonellae organisms that may be present in the eggs.

Meringues baked at moderate oven temperatures may be slightly sticky, as compared to those baked at high oven temperatures, but the moderate temperature produces an attractive evenly browned product that is safe to eat.

Two problems that may be encountered in soft meringues are "weeping" or leaking of liquid from the bottom of the meringue and "beading" which is the appearance of tiny droplets of syrup on the surface of the baked meringue as it stands [7, 10]. Weeping apparently results from undercooking the meringue. It can also occur as a result of underbeating the egg whites. Placing the meringue on a hot filling aids in achieving complete coagulation of the egg proteins. Beading is usually attributed to overcooking or overcoagulation of the egg white proteins. It can also result from failure to dissolve the sugar sufficiently when beating into the meringue.

Proportions for Hard Meringues

1 egg white	¹⁄₁₆ t cream of tartar
¼ c (50 g) sugar	f g salt
⅛ t vanilla	

Cream of tartar is added to the egg white and it is beaten until a soft foam begins to form. Salt and flavoring may be added at this point or even earlier. Sugar is added gradually and beaten into the egg white; beating is continued until the mass is very stiff. Spoonfuls are dropped on a baking sheet covered with heavy paper and the meringues are baked at a low oven temperature (about 250° F) for 40 to 60 minutes depending on the size of the meringues.

If a temperature lower than 250° F can be maintained for a longer time, the effect is one of drying instead of baking the meringue and gives even better results. Well-insulated ovens that hold the heat for several hours may be preheated, after which the heat is turned off entirely.

Desirable meringues of this type are crisp, tender, and white in appearance. If the meringues are used fresh the centers may be slightly moist but should not be gummy. If they are to be held for several hours, it is desirable to dry the centers. They may bake longer provided they are not becoming too brown or they may be allowed to remain in the oven until they are cool after the heat is turned off. Gumminess in hard meringues may result from the use of too much sugar, underbaking, too rapid baking, and too short a time of baking.

(For the use of eggs as emulsifiers, see pp. 177 and 349).

Microwave Cooking. Eggs and egg dishes cook quickly in a microwave oven. Heating them too fast or too long toughens them. Microwaves tend to cook the yolk somewhat faster than the white.

This problem is reduced by mixing the yolk and white together as with scrambled eggs or by surrounding the egg with liquid as in poaching. Eggs cannot be cooked in the shell by microwaves or they may explode. Eggs may be fried in a little fat if a browning dish is available.

Egg Substitutes

The food industry has responded to the desire of some consumers to have a low cholesterol egg product by marketing egg substitutes in both liquid and dry forms. Most of the available egg substitute products contain no egg yolk but have a high concentration of egg white (over 80 percent). To provide yolklike properties to the egg white mixture, various ingredients are used. These include, in different products, corn oil and nonfat dry milk; soy protein isolate, soybean oil, and egg white solids; and calcium caseinate, nonfat dry milk, and corn oil. A few products on the market do contain small amounts of egg yolk. Most of the egg substitutes are free or almost free of cholesterol and contain considerably less fat than whole egg. The fat in egg substitutes is also more unsaturated.

Egg substitutes have been compared to whole egg when used in various food products [6]. Custards made from egg substitute products showed less sag and spread than did whole egg custards. Yellow cakes prepared with egg substitutes were higher in volume than those made with whole eggs but were less desirable in flavor and overall acceptability. Scrambled whole eggs were also superior to the substitute products in flavor, tenderness, and overall acceptability.

Study Questions

1. a. Compare the chemical composition of whole egg, egg white, and egg yolk, indicating major differences.
   b. What major protein is found in egg white?
   c. What types of proteins predominate in egg yolk?
2. Describe the following parts of an egg and indicate the location for each:
   a. Cuticle or bloom
   b. Shell
   c. Outer membrane
   d. Inner membrane
   e. Air cell
   f. Thin white
   g. Thick white
   h. Chalazae
   i. Vitelline membrane
   j. Yolk
3. a. Compare the major characteristics of fresh and deteriorated eggs.
   b. How can freshness best be maintained in eggs during storage?

4. a. List the USDA consumer grades for eggs and describe the major characteristics of each grade.
   b. Describe the process by which eggs are graded.
5. a. Explain why eggs are usually pasteurized before freezing or drying.
   b. What special problem is usually encountered in the freezing of egg yolks and how may this problem be solved?
6. List several different uses for eggs in food preparation.
7. Egg proteins coagulate on heating and can, therefore, be used for thickening purposes in cooking. Describe the effect of each of the following factors on the temperature of coagulation:
   a. Source of egg protein (white or yolk)
   b. Rate of heating
   c. Dilution
   d. Addition of sugar
   e. Addition of acid
8. Describe the various changes or stages that occur as egg white is mechanically beaten to a very stiff dry foam.
9. Describe the effect of each of the following on the volume and/or stability of egg white foam:
   a. Thickness of the white
   b. Temperature of the white
   c. Type of beater used
   d. Type of container used
   e. Addition of salt
   f. Addition of acid
   g. Addition of sugar
10. Describe and explain an appropriate procedure for preparing:
    a. Poached eggs
    b. Soft cooked eggs in the shell
    c. Hard cooked eggs in the shell
    d. Fried eggs
    e. Omelets, plain or French and foamy or puffy
11. a. Describe appropriate procedures for preparing stirred custard and baked custard and explain why each step in the procedures is important.
    b. Why should precautions be taken to avoid overheating custards during preparation? Explain.
12. Describe major differences in preparation and use for soft and hard meringues.

References

1. Baker, R. C., J. Darfler, and A. Lifshitz. 1967. Factors affecting the discoloration of hard-cooked egg yolks. *Poultry Science* **46,** 664.
2. Baker, R. C., J. P. Goff, and J. F. Timoney. 1980. Prevalence of salmonellae on eggs from poultry farms in New York state. *Poultry Science* **59,** 289.
3. *Egg Grading Manual.* Agriculture Handbook No. 75. Washington, DC: U.S. Department of Agriculture, 1983.

4. *Eggs in Family Meals*. Home and Garden Bulletin No. 103. Washington, DC: U.S. Department of Agriculture, 1975.

5. Froning, G. W., and M. H. Swanson. 1964. Oiled versus unoiled eggs for short storage periods. 2. Some chemical and physical changes. *Poultry Science* **43**, 494.

6. Gardner, F. A., M. L. Beck, and J. H. Denton. 1982. Functional quality comparison of whole egg and selected egg substitute products. *Poultry Science* **61**, 75.

7. Gillis, J. N., and N. K. Fitch, 1956. Leakage of baked soft meringue topping. *Journal of Home Economics* **48**, 703.

8. Hanning, F. 1945. Effect of sugar or salt upon denaturation produced by beating and upon the ease of formation and the stability of egg white foams. *Iowa State College Journal of Science* **20**, 10.

9. Heath, J. L., and S. L. Owens. 1978. Effect of oiling variables on storage of shell eggs at elevated temperatures. *Poultry Science* **57**, 930.

10. Hester, E. E., and C. J. Personius. 1949. Factors affecting the beading and leaking of soft meringues. *Food Technology* **3**, 236.

11. *How to Buy Eggs*. Home and Garden Bulletin No. 144. Washington, DC: U.S. Department of Agriculture, 1975.

12. Irmiter, T. F., L. E. Dawson, and J. G. Reagan. 1970. Methods of preparing hard cooked eggs. *Poultry Science* **49**, 1232.

13. Kinner, J. A., and W. A. Moats. 1981. Effect of temperature, pH, and detergent on survival of bacteria associated with shell eggs. *Poultry Science* **60**, 761.

14. Kline, L., and T. F. Sugihara. 1966. Effects of pasteurization on egg products. *Baker's Digest* **40**, 40 (August).

15. Kohl, W. F. 1971. Pasteurizing egg whites. *Food Technology* **25**, 102 (November).

16. Kurisaki, J., S. Kaminogawa, and K. Yamauchi. 1980. Studies on freeze-thaw gelation of very low density lipoprotein from hen's egg yolk. *Journal of Food Science* **45**, 463.

17. Meehan, J. J., T. F. Sugihara, and L. Kline. 1962. Relationships between shell egg handling factors and egg product properties. *Poultry Science* **41**, 892.

18. Parsons, A. H. 1982. Structure of the eggshell. *Poultry Science* **61**, 2013.

Fats and Emulsions

Properties of Fats

In food preparation we are mostly concerned with one group of *lipids* or fat-like substances. These are called *neutral fats* or *triglycerides* and make up the major part of fats found in foods such as meat, cheese, butter, and margarine as well as in the more purified fats such as vegetable oils, shortenings, and lard.

The chemical structure of triglyceride molecules, showing how they contain three fatty acids combined with glycerol, is discussed on pp. 68–69. In common usage, fats are solid at room temperature whereas oils are liquid at room temperature but they are both made up of 99 percent triglyceride molecules.

The melting point of fats is greatly influenced by the types of fatty acids they contain. When fats contain a relatively high proportion of *saturated* fatty acids (such as palmitic and stearic acids shown on p. 69), they have a relatively high melting point and are usually solid at room temperature. In their chemical structure, saturated fatty acids do not have any double bonds between carbon atoms; the carbon atoms are holding all of the hydrogen atoms that they can hold. In other words, they are *saturated* with hydrogen. However, when fats contain a relatively high proportion of *unsaturated* fatty acids (such as oleic and linoleic acids shown on p. 69), they have a relatively low melting point and are oils at room temperature. Unsaturated fatty acids have one or more double bonds between carbon atoms to which more hydrogen could be added. They are, therefore, *unsaturated* with hydrogen. If fatty acids contain two or more double bonds, they are commonly referred to as *polyunsaturated*. Linoleic and linolenic acids are examples of polyunsaturated fatty acids. Polyunsaturated fats are fats containing a fairly large proportion of polyunsaturated fatty acids. Oils, such as corn, soybean, cottonseed, and safflower, are commonly called polyunsaturated fats.

All food fats are mixtures of triglycerides, containing different kinds of triglyceride molecules. Because of this they usually do not have a sharp melting point but melt over a range of temperatures. They also show wide variation in consistency and creaming properties.

Fats that are moldable and can be creamed (softened by being mixed with the incorporation of air) are said to exhibit *plasticity*. Plastic fats contain some triglyceride molecules that have associated together to form solid crystals and some liquid triglyceride molecules. The type and size of the crystals influence the performance of fats in baked products and pastry.

Fats are commonly used in baked products for their shortening or tenderizing power. Because they are insoluble in water they act to interfere with the development of firm masses or strands of the flour protein substance, gluten, actually shortening these strands and increasing tenderness. Fats are also used as major components of dressings for salads, as spreads on bread, and as a medium for transferring heat in frying.

Processing of Fats

Many foods, such as eggs, whole milk, and avocados, contain fat that is a component part of the food. This fat is, in a sense, invisible. Other fats commonly used in food preparation such as vegetable oils, lard, and butter, are separated from various materials or tissues and refined. They are purified or processed fats. Many oils come from seeds or fruits; lard comes from pork tissue; and butter comes from cream. Further processing may produce fats such as margarines and hydrogenated shortenings.

Butter

Butter is the fat of cream that is separated more or less completely from the other milk constituents by agitation or churning. The mechanical rupture of the protein film around the fat globules allows the globules to coalesce. Butter formation is an example of the breaking of an oil-in-water emulsion by agitation. The resulting emulsion that forms in butter itself is a water-in-oil emulsion, with about 18 percent water being dispersed in about 80 percent fat and a small amount of protein acting as emulsifier. Buttermilk remains after butter is churned from cream.

Butter is made from either sweet or sour cream. Butter from sour cream has a more pronounced flavor. The cream may be allowed to sour naturally or it may be acidified by the addition of a pure culture of lactic acid bacteria to pasteurized sweet cream. The latter method yields butter of better flavor and keeping quality as it excludes many undesirable types of microorganisms that may cause off flavor. Pasteurization also destroys pathogenic bacteria if present. Ripening of the cream after pasteurizing by the addition of acid-forming bacteria permits acid fermentation to occur.

After churning separates the butterfat from the other constituents, the mass is washed, salted, and worked to distribute the salt and to remove excess water or buttermilk. Some sweet-cream butter is marketed unsalted as sweet butter. Salted butter is preferred by most Americans, while sweet butter is used extensively in Europe and by European-trained chefs.

Coloring matter, if used, is added to the cream before churning. The season of the year and the demands of various markets for butter of different degrees of color affect the use of coloring matter. Butter produced when cows are on green feed is naturally more highly pigmented than butter produced when green feed is not consumed. Carotene is commonly added as a coloring agent.

USDA grade standards for butter have been set. They are U.S. Grade AA, U.S. Grade A, and U.S. Grade B. U.S. Grade AA butter must have a smooth, creamy texture and be made from high-quality fresh, sweet cream. U.S. Grade A butter rates close to the top grade [6]. U.S. Grade B butter is made from selected sour cream and may have a slightly acid flavor.

Butter flavor is complex and is the result of the combination of many flavor compounds. A substance called diacetyl, formed from bacterial action, is an important flavor component of butter.

Margarine

Margarine is made from one or more optional fat ingredients churned with cultured pasteurized skim milk. It is a water-in-fat emulsion and must contain not less than 80 percent fat according to the standard of identity for margarine that has been established by the U.S. Food and Drug Administration. Soybean and cottonseed oils, refined and partially hydrogenated to give the desired consistency, are extensively used in producing margarines. Oils may be blended with partially hydrogenated oils in such a way that the total polyunsaturated fatty acid content is higher than in ordinary margarines. If the first ingredient listed on the label is oil, rather than partially hydrogenated oil, the consumer may know that the polyunsaturated fatty acid content of the margarine is likely to be relatively high. Soft margarines with particularly high percentages of polyunsaturated fatty acids may be sold in small plastic tubs [4].

Other ingredients permitted in margarine by the federal standard of identity are vitamins A and D for nutritive purposes; diacetyl as a flavor constituent; lecithin, monoglycerides, and/or diglycerides of fat-forming fatty acids as emulsifying agents; artificial color; salt; citric acid or certain citrates; and sodium benzoate or benzoic acid as a preservative to the extent of 0.1 percent.

Oleomargarine was first developed in 1869 by a French chemist, Mege-Mouries, in response to the offer of a prize by Napoleon III for a palatable, nutritious, and economical alternate for butter. Beef fat was the chief constituent of the original margarine. Since that time many changes have occurred in the composition and processing of margarine to greatly improve the product. In addition to regular margarine and polyunsaturated fat margarines, the consumer may purchase whipped margarine containing nitrogen gas to increase the volume and decrease the density; liquid margarine in a squeeze bottle; and imitation diet margarine. Diet margarine contains a larger amount of water and a stronger emulsifying system than does regular margarine. It is called imitation because it does not meet the standard of identity established for margarine. Various federal and state restrictions that were previously placed on margarine have gradually been removed and public acceptance and consumption of this product have greatly increased over the years [7].

Lard

Lard, which is the fat that is separated from the fatty tissues of the hog by rendering, is one of the oldest of household fats. The quality of lard depends upon such factors as the part of the body from which the fat is obtained, the feed used for fattening the animal, and the rendering process. Leaf fat, which lines the abdominal cavity, is used to make the better qualities of lard. The lack of uniformity of lard and some of its physical properties, such as flavor, odor, grainy texture, and undesirability for making some baked products, such as cake, have resulted in a reduced use of lard by most Americans as other shortenings have become more available. Lard is susceptible to the development of rancidity and has antioxidants added to it in processing to increase its shelf life. Some lard samples may have relatively low smoking temperatures and have not been commonly used for frying. However, lards with high smoking points can be produced. The two most desirable properties of lard are its plasticity and its excellent shortening power.

Technology has provided methods for improving the quality, uniformity, and functional properties of lard. Improved rendering methods have been developed, one of which involves the division of the fatty tissues into fine particle size, after which flash heating is applied for 15 seconds. The product is then pulverized and centrifuged. This method gives a high yield and a bland and stable product at minimum cost.

Chemical modifications, such as interesterification, which brings about a change in the way the fatty acids are distributed on the glycerol molecules, have greatly improved the plasticity and creaming properties of lard for use in shortened cakes. Some of this lard may be combined with hydrogenated vegetable fat in a combination shortening or in margarine. Antioxidants are added to shortenings containing lard to improve their keeping quality.

Hydrogenated Shortening

The addition of hydrogen to unsaturated fats, thus converting oils into solid fats, is known as *hydrogenation*. A process for hydrogenation of vegetable oils was discovered more than 80 years ago and has since developed into one of the major chemical processes in the fat and oil industry. The fats produced are neutral in flavor, have a high enough smoking temperature to make them useful for frying, and have good shortening power. Hydrogenation involves a very complex series of chemical reactions where hydrogen is added to some carbon atoms as double bonds between the carbon atoms are broken. A catalyst such as finely divided nickel helps the reaction to go and conditions of temperature and pressure are carefully controlled. Unsaturated oils are hydrogenated only partially in order to produce a product with the desired plasticity or moldability. Complete hydrogenation would produce an undesirably hard fat. An inert gas is incorporated throughout the hydrogenated fat, which is chilled to produce the desired texture.

Hydrogenated fats may have emulsifiers, such as mono- and diglycerides, added to them. Small amounts of mono- and diglycerides may be produced during processing. The addition of emulsifiers to fats used in cakes makes possible the addition of higher proportions of sugar and liquid to fat, as may be desired for some cake formulas. The presence of mono- and diglycerides in hydrogenated shortenings, however, decreases the smoking temperature of the fat, thus making it somewhat less valuable for frying purposes. Special shortenings are used in commercial establishments for frying and for cake making. In the home, a general-purpose shortening is more commonly used.

Oils

The principal oils on the market are those from cottonseed, corn, soybeans, peanuts, and olives. Safflower oil is also available. The better grades of olive oil are unrefined but all other oils are refined. Any preference for olive oil is based largely on its flavor, which differs depending on the variety of olive used, its ripeness, and on various conditions of manufacture. Oils from other sources have come to be preferred by many people to the more expensive olive oil. All salad and cooking oils must be clearly and accurately labeled to enable the purchaser to know whether the oil is from a single source (peanut, corn, olive) or is a mixture of oils.

Oils may be removed from the oil-containing seeds by various pressing processes, by solvent extraction, or by a combination of these. A seed cake that is relatively high in protein remains after fat extraction and is often used for animal feed. The extracted oils are refined, bleached, and deodorized. Vegetable oils designed especially for use in salad dressings may be subjected to a process called *winterization*. This involves chilling the oil and removing from it the crystallized, more saturated fats which give it a cloudy appearance when stored at refrigerator temperatures.

Nutritive Value

Fats are valuable in the diet chiefly as energy foods. In the pure form, 1 pound of fat yields over 4,000 kilocalories, which is more than two times the kilocalories furnished by an equal quantity of purified carbohydrate or protein. Table 14-1 gives the approximate weight and measure of various fats and fat-rich foods required to furnish 100 kilocalories.

Fats are also valuable for the flavor and richness they give to food. They are generally retained in the stomach longer than proteins and carbohydrates and thus contribute to satiety (a feeling of fullness or absence of hunger). Some fats and oils contain the essential fatty acid, linoleic acid, and some fats are sources of the fat-soluble

Table 14-1 *Approximate Amounts of Various Fat and Fat-Rich Foods Required to Furnish 100 Kilocalories*

Food	Fat Content (%)	Weight (g)	Approximate Measure
Butter	80	13	1 T
Margarine	80	13	1 T
Hydrogenated fat	100	11	1 T
Lard	100	11	1 T
Salad oil	100	11	1 T
Bacon fat	100	11	1 T
Peanut butter	46	16	1 T
Cream, light	20	50	3 T
Cream, whipping	35	33	2 T or about double the volume if whipped

vitamins A, D, and E. The average vitamin A value for butter is about 15,000 International Units (IU) per pound. Margarines usually have 15,000 IU of vitamin A added per pound. Refined vegetable oils and hydrogenated shortenings contain little or no vitamin A.

Flavor of Fats

Some fats that are used for seasoning, table use, and salad dressings, possess distinctive and pleasing flavors. These include butter, bacon fat, olive oil, and margarines. Margarines have a certain amount of butterlike flavor because of the churning of the basic fats with cultured milk and the addition of the flavor substance diacetyl. In the choice of fats used for flavor purposes, the cost may also have to be considered. Corn, soybean, and cottonseed oils are commonly used to make satisfactory salad dressings but lack the flavor of the more expensive olive oil. Similarly, butter may be an expensive fat for use in cakes. Other fats, such as hydrogenated shortenings, make cakes of as good or perhaps even better a texture as butter because of emulsifying agents present and the greater percentage of fat, but obviously lack the flavor of butter.

The ability of fats to take up or dissolve certain aromatic flavor substances is frequently used in food preparation. Onions, celery, peppers, and other flavorful foods are cooked in fat to produce a savory fat that may immediately be incorporated into other foods or stored for future use. Aromatic fruit and other flavors are also dissolved by fat.

Rancidity

Rancidity is a special type of spoilage that commonly occurs in fats and fatty foods. It may develop on storage, particularly if the fats are highly unsaturated and the environmental conditions are conducive to chemical change in the fats. The chemical changes that result in rancidity are chiefly of two types: (1) hydrolytic and (2) oxidative.

Hydrolysis

Hydrolysis involves the breaking of chemical bonds and the addition, in the process, of the elements of water. In the hydrolysis of triglycerides, they are broken down into free fatty acids and glycerol. This reaction may be catalyzed, or made to occur, by an enzyme called *lipase*. The release of free fatty acids does not necessarily produce undesirable odors and flavors in fats except when they are *short chain* fatty acids, such as butyric and caproic acids. These fatty acids predominate in butter. They are volatile and are largely responsible for the very unpleasant odor and flavor of rancid butter. They may render butter inedible even when they are present in low concentrations. *Long chain* free fatty acids, such as stearic, palmitic, and oleic acids, do not usually produce a disagreeable flavor unless other changes, such as oxidation, also occur.

Oxidation

The characteristic unpleasant odor of fats in which oxidative rancidity has developed is difficult to describe but is widely recognized [5]. Oxidative rancidity may be caused by an enzyme called *lipoxidase* which is present in some foods. However, it most often results from a strictly chemical reaction that is self-perpetuating or a *chain reaction*. It is primarily the unsaturated fats that are susceptible to oxidative changes. Highly hydrogenated fats and natural fats that are composed largely of saturated fatty acids are relatively resistant to this type of chemical change. The currently accepted theory to explain the chemical oxidation of fat suggests that the addition of oxygen to carbon atoms next to a double bond in a fatty acid chain results in the formation of a product called a *hydroperoxide* as indicated by the following:

$$
\begin{array}{ccccc}
H & H & H & H & H \\
| & | & | & | & | \\
-C & -C & -C & = C & -C- \\
| & | & & & | \\
H & O & & & H \\
& | & & & \\
& O & & & \\
& | & & & \\
& H & & & \\
\end{array}
$$

Hydroperoxide formed on portion of long-chain fatty acid

Hydroperoxides themselves do not appear to have unpleasant rancid odors and flavors but these molecules readily break into pieces, producing smaller volatile substances that give the characteristic odors of rancid fat. As previously mentioned, the reaction is a chain reaction. Therefore, once a fat develops a slight rancid odor, the production of more pronounced rancidity occurs very rapidly. This type of rancidity is responsible for most of the spoilage of fats and fatty foods and may be a problem in dry foods containing only small quantities of fat, such as prepared cereals. When rancidity develops in fatty foods the fat soluble vitamins A and E that are present may also be readily oxidized.

Antioxidants and the Prevention of Rancidity.   Fats may be protected against the rapid development of rancidity by controlling the conditions of storage. Storage at refrigerator temperature along with the exclusion of light, moisture, and air aid in rancidity prevention. Because only certain rays of light catalyze the oxidation of fats, the use of colored glass containers that absorb the active rays protects fats against spoilage. Certain shades of green in bottles and wrappers and yellow transparent cellulose have been found to be effective in retarding rancidity in fats and fatty foods such as bacon. Vacuum packaging also helps to retard the development of rancidity. As containers of products such as peanut butter and hydrogenated shortening are used at home, one might compact the material and smooth off the surface or repackage it in a smaller container to reduce the amount of air in contact with the product.

Chemical substances called *antioxidants* may be added to fats to control the development of rancidity. Some compounds with antioxidant activity are naturally present in certain foods such as seeds. For example, tocopherols (vitamin E) are effective antioxidants found naturally in vegetable oils. Antioxidants act as oxygen interceptors in the oxidative process and break the chain reaction involved in the development of rancidity. They may thus greatly increase the shelf life of a fat or fatty food. The addition of antioxidants to fats to retard the development of rancidity has become an important practice commercially. Some of the substances approved for this purpose by the U.S. Food and Drug Administration include butylated hydroxyanisole (BHA), butylated hydroxytoluene (BHT), tertiary butyl hydroquinone (TBHQ), and propyl gallate. Some substances, such as citric acid, may be used along with antioxidants in foods as *synergists*. A synergist is something that increases the effectiveness of an antioxidant when used with it but is not as effective an agent when used alone. Metals, such as iron and copper, which may be present in trace amounts in foods, act as prooxidants in encouraging the development of oxidative rancidity. Some synergists may be effective because of their ability to bind or chelate the metals and prevent them from catalyzing the oxidation process. Binding or chelating agents are sometimes called *sequestering* agents.

The protection of fats against spoilage is important not only in connection with more or less purified fats but also with many other foods of high fat content, such as processed meats, whole-grain and dry-prepared cereal products, nuts, fat-rich biscuits and crackers, potato chips, and flour mixes.

Flavor Reversion.   A special type of oxidative deterioration is called *flavor reversion*. This involves a change in edible fats characterized by the development, in the refined material, of an objectionable flavor prior to the onset of true rancidity. Reversion may develop during the exposure of the fat to ultraviolet or visible light or by heating. A small amount of oxygen seems to be necessary for the reaction that is catalyzed by the presence of small amounts of metals such as iron and copper.

The kinds of off flavors that develop during reversion vary with the particular fat and with the conditions that cause the change. Reverted soybean oil has been described as "beany," "haylike," and, in the final stages, "fishy."

No fat is entirely free from a tendency to develop flavor reversion, but some oils, such as corn and cottonseed oil, are quite resistant to this type of deterioration. Soybean oil is very susceptible to flavor reversion. This may cause problems in food processing because soybean oil is so widely used in the preparation of edible fats. Soybean oil is known to contain traces of iron and copper, and the flavor of soybean oil is stabilized by the use of metal inactivators or sequestrants that tie up the trace amounts of iron and copper.

The chief precursors of the reversion flavor in oils are thought to be the triglycerides containing linolenic acid, although linoleic acid is probably also involved to some degree [13]. The fats that are most susceptible to reversion contain linolenic acid in larger amounts than do those fats that are relatively stable. The selective hydrogenation of soybean oil to decrease the amount of linolenic acid aids in preventing flavor reversion.

Frying

Frying may be accomplished in two ways: (1) pan-frying, in which a shallow layer of fat is used (Figure 14-1), and (2) deep-fat frying, in which the food could be submerged in fat (Figure 14-2). In the former method, a definite determination of the temperature of heating is difficult, if not impossible, because of the shallow depth of the fat. Smoking, however, is a definite indication that decomposition of the fat is occurring and should never be permitted.

In deep-fat frying, the use of a thermometer furnishes definite information as to the temperature of the fat and makes protection of the fat against overheating much easier. The use of a thermometer makes possible the holding of the fat at optimum temperatures for frying but care must still be exercised in applying heat. Electric deep fat fryers with mechanisms to thermostatically control the temperature may also be used. A test for approximate temperatures that has some value in case no thermometer is available involves measuring the time required to brown a cube of bread in the hot fat. Fats of a suitable temperature for thoroughly frying some raw foods, as well as for browning, require about 60 seconds to brown a cube of bread. Fats that are hot enough to fry cooked foods brown or to cook some raw, watery foods, brown a cube of bread in about 40 seconds.

14-1 *Pan-frying fish fillets.* (Courtesy of Lever Brothers Company)

14-2 *Frying chicken in deep fat.* (Courtesy of Lever Brothers Company)

Table 14-2 gives the commonly accepted range of temperatures used for deep-fat frying.

Small amounts of food should be fried at one time to avoid lowering the temperature of the fat excessively, thus increasing fat absorption by the food before browning can occur. The utensil that is used for deep-fat frying should be made of heavy metal to avoid marked fluctuation in temperature and should have straight sides and a relatively narrow diameter, which give a minimum surface for the volume of fat used. A frying basket is a convenient means of

Table 14-2 *Temperature Ranges for Deep-fat Frying**

Type of Product	Temperature of Fat	Approximate Time to Brown a 1-Inch Cube of Bread in Hot Fat
Doughnuts Fritters Oysters, scallops, and soft-shelled crabs	350°–375° F (177°–190° C)	60 seconds
Croquettes Eggplant Onions Cauliflower	375°–385° F (190°–196° C)	40 seconds
French-fried potatoes	385°–395° F (196°–201° C)	20 seconds

*From American Home Economics Association. *Handbook of Food Preparation.*

345

lowering the food into the fat and removing the food when it is cooked. A basket also avoids the need to handle some foods that are easily broken.

Wet foods, such as potatoes that have stood in cold water prior to frying, should be drained dry on a towel before frying. After frying, foods require draining on absorbent paper to remove excess fat.

It should be emphasized that frying fats are heated to comparatively high temperatures (Table 14-2) and are, therefore, potentially dangerous if improperly handled. Great care should be used to avoid spilling or splattering of these extremely hot liquids.

Changes in Fats Upon Heating

When fats are heated to very high temperatures, certain chemical and physical changes occur [10, 11]. For example, overheated fats will begin to give off smoke. The smoke point of a fat is defined as the temperature at which smoke comes continuously from the surface of the fat and this point is measured under standardized conditions as a specific temperature. Present in the smoke that comes from overheated fats is a substance called *acrolein*. Acrolein comes from the dehydration of glycerol and is highly irritating to the eyes and throat.

$$
\begin{array}{llll}
CH_2OH & & CH_2 & \\
| & & \parallel & \\
CHOH & \xrightarrow{\text{heat}} & CH & + \; 2 \; H_2O \\
| & & | & \\
CH_2OH & & C{=}O & \\
& & | & \\
& & H & \\
\text{Glycerol} & & \text{Acrolein} & \text{Water}
\end{array}
$$

The glycerol from which acrolein is produced comes from the breakdown of some of the triglyceride molecules of the fat to their component parts, three fatty acids and glycerol. The development of free fatty acids by this hydrolysis of some of the fat during frying contributes to a decrease in the smoke point as frying proceeds [1]. Suspended matter, such as flour or batter particles, lowers the smoke point. In addition, the greater the surface of the fat exposed to air, the more rapidly the smoke point will be lowered.

Fats to be used for frying should be chosen on the basis of their resistance to smoking at the temperatures used. The smoke point of a fat is partly a matter of its natural composition and partly a matter of the processing it has received. Most oils on the retail market are highly refined and deodorized and have relatively high smoke points above 228° C (442° F) (Table 14-3). Hydrogenated shortenings (without added emulsifier) may smoke within the range of 221° to 232° C (430° to 450° F). Shortenings that contain added mono- and diglycerides, which make them particularly suitable for shortened cakes, are less desirable for frying because the addition of these emulsifiers lowers the smoke point. In this case, the first smoke given off is not from the breakdown of the fat itself but is from the emulsifier. It is an interesting fact that on continued heating, as the emulsifier is decomposed, the smoke point may rise somewhat.

The ingredients in the product being fried will influence the changes in the frying fat. The presence of egg yolk in a batter or dough causes greatly increased darkening of the fat with continued use (Figure 14-3).

Questions have been raised concerning possible adverse nutritional or toxic effects when heated fats are used in the diet. Although fats can apparently be seriously damaged when heated to very high temperatures over long periods of time, under reasonably well-controlled conditions of frying, adverse effects are not apparent [3]. It is important to control frying temperatures, ideally with the use of a thermometer, so that the fat is not overheated. Fats should not be used for long periods of time without the addition of fresh fat. Much deep-fat fried food eaten by today's consumers is fried commercially. The fats in baked products appear to change very little under ordinary conditions of baking [9].

Table 14-3 *Smoking Temperatures of Some Fats**

Type of Fat	Smoke Point
Steam rendered lard	189° C (372° F)
Cottonseed oil	229° C (444° F)
Peanut oil	230° C (446° F)
Combination shortening I**	191° C (376° F)
Combination shortening II**	177° C (319° F)

*From [1].
**Contains interesterified lard plus vegetable fat and mono- and diglycerides.

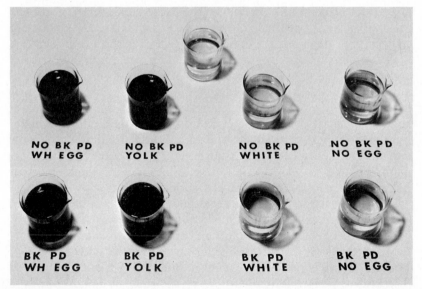

NO BK PD WH EGG   NO BK PD YOLK   NO BK PD WHITE   NO BK PD NO EGG

BK PD WH EGG   BK PD YOLK   BK PD WHITE   BK PD NO EGG

14-3 *Ingredients in the product being fried will influence the darkening of the frying fat. The sample of corn oil at the top center has not been used for frying. All other samples in the picture have been used for 8½ hours of continuous frying of fritter-type batters containing various combinations of egg and baking powder. The presence of egg yolk causes a marked darkening of the fat during frying. (BK PD = baking powder; WH EGG = whole egg; YOLK = egg yolk; WHITE = egg white.)*

Care of Frying Fat

A fat that is well adapted to frying may be used many times if it is cared for properly [12]. The selection of a fat of high smoking temperature is the first consideration. The avoidance of overheating is another important consideration. As previously stated, the use of a thermometer is the only means to know accurately the temperature of the fat. Even carefully heated fats, however, change to some extent with use. The addition of fresh fat to replace fat absorbed by food during frying increases the frying life of the fat.

Food particles remaining in used fat decrease the smoking temperature and may contribute to further darkening of the fat. After the fat has been used, all foreign matter should be strained from the fat and the fat should be stored in a cold place out of contact with light and air.

Fat Absorption

From the standpoint of both palatability and digestibility (rapidity of digestion) it is desirable to hold fat absorption by fried food to a minimum. The chief factors affecting the amount of fat absorbed are (1) the length of time of heating; (2) the amount of surface exposed to the fat; and (3) the character and composition of the food. The temperature of the fat indirectly affects the amount of fat absorbed during frying, because foods cooked at a lower temperature must be cooked for a longer period of time to achieve the desired amount of brownness. The longer the food remains in the fat, the greater is the absorption, in general. The greater the amount of surface area exposed to the fat, the greater is the fat absorption.

The proportion and kind of ingredients in doughnuts and fritters and various manipulative procedures affect fat absorption. Doughnuts containing a high percentage of sugar and of fat absorb more fat while frying than do doughnuts containing lesser amounts of sugar and/or fat. Doughnuts containing more lecithin (a phospholipid) were reported to absorb more fat than doughnuts with lesser amounts of lecithin [8]. The addition of egg, which contains phospholipids, to a fritter-type batter containing no additional shortening significantly increased fat absorption [2].

Doughnuts made from soft wheat flours and from soft doughs absorb more fat than doughnuts made from strong flours and from stiff doughs. The development of gluten by the extensive manipulation of the dough decreases fat absorption as compared with doughs in which gluten has not been developed. Rough dough surfaces caused by cracks or undermanipulation, or by allowing the dough to stick to the board, increase the surface area and therefore increase fat absorption.

For most fried food, high fat temperatures of 196° to 199° C (385° to 390° F) tend to produce too brown a crust by the time the food is completely cooked, although fat absorption is relatively low. Doughnuts fried at high temperatures are usually of comparatively small volume because the crust hardens before expansion is complete. The decreased volume may explain, in part, the lower fat absorption, since a low volume would mean exposing less surface area to the frying fat. Good color and volume in doughnuts can probably be achieved by frying them at a fat temperature in the range of 177° to 191° C (350° to 375° F).

The type of fat does not appear to significantly affect the amount of fat absorbed during frying. Under identical conditions of time, temperature, and type of food being fried, various fats commonly used for frying appear to be absorbed in similar amounts.

Emulsions

The term *emulsion* is applied to a liquid dispersed in another liquid with which it does not usually mix. Oil and water are examples of liquids that do not mix. A third substance, called an emulsifying agent, is necessary to keep one liquid dispersed in the other liquid on a permanent basis.

Prominent among natural food emulsions are milk, cream, and egg yolk. In all such foods the fat is divided into small particles or globules and dispersed throughout the watery portion of the food. As previously noted, the homogenization of whole milk further divides the naturally emulsified fat into particles that are so fine that they tend to remain in suspension and do not rise to the surface on standing as does the fat in nonhomogenized milk.

There are many foods that are examples of emulsions which have been formed in their preparation. In the formation of these food emulsions, work is necessary to divide the fat into tiny globules and thus increase its surface area tremendously. Shaking, beating, stirring, and grinding are some methods used to disperse one liquid in another. Mayonnaise and other salad dressings are examples of emulsions and are discussed in Chapter 9. Sauces, gravies, puddings, cream soups, shortened cake batters, and other flour mixtures in which the fat is dispersed are all classed as emulsions. Many emulsions are produced in the processing of foods such as peanut butter, confections, frozen desserts, sausages, and frankfurters. The dispersing medium may be water, milk, dilute vinegar, lemon or other fruit juice, or some similar liquid. The dispersed substance may be any of the commonly used food fats and oils. Some emulsions, such as margarine, have fat as the dispersing medium and water as the dispersed substance. Even though the fat is not always a liquid at ordinary temperatures of holding, the food system is still called an emulsion.

Temporary Emulsions

If oil and water alone are shaken together, an emulsion is formed, but on standing, the oil particles reunite and separate from the water. Emulsions of this kind are described as *temporary emulsions*. They must be used immediately or, if made in quantity and stored, they must be reshaken or beaten each time they are used. French dressing is the most common emulsion of this type used in food preparation. Most homemade French dressings separate readily. (See Chapter 9 for a discussion of French dressing.)

Permanent Emulsions

Permanent emulsions that can be held or stored without separation of the two immiscible liquids require an emulsifying agent or emulsifier to form a type of film around the dispersed droplets and prevent them from reuniting (see Figure 14-4). The term *stabilizer* is also used to describe the emulsifying agent in some food products. Various substances commonly used as emulsifiers or stabilizers in food products are egg yolk, whole egg, gelatin, pectin, starch paste, casein (milk protein), egg white, and fine powders, such as paprika or mustard. Commercially, a number of vegetable gums, such as carrageenan, are used as stabilizers. In batters such as cake batter several emulsifiers are present. These include egg, casein from milk, and gluten and starch from flour. Mono- and diglycerides are also present as emulsifiers in shortenings used for cakes. Mayon-

14-4 *An emulsion consists of one substance dispersed in another substance with which it is immiscible. An emulsifying agent surrounds each dispersed particle. Here is shown an oil in water emulsion.*

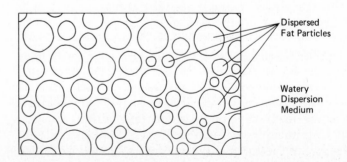

Dispersed Fat Particles

Watery Dispersion Medium

naise is an example of a permanent emulsion (see Chapter 9 for a discussion of mayonnaise). Actually, any food containing fat that is distributed throughout and does not appear on the surface as a separate layer is a permanent emulsion.

Two general types of emulsions are possible—an oil-in-water emulsion and a water-in-oil emulsion. Oil-in-water emulsions are more common in foods, but butter and margarine are examples of water-in-oil emulsions. The type of emulsion formed depends on the nature of the emulsifier. Because of their particular chemical structure, emulsifying agents are attracted to both water and oil and form a type of bridge between the two substances. But if the emulsifier is *more* attracted to the water, or more water soluble, it promotes the dispersion of oil in water. If the emulsifier is more oil soluble or more attracted to the oil, it tends to produce a water-in-oil emulsion. A photomicrograph of the fat-in-water emulsion of milk, both before and after homogenization, is shown in Figure 12-1, p. 272.

The breaking of emulsions or separation of the two phases may occur under certain conditions. In some cases the emulsion can be reformed.

Buying of Fats

It is important in purchasing fats for household use to keep in mind the specific uses for fats in food preparation and to select fats in accordance with one's needs and budget. Most consumers will probably not need to keep more than three or four household fats on hand.

Butter, because of its flavor, is sometimes preferred for table use as well as for use in some baked products and for the seasoning of some foods. Margarine serves a similar purpose, usually at a somewhat lower cost, although different brands of margarine vary widely in price. A blend of butter and margarine is also available. Margarines, particularly those types that are high in polyunsaturated fats, may be chosen over butter for health reasons. Some flavorful drippings, such as bacon fat, may be utilized for flavoring. If no oil dressings are made in the home, there may be no need to purchase oil unless the homemaker prefers to use oil for frying or for shortening. Most households usually require some shortening, but one general-purpose shortening may be found that can be used satisfactorily for both shortening and frying purposes. Lard is preferred by some for use in pastry or biscuits but usually requires modified methods of mixing to produce desirable results in shortened cakes.

The use of fats for shortening is considered in Chapter 18, Batters and Doughs.

Study Questions

1. For what general purposes are fats used in food preparation? Name at least four uses.
2. Explain at least one chemical reason why fats vary in their melting points so that some are liquid at room temperature while others are solid.
3. Most fats used in food preparation are separated from other tissues and refined or processed. For each of the fats listed below, briefly describe how they are produced. Also indicate for which of the general uses listed in question 1 each fat may be appropriate.
   a. Butter
   b. Margarine
   c. Lard
   d. Hydrogenated shortening
   e. Oil
4. a. Explain what happens when oils are hydrogenated and when they are winterized.
   b. What purposes do these processes serve in the production of food fats?
   c. What is a plastic fat? Give examples.
5. a. What is rancidity?
   b. Distinguish between hydrolytic rancidity and oxidative rancidity.
   c. Explain what probably happens when a fat is oxidized and becomes rancid.
   d. List several factors that may contribute to the development of rancidity. How can these be controlled?
   e. How does an antioxidant retard the development of rancidity?
   f. Name several antioxidants that may be added to or present in fatty foods.
6. a. What is pan-frying? What is deep-fat frying?
   b. Explain the importance of using a proper temperature in frying foods. What do smoke point and acrolein have to do with a proper temperature for frying?
   c. Give suggestions for the appropriate care of used frying fat.
   d. Discuss several factors that may influence the amount of fat absorbed by a food during frying.
7. a. What is an emulsion? What is necessary to produce a permanent emulsion?
   b. Give several examples of emulsions in natural foods and of emulsions in prepared or processed foods.
   c. Describe the difference between an oil-in-water emulsion and a water-in-oil emulsion.
8. Discuss some factors to consider in deciding which fats to purchase for household use.

References

1. Bennion, M., and F. Hanning. 1956. Effect of different fats and oils and their modification on changes during frying. *Food Technology* **10**, 229.
2. Bennion, M., and R. L. Park. 1968. Changes in frying fats with different foods. *Journal of the American Dietetic Association* **52**, 308.

3. Chang, S. S., R. J. Peterson, and C. Ho. 1978. Chemical reactions involved in the deep-fat frying of foods. *Journal of the American Oil Chemists' Society* **55,** 718.

4. Cochran, W. M., and R. J. Baeuerlen. 1981. Formulation innovations and other developments in shortenings, margarines and oils. *Baker's Digest* **55,** 16 (October).

5. Gray, J. I. 1978. Measurement of lipid oxidation: A review. *Journal of the American Oil Chemists' Society* **55,** 539.

6. *How to Buy Butter.* Home and Garden Bulletin No. 148. Washington, DC: U.S. Department of Agriculture, 1968.

7. Massiello, F. J. 1978. Changing trends in consumer margarines. *Journal of the American Oil Chemists' Society* **55,** 262.

8. McComber, D., and E. M. Miller. 1976. Differences in total lipid and fatty acid composition of doughnuts as influenced by lecithin, leavening agent, and use of frying fat. *Cereal Chemistry* **53,** 101.

9. Phillips, J. A., and G. E. Vail. 1967. Effect of heat on fatty acids. *Journal of the American Dietetic Association* **50,** 116.

10. Roth, H., and S. P. Rock. 1972. The chemistry and technology of frying fat. I. Chemistry. *Baker's Digest* **46,** 38 (August).

11. Roth, H., and S. P. Rock. 1972. The chemistry and technology of frying fat. II. Technology. *Baker's Digest* **46,** 38 (October).

12. Rust, M. E., and D. L. Harrison. 1960. Effects of method of care on the frying life of fat. *Food Technology* **14,** 605.

13. Smouse, T. H. 1979. Review of soybean oil reversion flavor. *Journal of the American Oil Chemists' Society* **56,** 747A.

15

Sweeteners and Sugar Cookery

Properties of Sugars

The sugar classification groups, monosaccharides and disaccharides, are described on pp. 64–66. The principal food sugars, their common sources, and products of hydrolysis are shown in Table 4-2 on p. 66.

Solubility

In the natural state, sugars occur in solution. Crystallization of sugar may occur from a sufficiently concentrated sugar solution and use is made of this fact in the production of commercial sugars from sugar cane and beets. The common sugars vary somewhat in their solubilities. Sucrose is the most soluble of the disaccharides, and lactose is the least soluble. Fructose is the most soluble of the monosaccharides and is more soluble than sucrose. At room temperature, the relative solubilities of the common sugars are fructose (most soluble), followed by sucrose, glucose, maltose, and lactose, in order of decreasing solubility. The solubility of all sugars in water is increased by heating. At a temperature of 20° C (68° F), 203.9 grams of sucrose may be dissolved by 100 grams of water, whereas at temperatures of 70° C (158° F) and 100° C (212° F), 320.5 grams and 487.2

grams of sucrose may be dissolved, respectively by the same amount of water.

A solution becomes *saturated* when it contains all of the dissolved solute (the dispersed substance) that it can take up at a given temperature when it is in contact with the undissolved solute. A solution is *supersaturated* when it holds more solute than is usually soluble at a particular temperature. Boiling sugar solutions, as they are cooled to room temperature, gradually become saturated and then supersaturated. Only by careful cooling and the avoidance of factors that promote crystallization can a solution be held in the supersaturated state. Since supersaturation is such an unstable state, crystallization eventually occurs and all excess of solute beyond saturation is precipitated or crystallized. Some substances require more time to crystallize from a supersaturated solution than others, unless agitation or seeding (adding a few already formed crystals) starts the precipitation of crystals. The sugars that are the most soluble, such as fructose, will be the most difficult to crystallize; those that are the least soluble, such as lactose, will crystallize most readily. In the making of candies, much concern must be given to the solubilities and ease of crystallization of sugars.

Melting Point and Decomposition by Heat

With the application of sufficient dry heat, sugars melt or change to a liquid state. Heating beyond the melting point brings about a number of decomposition changes. As sucrose melts at a temperature of about 160° C (320° F) a clear liquid forms that gradually changes to a brown color with continued heating. At a temperature of about 170° C (338° F) caramelization occurs with the development of a characteristic caramel flavor and brown color. This is a type of nonenzymatic browning. However, caramelization occurs with sugar alone, without the presence of protein substances having an amine group. It is a complex chemical reaction that is not very well understood. Caramel has a pungent taste, is often bitter, is much less sweet than the original sugar from which it is produced, and is noncrystalline. It is soluble in water. The extent and the rate of the caramelization reaction are influenced by the type of sugar being heated. Sucrose is the most commonly used sugar in food processing and, therefore, is the sugar most often involved in caramelization reactions. Galactose and glucose caramelize at about the same temperature as sucrose but fructose caramelizes at a temperature of 110° C (230° F) and maltose caramelizes at a temperature of about 180° C (356° F).

Absorption of Moisture

That sugars absorb moisture is clearly shown in many ways. Crystalline sugars become caked and lumpy unless they are stored in dry places. Baked flour mixtures that are rich in sugar take up moisture when surrounded by a moist atmosphere in tightly closed containers. Because of this tendency to absorb moisture from the atmosphere, sugars are said to be *hygroscopic*. Fructose is more hygroscopic than the other sugars commonly found in food. Therefore, higher moisture absorption occurs in products containing fructose, such as cakes or cookies made with honey, molasses, or crystalline fructose. These baked products remain moist noticeably longer than similar products made with sucrose.

Fermentation

Most sugars, except lactose, may be fermented or broken down by yeasts to produce carbon dioxide gas and alcohol. This is an important reaction in the making of bread and other baked products where the carbon dioxide leavens the product and the alcohol is volatilized during baking. The spoilage of canned or cooked products containing sugar may occur by fermentation.

Acid Hydrolysis

The disaccharides are hydrolyzed or broken down to their component monosaccharides by weak acids. Sucrose is easily hydrolyzed by acid but maltose and lactose are slowly acted upon. The end products of sucrose hydrolysis are a mixture of glucose and fructose. This mixture is commonly called *invert sugar*. The monosaccharides are not appreciably affected by acids.

The extent of hydrolysis is variable depending upon whether or not the solution is heated, upon the kind and concentration of acid used, and upon the rate and length of the time of heating. The application of heat accelerates the reaction and long, slow heating tends to bring about more hydrolysis than rapid heating for a shorter period of time. The higher the acidity the greater are the rate and extent of decomposition. Hydrolysis may occur incidentally, as in the cooking of acid fruits and sugar, or it may be brought about purposely as a means of improving the textures or consistencies of certain sugar products, such as fondant, where it is often produced by the addition of cream of tartar.

Enzyme Hydrolysis

Enzymes will also hydrolyze disaccharides. The enzyme *sucrase,* or *invertase,* may be used in the candy industry to hydrolyze some of the sucrose in cream fondant to fructose and glucose in order to produce soft, semifluid centers in chocolates. This enzyme is commonly added to the fondant layer around the fruit in chocolate-coated cherries. The enzyme must be added after the sugar solution is boiled and cooled so that the enzyme will not be destroyed, and is usually added during beating or when the fondant is molded for dipping. The fondant must be dipped in chocolate as soon as it is made and chocolate coatings must completely cover the fondant to prevent leakage as the enzyme acts on the sucrose. Because the enzyme acts best in an acid medium, the fondant is acidified.

Decomposition by Alkalies

The decomposition of sugars by alkalies also has significance in sugar cookery. Alkaline waters used in boiling sugar solutions may bring about some decomposition of sugars. The monosaccharides, which are only slightly affected by weak acids, are very markedly affected by alkalies. Both glucose and fructose are changed into many decomposition products both by standing and by being heated in alkaline solutions. The stronger the alkali solution the more pronounced are the effects on sugars. Sucrose, of the disaccharides, is the least affected by alkalies but the invert sugar formed from sucrose is readily decomposed. The decomposition products of glucose and fructose are brownish in color and, when the process is extensive, the flavor may be strong and bitter.

Fondant made with glucose or corn syrup is usually less white than fondant made with cream of tartar, an acid salt which hydrolyzes some of the sucrose to produce invert sugar, partly because the fondant mixture is more alkaline without the addition of acid and the decomposition of monosaccharides may occur. This is particularly true when hard water, which is alkaline, is used in the preparation of the fondant.

Other examples of cooked products may be cited to illustrate the color and flavor changes resulting from the decomposition of glucose and fructose: (1) baked beans are more brown in color and have a more caramelized flavor if made from glucose- and fructose-containing sugars rather than table sugar; and (2) cakes and cookies made from honey and baking soda invariably have a darkened color and strong flavor. These are complex food products, and browning may occur not only as a result of sugar decomposition by alkali but also because of the Maillard-type browning reaction involving the interaction of sugars and amino groups from proteins.

Sweetness

The flavor of purified sugars is described as sweet. Sweetness is a characteristic of certain substances that humans have always associated with pleasure. The degree of sweetness is affected by several factors, including concentration of the sweetener, temperature, pH (acidity), presence of other substances with the sweetener, and the sensitivity of the taster. Therefore, it is sometimes difficult to make consistent and reproducible comparisons of sweetness among the various sweeteners, including the common sugars. It has been generally suggested that, of the sugars, lactose is the least sweet, followed by maltose, galactose, glucose, and sucrose, with fructose being the most sweet [4]. However, these orders of sweetness do not hold at all temperatures nor in all products. For example, fructose was reported to give a sweeter lemonade than did sucrose when added in equal weights. But sugar cookies, white cake, and vanilla pudding were sweeter when made with sucrose as compared to fructose [3]. A maximum sweetness from fructose is most likely to be achieved when it is used with slightly acid, cold foods and beverages.

Nutritive Value

Pure sugar is only a source of energy for the body. Increasing the consumption of purified sugar products may contribute to unbalancing the dietary by proportionately decreasing the consumption of protein, minerals, and vitamins. In addition, the disguising of many natural food flavors by adding excessive amounts of sugar to foods results in a loss of variety and appreciation for individual food flavors.

The estimated per capita consumption of sucrose in the United States has been about 100 pounds per year. This figure remained essentially unchanged for more than 50 years but is now decreasing. However, the amount of corn sweeteners (glucose and corn syrup) used in the United States has been increasing since the 1960s, and at a more rapid rate in recent years, keeping the total consumption of sweeteners at about the same level [5]. Much of the glucose and corn syrup is used by food processors.

Molasses, which contains the natural ash of the plant juices from which it is made, furnishes some nutrients other than carbohydrate, such as a little calcium and iron. The unrefined sugars, however, are still essentially energy foods and, on the whole, cannot be relied on to furnish other nutrients in significant amounts.

Sugars have their proper place in the diet but both the quantity and the concentration of sweets must be considered from the standpoint of wholesomeness and adequate nutrition.

Crystalline or Solid Forms of Sugar

A white crystalline form of glucose is produced by the complete hydrolysis of corn starch. It can be obtained in various particle sizes, including powdered and pulverized, but is used chiefly in the food industry. The crystals sometimes found in honey are mostly glucose, the fructose remaining in the syrup. Crystalline fructose that is more than 99 percent pure is also available on the market [9]. It is being used in a variety of manufactured foods, including cake mixes and frozen reduced calorie desserts, although fructose is no lower in calories than other sugars. Crystalline lactose and maltose are available for special uses, but most of the crystalline sugar on the market is sucrose. Sucrose is extracted commercially from sugar cane or sugar beet but the source does not produce differences in quality. It is available in granulated, powdered, and loaf sugar forms and also as brown sugars of varying degrees of darkness or lightness.

Crystalline sucrose, called table sugar, plays a variety of roles in food systems. To the food scientist, sucrose is much more than a sweetener. For example, it affects the texture of many baked products, it improves the body and texture of ice creams, it is fermented by yeast to produce carbon dioxide gas which leavens breads, and it preserves jams and jellies by retarding the growth of microorganisms.

Many grades and granulations of refined cane or beet sugar are available. Finer granulations are more desirable for many culinary uses as they are more quickly soluble. Fine Granulated is the principal granulated sugar of commerce, but other classes, each more finely granulated than the preceding, are Extra-fine Granulated, Berry or Fruit or Fruit Powdered (this sugar is not powdered), and Coating. Sanding sugar is coarsely granulated sugar used for decorating purposes. In addition to sanding sugar, other grades of coarsely granulated sugars are available, each more finely granulated than the preceding ones: Coarse, Standard, Medium, and Manufacturers' Grade. These grades of sugar are for special uses where high temperatures must be used in cookery, such as in clear hard candies.

Powdered sugars are machine ground from the granulated sucrose obtained from sugar cane or sugar beets. Powdered sugars range from Coarse Powdered through Standard Powdered and a series of fine powdered sugars variously labeled according to the manufacturer but all using the letter *X*. Some labels seen on packages are XXXX or Confectioners'; 6X or Special XXXX, which is extrafine powdered sugar; and Confectioners' 10X Powdered, which is still finer. Powdered sugars usually contain small amounts of corn starch to prevent caking.

Loaf sugars are prepared by the pressing of wet sucrose crystals into a cake. When hard, the cake is cut into cube or tablet form, which is commonly designated *lump sugar*.

Brown sugars vary in color and flavor from the very light yellowish sugars to very dark brown ones. The lighter the color of the brown sugar the higher is the stage of purification and the less pronounced is the flavor. Brown sugar is made from cane sugar and contains some of the molasses from which the crystals were separated; hence some glucose and fructose as well as salts and flavor substances are present in brown sugar. Liquid brown sugar may also be available; the usual directions are to use one half as much of the liquid as the crystalline product, by measure, in recipes calling for brown sugar.

The high percentage of sucrose present in maple sap is not removed or purified but when it is sold as maple sugar sucrose is crystalline as a result of the concentration of the sap. The sap is more often concentrated only to the syrup stage.

Syrups, Molasses, and Honey

Corn syrups generally contain about 75 percent carbohydrate and 25 percent water. However, the proportions of the various sugars present in the carbohydrate portion may vary greatly, depending upon the manufacturing process and the proposed use of the product. Corn syrup has traditionally been prepared by using acid and high temperatures to hydrolyze corn starch. The carbohydrate of the resulting product is composed of from 10 to 36 percent glucose and from 9 to 20 percent maltose with the remainder consisting of higher sugars and dextrins [6, 7]. With the additional use of selected enzymes, such as *glucoamylase*, a corn syrup may be prepared that contains a much higher proportion of glucose and/or maltose. High glucose syrups have lower viscosity and higher sweetening power.

A high glucose corn syrup may be used to produce a high fructose corn syrup by the application of an enzyme called *glucose isomerase*. This enzyme catalyzes the chemical reaction that changes about half of the glucose in the mixture to the sweeter fructose. High fructose corn syrup (HFCS), which contains about 42 percent of the carbohydrate as fructose, was produced in the early 1970s [11]. Syrups containing up to 90 percent of the carbohydrate as fructose have since been prepared. High fructose corn syrup is used in the manufacture of soft drinks. It may also be used in the production of candies, preserves, and some baked products.

Molasses is the residue that remains after sucrose crystals have been removed from the concentrated juices of the sugar cane or beet. It contains not more than 25 percent water and not more than 5 percent mineral ash. The sugar, which may be present in amounts up to 70 percent, is a mixture of sucrose, glucose, and fructose, but is chiefly sucrose.

Sorghum is made from sorghum cane and is similar to molasses in appearance. The total sugar content is about 65 to 70 percent.

Maple syrup is the most highly prized of syrups used for culinary and table purposes. It is made by evaporation of the sap of the sugar maple to a concentration containing no more than 35 percent water. The special flavor that gives maple syrup its economic importance is not in the sap as it comes from the tree but is developed in the processing or cooking down of the sap into syrup. Organic acids present in the sap enter into the process of developing flavor by heat. It has been found that evaporating the sap at low temperatures through distillation or freeze-drying results in a syrup that is practically flavorless and colorless.

Honey is the nectar of flowers that is collected, modified, and concentrated by the honeybee. Honey contains about 75 percent of a mixture of glucose and fructose and 2 percent or more sucrose. As defined by the U.S. Food and Drug Administration, honey may not contain more than 8 percent sucrose; a higher percentage is taken as an indication of adulteration by added sucrose. Honey is the one natural food product in which fructose occurs in a higher percentage than glucose, the relative amounts being about 40.5 percent fructose and 34.5 percent glucose. The flavors of honey differ according to the characteristic esters that are present in the nectar of different flowers. Over half of the honey produced in this country is mild-flavored sweet clover, clover, or alfalfa honey. Honeys also come from orange and other citrus blossoms, wild sage, cultivated buckwheat, and the tulip tree. Much of the honey on the market is a blend of different floral types.

The color of honey may vary from white to amber or darker. The grades or qualities of honey are independent of color, but darker-colored honey generally has a stronger flavor than the white or light-colored product. It is also more acid, which has some significance in the determination of the amount of soda to neutralize the acidity of honey used as a partial substitute for sugar in flour mixtures.

Honey is stored in the comb by bees and in that form is marketed as section-comb honey. If extracted and strained from the comb, the honey is marketed as strained honey. About three fourths of the honey crop is sold as strained honey.

A process has been developed for producing dried honey. The prod-

Table 15-1 *Substitution Among Sugar and Syrup Products*

1 cup brown sugar = $\frac{1}{2}$ cup liquid brown sugar
1 cup honey = $1\frac{1}{4}$ cups sugar + $\frac{1}{4}$ cup liquid
1 cup corn syrup = 1 cup sugar + $\frac{1}{4}$ cup liquid

uct has a color and flavor that are quite close to that of the original honey. It has granular form, is free flowing, and has long shelf life. It may have sucrose added for the purpose of raising the temperature at which the dried product will soften thus making it more resistant to caking at high temperatures. Dried honey has applications in commercial baking, in confectionery, and in packaged dry baking mixes [2].

Table 15-1 lists some sugar and syrup substitutions that may be made in food preparation. Adjustment must be made for the liquid present in syrups.

Sugar Alcohols

Several sugar alcohols have been used in various processed foods. Two of these are sorbitol and xylitol, which are chemically similar to the sugars glucose and xylose, respectively. Sorbitol and xylitol occur naturally in a variety of plants including many fruits and vegetables. They perform several functions when used as food additives.

Sorbitol is considerably less sweet than sucrose (table sugar) and is, therefore, not generally used for its sweetening power. It is of value as a humectant to increase the water holding capacity of a food product. It is used in shredded coconut and marshmallows for this purpose. It also helps to control the crystallization of sugar in candies and maintain a smooth texture. Sorbitol has been used in certain "dietetic" cookies and candies for many years. It is more slowly absorbed from the intestinal tract than are the common sugars and may, therefore, have a lesser effect in raising the level of sugar in the blood after these foods are eaten. Sorbitol has a similar caloric value to glucose.

Xylitol is the sweetest of the sugar alcohols, being similar to sucrose in sweetness [1]. However, its sweetness is affected by its concentration, the degree of acidity, and the temperature of the food in which it is used. Xylitol is broken down or fermented only slowly by bacteria that are usually present on the teeth and, therefore, is not conducive to the development of dental caries as are the common sugars. It has been used as a sucrose replacement in certain cariogenic foods such as chewing gum and hard candies. The U.S. Food and Drug Administration has approved xylitol for special dietary uses but testing is continuing to completely establish its safety.

Sugar has been used to sweeten foods for many decades. But during the 1950s a concern about caloric intake and weight control emerged and has been steadily growing. The food industry has responded to this consumer concern with a wide variety of low- and reduced-calorie products. Noncaloric substitutes for sugar are necessary in the production of many low-calorie foods. Saccharin, which is approximately 300 times sweeter than sucrose, has been the most widely used artificial sweetener and has been the only one available during different periods of time. Safety testing on saccharin began long ago when it was first synthesized and has continued to the present time with controversial results. Because several studies showed that saccharin caused bladder tumors in rats, the U.S. Food and Drug Administration in 1977 proposed banning it for most uses. However, strong public protest influenced the U.S. Congress to impose a moratorium against any action to ban this substance. The moratorium must be extended periodically to allow its continued use.

In 1981 a new artificial sweetener, aspartame, was approved by the Food and Drug Administration for use in a variety of foods including beverages, cold cereals, gelatins, puddings, and dessert toppings. Aspartame is a synthetic compound comprised of two amino acids (building blocks of proteins). These amino acids are aspartic acid and phenylalanine [8, 10]. Individuals with phenylketonuria (PKU) should not use this product. Extensive testing has been done to assure the safety of aspartame for food use. This testing is continuing. Aspartame has the same caloric value as sugar but is at least 100 times as sweet and would thus provide only about one-tenth of a calorie for the same amount of sweetness in a teaspoon of sugar. A particular advantage of the use of aspartame is that it has no bitter aftertaste as does saccharin. In acid solutions, aspartame is not stable to high temperatures and loses its sweetening power. At 38° C (100° F) aspartame-sweetened beverages will retain a sweet taste for only about 1 month.

In the preparation of some of the concentrated sugar products, such as candies and frostings, many of the chemical and physical properties of sugar are of particular importance. The foundation for cooked frosting and candies is a boiled sugar solution. Some properties of solutions will, therefore, be discussed here.

Boiling Points and Solutions

The boiling point of a liquid may be defined as the temperature at which the vapor pressure of the liquid is equal to the atmospheric pressure that is resting on its surface. At the boiling point the vapor pressure of the liquid pushes against the atmospheric pressure to the extent that bubbles of vapor break and are released. Once boiling occurs, the temperature of the boiling liquid does not increase. An equilibrium is established.

The boiling point of a liquid varies with the altitude because atmospheric pressure is lower at high altitudes and higher at low altitudes. The boiling point of water at sea level, where atmospheric pressure is about 15 pounds per square inch or barometric pressure is 760 millimeters of mercury, is taken as a standard. Water boils at sea level at a temperature of 100° C or 212° F. At higher altitudes, water boils at temperatures lower than 100° C (212° F). For each 960 feet above sea level the boiling point of water drops 1° C or 1.8° F. In mountainous areas, the low boiling point of water seriously interferes with many cooking operations so that methods and formulas usually require modification for use in high altitudes.

The boiling point of water may be lowered artificially by the creation of a partial vacuum. This is accomplished by the withdrawal of part of the air and steam above a boiling liquid, thus lowering the air and steam pressure. Similarly, the boiling point may be elevated by an increase in air or steam pressure. The pressure cooker, which is a tightly closed utensil, increases pressure by preventing the vapor above the liquid from escaping. The pressure of the accumulated steam is thus added to that of the atmosphere above the liquid.

Anything that decreases the vapor pressure of a liquid will increase its boiling point. Substances in true solution, such as sugar or salt, which do not become volatile or gaseous at the boiling point of water, will decrease the vapor pressure of the water in which they are dissolved because these molecules displace water molecules on the surface of the liquid. The boiling point is thus increased because it takes more heat to raise the lowered vapor pressure to the point where it is equal to the atmospheric pressure (Figure 15-1). If dissolved substances ionize in solution, as does salt, they will decrease the vapor pressure, and therefore raise the boiling point of the water, to an even greater degree, the extent being dependent on the *number* of particles or ions formed. The larger the number of particles of solute in the solution, the more the vapor pressure is lowered and the higher is the temperature of boiling.

Boiling sugar solutions do not reach a constant boiling point as does water alone. As water evaporates and the remaining solution thus becomes more concentrated the boiling temperature increases. This process continues until all of the water is evaporated or the melting point of the sugar is reached, after which decomposition changes occur in the sugar. The boiling point of some pure sucrose solutions of various concentrations is given in Table 15-2. These figures are for sucrose solutions alone and do not apply to mixed

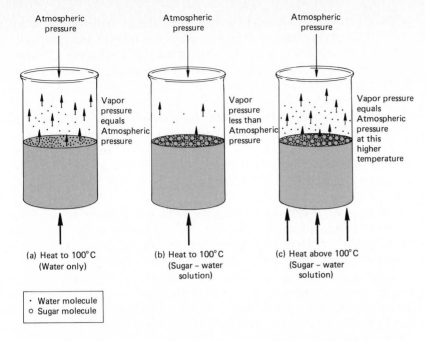

(a) Heat to 100°C
(Water only)

(b) Heat to 100°C
(Sugar – water solution)

(c) Heat above 100°C
(Sugar – water solution)

· Water molecule
∘ Sugar molecule

15-1 (a) *Pure water boils at 100° C (212° F) at sea level because its vapor pressure is equal to the atmospheric pressure at this point and an equilibrium is established.*
(b) *When sugar or other solute is dissolved in water, some of the sugar molecules displace water molecules on the surface and decrease the vapor pressure of the solution. Heating to 100° C does not increase the water vapor pressure enough to be equal to the atmosphere pressure at this point.*
(c) *More heat must be put into the solution in order to vaporize more water and increase the vapor pressure enough to equal the atmospheric pressure. Therefore, a sugar solution boils at a higher temperature than pure water. The higher the concentration of sugar or solute, the higher the boiling point.*

sugar solutions such as sucrose solutions containing corn syrup, glucose, or molasses, which are more commonly used in making candy than are pure sucrose solutions. Candy mixtures are, however, predominantly sucrose.

Inversion of Sucrose

The formation of equal amounts of glucose and fructose, called *invert sugar*, occurs when sucrose is hydrolyzed. Because a mixture of invert sugar and sucrose is more soluble than a sucrose solution alone, and thus less easily crystallized, the mixture allows the process of crystallization to be more easily controlled than when invert sugar is not present. Desirably small sugar crystals can thus be

Table 15-2 *The Boiling Points of Sucrose Solutions of Various Concentrations**

Percent Sucrose	10	20	30	40	50	60	70	80	90.8
Boiling point									
°F	212.7	213.1	213.8	214.7	215.6	217.4	223.7	233.6	266.0
°C	100.4	100.6	101.0	101.5	102.0	103.0	106.5	112.0	130.0

*From Browne's *Handbook of Sugar Analysis*. By permission of John Wiley & Sons, Inc.

produced in candies such as fondant and fudge. Although a small amount of invert sugar may be formed by the long slow heating of a simple sucrose solution, the reaction is accelerated by the presence of acid. Various acids may be used but the acid salt, cream of tartar, is probably preferable because its composition is fairly uniform and measurements may be quite accurate. Fondant made with cream of tartar is also snowy white. Invert sugar itself is very soluble and difficult to crystallize in comparison with sucrose. The amount of invert sugar formed in a boiled sugar solution is, therefore, important to the ease of crystallization of sugar from that solution. The presence of 43 percent invert sugar has been found to completely prevent crystallization.

The amount of inversion that occurs when sucrose is heated with water and acid varies greatly and is difficult to control. The rate of heating, the length of time of heating, and the quantity of cream of tartar used all affect the amount of invert sugar formed. Under household conditions, it is obviously difficult, if not impossible, to obtain uniform inversion. If too much acid is used, or if the period of heating is too long, too much inversion occurs with the result that the fondant is extremely soft or fails to crystallize at all. Usually about ¼ teaspoon of cream of tartar is used with 2 cups of sugar in fondant. It has been reported [12] that in fondant cooked to a temperature of 115° C (239° F) in 20 minutes, approximately ⅛ teaspoon cream of tartar with 200 grams (1 cup) sugar produced about 11 percent invert sugar in the finished fondant.

Glucose, fructose, or invert sugar may be added directly to sucrose solutions in candy making rather than producing invert sugar during cooking by the addition of a weak acid such as cream of tartar. The addition of these substances directly makes control of their quantity easier than trying to regulate the amount of invert sugar produced by sucrose hydrolysis. Corn syrup, which contains a high proportion of glucose, is sometimes used instead of cream of tartar in fondant mixtures made at home. The presence of glucose in the sucrose solution has a similar effect to invert sugar in increasing the solubility of the sucrose and allowing better control of the crystallization process so that small sugar crystals may be produced in the final product.

Calibrating and Reading the Thermometer

The first step in candy making is to calibrate the thermometer by taking the temperature of boiling water. At sea level this temperature is 100° C (212° F). At higher altitudes the boiling temperature will be lower (1° C for each 960 feet above sea level). If the thermometer does not show the proper temperature, an adjustment should be made by adding or subtracting, as appropriate, the difference in degrees between the expected and observed temperatures.

In taking the temperature of boiling sugar solutions, the bulb of the thermometer should be completely immersed in the solution but should not touch the bottom of the pan. In reading the scale, the eye should be on a level with the top of the mercury column.

Types of Candies from Boiled Sugar Solutions

Boiled sugar solutions may be so treated that they produce either *crystalline* or *noncrystalline* candies. Special textures result from the use of certain added substances, such as gelatin or egg white. The principal crystalline candies are fondant, chocolate fudge, and panocha. Noncrystalline candies may be chewy, such as caramels, or hard, such as butterscotch and brittles.

Crystalline Candies

Fondant. Fondant results from the cooking of a sucrose solution to a certain range of temperatures, after which the solution is cooled and beaten until crystallization occurs. A simple sucrose and water solution sometimes makes good fondant but surer and more satisfactory results are obtained by the addition of acid to accelerate inversion or by the direct addition of invert sugar, glucose, or corn syrup to aid in keeping crystals small.

Essential steps in the making of fondant include (1) complete solution of the crystalline sugar; (2) concentration of the solution to the desirable stage; and (3) prevention of crystallization until conditions are favorable for the formation of fine crystals.

Solution. Complete solution of sugar is accomplished by the addition of sufficient water to dissolve the amount of sugar used, by stirring, and by the use of a cover on the pan at the beginning of cooking to allow steam to dissolve any crystals that may remain on the sides of the pan. An alternative procedure to covering the pan for the purpose of dissolving crystals on the sides of the pan is to wash down the sides of the pan with a small piece of moistened paper towel or cheesecloth wrapped around a fork.

Undissolved crystals will cause seeding while the solution is cooling and start crystallization before it is desirable to have it start. The pan cannot remain covered throughout the cooking period as evaporation must occur to bring about the necessary concentration within a reasonable time period. Stirring the solution during cooking does not start crystallization. Stirring and vigorous boiling may, however, splash syrup on the sides of the pan above the level of the liquid where it may dry, drop into the cooling syrup, and start premature crystallization. The spoon used for stirring may also introduce dried crystals unless it is well rinsed between stirrings. It is desirable to wash down the crystals from the sides of the pan during the boiling period if more crystals form after the initial washing down.

Concentration. Table 15-3 gives the temperatures and tests of doneness for candies of various types.

As may be seen, the range of temperatures for final cooking of fondant mixtures at sea level is 112° to 115° C (234° to 240° F). The lower temperature gives a very soft fondant and the upper temperature gives a firmer, drier fondant for easier molding. A temperature of 112° C (234° F) may be a little low except for fondants for special uses (remelting) or for fondants containing corn syrup. When corn syrup is used in candy, definite stages of firmness are reached at slightly lower temperatures than when it is not used. For general use, 113° and 114° C (235° and 237° F) are the most satisfactory temperatures for fondants. The higher the temperature the lower is the water content and consequently the drier the fondant. When the

Table 15-3   *Temperatures and Tests for Syrup and Candies**

Product	Final Temperature of Syrup at Sea Level**		Test of Doneness	Description of Test
Syrup	110° C to 112° C	230° F to 234° F	Thread	Syrup spins a 2-inch thread when dropped from fork or spoon.
Fondant Fudge Panocha	112° C to 115° C	234° F to 240° F	Soft ball	Syrup, when dropped into very cold water, forms a soft ball that flattens on removal from water.
Caramels	118° C to 120° C	244° F to 248° F	Firm ball	Syrup, when dropped into very cold water, forms a firm ball that does not flatten on removal from water.
Divinity Marshmallows Popcorn balls	121° C to 130° C	250° F to 256° F	Hard ball	Syrup, when dropped into very cold water, forms a ball that is hard enough to hold its shape, yet plastic.
Butterscotch Taffies	132° C to 143° C	270° F to 290° F	Soft crack	Syrup, when dropped into very cold water, separates into threads that are hard but not brittle.
Brittle Glacé	149° C to 154° C	300° F to 310° F	Hard crack	Syrup, when dropped into very cold water, separates into threads that are hard and brittle.
Barley sugar	160° C	320° F	Clear liquid	The sugar liquefies.
Caramel	170° C	338° F	Brown liquid	The liquid becomes brown.

*From *Handbook of Food Preparation,* 7th ed. Washington, D.C.: American Home Economics Association, 1975.
**For each increase of 500 feet in elevation, cook the syrup to a temperature 1° F lower than the temperature called for at sea level. If readings are taken in Centigrade, for each 960 feet of elevation, cook the syrup to a temperature 1° C lower than that called for at sea level.

humidity is high, the use of higher temperatures is desirable, because more water is absorbed by fondant in damp weather. At altitudes above sea level, the final boiling temperatures should be lowered to the extent that the boiling point of water is decreased below 100° C or 212° F.

The testing of doneness for candy mixtures by measuring the temperature of the boiling solution is a method of estimating the concentration of sugar in the mixture. The final concentration of sugar is related, in general, to the consistency of the candy when it is completely prepared—the more concentrated the sugar solution, the firmer is the consistency of the finished candy. Another method of measuring doneness in the making of candies is by dropping a small portion of the boiling syrup into very cold water, allowing the syrup to cool, and evaluating its consistency. The results of the cold water tests of doneness are compared with the temperatures of cooking in Table 15-3.

The desired rate of cooking fondant mixtures depends partly on the proportions of ingredients used. Faster boiling is necessary if a high proportion of water is used in order to avoid too long a cooking period and consequently too great inversion in acid solutions. Violent boiling is usually to be avoided because of the larger amount of syrup that is splashed on the sides of the pan.

After boiling, the syrup is usually poured out on a smooth flat surface on which it can later be beaten. As the hot syrup cools, it becomes saturated and then supersaturated since it is holding in solution more solute (sugar) than is normally soluble at the lower temperatures. As has been previously stated, this is an unstable condition and crystallization readily occurs. Pouring the syrup should be done quickly without the pan's being scraped. Scraping, prolonged dripping from the pan, or jostling the poured syrup usually start crystallization. Uneven cooling may start crystallization in those portions of the syrup that first become supersaturated. If a thermometer is placed in the syrup to determine when the syrup is ready for beating, it should be read without its being moved in the syrup.

Crystallization. In making crystalline candies the aim is to produce a very smooth texture. Smooth texture results from the formation of many fine crystals rather than a few large crystals.

Conditions must be provided that favor the formation, within the supersaturated solution, of many nuclei or small clumps of molecules, which act as centers to begin crystal formation. Around these nuclei crystallization occurs. Some substances readily crystallize from a water solution with only a slight degree of supersaturation. With other substances, such as sugar, there must usually be a high degree of supersaturation before nuclei formation and crystallization start.

To produce many nuclei and fine crystals, control of conditions is necessary. Some of the conditions have been mentioned but may be summarized here along with others:

1. There must be no undissolved crystals of the solute. These may be present because (a) they were not completely dissolved in the beginning; (b) they formed during the boiling of the solution; or (c) they formed by agitation or other careless handling after the desired concentration of syrup was reached.

2. The presence of substances that interfere with crystallization is desirable but at an optimum level. In fondant, these substances may be added directly, as glucose, corn syrup, or invert sugar, or invert sugar may be formed by acid hydrolysis. In some other types of crystalline candies, such as fudge, fat, egg white, and milk may provide interfering substances. Adsorption of these substances on the surface of crystals retards the growth of crystals.

3. The temperature at which crystallization occurs affects the size of crystals, primarily because it affects the rate of crystallization. In general, the higher the temperature at which crystallization occurs, the faster the rate of crystallization and the more difficult it is to keep the crystals separated, resulting in larger crystals. Cooling to a temperature of about 40° C (104° F) before starting to beat the fondant favors the formation of more nuclei and finer crystals. The viscosity of the solution is also greater at lower temperatures, and high viscosity is a further aid in the production of fine crystals because it retards crystallization. Figure 15-2 shows the sizes of crystals formed in fondant beaten at different temperatures. The syrup may be cooled to so low a temperature that beating is impossible. Too low a temperature may also hinder the formation of many nuclei.

4. Agitation favors the formation of finer crystals than are produced when they form spontaneously. It is important to provide some form of agitation, such as beating, not only until crystallization starts but until it is complete. At that stage, the candy is stiffer and moldable.

Because it is desirable to knead out all lumps and form a smooth plastic mass as soon as crystallization occurs, rapid work is necessary at the completion of crystallization in order to prevent hardening and crumbling of the fondant before kneading is started (Figure 15-3). It is usually possible to see when the fondant is about to set in a more stiff mass. Its shiny appearance becomes dulled and it seems to soften temporarily. The softening is the result of the heat of crystallization being given off as the crystals form.

As crystalline candy stands after crystallization is complete, it becomes somewhat more moist and smooth and kneads more easily because some of the very small crystals dissolve in the syrup. This change during the initial period of storage is called *ripening*. Ad-

15-2 *Comparison of crystallization with various methods of making fondant.* (Courtesy of Dr. Sybil Woodruff and *Journal of Physical Chemistry*)

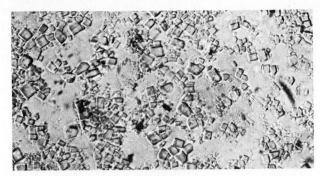

Crystals from fondant made with sugar, water, and cream of tartar; boiled to a temperature of 115° C (239° F) and cooled to a temperature of 40° C (104° F) before beating.

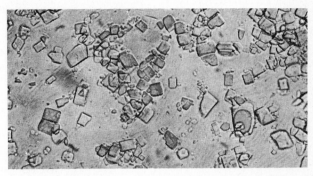

Crystals from fondant made with sugar and water with 7 percent glucose added; boiled to a temperature of 115° C (239° F) and cooled to a temperature of 40° C (104° F) before beating.

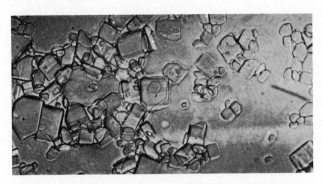

Crystals from fondant made with sugar and water only; boiled to a temperature of 115° C (239° F) and cooled to a temperature of 40° C (104° F) before beating.

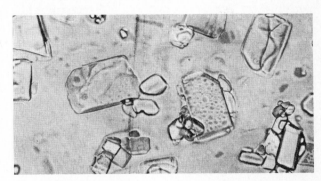

Crystals from fondant made with sugar and water only; boiled to a temperature of 115° C (239° F) and beaten immediately.

15-3 *Fondant being manipulated with a spatula after it has cooled to a temperature of 40° C (104° F). Some form of agitation is needed until crystallization is complete. As soon as crystallization is complete, fondant is quickly formed into a ball and kneaded until smooth.* (Courtesy of General Foods, Inc.)

sorbed substances that interfere with crystallization aid in retarding the growth of crystals during storage.

Proportions for Fondant

I. WITH CREAM OF TARTAR	II. WITH CORN SYRUP
2 c (400 g) granulated sugar	2 c (400 g) granulated sugar
¼ t cream of tartar	1 to 1½ T (21 to 39 g) syrup
1 c (237 ml) water	1 c (237 ml) water

Fudge. The principles of making fudge do not differ from those for making fondant. Usually the butter or margarine, the fat of chocolate, and the milk furnish the substances that interfere with crystallization. Acid is sometimes used, and corn syrup may be used. If brown sugar replaces part or all of the white sugar some invert sugar is introduced as part of the sugar, as well as some acid to help invert sucrose. Therefore, brown-sugar fudge (panocha) crystallizes less rapidly than white-sugar fudge. Fudge made from cocoa instead of chocolate should be cooked to a slightly lower temperature on account of its higher dextrin content. When crystallization is almost complete the glossy appearance of fudge will become dull and the whole mass will soften slightly as described for fondant (Figures 15-4 and 15-5).

Noncrystalline Candies

In noncrystalline candies one may prevent the crystallization of sugar by (1) cooking to very high temperatures so that the finished product hardens quickly before the crystals have a chance to form; (2) adding such large amounts of interfering substances that the crystals cannot form; or (3) a combination of these.

Brittles. Brittles are cooked to temperatures that are high enough to give a hard, brittle candy that solidifies before it has a chance to crystallize. The brown color and characteristic flavor of brittles results from nonenzymatic browning reactions, probably of both the Maillard type and the caramelization of sugar. The development of caramel also helps to prevent crystallization of sugar in the brittles since it is noncrystalline.

Some brittles are made merely by the melting and caramelizing of sucrose. Soda is sometimes a constituent of brittles and is added after cooking is completed. It neutralizes acid decomposition products and forms carbon dioxide gas, which gives a porous texture to the candy. The flavor is also made milder and less bitter by the use of soda. The degree of bitterness in a brittle depends on the extent of decomposition of the sugar. Brittles include butterscotch, nut brittles, and toffee. (See Figure 15-6.)

Combine sugar, salt, cream, milk, corn syrup, and margarine in a heavy saucepan.

Cook over medium heat, stirring constantly, until sugar is dissolved and mixture boils.

Continue cooking, stirring occasionally, until temperature reaches 114°C (238°F) or until a small amount dropped into very cold water forms a soft ball that flattens on removal from the water. Remove from heat and cool without stirring.

Beat until fudge begins to thicken and lose its gloss. Fold in nuts. Immediately spread into a buttered pan.

Cut into squares when cold. Chocolate fudge is made by adding unsweetened chocolate to the ingredients in the saucepan before starting to cook.

15-4 *Preparation of blonde fudge.* (Courtesy of Best Foods)

Fudge that has been beaten too long and has hardened in the pan.

Fudge beaten to the correct stage for pouring into a dish to harden.

Caramels. Caramels are firm noncrystalline candies containing large amounts of interfering substances, which are cooked to temperatures between those for crystalline and those for hard brittle candies. The added substances that interfere with crystallization are usually butter or margarine and viscous corn syrup or molasses which contain glucose, fructose, or invert sugar. Corn syrup also contains dextrins which do not crystallize. Acid hydrolysis may be used to produce invert sugar if preferred but more inversion is necessary for caramels than for fondant. Fats and proteins in milk or cream also aid in preventing crystallization. The final cooking temperature varies with the kind and proportion of ingredients.

The brown color of caramels is primarily the result of the nonenzymatic browning (Maillard) reaction. In this reaction glucose or lactose combines with the amino groups of the milk proteins. The color and flavor of caramels develop better with long, slow heating than with rapid cooking. The characteristic flavor of plain caramels may be modified somewhat by the addition of chocolate or molasses.

Taffy. Taffy may be made from a simple sucrose syrup with the addition of cream of tartar, vinegar, or lemon juice to invert part of the sucrose and prevent crystallization. Flavoring extracts may be added when the solution has cooled sufficiently for pulling. Glucose, corn syrup, or molasses may be used instead of acid. Taffies are harder candies than caramels and, therefore, require higher cooking temperatures.

Fondant Confections

The uses for fondants in confectionary are numerous. They may be made into bonbons, which are fondant centers dipped in melted fondant; or into fondant loaves, which have fruit and nut mixtures added. Centers for chocolates are commonly made from fondant. Fondant patties are made from melted fondant flavored and colored as desired. Candy cookbooks suggest many specific combinations of fondant with other ingredients.

Fondant Dipping. Fondant centers are prepared ahead of time from fondant of a suitable texture for molding. The molded centers are allowed to stand on waxed paper until they are firm and slightly hardened on the outside. The fondant for melting may or may not be of softer consistency than that used for molding. A small quantity of fondant—about 1 cup—is used for melting. This amount forms a sufficient depth to coat the centers easily yet not enough to become too coarse and granular before it can be used. The fondant is best melted over hot water, but for ease in using, a small shallow pan, suspended over another pan containing hot water, is preferable to a deep double boiler.

While melting, the solid fondant is broken up or turned frequently but with a minimum amount of agitation. The formation of coarse crystals by the stirring of a hot solution is as important here as in the making of the original fondant. While the fondant is melting, food colors in liquid or paste form may be applied on the point of a toothpick. Care should be taken to avoid adding too much color. Food flavors, if in the form of oils, must be added with equal care to avoid too strong a flavor. Extracts are more dilute.

After the fondant is melted, colored, and flavored, it requires cooling slightly to a consistency that will cling to the molded fondant during dipping. The molded pieces of fondant are quickly dipped into the melted fondant and are then placed on waxed paper in a cool environment to set.

Colors and flavors that are often used together are as follows:

Color	Flavor
Red	Oil of cinnamon or cloves
Green	Oil of lime
White	Oil of peppermint
Pink	Oil of wintergreen
Yellow	Oil of lemon
Orange	Oil of orange

Fondant Patties. Fondant patties are also made from melted fondant. After the melted fondant is colored and flavored it is dropped on waxed paper from a teaspoon. One-half to 1 teaspoonful may be used according to the size of patty desired. Speed is necessary in order to dip and pour the fondant before it begins to harden. If the melted fondant becomes too stiff to flow into a smooth patty, it should be remelted or have a very small amount of hot water added to it.

Chocolate Dipping

The chocolate used for ordinary culinary purposes is not generally suitable for dipping candies. Dipping chocolate is usually of fine quality and has sufficient cocoa butter to give a consistency that hardens satisfactorily with a smooth, glossy finish.

Centers to be coated with chocolate should be prepared several hours before dipping in order that they may be firm enough to handle easily. An exception is fondant centers to which invertase enzyme has been added. This type of fondant becomes softer the longer it stands.

Successful chocolate dipping depends largely on the following factors: (1) the use of a suitable chocolate; (2) the control of temperatures and avoidance of humid atmosphere; and (3) thorough stirring or handmanipulation of the chocolate while it is melting, cooling, and, so far as possible, while dipping. Manipulation of the chocolate ensures uniform blending of the cocoa butter with the other chocolate constituents and produces a more even coating on the finished chocolates.

Temperatures and Techniques. Room temperatures and humidity are well controlled in commercial chocolate dipping rooms. The temperature should be from 15° to 20° C (60° to 70° F). A clear, cool day of low relative humidity is desirable. Drafts should be avoided as uneven cooling affects the gloss and color of chocolates.

The even melting of the chocolate is facilitated by grating or shaving. A double boiler is a desirable piece of equipment to use as the chocolate should be melted over hot (not boiling) water. At high temperatures the cocoa butter tends to separate from the other constituents of chocolate. About 1 pound of chocolate gives a satisfactory quantity of melted chocolate with which to work. While the chocolate is melting, it should be stirred continuously. Stirring prevents uneven heating and overheating and maintains a uniform blend.

After the chocolate has melted and been taken to a temperature of about 49° C (120° F) for tempering, it should be continuously stirred while cooling to a temperature of about 28° C (83° F). The chocolate is then ready for dipping. The range of temperatures at which chocolates can be satisfactorily dipped is small; hence rapid dipping is necessary. Fondant centers may be dropped into the chocolate, coated, and lifted out with the use of a wire chocolate dipper or a two-tined fork. The coated chocolate is inverted on waxed paper. Another method of dipping chocolates is to pour the melted chocolate onto a marble-topped surface and stir it with the hand. Fondant centers may be rolled in the melted chocolate, the surplus chocolate removed by tapping the fingers lightly on the marble surface, and then the coated chocolate is dropped quickly on waxed paper. (See Figure 15-7.)

Defects of Dipped Chocolates. The chief defects of dipped chocolates are gray or streaked surfaces, a broad base on the dipped chocolate, or sticky spots on the surface. Gray surfaces are caused by unfavorable room temperatures, incorrect chocolate temperatures, direct drafts, excessive humidity, insufficient stirring of the chocolate, and too slow cooling of the chocolates. The surface of a defective chocolate appears dull and gray because the fat of the chocolate has

15-7

Chocolate is mixed until it reaches the correct temperature for dipping.

A fondant center is rolled in the chocolate and then placed on waxed paper in a cool room where the chocolate should set up or harden immediately.
(Photograph by Roger P. Smith and Ava Winterton)

not crystallized in a stable form. A broad base on the dipped chocolate results from dipping at too high temperatures or from failure to remove excess chocolate after dipping. Sticky spots result from leakage of the centers because of incomplete coating with chocolate. These spots are particularly likely to occur in chocolates made from fondants that liquefy on standing.

Study Questions

1. Sugars have many properties that are of importance in the preparation of candies and other sugar-containing foods.
   a. List the common sugars in order of their solubilities in water at room temperature and describe how the solubility of sugars is affected by temperature.
   b. Describe a saturated and a supersaturated solution and explain the significance of a supersaturated solution in making crystalline candies.
   c. What happens when sugar is heated in a dry state above its melting point? Why is this reaction of importance in food preparation?
   d. What is meant by hygroscopic? Which is the most hygroscopic sugar?
   e. Name the two monosaccharides that result from the hydrolysis of sucrose. What catalysts may cause sucrose hydrolysis? Describe examples of the importance of this reaction in food preparation, particularly in candy making.
   f. Describe examples from food preparation of the effect of sugar decomposition by alkali.
   g. Compare the common sugars for relative sweetness and discuss several factors that affect these comparisons. Under what conditions is fructose likely to taste most sweet?
2. Various types of sugars and syrups are available on the market. Describe the major characteristics of each of the following:
   a. Fine granulated sugar (sucrose)
   b. Powdered sugar
   c. Brown sugar
   d. Corn syrup
   e. High fructose corn syrup
   f. Molasses
   g. Honey
   h. Maple syrup
3. Describe major characteristics and potential uses for:
   a. Sorbitol
   b. Xylitol
   c. Saccharin
   d. Aspartame
4. a. What is the effect of sugar on the boiling point of water? Explain.
   b. Describe what happens as one continues to boil a sugar solution.
5. a. Name two major classifications for candies and describe the general characteristics of each type.
   b. Classify caramels, toffee, fondant, taffy, butterscotch, fudge, brittles, and panocha into the appropriate groups described in queston a.

6. Describe the basic steps involved in the preparation of crystalline candies such as fondant and fudge. Explain what is happening in each step and how crystallization is controlled.
7. Describe the basic steps involved in the preparation of brittles and of caramels. Explain how crystallization is prevented in each case.
8. Suggest several uses for basic fondant.
9. Describe and explain several precautions that must be observed for successful dipping of chocolates.

References

1. Emodi, A. 1978. Xylitol, its properties and food applications. *Food Technology* **32,** 28 (no. 1).
2. Glabe, E. F., P. W. Anderson, P. Goldman, and G. M. Murawski. 1965. Honey solids. *Baker's Digest* **38,** 71 (April).
3. Hardy, S. L., C. P. Brennand, and B. W. Wyse. 1979. Fructose: Comparison with sucrose as sweetener in four products. *Journal of the American Dietetic Association* **74,** 41.
4. Inglett, G. E. 1981. Sweeteners—a review. *Food Technology* **35,** 37 (no. 3).
5. Institute of Food Technologists' Expert Panel on Food Safety and Nutrition. 1979. Sugars and nutritive sweeteners in processed foods. *Food Technology* **33,** 101 (no. 5).
6. Keal, E. J. 1973. Sweeteners for baked foods. *Baker's Digest* **47,** 80 (October).
7. Koivistoinen, P., and L. Hyvönen. *Carbohydrate Sweeteners in Foods and Nutrition.* New York: Academic Press, 1980.
8. Lecos, C. *The Sweet and Sour History of Saccharin, Cyclamate, Aspartame.* HHS Publication No. (FDA) 81-2156. Rockville, MD: Department of Health and Human Services.
9. Lineback, D. R., and G. E. Inglett, editors. *Food Carbohydrates.* Westport, CT: Avi Publishing Company, Inc., 1982.
10. O'Brien, L., and R. C. Gelardi. 1981. Alternative sweeteners. *Chemtech* **11,** 274.
11. Saussele, H., Jr., H. F. Ziegler, and J. H. Weideman. 1976. High fructose corn syrups for bakery applications. *Baker's Digest* **50,** 32 (February).
12. Woodruff, S., and H. Van Gilder. 1931. Photomicrographic studies of sucrose crystals. *Journal of Physical Chemistry* **35,** 1355.

16
Frozen Desserts

Frozen desserts include sherbets, ices, ice creams, ice milks, and mousses although there is some confusion in the names given to various frozen mixtures. Frozen desserts, particularly ice creams, are among the most popular desserts in the United States. Most of the ice cream used in this country is commercially manufactured, although some ice cream is still prepared at home. Electrically operated ice cream freezers are available for home use.

In the making of commercial ice creams, mixes are scientifically blended and frozen to obtain optimum flavor, texture, and body. Homemade ice creams differ from the commercial products, generally containing fewer stabilizers and increasing less in volume when frozen. Even though homemakers may not often prepare ice cream at home, they might profit by a better understanding of the various factors that influence the flavor, texture, and body of ice cream made either commercially or at home and by a recognition of the standards of identity and composition in frozen desserts.

All types of frozen desserts are crystalline products in which water is crystallized as ice. In many of these products the aim is to obtain fine crystals that give a product that has a smooth texture. However, others, such as ices served as meat accompaniments, are expected to be rather crystalline in texture. Many of the same general factors that tend to produce fine crystals in crystalline candies, where the crystals are sugar, also tend to produce fine ice crystals in frozen desserts.

Body

The term *body* as used in connection with frozen desserts implies firmness or resistance to rapid melting. Homemade ice creams usually have less body than commerical ice creams because stabilizers used in the commercial products often add body. Homemade ice creams generally melt faster in the mouth and give the impression of being lighter desserts although they may actually be richer mixtures than many commercial ice creams.

Texture

Texture refers to fineness of particles, smooth quality, and lightness or porosity. The size and distribution of ice crystals is a major factor influencing the texture of frozen desserts. Substances that interfere with large crystal formation, such as fat and certain stabilizers, help to produce fine, smooth texture in frozen desserts. Tests of consumers preference show that consumers generally like a smooth, fine-grained ice cream.

Overrun or Swell

By *overrun* is meant the increase in volume of a frozen dessert that results from the beating of air into the mixture during freezing. Homemade ice creams usually have no more than 30 to 40 percent overrun, whereas commercial ice creams have at least 80 percent overrun and sometimes 90 to 100 percent. Federal standards have suggested a minimum weight of 4.5 pounds per gallon of ice cream. Too great an overrun results in a frothy, foamy ice cream, whereas too little air produces an ice cream of heavy, coarse texture. The higher percentage of overrun in commercial ice creams in comparison to homemade products results from a better control of freezing conditions, such as the rate of freezing and the stage of hardness at which the freezing is discontinued. Homogenization increases the viscosity of the mix, which favors a better retention of air.

The classification of frozen desserts, particularly homemade products, may be a little difficult because of the large variety of recipes or combinations of ingredients used. Commercial frozen desserts, however, are subject to state regulations and to federal regulations if they enter interstate commerce. These regulations are particularly designed to control the milk fat content.

There are four main types of frozen desserts: ice creams, ice milks, sherbets, and water ices [2]. Commercial ice creams made according to traditional formulations contain milk fat or butterfat, milk solids, sugar, flavoring, and a small amount of stabilizers. The stabilizers permitted under federal ice cream standards include agar, algin, gelatin, lecithin, sodium carboxymethylcellulose, Irish moss or carrageenan, gum acacia, and several other vegetable gums.

The U.S. Department of Agriculture has established a standard of composition for ice cream. Ice cream manufacturers may use a USDA symbol on their ice cream labels if they have met specified USDA requirements. Under the standard, ice cream must contain at least 1.6 pounds of total solids per gallon and weigh at least 4.5 pounds per gallon. It must contain at least 20 percent total milk solids, at least 10 percent milk fat, and at least 6 percent milk-solids-not-fat. Whey can be no more than 25 percent of the milk-solids-not-fat. Ice cream may or may not contain small amounts (up to 1.4 percent) of egg yolk solids. French ice cream or frozen custard must contain more than 1.4 percent egg yolk solids. If ice cream contains a comparatively large amount of bulky ingredients, such as chocolate syrup, nuts, and fruits, the minimum milk fat requirement is reduced to 8 percent and the minimum total milk solids decreased to 16 percent. Ice milk resembles ice cream except that the federal recommendation for minimum milk fat is 2 to 7 percent.

Commercial water ices are water-sugar syrups combined with fruits, fruit juices, or other flavoring materials and a small amount of gelatin, egg white, vegetable gum, or other stabilizer added to give body and smooth texture. Commercial sherbets are similar in ingredients to water ices except that they contain some dairy product such as milk or cream. Sherbets contain not less than 1 percent and not more than 2 percent milk fat and between 2 and 5 percent total milk solids.

Synthetic or imitation ice cream, often called *mellorine*, is similar in appearance and eating properties to ice cream but the fat ingredient is not milk fat. It is usually a vegetable fat but animal fats other than milk fat may also be used. Mellorine is less expensive to produce than ice cream and generally sells for less.

Either ice creams or ice milks may be sold in a soft form. The composition of soft ice creams or ice milks is similar to the regular forms, but they are not hardened or stored. State regulations may vary concerning the sale of soft-serve products.

Homemade frozen desserts may be variations of the following.

Water Ice. Water ice is a water-sugar syrup with fruit juice added. A stabilizer may be included.

Sherbet.   Sherbet is a milk-sugar syrup with fruit juice added, with or without a stabilizer.

Frappé.   A frappé is a frozen dessert frozen to a mush with a high percentage of salt used in the freezing mixture to give a coarse granular texture.

Ice Cream.   Ice cream is light cream (18 or 20 percent fat) that is sweetened and flavored. It may be modified in flavor by the addition of fruits, chocolate, chopped nuts, and the like. A custard mixture (often made with egg yolks) may be used. It may also contain stabilizers such as gelatin or a cooked starch paste.

Mousse.   Mousse is sweetened and flavored whipped cream. It may contain a small amount of gelatin and is usually frozen without stirring.

Biscuit.   Biscuit is similar to mousse but frozen in individual forms.

Freezing Points of Liquids

The Freezing Process

Pure liquids have characteristic freezing points at constant pressure. The freezing point is the temperature at which the vapor pressures of the pure liquid and its pure solid substance are equal and the liquid and solid forms remain together in equilibrium. The melting point and freezing point are identical. Because a liquid can be supercooled to a temperature below its freezing point before freezing occurs, it is not altogether accurate to describe the freezing point as the temperature at which the liquid changes to a solid.

Water freezes at a temperature of 0° C (32° F) at a pressure of 760 millimeters of mercury. After freezing, the temperature of ice may be lowered below 0° C (32° F). If the temperature of the surroundings is lower than 0° C (32° F), the ice as well as the air eventually reaches the lower temperature. Water expands in freezing to occupy more space than it did in the liquid form. The swelling or increased volume of frozen desserts is partly a result of the fact that watery mixtures expand in freezing and partly a result of the incorporation of air in those mixtures that are agitated during freezing.

Substances dissolved in a liquid to form a true solution cause the freezing point of the solution to be lower than the freezing point of the pure liquid. A sugar solution, which is the basis for frozen desserts, has a lower freezing point than pure water. The higher the concentration of the solution the lower is the freezing point. Ices and sherbets that contain acid fruit juices usually have a higher percentage of sugar than ice creams. They require a lower temperature to freeze and are actually colder when frozen than are most ice creams.

Freezing Mixtures

A freezing mixture as used in the ordinary ice cream freezer is ice combined with some soluble salt. The salt is usually sodium chloride (NaCl) because it is relatively inexpensive and readily available. One can lower the freezing point of the coarse salt-ice mixture by increasing the proportion of salt to ice until the saturation point for a salt in a water solution is reached. The lowest temperature possible in a brine from a salt and ice mixture is about $-21°$ or $-22°$ C ($-6°$ to $-8°$ F). Few dessert mixes require a temperature lower than $-8°$ to $-10°$ C ($14°$ to $18°$ F) in order to freeze.

When ice and salt are mixed, the surface of the ice is usually moist and dissolves some of the salt. The vapor pressure of the concentrated salt solution formed on the surface of the ice is lower than that of the ice itself. In an attempt by the system to establish equilibrium more ice melts. More salt then dissolves and the process is repeated. As the ice melts, it absorbs heat and the rapid melting of ice that occurs when salt is added increases the absorption of heat. Also, heat is absorbed as the salt dissolves in the film of water on the surface of the ice. The heat is taken from the brine, the air, or from the mixture to be frozen. As heat is absorbed, the temperatures of the brine and of the mixture to be frozen are lowered. The mixture to be frozen is thus rapidly lowered in temperature until its freezing point is reached. At the freezing point of the dessert mixture, ice crystals begin to form and precipitate out. The removal of some water as ice causes the remaining unfrozen mixture to become more concentrated, with a lower freezing temperature than the original dessert mixture. Thus, as freezing proceeds, the freezing temperature is gradually lowered just as boiling a sugar solution, with the evaporation of water, produces a gradual increase in the boiling temperature of the mixture.

Proportions of Salt to Ice. The proportions of salt to ice that are used in freezing a frozen dessert may vary according to the concentration of the mixture to be frozen, the texture desired in the finished dessert, the rate of freezing desired, and whether or not the mixture is stirred while freezing. When freezing is done with stirring, a proportion of salt to ice that is efficient for home freezing is about one part coarse salt to six parts finely chopped ice by weight. A proportion of one part salt to six parts ice by weight is equivalent to about one to twelve by measure. For faster freezing, a proportion of about one part salt to eight parts ice, by measure, is also satisfactory. The higher the percentage of salt, the shorter is the time required for freezing. However, if freezing is too rapid, not enough time is allowed to keep the ice crystals separated and small while stirring and the crystals of ice formed may be large enough to produce a granular texture.

If desserts are frozen without stirring, that is, packed in the freezing mixture, the proportion of salt to ice is about one to two by measure. Mixtures frozen without stirring require a longer time and a colder temperature to freeze than do stirred mixtures. Removal of heat from the center of the mass may be difficult in unstirred frozen desserts because they are high in fat and have air beaten into the heavy cream that is usually used as a basis of the mixture, and both cold fat and air are poor conductors of heat.

The fineness of the division of salt and ice is also a factor influencing the rate of freezing in the preparation of frozen desserts. Finely crushed ice has more surface exposed to the action of salt than does coarsely chopped ice and hence melts faster. Fine salt dissolves more rapidly, but because of its lumping and collecting in the bottom of the freezer, it is less desirable to use than coarse or crushed rock salt.

Ice Cream Freezers

Construction. Figure 16-1 shows a diagram of an ice cream freezer. The outer container of the freezer is usually made of a mate-

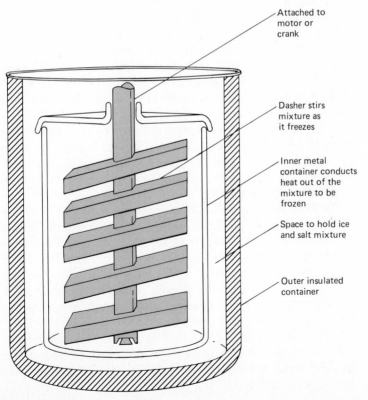

Attached to motor or crank

Dasher stirs mixture as it freezes

Inner metal container conducts heat out of the mixture to be frozen

Space to hold ice and salt mixture

Outer insulated container

16-1 *Structure of an ice cream freezer.*

rial, such as styrofoam or wood, that conducts heat poorly. This minimizes the absorption of heat from the air. The goal is to have heat absorbed from the mixture to be frozen by the ice as the ice melts. The container that holds the ice cream mixture inside the outer container is made of metal, which permits the rapid absorption of heat from the ice cream mixture. A paddle or dasher inside the metal can agitates the ice cream mixture as the freezer is turned, thus incorporating air. The dasher scrapes the mixture from the side walls, thus permitting a new layer of mixture to come in contact with the can. Agitation also tends to form many nuclei on which ice crystals may form, which favors small crystal formation.

Rate of Turning the Freezer. Slow agitation of the ice cream mixture is desirable at the beginning of the freezing period until the temperature of the freezing mixture is lowered below the critical churning temperature. At a temperature of 4.5° C (40° F) or above, agitation tends to form clumps of butterfat, resulting in a buttery ice cream or in actual butter formation. There is no advantage in fast turning of the freezer until the temperature of the mixture is reduced to about 1° C (34° F) as little air is incorporated until the mixture is cooled. If the ice cream mixture is precooled before being placed in the freezer, fast turning may be used from the beginning of the freezing operation. Rapid agitation after the mixture is chilled not only incorporates much air but favors the formation of many nuclei and fine ice crystals. It is difficult to obtain fine crystals in ice creams that are frozen without stirring because only a relatively few nuclei for ice crystal formation are present and large crystal growth can occur. Rapid agitation and a relatively gradual lowering of the temperature of the ice cream mixture favor the formation of many nuclei and, thus, small crystals.

In quick-freezing procedures that may be practiced commercially, many nuclei and small crystals are formed because of the extremely low temperatures used [1]. The shortness of the time of freezing prevents the growth of crystals. Quick freezing cannot be used in household practices.

Packing the Freezer. Before packing the outer freezer container with an ice and salt mixture at the beginning of the freezer period, the freezer should be tested to see that it is in good working order. The mixture to be frozen should occupy only about two thirds of the capacity of the inner metal can in order to allow for overrun or swell during freezing. After the paddle or dasher is adjusted, the space between the inner can and the outer container is best filled about half full with crushed ice before any salt is added. This tends to prevent the salt from collecting in the bottom of the freezer. Slow turning of the freezer is usually necessary to keep the can from freezing solidly to the bottom of the freezer. The remainder of the ice and salt needed to fill the freezer may be added alternately. The brine formed is not drained off. It is also possible to mix the crushed ice and salt together before adding it to the freezer, but the first cooling effect obtained when the salt is added to the ice is lost. When the mixture is frozen, the crank turns with difficulty. The lid may be removed, the dasher taken out, and the ice cream pressed down solidly in the can. The hole in the inner metal can top is corked to prevent the salty freezing mixture from getting into the can, and the excess brine is drained off. If the frozen dessert is to be used soon, the freezer may be packed with a freezing mixture containing a higher percentage of salt than that used for freezing. The hardening of the dessert to a consistency desirable for serving is thus accomplished more rapidly. If the ice cream is to stand for a longer time before serving, the same mixture used for freezing may also be used for packing the frozen dessert.

Factors Affecting Flavor, Texture, and Body of Ice Cream

Fat

Milk fat is one of the chief factors affecting the flavor of ice cream. Because cream is the most costly ingredient in ice cream, commercial ice creams may contain less milk fat than homemade products. An optimum amount of milk fat improves body and texture giving a firm, smooth product. Too much milk fat gives a hard ice cream. Homemade ice creams with a high content of milk fat may have a tendency to churn, giving agglomerated particles of butter. The homogenization of commercial ice cream mixes helps to avoid this. Commercial ice creams usually contain 10 to 14 percent milk fat. The amount of milk fat influences the viscosity of the mix and affects the incorporation of air. A moderate viscosity is desirable. A very viscous mixture resists the incorporation of air as does a very thin, nonviscous mixture. The air cells are desirably small and the texture is smooth in a mixture with optimum viscosity.

Nonfat Milk Solids

One of the chief points of difference between homemade and commercial ice creams is the amount of nonfat milk solids present. Homemade ice creams usually are not reinforced with milk solids although some may be added. Unless they are reinforced, homemade ice creams probably contain not more than 6 percent milk serum solids as compared with an average of about 9 or 10 percent in commercial ice creams. A relatively high percentage of milk solids reduces the free water content of ice cream and improves its texture by encouraging finer ice crystal formation. Commercial ice creams may be reinforced with milk solids by the use of evaporated skim milk or nonfat dry milk.

Too high a percentage of nonfat milk solids gives a sandy ice cream resulting from the crystallization of lactose at the low temperature of holding. Twelve percent or more of milk solids introduces 6 percent or more of lactose and results in gritty or sandy ice cream. Eleven per cent serum solids is about the upper limit to prevent a sandy product.

Sugar

Sugar is used in ice cream chiefly for flavor. Consumer preference is for a fairly sweet ice cream (one containing about 14 or 15 percent sugar or approximately one-sixth by weight) [3]. An excess of sugar lowers the freezing point and retards freezing. It also lowers the overrun.

Stabilizers

As previously mentioned, a number of different stabilizers may be used in commercial ice cream in amounts up to 0.5 percent. They usually absorb water and interfere somewhat with ice crystal formation, helping to keep the crystals small, and give body to the mixture [4]. A good quality of ice cream should melt to about the consistency of thick cream. Egg added to an ice cream mix increases viscosity and aids in the incorporation of air. Chocolate ice cream is especially improved by the use of egg yolk.

Fruit Ice Creams

Fresh unsweetened fruits may be added to ice creams but should have sugar added to them before they are used. For strawberries, 2 pounds of berries require about 1 pound of sugar for good flavor. Other fruits may require different amounts of sugar, depending on the acidity of the fruit. To avoid hard particles of frozen fruits in ice cream, the fruit should be finely crushed or run through a strainer. Three fourths to 1 pound of fruit in about 2 quarts of mixture is a desirable amount to use.

Chocolate Ice Cream

Cocoa is preferred to chocolate in the ice cream industry as a means of adding chocolate flavor to ice cream because of the greater ease of blending. A chocolate liquor may be made from ¾ cup of cocoa, ½ cup of sugar, and 1 cup of water. The cocoa and sugar are mixed together. Enough water is added to form a smooth paste; then the remaining water is added. The mixture is heated to boiling before cooling and using for 2 quarts of plain mix.

Other Added Materials

Finely crushed mint stick, English toffee, and chocolate chips, as well as chopped nuts or crushed dry macaroons, may be added to plain ice cream to give a variety of flavors. About 4 ounces of material to 2 quarts of mixture is sufficient for good flavor.

Preparation of Frozen Desserts

Commercial ice cream mixes are pasteurized and homogenized. The latter process finely divides the fat particles, thus producing a more homogeneous and smooth mixture. If homemade ice cream is made from pasteurized products the mixture does not require pasteurization, although heating in a double boiler for 15 to 20 minutes at a temperature of 63° C (145° F) blends ingredients thoroughly and may be an extra precaution from a health standpoint. After heating, the mixture should be cooled quickly to a temperature of 13° C (55° F) or below. A smoother ice cream and improved flavor result from aging or holding the mix for 3 or 4 hours at low temperature before freezing.

If gelatin is used in a frozen dessert, it may be mixed with the sugar and added to the liquid when the latter has reached a temperature of 43° C (109° F). The entire mixture is then heated further. If egg yolks are used, they may be mixed with the sugar to form a smooth paste, which is then mixed with the liquid and heated. Flavoring and coloring are added just before freezing.

Freezing Without Stirring

The freezing compartment of a refrigerator provides a temperature low enough for freezing as well as holding frozen mixtures. Some refrigerators are equipped with devices for stirring the mixture as it freezes. Without stirring, the rate of freezing is retarded and ice crystals tend to be larger than when stirring occurs.

Mixtures that can be frozen most successfully without stirring are those rich in fat, such as whipped cream products, or mixtures containing gelatin, custard, egg white, evaporated milk, or a cooked starch base. These substances interfere with the formation of large ice crystals. Because the desserts are not stirred to incorporate air, air must be beaten into cream or egg white prior to freezing. Partially frozen mixtures may be removed from the freezing trays and beaten once or twice during the freezing period. Air cells tend to interfere with coarse crystal formation.

Egg Whites. Egg whites provide the best medium for adding air to the mixture before it is frozen. Two methods may be used for adding them to refrigerator ice creams: (1) a syrup is made by the boiling of the sugar with water or fruit juice until the syrup spins a thread. The hot syrup is poured over the beaten egg whites with additional beating and, after cooling, the egg mixture and whipped cream are combined; (2) the egg whites are beaten stiff and the granulated sugar is beaten in to form a stiff, fine-textured meringue, which is then combined with the whipped cream. Mixtures prepared in this way do not require beating during the freezing period.

Gelatin. Too much gelatin gives a hard or gummy dessert. Thin cream or rich milk may have gelatin added to the extent of 1 tablespoon per pint. (See pp. 503–507 for a method of combining gelatin with liquid.) When the mixture becomes syrupy, it may be beaten very stiff.

Custard. Custards thickened with egg yolk or whole egg may be used in ice creams. The cooked custard must be well chilled before being combined with whipped cream. Three-fourths cup of custard is the maximum amount that will combine with a cup of whipping cream to give a smooth ice cream.

Time Required for Freezing. The time required for freezing refrigerator desserts depends on the quantity being frozen, on the composition of the mixture, and on the degree of cold. About 4 to 6 hours may be needed and the cold control is best set on the lowest temperature. When the mixture is frozen without stirring, freezing as quickly as possible aids in the production of many small ice crystals. Faster freezing occurs if the mixture is stirred occasionally in the tray to permit unfrozen portions to come in contact with the tray.

Sanitary Quality of Frozen Desserts

Ice cream is a favorable medium for the development of microorganisms including pathogenic organisms. Because freezing does not destroy but only inhibits the growth of bacteria, contaminated ice creams may be responsible for causing a variety of diseases if improperly handled.

The prominent causes of a high bacterial count in frozen desserts are contaminated equipment; contaminated ingredients, especially those ingredients, such as nuts, fruits, coloring, and flavoring, that are not added prior to pasteurization; failure to pasteurize the mix or to use pasteurized dairy products; and carelessness in the freezing process.

Food Value of Frozen Desserts

The higher the percentage of milk constituents in frozen desserts, the more important is the contribution of protein, minerals, and vitamins. Those desserts with a high butterfat content are obviously of higher caloric value and higher vitamin A content than are those with a low percentage of fat. Frozen desserts, in order to taste desirably sweet, must have a higher sugar content than most other types of desserts because of the dulling effect of cold temperatures on taste sensations. Fruit ices and sherbets, because of their acidity, also require a fairly high sugar content. Vitamins are probably unaffected by freezing.

Study Questions

1. Describe the major characteristics of a well prepared frozen dessert such as ice cream or sherbet.
2. Describe identifying characteristics of each of the following:
   a. Sherbet
   b. Water ice
   c. Ice cream
   d. Ice milk
   e. Mousse
   f. Mellorine
3. Explain how a mixture of ice and salt is able to act as a freezing mixture to freeze frozen desserts.
4. Describe an appropriate procedure for preparing homemade ice cream in an ice cream freezer. Explain what is happening at each step.
5. What is the effect of each of the following on the flavor, texture, and/or body of a frozen ice cream?
   a. Milk fat
   b. Nonfat milk solids
   c. Stabilizers
   d. Whipping in air (overrun)
6. What procedures should be used when freezing a frozen dessert without stirring and why?

References

1. Arbuckle, W. S. *Ice Cream*, 3rd ed. Westport, CT: Avi Publishing Company, Inc., 1977.
2. Code of Federal Regulations. Definitions and Standards Under the Federal Food, Drug, and Cosmetic Act: Frozen Desserts. Title 21, Part 20.
3. Pangborn, R. M., M. Simone, and T. A. Nickerson. 1957. The influence of sugar in ice cream. I. Consumer preferences for vanilla ice cream. *Food Technology* **11**, 679.
4. Thomas, E. L. 1981. Structure and properties of ice cream emulsions. *Food Technology* **35**, 41, (no. 1).

17

Cereals and Starch

Cereals and Cereal Cookery

Definition and Uses

Cereals are seeds of the grass family. The most important cereals for food use are wheat, corn (maize), rice, oats, rye, and barley. Grain sorghums, which are also cultivated in the United States, are used chiefly for animal feed but starches are extracted from them for commercial food use.

The cereal grains are widely used for the making of breakfast foods, flours, meals, breads, alimentary pastes, and starches. Thus, it is obvious that the term *cereal* is not limited to breakfast foods but applies to a large group of foods made from the grains. The ease with which grains may be produced and stored, together with the relatively low cost and considerable nutritive value of many cereal foods, has resulted in the widespread use of grain products throughout the world.

Composition and Structure

All whole grains have similar structures, being composed of outer bran coats, a germ, and a starchy endosperm portion as shown in Figure 17–1.

Cereal products vary in composition depending on the part or parts of the grain used. The chaffy coat that covers the kernel during growth is eliminated when grains are harvested. The outer layers of the kernel proper, which are called the *bran*, constitute about 5 percent of the kernel. The bran has a high content of fiber and mineral ash. As milled, it may also contain some germ and the aleu-

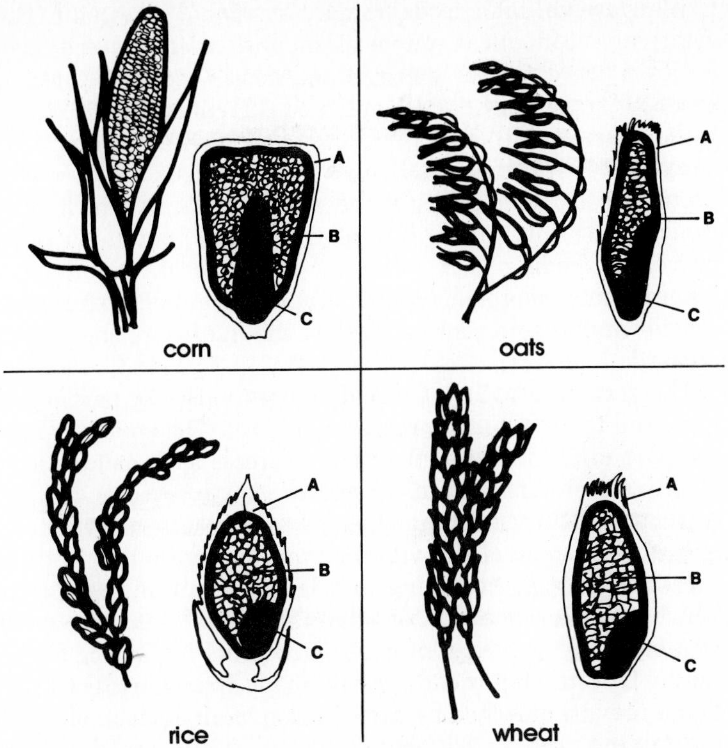

17-1 *Several common grains have similar structures. They are used to make a variety of breakfast cereals.* (Courtesy of Cereal Institute, Inc.)

corn

oats

rice

wheat

A BRAN consists of several thin outer layers of the grain kernel and is its protective coat.

B ENDOSPERM is the stored food supply for the new plant which develops as the kernel germinates. It comprises about 85% of the kernel.

C EMBRYO or GERM is the miniature plant which enlarges and develops after the kernel germinates.

rone layer usually adheres to the bran during milling. The *aleurone* is a layer of square cells located just under the bran layers of the kernel. These cells are rich in protein, phosphorus, and thiamin, and also contain some fat. The aleurone layer makes up about 8 percent of the whole kernel.

The *endosperm* is the large central portion of the kernel and constitutes about 83 percent of the kernel. It contains most of the starch, as well as most of the protein of the kernel, but very little mineral matter or fiber, and only a trace of fat. The vitamin content of the endosperm is generally low.

The *germ* is a small structure at the lower end of the kernel, that usually makes up 2 to 3 percent of the whole kernel. It is rich in fat, protein, ash, and vitamins. When the kernel is broken, as it is in certain processing procedures, and the fat is exposed to oxygen in the air, the storage life of the grain is greatly reduced since the fat may become rancid. The broken or milled grain is also more susceptible to infestation by insects.

Nutritive Value and Enrichment

Cereals are valuable foods from a nutritional viewpoint. They are a relatively economical source of energy, chiefly in the form of the complex carbohydrate starch; a significant source of protein; a good source of indigestible fiber; and a consistent source of key vitamins and minerals. Although the proteins of cereal grains are generally of relatively low biological value, when cereals are used with other protein foods which supply the amino acids in which cereals are limited, the nutritive value of the cereal protein is greatly improved. In feeding the populations of the world, various cereals and legumes may supplement each other in the diet with respect to essential amino acid content so that the quality of the protein is increased.

The nutritive value of cereals varies with the part of the grain used and the method of processing [1, 10]. The endosperm, which is the part used in refined flours and cereals such as farina, contains chiefly starch and protein. Therefore, refined cereals and flours furnish very little more than these two nutrients unless they are enriched with some of the vitamins and minerals lost in milling.

Enriched flour, according to a legal definition, is white flour to which specified B vitamins (thiamin, riboflavin, and niacin) and iron have been added. Optional ingredients include calcium and vitamin D. Enriched bread may be made from enriched flour or the bread may be enriched by the addition of an enrichment wafer during mixing. The enrichment of bakers' white bread and rolls was made compulsory by the federal government in 1941 as a war measure to improve the nutritional status of the people in the United States. After World War II, enrichment became a voluntary matter. Many states have since passed laws requiring that various refined cereal products and flours sold within their boundaries be enriched. Quantities of nutrients required by the federal Food and Drug Administration for flour and bread that are labeled *enriched* are given in Table 17–1. The enrichment of white flour does not make this product nutritionally equivalent to whole-grain flour because only a few of the nutrients that are lost in milling are replaced by the enrichment process. Other vitamins and minerals are present in the whole grain that are not included in the enrichment mixture. Whole-grain products are particularly valuable as dietary sources of iron, phosphorus, thiamin, and vitamin B_6, as well as fiber. Many

Table 17–1 *Enrichment Standards Compared with Whole Wheat Flour* (milligrams per pound)*

	Thiamin	Riboflavin	Niacin	Iron
Whole wheat flour	2.49	0.54	19.7	15.0
Enriched white flour	2.0 to 2.5	1.2 to 1.5	16 to 20	13.0 to 16.5
Enriched bread, rolls, or buns	1.1 to 1.8	0.7 to 1.6	10 to 15	8.0 to 12.5

*One pound of flour is usually equivalent to 1½ pounds of bread.

breakfast cereals are highly fortified with vitamins and minerals.

Most all-purpose flour sold for consumer use is enriched. However, in states where the enrichment of flour and bread is not required by law, much bread, rolls, and sweet rolls may not be enriched. Enrichment does markedly increase the B vitamin and iron content of bread and flour over that in the unenriched product and should be demanded by the consumer. Probably the most effective means of ensuring that only enriched products are sold is to educate the consumer to their importance so that the consumer refuses to buy the unenriched items.

Common Cereal Grains

Wheat.   Wheat is one of the most widely cultivated plants on earth. Every month of the year a crop of wheat is maturing at some place in the world. Cultivation of this grain goes back to the early history of man. There are several thousand different varieties of wheat. Plant breeders have created new wheat varieties with high yields and strong disease resistance that have contributed to a so-called "green revolution" in many parts of the world [12]. A new cereal, called *triticale,* has been produced by cross-breeding wheat and rye. Triticale generally has higher protein content and better amino acid balance than wheat and may be a valuable source of nutrients for many peoples of the world. Certain varieties of triticale have been shown to produce acceptable breads and noodles [6, 11, 15].

Wheats are commonly milled into flour, and wheats used for flour are often classified in terms of their "hardness" or "softness." Hard wheat varieties are higher in protein content than are soft wheats and usually have greater baking strength in terms of being able to produce a loaf of bread with a large volume and fine texture. Wheat flour is uniquely suitable for bread-making because of its content of specific proteins that develop strong, elastic properties in a dough. No other cereal grain equals wheat in bread-making qualities. Classes of wheat, milling, and flour are discussed in more detail in Chapter 18.

Durum wheat is a very hard, non–bread-making wheat of high protein content. It is grown chiefly for use in making macaroni and other alimentary pastes.

Bulgur is wheat that is first boiled and then dried. A small amount of the outer bran layers is removed and it is then usually cracked. It is an ancient form of processing wheat, having been used in biblical times. Bulgur is often found in the gourmet food sections of supermarkets. Armenian restaurants commonly serve cooked bulgur in the form of pilaf [13].

Wheat is also used for the production of wheat starch and in large quantity for the making of various types of breakfast cereals. A comparison of composition and nutritive value for various cereals is given in Appendix C.

Corn. Corn is a native American plant. Early settlers in the New World were introduced to the uses of corn by the American Indians. The United States now produces almost half of the world's corn crop. Corn is a major food for the peoples of Mexico and Central America and is a very popular product in the southern United States.

The corn kernel has a great variety of uses in food products. It is made into hominy, which is the corn kernel endosperm freed from the bran and germ (see Figure 17–2). The whole endosperm of hominy is broken into fairly small pieces to make hominy grits. Corn is also milled into cornmeal. Both white and yellow are used for making cornmeal, a granular product made either without the germ and most of the bran, or with all of the kernel except the larger bran particles. The latter is the old process of making cornmeal. Like all other whole cereal products, cornmeal that contains the germ deteriorates more rapidly than that made without the germ because of the high fat content of the germ. Refined cornmeal and hominy grits may be enriched. Hominy grits are often served as a breakfast cereal in the southern United States.

Corn is used in the production of various breakfast foods and for corn flour, which is used mainly in commercial flour mixes. Corn oil is extracted from the germ of the corn kernel. Corn oil contains a high proportion of polyunsaturated fatty acids. Corn syrups and glucose are made by the hydrolysis of corn starch. The principal starch used in the United States for culinary purposes is corn starch. Other starches, such as wheat, potato, rice, tapioca, and arrowroot, are available and may have specialized uses in cookery, depending on desired characteristics.

17-2 *Hominy is the endosperm of the corn kernel, freed from bran and germ.*

Rice. Considered as a world crop, rice is one of the most used of all cereals and is the major food of many peoples living in Asia. Rice is also grown in southern United States and California. New varieties of rice with high yields and disease resistance have been developed to increase world food production. Rice is one of the cereals commonly used in the manufacture of breakfast foods.

Cultivated rice is available as white or polished rice, which is the starchy endosperm of the rice grain, the bran coats and germ having been rubbed off by an abrasive process. The polishing process also removes more than half of the minerals and most of the vitamins from the kernel. White rice may be enriched, often as a powdery material on the surface of the grain. In this case, it is particularly important that the rice not be washed before cooking or rinsed after cooking to avoid loss of the enrichment nutrients. Brown rice has only the outer husk or chaffy coat removed from the kernel.

There are several thousand known varieties of rice but they may be divided into three main groups: short-, medium-, and long-grain varieties (Figure 17–3). The long-grain kernels tend to separate and are light and fluffy when cooked. The cooked shorter grains tend to cling together more. Preferences differ in different cultures for fluffy versus sticky rice. One cup of uncooked regular polished rice will yield about 3 cups of cooked rice.

Grains of rice may be parboiled before milling by a special steam-pressure process. This process gelatinizes the starch and changes the cooking characteristics of the rice. Parboiled rice, also called converted rice, requires longer cooking than regular white rice. Parboiling improves the nutritive value of milled white rice because the heating process causes migration of vitamins and minerals from the outer coats to the interior of the kernel and they are retained after milling. The keeping quality of parboiled rice is improved over that of the untreated grain. Precooked rice is a long-grain rice that has been cooked, rinsed, and dried by a special process. It requires very little preparation. One cup of precooked rice will yield 2 cups of cooked rice. Rice flour and rice starch are manufactured but have limited culinary uses in the United States by the home preparer of foods.

Wild rice is not true rice but is the hulled and unmilled grain of a reedlike water plant. It is available in limited quantity and is, therefore, usually relatively expensive. It is prized for its unusual flavor. Like many whole-grain cereals it has relatively poor keeping quality especially in warm weather.

Oats. Oats are used in the United States chiefly in the making of oatmeal, which term is applied to both rolled oats and ground or cut oats. The husk clings very tightly to the oat kernel. The outer hull is removed, but most of the germ and bran remain with the endosperm when the grain is processed. Rolled oats of commerce, therefore,

17-3 *Varieties of rice: short-, medium-, and long-grain.* (Courtesy of The Rice Council)

contain nearly the whole oat kernel. Because of the retention of most of the germ, rolled oats are higher in fat than most other cereals, and are also a good source of thiamin and other B vitamins and iron. The oat kernels with hulls removed are called *groats*. Rolled oats are made by passing the groats through rollers to form flakes. For quick-cooking rolled oats the groats are cut into tiny particles that are then rolled into thin, small flakes. Regular rolled oats are rolled without cutting.

Oatmeal is a commonly used breakfast cereal. Rolled oats are used in many recipes for breads, muffins, cookies, and cakes, and they may also be used in a topping mixture for fruit cobblers.

Rye. Rye is grown and used in the United States chiefly as a flour-making grain. It is used much less than wheat but it more nearly approaches wheat in flour quality than do other grains. Rye flour is available in three grades: white, medium, and dark. Rye is seldom used as a breakfast food.

Barley. Pearled barley, which is the whole grain with hull and bran removed, is the chief form in which this grain is used in the United States. Pearled barley is used in soups. Some barley flour is also available and may be used in breakfast cereals and in baby foods. Sprouted barley is a source of malt, which is rich in the enzyme amylase. This enzyme hydrolyzes starch to dextrins and maltose.

Buckwheat. Buckwheat is not a seed of the grass family. It is the seed of an herbaceous plant, but because it contains a glutenous substance and is made into flour it is commonly considered with grain products. Fine buckwheat flour has little of the thick fiber coating included, and in that respect it is similar to refined white flour. It is prized for its distinctive flavor and is commonly used in the making of griddle cakes. The volume of buckwheat flour sold in the United States is relatively small.

Breakfast Cereals

Breakfast foods made from cereal grains vary widely in composition depending on the kind of grain, the part of the grain used, the method of milling, and the method of processing. Several processes are used in the production of prepared cereals. They may be puffed, shredded, flaked, made into granules from a baked dough, or made into a dough and extruded through a die under pressure (see Figure 17–4). Mixtures of cereals or cereal flours are often used and various shapes and sizes of cereal particles result. Breakfast foods may be raw, partially cooked, or completely cooked. Some have added substances, such as sugar, syrup, molasses, or honey. Some of the carbo-

GRAINS INTO BREAKFAST CEREALS

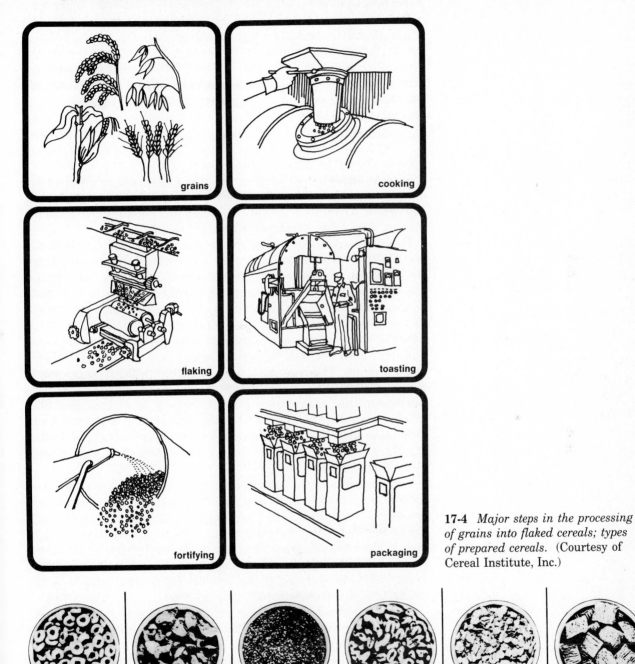

grains

cooking

flaking

toasting

fortifying

packaging

17-4 *Major steps in the processing of grains into flaked cereals; types of prepared cereals.* (Courtesy of Cereal Institute, Inc.)

extruded | flaked | granulated | puffed | rolled | shredded

399

hydrate may be changed by the use of malt or some may be partially dextrinized by dry heat.

Raw cereals that are cooked in the home may be in various forms: whole grains, cracked or crushed grains, granular products made from either the whole grain or the endosperm section of the kernel, and rolled or flaked whole grains. The finely cut flaked grains will cook in a shorter period of time and are called *quick cooking*. Disodium phosphate is sometimes added to farina for quick cooking. It changes the pH of the cereal, making it more alkaline, and causes it to swell faster and cook in a shorter time. An enzyme that breaks down proteins may be utilized during the processing of a cereal, such as farina, to make it quick cooking.

Instant cereals, including farina and rolled oats, are marketed. The starch in these cereals has been pregelatinized by prior cooking. Therefore, when boiling water is added and the mixture is simply stirred, the cereal is ready for consumption.

The number and variety of ready-to-eat cereals on the market in the United States have increased tremendously in recent years. Ready-to-eat cereals include granulated, flaked, shredded, puffed, toasted, seasoned, and sugar-coated products in a wide variety of shapes and sizes. Much advertising of these cereal products is done in the mass media and is particularly aimed at young children. Many of these cereals are fabricated into special shapes and forms and have been enriched or fortified with a wide variety of vitamins and minerals. Vitamins are added at stages in the process beyond which they are not subject to destruction. Congressional committees have heard testimony concerning the merits of various cereals as marketed in an effort to develop legislation that will protect the consumer from misleading labeling and advertising. No federal standard of identity has yet been developed for breakfast cereals other than farina.

The large number of cereal products on the market may be cause for confusion in the buying and use of cereals. Advertising and high-pressure salesmanship are sometimes invoked to induce homemakers to buy this or that cereal product. Too much food money may be spent for products that are no better nutritionally than many others which are available at a fraction of the cost. A large amount of sugar, up to 35 percent of the product by weight, is used in the production of many prepared cereals.

In general, the more processing that is done to a breakfast cereal and the more ingredients that are added, the higher is the retail price. Cereals cooked in the home are usually much less costly than the ready-to-eat cereals and presweetened ready-to-eat cereals are often more expensive than the unsweetened products. Individuals with low incomes who may need to use a high percentage of cereal products in the diet or those who are interested in higher fiber and lower sugar products would do well to choose more often the less processed cereals in preference to the more convenient ready-to-eat cereals. Whole grain or enriched cereals should always be purchased instead of unenriched refined products.

Cooking of Breakfast Cereals

The main purposes of cereal cookery are to improve palatability and digestibility. So far as is known, early man consumed cereals as whole grains with no preliminary preparation. Later, heat was applied in the parching of grains, and the improved palatability resulted in the use of the parching method as an accepted cookery process for cereals. Still later came the addition of water before the application of heat.

Cereal cookery is fundamentally starch cookery because starch is the predominant nutrient of cereals. Other factors involved are (1) fiber, which is chiefly exterior bran layers, and (2) protein, which is also a prominent constituent of cereals. Until softened, or unless disintegrated mechanically, bran may interfere with the passage of water into the interior of the kernel and presumably may retard the swelling of starch in contact with water. If cellulose is finely ground, its affinity for water is greatly increased. The temperatures necessary for starch cookery are more than adequate for cooking the protein of the cereal [4].

Technique for Combining Cereal and Water. In the cooking of cereals attention must often be paid to the technique of combining the cereal with water. Particularly if the cereal is in finely divided form, it is added in a way to avoid lumping so that a uniform gelatinous mass is formed on heating. All of the cereal particles should be equally exposed to water and heat. If lumps form, dry material remains inside a gelatinous external coating. The following two methods are commonly used to combine cereal with water. (Salt is usually added to the boiling water before the cereal is combined with it.)

1. Gradually pour the dry cereal into boiling water. Slight stirring may be required but if the water does not cease boiling, stirring may be unnecessary.
2. Wet the cereal with cold water before adding it to the boiling water. Wetting tends to hold the particles apart.

The effect of excess stirring is to break up cereal particles so that they lose their identity. Even granulated cereals may be broken up to form a more gummy mass than would result from being heated with the minimum amount of stirring.

Temperatures and Time Periods. Adequate temperatures for cereal cookery are obtainable and the process may be better controlled if the cereal is placed in a double boiler after it has been added to the boiling water. When the water in the lower compartment is kept boiling the temperature in the top is about 85° C (185° F). However, cereals may also be cooked over direct heat using low to moderate temperatures. Cooking times will be somewhat less over direct heat than in a double boiler.

The principal factors that appear to affect the time required for the cooking of cereals are the size of the particle, the amount of water used, the presence or absence of the bran layer, the temperature, and the method used. Finally granulated endosperm cereals and precooked cereals cook in less time than whole or cracked and completely raw cereals. Whole wheat is available in some areas and may be used as a breakfast cereal. If it is soaked before cooking, it cooks in less time than if cooked without soaking, but in any case 1 to 2 hours of cooking will be needed to soften the bran and completely gelatinize the starch granules. Soaking is best started in 2 cups of boiling water per cup of wheat. If the mixture is heated just to the boiling point after the grain is combined with the water, in a hot-soak method, undesirable fermentation is less likely to occur during a soaking period of several hours. The grain is cooked in the water in which it is soaked, more water being added if needed.

Proportions of Water to Cereal. Proportions of water to cereal vary according to the type of cereal, the quantity cooked, the method of cooking, and the length of time of cooking. The consistency desired in the finished cereal is also a factor affecting the amount of water used. The majority of persons appear to prefer a consistency that is fairly thick but not too thick to pour. The amount of water must be adequate to permit swelling of the starch granules. If the consistency is then too thin, further cooking may be necessary for the purpose of evaporation. If cereals are cooked for the entire time at boiling temperature, evaporation is greater than if the cereal is started at boiling temperature and finished in a covered double boiler.

Table 17–2 gives the common proportions used for various types of cereal breakfast foods. The amount of salt is based on the dry

Table 17-2 *Approximate Proportions of Water to Cereal for Cooked Breakfast Foods*

Type of Cereal	Water (Cups)	Cereal (Cups)
Rolled or flaked	2 or 2½	1
Granular	4 or 5	1
Cracked grain	About 4	1
Whole grain	About 4 unless grain was soaked for several hours	1

Cooking of Rice

The problem in rice cookery is one of retaining the form of the kernel while at the same time cooking the kernel until it is completely tender. It is usually suggested that rice be cooked with amounts of water that will be fully absorbed during cooking. Rice needs no more than about twice its volume of water, and regular rice increases to about three times its volume in cooking. One-half teaspoon of salt per cup of uncooked rice is usually used for seasoning.

If cooked by the boiling method, the rice is started in two to two and one-fourth times its volume of boiling water, brought back to a boil, and then covered and finished over reduced heat. Fifteen to 20 minutes are usually required, although converted rice takes a little longer time. If cooked in a double boiler, the volume of water may be reduced to 1¾ cups per cup of rice. After the water is brought back to a boil over direct heat, the top of the double boiler is placed over boiling water and the covered rice is cooked about 45 minutes or until tender.

For oven cooking, about the same amount of boiling water is needed as for the boiling method because a longer time is required for cooking in a closed baking dish at a temperature of 350° F— about 35 minutes. Rice may be cooked in milk with the use of the double-boiler method. Cooking rice in chicken or beef broth may also give a desirable flavor.

Precooked rice can be prepared very quickly. It requires only the addition of boiling water, the bringing of the mixture back to a boil, removing it from the source of heat, and allowing it to stand closely covered until the rice swells.

Brown rice may be cooked by the same methods used to cook white rice, but it requires about twice as long to cook. Brown rice may be soaked for an hour in tepid water to soften the bran and to shorten the cooking period. It does not tend to become sticky in cooking. Precooked brown rice is also available. Wild rice is usually cooked in salted water and requires about 20 to 25 minutes to cook tender.

The browning of rice in a small amount of hot fat preliminary to cooking in water converts part of the starch to dextrins. Swelling is also somewhat decreased but the rice develops an interesting color and flavor that makes the method a desirable one to use as a basis for Spanish rice, as rice pilaf, or as a side dish.

Minerals in hard water in some sections of the country produce in cooked rice a grayish-green or yellowish color. One-fourth teaspoon of cream of tartar or 1 teaspoon of lemon juice added to 2 quarts of water will produce a white cooked rice.

Pastas

The term *pasta* or *alimentary paste* is applied to macaroni, spaghetti, vermicelli, noodles, and other similar products (Figure 17–5). The primary ingredient utilized in the making of pastas is a coarsely ground flour from durum wheat called *semolina*. Macaroni products originated in the Orient many years ago and were brought

17-5 *Pasta comes in many shapes and sizes.* (Courtesy of Wheat Flour Institute)

to Italy by Venetian traders and explorers in the middle ages. The Italians adopted pasta as their national dish. From Italy, the popularity of pasta spread throughout Europe. European immigrants to the United States introduced the process of making macaroni, spaghetti, and egg noodles to this country before the Civil War. For many years these products were made in the home, although industrial production of pasta had developed in America by 1900. To supply durum wheat for pasta manufacture, the growing of this variety of wheat was introduced in the early 1900s to the farmers of the Dakotas and the nearby states, where climatic conditions are well suited to its cultivation. This assured an ample supply of durum wheat for American macaroni production.

In the commercial manufacture of pastas, measured amounts of flour and water are automatically fed into a mixer, which thoroughly blends the ingredients into a dough. After mixing, the dough is transferred through another compartment into a cylinder. The lower end of the cylinder is fitted with a thick disc or "die" with openings that produce the desired size and shape of pasta. As the dough is forced through the openings by tremendous pressure, various shapes are formed. Cutting blades cut the strands to desired lengths. Macaroni is a short tube form, spaghetti is usually a long rod, vermicelli is a tiny, thin rod, and noodles are flat strips. A wide variety of other shapes are made, including shells and alphabet letters.

The pastas are automatically placed on drying trays. The drying process is carefully controlled to maintain the optimum temperature and humidity necessary to prevent the development of chips and cracks in the pastas.

Optional ingredients in macaroni products, according to the federal standards of identity, include eggs and various seasonings. Eggs are commonly added to noodles. In egg noodle products, whole eggs or egg yolks are added to the flour and water mixture to form a soft dough. The dough is run between rollers until it is of the desired thickness. The sheet of dough is then automatically cut into ribbons of the desired width or into other shapes. The cut dough is then carefully dried.

Durum flour is available in some areas for use in the home production of pasta. Pasta machines or pasta attachments to food processors are becoming popular.

High-protein macaroni products have been developed that contain 20 to 25 percent protein on a dry weight basis. Soy and corn flour are often combined with wheat flour in the production of these protein-fortified, enriched macaroni-type products. Nonfat dry milk may also be used. The U.S. Department of Agriculture has issued specifications for the use of these products as alternatives for meat in school food service.

The cooking of macaroni, spaghetti, and other pastas is done by adding the pasta to boiling water that is usually salted. Approximately 2 to 3 quarts of boiling water are used for 8 ounces of pasta product. Pasta that is to be served without further preparation is cooked, uncovered, and occasionally stirred, until it is tender yet firm. The standard for final cooking is called *al dente* (meaning, to the tooth). Because of the very high protein content of the flour used in the manufacture of pastas of good quality, little difficulty is encountered in retaining their form on cooking. If the pasta is to be further baked or simmered with other ingredients, it is cooked until it is almost tender. Cooking will be completed after the pasta is combined with the other ingredients. When the boiling process is completed, the pasta should be drained thoroughly in a colander or strainer. Enriched pasta should not be rinsed in water after cooking because this process increases the loss of vitamins and minerals. If cooked macaroni must be held awhile before serving, it may be placed over hot water in a strainer. Steam will keep the product hot and moist without further cooking. Stickiness will be reduced by this procedure as compared to overcooking the product.

The variety of dishes that may be prepared with macaroni products is almost endless. These include soups, salads, main dishes, and meat accompaniments.

Starch

Composition and Structure

Starch is a storage form of carbohydrate with the molecules of starch being deposited in tiny units called granules within the cells of plants. The sizes and shapes of granules differ in starches from various sources but all are microscopic in size. Photomicrographs of starch granules from several sources are shown in Figure 17–6.

The parts of plants that serve most prominently in the storage of starch are seeds, such as cereal grains and legumes, and roots and tubers, such as parsnips, potatoes, and sweet potatoes. Starches are derived from the tropical cassava root (marketed as tapioca) and from the pith of a tropical palm (marketed as sago).

Starch is a polysaccharide made up of hundreds or even thousands of glucose molecules joined together. Molecules of starch are of two types, called fractions: amylose and amylopectin. The amylose, which is a long chain-type molecule, contributes gelling characteristics to cooked and cooled starch mixtures. A gel is rigid to a certain degree and will hold a shape when molded. Amylopectin is a highly branched, bushy kind of molecule that provides cohesive or thickened properties but does not contribute to gel formation. Most starches are mixtures of the two fractions. Corn, wheat, rice, potato, and tapioca starches contain 24 to 16 percent amylose with the remainder being amylopectin. The root starches of tapioca and potato, are lower in amylose content than are the cereal starches of corn, wheat, and rice. Certain strains of corn, rice, grain sorghum, and barley have been developed that are practically devoid of amylose. These are called *waxy* varieties because of the waxy appearance of the cut grain. They contain only the amylopectin fraction of starch and are nongelling because of the lack of amylose.

Starches from different sources behave differently because of their varying composition and molecular structure. The natural differences that occur are sometimes augmented by some deliberate chemical modification made by starch chemists in the laboratory or processing plant [16]. A tremendous change has occurred in recent years in the manufacture and modification of starches from various sources in order to furnish starches for industry and the home that are suitable for various uses. Many specialty starches are available mainly for industrial use, but the homemaker profits by the use of these starches in foods, confections, laundry products, textiles, and other products. Examples of some of the products made from these modified starches are the instant pudding mixes in which the precooked starch reconstitutes in cold liquid to yield a pudding of excellent texture and flavor; the frozen pudding that is stable to freezing temperatures and maintains a desirable texture and consistency on thawing; the canned pudding that remains a good quality product even though it is subjected to high temperatures during the canning process; and the frozen fruit pie fillings that are stable to freezing and, in addition, maintain a soft thickened texture after baking and standing.

Waxy varieties of starch, particularly waxy rice, give a more stable sauce for any frozen creamed foods than a sauce made from ordinary corn or wheat starch. The naturally produced waxy starches are further modified to decrease their undesirable stringiness and yet retain their desirable nongelling characteristic. Thus, a starch made from modified tapioca is ideal as a thickening for fruit pie filling. It is sparkling clear, fluid, and free from stringiness. Modified starches are tailor-made for specific uses in many convenience foods.

Starch may be broken down or hydrolyzed. Complete hydrolysis produces glucose. Intermediate steps in the breakdown yield large chunks of starch molecules called dextrins (polysaccharides), sugars called oligosaccharides which contain several glucose units, and maltose, a disaccharide with two glucose units. Starch hydrolysis may be catalyzed or brought about by the action of enzymes, called *amylases,* or by acid.

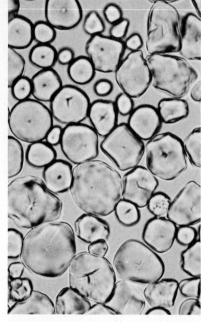 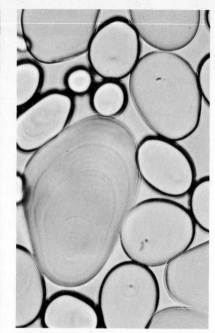

17-6 *Photomicrographs of starch granules from 4 different plant sources (magnified 700X). (Courtesy of Eileen Maywald, Corn Products Company)*

Corn starch   *Potato starch*

Starch Cookery

Effect of Dry Heat. When dry heat is applied to starch or starchy foods, the starch becomes more soluble in comparison to unheated starch and has reduced thickening power when made into a cooked paste. Some of the starch molecules have been broken down to dextrins in a process that is sometimes called *dextrinization.* Color and flavor changes also occur when starch-containing foods are subjected to high temperatures with dry heat. A nonenzymatic browning occurs and a toasted flavor, which may turn to a burned flavor if the process is continued, develops. Brown gravy is usually relatively thin in consistency if the flour is browned in the process of making the gravy. Some white flour used with the browned flour is necessary in order to get a thick gravy. Dry-heat dextrins, known as *pyrodextrins,* are formed in the crust of baked flour mixtures, on toast, on fried starchy or starch-coated foods, and on various ready-to-eat cereals.

Effect of Moist Heat. The starch granule is completely insoluble in cold water. A nonviscous suspension of starch is formed in which the granules gradually settle to the bottom of the container. On cooking, a colloidal dispersion of starch in water is produced. The resulting thickened mixture is called a starch paste. Some cooked

(handwritten margin notes: reduced thickening power / starch molecules have been broken down Dextrinization / Browning + toasted occur flavor)

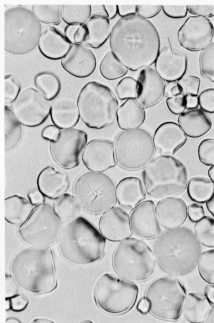
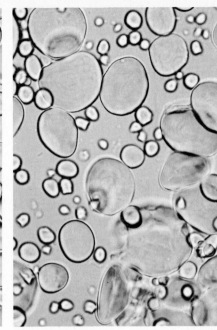

Potato starch under polarized light

Tapioca starch

Wheat starch

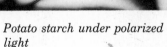

starch pastes are opaque or cloudy and some are more clear in appearance. In general, the pastes made with cereal starches, such as those of corn and wheat, are cloudy in appearance whereas those made from root starches, such as potato and tapioca, are more clear.

When starches are heated with water the granules absorb water and swell and the dispersion increases in viscosity or thickness until a peak thickness is reached. The dispersion also increases in translucency to a maximum as heating continues. The term *gelatinization* is used to describe these changes [8]. The changes are gradual over a temperature range that is characteristic for a particular starch. The granules of any starch are of varying sizes and do not swell at the same rates. Large granules swell first. Potato starch, with its generally larger granules, begins to gelatinize at a lower temperature than corn starch. In any case, gelatinization is usually complete at a temperature of 88° to 92° C (190° to 194° F). Figure 17–7 shows the stages of gelatinization for corn starch.

Continued heating under controlled conditions after gelatinization is complete results in decreased thickness. Boiling or cooking starchy sauces and puddings in the home for longer periods of time usually does not produce thinner mixtures, however, because the loss of moisture by evaporation is usually not controlled. The loss of

17-7 *Photomicrographs showing the gelatinization of corn starch granules (magnified 575X) as cooking proceeds. (Courtesy of Corn Products Company)*

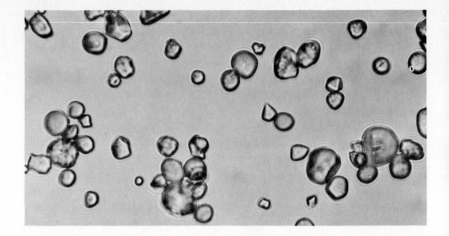

Uncooked corn starch.

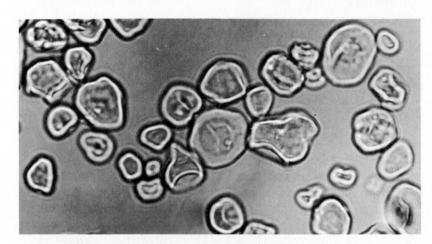

Corn starch cooked to 72° C. Note that the granules are swollen but not ruptured.

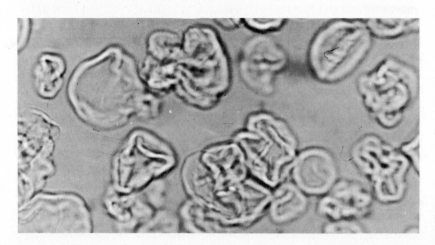

Corn starch cooked to 90° C. Note that some of the granules appear to be ruptured; this is accompanied by a loss of viscosity of cooked starch paste.

410

moisture, resulting in increased concentration of the starch, causes increased thickness and counterbalances the first process.

Elbert [5] points out that the term *gelatinization* has been used without a consistent definition. It has been defined differently by various researchers and has included the degree of swelling, hot starch paste viscosity, translucency, and *loss of birefringence,* which is loss of a Maltese-cross appearance of the granules under a polarizing microscope (Figure 17–6).

Gel Formation and Retrogradation. As a starch-thickened mixture cools after gelatinization is complete, bonds apparently form between the molecules of starch in the mixture. Bonds forming between the branches of the bushy amylopectin molecules are very weak and have little practical effect on the rigidity of the starch product. However, bonds between the long-chain amylose molecules are relatively strong and form readily. This bonding produces a three-dimensional network that results in the development of a gel, with the amylose molecules forming a network which holds water in its meshes. The rigidity of the starch mixture is increased. Gel formation or *gelation* is a different process from gelatinization. Gelation takes place on cooling the starch paste after the starch granules have been gelatinized. Gel formation in cooked starch pastes is a gradual process that continues over a several hour period as the paste cools. Waxy varieties of starch without amylose do not form gels. Starches, such as corn starch, containing relatively large amounts of amylose, form firmer gels than starches with a somewhat lower concentration of amylose.

As starch-thickened mixtures continue to stand after gel formation is complete, additional bonds are formed between the straight-chain amylose molecules. Some of the amylose molecules become aggregated in a particular area in an organized, crystalline manner. As these amylose molecules pull together, the gel network shrinks, and water is pushed out of the gel. This process of "weeping" from a gel, called *synersis,* is a result of the increased association of starch molecules as a starch gel ages. This increased association of amylose molecules in starch gels is called *retrogradation* (Figure 17–8).

Factors Requiring Control in Starch Cookery. In order to obtain uniformity in the cooking of starch pastes, certain conditions must be standardized and controlled. These conditions are as follows:

1. Temperature of heating.
2. Time of heating.
3. Intensity of agitation or stirring.
4. Acidity (pH) of the mixture.
5. Addition of other ingredients.

Temperature and Time of Heating. Gelatinization is a change that occurs over a range of temperatures. More concentrated disper-

17-8 *A diagram representing the gel formation and then retrogradation of a starch dispersion. (a) Solution; (b) gel; (c) retrograded. (From Elizabeth Osman. "Starch and Other Polysaccharides." In* Food Theory and Applications. *Pauline C. Paul and Helen H. Palmer, editors. Copyright 1972, John Wiley & Sons, Inc. Reprinted by permission of John Wiley & Sons, Inc.)*

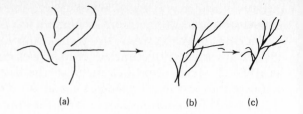

(a) (b) (c)

sions show higher viscosity at lower temperatures than do less concentrated dispersions because of the larger number of granules that swell.

Starch pastes may be prepared most quickly by bringing them to a boiling temperature over direct heat, with constant stirring as they thicken, and simmering them for approximately one minute. Longer cooking to improve the flavor is not necessary. Under carefully controlled conditions starch pastes that are heated rapidly are somewhat thicker than similar pastes that are heated slowly [9].

Agitation or Stirring. Stirring while cooking starch mixtures is desirable in the early stages in order to obtain a smooth product of uniform consistency. However, if agitation is too intense or continued too long, it accelerates the rupturing of the starch granules, decreases viscosity, and may give a slick, pasty mouthfeel. Stirring should, therefore, be minimized.

Acidity (pH). A high degree of acidity appears to cause some fragmentation of starch granules and hydrolysis of some of the starch molecules, thus decreasing the thickening power of the starch granules [7]. In cooked starch mixtures containing fruit juices or vinegar, such as fruit pie fillings and salad dressings, the acidity may be high enough (pH below 4) to cause some thinning. Specially prepared modified starches that are resistant to acid breakdown are used in commercial food processing where this may be a problem. When a high concentration of sugar is also present in a starch paste, the sugar may help to decrease the effect of acid since sugar limits the swelling of starch granules and the starch molecules are, therefore, not as available for hydrolysis by acid. Proportions of ingredients in home recipes for acid-starch products, such as lemon pie filling, have been adjusted to compensate for the usual effects of acid and sugar so that a desirable consistency results. Acid juices, such as lemon juice, can also be added after the starchy paste has been cooked. This limits the contact that the acid has with starch molecules, particularly during gelatinization.

Addition of Other Ingredients. Various other ingredients are commonly used with starch in the preparation of food. Some ingredients have a pronounced effect on the gelatinization of starch and on the gel strength of the cooled mixture. Sugar is one ingredient that is used in many starchy mixtures. It raises the temperature at which a starch mixture gelatinizes [2, 3, 14]. If sugar is used in a relatively large amount it delays the swelling of the starch granules and decreases the thickness of the paste. It does this at least partially by competing with the starch for water. If not enough water is available for the starch granules they cannot swell sufficiently. If a recipe calls for a large amount of sugar, only part of the sugar need be added before cooking. After the starch has been gelatinized the remainder of the sugar may be added with much less effect on viscosity.

High concentrations of sucrose are more effective in delaying swelling or gelatinization than are equal concentrations of monosaccharides such as glucose and fructose. At a concentration of 20 percent or more, all sugars and syrups cause a decided decrease in the gel strength of starch pastes.

Fats have been shown to lower the temperature at which the maximum viscosity of cooked starch pastes occurs. Milk, eggs, and flour proteins also appear to affect gelatinization of starch in various ways.

Combining Starch with Hot Liquid. One potential difficulty encountered in starch cookery is the result of the tendency of starch particles to clump or form lumps. Before hot liquids are combined with starch, the particles of starch must be separated in some way in order to bring about a uniform dispersion of well-hydrated starch granules. This can be accomplished by dispersing the particles with melted fat, by blending the starch with sugar, or by making a paste of starch with cold water before adding it to hot liquid.

White Sauces. A white sauce is a starch-thickened product made from fat, flour, and milk with seasonings. White sauces are used in the preparation of a variety of dishes including creamed eggs, fish, and vegetables; cheese sauce; cream soups; soufflés; croquettes; and certain casserole mixtures. The finished sauce should be smooth and satiny in appearance and free of lumps. The consistency is dependent upon the amount of starchy agent used. Table 17–3 gives proportions for white sauces of various consistencies and suggested uses.

Ingredients for a white sauce may be mixed in different ways as long as a smooth, creamy product results. Most commonly the fat is

Table 17–3 *Proportions of Ingredients and Uses for White Sauce*

Sauce	Fat	Flour	Milk	Salt	Pepper	Uses
Thin	1 T (14 g)	1 T (7 g)	1 c (237 ml)	¼ t (1.5 g)	fg	Cream soups
Medium	2 T (28 g)	2 T (14 g)	1 c	¼ t	fg	Creamed vegetables and meats; casseroles
Thick	3 T (42 g)	3 T (21 g)	1 c	¼ t	fg	Soufflés
Very thick	4 T (56 g)	4 T (28 g)	1 c	¼ t	fg	Croquettes

melted and the flour and salt stirred into it. This separates the starch granules so that lumping is less likely when hot liquid is added. The fat-flour mixture is called a *roux* and may be cooked until bubbly. Hot milk is then added with constant stirring and the sauce is brought to boiling over direct heat. A double boiler may also be used but cooking is slower.

An alternative method for preparing white sauce involves mixing the flour with some of the cold milk to form a paste. The remainder of the milk is then added and the mixture cooked over direct heat until it boils. At this time the fat and seasonings are added (if butter is the fat, the volatile flavor may be better retained with this method). Instantized flour has a lesser tendency to form lumps when mixed with liquid than does noninstantized flour and may be conveniently used in the making of white sauce.

Cream Soups. Cream soups may vary in consistency but the usual thickness corresponds to that of thin white sauce. One tablespoon of flour is used for each cup of liquid, which may be part milk and part vegetable cooking water or meat broth and vegetable pulp. Combined vegetable waters sometimes give a soup of better flavor than the water from a single vegetable.

If starchy vegetables are used for pulp the amount of flour must be reduced to about one half the usual amount, but fat must also be reduced or the fat, lacking flour enough to hold it in suspension, will float on top of the soup. Some flour is desirable for starchy soups, such as potato or dried bean soup, to hold the pulp in suspension.

If green vegetable pulp is added to the cooking water, care must be used to avoid too large a quantity of pulp which may detract from the appearance of the soup. In preparing a cream soup, a medium white sauce may be made from milk, fat, flour, and seasonings. An amount of vegetable juice and pulp equal to the milk used is then heated and added to the sauce, thus diluting the mixture to the consistency of thin white sauce.

If acid juices, such as tomato, are used, the acid is added gradually to the white sauce at serving time to minimize the tendency to curdle if combined too far in advance. Soda is not a necessary ingredient in the making of cream of tomato soup and its use is not recommended because it may increase the alkalinity of the soup so much that ascorbic acid and some of the B vitamins are essentially destroyed by oxidation. The use of soda may also seriously mar flavor if an excess is used.

Thickening the tomato juice by making a tomato sauce of the tomato juice, fat, and flour instead of making a white sauce is preferred by some persons and is a common practice commercially. Probably the same precautions should be observed as to the time and manner of combining the tomato sauce with the hot milk.

Starch Desserts. The corn starch pudding is probably the most commonly used pudding of this class, although a similar dessert may be made with other cereal starches and tapioca or sago as the thickening agents. The consistency of starchy puddings may vary according to personal preference. If one desires that the pudding be stiff enough to form a mold, it should be as soft as possible while still holding its form when unmolded. Others may prefer the pudding to be of a softer consistency so that it must be spooned into individual dishes. Tapioca and sago puddings are usually of a more desirable eating quality if they are relatively soft.

The preparation of puddings and pie fillings often combines starch and egg cookery in the production of a creamy mixture. The product is thickened with starch before the egg is added because starch tolerates higher temperatures than does the egg. Therefore, a pudding is first prepared in the same manner as a corn starch pudding containing no egg. After starch gelatinization is complete, a small amount of the hot starchy mixture may be added to the egg. This dilutes the egg so that it will not coagulate in lumps when it is added back to the bulk of the hot mixture. Alternatively, a small amount of cold milk may be withheld in the beginning of the preparation and mixed with the egg to dilute it. This milk-egg mixture is then added all at once to the hot starchy pudding mixture, to produce a smooth creamy product.

Starchy puddings containing an egg should be cooked sufficiently after the addition of the egg to coagulate the egg proteins. If this is not done, the pudding may become thin on standing. The temperature of the pudding after the egg is added should not reach boiling, if a fairly large amount of egg is used, as this may result in curdling of the egg with a consequent grainy texture of the pudding.

Basic Formula for Corn Starch Pudding

2 to 3 T (16 to 24 g)	
corn starch	2 c (474 ml) milk
¼ c (50 g) sugar	1 t vanilla
⅛ t salt	1 egg or 2 egg yolks (optional)

Mix sugar, salt, and starch. Add ½ c cold milk gradually to form a smooth paste. Heat remaining milk in a saucepan and add the starch-sugar paste to the hot milk with constant stirring. Cook the mixture over direct heat, stirring constantly, until the mixture boils; continue simmering for 1 minute. Remove from heat and add vanilla. Chill. If egg is used in the pudding, add a small amount of the hot boiled mixture to the slightly beaten egg; then add this back to the hot mixture in the saucepan. Cook over moderate heat for 3 or 4 minutes. After cooking is completed, add vanilla. Chill.

The mixing of sugar and then cold milk with the starch separates the starch particles and prevents lumping. Numerous additions or substitutions may be made to change the flavor of the basic formula for corn starch pudding. These include the addition of chocolate or cocoa, caramelized sugar, shredded coconut, nuts, maple syrup, or diced fruits. Recipe books should be consulted for specific directions for preparing the variations.

Microwave Cooking. Corn starch or flour thickened sauces may be prepared in the microwave oven. In making a white sauce, a mix may first be prepared using instant nonfat dry milk, flour, and salt, with butter or margarine cut-in to the mixture. This mix may be combined with water in appropriate proportions and cooked on high for thorough heating and thickening, stirring often to eliminate lumps. Alternatively, the fat may be melted, the flour and salt stirred in, and the roux cooked briefly before adding the milk and cooking on high power as described above.

Study Questions

1. Name the most important cereal grains that are used for food.
2. The structure of all grains is somewhat similar.
   a. Name three major parts of a grain and describe the general chemical composition of each part.
   b. What is the aleurone of a cereal grain? Describe its general composition and indicate where it usually goes during the milling of grain.
3. a. What is meant by enrichment of cereals and flours? What nutrients must be added to meet the standards of the federal government?
   b. Compare the general nutritional value of refined unenriched, enriched, and whole grain cereal products.
4. Cereal grains are often processed in preparation for use.
   a. Indicate which grains are commonly used for each of the following processes and briefly describe the processes involved in preparing each grain for each use that is appropriate for that grain.
      (1) Uncooked breakfast cereals
      (2) Prepared breakfast cereals
      (3) Flour
      (4) Meal
      (5) Hominy
      (6) Grits
      (7) Alimentary pastes
5. a. What are the main purposes for cooking cereals?
   b. Suggest appropriate methods for cooking each of the following cereal products and explain why these methods are appropriate:
      (1) Granular cereals such as farina and cornmeal
      (2) Rolled oats
      (3) Rice
      (4) Macaroni or spaghetti

6. Starch is a storage form of carbohydrate deposited as granules in plant cells.
   a. Describe the appearance of starch granules when viewed under a microscope; how do the size and shape of starch granules differ from one plant source to another?
   b. Name the two fractions of starch and explain how they differ in structure.
   c. What products are produced as starch is hydrolyzed and what may catalyze this process?
7. Briefly describe what happens when starch granules are heated in water. What is this process called?
8. Many starch-thickened mixtures become stiff or rigid on cooling.
   a. What is this process called and what happens in the starch mixture to bring it about?
   b. How does the amount of amylose in the starch affect the rigidity and why?
   c. What is meant by retrogradation of a starch paste?
   d. What is syneresis and why may it occur in cooked starch mixtures?
   e. Which of the common starches will form the stiffest and which the softest pudding when used in equal amounts? Explain.
9. Distinguish between gelatinization and gelation of starch mixtures.
10. Why is gravy made from browned flour usually thinner than gravy made from the same amount of unbrowned flour? Explain.
11. Describe the general effect of each of the following on the thickness of a cooked starch mixture:
    a. Rate of heating
    b. Excessive stirring
    c. Addition of sugar
12. Describe three ways to keep powdery starches from lumping when they are added to hot liquid. Explain what is happening in each case.
13. Describe appropriate methods for preparing each of the following items and explain why these methods should be successful:
    a. White sauce
    b. Cream of vegetable soup
    c. Cream of tomato soup
    d. Corn starch pudding
    e. Corn starch pudding with egg

References

1. Anderson, R. H., D. L. Maxwell, A. E. Mulley, and C. W. Fritsch. 1976. Effects of processing and storage on micronutrients in breakfast cereals. *Food Technology* **30** (No. 5), 110.
2. Bean, M. L., and E. M. Osman. 1959. Behavior of starch during food preparation. II. Effects of different sugars on the viscosity and gel strength of starch pastes. *Food Research* **24**, 665.
3. Bean, M. M., and W. T. Yamazaki. 1978. Wheat starch gelatinization in sugar solutions. I. Sucrose: Microscopy and viscosity effects. *Cereal Chemistry* **55**, 936.

4. *Cereals and Pasta in Family Meals.* Home and Garden Bulletin No. 150. Washington, DC: U.S. Department of Agriculture, 1979.

5. Elbert, E. M. 1965. Starch: Changes during heating in the presence of moisture. *Journal of Home Economics* **57,** 197.

6. Haber, T., A. A. Seyam, and O. J. Banasik. 1976. Hard red winter wheat, rye and triticale. *Baker's Digest* **50,** 24 (June).

7. Hansuld, M. K., and A. M. Briant. 1954. The effect of citric acid on selected edible starches and flours. *Food Research* **19,** 581.

8. Holmes, Z. A., and A. Soeldner. 1981. Macrostructure of selected raw starches and selected heated starch dispersions. *Journal of the American Dietetic Association* **78,** 153.

9. Holmes, Z. A., and A. Soeldner. 1981. Effect of heating rate and freezing and reheating of corn and wheat starch-water dispersions: *Journal of the American Dietetic Association* **78,** 352.

10. Lachance, P. A. 1981. The role of cereal grain products in the U.S. diet. *Food Technology* **35,** 49 (no. 3).

11. Rao, D. R., G. Patel, and J. F. Nishimuta. 1980. Comparison of protein quality of corn, triticale and wheat. *Nutrition Reports International* **21,** 923.

12. Reitz, L. P. 1970. New wheats and social progress. *Science* **169,** 952.

13. Smith, G. S., E. J. Barta, and M. E. Lazar. 1964. Bulgur production by continuous atmospheric-pressure process. *Food Technology* **18,** 89.

14. Spies, R. D., and R. C. Hoseney. 1982. Effect of sugars on starch gelatinization. *Cereal Chemistry* **59,** 128.

15. Wu, Y. V., K. R. Sexson, and J. S. Wall. 1976. Triticale protein concentrate: Preparation, composition, and properties. *Agricultural and Food Chemistry* **24,** 511.

16. Wurzburg, O. B., and C. D. Szymanski. 1970. Modified starches for the food industry. *Agricultural and Food Chemistry* **18,** 997.

18

Batters and Doughs

Batters and doughs, sometimes called *flour mixtures,* include a large variety of baked products, such as muffins, biscuits and other quick breads, pastry, shortened and unshortened cakes, cookies, and breads. Producing the end result that is desired in these flour mixtures is dependent on such factors as accuracy in measurements or weights (see Chapter 5), skill in manipulation, control of oven or other temperatures, and information about the kinds and proportions of ingredients and the temperatures that are optimal for given mixtures. It is important to learn what characteristics are generally preferred in various baked products and what proportions of ingredients and techniques of mixing might be used to achieve these characteristics. However, a so-called standard product may vary from one group of individuals to another, depending upon preferences. A knowledge of basic ingredients and their effects and of basic methods of mixing and their effects should be valuable in learning to produce any standard desired.

Ingredients

The principal ingredients used in foundation formulas for doughs and batters are flour, liquid, fat, egg, sugar, leavening agent, and salt. Flavoring substances are added to some types of mixtures.

Flour

White wheat flour is defined by the U.S. Food and Drug Administration as a food made by the grinding and sifting of cleaned wheat

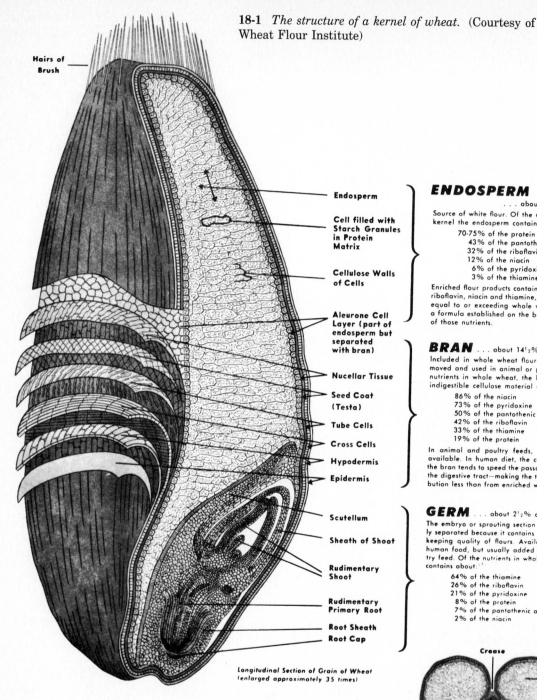

18-1 *The structure of a kernel of wheat.* (Courtesy of Wheat Flour Institute)

Hairs of Brush

Endosperm

Cell filled with Starch Granules in Protein Matrix

Cellulose Walls of Cells

Aleurone Cell Layer (part of endosperm but separated with bran)

Nucellar Tissue

Seed Coat (Testa)

Tube Cells

Cross Cells

Hypodermis

Epidermis

Scutellum

Sheath of Shoot

Rudimentary Shoot

Rudimentary Primary Root

Root Sheath

Root Cap

Longitudinal Section of Grain of Wheat (enlarged approximately 35 times)

ENDOSPERM

. . . about 83% of the kernel
Source of white flour. Of the nutrients in the whole kernel the endosperm contains about:

70-75% of the protein
43% of the pantothenic acid
32% of the riboflavin   B-complex
12% of the niacin   vitamins
6% of the pyridoxine
3% of the thiamine

Enriched flour products contain added quantities of riboflavin, niacin and thiamine, plus iron, in amounts equal to or exceeding whole wheat — according to a formula established on the basis of popular need of those nutrients.

BRAN . . . about 14½% of the kernel

Included in whole wheat flour but more often removed and used in animal or poultry feed. Of the nutrients in whole wheat, the bran, in addition to indigestible cellulose material contains about:

86% of the niacin
73% of the pyridoxine
50% of the pantothenic acid
42% of the riboflavin
33% of the thiamine
19% of the protein

In animal and poultry feeds, these nutrients are available. In human diet, the cellulose material of the bran tends to speed the passage of food through the digestive tract — making the total nutritive contribution less than from enriched white flour products.

GERM . . . about 2½% of the kernel

The embryo or sprouting section of the seed, usually separated because it contains fat which limits the keeping quality of flours. Available separately as human food, but usually added to animal or poultry feed. Of the nutrients in whole wheat, the germ contains about:

64% of the thiamine
26% of the riboflavin
21% of the pyridoxine
8% of the protein
7% of the pantothenic acid
2% of the niacin

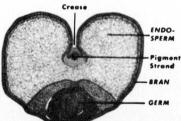

Crease

ENDO-SPERM

Pigment Strand

BRAN

GERM

Cross Section View

(Figure 18-1). The flour is freed from the bran and germ to such an extent that certain specifications as to moisture, ash, and protein content may be met. Flour, the basic ingredient of batters and doughs, provides structure and body in baked flour products because of its protein and starch content.

Milling. The milling of white flour is a process of separation of the endosperm from the bran and germ and subdividing it into a fine flour. Specific procedures in milling may vary from one mill to another. A simplified chart showing the major steps in milling is shown in Figure 18-2. The three main portions of the wheat kernel are divided approximately as follows: 83 percent endosperm, 14.5 percent bran layers (including the aleurone layer), and 2.5 percent germ [10]. When no separation of these main portions is made, the flour resulting from the milling process is called *whole wheat, entire wheat, or graham.*

White flours were formerly made by sifting wheat ground in a stone mill, but this method of separation yielded a flour that was less white and of poorer baking quality than flour made in a modern roller mill. In the modern milling process the wheat passes through a series of rollers. The first sets of corrugated rolls crush the grain and detach the endosperm from the bran. That portion of the endosperm that is separated and pulverized is sifted after each crushing.

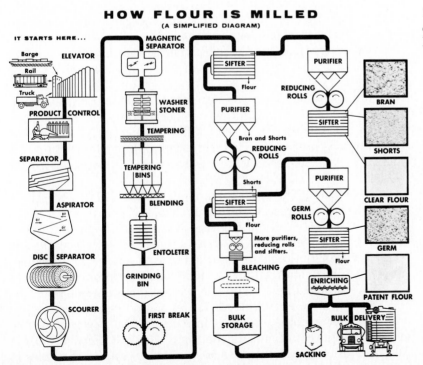

HOW FLOUR IS MILLED
(A SIMPLIFIED DIAGRAM)

18-2 *Steps involved in the milling of flour.* (Courtesy of Wheat Flour Institute)

The flours resulting from the first siftings are known as *break flours* of which there are about five streams.

The small pieces of the inner portion of the kernel, which are granulated with difficulty, are known as *middlings*. After their separation from the bran, the middlings are fed through a series of smooth rolls that further reduce the size of the particles and produce fine flour. About six to eight streams of flour are obtained from the rolling and sifting of the purified middlings.

Various grades and types of flours are made from the many streams of flour resulting from the roller process. The streams vary in their protein content. The break flours and those from the last reductions of the middlings are inferior to the other streams of flour for baking purposes.

Because the endosperm represents about 83 percent of the total kernel, theoretically about that much white flour should be obtained by milling, but in actual practice only 72 to 75 percent is separated as white flour. The kind and composition of flour depend on the class of wheat used, on the conditions under which the wheat is grown, and on the method of fractionation. The separation of endosperm from bran and germ is neither a simple nor an extremely efficient process. The inner bran layers and the germ are tightly bound to the endosperm, and it is impossible to make a complete separation. The usual 72 to 75 percent extraction produces white flour containing essentially no bran and germ and exhibiting good baking properties. In times of national emergency the usual percentage of extraction has been increased as a conservation measure. It has been suggested that the extraction rate of white flour could be increased regularly up to 80 percent without sacrificing baking quality [12].

A milling method based on separation of flour particles by air currents called *air classification* has been developed. The various fractions obtained in this process differ in composition and, therefore, in baking properties. This method of milling offers promise for the ready production of both high- and low-protein flours for specific uses.

A final stage in the production of white flour is often bleaching and/or maturing. Freshly milled, unbleached flour is yellowish in color chiefly because of the presence of carotenoid pigments. When used for baking bread this flour gives a somewhat lower volume and a less fine texture than does bleached or aged flour. Aging involves simply holding or storing the flour for several weeks or months until the color becomes lighter and the baking qualities improve. The addition of certain chemical substances to the freshly milled flour produces effects similar to aging in a much shorter period of time and saves the cost of storing the flour. The U.S. Food and Drug Administration permits the use of specified chemical substances in the bleaching and maturing of white flour. These include benzoyl peroxide, which is primarily a bleaching agent, and chlorine dioxide, chlorine, and acetone peroxides, which have both a bleaching and a maturing or improving effect. Azodicarbonamide may be added to flour as a maturing agent but does not react until the flour is made into a dough. The maturing or improving effect appears to be a complex reaction involving flour proteins, possibly oxidizing them in some way. Flour that has been treated with any of these chemicals must be labeled "bleached." Both bleached and unbleached flours are available to the consumer on the retail market.

Classes of Wheat. Wheats may be classified on the basis of the time of planting or the growing season, on the color of the kernel, and on the "hardness" or "softness" of the kernel. Wheats that are planted in the spring and harvested in the fall are called *spring wheats,* whereas those that are planted in the fall and harvested the following summer are called *winter wheats.* Since these wheats remain in the ground all winter, they are grown in areas with relatively mild winters. Some wheat kernels have a reddish appearance and are called *red wheats,* whereas others are white. A hard wheat has a hard, vitreous kernel, whereas a soft wheat appears to be more powdery. Hard wheats are usually higher in protein than are soft wheats and the protein has more baking strength when flour from this wheat is made into dough. Spring wheats include hard red varieties, hard white and soft white varieties, and durum wheats, which are used only for the production of macaroni products. Winter wheats may be hard, semihard, or soft. Hard winter wheats have a fairly strong quality of protein and are suitable for bread-making purposes.

The geographical areas in which most of the hard spring wheats are produced are the north central part of the United States and western Canada. Hard winter wheats are grown mainly in the south central and middle central states. Soft winter wheat is grown east of the Mississippi River and in the Pacific Northwest. Because climatic and soil conditions affect the composition of wheat, it is to be expected that wide variations may occur within these classes.

Grades of Flour. The miller grades white flours on the basis of the flour streams going into them. *Straight grade* theoretically should contain all the flour streams resulting from the milling process but actually 2 to 3 percent of the poorest streams is withheld. Very little flour on the market is straight grade. *Patent* flours come from the more refined portion of the endosperm and may be made from any class of wheat. They are divided into *short patent,* which includes 60 to 80 percent of the total flour; *medium patent* with 80 to 90 percent; and *long patent* with 90 to 95 percent. Most patent flours on the market include about 85 percent of the straight flour. *Clear grade* is made from streams withheld in the making of patent flours.

Clear grade flours may be used in various flour products such as pancake mixes.

Types of Wheat Flour.   It is important to understand the differences in wheat flours in order to use them most effectively. Within certain limits, various types of flour may be interchanged in different recipes by altering the proportions of the nonflour constituents of the mixture. The composition and nutritive value of some wheat flours is given in Appendix C.

Whole Wheat Flour.   Whole wheat flour may also be called *graham* flour or entire wheat flour. It is the product prepared from cleaned wheat in such a manner that the proportions of the natural constituents of wheat are not altered. It contains essentially the entire wheat kernel and may be ground to different degrees of fineness. The keeping quality of whole wheat flour is lower than that of white flour because it contains fat from the germ that may become oxidized on storage.

Bread Flour.   Bread flour is a white flour made chiefly from hard wheat. It contains a relatively high percentage of protein that will develop into gluten with very strong, elastic properties when the flour is made into a dough. Bread flour has a slightly granular feel when it is touched and does not form a firm mass when pressed in the hand. It may be bleached or unbleached. Bread flour is used by the commercial baker for yeast breads and is also available for use in the home. It produces breads with relatively high volume and fine texture.

All-Purpose Flour.   All-purpose flour is sometimes called *family* flour or *general-purpose* flour. It is a white flour usually made from a blend of wheats to produce a protein content that is lower than that of bread flour. It contains enough protein that it can be satisfactorily used for making bread and rolls at home and it can also be used for making quick breads. The gluten that develops in doughs made from all-purpose flour is less strong and elastic than that produced in bread flour doughs. All-purpose flour may be used for making pastry, cookies, and certain cakes. It usually has too high a protein content to make a delicate fine-textured cake.

Pastry Flour.   Pastry flour is a white flour that is usually made from soft wheat and contains a lower percentage of protein than is found in all-purpose flour. Its chief use is for baking pastries and cookies, and it is used primarily in the commercial baking industry.

Cake Flour.   Cake flour is prepared from soft wheat and is so finely milled that it feels soft and satiny to the touch, forming a firm mass when pressed in the hand. It usually contains only the most highly refined streams of flour from the milling process and is a short patent grade of flour. The protein content of cake flour is very low in comparison to other types of flour and it is usually highly bleached with chlorine. The high starch content and weak quality of gluten produced from cake flours makes it desirable chiefly for the preparation of delicate, fine-textured cakes.

Instantized Flour. Instantized flour is also called *instant, instant-blending,* or *quick-mixing* flour. It is a granular all-purpose flour that has been processed by moistening and then redrying the flour in order to aggregate small particles into larger particles or agglomerates. The agglomerated particles are of relatively uniform size and do not pack. Therefore, this flour does not require sifting before measuring. It flows freely without dust, is easily measured, and blends more readily with liquid than does regular flour. Some changes should be made in formulas and preparation procedures when this flour is substituted for regular flour in baked products to assure good quality in the finished product.

An evaluation was made of ten baked products using two brands of instantized flour and a regular all-purpose flour [8]. In general, the volume of instantized flour had to be adjusted by removing 2 tablespoons per cup of measured flour to ensure a good quality baked product. Yeast rolls, popovers, and pastry made with instantized flour scored below acceptable quality, however, even when adjustments were made for the amount of flour.

Self-rising Flour. Self-rising flour has had leavening agents and salt added to it in proportions desirable for home baking. Monocalcium phosphate is the acid salt most commonly added in combination with sodium bicarbonate (baking soda) as leavening ingredients. Self-rising flours are commonly used in the southern United States where quick breads, such as baking powder biscuits, are frequently prepared.

Gluten Flour. Wheat flour is mixed with dried extracted gluten to form gluten flour. This flour has a protein content of about 41 percent in comparison to the 10 to 14 percent protein content of wheat flour. The gluten is extracted by a gentle washing of a flour-water dough and is dried under mild conditions to minimize the effects on the baking characteristics of the gluten. Gluten flour is used primarily by the baking industry to adjust the protein level in various doughs.

Gluten. The proteins of wheat are very important in determining the functional properties of wheat flour doughs and have been under study for many years. [4, 6, 11]. A variety of proteins has been extracted from wheat. Some of these are the more soluble albumins and globulins that do not appear to play major roles in baking. About 85 percent of the proteins of white flour are relatively insoluble. In early research the insoluble wheat proteins were separated into two fractions called *gliadin* and *glutenin*. When flour is moistened with water and thoroughly mixed or kneaded, these insoluble proteins form *gluten*. Gluten is primarily responsible for the viscous and elastic characteristics and high loaf volume of wheat flour

18-3 *Gluten may be extracted from a flour-water dough by washing carefully with cold water to remove the starch. A comparison of the amount and characteristics of gluten from various flours may thus be made. Pictured are samples of unbaked and baked gluten. Left, cake flour; center, all-purpose flour; right, bread flour. (Courtesy of Wheat Flour Institute)*

doughs. Gluten may be extracted from a flour and water dough that has been vigorously kneaded by a thorough washing with water to remove the starch (Figure 18-3). The moist gluten thus extracted has elastic and cohesive properties something like chewing gum. When gliadin and glutenin are separated from each other, the gliadin is found to be a syrupy substance that may bind the mass together and the glutenin exhibits toughness and rubberiness that probably contributes strength (Figure 18-4). Later research on flour proteins has shown that gliadin and glutenin each consist of several components or subunits of different molecular weights. Glutenin is a much larger molecule than gliadin. High-molecular-weight glutenin molecules may have subunits bound together by the formation of disulfide bonds (—S—S—) between the protein chains. During the mixing of a dough the long strands of glutenin evidently become aligned in the direction of mixing and associated with gliadin molecules to form a strong elastic uniform film that envelops the starch granules in the dough. Interactions in the dough probably also occur between gluten proteins and lipids and possibly other dough components. The nature of these interactions continues to be studied.

In yeast breads gluten is developed to its maximum strength to make possible a high volume and fine texture. In other baked products, such as shortened cakes, gluten development is retarded so that a more tender product will result.

Other Wheat Products. *Cracked wheat,* although not a flour, is extensively used in baking breads and quick breads. It should be soaked in double its volume of water for 24 hours before being used. Cracked wheat may be combined in varying proportions with whole wheat or white flour. Rolled wheat is also used in making cookies and quick breads.

Wheat germ, which contains essentially all of the fat from the wheat kernel, is available as yellowish tan flakes either toasted or

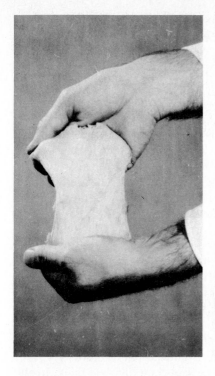  

18-4 *The different properties of glutenin (left), gliadin (center), and gluten (right) are illustrated.* (Courtesy of *Baker's Digest* and R. J. Dimler)

unheated. It is often vacuum packed to prevent oxidative changes that may occur in the fat. Wheat germ is a good source of B vitamins, iron, and other nutrients and may be added to both yeast and quick breads. The vitamin potency of wheat germ is not appreciably decreased by baking in the yeast breads that contain it. However, the germ has been found to exert a deleterious effect on the baking quality of flour. For this reason, a relatively strong flour is best used with it and the germ may be substituted to the extent of one-fifth to one-third of the flour.

Flours and Meals Other Than Wheat Flour. Flours other than wheat are commonly used in quick breads as well as in yeast breads.

Rye Flour. Rye flour is obtained by sifting rye meal. It has some gluten-forming properties but it contains chiefly gliadin with only small amounts of glutenin. Therefore, bread made from rye flour, although not necessarily soggy or heavy, is more compact than bread made with wheat flour. Some white flour is often combined with rye flour in making bread to yield a lighter, more porous product than is possible with rye flour alone.

Barley Flour. Barley flour contains *hordein,* a protein with properties similar to gliadin. Although the flour can be used fairly successfully in flour mixtures, the flavor of the flour has been a factor limiting its use.

Cornmeal and Corn Flour. Cornmeal, a granular product made

427

from either white or yellow corn, is commonly used in several types of quick breads. Its chief protein, *zein*, has none of the properties of the gluten of wheat. If a crumbly product is to be avoided, cornmeal must be combined with some white flour, preferably all-purpose flour, to bind it. Corn flour has the same properties as cornmeal except that it is finer. It is used chiefly in commercial pancake mixes and prepared cereals.

Miscellaneous Flours. Although other flours are available they are used less often, either because they lack gluten or some similar constituent or because they are little known except in certain areas. *Rice flour* is fundamentally rice starch. *Potato flour* is used in some countries and, like rice flour, is chiefly starch. Potato and soy flours may be used by those who have an allergy to wheat. *Soy flour* is made from soybeans, which are legumes. Although soy flour is high in protein, the protein has none of the characteristics of gluten and the flour must be used with a strong or moderately strong wheat flour for good results in baking. The chief advantage of using soy flour is the contribution it makes in increasing the protein value of the product. When 20 percent soy flour is used in yeast bread, the protein content may be increased by as much as 50 percent. The flavor is pleasing if the quantity of soy flour substituted is not too high. A manufacturing process has produced two types of soy flour in which the oil is removed, refined, and then blended back, in the proper amounts, into the flour as a fine spray. The soy oil is thus free to mix readily with other ingredients. These flours are low fat (4 percent soy oil) or high fat (14 percent oil). Yeast breads made with 20 percent soy flour are somewhat dark in color and have texture qualities comparable to whole wheat breads. Federal standards for commercial white breads permit the use of 3 percent soy flour as an optional ingredient.

Buckwheat flour does not have the same baking properties as does wheat flour. The principal use of buckwheat is in pancakes or waffles. Some of the pancake batters are fermented to increase the flavor.

Triticale flour, made from the cereal that is a cross between wheat and rye, may be used to make yeast bread of satisfactory quality. Its flavor has been reported to be like that of a very mild rye bread [7].

Leavening Agents

To leaven means to "make light and porous." Most present-day flour mixtures are leavened. This is done by the incorporation or formation in the product of a gas that expands during preparation and subsequent heating. There are three major leavening gases—air, steam, and carbon dioxide. In some flour mixtures one of the leavening gases predominates, whereas in other products two or three of the gases play important roles.

Air is incorporated in flour mixtures by beating eggs; by folding and rolling doughs, such as puff paste; by creaming fat and sugar together; or by beating batters. In common practice, some air will be incorporated into all flour mixtures.

Steam is probably produced in all flour mixtures to a certain degree since all flour mixtures contain water and are usually heated to the vaporization temperature of water. However, those products that are leavened almost entirely by steam are popovers and cream puffs. These mixtures have a high percentage of liquid and are started to bake at a high oven temperature, which rapidly forms steam. Since one volume of water increases to more than 1,600 volumes when converted into steam, it has tremendous leavening power. The water that is available for conversion to steam may be added as liquid or as a component of other ingredients, such as eggs. Egg whites contain enough water to furnish two to three times more expansion in baking angel food cakes than the air that was added by beating. Even stiff doughs, such as pie crust, are partially leavened by steam.

Carbon dioxide may be produced in a flour mixture either by a biological process or by a purely chemical reaction.

Biological Production of Carbon Dioxide. Carbon dioxide is produced by the action of yeast and certain bacteria on sugar. This process is called *fermentation* and carbon dioxide is a by-product of the overall reaction. Yeast ferments sugar to form ethyl alcohol and carbon dioxide. The alcohol is volatilized by the heat of baking. This fermentation is catalyzed by a mixture of many enzymes produced by the yeast cells. Sugar is usually added to yeast-flour mixtures to speed up fermentation and the production of carbon dioxide gas. If no sugar is used, yeast can form gas slowly from the small amount of sugar that is present in flour and from the maltose produced by the amylase enzyme of flour as it breaks down starch. The maltose formed from starch hydrolysis is further broken down to glucose by the maltase enzyme that is produced by yeast. The use of yeast in leavening is further discussed in connection with yeast breads in Chapter 20. Certain bacteria may also produce leavening gas in flour mixtures. One type used produces hydrogen and carbon dioxide gases in salt-rising bread. Although the organisms occur normally in the cornmeal used to make the sponge for salt-rising bread, they have also been isolated and put on the market as starter for this type of bread. Sour dough bread also uses bacteria in producing leavening gas.

Chemical Production of Carbon Dioxide. Sodium bicarbonate (baking soda) in a flour mixture will give off carbon dioxide (CO_2) gas when heated in accordance with the reaction:

$$2 \, NaHCO_3 + heat \longrightarrow Na_2CO_3 + CO_2 + H_2O$$

Sodium   Sodium   Carbon   Water
bicarbonate   carbonate   dioxide

However, the sodium carbonate (Na_2CO_3) residue from this reaction has a disagreeable flavor and produces a yellow color in light-colored baked products. Brown spots may also occur in the cooked product if the soda is not finely powdered or is not uniformly distributed throughout the flour.

To avoid the problem of a bitter, soapy-flavored residue in the baked product, sodium bicarbonate is combined with various acids. The flavor of the residue is dependent upon the kind of acid involved in the reaction. The salts formed with many acids have not been found to be objectionable in flavor. Some food substances that contain acids and may be combined with soda in flour mixtures, releasing carbon dioxide gas, are:

1. Buttermilk or sour milk (containing lactic acid).
2. Molasses (containing a mixture of organic acids).
3. Brown sugar (which has a small amount of molasses coating the sugar crystals).
4. Honey.
5. Citrus fruit juices (containing citric and other organic acids).
6. Applesauce and other fruits.
7. Vinegar (containing acetic acid).

The optimum amount of soda to combine with an acid food in a recipe depends on the degree of acidity of that food. However, the acid-containing foods listed above vary in acidity and yield variable results when combined with soda. The usual amount of soda to combine with 1 cup of buttermilk or fully soured milk is ½ teaspoon. Less soda is required for milk that is less sour. Because the pronounced flavor of molasses may mask any undesirable flavor resulting from an excess of soda, up to 1 teaspoon of soda is often recommended to be used with 1 cup of molasses but less may be used. The acidity of honey and of brown sugar is too low to allow their use in flour mixtures as the only source of acid to combine with soda.

Cream of tartar is an acid salt (potassium acid tartrate) and may be combined with soda to produce carbon dioxide gas when the mixture is moistened. The salt that is left as a residue in this reaction (sodium potassium tartrate) is not objectionable in flavor. The chemical reaction between cream of tartar and soda is as follows:

$$HKC_4H_4O_6 + NaHCO_3 \longrightarrow NaKC_4H_4O_6 + CO_2 + H_2O$$

cream of   sodium bi-   sodium   carbon   water
tartar   carbonate   potassium   dioxide
                               tartrate

Baking powders were developed as one of the first "convenience" foods. They contain mixtures of dry acid or acid salts and baking soda with starch added to standardize the mixture and help stabilize the components so that they do not react prematurely. Baking powders have been classified into different groups or types depending upon the acid constituent used. However, all types are not available to the consumer.

The type of baking powder that is generally available for home use is called *SAS-phosphate* baking powder. It is a double-acting baking powder, which means that it reacts to release carbon dioxide gas at room temperature when the dry ingredients are moistened and reacts again when heat is applied in the process of baking. SAS-phosphate baking powder contains two acid substances that each react with soda to release carbon dioxide gas at different times in the baking process. One of the acids is a phosphate, usually calcium acid phosphate. This acid salt reacts with soda at room temperature as soon as liquid is added to the dry ingredients. This causes the batter or dough to become somewhat light and porous during the mixing process. The other acid substance is sodium aluminum sulfate (SAS). It requires heat as well as moisture to complete its reaction with soda. Therefore, additional carbon dioxide gas is produced during baking.

The reactions of calcium acid phosphate and baking soda are very complex and difficult to write. A number of different salts are probably produced in this reaction and they may interact with each other.

$$CaH_4(PO_4)_2 + NaHCO_3 \longrightarrow \text{insoluble calcium phosphate salts} + \text{soluble sodium phosphate salts} + CO_2 + H_2O$$

calcium acid phosphate   sodium bicarbonate   carbon dioxide   water

Sodium aluminum sulfate apparently reacts in two stages. The first reaction is with water and results in the production of sulfuric acid as heat is applied, after which the sulfuric acid reacts with soda to produce carbon dioxide gas, according to the following equations:

$$(1)\ Na_2SO_4 \cdot Al_2(SO_4)_3 + 6\ H_2O \xrightarrow{\text{Heat}} Na_2SO_4 + 2\ Al(OH)_3 + H_2SO_4$$

sodium aluminum sulfate   water   sodium sulfate   aluminum hydroxide   sulfuric acid

$$(2)\ 3\ H_2SO_4 + 6\ NaHCO_3 \longrightarrow 6\ CO_2 + 6\ H_2O + 3\ Na_2SO_4$$

sulfuric acid   sodium bicarbonate   carbon dioxide   water   sodium sulfate

All baking powders are composed of soda plus an acid ingredient. Different acid components may be used by the food industry for baking powders employed as ingredients in dry flour mixes. According to federal law, all types of baking powders must contain at least 12 percent available CO_2 gas. Those powders manufactured for home use generally contain 14 percent, and some powders for commercial use have 17 percent available gas. Baking powder containers should always be kept tightly covered to avoid the absorption of moisture that causes the acid and alkali constituents to react prematurely with the loss of some carbon dioxide.

All baking powders leave residues in the mixture in which they are used. The sodium sulfate (Na_2SO_4) residue from the SAS-phosphate baking powder has a somewhat bitter taste that may be objectionable to certain individuals. Some people are more sensitive than others to this bitter taste.

An optimum amount of baking powder is desirable for any baked product. If too much baking powder is used, the cell walls of the flour mixture are stretched beyond their limit to expand and they may break and collapse. If too little baking powder is present, insufficient expansion will occur and a compact product will result. Use of the minimum amount of SAS-phosphate baking powder that will leaven satisfactorily is particularly desirable because of the bitter residue formed with this baking powder. Between 1 and 1½ teaspoons of baking powder per cup of flour should be adequate for the leavening of most flour mixtures.

Methods of Adding Baking Powder and Soda. Dry chemical leavening agents are usually sifted with the flour and are not allowed to become wet until the gas-forming reaction is required. Older recipes using soda and sour milk or molasses sometimes specify that the soda be mixed with the sour milk or molasses. Because of the high viscosity of molasses, gas tends to be lost slowly from a mixture of soda and molasses, but because as much gas as possible should be retained in the flour mixture the better method probably is to sift the soda with the flour.

It is expected that carbon dioxide gas will be more rapidly lost from a mixture of buttermilk and soda than from a batter made by mixing the soda with dry ingredients and then adding the buttermilk. However, students in laboratory classes have compared the volumes of chocolate cakes containing soda and buttermilk when the soda was either sifted with the dry ingredients or added directly to the buttermilk and have found that, if the soda-buttermilk mixture is added immediately to the batter, the volumes of the finished cakes are quite similar. Allowing the soda-buttermilk mixture to stand before adding it to the batter results in a loss of cake volume. The method of dissolving soda in water before adding it to a flour mixture is not objectionable provided that the water solution is mixed with the dough or batter rather than with the buttermilk. A water solution is probably unnecessary today because soda is more finely powdered than formerly. Coarse soda tends to leave brown spots in the finished product unless dissolved.

Substitutions of Chemical Leavening Agents. Buttermilk and soda may be substituted for sweet milk and baking powder and vice versa in many recipes for baked products. One-half teaspoon of soda and 1 cup of buttermilk or fully soured milk produce an amount of leavening gas about equivalent to that produced by 2 teaspoons of baking powder. Other approximately equivalent substitutes include ½ teaspoon of baking soda plus 1¼ teaspoons cream of tartar and ½ teaspoon baking soda plus 1 cup molasses. Sweet milk can be made sour by taking 1 tablespoon vinegar or lemon juice and adding enough sweet milk to make 1 cup or by adding 1¾ teaspoons cream of tartar to 1 cup sweet milk. An example of making a substitution in a recipe is the following.

Original Recipe	Recipe with Substitution of Soda and Sour Milk
2 c (230 g) flour	2 c (230 g) flour
1 c (237 ml) sweet milk	1 c (237 ml) buttermilk
	½ t (2 g) soda
3 t (9.6 g) SAS-phosphate powder	1 t (3.2 g) SAS-phosphate powder

Fat

Fat As Shortening. Fat is added to flour mixtures chiefly for its shortening or tenderizing effect. Fat produces its tenderizing effect by coating flour particles and by forming layers or masses that physically separate different strands of gluten and prevent them from coming together. To shorten effectively, a fat must have the capacity to coat or spread well and to adhere well to flour particles.

It is difficult to make definite statements concerning the comparative shortening power of various fats because many factors have been shown to modify the effect of fats in different mixtures. For example, the manner in which a fat is distributed in a mixture, the extent of distribution, the temperature of the fat and of the mixture, the presence or absence of emulsifying agents in the mixture, the type of mixture, and the method and extent of mixing, as well as the method by which the fat itself has been processed, may have an effect on the shortening power of the fat.

Smoothness of the batter and desirable texture in some finished baked products, such as shortened cakes, are related to the emulsification of the fat in the batter. The presence of some mono- and diglycerides in the fat increases the degree of emulsification of the fat, allowing it to be dispersed in small particles throughout the batter. The addition of emulsifiers to shortened cake batters has been shown to give increased cake volume and finer texture than usually results without the use of emulsifiers.

The *plasticity* of a fat, which is its capacity to be molded or shaped, may be related to its shortening power. In a plastic fat, some of the triglyceride molecules are present in a liquid form and some are crystallized in a solid form. The fact that there are both solid and liquid phases in the fat makes it possible to mold and shape the fat rather than having it fracture or break when force is applied to it. Fats that are more plastic are more spreadable and, presumably, can spread over a greater surface area of flour particles than can less plastic fats. The temperature of fat affects plasticity. At a temperature of 18° C (64° F) butter is less plastic than at a temperature of 22° to 28° C (72° to 83° F). At higher temperatures, butter tends to become very soft or completely melted.

With the use of a shortometer, an instrument that measures the weight required to break a baked wafer, a number of tests of the shortening value of fats have been made on pastry. The results of these tests have been somewhat variable but, in many cases, lards have been shown to have more shortening power than most hydrogenated fats, butter, and margarine. Oils that are high in polyunsaturated fats usually give more tender pastries than lards. One explanation that has been offered is that these oils cover a larger surface area of flour particles per molecule of fat than do fats containing a relatively high proportion of saturated fatty acids. However, further research is needed to clarify the relationship of the degree of unsaturation to the shortening power of fats.

With other proportions and other conditions standardized, the higher the concentration of fat in a mixture the greater is the shortening power. This point deserves consideration in the substitution of one fat for another. Butter and margarines contain approximately 82 percent fat and about 16 percent water. Lard, hydrogenated fats, and oils contain essentially 100 percent fat. Disregarding other factors that appear to affect the shortening power of fats, the mere substitution of an equal weight of a fat of higher fat concentration for one of lower concentration affects the tenderness of baked flour mixtures.

Fat in Leavening. Plastic fats appear to play important roles in some flour mixtures in the trapping of air bubbles that later contribute to the texture of the finished product. This role of fat may be particularly important in the preparation of shortened cakes. It has been suggested that creaming fat and sugar crystals together and also vigorous beating of fat-containing batters cause air cells to be entrapped in the mixture. Fats that incorporate air readily and allow it to be dispersed in small cells are said to have good creaming properties.

Liquids

Liquids have various uses in flour mixtures. They hydrate the starch and gluten and dissolve certain constituents, such as sugar, salts, and baking powder. It is only when baking powders are wet that the evolution of carbon dioxide gas is started. The typical structure or framework of doughs and batters is not formed until the protein particles become hydrated. The gelatinization of starch during baking requires moisture.

Various liquids may be used in flour mixtures, including water, potato water, milk, fruit juices, and coffee. The water content of eggs is also a part of the total liquid.

Eggs

Eggs may be used as a means of incorporating air into a batter. The incorporation of air is possible because egg proteins coagulate on beating and give some structure or rigidity to the cell walls surrounding the air bubbles. Egg whites can form a particularly stable foam. As they are beaten, the cell walls become increasingly thinner and more tender up to an optimum point. Beaten egg whites may be folded into a batter.

Egg yolks add flavor and color to flour mixtures. They also aid in forming emulsions of fat and water because of their content of lipo-proteins that act as effective emulsifying agents. Because egg proteins coagulate on heating, the addition of eggs to flour mixtures increases the rigidity of the baked product.

Sugar

Sugar is used in many flour mixtures for sweetening purposes. Sugar also contributes to the browning of outer surfaces. Caramelization of sugar occurs at the high oven temperatures as the surface of the products becomes dry. In yeast mixtures, sugar is a readily available food for the yeast plant. Sugar has a tenderizing effect because it interferes with the development of gluten in a batter or dough. It may do this by tying up water so that less water is available for the gluten and more manipulation is necessary to develop gluten than when sugar is not present. The volume of many flour mixtures is increased by the addition of optimal amounts of sugar because the gluten structure is tenderized and expands more easily under the pressure of leavening gases. Sugar probably also contributes to the formation of a fine texture in many baked products [9]. Sugar elevates the coagulation temperature of egg proteins. This fact is especially important in the making of sponge-type cakes containing relatively large amounts of egg. Sugar also increases the temperature at which starch gelatinizes. This is of particular importance in high sugar products such as cakes.

Brown sugar imparts a distinctive flavor to baked foods and yields products that tend to remain moist longer than those made with granulated sugar. Measured lightly, brown sugar weighs less per cup than granulated sugar. Brown sugar should be packed firmly in the cup or be substituted by weight for granulated sugar.

Classification of Batters and Doughs

Flour mixtures vary in thickness depending largely on the proportion of flour to liquid. Based on thickness, flour mixtures are classed as batters or doughs.

Doughs

Doughs are thick enough to be handled or kneaded on a board. Most doughs are rolled in the final stages of preparation, although yeast dough is not usually rolled except for the shaping of certain types of rolls. Doughs may be soft (just stiff enough to handle) or stiff. Soft doughs contain about ⅓ cup of liquid per cup of flour. A stiff dough may contain only ⅛ cup of liquid per cup of flour. Examples of soft dough products include baking powder biscuits, rolled cookies, yeast bread, and rolls. Pie crust is an example of a stiff dough.

Batters

Batters are classified into pour batters and drop batters. There is considerable variation within each group, some pour batters being very thin, whereas others pour with difficulty. A pour batter contains ⅔ to 1 cup of liquid per cup of flour. A drop batter usually has ½ to ¾ cup of liquid per cup of flour. In batters containing approximately 1 part of liquid to 2 parts of flour, gluten development readily occurs on mixing. Popovers and thin griddle-cake and shortened-cake batters are examples of pour batters. Some drop batters are stiff enough to require scraping from the spoon. Drop batters include muffins, many quick breads, and various kinds of cookies. A batter containing yeast is called a *sponge*.

In general, it may be stated that the objectives in the mixing of doughs and batters include (1) uniform distribution of ingredients, (2) minimum loss of the leavening agent, (3) optimum blending to produce characteristic textures in various products, and (4) optimum development of gluten for various products.

Many different methods may be employed for the mixing of batters and doughs. However, there are three basic methods of mixing that may be adapted for use with a variety of products.

General Methods for Mixing Batters and Doughs

The Muffin Method

In the muffin method dry ingredients are sifted together into the bowl used for mixing. The eggs are beaten and the liquid and melted fat (or oil) are added to the beaten eggs. The liquid ingredients are then blended with the dry ingredients with varying amounts of stirring depending on the mixture.

For thin mixtures, such as popovers, thin griddle cakes, and thin waffle mixtures, lumping may be prevented by adding the liquid ingredients somewhat gradually to the dry ingredients. The overstirring of thicker batters, such as thick waffle mixtures and muffins, may, however, be prevented by the addition of the liquid ingredients *all at once* to the dry ingredients. Thicker batters are stirred only until the dry ingredients are dampened.

The Pastry or Biscuit Method

In the pastry or biscuit method the dry ingredients are sifted together. Fat is cut in or blended with the dry ingredients and liquid is then added to the fat-flour mixture. Although this method is used mainly for pastry and biscuits, it is also appropriate for other flour mixtures. The techniques of handling the dough after the addition of liquid differ for pastry and biscuits. Biscuits are generally mixed more thoroughly and are lightly kneaded before they are rolled out and cut into the desired shapes.

The Conventional Method

Although cakes may be mixed by more than one method, the conventional method is usually understood to mean the conventional way in which fat and sugar are creamed together, beaten eggs added, and dry and liquid ingredients alternately blended with the fat-sugar-egg mixture. This method may also be used for making cookies and various quick breads as well as other flour products.

Yeast bread, cream puffs, and the sponge-type of cake are mixed by special methods that are applicable only to those products. Whatever the method, the optimum amount of manipulation varies with the type of product, with the character and proportion of the ingredients used, and with the temperature of the ingredients.

Structure of Batters and Doughs

In the mixing of batters and doughs a definite structure is obtained. The structure varies according to the kind and proportion of ingredients used but, in all mixtures except those of high liquid content, the gluten particles on becoming hydrated tend to stick together, forming a continuous mass that spreads out into a network. Some constituents, such as salts and sugar, tend to be partially or completely dissolved in the liquid. The starch granules from the flour tend to be imbedded in the gluten network. Some constituents may act as emulsifying agents by separating or dividing the fat in the mixture into particles of varying fineness. The temperature as well as the physical and chemical state of the ingredients will partially determine the degree of dispersion of the emulsion. Melted fats or oils may behave differently from solid fats in certain doughs and batters.

The texture of the finished product is very largely dependent upon the structure obtained in the mixing of the dough or batter. Texture is a combination of such characteristics as the distribution of cells, the thickness of cell walls, the character of the crumb (elastic, crumbly, velvety, or harsh), and the grain (the size of the cells). Optimum texture cannot be expected to be the same for all products, because of the variation in the kinds and amounts of constituents used. Typical textures for different baked products are discussed with those products in later chapters. Variations from typical textures and possible causes for variation are also considered.

When all the factors that affect texture are considered, it is not surprising that products made from the same formula may differ with different bakings. Although a certain degree of control of materials, manipulation, and temperatures is possible, it is difficult in practical home baking always to control all factors that play a part in determining the quality of the end products obtained.

Dry Flour Mixes

A wide variety of flour-based mixes is on the shelves of the modern supermarket. Excellent directions for the use of these prepared mixes tend to ensure uniform, good quality finished products. In addition to flour, they may contain leavening, salt, fat (sometimes powdered shortening), nonfat dry milk, dried eggs, sugar, and flavoring ingredients, such as dried extracts, cocoa, ginger, and dried molasses, depending upon the type of mixture. Some mixes are yeast mixtures for making fermented bread or rolls.

A number of additives, such as emulsifiers, antioxidants, and whipping aids, have contributed to the success of prepared flour mixes. Mixes are convenient time-savers and they may cost no more (and sometimes even less) than a home-prepared product. Costs must be determined on an individual basis, however, and are sometimes difficult to compare because of differences in ingredients and yields. (Cost of convenience foods is discussed in Chapter 2.)

Many different flour mixes may also be made at home, saving time by the measuring and mixing of at least part of the ingredients all at one time. The making of mixes at home is discussed in Chapter 2. However, homemade mixes, without the techniques available in the production of commercial mixes, do not have as long a shelf life. They should be adequately packaged and stored at cool temperatures. Commercial mixes usually contain a leavening acid that dissolves slowly, such as anhydrous monocalcium phosphate or sodium acid pyrophosphate, to prevent the premature reaction of the baking powder during storage. Also, off flavors do not readily develop in the mixes with these acids.

Baking at High Altitudes

Some balancing of ingredients as well as variation of baking temperature may be necessary at high altitudes. Because the atmospheric pressure is less, the leavening gases in baked products meet less resistance and are apt to overexpand, especially during the early part of baking. This overexpansion may stretch the cells to the extent that they break and then collapse, producing a coarse texture and decreased volume [2].

Corrections in recipes that are standardized for use at sea level may involve decreasing the leavening agent or strengthening the cell walls by decreasing the sugar or adding more flour. Increased liquid may also be added because of greater loss by evaporation. Oven temperatures may be increased. However, definite rules cannot be strictly applied in all recipe adjustments because of the varying proportions of ingredients in recipes. Each recipe needs to be tested individually. The Colorado State University Experiment Station has conducted research on baking at high altitudes and has developed cake recipes for altitudes up to 10,000 feet [5]. The University of Wyoming Experiment Station has also published tested recipes for high altitudes [3].

Table 18-1 *Adjustments for Shortened Cakes**

Adjustment	3,000 Feet	5,000 Feet	7,000 Feet
Reduce baking powder For each teaspoon, decrease:	$\frac{1}{8}$ t	$\frac{1}{8}$–$\frac{1}{4}$ t	$\frac{1}{4}$ t
Reduce sugar For each cup, decrease:	0–1 T	0–2 T	1–3 T
Increase liquid For each cup, add:	1–2 T	2–4 T	3–4 T

*From *Handbook of Food Preparation,* 7th ed., Washington, D.C.: American Home Economics Association, 1975.

Altitude corrections are not necessary for pastry and cream puffs. Yeast products may require shorter rising periods. Muffins and biscuits can usually be made at higher altitudes with little change in recipes although a slight decrease in baking powder might be desirable at altitudes above 5,000 feet. Because cakes have a very delicate structure, they are more affected by altitude than most other baked products. Decreasing amounts of sugar and increasing amounts of flour may be used in angel food and sponge cakes as altitude increases. The American Home Economics Association, in the *Handbook of Food Preparation,* suggests the adjustments for shortened cakes given in Table 18-1.

Study Questions

1. a. What is meant by the milling of flour?
   b. How is white flour produced?
   c. How is whole-wheat or graham flour produced?
   d. How do hard and soft wheat flours generally differ in characteristics and composition?
   e. Name three grades of white flour and indicate which is usually found on the retail market.
2. For each of the following types of flour, describe general characteristics and uses in food preparation:
   a. Bread flour
   b. All-purpose flour
   c. Pastry flour
   d. Cake flour
   e. Instantized flour
   f. Self-rising flour
3. About 85 percent of the proteins in white wheat flour are relatively insoluble and play an important role in developing the structure of baked products.
   a. Name the two wheat flour proteins that develop into gluten with moistening and mixing or kneading.

b. Describe the characteristics of wheat gluten and discuss its role in the preparation of baked flour mixtures.

4. a. What is meant by the word *leaven*?
   b. Name three leavening gases that are commonly present in baked products.
   c. Describe several ways in which air may be incorporated into a batter or dough during preparation.
   d. Explain why steam is such an effective leavening gas and name two products that are leavened primarily by steam.

5. Carbon dioxide (CO_2) gas may be produced by biological and by chemical means.
   a. Describe how CO_2 may be produced biologically in baked products.
   b. Describe examples of the chemical production of CO_2 in flour mixtures.

6. Although CO_2 will be released when soda is heated in a moist environment, explain why it cannot satisfactorily be used for leavening in baked products without an accompanying acid.

7. Baking powders always contain at least two active ingredients. Name them. Which one is responsible for the production of CO_2?

8. Name several acid foods that are commonly used with soda in baked products.

9. Generally the only type of baking powder available to the consumer is SAS-phosphate baking powder.
   a. Explain why this baking powder is called double-acting.
   b. Name the active ingredients in this baking powder.
   c. Explain how the active ingredients participate in the production of CO_2 gas.

10. a. How much soda is usually used with 1 cup of buttermilk in a baked product?
    b. How much baking powder is usually used per 1 cup of flour to leaven a baked product?

11. Briefly describe the general role of each of the following ingredients in baked flour mixtures:
    a. Fat
    b. Flour
    c. Liquids
    d. Eggs
    e. Sugar

12. What are batters? Doughs? Give examples of each.

13. Describe each of the following general methods of mixing batters and doughs and give examples of baked products commonly prepared by each method:
    a. Muffin method
    b. Pastry or biscuit method
    c. Conventional method

14. a. Why do some adjustments need to be made in baked products when they are prepared at high altitudes? Briefly discuss this.
    b. Suggest appropriate adjustments for shortened cakes that are baked at high altitudes when using recipes standardized at sea level.

References

1. American Home Economics Association. *Handbook of Food Preparation,* 8th ed. Washington, D.C. 1980.
2. Barmore, M. A. *The Influence of Various Factors Including Altitude in the Production of Angel Food Cake.* Colorado State University Experiment Station Technical Bulletin No. 15, 1936.
3. Boyd, M. S., and M. C. Schoonover. *Baking at High Altitude.* University of Wyoming Agricultural Experiment Station Bulletin No. 427. Laramie, WY 1965.
4. Butaki, R. C., and B. Dronzek. 1979. Comparison of gluten properties of four wheat varieties. *Cereal Chemistry* **56,** 159.
5. Dyar, E., and E. Cassel. *Mile-High Cakes: Recipes for High Altitudes.* Colorado Agricultural Experiment Station Bulletin No 404-A. Fort Collins, CO 1958.
6. Khan, K., and W. Bushuk. 1978. Glutenin: Structure and functionality in breadmaking. *Baker's Digest* **52,** 14 (no. 2).
7. Lorenz, K. 1972. Food uses of triticale. *Food Technology* **26,** 66 (no. 11).
8. Matthews, R. H., and E. A. Bechtel. 1966. Eating quality of some baked products made with instant flour. *Journal of Home Economics* **58,** 729.
9. Myhre, D. V. 1970. The function of carbohydrates in baking. *Baker's Digest* **44,** 32 (no. 3).
10. Pomeranz, Y., and M. M. MacMasters. 1968. Structure and composition of the wheat kernel. *Baker's Digest* **42,** 24 (no. 4).
11. Wall, J. S. 1967. Origin and behavior of flour proteins. *Baker's Digest* **41,** 36 (no. 5).
12. Watson, C. A., W. C. Shuey, R. D. Crawford, and M. R. Gumbmann. 1977. Physical dough, baking, and nutritional qualities of straight-grade and extended-extraction flours. *Cereal Chemistry* **54,** 657.

19

Quick Breads

Traditionally, *quick breads* have included a variety of products that may be prepared without the rising or proofing time required by yeast breads. Quick breads are often served warm. Examples of quick breads are popovers, pancakes or griddle cakes, waffles, muffins, biscuits, coffee cakes, and loaf breads made with baking powder as a leavening ingredient. Cream puffs may also be classified with quick breads. Table 19-1 gives basic proportions of ingredients for various quick breads. Ingredients are balanced to produce the type of product desired. Structural ingredients, such as flour and egg, are balanced against tenderizing ingredients, such as sugar and fat, so that the product will have form yet be appropriately tender. The consistency of the batter or dough is generally determined by the ratios of ingredients.

Popovers

Popovers contain a relatively high proportion of liquid and are leavened chiefly by steam that is produced by the use of a hot oven temperature in the early stages of baking. They are usually mixed by the muffin method. (The muffin method is described in Chapter 18.)

Although either pastry or all-purpose flour may be used for making popovers, the crusts are usually more rigid when all-purpose flour is used. Because of the high percentage of moisture in the batter, the gluten particles on becoming hydrated tend to float in the liquid. Because the gluten particles do not adhere to each other sufficiently

Table 19-1 *Proportions of Ingredients for Quick Breads*

Product	Flour	Liquid	Eggs	Fat	Sugar	Salt	Baking Powder	Soda
Popovers	1 c	1 c	2 to 3	0 to 1 T		¼ to ½ t		
Cream puffs	1 c	1 c	4	½ c		¼ t		
Muffins	1 c	½ c	½ to 1	1 to 2 T	1 to 2 T	½ t	1½ to 2 t	
Waffles	1 c	⅔ c	1 to 2	3 T	1 t	½ t	1 to 2 t	
Pancakes								
Sweet milk	1 c	⅔ c	1	1 T	1 t	¼ to ½ t	1 to 2 t	
Thick buttermilk	1 c	1 c	1	1 to 2 T		¼ to ½ t	¼ to ½ t optional	½ t
Thick sour cream	1 c	1 c	1			¼ to ½ t	¼ to ½ t optional	½ t
Biscuits	1 c	Rolled ⅓ c Dropped ⅓ to ⅜ c		2 to 3 T		½ t	1½ to 2 t	

to form a continuous mass, the batter may be stirred much or little without appreciably affecting the finished product. The batter should be smooth and free from lumps. With so small an amount of flour, the liquid is best added gradually at first until the lumps are stirred out.

Egg is an essential constituent in popovers to give them structure. The floating gluten particles do not form a mass of sufficient continuity to expand under the pressure of the steam formed during baking. With no egg, the popover is heavy and has a very small volume; with two eggs per cup of flour enough extensible and coagulable material is furnished to form rigid walls. If the eggs are small or if pastry flour is used, three eggs per cup of flour give more desirable results than two eggs. Fat serves little purpose in popovers. It tends to float on top of the thin batter, and thus chiefly affects the top crust. If as much as 1 tablespoon of fat is used the top crust may have a flaky appearance.

Baking Popovers

Muffin pans (preferably deep ones) or heat-resistant glass cups may be used for baking popovers and are greased to keep the popovers from sticking. If iron pans are used, baking may be speeded up if the pans are warm because iron requires more time to become hot than does tin or aluminum. Since steam is the chief leavening agent in popovers, a hot oven temperature (450° F) is required to form steam quickly. If baked for the whole time at a hot temperature, the crusts may become too brown in the time required to form rigid

19-1 *Well-made popovers have a large volume and a moist, hollow interior.* (Photographs by Roger P. Smith)

walls that will not collapse when the popovers are removed from the oven. Browning in popovers is apparently produced primarily by the Maillard reaction, which involves a combination of protein and sugar. The amount of sugar in the milk is probably sufficient for this reaction to occur. Dextrinization of flour may also contribute to browning. The oven may be hot for 15 minutes and then be reduced to a temperature of 375° F for the remainder of the time, about 45 minutes.

Characteristics

Popovers rise high and may have very irregular shapes. They are hollow and have thick crusty walls (Figure 19-1). Because of the high percentage of liquid in the mixture, the interior is moist but has no similarity to raw dough. Crusts should not be so brown that their flavor is undesirable.

Causes of Failure

Probably the chief cause of failure in making popovers is insufficient baking. The popovers are not necessarily done when brown and may collapse upon removal from the oven if the egg proteins are not adequately coagulated. However, the popovers will not rise sufficiently unless they are baked in a hot oven for the first part of baking so that steam may be generated. An inadequate amount of egg in the formula may also result in decreased volume.

Cream Puffs

Cream puffs contain the same proportion of liquid to flour as do popovers and are leavened primarily by steam, but the amount of fat used is eight times as much. Cream puffs are, therefore, considerably more tender than popovers. A large proportion of egg is used in cream puffs to emulsify the high percentage of fat. The method of mixing the cream puff batter is unique for this product. The fat is melted in the hot water and the flour added all at once with vigorous stirring. Heating is continued until the batter is smooth and forms a stiff ball. Gelatinization of the starch occurs during this cooking process. The mixture is then cooled slightly and the eggs added (either one unbeaten egg at a time, or one-third of the beaten eggs at one time). The mixture is beaten thoroughly after each addition of egg. The eggs contain lipoproteins which act as emulsifying agents to divide the fat into small particles throughout the mixture. At this stage, the batter is smooth, stiff, and glossy. The egg also plays a role in obtaining a large volume because the proteins aid in the stretching process and are coagulated by heat to contribute to the rigid structure in the final product. Even though the cream puff batter is stiff, it may be beaten without danger of toughening the puffs because the high percentage of fat and water in relation to flour interferes with the development of gluten and prevents it from forming a tenacious mass.

Baking

The cream puff batter is dropped in mounds on an ungreased baking sheet with some room between mounds allowed for expansion during baking. A high oven temperature (450° F) is necessary to form steam quickly and bring about the puffing or expansion of the batter. The high temperature may be maintained throughout the baking period providing that overbrowning does not occur. The baking time is decreased to about 30 to 35 minutes if a high tempera-

19-2 *Cream puffs.* (Photograph by Roger P. Smith)

ture is used continuously. If a temperature of 450° F is used for 15 minutes, followed by a temperature of about 375° F for the remainder of the baking time, about 45 minutes total baking time will be required.

The puffs should feel rigid and should not collapse on removal from the oven. Puffs are not necessarily done when brown. The hollow center in cream puffs may be filled with a variety of mixtures from chicken or tuna salad to sweet custards, puddings, or ice cream. Smaller puffs are generally used for hors d'oeuvres and larger ones for desserts.

Characteristics

The puffs are usually irregular on the top surface, although the surface may vary depending upon the consistency of the batter before baking. The walls are rigid but tender because of the high fat content. The center of the puff is hollow and moist. Some of the moist interior strands may be removed, if desired, and the puff dried out in the oven. The crust should not be brown enough to have an undesirable color and flavor (Figure 19-2).

Causes of Failure

As in the making of popovers, one possible cause of failure in making cream puffs is insufficient baking. If the walls of the puffs are not rigid they will collapse on removal from the oven. Another possible cause of failure is the excessive evaporation of moisture during the cooking of the paste, which alters the proportions of the ingredients. Excessive evaporation may be caused by (1) boiling the water and fat too long before adding the flour; and (2) overcooking the flour-fat-water mixture. Overcooking also decreases the amount of fat that becomes emulsified while the mixture is being cooked. Because more of the fat forms in layers, it tends to separate from the mixture. The batter, after the eggs have been added, will appear oily and separated instead of shiny and viscous, and the fat will ooze from the puffs during baking. Inaccurate measurements may so increase the percentage of fat in the mixture that the results will be similar to those obtained by overcooking.

Pancakes

Pancakes are more variable both in the proportion of flour to liquid and in the characteristics of the finished product than are most flour mixtures. The cooked cakes may be thin and moist or thick and

19-3 *Pancakes or griddle cakes may be made thin and moist (left) or thick and porous (right).*

porous according to the proportions of the ingredients used (Figure 19-3).

Pancake mixtures contain flour, liquid, leavening agent, and salt. Egg is usually used but may be omitted. Cakes are more tender if they contain fat but it is possible to omit fat. Sugar may be used as an aid in browning, because of its caramelization, and may slightly modify the flavor. If thick buttermilk or sour cream is used, the proportion of flour to liquid ingredients may be about one to one. Shortening may be omitted in cakes made from cream because the cream contains fat. In sweet-milk cakes the amount of flour may be 1⅓, 1½, or 1¾ cups per cup of liquid, depending on the type of flour used and on the thickness of cake desired. Pancakes are usually mixed by the muffin method described in chapter 18. The stiffer the batter, the less the batter should be stirred to avoid toughening the cakes by developing the gluten.

Pancakes are leavened by carbon dioxide gas produced either from baking powder or a sour milk and soda combination. Overstirred pancakes may be soggy because of the loss of carbon dioxide by stirring and may show some tunnel formation. Thin batters tend to lose more carbon dioxide gas on standing than do thicker batters. More baking powder may be required if batters are to stand for some time than if they are baked immediately.

Cooking Pancakes

Much of the success in making pancakes depends upon the temperature of the griddle. If the griddle is appreciably below the appropriate temperature, the pancakes will cook so slowly that they lose leavening gas and do not expand sufficiently to produce light, porous cakes. They also do not brown desirably. Browning in pancakes is primarily the result of the Maillard reaction. Too hot a griddle may burn the cakes before they are sufficiently done. Even if the griddle is not hot enough to cause burning, it may produce very uneven browning and a compact texture from too rapid cooking. the temperature of the griddle may be tested by cooking a few drops of batter on it.

Ordinary griddles may be used without greasing provided that the batter contains 2 or more tablespoons of fat per cup of liquid used. Specially coated cooking surfaces may be used without greasing.

A uniformly heated griddle is essential if the griddle cakes are to brown uniformly. Large griddles over small flames may be practically cold in the outer areas. As cakes cook on a griddle of a desirable temperature, bubbles of gas expand and some of them break at the surface. When the edges of the pancakes appear slightly dry they should be turned. If the entire surface becomes dry, the cakes will not brown evenly on the second side after turning. After being turned, the cakes rise noticeably and become slightly higher in the center. They do not form peaks, however, unless the mixture is very stiff or was greatly overstirred. Pancakes are done when browned on the second side. Although pancakes may sometimes be turned a second time provided that they are about done when turned, more desirable cakes usually result from one turning.

Waffles

Waffle mixtures are similar to pancake mixtures except that they contain more egg and more fat. They are leavened by carbon dioxide gas, usually from baking powder. Because tenderness and crispness rather than a breadlike quality are desirable in waffles, a flour of relatively low gluten content and weak gluten quality is a good choice for making waffles. By using a sufficient amount of fat and by avoiding overstirring, one can use a stronger flour successfully, but stronger flour tends to yield a tougher, breadlike waffle. Waffles of excellent quality usually result when the batter is mixed by a modified muffin method that involves separating the eggs and adding the beaten egg whites last. However, the whole beaten egg may be used successfully in the muffin method for mixing waffles.

The proportion of flour may vary from about $1\frac{1}{3}$ to $1\frac{3}{4}$ cups per cup of liquid. If optimum stirring is used with each consistency of batter and if all batters are baked under equally good conditions, there seems to be little difference in the waffles obtained. Thinner batters lose their leavening gas more quickly and it is more difficult, without loss of air, to blend beaten egg whites with batters of thin consistency but ease of pouring is a point in favor of somewhat thinner batters. Very thin batters made with 1 cup of flour per cup of liquid are too thin to fill the waffle iron sufficiently to bake the waffle crisp and brown on both sides. Crispness is partly dependent upon the depth of batter that the waffle iron holds. A thicker waffle has a tendency to be less crisp than a thin waffle. The temperature of the waffle iron is also a factor in producing a good waffle. Slow baking yields a waffle that is hard rather than crisp and tender.

Some waffle mixtures that are to be used as dessert or as short-cake are richer in fat than the proportions suggested in Table 19-1. They often contain sugar and may contain cocoa or molasses. Such mixtures require longer, slower baking than do batters with no sugar in order to be crisp and done without scorching. Caramelization of the sugar contributes to browning.

Baking Waffles

Most newer electric waffle irons are specially coated and do not require greasing. If they are either too hot or insufficiently heated, the waffles will stick. Also, if there is not enough fat in the batter the waffles are likely to stick. Most irons have an automatic heat control and have an indicator to show when the iron is hot enough for baking.

Muffins

Muffins usually contain flour, leavening, salt, sugar, fat, egg, and liquid. Sugar may be omitted and muffins may be made without egg, but better flavor and texture result from including both ingredients. Muffins are leavened by carbon dioxide gas, usually produced from baking powder. Structure is provided by the flour components, starch and some gluten, and by egg proteins as they coagulate on heating.

Mixing Muffins

Muffins are generally mixed by the muffin method. The fat, if solid, is melted and combined with the liquid ingredients which are then added, all at once, to the dry ingredients. The proportion of flour to liquid in a muffin mixture is approximately two to one. The amount of stirring is more important for muffins than for most mixtures blended by the muffin method. The gluten forms most readily when a two-to-one proportion of flour to liquid is used and is readily overdeveloped with too much stirring. Peaks and tunnels tend to form in the overstirred muffin. A muffin mixture made from wheat flour, particularly a flour of fairly strong gluten quality, should be stirred only enough to blend the liquid and dry ingredients. Dry flour lumps must be dampened but a properly manipulated muffin batter appears lumpy and drops sharply from the spoon. With overstirring, the batter becomes smooth and tends to string from the spoon (Figure 19-4). The muffins tend to increase slightly in volume with moderate overstirring but decrease in volume with further stirring. Carbon dioxide gas is probably lost with excessive stirring. A crust then forms on the overmixed muffin during baking before additional carbon dioxide gas is produced by the heat of the oven. As the gas is produced it is forced through the softer center of the muffin and contributes to tunnel formation.

Figure 19-5 shows the effects on baked muffins of overmixing the batter. Although the texture of a well-made muffin is uniform, the grain is not fine and the cell walls are of medium thickness. A more compact texture is associated with peaks or knobs and tunnels in an overmanipulated muffin. With extreme overmanipulation, sogginess may occur and, owing to the loss of much gas, few tunnels may form.

Muffins containing relatively large amounts of fat may be mixed by the conventional method. Such muffins are more cakelike in texture and are sweeter and more tender than plain muffins. Because sugar and fat interfere with the development of gluten in the batter, the effects of increased mixing or stirring are less pronounced than in a plain muffin and tunnel formation less likely [1].

Variations in Muffins

A great variety of muffins may be made if cornmeal, bran, or whole-wheat flour are substituted for part of the white flour. Also nuts, dates, blueberries, or bits of crisp bacon may be added to the batter while it is being mixed. Muffins that contain proportionately more sugar and/or fat may have a finer, more even texture than plain muffins. However, a sweet muffin may not be as acceptable to some people when used as a bread accompaniment to the main course of a meal.

Bran and cornmeal muffins can tolerate more manipulation without undesirable results than can muffins made entirely of all-purpose wheat flour. Bran interferes with the development of gluten and cornmeal does not contain gluten proteins. In the making of bran muffins, flavor may be improved by first soaking or hydrating the bran in the liquid before combining it with the other ingredients. The substitution of wheat or corn bran for up to 25 percent of the weight of the flour still allows for an acceptable muffin while increasing the fiber content to a considerable degree [2].

19-4 *A properly mixed muffin batter results when dry ingredients are just moistened. The batter is pebbly and not smooth in appearance.*

An overmixed muffin batter in which gluten has partially developed is smooth and cohesive.

19-5 *External and internal characteristics of well-made muffins (left) and overstirred muffins (center and right).* (Courtesy of Ohio State University)

Baking Muffins

Pans should be prepared before the muffins are mixed as the batter becomes full of gas bubbles and rises perceptibly if allowed to stand in the mixing bowl while the pans are being prepared. Cutting into the batter later to fill muffin pans permits gas to escape and decreases the volume of the finished muffins. The bottoms of the pans should be greased but the greasing of the side walls is optional. The muffin structure may receive some support from clinging to ungreased sides of the muffin pan as the batter rises in baking. However, muffins may be removed from the pans more easily when the sides are greased.

An oven temperature of about 400° F is satisfactory for baking muffins in about 20 to 25 minutes. A product leavened by carbon dioxide gas must be allowed to rise before crust formation occurs. For that reason a very hot oven must be avoided. A temperature slightly under 400° F is satisfactory if sufficient time is allowed for baking. Browning appears to be chiefly the result of the Maillard reaction but the caramelization of sugar may also contribute.

Biscuits

Biscuits usually contain flour, fat, milk, baking powder, and salt. Soda and buttermilk, either the fresh cultured product or dried churned buttermilk, may be used instead of sweet milk and baking powder for the leavening of biscuits. Dried churned buttermilk contains phospholipids which act as emulsifiers and aid in the fine dis-

Make soft but stiff, dry dough.

Knead dough lightly.

Roll to about ½-inch thickness.

tribution of fat in baked products. Since cultured buttermilk is usually made from fluid skim or lowfat milk, it does not have the same composition as churned buttermilk.

Biscuits are mixed by the biscuit or pastry method which involves cutting a solid fat into the flour, baking powder, and salt mixture before adding milk and stirring. The dough for rolled biscuits should be a soft, rather than a stiff, dry dough. Biscuit dough that is patted or rolled with no preliminary kneading yields biscuits that are very tender and have crisp crusts but that are coarse in texture, small in volume, and have slightly rough crust. Kneading lightly, using ten to thirty strokes (depending on the amount of stirring used to mix the dough), produces a biscuit of fine texture that gives evidence of layering when broken open (Figure 19-6). It also rises to a larger volume than an unkneaded biscuit (Figure 19-7). The flakiness, which is seen as easily separated sheets of dough, results from the distribution of fat particles coated with dough. The fat melts on baking and leaves spaces between the sheets of dough. The top crust is smoother and the general external appearance is better in slightly kneaded biscuits than in unkneaded ones. Overkneading produces a compact, toughened product.

Dropped biscuits are irregular in shape, and are tender and slightly coarse in texture. They usually have crisp crusts.

Cut and transfer to baking sheet.

19-6 *Steps in making rolled biscuits.* (Courtesy of General Foods, Inc.)

Baking Biscuits

The baking sheet requires greasing for dropped biscuits but not for rolled ones. Rolled biscuits, may be placed on the baking sheet about 1 or 1½ inches apart if crusty biscuits are desired. Otherwise, no space need be allowed between biscuits. A hot oven (425° to

19-7 *The proper amount of kneading improves the volume and quality of baking powder biscuits. The biscuit on the left was prepared from unkneaded dough while the one on the right was made from dough kneaded 15 times before rolling and cutting.*

450° F) for about 15 minutes is satisfactory for baking biscuits. The hot oven produces steam that aids in separating sheets of dough as the fat melts.

Study Questions

1. For each of the following products describe:
   a. The usual ingredients
   b. The usual method of mixing
   c. Any special precautions to be observed in their preparation or potential problems to be avoided
   Products
   (1) Popovers
   (2) Cream puffs
   (3) Pancakes
   (4) Waffles
   (5) Muffins
   (6) Biscuits
2. What characterizes a quick bread?

References

1. Matthews, R. H., M. E. Kirkpatrick, and E. H. Dawson. 1965. Performance of fats in muffins. *Journal of the American Dietetic Association* **47,** 201.
2. Polizzotto, L. M., A. M. Tinsley, C. W. Weber, and J. W. Berry. 1983. Dietary fibers in muffins. *Journal of Food Science* **48,** 111.

20
Yeast Breads

The making of bread is one form of food processing that has become a highly specialized industry. A wide variety of bread products is available on the market. Most families buy bread rather than make it at home. However, the making of bread at home can be a rewarding experience. The serving of hot bread, made at home, makes any meal a special one. In families of low-income levels, where a higher-than-average consumption of cereals, including bread, is necessary, home production of bread is one way to increase bread consumption. However, making bread at home takes a certain amount of time for which planning must be done. Well-made bakers' bread is of good uniform quality but its moisture content is generally high and it is often extremely compressible. A good quality homemade bread is often conceded to be superior in flavor and in eating quality, particularly when it is very fresh. Homemade bread tends to stale more quickly than does commercially produced bread.

Characteristics of Yeast Breads

The texture of bread should be fine, the cell walls thin, and the grain uniform. Cells tend to be slightly elongated rather than round, although the shape of the cell varies. The crumb is elastic and thoroughly baked so that it does not form a gummy ball when it is pressed between the fingers. The fresh crumb should spring back quickly if it is touched with the finger (Figure 20-1).

A well-shaped loaf of bread has a rounded top and is free from rough, ragged cracks on the sides. The *shred* on the sides of the loaf

20-1 *Homemade bread with a relatively high volume and fine texture may be made using white all-purpose flour (left) and whole wheat flour (right).*

where the dough rises is smooth and even. Careful and uniform shaping of the loaf and placing the shaped dough in the center of the baking pan contribute to the production of a well-shaped baked loaf of bread. However, abnormalities in shape have numerous causes in addition to problems created by the way the dough is shaped. Such factors as the stiffness of the dough, the strength of the gluten, the extent of fermentation and proofing, the baking temperature, and the position in the oven may all affect the shape of the loaf as well as its volume and texture. Bread of good quality is light, having a large volume in relation to the weight of the loaf.

If a loaf has been allowed to proof too long before being placed in the oven, the cells will be overexpanded and collapse somewhat. This may result in a loaf of bread that is flat or sunken on top and has overhanging eaves on the sides, somewhat like a mushroom shape. The texture of this loaf is coarse with an open grain and crumbly character (Figure 20-2). If a loaf has not proofed long

20-2 *A loaf of bread that has proofed too long in the pan before being baked. The texture is open and coarse and "eaves" are seen on the sides of the loaf.*

20-3 *A loaf of bread that did not rise sufficiently in the pan before being baked. A ragged crack appears on the end and side where the dough rose unevenly during the process of baking. The volume is relatively low and the texture rather coarse.*

enough before being placed in the oven, it may have wide cracks on the sides of the baked loaf because the crust structure will have set before sufficient expansion of the loaf has occurred. The texture of this loaf of bread may be somewhat compact (Figure 20-3).

Ingredients

The essential ingredients for yeast-leavened dough are flour, liquid, yeast, and salt, which is very important in regulating the yeast activity. The other constituents added (sugar and fat) affect texture and flavor.

Yeast

Yeast is a microscopic one-celled plant that provides carbon dioxide gas which leavens bread. It does this by a process called *fermentation*. (See p. 429 for a discussion of yeast in leavening.) The species of yeast that is purposely added to bread dough is *Saccharomyces cerevisiae*. Strains of this microorganism are carefully selected in relation to their carbon dioxide-producing power and are grown to develop desirable characteristics for baking. Many enzymes, produced by the yeast cells, are responsible for the fermentation or breakdown of sugar that yields carbon dioxide and ethyl alcohol.

Yeast is marketed as compressed yeast or as dry active yeast. *Compressed yeast* is composed chiefly of moist living cells pressed into cake form with a small amount of starch as a binder. Compressed yeast is perishable and must be kept refrigerated. It will remain fresh for only a few days. A fresh sample is creamy white in color, is moist but not slimy, crumbles easily, and has a distinctive odor. When stale, the yeast may become slimy and brown in color and may develop a strong or off odor. Very little compressed yeast is now found on the retail market.

Dry yeast is made from an active strain of yeast, dried in fine granular form, packaged in metal foil, and sealed in an atmosphere of nitrogen to exclude air. The conditions that contribute to its loss of viability are mainly air, moisture, and warm temperature. Although dry yeast will keep fairly well at room temperature, it is better kept cold for longer viability. Dry yeast keeps well for several months but is dated in order to ensure the best results in its use. Some dry active yeast has very fine granules that require no preliminary softening in liquid. This yeast may be mixed directly with the dry ingredients in making yeast-leavened products. A finely granulated yeast that rises faster than regular dry active yeast is also available.

Compressed yeast must be softened in lukewarm liquid (29°C or 85°F) so that it will blend with other dough ingredients. It may be softened either in a small amount of water or in the total amount of liquid used in the dough. If dry active yeast is softened in water before blending with other dough ingredients, the temperature of the water should be quite warm—43° to 46°C (110° to 115°F). This allows proper reconstitution of the yeast without a loss of cell contents. Softening dry active yeast at lower temperatures results in diffusion of cell contents into the liquid to the detriment of yeast activity during the dough fermentation period.

High-quality yeast leavened products may be prepared using either dry active or compressed yeast. The major differences in use involve keeping quality, compressed yeast being much more perishable, and temperature for softening in liquid, dry active yeast requiring a higher temperature.

A *starter* is some of the sponge from a previous baking saved for future use (to replace yeast). It has sugar added as food for the yeast plant and should be used frequently (once or twice a week) to keep the yeast cells alive and to prevent undesirable flavor changes. Sourdough starters may be prepared initially by the mixing of equal volumes of milk or water and flour and the exposing of the mixture to air so that wild yeast cells may inoculate it. After 2 to 5 days the mixture should be sour and bubbly and ready to use in a variety of recipes. Both wild yeasts and bacteria probably contribute to the formation of gas and flavor substances in sourdough starter.

Liquid yeast usually is made from potato water, sugar, and yeast. Like starter it must be used frequently to avoid spoilage. Both starter and liquid yeast are more uncertain sources of yeast cells than compressed and dry yeast. Their chief advantages are convenience and economy in families where bread is baked frequently or where markets are not easily available for the purchase of yeast. However, a sourdough starter may be used because of its flavor.

The carbon dioxide gas produced during yeast fermentation causes the bread dough to expand or rise. Ethyl alcohol is volatilized during baking. By-products of the fermentation reaction also include many flavor substances. Organic acids, amino acids, and other substances produced during fermentation participate in complex reactions that result in characteristic bread flavor.

The amount of yeast used may be altered within limits according to the amount of time to be used for the bread making process. Small amounts of yeast, such as ¼ to ⅓ cake or package per 1 cup liquid, are satisfactory if given enough time. With small amounts of yeast, the sponge method of mixing permits more rapid growth of yeast. Excess yeast causes an undesirable odor and flavor in bread. Coarse texture, gray color of crust and crumb, and loaves of distorted shapes may also result from a great excess of yeast and too rapid fermentation. Bread can be made in about 2½ hours using 1 cake or package of yeast per 1 to 1¼ cups of liquid if one is in a hurry. For ordinary use, however, the smallest amount of yeast that will serve the purpose is desirable.

Flour and Liquid

Wheat flour is unique in that it has the necessary components to produce bread of high volume and fine texture with a cohesive, elastic crumb. This is because the flour provides the proteins that, when hydrated and mixed, produce gluten. Gluten is responsible for extensibility and elasticity in the dough. After the gluten structure has been expanded by gas cells, heat coagulates the gluten proteins and sets the structure. Because of the weakening effect of fermentation on gluten, the flour best adapted to the making of bread is one of strong gluten quality. A weak gluten becomes so highly dispersed that a bread of poor volume and quality is likely to result. If soft wheat flours are used for bread, variations in proportions, method, and technique are necessary in order to obtain a good product. A high-protein bread flour is used in commercial bread making and is available for home use but acceptable bread can also be prepared from all-purpose flour.

Liquid is essential in bread dough to hydrate flour proteins and contribute to the development of gluten. In addition, it is essential for the partial gelatinization of starch, which makes an important contribution to bread structure [4]. Other components are also dissolved or dispersed in the liquid. The liquid used in making bread may be milk, water, potato water, or whey. If the liquid is milk, it should be scalded, which is a process that destroys some enzymes or changes some proteins so that an undesirable softening of the dough does not occur during fermentation. A small quantity of mashed potato may also be added to bread dough. Potato water and cooked potato introduce gelatinized starch into the mixture, which favors fermentation, and also enhances the keeping quality and flavor of the baked bread. Milk and whey increase the nutritive value of bread to some extent.

The amount of flour required to make a pound loaf of bread is approximately ¾ of a pound or 3 cups. The amount depends chiefly on the hydration capacity of the flour proteins. Strong flours with a high protein content have a higher hydration capacity than do flours of lower protein content and the quantity of high protein flours required is slightly smaller. Thus, the amount of liquid used in making bread varies with the hydration capacity of the gluten-forming proteins in the flour. For good bread flours about 60 to 65 percent of the weight of the flour as liquid gives a dough of the best consistency. In terms of measurements, 65 percent of the weight of the flour is approximately 1 cup of water for a 1-pound loaf.

Weak flours have a low imbibition capacity and, therefore, require a lower percentage of moisture. If milk is used, a higher proportion of it is needed because of the 12 to 14 percent of milk solids present.

Beyond the amount of liquid required to achieve maximum loaf volume, additional absorption of water produces a less tenacious or more tender gluten, which results in decreased loaf volume. Too small a proportion of moisture may not provide enough water for optimal gluten development and may result in decreased loaf volume of the finished bread.

Sugar

Sugar, although not an indispensable ingredient in a bread formula, plays several roles in breadmaking. It increases the rate of fermentation by providing readily available food for yeast so that the bread rises in a shorter period of time. If larger amounts of sugar are used, however, as in sweet rolls, the action of the yeast is somewhat repressed and the fermentation and proofing periods must be longer. Flavor (primarily sweetness), texture, and browning are also affected by the use of sugar, although the browning of bread is primarily the result of the Maillard reaction in which table sugar (sucrose) does not participate. Sugar in bread dough comes from three sources: (1) that present in the flour; (2) that produced by the action of enzymes hydrolyzing starch; and (3) that added as an ingredient [10].

For loaf breads, 2 teaspoons to 1½ tablespoons of sugar per 1-pound loaf are common amounts used. Doughs for rolls usually con-

Fat

Fat is used in bread commercially to facilitate the handling of the dough, to increase the keeping quality of the bread, and to improve loaf volume and crumb grain [8]. The tenderness of the bread is also increased. Liquid oils do not perform the same functions that allow an increase in volume as do solid shortenings. However, the commercial baker can combine various conditioners and softeners with liquid oil and produce a bread of acceptable quality [3].

For loaf breads, 1 to 1½ tablespoons of fat per 1 pound loaf are sufficient to improve tenderness, flavor, and keeping quality. Two to 4 tablespoons or more per cup of liquid may be used in roll dough for increased tenderness.

Salt

Salt is added to bread dough for flavor, but it also has other effects. Salt retards yeast fermentation and, therefore, increases the time required for bread dough to rise. Salt has a firming effect on gluten structure. Bread made without salt is often crumbly in texture and may easily become overlight.

The amount of salt needed for a good flavor of bread is approximately 1 teaspoon per 1 pound loaf. The amount may vary from less than 1 to 1½ teaspoons without detrimental effects. An excess of salt is to be avoided from the standpoint of both texture and flavor.

Mixing and Handling

Two basic methods of mixing yeast bread are the straight-dough method and the sponge method. The batter method may also be used for some breads.

Straight-Dough Method

In mixing yeast bread by the straight-dough method, the liquid is generally warmed with the sugar, salt, and softened fat. If scalded milk is used, it must be cooled to the proper temperature before yeast is added. Yeast may be softened in a small amount of warm water and added to the liquid mixture or it may be softened in the total liquid. The temperature of the liquid used for softening should be appropriate for the type of yeast used as previously discussed. Finely granulated dry active yeast may be stirred with part of the flour. About a third of the flour is then blended with the liquid ingredients and vigorously mixed. Beating the batter blends ingredients uniformly and starts the development of gluten, and also incorporates air cells. The remainder of the flour is added gradually to form a dough that is then transferred to a floured board for kneading. The dough is kneaded (see following section, Kneading) until it has a smooth, satiny outside surface. It is next placed in a clean mixing bowl and allowed to rise until it is at least doubled in bulk, after which it is lightly punched down. It may then be either allowed to rise a second time or be molded into loaves or rolls. If special bread mixers are available, the entire mixing process may be done by machine.

The number of risings may vary with the strength of the flour. Doughs made from strong gluten flours may be allowed to rise more times than doughs made from flours with lower protein content before the dough is placed in the pans. Weak glutens tend to become too highly dispersed with too long a fermentation period. A more thorough mixing of the bread alters the quality of the gluten so that a shorter fermentation time gives as good a volume and quality of loaf as may be obtained by a shorter preliminary mixing and a longer fermentation period (more risings).

Sponge Method

A sponge consisting of liquid, sugar, yeast, and part of the flour is mixed as in the straight-dough method. When the mixture has stood until it is light and full of gas bubbles, it is then made into a dough by the addition of slightly cooled melted fat, salt, and the remainder of the flour. The dough is kneaded and allowed to rise until at least double its original volume, after which it is molded and placed in baking pans.

Batter Method

Breads may be made from batters containing less flour than doughs. The straight-dough method may be modified to eliminate the kneading and shaping steps. The batters are allowed to rise at least once in the bowl and/or in the baking pan, depending upon the recipe being followed. These unkneaded breads usually have a more open grain and uneven surface than kneaded breads and lack the elasticity of the crumb, but require less time in preparation.

Commercial Processes

Many technological advances have been made in the baking industry in recent years. Pure yeast cultures and standardized ingredients are available. Powerful mixers; fermentation rooms; dough dividers; and automatic proofing, baking, and wrapping systems are used. Bread may be made by a continuous dough-mixing process that uses a very high-speed, short-time mixing period substituting for a long fermentation period. A no-fermentation process is also available [5] that involves the addition to the bread dough of a mixture of amino acids and organic acid salts that produce typical bread flavor during baking. If the fermentation period is eliminated in commercial bread production, a large savings in time and labor costs results.

Kneading

Kneading of bread dough is essential for the development of strong elastic gluten strands from flour of relatively high protein content. Skillful handling of the dough ball is necessary at the beginning of kneading. The mass may rather easily be collected into a ball of dough that, with proper handling, tends to remain smooth on the outer surface in contact with the board. All wrinkles and cracks are best kept on the side in contact with the hands to minimize the tendency for the dough to stick to the board. Wet spots on the outside surface may require frequent coating with flour until the dough becomes elastic enough to knead easily.

The kneading movement is a rhythmical one in which the fingers are used to pull the mass over into position for kneading and the lower part of the hand is used for applying pressure to the dough. Forcing the fingers into the dough or using too heavy a pressure tends to keep the mass of dough sticky and difficult to handle. See Figures 20-4 and 20-5.

20-4 *Dough development. Left, dough barely mixed; center, dough partially developed; right, dough developed.* (Courtesy of Wheat Flour Institute)

Fold the dough over from the far side toward you.

Firmly push the dough away, using the heels of the hands.

Turn the ball of dough ¼ of a turn and repeat the steps from the first folding.

Kneading should be thorough, and it is unlikely that bread dough will be overkneaded by hand. Various mixers are available having motors powerful enough to mix bread dough completely, thus eliminating the necessity of kneading by hand. The manufacturers' directions should be followed in the use of these mixers. Handling of doughs after fermentation has been completed should be done lightly to avoid the pressing together of the thin filaments of gluten that are formed.

Care must be used during kneading to avoid the incorporation of excess flour into the mixture, which results in too stiff a dough. With the development of a good kneading technique it is surprising how little flour need be used on a board for the handling of any kind of dough. Later handling can be done with practically no flour because of the increased extensibility of the dough after fermentation.

During the kneading process the swollen particles of the proteins, *gliadin* and *glutenin,* adhere to each other and become aligned in long elastic strands. Starch granules from the flour are entrapped in the developing gluten. The development of gluten during kneading is important to provide structure and strength for the dough and the finished loaf of bread.

Fermentation and Proofing

Fermentation, which involves the breaking down of sugar to smaller molecules, particularly carbon dioxide and alcohol, occurs primarily during the rising periods in the preparation of yeast breads. It is catalyzed by many different enzymes from the yeast cells and is a complex process. Other enzyme action also occurs in bread dough. A starch-splitting enzyme, called *amylase,* is present in the flour and may also be added in commercial bread making. This enzyme catalyzes the hydrolysis of starch to dextrins and maltose. Gelatinized starch is more easily broken down by amylase than is uncooked starch. Therefore, mixing some scalded flour or cooked potato in the dough favors the enzyme action. There may also be some action of proteases in bread dough. These enzymes hydrolyze proteins to peptides and amino acids. If the proteases are too active, they may hydrolyze too much of the protein and produce harmful effects, such as poor texture and decreased volume. Slight action of protease may be beneficial. Acidity increases in bread dough during fermentation. The increase in acidity is largely attributed to the carbon dioxide but organic acids, chiefly acetic and lactic, are also formed. Advantageous effects of a certain degree of increased acidity are the promotion of fermentation and amylase activity, and the holding in check of some unwanted organisms.

The changes in gluten quality during fermentation are partly attributed to the increased acidity. Greater dispersion of the gluten with loss of elasticity and tenacity occurs as acidity increases. The action of proteases may possibly be a factor in the softening of the gluten, although this is not well understood. The stretching of the dough under the pressure of gas appears also to have a modifying effect on the gluten.

The optimum amount of fermentation varies with flours of different gluten strength and of different amylase activity. Bread must be baked before gluten strands become so thin and weak that they break, thus allowing carbon dioxide gas to escape. Overfermentation with excessive loss of gas results in poor oven spring and is likely to give a loaf that is flat or sunken on top.

Overfermented bread also has a coarse grain and thick cell walls and may have a sour odor and flavor and a crust that does not brown well. The volume is small and the loaf is heavy and compact. Weak glutens are more easily overfermented than are strong glutens, which not only tolerate but require more fermentation in order to yield bread of a good quality. Underfermentation produces bread that has thick cell walls and is heavy, small in volume, and less tender than bread that has fermented sufficiently to bring about a desirable dispersion of the gluten.

Fermentation can take place over a wide range of temperatures, but the best flavor is probably developed at a temperature of 26° to 32° C (79° to 90° F). Cold inhibits yeast activity and a temperature of about 55° C (130° F) destroys yeast plants. Warm temperatures may favor the growth of organisms that produce undesirable flavors in bread.

Dough that is exposed to air develops a crust or film that must later be thrown away to avoid the formation of heavy streaks throughout the dough. To avoid crust formation, a cabinet may be devised by the placing of the bowl containing the dough in a pan of warm water that is closely covered with another pan of the same size. The vaporization of moisture from the surface of the water maintains a humidity that keeps the bread surface from drying out. Alternatively, the surface of the dough may be lightly greased and the bowl covered with a plastic wrap. Fermentation is usually continued until the dough has risen to 2 to 2½ times its original volume.

After the dough has undergone fermentation and is molded into a loaf and placed in a baking pan, it is allowed to rise again. This final rising in the pan is called *proofing*. Proofing should be terminated when the loaf has approximately doubled in size and the dough does not spring back when lightly touched.

Baking Bread

As heat is applied to the bread during baking, gas production and expansion are greatly accelerated, which results in a sharp rising of the dough for the first few minutes of the baking period. This is called *oven spring*. The temperature of the interior of the loaf gradually rises until a temperature is reached that destroys yeast plants and enzymes and stops fermentation. Alcohol is volatile and is almost completely driven off during the baking of bread. The maximum temperature of the interior of the loaf is approximately the boiling point of water, but as moisture evaporates from the exterior surface and crust formation occurs, the temperature of the crust becomes higher than that of the crumb.

Gluten undergoes a gradual change in properties over a rather wide range of temperatures—50° to 80° C (122° to 175° F)—and finally becomes firm as it coagulates. Partial gelatinization of starch occurs during baking. Starch absorbs only about one third of its weight of water at room temperature, but because it constitutes about four fifths of flour, it is responsible for about half the total water absorption of flours when made into dough. As the gluten loses water during baking and the starch swells with the imbibition of additional water during heating, at least a partial gelatinization of the starch is made possible [7]. In fresh bread the gluten holds less and the starch holds more water than in the uncooked dough. The partially gelatinized starch contributes to bread structure as it is embedded within strands of coagulated gluten proteins. The nonenzymatic browning or Maillard reaction appears to be chiefly responsible for the brown crust color in baked bread. The browning reaction probably also contributes to bread flavor.

Greasing the bottoms of pans is an aid in removing the baked bread from the pan. The greasing of side walls is optional, but a somewhat larger volume of loaf may result from allowing the dough to cling to the side walls while rising.

Baking temperatures and time periods vary according to the type of dough and size of mass to be baked. Whether a hot or moderate oven is used at the beginning depends upon the extent of rising before the bread is placed in the oven. Bread that has risen approximately double its bulk should go into a hot oven (400° to 425° F) to set the structure of the bread and prevent too much rising in the oven. Bread that has risen less than double its bulk may be allowed to continue rising in the oven by the use of a more moderate oven temperature (375° to 400° F). The oven temperatures should be hot enough to avoid overfermentation in the oven with the possible falling of the bread before the yeast destruction occurs, but too hot an oven sets the bread before optimum oven spring occurs, thus reducing the final volume and affecting the texture.

One-pound loaves may bake 35 minutes at a temperature of 400° F or may bake for about 15 minutes at a temperature of 425° F and for an additional 30 to 45 minutes at 375° F.

White bread is generally not acceptable when cooked by microwaves because of the lack of crust formation. However, relatively dark breads, such as rye and whole wheat, have been satisfactorily prepared in the microwave oven with very little additional heating in a hot conventional oven. Yeast dough may be proofed in the microwave oven fairly well, speeding up the rising. Brown-and-serve rolls are successfully prepared by the use of microwaves. They are browned in a hot conventional oven before being served.

Rolls

Rolls usually contain somewhat larger amounts of fat and sugar than are generally found in bread. Eggs may also be added, although satisfactory roll dough may be made without eggs. The eggs may be beaten lightly and added in the early stages of making the dough. Because an egg adds about 3 tablespoons of liquid, either the liquid should be decreased by that amount or extra flour will be required to form a dough that can be handled.

Although any roll dough may be held in the refrigerator for 1 or 2 days before baking, refrigerator rolls are probably best made from a dough of slightly different proportions from plain rolls. Refrigerator rolls have only a moderate amount of yeast to avoid overfermentation, and slightly more than the usual amount of sugar to serve as food for the yeast during the period of about a week that the dough may be held before baking. The rolls may or may not contain egg. When the rolls are first mixed they are kneaded and allowed to undergo one fermentation, after which they are punched to release gas and stored closely covered at refrigerator temperature to be used as needed. If the dough rises appreciably during holding, it is punched from time to time to release gas. When needed, part of the dough is removed from the refrigerator, shaped into rolls, and allowed to rise in a warm room until it doubles in bulk. This may require 2 to 3 hours depending on the temperature of the dough and the room.

Rolls usually require 20 to 25 minutes of baking at a temperature of 425° F. Pan rolls require a longer baking time than do single rolls separated on a baking sheet or in muffin pans. A pan of rolls may require almost as much baking time as a pound loaf of bread.

Whole- and Mixed-Grain Breads

Contrast in the flavor and texture of breads is made possible by the use of a variety of grains in various forms. Flours, meals, and flakes may all be used. Whole-grain flours contain essentially all of the vitamins and minerals present in the unmilled grain and thus offer nutritional advantages over highly milled flours.

Whole-wheat bread is prepared with the use of whole-wheat flour. All of the flour in the bread may be whole-wheat or varying proportions of white and whole-wheat flour may be used. The procedure for mixing, fermenting, and baking whole-wheat dough is similar to that described for white bread dough, although the kneading does not have to be as extensive. The small particles of bran in whole-wheat flour interfere with the development of gluten and even extensive kneading does not overcome this effect. The volume of the finished loaf of whole-wheat bread is, therefore, usually somewhat less than that of white bread. If the whole-wheat flour is very finely ground, however, the volume of the bread made from this flour may approach that of white bread.

With an emphasis on the need for increased fiber in the diets of

Americans, the baking industry has developed ways of adding extra bran to breads without sacrificing quality [9, 11]. Vital wheat gluten and certain conditioners can be used to counteract the deleterious effects of up to 15 parts of bran per 85 parts of flour. Bran flakes or prepared bran cereals may be used at home as added ingredients in wheat bread or rolls to provide additional fiber.

Some wheat flour is needed in all yeast breads in order to provide gluten for bread structure and lightness. Flours milled from grains other than wheat may be combined with wheat flour to give varied and flavorful baked products. Rye flour comes closest of all the grains to wheat in terms of gluten-forming properties, but rye flour alone does not make a light loaf of bread. Rye yeast bread generally contains some wheat flour. Approximately equal portions of rye and wheat flour yield good results.

The germ of wheat or other grains is a good source of protein, vitamins, and minerals. However, the germ contains a reducing substance that has a detrimental effect on bread volume. Heat treatment inactivates this substance and heat-treated wheat germ may be added to bread in amounts up to 15 percent of the weight of the flour with no deleterious effect on bread volume.

Soy flour increases the protein content of breads and has been used commercially to make high-protein breads. Additives are commonly used by the commercial baker to overcome the adverse effects of soy flour on the absorption, mixing, and fermentation of dough. However, bread containing about ⅓ cup of soy flour to 5 cups of all-purpose flour can be satisfactorily made at home. This bread may be made higher in protein by the use of extra nonfat dry milk solids.

Other grains that may be used in bread making, in combination with wheat flour, include oatmeal, cornmeal, barley flakes, and buckwheat flour. Molasses and honey are often used as the source of sugar in whole grain breads to contribute flavors that blend well with whole grain products. The relatively coarse textures and dark colors of some of the specialty breads lend variety to meals.

Staling of Bread

Staling refers to all of the changes that occur in bread after baking. These include increasing firmness of the crumb, decreasing capacity of the crumb to absorb moisture, loss of flavor, and development of a leathery crust. Changes that can be detected in the laboratory in the starchy portion of bread have lead to the conclusion that starch is somehow responsible for staling. It is also possible that the amylopectin fraction of starch is more involved in staling than is amylose. However, the complex processes related to staling are not fully understood even though they have been studied for many years [1, 2,

6]. Fat in the bread formula helps to retard staling. Softeners added by the commercial baker have a similar effect.

If stale bread is reheated to a temperature of 50° to 60° C (122° to 140° F) or above, the staling is reversed and the bread acquires the characteristics of fresh bread. The soluble fraction of the starch that decreased during staling is increased. The process can be reversed several times until the bread has lost too much moisture. In the practical application of this freshening process, moisture may even be supplied if rolls are covered with a slightly dampened cloth or paper toweling while heating. Freezing also seems to reverse the staling process. Freezing combined with heating to thaw the frozen product brings about considerable freshening of stale bread products. This process can be quickly accomplished in a microwave oven. Bread stales more rapidly when held at refrigerator temperatures than it does when stored at room temperature. However, refrigeration retards mold growth on bread.

Rope in Bread

Rope is a bacterial contamination that can originate in the flour bin or in the various constituents used to make the bread. The spores of this bacterium are not destroyed in baking and within a few days the interior of the loaf becomes sticky and may be pulled into "ropes" of a syrupy material. The odor of the loaf becomes foul and somewhat like the aroma of overripe melons. Bread is inedible when rope has developed extensively. The cure consists mainly of eliminating the source of the bacteria although acidifying the dough to a pH of 4.5 or lower will prevent rope development. Sour milk or buttermilk may be substituted for one fourth to one half of the total liquid, or approximately 1 tablespoon of distilled vinegar per quart of liquid may be added. This does not change the flavor of the bread. Commercially, calcium or sodium propionate is commonly used in bread to retard molding. This also is effective in preventing rope.

Study Questions

1. Describe desirable characteristics of yeast bread.
2. Explain the role played by each of the following ingredients in making yeast bread at home:
   a. Yeast
   b. Flour
   c. Liquid
   d. Sugar
   e. Fat
   f. Salt
3. Compare the similarities and differences between compressed yeast and

dry active yeast as they are used for the preparation of yeast breads in the home.

4. Compare bread flour and all-purpose flour in terms of mixing, handling, and expected outcome when making yeast bread at home.
5. What steps are involved in mixing yeast bread by the straight-dough method? The sponge method? The batter method?
6. Explain why kneading is such an important step in the preparation of yeast bread at home.
7. What is meant by fermentation of yeast dough and by proofing? What important things occur during these processes?
8. a. Describe changes that occur during the baking of yeast bread.
   b. What is meant by "oven spring?"
   c. Why is it important to bake bread at precisely the right time after proofing in the pan?
9. How do ingredients and their proportions generally differ between rolls and bread?
10. a. What changes occur as bread stales?
    b. Which component of bread appears to be responsible for staling?
    c. How may somewhat stale bread be refreshened?
11. What is *rope* in bread and how may it be controlled?

References

1. D'Appolonia, B. L., and M. M. Morad. 1981. Bread staling. *Cereal Chemistry* **58,** 186.
2. Dragsdorf, R. D., and E. Varriano-Marston. 1980. Bread staling: X-Ray diffraction studies on bread supplemented with alpha-amylases from different sources. *Cereal Chemistry* **57,** 310.
3. Hartnett, D. I., and W. G. Thalheimer. 1979. Use of oil in baked products—Part I: Background and bread. *Journal of the American Oil Chemists' Society* **56,** 944.
4. Hoseney, R. C., D. R. Lineback, and P. A. Seib. 1978. Role of starch in baked foods. *Baker's Digest* **52,** 11 (no. 4).
5. Johnson, J. A., and C. R. S. Sanchez. 1972. New no-fermentation process controls bread flavor and costs. *Baker's Digest* **46,** 30 (no. 4).
6. Knightly, W. H. 1977. The staling of bread. *Baker's Digest* **51,** 52 (no. 5).
7. Marston, P. E., and T. L. Wannan. 1976. Bread baking. *Baker's Digest* **50,** 24 (no. 4).
8. Pomeranz, Y. 1980. Molecular approach to breadmaking—An update and new perspectives. *Baker's Digest* **54,** 26 (no. 1).
9. Pomeranz, Y. 1977. Fiber in breadmaking. *Baker's Digest* **51,** 94 (no. 5).
10. Pomeranz, Y., and K. F. Finney. 1975. Sugars in breadmaking. *Baker's Digest* **49,** 20 (no. 1).
11. Shogren, M. D., Y. Pomeranz, and K. F. Finney. 1981. Counteracting the deleterious effects of fiber in breadmaking. *Cereal Chemistry* **58,** 142.

21
Cakes and Cookies

Cakes

Cakes are commonly classified as (1) shortened cakes or cakes containing fat and (2) unshortened cakes or cakes with no fat. The chiffon cake has characteristics of both shortened and unshortened cakes but might be classified as a modification of an unshortened cake. A chiffon cake usually contains a larger proportion of egg than does a shortened cake, but it does contain fat in the form of oil.

Shortened Cakes

Shortened cakes are of two types—the pound cake and the standard shortened cake. The pound cake, as commonly prepared, has no added leavening agent except for the air incorporated in the creaming of the fat and sugar and in the beaten eggs. Steam has been found to be responsible for about half the expansion during baking provided that the air cells are retained, the theory being that moisture evaporates into the air cells and the vapor expands during baking. In commerical pound cakes, improved textures have resulted from the addition of a small amount of baking powder.

The standard shortened cake is leavened chiefly by carbon dioxide gas from baking powder or from soda and buttermilk. Air incorporated in the plastic fat or in the beaten eggs or egg whites also aids in leavening the mixture.

The textures of the two types of shortened cakes are different. Pound cakes have a close grain and are somewhat compact in character yet are very tender. They should not be heavy or soggy but they lack the soft, light, velvety crumb of a well-made shortened cake. A good standard shortened cake has a fine grain, cells of uniform size, thin cell walls, and a crumb that is elastic rather than crumbly. Crusts should be thin and tender. Top crusts should be smooth or slightly pebbly and have top surfaces that are only slightly rounded.

Proportions of ingredients vary widely for ordinary shortened cakes. Mixtures may be classed as lean or rich depending largely on the relationship of fat and sugar, the tenderizing ingredients, to the ingredients that give structure, such as flour and egg. One has but to study and experiment with the many proportions given for cakes to realize that numerous variations are possible [3]. Maximum and minimum quantities doubtless exist for most of the essential ingredients for cake but it is not yet known what all of these are. Specific ingredients can be increased or decreased within certain limits without producing undesirable results. But change in proportion often requires change in manipulation.

The optimum amount of stirring that produces the best results from one set of proportions or a definite quantity of mixture can usually not be applied to another set of proportions or a smaller or larger quantity of mixture.

Ingredients in Shortened Cakes. Usual ingredients in a standard shortened cake include sugar, fat, egg, liquid, leavening agent, salt, and flour. A proper balance between the tenderizing effects of sugar and fat and the firming or structural effects of flour and egg are particularly important in shortened cakes [9].

Sugar adds sweetness to a shortened cake, but it also has an important effect on texture and volume. It interferes with gluten development from the flour and has a weakening effect on the structure of the cake. It probably affects gluten development because it attracts and holds water that would otherwise be absorbed by the gluten proteins. It is only when the proteins of flour become sufficiently hydrated to adhere to each other that gluten is developed. Sugar also raises the temperature at which starch gelatinizes. Starch is an important part of the structure of a cake.

It has been suggested that the resistance to movement of a cake batter during baking, referred to as cohesive forces, influences the development of the structure of the finished cake. Various ingredients affect these cohesive forces in different ways. Sugar, added in increasing amounts up to an optimum quantity, decreases the cohesive forces and allows the batter to move more freely. The volume of the cake, therefore, increases [11]. As sugar is increased in a formula, stirring must also be increased to develop the gluten sufficiently to overcome the weakening effects of excess sugar. Without increased stirring, an increase in the percentage of sugar in a cake causes the cake to fall and produces a coarse texture and thick cell

21-1 *A cake containing too much sugar may fall in the center and have a coarse, gummy texture.*

walls. Both crust and crumb are gummy and the crust may appear rough, sugary, and too brown (Figure 21-1).

Sucrose or table sugar is the sugar that has most commonly been used in cakes. The use of fructose and glucose has been studied and differences in their effects have been noted [2, 13]. The temperature at which starch gelatinizes in cake batters appears to be an important factor in determining cake volume and contour. More fructose and glucose then sucrose are required in a formula to attain the same starch gelatinization temperature. Adjustments must be made in ingredient proportions when different sugars are used. Cakes made with fructose also tend to be darker in color because the browning reaction is more pronounced.

The optimum amount of egg in a given mixture produces finer cells and thinner cell walls than are obtained with a lower or higher percentage of egg. The volume of the cake is also likely to be larger. An excess of egg gives a rubbery, tough crumb although the method of adding the eggs may modify the effects. With beaten egg whites added last, the effects of increased egg are less noticeable. The cohesive forces in a baking cake batter are increased as egg white is added in increasing amounts [11].

Increasing the fat in a shortened cake increases tenderness. Fat weakens structure and tends to decrease volume when added beyond an optimum amount. Cohesive forces decrease with increasing amounts of fat [11].

In substituting a shortening containing 100 percent fat for butter or margarine (which are 82 percent fat) in a formula that has a fairly high fat content, it is best to use only 82 percent as much fat. It is not necessary to make this reduction in amount when substituting shortening for butter or margarine in a lean cake mixture. Fat of good creaming quality yields a cake of better texture than do soft or liquid fats unless the methods of mixing are altered. In comparing various fats, butter has been reported to make cakes that scored highest for tenderness and velvet-like texture while hydrogenated

474

shortening produced cakes with the highest rating for evenness of grain [10].

In addition to tenderizing, plastic or moldable fats aid in incorporating air into the batter. Most hydrogenated fats contain some inert gas as they are marketed. Creaming fat and sugar together adds additional air bubbles to the fat. It has been suggested that the air bubbles incorporated into fat during creaming act as a base for the distribution of leavening gas (carbon dioxide, particularly) during mixing and baking. Additional research with microscopic studies on freeze-dried cake batters [12] showed that the air bubbles were not necessarily incorporated in the fat but were distributed throughout the watery phase of the batter. The fat probably still plays an important role, however, in the trapping of air bubbles in a batter mixture.

Emulsifying agents in cake batter cause the fat to be distributed more finely throughout the mixture. When optimum amounts of emulsifier are used with the fat, the cohesive forces in the cake batter are decreased, the batter moves or flows readily during baking, and the volume of the finished cake is increased. The texture is also fine and even (Figure 21-2). Hydrogenated shortenings on the market generally contain small amounts of the emulsifiers mono- and diglycerides (about 3 percent). In commercial baking, emulsifiers used with liquid oil can overcome the undesirable results of using a liquid rather than a plastic fat in making shortened cakes [8].

Too little baking powder in a cake gives a compact, heavy cake. Increasing baking powder increases cake volume until the optimum quantity is reached. Beyond that, volume decreases and the cake falls. A coarse texture and a harsh gummy crumb may also result from an excess of baking powder. Cake made from SAS-phosphate powder may be disagreeably bitter if large amounts are used. Less baking powder is needed to produce the best volume and texture if more air is incorporated into the cake by means of the creamed fat-sugar mixture or the beaten egg whites.

Too little flour may affect cake similarly to an excess of fat or

21-2 *The volume and quality of a shortened cake improves when an emulsifier is used.* (Courtesy of *Food Engineering* and C. D. Pratt, Atlas Powder Co. Photograph by R. T. Vanderbilt Co.)

sugar. The structure is weak and the texture is coarse. The cake may fall. Excess flour, on the other hand, produces a compact, dry cake in which tunnels may form readily. Tunnels, however, may form in a cake of good proportions if the mixture is overmanipulated or is baked at too high a temperature. Flour contributes structure to shortened cakes. Cakes made with all purpose flour are generally lower in volume and have a more coarse texture than similar cakes made with cake flour. Cake flours are usually highly bleached with chlorine gas. This chlorination of cake flours apparently alters some of the lipids in the flour and produces an increase in cake volume [7]. The gelatinized starch is probably more important to structure than is the small amount of gluten developed from cake flour.

The liquid ingredient in cakes dissolves the sugar and salt and makes possible the reaction of baking powder. It disperses the fat and flour particles and hydrates the starch and protein in the flour, allowing for starch gelatinization and gluten formation. Liquid provides some steam which helps to leaven the cake. Various liquids may be used, including milk, water, and fruit juices. Too much liquid produces a moist cake of low volume. Salt is used in cakes for flavor. Large amounts are not necessary.

A very satisfactory plain standard cake has, by measure, one third as much fat as sugar, two thirds as much milk as sugar, and about three times as much flour as liquid. A cake with that general proportion is as follows:

Cake Formula

Sugar	1½ c
Fat	½ c
Milk	1 c
Cake flour	3 c
Eggs	2
Salt	½ t
Baking powder	3 t
Flavoring	1 t

Methods of Mixing. A variety of methods may be used for combining the ingredients in shortened cakes. A few of the commonly used methods are described here.

Conventional Method. This method consists of creaming a plastic fat, adding the sugar gradually to the fat with continued creaming, adding the eggs or egg yolks to the fat-sugar mixture, and beating until the mixture is well blended and very light. The dry ingredients are sifted together and are added alternately with the milk in about four portions. The egg whites may be beaten separately until stiff but not dry and quickly folded into the batter at the end of mixing in order to avoid excessive loss of gas.

Flavoring extract may be added: (1) to the creamed mixture; (2) to the milk; or (3) while the dry and liquid ingredients are being added. The conventional method of mixing is more time consuming than the other methods described. It should produce a fine-textured cake and may be conveniently used when mixing cakes by hand.

Conventional Sponge Method. This method is used in lean cake mixtures where the amount of fat is not sufficient to produce a light creamed mass when all the sugar is added to the fat. To avoid the dry, crumbly character of the fat-sugar mixture, about half of the sugar is reserved to be beaten with the eggs until the mixture is very stiff. The rest of the sugar is creamed with the shortening and the liquid and dry ingredients added alternately to this sugar-fat mixture. The beaten egg-sugar mixture is then folded into the batter at the end of mixing. It may be added, however, that a surprisingly large amount of sugar can be creamed with a small or moderate amount of fat if the fat is at the most favorable temperature for creaming (24°–29° C or 75°–85° F) and if the addition of sugar is gradual. A good cake can be made from oil by the use of the conventional sponge method.

Muffin Method. In the muffin method the eggs, milk, and melted fat are mixed together and added all at once to the sifted dry ingredients. This method is simple and rapid and is particularly useful for lean formulas where the cake is to be eaten while still warm.

Quick-Mix Method. This method has been known by several names, including single-stage, one-bowl, and one-mix, as well as quick-mix. It requires a change in the proportions of ingredients from those that are satisfactory for the conventional method of mixing. A higher ratio of sugar and liquid are used with the quick-mix method and the shortening should contain an emulsifying agent. All of the ingredients, particularly the fat, should be at room temperature so that the ingredients can be readily dispersed. Use of this method is difficult if mixing is to be done by hand. An electric mixer is desirable. However, commercial cake mixes, which use the one-bowl method of mixing, may be made by hand with the counting of mixing strokes rather than time in minutes. The quick-mix method used with an appropriate formula yields a fine-grained, tender, moist cake with good volume that remains fresh for a relatively long period of time.

The mixing of the batter is usually completed in two stages (Figure 21–3):

Stage I

Sift all dry ingredients into bowl used for mixing.
Add all fat, part of liquid, and flavoring or add all fat, liquid, and flavoring.
Beat for a specified time.

21-3 *A one-bowl, two-stage method of mixing a shortened cake.* (Courtesy of Kitchens of Betty Crocker, General Mills, Inc.)

(1) Grease the bottom and sides of the pan and dust with flour before beginning to mix the cake.

(2) Add shortening, two thirds of the liquid, and flavoring to the blended dry ingredients.

(6) Place the pans on the middle rack at least 1 inch from the sides of the oven. The pans should not touch.

(7) After minimum baking time, touch the center lightly. If no imprint remains, the cake is done. Or insert wooden pick in center. If it comes out clean, the cake is done.

(3) Blend in a mixer at low speed to moisten ingredients. Beat 2 minutes; scrape the bottom and sides of bowl often. Undermixing gives a coarse texture.

(4) Add the remaining liquid and un-beaten eggs. Beat 2 minutes more; scrape the sides and bottom of bowl often.

(5) Pour the batter into prepared pans. The batter should be divided evenly between the layer pans.

(8) Allow the cakes to cool 10 minutes on the wire racks before removing from the pans. If the cakes are left in the pans too long, they will steam and become soggy.

(9) The finished cake has a moist, velvety crumb and good volume.

Stage II

Add unbeaten eggs or egg whites and remaining liquid if part of the liquid was withheld in the first stage.
Beat for a specified time.

In some recipes, the baking powder may be omitted from the first stage and stirred in quickly (all by itself) between the two stages. For uniformity of blending, the bowl requires frequent scraping from both the sides and the bottom of the bowl during the mixing.

Effects of Under- and Overmanipulation. It appears that the amount of mixing needed for producing the best cake texture varies with the proportion of ingredients and the quantity of batter. The temperature of the ingredients is also a factor as is the quantity of baking powder and the time of adding the baking powder. The thoroughness of creaming the fat-sugar-egg mixture affects the extent of subsequent mixing. Thorough creaming makes possible a wider range in the amount of mixing that will produce a good texture. A good creamed mixture is light and spongy but has enough body to prevent an oily, pasty, or frothy mass. When eggs are added to the creamed fat and sugar, the mass becomes softer but should retain enough air to remain light. When the fat-sugar mixture separates into large flecks or curds upon the addition of the eggs, the resulting cake usually has a coarser texture than does the cake produced from an uncurdled batter. A more stable emulsion may result from adding eggs gradually to the fat-sugar mixture.

Mixing a cake batter barely enough to dampen the dry ingredients may yield a cake of good volume, but the texture is coarse and the cell walls are thick. The optimum amount of stirring gives the optimum volume of cake and the texture is uniform, the cells are small, and the cell walls are thin. Stirring beyond the optimum amount tends to produce a compact cake of smaller volume. The texture may be fine but tunnels are likely to be formed. When cakes are greatly overstirred, they become heavy or soggy. Cakes stirred close to the optimum amount tend to be slightly rounded on top. Certain rich mixtures may show a concave surface if they are understirred. As stirring is increased, peaks tend to form and the side walls of the cake are not so high as in the cakes stirred the optimum amount. If cakes are cut or broken where the peaks occur, long tunnels will be found.

The fact that cake mixtures contain more sugar and fat than most other flour mixtures decreases the tendency for toughness to result from stirring. Gluten development is retarded by sugar and fat. But more than the optimum amount of stirring may appreciably toughen cakes, especially those made from lean mixtures and from flours of stronger gluten quality.

Chocolate Cakes. Because of the starch content of cocoa and chocolate, a smaller percentage of flour than used in a yellow cake gives a more desirable chocolate cake. With the same proportions of flour, fat, and sugar as used in plain shortened cakes, chocolate cake batters tend to be undesirably stiff and the cakes are dry with a tendency to crack on top. Chocolate cake recipes usually contain relatively high percentages of sugar or fat or both, however, and the proportion of flour may approach that usually used in other short-ened cakes. Cocoa has a greater thickening effect than chocolate because the percentage of starch in cocoa is about 11 percent as compared to 8 percent in chocolate. From the standpoint of flavor, color, and thickening effect, best results are usually obtained by using about two thirds, by weight, as much cocoa as chocolate in a recipe. This amounts to about 3 to 3½ tablespoonfuls of cocoa as a substitute for 1 ounce of chocolate.

The acidity of chocolate is not sufficiently high to necessitate the use of soda unless buttermilk is used in the cake mixture. The color of chocolate cakes gradually changes from a cinnamon brown to a mahogany red color as the acidity decreases and the alkalinity in-creases. Devil's food cakes, which are characteristically mahogany red in color, contain enough soda to produce an alkaline pH in the batter. The characteristic chocolate flavor is decreased with increas-ing amounts of soda and more alkalinity in a chocolate cake.

Preparation of Pans. If the baking pans are prepared before the cake batter is mixed, the batter can then be transferred to them immediately after mixing. Allowing the batter to stand in the mix-ing bowl for more than 15 to 20 minutes before placing it in the baking pans is undesirable since transfer of the batter at this point may have adverse effects on the volume and texture of the baked product. Pans may be greased on the sides and bottoms or the sides may be left dry. Cake volume may be somewhat greater if the sides of the pans are not greased because the cake structure is supported by clinging to the sides. Because cake mixtures sometimes stick to the bottom of the pan even when the pan is greased, it is desirable to cut a piece of paper, waxed or unwaxed, to fit the bottom of the pan. After the paper is in place in the greased pan it is greased on the top surface, which will come in contact with the cake. Flouring the greased bottom of the pan is an aid in removing the cake from the pan but the flour coating should be very light.

Baking Temperatures. The oven temperatures commonly used for baking shortened cakes range from 350° to 375° F. The optimal temperature may vary with the cake formula. Some data indicate that plain cakes increase in volume and in total cake scores (includ-ing such characteristics as texture, tenderness, velvetiness, and eat-ing quality) up to a temperature of 365° F but decrease at a tempera-ture of 385° F. Chocolate cakes, which have often been baked at lower temperatures than other shortened cakes on the theory that chocolate scorches easily, also show increased volume and total cake scores when baked at higher temperatures—loaf cakes at 385° to 400° F and layer cakes at 400° F. High temperatures are sometimes not recommended because of the excessive browning and humping of the top even though improved volume and total cake scores are obtained up to a temperature of 435° F.* The browning of cakes is apparently the result of both the Maillard reaction and the caramelization of sugar.

The better results obtained with higher temperatures would seem to indicate that a more rapid coagulation of cake batter in relation to the rate of gas formation and gas expansion prevents the collapse of cells. Such collapse results in coarse grain and thick cell walls in the baked cake.

Cooling the Cake Before Removal from the Pan. Although a cake sets or develops a certain degree of firmness when fully baked, it is recommended that cakes not be removed from the pan until the interior reaches a temperature of about 140° F to become firm enough to handle without damage to the structure of the cake. Allowing the baked cake to stand about 10 minutes before removal from the pan is usually sufficient for this temperature to be reached.

Microwave Baking. Flour mixtures do not form a brown crust when cooked by microwaves. Since cakes are usually frosted, the lack of crust formation is of less importance from the standpoint of appearance for cakes than for some other baked products. However, the flavor associated with browning is not developed. A browning unit in the microwave oven may aid in browning the top surface of the cake. Wax paper laid over the surface of cake batters before cooking gives them a smooth surface.

Many cake mixes may be satisfactorily cooked in a microwave oven. The volume of the cakes may be larger than when they are baked in a conventional oven and the sides of the cake are softer. The cake may be placed for a few minutes in a conventional oven at 400° F for crusting after cooking by microwaves.

Unshortened Cakes

Unshortened cakes are of two types: (1) the white angel food which is made from egg whites and (2) the yellow sponge which is made from the whole egg.

Angel Food Cake. Angel food cakes are often made using commercial mixes in which the egg white foam is stabilized by the addition of a whipping aid. However, good quality cakes can also be

*Cook, thesis, Iowa State College.

made at home using fresh egg whites. Without the incorporation and retention of air, proper expansion and a typical texture do not develop in the baking of unshortened cakes. Air accounts for approximately half of the leavening in angel food cakes. But steam also plays an important role in the leavening of this product. Steam that is formed from the vaporization of the water of egg white brings about two or three times the expansion in baking angel food cake as is accounted for by the expansion of air.

Characteristics. An angel food cake should be porous or spongy, the volume large, and the cell walls thin (Figure 21–4). Tenderness and moistness are desirable qualities. The size of the cells varies but large cells are not objectionable if the cake has all the other desirable characteristics. If the cell walls are thick and the cake lacks tenderness and a feathery quality, large cells are then objectionable.

Egg Whites. Egg whites incorporate air as they are beaten to form a foam. Proteins are coagulated by the mechanical forces of beating to stabilize the foam. The reader should review the part of the chapter on Eggs and Egg Cookery that deals with factors affecting the production of egg white foams (pp. 318–321). Egg whites also contain heat-coagulable proteins that give structure to baked angel food cakes. Fresh eggs are preferable to older eggs for making angel cakes because the fresh whites are thicker and produce a more stable foam.

Angel cakes of good to very good quality have been made using egg whites dried by various methods—foam-spray-dried, freeze-dried, and spray-dried. These cakes were slightly less tender and flavorful than cakes made with frozen egg whites [6].

Flour. Cake flour, because of its low percentage of protein, its weak quality of gluten, and its fine granulation, gives a more tender, delicate angel food cake than does flour of stronger gluten quality. Flour increases the strength of the cake crumb and contrib-

21-4 *An angel food cake of good quality has high volume and thin cell walls.*

utes to the structure. As the amount of sugar is increased, the flour also, within certain limits, must be increased to give a satisfactory ratio of sugar to flour so that sufficient structure is maintained in the cake.

Sugar. A sugar of fine granulation is best for producing fine texture. Sugar elevates the coagulation temperature of egg proteins, and if it is used in excess, sugar may retard coagulation to such an extent that the cake may collapse. Sugar interferes with gluten development and therefore tends to produce a more tender and fragile cake when used in increasing amounts. Sugar also increases the temperature for starch gelatinization and thus affects the development of cake structure. The higher the percentage of sugar the greater is the tendency toward a sugary crust. Sugar has a stabilizing effect on the egg white foam and allows more beating without overcoagulation of the egg white proteins. Sugar, of course, also sweetens the cake and aids in browning.

Cream of Tartar. Cream of tartar is an important constituent of angel cake because of its beneficial effect on color, volume, and tenderness. The anthoxanthin pigments of flour are yellowish in an alkaline medium but are white in an acid or neutral medium. Also, the Maillard or browning reaction between sugars and proteins is less likely to occur in an acid than an alkaline medium. Therefore, the presence of cream of tartar (an acid) produces a whiter cake. It also stabilizes the egg white foam so that heat may have time to penetrate and bring about coagulation without the collapsing of the foam. Large air cells and thick cell walls (coarse grain) are the effects of an unstable foam that has partially collapsed. Cream of tartar prevents extreme shrinkage of the cake during the last part of the baking period and during the cooling period. The use of cream of tartar also produces a more tender cake. The optimal proportion is about 1 teaspoon per cup of egg whites.

A formula for angel food cake is as follows:

Egg whites 1 c	Cream of tartar 1 t
Sugar 1¼ c	Salt ¼ t
Cake flour 1 c	Flavoring 1 t

The ratio of sugar to flour in this cake formula is an appropriate one for tenderness yet not high enough to cause the collapse of the cake.

Mixing the Cake. The whites may be beaten with an electric mixer, a rotary beater, or a wire whisk. The latter usually gives a somewhat larger volume of cake but the cells are also larger. A fine division of air cells is important in the production of a fine-grained cake of large volume. However, the overbeating of egg whites for angel cake is one of the causes of poor products. Overbeating contributes to dryness and a lack of extensibility in the films surrounding the air bubbles. The air cells break and collapse, which results in a cake with low volume, thick cell walls, and coarse texture.

Both sugar and cream of tartar have a stabilizing effect on the egg white foam and contribute to the production of a large volume in the finished cake. The whites should be stiff but the peaks and tails that form should bend over slightly instead of standing rigid and upright.

Egg whites beat more easily to a foam of large volume when they are at room temperature than when they are beaten at a lower temperature. Therefore, eggs to be used in angel cake should be removed from the refrigerator some time before they are to be beaten. Cream of tartar is added to the egg whites and they are beaten until a foam begins to form. Sugar may be beaten into the whites as they are being whipped or it may be added by folding after the egg whites are completely beaten. In the first case, the sugar is added gradually as for meringue, starting after the cream of tartar is added. Beating the sugar into the whites is known as the *meringue* method and is preferable if an electric mixer is used. Beating some sugar into the egg-white foam seems to have a greater stabilizing effect on the cake than folding all of the sugar in with the flour. Regardless of the method used for adding sugar, about 2 tablespoons of sugar at a time are sifted over the surface of the egg whites. Adding either sugar or flour in too large portions results in the loss of air and often in the uneven blending of the sugar or flour.

After the sugar is added, the flour is gently folded into the mixture. If an electric mixer is being used, it should be turned down to the lowest speed setting. A part of the sugar may be reserved to mix with the flour. The flour mixed with some sugar unquestionably folds into the mixture more easily but usually a better cake is obtained when as much of the sugar as possible is added to the egg-white foam before the addition of any flour. The thorough mixing of sugar with the egg white gives a product into which the flour blends easily.

The number of strokes needed by different individuals for folding the flour varies. Thorough blending is necessary, but overmanipulation results in a loss of air and in decreased tenderness.

The flavoring extract may be added after the whites are partially beaten. Adding the extract at this stage allows it to become thoroughly distributed without the necessity for overmanipulation later. In no case is it desirable to add extract at the end of mixing because the extract is either incompletely blended with the batter or extra manipulation is needed to blend it uniformly. Alternatively, extract may be added while sugar or flour is being folded into the mixture. The salt may be added toward the end of the beating of the foam and before the addition of flour because salt may have a slight destabilizing effect on the egg white foam if added earlier.

Preparation of Pans. Pans are not greased for either type of sponge cake. It is desirable to have the mixture cling to the sides of the pan until it is coagulated by the heat of the oven. After baking, the pan is inverted and allowed to stand until the cake is thoroughly cooled.

Baking Temperatures. Early workers recommended low oven temperatures from 250° to 325° F for baking angel food cakes. Barmore [1] found that a temperature of 350° F gave more tender cakes of larger volume and with thinner cell walls than did lower oven temperatures. The cakes baked at a temperature of 350° F were also more moist as the longer time required at the lower temperature evaporated more moisture. Other work has suggested that a wide range of temperatures is possible if the minimum time required to bake the cake is used. Longer baking tends to toughen the cake whatever the temperature used, but greater toughening occurs with longer baking at higher temperatures. Temperatures of 300° to 425° F have been used. Baking at high temperatures tends to give a slightly smaller volume and browner crust than baking at lower temperatures, but if the minimum time is used, the cake is very moist. Elgidaily and co-workers [5] reported that angel cakes from commercial mixes that were baked at temperatures of 350° F and 375° F scored higher in all quality characteristics than did those baked at temperatures of 400° F and 425° F. Compact layers formed as a result of partial collapse of the structure after the cakes baked at temperatures of 400° F and 425° F were removed from the oven. It has been suggested that using an oven temperature of 375° F to start baking angel food cakes made from commercial mixes and turning the temperature down to 350° F, then 325° F, and 300° F at 10-minute intervals gives tender baked cakes of very high volume.

When the baking cake begins to shrink it may be tested with a toothpick or cake tester. If moist or sticky crumbs cling to the tester, the cake requires longer cooking.

Sponge Cakes. The usual ingredients and proportions for yellow sponge cake are as follows:

Eggs 6	Water 2 T
Sugar 1 c	Lemon juice 1 T
Cake flour 1 c	Grated lemon rind 1 T
Salt ¼ t	(lightly measured)

Methods of Mixing. Yellow sponge cakes may be made by either separated or whole egg methods. In the whole egg method the eggs are beaten until they are foamy with an electric mixer or a rotary beater. The water, lemon juice, and lemon rind are then added and the mixture is beaten until it is as stiff as it is possible to make it. (This mixture can be made very stiff.) The sugar is added gradually and beaten into the mixture with the rotary or electric beater. The flour and salt are mixed together and then sifted over the surface about 2 tablespoons at a time and folded into the egg mixture until well blended.

This method is desirable where a very small recipe is prepared. It gives no better cake than a method in which egg whites and yolks are separated but there is difficulty in beating one or two separated egg yolks as thoroughly as they should be beaten for best results.

In one separated egg method the egg yolks are partially beaten. The sugar, salt, water, lemon juice, and lemon rind are added and the whole mass is beaten until very stiff. The flour is folded lightly into the mixture, after which the stiffly beaten egg whites are folded in [4]. Alternatively the stiffly beaten mixture of yolks, sugar, water, lemon juice and rind, and salt is combined with the beaten egg whites before the flour is folded into the mixture.

In a meringue method the sugar is boiled with about three fourths the volume of water to a temperature of 118° C (244° F). It is then poured gradually over the beaten egg whites with constant stirring until a stiff meringue is formed. The egg yolks, lemon juice, lemon rind, and salt are beaten together until very stiff. The yolk mixture is folded into the whites and the flour is then gradually folded in.

Baking temperatures for sponge cakes are similar to those used for angel food cakes. Sponge cakes are toughened by overbaking.

Certain types of emulsifiers may be used by the commercial baker of sponge cakes. These allow the use of a simplified one-stage mixing procedure and result in a lighter cake of uniform grain, greater tenderness, and longer shelf life.

Cookies

Fine texture and velvety crumb are less prominent characteristics of cookies than of cakes and less skill is, therefore, often required to prepare them. However, the rolling of cookie dough is often challenging, particularly for the inexperienced person.

Classification

Cookies are of four basic types: the rolled cookie, which when baked may form either a crisp or a soft cookie depending on the proportions of the ingredients; the dropped cookie, which is made from a stiff batter that may be dropped or scraped from the spoon; the bar cookie, which is often a cake-type mixture baked in a thin sheet and later cut into squares or bars; and the so-called icebox cookie, which is made from a mixture so rich in fat that the dough is difficult if not impossible to roll. It is chilled in the refrigerator to harden the fat and is then sliced from the roll or mold and baked.

Ingredients

Formulas for cookies are as varied as are those for cakes and some of the same principles apply in mixing them. In general, the same ingredients that produce good cakes also produce good cookies. Cake flour is usually not necessary because few cookies have a soft, velvety crumb or the texture of good sponge or shortened cakes. All-purpose flour is satisfactory for most cookies.

The crisp cookie is usually made from a mixture that is rich in fat or sugar or both. Many rolled-cookie recipes have very little or no liquid. Because large volume is not desired in rolled cookies, the mixtures contain little or no leavening agent other than air incorporated in the creamed fat-sugar mixture.

Mixing and Handling

The conventional method is used for mixing most cookies but beaten egg whites are seldom added last. Cookies of the sponge type are made by sponge cake methods.

Doughs for rolled cookies are usually as soft as can be handled and rolled. Stiffer doughs and those rehandled and rerolled give dry, compact cookies. Many cookie mixtures other than icebox cookies must be chilled to facilitate rolling. Rolling only a portion of the dough at one time prevents continued rerolling. All trimmings may then be collected at the end for rerolling. Rolling between sheets of heavy waxed paper is a method sometimes used, but the usual method is to roll the dough on a floured board. Care must be used to avoid incorporating much extra flour into the dough while rolling it and to avoid having the cookie covered with excess flour when it is ready for baking. Usually excess flour remains on the cookie after baking and mars the external appearance and flavor.

The thickness of rolled dough ready for cutting is usually ⅛ or 3/16 of an inch. If the dough is to be used for cutouts, especially large ones, it is good to roll it to ¼ inch thickness. In the removal of cut cookies from the board to the baking sheet the side, rather than the end, of a knife or spatula usually avoids marring the shape of the cookie. Sticky cookie dough, however, and dough that is rolled tightly to the board are difficult to remove by any method.

Dropped cookie mixtures vary in consistency depending on the finished product desired. Some mixtures are meant to spread into a round flat cookie of about ⅜ inch to ½ inch thickness after baking.

Such mixtures give softer cookies than does the average rolled dough. Other dropped cookies are meant to hold their form. Judgement and acquaintance with the recipe are necessary in order to avoid too stiff or too soft a mixture. A mixture that is stiff enough to hold its form almost completely while baking usually produces a dry, breadlike cookie that may crack on top while baking. A cookie that only partially holds its shape during baking is usually of a more desirable texture and eating quality and has a better appearance. The type of mixture partially determines how stiff it may be without producing undesirable results. A mixture very rich in fat can be stiffer than a leaner mixture. Practically all mixtures will be stiff enough to require scraping rather than dropping from the spoon if they are expected to hold their form fairly well. Flour of strong gluten quality tends to give a dry breadlike drop cookie if the mixture is very stiff before baking.

Baking Cookies

Baking sheets rather than cake pans are more efficient for baking most cookies as there are no high side walls to interfere with the circulation of heat. Cookies baked in pans with high sides may cook until done but brown little or none on top. Bar cookies are usually baked in cake pans with sides. Baking sheets require no greasing for rolled or icebox cookies but do require greasing for dropped batters or cookie bars.

Rolled cookies spread little in baking so that little space is needed between them. Icebox cookies spread somewhat more and dropped cookies must have space to spread.

Study Questions

1. Shortened cakes are of two types. Name them and describe distinguishing characteristics of each.
2. Describe the usual role and the effect of an excessive amount for each of the following ingredients in the production of a shortened cake:
   a. Sugar
   b. Egg
   c. Fat
   d. Baking powder
   e. Liquid
   f. Flour
3. What role is played by an emulsifier in a shortened cake batter and what effect does it have on the finished product?
4. Briefly describe each of the following methods for mixing a shortened cake and explain advantages or disadvantages of each method:
   a. Conventional

    b. Conventional sponge
    c. Muffin
    d. Quick mix
5. Describe the effects of under- and overmixing a shortened cake batter. What factors affect the desirable amount of mixing to be done?
6. Why is it important to prepare the pans for a shortened cake batter before the batter is mixed? Explain.
7. Suggest an appropriate temperature for baking a shortened cake and explain why this temperature is recommended.
8. Why should a shortened cake be allowed to stand for about 10 minutes after baking before removal from the pan?
9. Name and describe characteristics of two types of unshortened cakes.
10. Describe the usual role of each of the following ingredients in angel food cake:
    a. Egg whites
    b. Sugar
    c. Cream of tartar
    d. Flour
11. a. Describe appropriate methods for mixing angel food and sponge cakes.
    b. Point out precautions that should be taken in the mixing of unshortened cakes in order to ensure finished cakes of good quality.
12. Suggest appropriate baking temperatures for angel food and sponge cakes.
13. How should angel and sponge cakes be cooled after baking and why?
14. a. Describe four basic types of cookies.
    b. Suggest some precautions that are necessary in the preparation of rolled cookies of good quality.
    c. What types of baking pans are generally recommended for cookies and why?

References

1. Barmore, M. A. *The Influence of Various Factors Including Altitude in the Production of Angel Food Cake.* Colorado State University Experiment Station Tecnical Bulletin No. 15. 1936.
2. Bean, M. M., W. T. Yamazaki, and D. H. Donelson, 1978. Wheat starch gelatinization in sugar solutions. II. Fructose, glucose, and sucrose: Cake performance. *Cereal Chemistry* **55,** 945.
3. *Breads, Cakes, and Pies in Family Meals.* Home and Garden Bulletin No. 186. Washington, D.C.: U.S. Department of Agriculture, 1979.
4. Briant, A. M., and A. R. Willman, 1956. Whole-egg sponge cakes. *Journal of Home Economics* **48,** 420.
5. Elgidaily, D. A., K. Funk, and M. E. Zabik. 1969. Baking temperature and quality of angel cakes. *Journal of the American Dietetic Association* **54,** 401.
6. Franks, O. J., M. E. Zabik, and K. Funk. 1969. Angel cakes using frozen, foam-spray-dried, freeze-dried, and spray-dried albumen. *Cereal Chemistry* **46,** 349.

7. Gaines, C. S., and J. R. Donelson, 1982. Contribution of chlorinated flour fractions to cake crumb stickiness. *Cereal Chemistry* **59,** 378.

8. Hartnett, D. I., and W. G. Thalheimer. 1979. Use of oil in baked products—Part II: Sweet goods and cakes. *Journal of the American Oil Chemists' Society* **56,** 948.

9. Lawson, H. W. 1970. Functions and applications of ingredients for cake. *Baker's Digest* **44,** 36 (no. 6).

10. Matthews, R. H., and E. H. Dawson. 1966. Performance of fats in white cake. *Cereal Chemistry* **43,** 538.

11. Paton, D., G. M. Larocque, and J. Holme. 1981. Development of cake structure: Influence of ingredients on the measurement of cohesive force during baking. *Cereal Chemistry* **58,** 527.

12. Pohl, P. H., A. C. Mackey, and B. L. Cornelia. 1968. Freeze-drying cake batter for microscopic study. *Journal of Food Science* **33,** 318.

13. Volpe, T., and C. Meres. 1976. Use of high fructose syrups in white layer cake. *Baker's Digest* **50,** 38 (no. 2).

22
Pastry

Pastry includes a variety of products made from doughs containing medium to large amounts of fat mixed in such a way as to produce flakiness. Examples of pastry include:

1. Plain pastry or pie crust used to make all types of tarts, turnovers, and dessert pies—single- and double-crust fruit pies (Figure 22-1); custard-type pies baked in the shell; and soft starch-thickened cream pies and gelatin-based chiffon pies in which the fillings are added after the pie shells are baked.
2. Plain pastry used as a carrier of high-protein foods to be served as a main dish—various types of meat, poultry, and fish pies with single or double crusts; patty shells to hold chicken á la king and similar types of creamed mixtures; and quiches, pies with a variety of ingredients, such as bacon, ham, Swiss cheese, onions and other vegetables, baked in a custard-type filling (Figure 22-2).
3. Puff pastry—flaky layers of light, buttery dough used to make crisp, sugar-glazed and cream-filled French pastry or flaky sweet rolls called Danish pastry (Figure 22-3). Puff pastry is made by rolling chilled butter in a well-kneaded flour and water dough; then folding and rerolling several times to make many thin layers of dough separated by thin layers of butter. During the baking butter melts and permeates the dough.

This chapter will focus on the making of plain pastry.

22-1 *A lattice-top fruit pie.* (Courtesy of Sun-Maid Raisin Growers of California)

Plain pastry contains only flour, fat, salt, and water. Either pastry or all-purpose flour may be used, pastry flour requiring less fat for optimum tenderness. However, pastry flour is used primarily by the commercial baker. Because of the larger amount of gluten formed with all-purpose flour, about ⅓ cup of fat per cup of flour may be needed to produce a tender crust. This proportion is, however, dependent also upon the kind of fat used and the skill of the handler. The amount of water required will vary with the hydration capacity of the gluten, the amount and type of fat, the temperature of ingredients, and the individual technique of handling. An excessive amount of water added in the making of pastry dough allows the hydration and development of more gluten than is desirable for optimum tenderness. Toughness of pastry is, therefore, increased by too much water in the dough. Too little water produces a dry dough that

22-2 *A quiche may contain bacon, Swiss cheese, and vegetables in a custard mixture that is baked in a pastry shell.*

493

22-3 *Puff pastry may be utilized to produce a variety of tantalizing products. In the center front is an apple turnover; behind this, the thin flakes of the pastry may be seen in elephant ears; three creme-filled French pastries are on the right; and at the top of the picture is a small Danish pastry.*

is crumbly and difficult to handle. The amount of liquid should be sufficient to barely form a dough that is not wet and sticky [4].

Fat is responsible for tenderness in pastry by spreading over the particles of flour and retarding their hydration. Fats vary in their tenderizing properties [3]. Liquid oils spread more than do plastic fats and usually have greater tenderizing power. Softer plastic fats spread more readily than harder fats. Butter and margarine contain only about 82 percent fat and, therefore, have less tenderizing power than 100 percent fats such as lard and hydrogenated shortening when substituted on a weight basis. A cup of lard weighs more than a cup of hydrogenated shortening because the shortening has been precreamed and contains an inert gas to make it lighter. In addition to the role of fat in tenderizing, plastic fats, in particular, play an important part in the development of flakiness in pastry.

Plain pastry is leavened primarily by steam, which is produced by baking in a hot oven. Leavening in this product is not extensive, however.

Very hard fat, direct from the refrigerator, and iced water are not necessary in the making of pastry. The fat should be cold enough to be firm rather than pasty or oily but plastic enough to be measured accurately and to blend with the flour. In warm weather, some chilling of fat may be necessary. Likewise, some chilling of water may be required, but both water and fat at room temperature will give good results.

Characteristics of Pastry

Pastry is usually preferred if it is tender but does not break too easily when served, and if it is flaky with a blistered surface, slightly crisp, evenly and lightly browned, and pleasantly flavored. Flakiness may be described as thin layers of baked dough separated by open spaces. Some of the factors that have been found to affect flakiness are (1) character of the fat used (solid versus melted or liquid fat); (2) the consistency of solid fat; (3) the type of flour used; (4) the proportion of water; (5) the degree of mixing; (6) the method of mixing; and (7) the number of times the dough is rolled.

Flakiness is thought to result from the process in which small particles of fat are coated with moistened flour or dough and then flattened into thin layers when the dough mixture is rolled out. On baking, the fat melts, is absorbed by the surrounding dough, and leaves empty spaces between thin layers of the baked dough. Solid fats yield a flaky crust more easily than do melted or liquid fats. However, flaky pastry can be produced with melted fats or oils. Liquid fats tend to blend so completely with flour that they produce a very short and crumbly crust if used in the same proportion as solid fats. When making pastry with oil, the liquid fat and water may be shaken together to form a temporary emulsion that is then quickly added to the flour and salt mixture with light mixing. Or the oil may be sprinkled over the flour and salt mixture, lightly mixed, and the water added last. Either method will produce a satisfactory pastry that is usually somewhat flaky.

Firm fats that remain in layers when rolled yield a flakier crust than do soft fats. The method used in making puff pastry, in which the fat is reserved to be rolled between the layers of dough, increases flakiness. Merely rerolling increases flakiness, but unless the percentage of fat in the mixture is high, rerolling may also develop the gluten sufficiently to increase toughness. Rerolling as a means of increasing flakiness is valuable chiefly for puff pastry.

A regular pastry flour may yield a very flaky crust, but flakiness increases with the strength of gluten. Toughness may also increase with the use of a stronger flour unless additional fat is used and greater care is taken in manipulation. Because tenderness is one of the most desirable characteristics of good pastry, it requires at least as much consideration as flakiness. Adjustments in ingredients and techniques of handling must be made so that both flakiness and tenderness are achieved.

Techniques of Mixing

Fat may be cut into the flour with a pastry blender or with a knife or spatula. It may be lightly blended with the fingers. Electric mixers or food processers may also be used both to mix the fat with the flour and to mix the liquid with the fat-flour mixture in the final stages of dough preparation. A reasonably uniform blending of fat with flour produces a more uniformly tender crust, but fat particles may be somewhat variable in size. Those who favor a relatively coarse division of fat in the flour and salt mixture do so on the theory that

22-4 *Preparation of pastry.* (Courtesy of Kitchens of Betty Crocker, General Mills, Inc.)

(1) After measuring the flour and salt and mixing them together in the mixing bowl, cut in the shortening with the use of a pastry blender.

(2) Sprinkle the water, a table-spoonful at a time, over the flour-fat mixture.

(6) Divide dough approximately in half; round up larger part on lightly floured cloth-covered board.

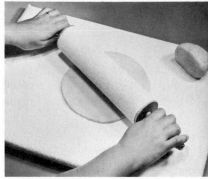

(7) Roll out not quite ⅛-inch thick.

flakiness is increased by the rolling of larger fat masses into thin layers. A very flaky crust may be obtained, however, with a uniform distribution of fat.

Unless sufficient water is added, the baked crust will be too tender and crumbly. As previously mentioned, too much water can toughen the pastry. Gluten may form to a greater than desirable extent when water is used in excessive amounts [2].

Several methods of mixing pastry, other than the traditional pastry method (shown in Figure 22-4), have been suggested. A satisfactory pastry product may be obtained by using any one of these methods.

A modified method of mixing pastry has been developed in which ¼ cup of a 2-cup portion of flour is reserved to be mixed with liquid

(3) Mix lightly with a fork until all the flour is moistened.

(4) Gather the dough together with the fingers and press into a ball.

(5) A canvas-covered board and a stockinette-covered rolling pin prevent sticking of pastry while it is being rolled out.

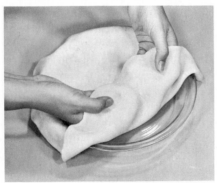

(8) Keep the pastry circular and roll it about 1 to 2 inches larger than the pie pan.

(9) Fold the pastry in half. Quickly transfer to a pie pan and unfold.

(10) Fit the pastry carefully down into the pan. Avoid the trapping of air underneath the dough. Trim off the overhanging edges. Place the filling in a pastry-lined pan. Roll out the other part of the dough for the top crust.

to form a paste. After the fat and the remainder of the flour have been combined as described, the paste is added all at once and blended with the fat-flour mixture.

In a hot water method of mixing pastry, solid fats may be melted by stirring them into boiling water; this mixture is then stirred into the flour and salt. If oil is used as the fat it may be shaken with water and added in a similar manner. Alternatively, the oil may be sprinkled on the flour-salt mixture and then stirred into it. The water may be added as in the traditional method. Pastry made by the hot water and oil methods may be somewhat less flaky than pastry made by the traditional method.

Pastry may also be made by a modified puff pastry method: about 2 tablespoons of the fat-flour mixture are removed before the liquid is added. After the pastry has been rolled out this fat-flour mixture is sprinkled over the dough. The dough is rolled up like a jelly roll and cut into two pieces. One piece is placed on top of the other and they are then rerolled for the pie pan. This method tends to increase flakiness in pastry.

Rolling Pastry

Pastry may be rolled as soon as it has been mixed, but allowing the dough to stand for a few minutes increases the extensibility or elasticity of the dough, making it easier to handle or to roll. For ordinary pie crust, the dough is rolled to about ⅛ inch thickness. Enough flour is required for the board to keep the crust from sticking but a minimum amount should be used to avoid toughening the pastry. Occasional lifting of the crust while rolling also tends to prevent sticking. The dough may be rolled on a canvas-covered board, into which a small amount of flour has been rubbed, or between two layers of waxed paper. Crusts that are rolled very thin become too brown when baked as pie shells and break in handling or in serving. If they are used for fruit pies, they may break while baking and allow juices to flow out.

Crusts are rolled into a circular shape and the dough for a lower crust or a pie shell should be about 1 to 2 inches greater in diameter than that of the top of the pan, which will allow for variable pan depth (Figure 22-4). Each crust should be rolled separately to avoid excessive rolling of dough, which may toughen the pastry. Rolled pastry may be frozen before baking as a convenience food [1] or the baked shells may be frozen.

Although pie shells tend to shrink somewhat in baking, excessive shrinkage may be prevented if the dough is not stretched when it is fitted into the pan. Having enough dough to permit building up a rim or a frilled edge is also an advantage if shrinking occurs. Overdevelopment of the gluten by rerolling may result in greater shrinkage during baking than occurs when gluten is not developed to an appreciable extent.

The formation of large blisters in pastry shells during baking may be prevented by forcing air from under the dough while fitting the dough into the pan and by pricking the dough adequately with the tines of a fork before baking. Crusts that are to have fillings cooked in them are never pricked.

Top crusts for fruit pies are less likely to break under the pressure of steam if small openings are made near the center for the escape of steam. Large gashes should be avoided as they are unattractive and permit the loss of juices. Top crusts adhere more closely to lower crusts if the latter are moistened before the crusts are pressed together.

Plain pastry that is baked prior to adding the filling is baked at a hot oven temperature (425° to 450° F). This allows rapid production of steam that separates the layers of dough which are formed as the fat particles melt. Baking is continued until the surface is delicately browned, which probably occurs chiefly as a result of the Maillard reaction. Baking temperatures are adjusted according to the types of fillings that are cooked in pastry shells. The filling must be adequately cooked before the crust becomes too brown. The soaking of bottom crusts by fruit and custard fillings sometimes creates problems in baking.

Preventing Soaked Crusts

Many methods have been suggested and tried for the prevention of soaked crust in fruit, custard, and pumpkin pies. Some methods such as partially baking the crust, coating the crust with raw egg white, or heating the crust until the egg white is coagulated, have no value. A partially baked crust becomes more soaked than one that is not baked, and also tends to be heavy to soggy. Raw egg white, being soluble in water, blends with the filling, thus offering no protection against the soaking of the crust. Some of the methods for fruit pies that do protect crusts are coating the upper surface of the lower crust with melted butter, using a hot oven temperature for the first 15 minutes of baking, and thickening the filling before placing it in the pastry-lined pan. The latter method has the added advantange of making possible a known consistency of juice before the pie is baked. It is even more difficult to prevent the soaking of the crusts of custard and pumpkin than of fruit pies. The lower baking temperatures used for egg mixtures prolong the baking time and permit increased soaking before the pie is done. A method that has been suggested to improve the crusts of custard pies is chilling the pastry for 1 hour before adding the filling, and using a high oven temperature (450° F) for the first 10 minutes of baking. Increasing the percentage of egg in the mixture (three eggs per pint of milk) lowers the coagulation temperature of the egg proteins and increases the ease of coagulation for the mixture. Scalding the milk used for the filling also shortens coagulation time. A coagulated custard will not penetrate the crust as readily as the uncooked mixture. An overcooked custard may exude sufficient water to provide a very wet crust.

Microwave Cooking

Piecrust usually is not well cooked in a microwave oven alone. For one-crust pies, the pastry shell may be baked in a conventional oven and the filling cooked in a microwave range. Commercial pie filling mixes are easily prepared by mixing the pack contents with milk and cooking on a high power setting for 2 to 3 minutes with periodic stirring. The bottom crust of a two-crust pie may be cooked by microwaves on a medium setting for 7 to 9 minutes, the uncooked filling added, the top crust placed on, and the pie again cooked. The pie should be turned midway in the cooking period. If a broiling unit is not available for browning, the pie may be finished by baking for 10 to 15 minutes in a hot conventional oven. Meringues can be cooked by microwaves but must be browned by the use of a conventional heating unit.

Study Questions

1. Describe the role of each of the following ingredients in the preparation of good quality pastry:
   a. Flour
   b. Fat
   c. Water
2. Describe desirable characteristics of good quality pastry.
3. a. Suggest an appropriate proportion of fat to flour for making pastry.
   b. Explain how the type of fat and the type of flour used might affect these proportions.
4. a. Describe several procedures for mixing pastry.
   b. What techniques of mixing are likely to produce the most flaky pastry and why?
5. Describe a satisfactory procedure for making pastry with oil. How will the characteristics of this pastry compare with one made with a solid fat?
6. What is the effect of each of the following on tenderness of pastry?
   a. Type of fat used
   b. Type of flour used
   c. Technique of mixing and handling
7. Suggest an appropriate temperature for baking plain pastry and explain why this temperature may be recommended.
8. How might one prevent or minimize the soaking of bottom crusts of custard and fruit pies during baking?

References

1. Briant, A. M., and P. R. Snow. 1957. Freezer storage of pie shells. *Journal of the American Dietetic Association* **33**, 796.
2. Hirahara, S., and J. I. Simpson. 1961. Microscopic appearance of gluten in pastry dough and its relation to the tenderness of baked pastry. *Journal of Home Economics* **53**, 681.
3. Matthews, R. H., and E. H. Dawson. 1963. Performance of fats and oils in pastry and biscuits. *Cereal Chemistry* **40**, 291.
4. Miller, B. S., and H. B. Trimbo. 1970. Factors affecting the quality of pie dough and pie crust. *Baker's Digest* **44**, 46 (no. 1).

Gels and Gelatin

23

A gel is a special kind of structure that might be described as being somewhere between a solid and a liquid. A number of different food products represent gels. Examples include most starch-thickened puddings and pie fillings, egg custards, and fruit jellies. Each of these products is discussed in other chapters. Gelatin mixtures also have the capacity to form gels, and gelatin salads and desserts are very familiar menu items. All gels have certain characteristics in common. In this chapter some of these common characteristics will first be described. The remainder of the chapter will be devoted to a discussion of gelatin and its use in food preparation.

Gel Structure and Characteristics

Gels are composed mainly of fluid but they behave much like rigid solids. These interesting characteristics appear to be the result of their special type of structure. Gels contain long, thin chain-like molecules, called polymers, that are joined together or cross-linked at random spots to produce a three-dimensional structure something like a pile of dry brush (Figure 23-1). This polymer network is immersed in a liquid medium to which it is attracted. The liquid, in a sense, is trapped by the chain-like network. The liquid keeps the polymer network from collapsing into a compact mass and the network keeps the liquid from flowing away. Gels are sometimes described as mixtures which hold the shape of the container after they are removed from it. However, they may vary from very soft gels to fairly rigid solids [2]. Most food gels are relatively soft but are resilient or elastic.

23-1 *When a gel is formed, a network of long, thin molecules traps liquid in its meshes.*

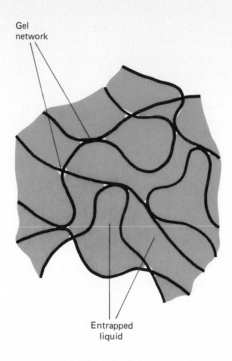

Gel
network

Entrapped
liquid

Environmental conditions may affect the characteristics of many gels. Gels may shrink or swell with changes in temperature. They may also be affected by pH (degree of acidity). Many food gels are liquified or melt over a relatively narrow temperature range. The melting and solidifying is a reversible process in gels such as gelatin mixtures. Gels often exhibit *syneresis* which is a weeping or exudation of liquid from the rigid gel. This may occur in certain gels such as egg mixtures when they are overcooked and in some starch and gelatin gels when they are stored in the refrigerator for a few days.

Gelatin

Manufacture of Gelatin

Gelatin is a product obtained by the hydrolyzing or breaking down of certain connective tissues of animals. The chief sources of commercial gelatin are animal hides or skins and bones. Collagen (a protein) is found in the inner layer of skin and in bone and may be converted into gelatin [1]. The conversion of collagen to gelatin is, in fact, a fundamental part of the cookery of less tender cuts of meat.

The conditions under which edible gelatin is manufactured are such as to ensure a product of high sanitary quality [3]. The dry form in which gelatin is marketed also favors a low bacterial count. However, because gelatin in the hydrated state is a favorable medium for bacterial growth it should be protected as are other perishable foods by adequate refrigeration.

Gelatin is marketed in both granular and pulverized form. A fine division of the gelatin allows it to be dispersed more easily in hot water. Gelatin mixes, which include sugar, acid, coloring, and flavoring substances, usually contain pulverized gelatin. A good quality of plain gelatin should be as nearly flavorless and odorless as possible.

Uses for Gelatin

Edible gelatin is used as a gelled base for desserts and salads and as an emulsifying or stabilizing agent in frozen desserts. It is also used in the making of some candies such as marshmallows. Gelatin is a very efficient gelling agent for foods. As little as one to two parts of gelatin in ninety-eight to ninety-nine parts of water may produce a moldable gel.

Nutritive Value

Gelatin is a protein food and is derived from animal sources, yet it is a protein of low biological value because of its lack of several essential amino acids, particularly tryptophan. Regardless of the quality of protein, the amount of gelatin required to form a gel is so small (1 tablespoon per pint of liquid) that its nutritive contribution is insignificant. One tablespoon of granulated gelatin furnishes about 30 kilocalories and 9 grams of protein.

Some gelatin desserts and salads may be a means of using significant amounts of fresh fruits and vegetables in the diet, but it is the added foods rather than the gelatin that are nutritionally valuable.

Preparation of Gelatin Mixtures

Hydration or Swelling.   Gelatin swells or becomes hydrated when soaked in cold water. Water molecules are attracted to the gelatin molecules and form a water shell around them. This aids in dispersing the gelatin in hot water.

The ease, rapidity, and extent of swelling depend on several factors. If the gelatin is finely granulated or pulverized, more surface is exposed to the water. Consequently, the rate of swelling is increased. The directions on the packages of most gelatin mixes suggest omitting the soaking in cold water and adding boiling water directly to the pulverized gelatin which has previously been mixed with sugar and flavorings.

The degree of acidity or alkalinity, the kinds of salts present, and the presence of sugar all influence the swelling of gelatin. Because the fruit acids and sugar used for flavor are usually not added until after the swelling and dispersing of unflavored gelatin have occurred, they are not of importance in the preparation of gelatin dishes other than those made from gelatin mixes. Sugar and certain salts inhibit swelling, whereas other salts accelerate it.

Dispersing Gelatin. When the temperature of soaked gelatin is elevated to 35° C (95° F) or above, the gelatin molecules separate or disperse. Some hot liquid may be added to the hydrated gelatin to disperse it, after which the remaining liquid may be added cold; or the hydrated gelatin may be suspended over hot water until dispersion takes place, after which all remaining liquid may be added cold. Adding all the remaining liquid as boiling liquid is unnecessary and is undesirable for two reasons: (1) more time is required to cool the mixture; and (2) some volatile flavor substances are lost with high temperatures.

Gelation. Gelation means gel formation or the setting or stiffening of a gelatin dispersion. Gelation does not occur at a fixed or clearly defined point but is a gradual process. It evidently involves the joining or linking together of gelatin molecules in various places to form the three-dimensional "brush-heap" structure that is typical for gels.

Effect of Temperature. Different samples of gelatin set at different temperatures, but all require cooling below the temperature of dispersion (35° C or 95° F). Gelatins that require a low temperature in order to solidify tend to liquefy readily when brought back to room temperature. Also, gelatin dispersions that have set quickly because they were subjected immediately to very low temperatures will melt more readily at room temperature than similar gelatin mixtures set at somewhat higher temperatures.

It is possible, because of rapid cooling, for a gelatin dispersion to remain liquid at temperatures that would ordinarily be low enough for gelation. It is sometimes necessary, because of time schedules, to chill gelatin dispersions rapidly and to hold them at low temperatures for quick setting. Sometimes ice cubes are added as part of the cold water to speed up the setting process. If more time is allowed, however, gelation occurs at a higher temperature. It is also true that it occurs more quickly at a cold temperature if the gelatin dispersion stands at room temperature for a time before being chilled. Temperatures required for the solidification of a gelatin dispersion vary from less than 10° C (50° F) to around 14° to 16° C (57° to 61° F).

Effect of Concentration. The concentration of the gelatin used affects not only the firmness of the gel but also the rate of setting.

Under home conditions, the usual percentage of gelatin in a gelatin mold of good texture is about 1.5 or 2.0 percent, depending on the ingredients used in the mixture. One tablespoon (7 grams) of un-flavored gelatin per 2 cups of liquid gives a gelatin concentration of about 1.5 percent. Beating the gelatin dispersion to a foam or sponge increases the volume sufficiently to decrease the firmness of the gel. A higher concentration of gelatin is thus required to produce a firm texture of sponge. Very weak dispersions of gelatin, such as those used in ice creams, will eventually set if given a long period of time and a low temperature. If excess gelatin is used in ice cream, gum-miness increases with longer storage.

Gels become stiffer with longer standing. Unless a relatively high concentration of gelatin is used, it is usually desirable to allow gela-tin mixtures to stand several hours or overnight at a low tempera-ture in order to develop optimum stiffness.

Effect of Acid. The fruit juices and vinegar that are frequently added to the gelatin mixtures used for desserts or salads increase the acidity of the dispersions. Too high a concentration of acid may prevent gelation or may cause the formation of a soft gel even when a fairly high concentration of gelatin is present. The use of lemon juice or vinegar produces a more pronounced effect on gelation than does tomato juice or some other fruit juices of lower acidity. Two tablespoons of lemon juice as part of 1 cup of liquid is usually enough for good flavor unless the dispersion is to be beaten to a foam. In this case, the flavor is diluted. This dispersion will form a more tender gel than one made without acid and yet is usually satis-factorily stiff even when no extra gelatin is added. Chopped vegeta-bles or diced fruits added to a gelatin dispersion may mechanically break up the gel or prevent its setting into a firm mass. If, in addi-tion, sufficient acid is used to give good flavor, the resulting gel may be much too weak to be desirable. The use of a somewhat higher concentration of gelatin may be necessary under such circum-stances. The time required for acid gelatin dispersions to set is greater than that required for neutral ones.

Effect of Salts. Gel strength is increased when milk is used as a liquid in gelatin mixtures. The effect of milk is probably the result of the salts that are present in milk. Even hard water that contains minerals produces a firmer gel than does distilled water.

Effect of Sugar. Sugar weakens a gelatin gel and retards the rate of setting. Usual recipes for gelatin mixtures have been adjusted so that the weakening effect of sugar is counterbalanced by the firming effect of increased gelatin concentration.

Effect of Raw Pineapple. The enzyme bromelin in fresh pineapple is a proteinase that digests or hydrolyzes protein. If it is not de-stroyed by heat before the pineapple is added to a gelatin dispersion, bromelin breaks down gelatin molecules so that they cannot form a gel. Since the heat of processing has destroyed the enzyme in canned pineapple pieces or juice, these products can be satisfactorily used in gelatin mixtures. Freezing does not affect the activity of the enzyme, however, and frozen pineapple cannot be used in a gelatin gel. Some other fruits, such as kiwi, also contain proteinases.

Types of Gelatin Desserts and Salads

Foams and Sponges. A gelatin dispersion may be beaten to form a foam. It increases two or three times its original volume, depending largely on the stage at which the dispersion is beaten. If beating is not started until the gelatin begins to set, the volume obtained will be small, and finely broken bits of solidified gelatin will be evident throughout the mass. The best stage for beating is when the dispersion is about the consistency of whipping cream or thin egg whites. The gelatin mixture is elastic and stretches to surround the air bubbles. Beating is continued until the mass is very stiff, in order to avoid the formation of a clear layer in the bottom of the mold. However, it may be necessary to stop and chill the beaten mixture again in the middle of beating because just the friction of continued beating can warm the mixture enough to thin it. On standing, the gelatin sets and stabilizes the foam. An increase in gelatin, sugar, and flavoring is required if the gelatin dispersion is to be beaten to a foam because the increased volume of a foam dilutes these ingredients.

Fillings for chiffon pies have gelatin as a basic foam stabilizer. In the preparation of most chiffon fillings, a custard mixture containing egg yolk and sugar is thickened with gelatin. Whipped egg whites and possibly whipped cream are folded into the mixture. The gelatin sets and stabilizes the egg and/or cream foam.

To form a sponge, after beating the syrupy gelatin mixture until it is thick and foamy, whipped egg white is beaten into the mixture. The sponge may be poured into molds and should be refrigerated until it solidifies.

Bavarian Cream. Gelatin mixtures that have stood long enough to be thickened and syrupy may have fruit pulp added and whipped cream folded into them to make Bavarian creams. Charlottes are similar to Bavarian creams but may contain a large proportion of whipped cream and are usually molded with lady fingers. Whipped evaporated or dried milks are sometimes substituted for whipped cream in gelatin desserts.

Fruit and Vegetable Gelatin Mixtures. Gelatin mixtures should stand until they are thickened and just ready to form a gel before fruits or vegetables are added to them. The thickening will disperse the added pieces evenly.

To unmold a gelatin gel, the mold containing the gel should be dipped for a few moments in lukewarm (not hot) water. One side of the gel should then be carefully loosened with a knife to allow air to come between the gel and the mold. The gel should then slide easily from the mold. The mold may be very lightly oiled before the gelatin mixture is placed in it in order to facilitate removal of the gel.

Study Questions

1. Gels of various types have common characteristics.
   a. Give several examples of food products that are gels.
   b. Describe the theoretical structure of a gel.
   c. What is syneresis?
2. What is gelatin? What is its source commercially?
3. In what forms is gelatin usually sold on the market?
4. How should unflavored gelatin be treated and why as it is used in the preparation of gelatin gels.
5. Describe what probably happens as gelatin forms a gel.
6. What is the effect of each of the following on the gelation of gelatin gels?
   a. Temperature
   b. Concentration of gelatin
   c. Addition of acid
   d. Addition of sugar
   e. Addition of raw pineapple
7. Describe major characteristics of each of the following gelatin mixtures:
   a. Foams
   b. Sponges
   c. Bavarian creams

References

1. Gross, J. 1961. Collagen. *Scientific American* **204,** 121 (no. 5).
2. Tanaka, T. 1981. Gels. *Scientific American* **244,** 124 (no. 1).
3. Ward, A. G., and A. Courts, editors. 1977. *The Science and Technology of Gelatin.* New York: Academic Press.

24

Coffee, Tea, and Cocoa

Coffee

The coffee plant is said to be a native of Abyssinia (now Ethiopia) and other parts of tropical Africa. It was introduced into Arabia in the fifteenth century and, later, both the growing of the plant and the custom of coffee drinking spread throughout the Eastern Hemisphere and to the Americas. Coffee was introduced into Java by the Dutch in the seventeenth century and later into South America. Brazil has become the largest coffee-producing country in the world. Central America, Colombia, Hawaii, and Puerto Rico have favorable climatic conditions for growing a fine grade of mild coffee.

The Coffee Plant

The coffee plant grows from 6 to 20 feet high depending on the species, the country in which it is grown, and the local custom of pruning. There are many varieties of coffee, but only a few are grown for commercial use. The original species native to Ethiopia and the one that is most commonly grown is *Coffea arabica,* but grown in different soils, altitudes, and climates this species takes on different characteristics. Arabica, which is now grown chiefly in Central and South America, has a fine full flavor and aroma. A second hardy variety commonly grown in Africa is *C. robusta.* Robusta coffee shrubs are best suited to growing at low elevations

508

(about 1,000 feet) and the beans are not as flavorful or as acid tasting as those from arabica coffee plants. The evergreen coffee plant bears white flowers, which give place to the fruit. When ripe, the fruit resembles a small cherry with the dark red pulp covering two oval beans, which grow with the flat sides together (Figures 24-1 and 24-2). The beans or seeds are the part used to make the coffee beverage.

Preparation and Blending of Beans

In the curing process that prepares the coffee beans for market, the cherries may be either dried for 2 to 3 weeks in the sun, or soaked, depulped, washed, and dried by machine. One curing process—the washed coffee process—makes use of pectic enzymes on selectively picked cherries to replace spontaneous fermentation.

The skin, pulp, parchment, and silverskin are all removed leaving the cleaned beans that are light green or blue-green in color. The green beans are then classified into six different sizes and graded to eliminate unripened and discolored beans, sticks, small stones, and other foreign matter. Next they are packed into jute or fiber bags and shipped to various markets. Green coffee may be stored for prolonged periods with no adverse effects.

Each variety of coffee has its own flavor and other characteristics. Coffee that is available to the consumer-buyer is usually a blend that may contain as many as five or six different varieties of coffee beans from as many countries. The blends are controlled for flavor, aroma, color, and strength or body of the beverage from the roasted bean. Blending is done by "creative artists" of the coffee world, who choose beans that will combine to eventually produce desirable brews and yet not be too expensive. Once a blend combination has been developed, it is continuously produced so that one brand of coffee will always have the same flavor and aroma.

Effects of Roasting

Green coffee beans have little flavor and aroma but these are developed by roasting. The beans expand to half again their original size and become more porous. The dull-green color changes to brown. Coffee roasts are classified according to the color of the roasted bean into the following: light roast, medium roast, dark roast, and Italian or French roast. The latter is very dark. A lighter roast is preferred by most Americans.

Moisture is lost during roasting, carbon dioxide gas is formed, and sugar is decomposed. Changes in the sugar, possibly in combination

24-1 *Flowers and fruit of the coffee tree.* (Courtesy of American Can Co.)

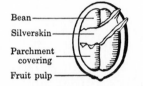

24-2 *Coffee berry with half of the fruit pulp removed.* (Courtesy of American Can Co.)

Bean
Silverskin
Parchment covering
Fruit pulp

with other substances, contribute much to the color of the beverage produced from the roasted beans.

Carbon dioxide gas appears to be lost gradually from roasted coffee on standing but is better retained in the bean than in ground coffee. Carbon dioxide is a desirable constituent of coffee both from the standpoint of the keeping quality and the retention of flavor and aroma substances. Flavor and aroma substances may be in some way tied up with the gas, or the presence of the gas may tend to prevent undesirable oxidation reactions on certain coffee constituents. At any rate, the loss of carbon dioxide is closely associated with loss of flavor and aroma.

Composition of Coffee

The constituents of coffee that are of significance in the making of the beverage include acids, volatile substances, bitter substances, and caffeine, which is desired by those who seek stimulation from the beverage but which is not desired by others who enjoy the flavor but not the stimulating effect of coffee. Ninety-five percent of the extract from green coffee beans has been accounted for in terms of well-known chemical compounds—proteins or amino acids, sugars, ash, acids, and others.

Organic Acids. Several organic acids are present in aqueous coffee extracts, including acetic, pyruvic, caffeic, chlorogenic, malic, citric, and tartaric. The predominant acid present is chlorogenic, which is somewhat sour and slightly bitter. It has been suggested that, in general, the more acid-tasting the coffee, the better are the aroma and flavor [7]. Coffee acidity is apparently affected by many factors including variety, altitude at which the plant is grown, processing of the fruit, age of the beans, and the degree of roasting of the beans.

Volatile Substances. Many of the volatile constituents contributing to the aroma of coffee have been identified [8]. Sulfur compounds and phenolic compounds are some of the main contributors to the characteristic aroma of coffee. Since many of the flavor substances in coffee are volatile or are changed by heat, too long a heating period at too high a temperature may remove or destroy the characteristic flavor and aroma. Long heating even at a low temperature may have the same effect. Reheating coffee beverage has been shown to decrease organoleptic acceptance by a judging panel at the same time that a loss of volatile substances was shown by gas chromatographic techniques [6]. Products from the decomposition of sucrose contribute some aroma, as well as bitterness and sourness, and are responsible for much of the color of the beverage.

Bitter Substances. Bitterness in coffee becomes more pronounced as the polyphenol content increases. Polyphenol solubility apparently increases with temperature and a boiling temperature releases polyphenols readily from the coffee bean. Caffeine contributes to bitterness. Also present in coffee are other substances that can produce distinctly bitter tastes.

Caffeine. Caffeine is one of a group of chemical compounds called methylxanthines occurring naturally in many species of plants, including the coffee bean. It produces the stimulating property of coffee and also contributes to bitterness. The caffeine content of brewed coffee varies from 110 to 150 mg per 5-ounce cup, depending upon the sample of coffee and the method of brewing [4]. Instant coffee has been reported to contain only 66 mg per serving [2].

By a chemical process, most of the caffeine can be removed from the green coffee bean to give what is called *decaffeinated coffee*. The solvents used to remove caffeine probably affect the flavor of the coffee to some extent, although a fresh sample of decaffeinated coffee has good flavor.

Coffee Substitutes and Adulterants

Coffee substitutes are parched cereals and/or roots that owe their flavor largely to the various products formed by heating. Coffees may have been adulterated in the past by adding ground cereal products to ground coffee. Chicory was also used as an adulterant. A blend of chicory with coffee is preferred by some nationalities and if purchased knowingly cannot be considered an adulteration. Chicory gives a darker color to the beverage but lacks the characteristic coffee flavor and aroma. It possesses no stimulating effect as does caffeine.

Coffee Staling

One of the most important factors affecting the quality of the coffee beverage is the freshness of the coffee used. Coffee is best when it is freshly roasted and deteriorates on standing. Because ground coffee becomes flat or stale more rapidly than coffee in the bean, and because coffee exposed to air changes more rapidly than coffee not so exposed, the chief cause of staleness has been assumed to be the oxidation of certain coffee constituents. However, the oxidation theory seems to be inadequate to explain all changes that are brought about in stale coffee. The fat of coffee apparently does not become rancid in the short time required for coffee to become stale.

Moisture has a very pronounced effect in decreasing the storage life of coffee. Tests on extracted volatile substances show that if the substances are sealed in a vacuum tube, changes are retarded; if the substances are exposed to air, changes occur rapidly; and if they are exposed to moisture, the changes are still more pronounced.

The effect of oxygen on roasted coffee is very rapid during the first 3 weeks and is thought to affect mainly the flavor constituents. After the first 3 weeks, the oxygen probably combines with the oils of the coffee, which results in the development of true rancidity several months later.

The proper sealing of roasted—especially ground—coffee is fundamental. The vacuum type of package from which air is removed before sealing affords more protection than other types of packages. Flavor deterioration in vacuum-packed coffee depends on the extent to which air is removed from the container. Another development involves the use of carbon dioxide gas under pressure in cans after the air is removed. It has been suggested that vacuum packed roasted and ground coffee in cans at a moisture content of 5 percent or less can be expected to have a storage life of at least 2 years [1]. Because of the rapid loss of flavor after grinding and exposure to the air, markets may have facilities for grinding coffee at the time of purchase.

After a container of vacuum packed coffee is opened, it should be stored, tightly covered, in a cool place, preferably at a temperature as low as 4° C (40° F), to retard staling. Moisture is particularly detrimental to the maintenance of coffee freshness. Contact with moist air should be kept at a minimum.

Preparation of Coffee Beverage

Grind and Quality of Coffee Used. Coffee may be ground to different degrees of fineness. Finely ground coffee, because of the greater surface exposed to water, gives more flavor per given weight than do coarser grinds. It has been recommended that only a fine grind should be used in a vacuum coffee maker; a medium grind or drip grind should be used for making coffee in a drip pot; and a coarse or regular grind is appropriate for use in a percolator. However, terminology on grinds differs and the effect of grind on beverage quality is not clearcut.

Good grades of coffee are characterized by a sharp, more desirable flavor as compared with the flat, neutral flavor of poor grades. A middle grade of coffee, purchased and used fresh, yields a better beverage than a high grade that is stale.

Methods. Instant coffee has gained wide acceptance because of its convenience but it has not replaced brewed coffee. Good coffee may be brewed by several methods (Figure 24-3). In each method it is important to control the temperature of the water and the time

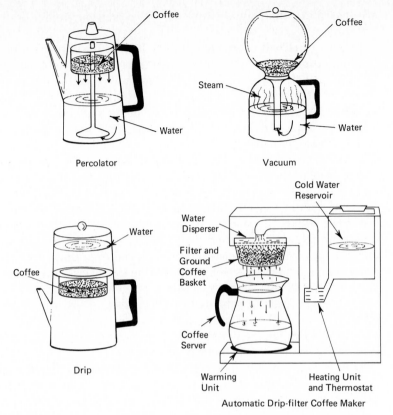

Coffee

Water

Percolator

Steam

Coffee

Water

Vacuum

Water

Coffee

Drip

Cold Water
Reservoir

Water
Disperser

Filter and
Ground
Coffee
Basket

Coffee
Server

Warming
Unit

Heating Unit
and Thermostat

Automatic Drip-filter Coffee Maker

that the coffee is in contact with the water. The temperature of the water should be at least 85° C (185° F) to extract a desirable amount of soluble solids. However, it should not be hotter than 95° C (203° F) to avoid extraction of excessive amounts of bitter substances and loss of many volatile flavor substances.

The amount of coffee used in relation to the water determines the initial strength of the brew. From 1 to 3 tablespoons of coffee per cup (8 ounces) of water will give brews ranging from weak to very strong. From 1⅓ to 1½ tablespoons of coffee per cup of water give a medium strength brew.

Filtration. The drip or filtration method is probably the most easily and successfully used by a majority of persons. By this method, the water filters through the coffee into a lower compartment of the coffee maker. The drip pot consists of an upper compartment, which is perforated, and a lower compartment, which is a receiver for the filtered beverage. The perforations of the upper compartment are covered with thin filter paper or with cheesecloth to prevent the passage of coffee into the beverage. If the perforations are too small, the rate of filtration is too slow to yield a desirable beverage.

The drip method probably extracts less of the bitter substances than do other methods. If not allowed to boil or not held too long in being kept hot, coffee made by the drip method retains more of the flavor constituents than coffees made by other methods. Probably all methods extract a high percentage of the caffeine.

Another type of pot for the filtration method is the vacuum coffee maker. The upper compartment, which holds the coffee, has an open tube that extends almost to the bottom of the lower compartment. Coffee is usually prevented from passing into the lower compartment by the use of a cloth-covered disk, which is held in place over the tube opening. Some models have a glass rod that fits the tube opening instead of the disk. Water is placed in the lower compartment and the pot is heated until most of the water rises into the upper compartment. The pot is then removed from the source of heat until the water filters through the coffee and passes back into the lower compartment. The upper compartment is then removed and the beverage carefully reheated to a desirable temperature for serving. The chief difficulty in the use of this method is that the coffee may not be hot when served or that in being kept hot it may boil, thus losing much of the flavor and aroma.

Percolation. In this method, the heated water is forced upward through a tube into the coffee compartment. The water filters through the coffee several times before the beverage becomes of desirable strength. The water is probably not actually at the boiling point when it is in contact with the coffee but the beverage is close to the boiling point when it is ready to be served. Unless the construction of the pot is good and the time of percolating is carefully controlled, much of the flavor and aroma may be lost by this method. The time required varies with the speed of percolation and with the quantity of coffee made. Usually 6 to 8 minutes is adequate to make 4- to 6-cup portions of coffee.

Steeping. Although coffee made by this method is sometimes described as boiled, the beverage made by heating the coffee and water together is more desirable in flavor if it is not actually allowed to boil. Steeping (extracting flavor below the boiling point) extracts much less of the bitter substances from coffee than does boiling. Coffee boiled 1 minute is distinctly more bitter than coffee heated from a temperature of 85° (185° F) to 95° C (203° F). This method may be convenient for use on picnics and camping excursions. If egg white is mixed with the coffee before water is added, the temperature must go high enough to coagulate the dilute solution of egg in order to clarify the beverage. The flavor of boiled coffee made with egg is more bland than of that made without egg because of the combination of egg albumin with the polyphenol compounds. The length of time of steeping varies with the temperature of water mixed with the coffee and with the fineness of the coffee grind. Hot water is preferable to use because the time required for making the beverage is shorter than when cold water is used. Short infusion periods usually yield better flavored coffee than do longer periods.

Other Factors That Affect Coffee Beverage.

Material from Which the Pot is Made. Tin is the least desirable of metals for coffee pots but even silver has an influence on the flavor of the beverage. Some metals form compounds with caffeine and probably with other constituents of coffee. Metallic pots impart a metallic flavor to coffee. Pots made of glass, earthenware, or enameled ware may be used. Stainless steel is resistant to attack and, therefore, its effect on the flavor of coffee is negligible. Chrome and nickel plating show no staining or corrosion when used in a coffee pot.

Water. Soft water or water of low hardness gives coffee a more desirable flavor than does very hard or alkaline water. Water having a high carbonate or bicarbonate content and water that has passed through an ion-exchange softening system (thus high in sodium ions) will not filter through coffee in a drip or vacuum pot as rapidly as naturally soft water. This means increased time of contact with the coffee and an increased amount of material extracted that can be objectionable. Experimental coffee was prepared using solutions of 8 minerals each at 750 parts per million [5]. Those containing carbonates were the least desirable, having flat, insipid characteristics. Coffee prepared from distilled water was excessively sour. Changes in the visual characteristics of the coffee were observed with the various kinds of water used.

Temperature. Probably 85° to 95° C (185° to 203° F) are optimum temperatures for brewing a good coffee beverage. Boiling gives a distinctly bitter beverage. Polyphenol substances are more soluble at boiling temperature than at a temperature of 95° C (203° F). The longer the heating period even at lower temperatures, the higher is the percentage of bitter substances dissolved and the greater is the loss of flavor substances. The caffeine is nearly all dissolved at a temperature of 85° to 95° C (185° to 203° F) and the flavor substances are not lost as much as at higher temperatures. Boiling water may be used to start the preparation of coffee because the temperature at once drops when the water comes in contact with the coffee and the pot.

Cleanliness of Pot. A clean coffee pot is one of the essentials in the making of a good coffee beverage. Washing the pot with hot soapy water or scouring is necessary in order to remove the oily film that collects on the inside of the coffee pot. Thorough rinsing is essential. A pot that retains a stale coffee odor is not a clean pot and will mar the flavor of the best made coffee.

Iced Coffee. A sparkling iced beverage that possesses the maximum amount of flavor is made by pouring a freshly made, strong coffee infusion over crushed ice in a glass. Strong infusions, whether combined hot or cold with ice, are made with a larger than usual amount of coffee per cup of water rather than by longer than usual infusion periods. Long infusion periods decrease flavor and aroma and increase bitterness.

Instant Coffee Products

Instant or soluble coffee is very convenient to use. It is composed of dry, powdered, water-soluble solids produced by dehydrating very strong, brewed coffee, which is often percolated under vacuum to minimize the loss of flavor substances. It may have some carbohydrate added. The flavor of instant coffee is similar to that of freshly brewed coffee but the aroma is usually somewhat lacking in comparison with the fresh-brewed beverage.

Some soluble coffees are freeze-dried. In this process the strong, brewed coffee is first frozen and then dried by vaporization in a vacuum. Like instant coffees produced by other methods, the freeze-dried products are reconstituted by adding boiling water according to directions on the package. Soluble coffees should be kept packaged in water- and air-tight containers because they are hygroscopic and tend to absorb moisture.

Tea

Tea is a widely used beverage produced from the dried shoots of an evergreen shrub of the species *Thea*, chiefly *Thea sinensis*. The principal tea-producing areas of the world are India, Sri Lanka, China, Indonesia, and Japan. Teas vary according to the age of the leaf, the season of plucking, the altitude, the soil, and climatic conditions, as well as the method of manufacture.

The Tea Plant

The tea plant is pruned and cultivated to produce many young shoots. Pluckings extend over a period of several months, the spring and early summer leaves yielding better tea than late summer and autumn pluckings. Grades of tea are largely determined by the location and size of the leaf. The young unopened leaf buds at the tip of the shoot rank first in quality. Quality decreases as the size of the leaf increases toward the lower end of the shoot (Figure 24-4). The

quality of tea is also influenced by the climate and soil where the tea is grown and by the processing.

Processing of Tea

There are three principal types of tea depending upon the method of processing the leaves. These are green, black, and oolong. Any size of leaf may be made into any one of these types of tea.

Black Teas. Most of the tea consumed in the United States is black tea. In its manufacture, the leaves are withered and rolled to break tissues and release juices and are then held and allowed to undergo oxidative changes catalyzed by enzymes in the leaves. After this they are heated and dried. The process of holding is called *fermentation*. During fermentation, polyphenolic substances are oxidized and some new phenolic products result. The color of the leaf changes to black. The beverage made from black tea has an amber color, is less bitter and astringent than green tea, and has a rich aroma and flavor.

Generally, the best grade of black tea is Broken Orange Pekoe. Other grades include Broken Pekoe (used as a filler in blends), Orange Pekoe, Pekoe, Souchong, Fannings, and Dust. Teas from various countries are blended to give uniform flavor, strength, and color.

Green Tea. Green tea, which is produced in Japan, is made by first steaming the leaves to inactivate the enzymes. Steaming is then followed by rolling and drying. The leaf retains much of its original green color, especially the finer leaves. The older leaves often have a blackish gray color. The beverage made from green tea has a greenish-yellow color and is distinctly bitter and astringent. It has little aroma and flavor as compared with black tea because the preliminary steaming destroys the enzymes that produce flavor substances during the fermentation of black tea. Less than 5 percent of the world's tea is made into green tea. Grades of green tea include Gunpowder, Young Hyson, Hyson, and Imperial.

Oolong Tea. Oolong tea is a partially fermented tea. The fermentation period is too short to change the color of the leaf completely; it is only partially blackened. The beverage is intermediate between those produced from green and black teas.

Market Forms of Tea

There is a wide variety of teas available on the market. Much of the tea sold in the average supermarket is in the form of tea bags for convenient brewing. Some of these contain decaffeinated tea. Many scented or flavored teas are marketed. These teas contain such flavorings as oils of peppermint, strawberry, orange, or lemon; spices such as cinnamon or cloves; blackberry leaves; and licorice root.

Instant teas are dried products prepared from brewed teas. These teas are particularly useful for preparing iced tea. One simply disperses the tea in cold water, adds ice, and serves. Instant tea mixes already contain sugar and flavoring such as lemon. These mixes are also available as low calorie products sweetened with aspartame or saccharin.

A number of herb teas are available in many supermarkets. They often contain a mixture of several dried products such as strawberry leaves, apples, hibiscus flowers, rosehips, peppermint, ginger, nutmeg, cinnamon, chamomile, and alfalfa.

Composition

The alkaloid substance that gave tea its stimulating property was formerly designated *theine,* but the substance has been shown to be identical with caffeine. The tea beverage contains somewhat less caffeine than does coffee but the content depends upon the method of brewing. Tea has been reported to contain from as little as 9 to as much as 50 mg of caffeine per 5-ounce cup [2, 4]. Herb teas generally do not contain caffeine.

The flavor of tea is influenced by the presence of considerable quantities of polyphenolic substances that are particularly responsible for astringency. Some of the polyphenols are changed in the oxidation process that takes place when black tea is fermented and contribute to the characteristic aroma and flavor of this tea. The degradation of other substances, including linolenic acid, amino acids, and carotenes, during the process of manufacturing black tea may also contribute to flavor and aroma.

Preparation of Tea Beverage

Water. Soft water is as preferable to hard alkaline water in making tea as it is in making coffee. The polyphenol substances in tea may interact with certain salts in hard water to produce an undesirable precipitate. The water should be freshly boiled with still enough oxygen in it to prevent the flat taste that results from the loss of dissolved gases by boiling.

The Teapot. Metallic pots impart a metallic taste to the tea beverage. Glass, earthenware, enameled ware, or other vitrified ware is recommended for making tea because of the large amount of polyphenolic substances in tea.

Temperature. Temperatures slightly under boiling are less likely to volatilize flavor and aroma substances than is boiling temperature. Boiling water is quickly reduced in temperature, however, when poured over tea leaves. A lid on the teapot helps to retain heat and prevent the escape of volatile substances. The optimum time of contact between hot water and tea will vary somewhat with the temperature of the water. A steeping period of 2 to 6 minutes is appropriate at a temperature between 85° and 93° C (185° and 199° F).

Methods. The soluble substances of the tea leaves are extracted in the beverage. Most persons object to bitterness in beverages and because the polyphenol content of tea is fairly high, too long steeping, especially at a temperature at or near the boiling point, extracts more bitter polyphenol substances than is desirable. These substances are more soluble in boiling water than in water under the boiling temperature. Flavor substances and caffeine are readily extracted by short infusion periods. The aim in making tea is to extract the maximum flavor with a minimum of polyphenol compounds. Strong beverages of good flavor require more of the beverage-making constituents rather than long infusion periods. The latter result in bitter beverages having a disagreeable flavor.

What constitutes a desirable strength of tea beverage is largely a matter of individual opinion. The usual proportion of tea per cup of water is about 1 teaspoon, although when steeping periods are prolonged or when the quantity of beverage made is larger, as little as ½ to ¾ of a teaspoon gives a better beverage.

Tea-ball Method. The tea-ball method in which water at the boiling temperature or just under boiling is poured over tea in a cheese-cloth or paper bag, or a silver ball, is one of the most desirable methods of making tea. The ball or bag, may be allowed to remain in contact with the water until the desired strength is obtained, after which it is removed. A modification of this method is often used for making tea in large quantity. The measured tea is placed in a wire strainer and the hot water is poured once through the tea.

Steeping. Another method consists of placing the measured tea in a preheated pot and pouring the boiling water into the pot. The pot is then covered and allowed to stand in a warm place until the desired strength is obtained. Steeping periods usually range from 2 to 4 minutes, depending on the temperature and the strength desired. If the maximum quantity of tea is used, 4 minutes may give a somewhat bitter beverage. The tea should be poured from the grounds immediately to avoid excess bitterness in later portions of tea served from the pot.

Iced Tea. Iced tea, a favorite drink in the United States, is best made from a larger proportion of tea to water than is usually used for hot tea because melting ice dilutes the beverage. Long steeping to brew a beverage strong enough to stand dilution extracts too many polyphenol substances. It is believed that a cloudy beverage may result from a complex formed between caffeine and some of the polyphenol substances. This complex formation may occur more readily in iced than in hot tea and is encouraged when larger amounts of polyphenol substances are present. Diluting strong infusions while they are hot is an aid in preventing cloudiness.

For sweetening iced tea with sugar, it is desirable to use an extra-fine granulation that is quickly soluble.

If mint flavor is desired in iced tea, the mint leaves may be crushed and added to the tea leaves before the boiling water is added, or a sprig of mint may be served in the glass of iced tea.

The lightening of tea with added lemon is the result of the change of color of oxidized polyphenol compounds in an acid medium. These substances tend to be dark-colored in an alkaline medium.

Cocoa and Chocolate

Cocoa and chocolate are made by grinding the seeds of pods of the cacao tree. The pods are 4 to 7 inches in diameter, having thick leathery rinds containing seeds inside in rows. The seeds are embedded in a white or pinkish pulp (Figure 24-5).

The seeds are first fermented to decrease the bitter taste, after which they are roasted, shelled, and cracked. Roasting develops flavor. There are many varieties of cacao beans or seeds and the great

24-5 *Cacao pods have a semiwoody shell that does not readily yield to the blow of a cutlass. One or two well-aimed blows from an expert, or perhaps three or four from a less experienced worker, are usually required before the contents of the pod are laid bare. Pods carry anywhere from 20 to 50 beans.* (Courtesy of the Nestlé Co.)

variation in flavor, color, and other characteristics that exist in cocoa and chocolate products is explained on the basis of the varieties of seeds used to make them.

The cracked seeds are known as *nibs* and usually there is some blending of the nibs of different varieties of cacao before the nibs are ground. If no fat is removed from the nibs before grinding, the temperature maintained during grinding (32° C or 90° F) and the high fat content result in a fluid mass that is run into molds, where it hardens, producing cake chocolate. For some types of chocolate, milk solids, cocoa butter (the fat from cacao beans), sugar, and flavoring are added before the liquor is molded.

When the liquor is to be used for making cocoa some of the fat is removed by pressure. If sufficient fat is removed, the ground product is a powder instead of a paste.

Cocoas may be divided into two main classes: natural-process, and Dutch-process. Some chocolate is also Dutch-processed. Dutch-processing consists of treating the nibs with alkali, the object being to increase the reddish color and the solubility. The latter effect is accomplished to only a slight degree. The color of Dutched cocoa is distinctly darker than that of natural-process cocoa, and the characteristic chocolate flavor is diminished by the alkali treatment. The pH of Dutch-processed cocoa is 6.0 to 8.8 and that of natural-process cocoa is usually 5.2 to 6.0. The color of products such as chocolate cake may range from cinnamon brown to deep mahogany red as the pH changes from acid to alkaline (see p. 481). A number of instant cocoa mixtures are available, which contain sugar, flavorings, emulsifiers, and sometimes nonfat dry milk. Instant cocoa mixtures sweetened with aspartame and/or saccharin are also produced for the low calorie market.

Composition of Cocoa and Chocolate

Fat. According to the U.S. Food and Drug Administration standard of identity, chocolate contains not less than 50 percent and not more than 58 percent by weight of cacao fat. The high fat content of chocolate produces a richer beverage than one made from cocoa. Cocoas may vary in fat content. Breakfast cocoa is a high-fat cocoa and must contain at least 22 percent of cacao fat.

When cocoa is substituted for chocolate, particularly in baked products, approximately 3 tablespoons of cocoa plus 1 tablespoon of fat are considered to be equivalent to 1 ounce of chocolate.

The fat of chocolate contributes much to its eating quality because it has a sharp melting point that is close to body temperature. This results in rapid melting of the chocolate in the mouth with a smooth, velvety feel and the release of flavor substances. The dipping of chocolate is discussed in Chapter 15, Sweeteners and Sugar Cookery.

Starch. Cocoa contains about 11 percent starch and chocolate contains about 8 percent starch. In preparing a beverage from cocoa and chocolate, a method that cooks the starch results in a more homogeneous beverage in which there is less tendency for the cocoa or chocolate to settle out than does a method of preparation in which no heat is applied. Starch is an important constituent of cocoa and chocolate when the latter are used in flour mixtures. The thickening effect must be taken into account in the amount of flour used. If cocoa is substituted directly on the basis of weight for chocolate it thickens more than does chocolate.

Flavor Substances. The exact identity of the many flavor substances in chocolate and cocoa has not been fully established, although it is known that they are partly volatile substances. The flavor of chocolate and cocoa undergoes marked changes when these substances are heated to high temperatures, especially without water. Bitter, disagreeable flavors are developed and scorching occurs easily.

Phenolic Substances. Phenolic substances in the cacao bean are evidently highly important constituents from the standpoint of color and flavor. Phenolic compounds undergo oxidation to form compounds of reddish-brown color. These substances are insoluble in water. Some of the astringent substance of the fresh unfermented bean has an extremely bitter taste. This substance undergoes a change during fermentation and is present to a very small extent in the fermented bean.

Theobromine and Caffeine. Cocoa and chocolate contain the alkaloid substances *theobromine* and caffeine, but chiefly the former [3]. Theobromine is a milder stimulant than caffeine. The caffeine content of cocoa beverage prepared with Dutch process cocoa was reported to range from 10 to 17 mg per cup [2].

Effect of Heat and Moisture

Heat and moisture rapidly destroy the gloss on the outside of a cake of chocolate. A mottled or gray surface known as *bloom* may develop. This bloom is probably caused by melting of some of the fat and the recrystallization of the melted fat in a different form at the surface of the chocolate. The use of proper tempering temperatures and time periods during the manufacturing process, and the use of stabilizers and modifiers, have resulted in the retardation of bloom formation. However, the avoidance of high storage temperatures is still of importance in maintaining the quality of chocolate.

The ideal temperature and humidity for storing cocoa is around 16° to 21° C (61° to 70° F) and 50 to 65 percent relative humidity. Cocoas tend to lump and lose their brown color if they are stored in too moist an atmosphere or at too high a temperature. Although the flavor of chocolate products is usually not impaired by bloom or lumping, the products appear stale and the mouth-feel of solid sweetened chocolate may be granular. Milk chocolate absorbs flavors and odors and should be stored where this cannot happen.

When chocolate is melted care must be used to avoid overheating, which may produce a firm, lumpy mass that will not blend with other ingredients. A low to moderate temperature should be applied to chocolate that has been shaved or chopped into pieces. Heating the chocolate over hot water lessens the danger of overheating. The use of chocolate in coating confections is discussed on pp. 376–378.

Methods for Making Beverage

A quick method of pouring hot liquid over a cocoa-sugar mixture in the cup does not cook the starch sufficiently to prevent the cocoa from settling out. With instant cocoa mixes the addition of a stabilizer or emulsifier may help keep the particles dispersed. Preparation of the beverage by either a syrup or a paste method should produce more desirable body and flavor than usually results from simply pouring hot liquid over a cocoa-sugar mixture.

Syrup Method

COCOA	CHOCOLATE
2 t to 1 T cocoa	⅓ ounce chocolate, shaved fine
2 t to 1 T sugar	1 to 1½ T sugar
¼ c water	⅓ c water

Make a syrup by boiling either of these two lists of ingredients for 2 or 3 minutes. Evaporation will reduce the volume. Add ¾ cup of hot milk. The syrup can be made in quantity and stored in the refrigerator.

Paste Method

½ T cornstarch	1 ounce chocolate (or 3 T cocoa)
⅓ c water	2 T sugar

Boil for 2 or 3 minutes. Combine with 2 cups of hot milk. The purpose of the cornstarch is to give a beverage with more body and to prevent more satisfactorily any tendency of the cocoa to settle.

Because milk is a prominent constituent of cocoa or chocolate beverages, scum formation may occur. It can be retarded by covering the pan or by beating the mixture to produce a light foam. High temperatures, which may scorch both the milk and chocolate, should be avoided. (See Chapter 12, Milk and Milk Products.)

Nutritive Value of Cocoa and Chocolate Beverages

Because cocoa and chocolate beverages are usually made with milk, they have a food value similar to milk in proportion to the amount of milk used. Unlike tea leaves and coffee grounds, which are strained from the beverages, cocoa and chocolate remain in the beverage, thus adding fat and starch to the milk to increase the caloric value.

Study Questions

1. From what is coffee made and how is it processed to make it ready for use in preparing a beverage?
2. List the constituents of coffee that contribute to its quality as a beverage and describe the contributions each constituent makes.
3. Describe conditions that will aid in preserving freshness in coffee, both in the bean and ground.
4. a. Describe three methods for preparing coffee.
   b. What types of material are preferable for coffee pots and why?

    c. How does the type of water used affect coffee quality?

    d. Why should coffee not be boiled? Explain.

    e. How is instant coffee produced?

5. Describe differences in processing and characteristics of black, green, and oolong teas.

6. a. Describe two appropriate procedures for the preparation of tea.

    b. Discuss the importance of the type of water, the teapot, and the temperature in the preparation of tea of good quality.

    c. Discuss several factors that are important in the preparation of iced tea.

7. What is the source of chocolate and cocoa and how are they processed?

8. a. How do natural-process and Dutch-process cocoa differ?

    b. How do chocolate and breakfast cocoa differ in fat and in starch content?

    c. How might cocoa be appropriately substituted for chocolate in a recipe?

9. What is responsible for the development of a whitish or gray mottled surface on chocolate that has been stored? Explain.

10. Suggest a satisfactory method for preparing cocoa beverage and explain why this is a good method.

References

1. Adinolfi, J. 1981. How long is coffee's shelf life? *Food Technology* **35,** 42 (no. 6).

2. Bunker, M. L., and M. McWilliams. 1979. Caffeine content of common beverages. *Journal of the American Dietetic Association* **74,** 28.

3. DeVried, J. W., K. D. Johnson, and J. C. Heroff. 1981. HPLC determination of caffeine and theobromine content of various natural and red dutched cocoas. *Journal of Food Science* **46,** 1968.

4. Institute of Food Technologists' Expert Panel on Food Safety and Nutrition. 1983. Caffeine. *Food Technology* **37,** 87 (no. 4).

5. Pangborn, R. M., I. M. Trabue, and A. C. Little. 1971. Analysis of coffee, tea and artificially flavored drinks prepared from mineralized waters. *Journal of Food Science* **36,** 355.

6. Segall, S., C. Silver, and S. Bacino. 1970. The effect of reheat upon the organoleptic and analytical properties of beverage coffee. *Food Technology* **24,** 54 (No. 11).

7. Sivetz, M. 1972. How acidity affects coffee flavor. *Food Technology* **26,** 70 (no. 5).

8. Vitzthum, O. G., and P. Werkhoff. 1974. Oxazoles and thiazoles in coffee aroma. *Journal of Food Science* **39,** 1210.

25
Microwave Cooking

Microwave energy has been available for use in the heating and cooking of foods since the 1950s. The first manufactured models of microwave ovens, however, were large, heavy, expensive, and required special wiring. There have been many changes in recent years in the type and cost of equipment available on the U.S. market for microwave cooking, and microwave ovens are being purchased in increasing numbers for home use. In 1969 there were an estimated 40,000 microwave units in use in the United States. This figure had increased to over 9 million by 1978 [6]. With the widespread use of microwave cooking has come an interest by the food industry in producing food products designed for microwave preparation.

Although the microwave oven is used in the home to cook a wide variety of foods, its predominant use remains that of warming up or defrosting. A survey of microwave usage in the Phoenix area [6] found that 36.2 percent of the use was for this purpose. This same survey also noted that the amount of organized instruction on the use of the microwave oven was a major determinant in the satisfaction experienced in the results of microwave cooking. Those who had received one or more days of instruction were more consistently satisfied with the results. In addition to home use, the microwave oven is used in many operations in the food-processing industries and in food-service systems, such as hospital food-service where foods may be cooked, chilled, and reheated in the microwave oven just before serving [3].

The cooking of vegetables, meats, and some starch and flour mixtures by microwaves is discussed in Chapters 7, 10, 17, 20, 21, and 22. General principles of microwave cookery are included in this chapter.

Action of Microwaves in Heating

Microwaves are high-frequency waves, falling between light waves and radio waves in frequency, that are generated in a vacuum tube called a *magnetron*. The magnetron converts alternating electric current from a household circuit into electromagnetic energy radiation. A stirrer blade in the top of the oven helps to distribute the waves produced.

The Federal Communications Commission has assigned certain frequencies for microwave cooking to avoid interference with communication systems that operate close to the frequencies used for microwave ovens. The assigned frequencies for microwave ovens are 915 and 2450 megahertz (million cycles per second). The higher the frequency, the shorter is the wavelength and the more shallow is the depth of penetration of the waves into the food being cooked. At a frequency of 2450 megahertz, the wavelength is approximately 4.8 inches, whereas at a frequency of 915 megahertz, the wavelength is about 13.5 inches long. The shorter wavelengths produce more uniform heating and better results for small items being cooked. Microwave cooking may be satisfactorily accomplished at either frequency, however.

Microwave ovens may have variable power features that allow cooking on "high" or on "simmer." A radiation safety standard for the manufacture of microwave ovens is enforced by the U.S. Food and Drug Administration. The standard limits the amount of microwaves that can leak from an oven throughout its lifetime [5].

Microwaves are absorbed by the food in the oven. This energy entering the food causes the molecules in the food to vibrate as a result of the rapid movement that occurs as they keep reversing their positions in order to realign themselves in the rapidly changing microwave field. This vibration produces friction that creates heat within the food, thereby cooking it. Further distribution of the heat, particularly toward the center of a relatively large mass of food, may occur by conduction.

The short, straight microwaves are reflected by metals. The metal walls of a microwave oven reflect and thus contain the microwaves within the oven cavity. Microwaves reach the food that is to be cooked both directly from the magnetron unit and indirectly by reflection from the metal walls.

One of the great advantages of using a microwave oven is the speed with which cooking may be accomplished, which results in considerable savings of time in cooking. Microwave cooking is two to ten times faster than with the use of conventional methods, depending on the volume and type of food being cooked. The microwave oven is generally not designed for quantity cookery, and the time of cooking must be lengthened as the quantity of food cooked is increased. One potato, for example, may cook in 4 to 6 minutes in a microwave oven, whereas four potatoes will require 16 to 19 minutes to cook.

The relationship between the quantity of food to be prepared in a microwave oven and the total cooking time appears to be a simple, linear one. Almost without exception, the total cooking time will be the time for a particular unit of food (such as an egg, an ear of corn, or a pound of meat) times the number of units to be cooked together.

The microwave oven has a real advantage in the saving of energy. On tests with a variety of food types and menus cooked in a microwave oven and on the surface units and oven of a conventional electric range, it has been shown that the microwave oven consumed less energy in 100 of 127 tests [8]. In other studies of energy use with various cooking methods, surface cooking and microwave cooking were comparable and cost the least, followed by broiling and baking [9]. There is an additional saving of energy from microwave cooking through the lesser amount of dishwashing that is usually required. Energy efficiency will probably become an increasingly important consideration in evaluating cooking methods [7].

Another advantage of microwave cooking is that only the food is heated during cooking. The oven itself does not become hot. The nonmetal materials used to hold the food during cooking do not become hot, except when cooking periods are relatively long and some heat is conducted from the food to the container in which it is held.

A limitation of the microwave oven is that foods cooked in short periods of time do not become brown on the surface as do many foods that are baked or roasted in a conventional oven or cooked in a skillet. With many baked products, particularly, a browned surface is very desirable. A loaf of bread without a crisp, golden-brown crust does not have the same appeal as one that possesses these characteristics. To overcome to some degree the problems created by lack of browning, some earlier microwave oven models included a regular broiler unit in the top of the oven that could be operated without interfering with the movement of the microwaves. The element could be used only briefly because the oven became too hot. Some companies have combined a conventional electric oven with a microwave oven in the same compartment, whereas others have provided conventional electric ovens as part of a cooking center. A microwave-convection oven combination is also available.

Another innovation is a browning grill, which is a platelike object of a special composition (patented by Raytheon Company in 1958), having the ability to absorb microwave energy and become heated up to a temperature of approximately 232° to 288° C (450° to 550° F). The food is placed on the browning grill. The grill with the food on it is then put in another container for cooking in the microwave oven so that the hot browning grill does not need to be handled when food is removed from the oven. Special browning skillets contain a special material built into the bottom with the same ability to absorb the microwaves and convert them to heat. An infrared-type element has also been included in some ovens to produce browning.

Microwave cooking has special advantages in reheating precooked foods and in thawing frozen foods, both individually packaged and packaged in meals. In a survey of microwave owners it was found that they generally preferred their microwave ovens to conventional appliances for cooking convenience meat items, casseroles, and all types of vegetables [4]. The microwave oven not only reheats precooked foods more quickly than conventional cooking but a reheated or leftover flavor is also avoided. Conventional appliances were generally preferred by microwave oven owners for cooking large cuts of meat and for baked products.

The advantages of microwave cooking will undoubtedly increase in the future as more is learned about its practical use. With changing patterns of living and the use of more precooked and frozen foods, many of which are designed with the microwave oven in mind, the speed and convenience of microwave cooking will probably be found even more desirable.

Containers Used in Cooking

Glass, paper, ceramic, and most plastic materials are transparent to microwaves and allow them to pass through. Thus these materials are useful as containers to hold the food that is to be cooked. Since metals reflect microwaves, when they are used as containers to hold the food the heating is likely to be uneven. It is also possible that the magnetron unit itself may be damaged. However, the Aluminum Foil Container Manufacturers Association has suggested a method that may be used to satisfactorily heat frozen foods packaged in aluminum foil containers [1]. This procedure involves (1) removing the foil container from the carton and taking off the lid; (2) returning the container to the carton, leaving one end-flap partially open to eliminate the risk of arcing; and (3) placing the carton in the microwave oven and heating.

A variety of wide-mouth glass containers containing various commercially prepared foods such as spaghetti sauce and baked beans that were canned in the jars have been tested for reheating in the microwave oven [10]. The test results indicated that consumer microwave reheating of these commercially canned foods in the wide-mouth glass containers is feasible. Closures should be removed before heating and the jar opening covered with plastic wrap or waxed paper to avoid splattering. To assure uniform heating, the contents should be stirred at least once midway through heating.

General Cooking Methods with Microwave Energy

Most foods that are to be cooked in microwave ovens are prepared very much as they are for conventional cooking. There are some slight differences in the cooking procedures, however. Containers used for cooking must be properly selected from materials that transmit microwaves.

The cooking time is directly related to the volume of food being cooked by microwave energy. The larger the food item, the longer it will take to cook. There will also be slightly more cooking on the outside than on the inside of the food because microwave energy decreases as it goes deeper inside a food. Large volumes of food, such as roasts of meat, will brown during cooking in a microwave oven because cooking time is relatively long, but smaller quantities of food cooked for short periods of time will need to be browned by some means other than the use of microwave energy. The optimum time for cooking should not be overextended. Drying out of food occurs very rapidly with only slight overcooking when using microwaves.

Power is unevenly distributed in the microwave oven. Because of this, foods need to be turned around, turned over, stirred, or relocated in the oven at various times during cooking. Items such as individual potatoes, custard cups, etc. should be placed in a circle. Some microwave ovens contain a revolving carousel. Parts of a food may be shielded with small amounts of metal foil to prevent overcooking.

Cooking will continue in a food for several minutes after it is removed from the microwave oven. This should be taken into account when cooking time is determined. Some foods may be cooked in the microwave oven directly from the frozen state. However, for frozen foods with large volumes, such as whole poultry, a short thawing period in the microwave oven should be followed by a few minutes of standing out of the oven to allow the temperature to be equalized throughout the food before cooking is continued.

Some foods cannot be successfully prepared in a microwave oven at the present time. These include soufflés and angel food cakes. Special instructions and recipes are available from the manufacturers of microwave ranges and should be followed in the use of their particular models. It is especially important to follow directions in the manufacturer's booklet on use and care for good, safe results with the microwave oven.

Microwave ovens are widely used, in both homes and institutions, for the reheating of fully cooked plated meals. Individual meal items should be chosen and grouped so that they will be compatible in terms of rapidity and uniformity of heating. Placement on the plate is also important for optimal heating and maintenance of quality in the heated meal. Dense meal items heat slowly and with some difficulty. These include baked potatoes, mounded mashed potatoes, lasagna more than ½ inch thick, cabbage rolls, stuffed peppers, and thickly sliced meat or fish. Examples of meal items that heat more rapidly and easily include piped, extruded, spaghettilike mashed potatoes; mashed potatoes with the center pressed down and a butter pat placed in the depression; very light and fluffy stuffing for stuffed peppers or a center in the pepper composed of toast sticks or pastry; thinly sliced meats, centered on the plate with gravy draining over the meat; and thinly portioned fish without sauce.

In a rectangular dish, the faster heating locations are at the corners or ends and the center heats slower. Denser, thicker, solid items, such as steaks and chops, should be placed at the sides. Subdivided vegetables or loose rice and pasta should be placed in the center.

Study Questions

1. What are microwaves and how do they produce heat when absorbed by food?
2. Discuss several advantages and limitations to the use of microwave ovens in the home.
3. What containers should be used to hold food when cooking in the microwave oven. Explain your answer.
4. What relationship does the cooking time have to the volume of food cooked in a microwave oven?
5. Why should foods be stirred or turned at intervals during cooking in a microwave oven?
6. What precautions should be taken when reheating fully cooked plated meals in a microwave oven and why?

References

1. AFCMA promotes microwave cooking in aluminum foil containers. 1981. *Food Technology* **35,** 99 (no. 11).
2. Cipra, J. S., and J. A. Bowers. 1971. Flavor of microwave- and conventionally-reheated turkey. *Poultry Science* **50,** 703.
3. Dahl, C. A., and M. E. Matthews. 1980. Effect of microwave heating in cook/chill foodservice systems. *Journal of the American Dietetic Association* **77,** 289.
4. Drew, F., K. S. Rhee, and A. C. Stubbs. 1977. Microwave ovens. *Journal of Home Economics* **69** 31, (no. 1).

5. Food and Drug Administration. *Microwave Oven Radiation*. HHS Publication No. (FDA) 80-8120. Washington, DC: U.S. Department of Health and Human Services, 1982.

6. Gast, B., G. J. Seperich, and R. Lytle. 1980. Beef preparation expectations as defined by microwave user survey—a marketing opportunity. *Food Technology* **34,** 41 (no. 10).

7. Mandigo, R. W., and T. J. Janssen. 1982. Energy-efficient cooking systems for muscle foods. *Food Technology* **36,** 128 (no. 4).

8. McConnell, D. R. 1974. Energy consumption: A comparison between the microwave oven and the conventional electric range. *Journal of Microwave Power* **9,** 341.

9. Rhee, K. S., and F. Drew. 1977. Energy consumption and acceptability comparison of cooking methods and appliances for beef patties. *Home Economics Research Journal* **5,** 269.

10. Shapiro, R. G., and J. F. Bayne. 1982. Microwave heating of glass containers. *Food Technology* **36,** 46 (no. 2).

26

Food Preservation

When foods spoil, they undergo chemical and physical changes that may render the food inedible or hazardous to eat. The two chief causes of food spoilage are the growth of microorganisms, including bacteria, yeasts, and molds, and the action of enzymes that occur normally in the food. Additional causes of spoilage include nonenzymatic reactions in food, such as oxidation and desiccation (drying out); mechanical damage, such as bruising; and damage from rodents and insects.

Causes of Food Spoilage

Microorganisms

In order to grow or multiply in number, all microorganisms need a source of nutrients, sufficient moisture, a favorable temperature, and an appropriate pH (Figure 26-1). Because, in a consideration of food preservation, it is impossible to eliminate available food as a factor in microbial growth, attention must be given to the control of other conditions that encourage microbial growth.

Molds. Molds are multicellular, filamentous fungi usually giving a fuzzy or cottony appearance when they grow on foods. They may be white, dark, or of various colors. Spores are produced by molds, usually asexually, in large numbers for purposes of reproduction. They are small, light cells that are resistant to drying and are easily spread through the air to alight on any exposed food. Given favorable conditions and enough time the spore may then grow on the food.

Molds are able to utilize many different kinds of substances, from

26-1 *Approximate growth limit for microorganisms; and relationships between pH and processing temperature.* (Courtesy of Ball Brothers Co.)

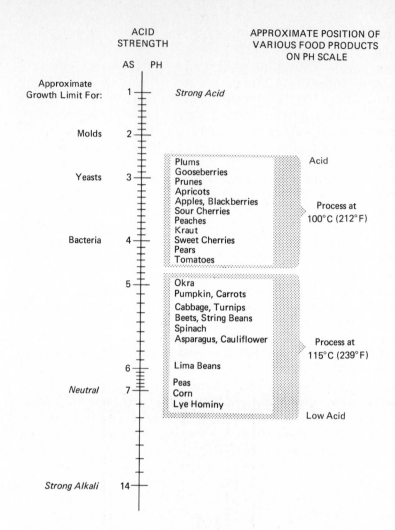

ACID STRENGTH

APPROXIMATE POSITION OF VARIOUS FOOD PRODUCTS ON PH SCALE

AS PH

Approximate Growth Limit For:

1 — Strong Acid

Molds — 2

Yeasts — 3

Plums
Gooseberries
Prunes
Apricots
Apples, Blackberries
Sour Cherries
Peaches
Kraut
Sweet Cherries
Pears
Tomatoes

Acid

Process at 100°C (212°F)

Bacteria — 4

5 —

Okra
Pumpkin, Carrots
Cabbage, Turnips
Beets, String Beans
Spinach
Asparagus, Cauliflower

Process at 115°C (239°F)

6 —

Lima Beans

Neutral — 7

Peas
Corn
Lye Hominy

Low Acid

Strong Alkali — 14

very simple to complex, for food. In general, they are aerobic, requiring oxygen for growth. They can also grow over a wide range of pH, from quite acid to fairly alkaline (pH 2.0 to 8.5). They grow most rapidly at temperatures of 20° to 35° C (68° to 95° F) and in a moist, still atmosphere. However, they may grow with very little moisture. Low temperatures retard their growth but molds may still grow at ordinary refrigerator temperatures of 7 to 10° C (45 to 50° F). A boiling water temperature destroys both molds and their spores. Temperatures somewhat below that of boiling water (71° to 82° C or 160° to 180° F) will readily destroy vegetative mold cells and will also destroy spores if the temperature is maintained for a sufficient time. The time is variable, depending on other conditions. Some molds will not grow in bright sunlight but others grow in either darkness or light.

In general, molds require less moisture than most yeasts and bacteria, and because they are also adaptable to many conditions of acidity and temperature they are commonly involved in the spoilage of food. Molds will grow on sweet foods, such as jellies or jams. They commonly occur on meats (even cured meats), on cheese, milk, and other protein foods. They also grow on fresh fruits, vegetables, and on cereal products.

For many years it was thought that molds were probably not harmful. However, certain molds, such as *Aspergillus flavus,* growing on cereal grains and on peanuts have been found to produce toxins that have caused illness and death in animals and humans [1]. The toxin produced by *Aspergillus flavus* is called *aflatoxin* but the term *mycotoxin* is used to designate toxins produced by any molds.

Some molds play valuable roles in food production. Certain cheeses, such as Roquefort and Camembert, are ripened by molds. Molds are also used for the commercial production of some enzymes, such as amylase for breadmaking, and for the production of citric acid. They are also used in making certain Oriental foods, such as soy sauce.

Yeasts. Yeasts are unicellular plants, also called fungi. They are usually aerobic and may play both useful and harmful roles in foods. Yeast fermentations, chemical changes in which enzymes produced by the yeast cells break down sugars into smaller molecules, are important in the production of such foods as bread, vinegar, beer, and wine. Yeasts are also grown for food and for the production of some enzymes. Yeasts are undesirable when they grow and ferment fruits, fruit juices, syrups, honey, molasses, and the like. Moist, sugar-containing foods, especially those that are slightly acid, such as fruit and fruit juices, are particularly susceptible to spoilage by yeasts. The optimum pH for yeast growth is 4.5 to 6.5 [7]. Fermenting foods are full of carbon dioxide gas bubbles. Yeasts grow most rapidly at temperatures of 20° to 38° C (68° to 100° F). As in the case of molds, temperatures somewhat below the boiling point of water may be adequate for the destruction of yeasts if the time of heating is extended. Yeast growth is inhibited by low temperatures and may be checked entirely in a concentrated sugar solution (65 percent or greater). The boiling temperature of water destroys yeast cells and spores.

Bacteria. Bacteria are of many types and are widely distributed in air, soil, water, and in foods. Some types of bacteria produce substances of desirable flavor and are cultivated for their beneficial action. The lactic acid of buttermilk, sauerkraut, fermented pickles, cheese, yogurt, and butter (when made from sour cream) is an example of a desirable flavor substance formed by bacterial action. However, other products of bacterial decomposition bring about the spoilage of foods, causing them to become inedible or even highly toxic.

Under conditions favorable for their growth, bacteria multiply rapidly. Favorable conditions usually include 25 to 30 percent available moisture and temperatures from 20° to 55° C (68° to 131° F). Some types of bacteria have an optimal temperature for growth that is above 45° C (81° F) and are called *thermophilic;* those having a low optimal temperature, such as refrigerator temperatures or below, are called *psychrophilic.* Psychrophilic bacteria may cause particular problems in the cold storage and freezing of foods, whereas thermophiles may create problems in the canning industry. Bacteria with an optimal growth temperature of 20° to 45° C (68° to 81° F) are called *mesophilic.* If bacteria require air or oxygen they are called *aerobic;* if they do not require oxygen and grow better in its absence they are called *anaerobic. Facultative* bacteria are capable of growing either with or without free oxygen. Each bacterium also has its own optimal pH or degree of acidity for growth, but most bacteria grow best at a pH near neutrality. Heat in the presence of acid is highly destructive to bacteria. Therefore, in acid foods, the temperature of boiling water maintained for a relatively short period of time is adequate for the destruction of bacteria. Foods of low acid content or high pH (those of lower acidity than is represented by a pH of 4.5) are more difficult to preserve than are foods with a low pH because bacteria and their spores are more resistant to destruction in these low acid surroundings [4].

Some bacteria, such as those of the genera *Bacillus* and *Clostridium,* form endospores or spores. These spores are much more resistant to heat and other destructive agencies than are the vegetative cells. Bacteria in the vegetative state may be readily destroyed in moist foods at the boiling temperature of water for relatively short periods of time. Spores, however, particularly in low acid food, require temperatures higher than boiling water for their destruction in reasonable time periods. Pressure cookers or pressure canners are used to achieve these higher temperatures.

Enzymes

Enzymes have been described briefly in Chapter 4, p. 74. Enzymes are present in many foods that are commonly preserved in the home. Unless undesirable enzyme action is controlled or the enzymes are destroyed (usually by heating), they may be responsible for certain unwanted chemical changes in preserved foods.

All methods used for preserving foods are based upon the general principle of preventing or retarding the causes of spoilage—microbial decomposition, enzymatic and nonenzymatic chemical reactions, and damage from mechanical causes, insects, and rodents. When the growth of microorganisms is only retarded or inhibited, preservation is temporary. When spoilage organisms are completely destroyed and the food is protected so that no other microorganisms are permitted to reinfect it, more permanent preservation is achieved. No method of food preservation will improve the original quality of a food product. If a preserved food is to be satisfactory, then fresh, flavorful produce at an optimal stage of ripeness or maturity must be used.

Preservation by Temperature Control

Unfavorable temperatures for microbial growth include (1) cold temperatures, which chiefly inhibit growth although some destruction of microorganisms occurs at very low temperatures, and (2) hot temperatures, which destroy microorganisms. With chilling temperatures, the length of time that the food will remain wholesome varies with the temperature and with the type of food. In home refrigerators, at 7 to 10° C (45 to 50° F), most foods keep for a few days only. In cold storage warehouses the length of time is increased. Here the temperature is low and the humidity is controlled, both of which conditions favor preservation.

Freezing may preserve foods for long periods of time provided the quality of the food is good to begin with and the temperature of storage is below the actual freezing temperature of the food. Some microorganisms are destroyed during the freezing process and subsequent storage but the chief preservative effect of freezing lies in the inability of microorganisms to grow at freezing and below freezing temperatures. Enzyme action is also retarded at freezing temperatures. However, in certain products, such as vegetables, enzyme action may still produce undesirable effects on flavor and texture during freezing. The enzymes, therefore, must be destroyed by heating or blanching before the vegetables are frozen.

Hot temperatures preserve by destroying both microorganisms and enzymes. Yeasts, molds, and enzymes are readily destroyed at the boiling temperature of water. The heating must be maintained for a long enough time to permit all parts of the food to reach the necessary temperature. Heat penetration is sometimes slow in such foods as partially ripe pears or peaches. Bacteria are less readily destroyed than are yeasts, molds, and enzymes, the vegetative or active cells being more readily destroyed than spore forms. Many bacterial spores are very resistant to heat. Canning as a method of food preservation involves essentially the complete destruction of microorganisms and their spores and enzymes by high temperatures and then sealing to prevent the recontamination of the food [5]. The food in this case is essentially sterilized. Pasteurization of food products such as milk and eggs that are to be frozen or dried involves use of temperatures that are lower than those required for sterilization. All pathogenic or disease-producing microorganisms are destroyed but not all of the other microorganisms present are eliminated. This is a more temporary preservation than is sterilization and canning.

Preservation by Moisture Control

The reduction in moisture content is one of the oldest methods of preserving foods [6]. As practically applied, the food is dried in the sun or by air current and artificial heat until the moisture content of the food is reduced to an amount that will inhibit the growth of microorganisms. The actual percentage of moisture is variable but is usually under 30 percent. Some dehydrated foods, such as dried potato slices, may contain only 2 to 3 percent moisture. Foods, such as many commercially dried fruits with an intermediate moisture content, about 15 to 35 or 40 percent, may have low enough water activity for preservation yet are pleasant to eat directly without rehydration [3].

Freeze-drying involves the removal of water from a product, while it is frozen, by *sublimation* under a vacuum. Sublimation means that ice is changed directly to vapor without going through the liquid stage. This is an expensive process because of the equipment involved. Therefore, it is more commonly used for the dehydration of relatively expensive foods, such as seafood and meats, that can more easily absorb the added cost than can less expensive products such as vegetables.

Preservation by Added or Developed Substances

Adding some chemical substances, called *preservatives,* to a food product is another method of inhibiting the growth of undesirable microorganisms. In some cases, acid, as a preservative, may be developed in foods by the use of favorable bacteria in pickling processes. The common preservatives, sometimes called *household preservatives,* are salt, sugar, acid, spices, and smoke. The phenols of wood smoke exert the preservative action. Ground cinnamon and cloves are more valuable than nutmeg and allspice in quantities that can be used without marring flavor, but spices themselves are often responsible for introducing bacteria into foods. Oils of spice are sterile and have a more inhibitory effect on microbial growth than do ground spices. Acids, such as acetic acid in vinegar, and salt are commonly used in pickling vegetables. In pickle and sauerkraut fermentations, lactic and other acids are produced by certain bacteria. Sugar in large amounts is used in the production of jellies, jams, and preserves.

Other preservatives may be used in small amounts in the commercial processing of foods. The U.S. Food and Drug Administration must approve any preservatives that are used in the foods entering interstate commerce. Thorough testing for safety is required of these chemical additives before they can be used. Foods produced and sold within a state come under the jurisdiction of state regulatory agencies. Benzoate of soda, used in very small amounts in some margarines, and sulfur dioxide, used to prevent the discoloration of dried fruits, such as apricots, apples, and pears, are examples of preservatives that may be added to foods.

Use of Ionizing Radiation

Other Food Preservation Techniques

Although a large amount of research, much of it government-sponsored, has been carried on in the past 20 to 25 years to determine the desirability of using ionizing radiation as a means of preserving foods, this method is not yet acceptable for general use [4]. Food irradiation is considered to be a food additive and the U.S. Food and Drug Administration must approve any irradiated food before it can be marketed. The testing for safety that is required is very extensive. Approval has been given for the use of radiation in the disinfestation of wheat grains and for the sprouting inhibition of potatoes.

The radiation preservation of food is considered to be a "cold" process because there is only a slight rise in the temperature of the food irradiated. Adverse changes in flavor and texture by heat are thus avoided. Radiation at levels above 1 *megarad* (a unit for measurement of radiation) has the potential for use in preserving meats, fish, poultry, and other highly perishable foods for long term without refrigeration. Doses of radiation below 1 megarad may extend the refrigerated storage life of perishable foods, may destroy food poisoning salmonellae organisms in frozen animal products, may destroy insects in cereal grains, and may extend the shelf life of fresh fruits and vegetables by destroying molds and yeasts. Radiation at lower levels may pasteurize (destroy pathogens and reduce the level of microorganisms) while sterilization (complete destruction of microorganisms) occurs at high dosages.

When considering the wholesomeness of irradiated food it is necessary to be assured that (1) there is no radioactivity in the irradiated food; (2) all pathogenic microorganisms have been destroyed; (3) no toxic radiation products are produced; and (4) there are no unacceptable losses in nutritive value [4]. After many years of testing, an international review committee from the World Health Organization has concluded that food products irradiated to an average dose of up to 1 megarad are wholesome. The U.S. Food and Drug Administration is working with industry and other interested groups on recommendations for the radiation processing of various foods.

Use of Antibiotics

Research has been reported concerning the possible use of antibiotics in food preservation. Many antibiotic substances have been tested on raw foods to determine their effect on the storage life of foods at refrigerator temperatures. Aureomycin (chlortetracycline) and Terramycin (oxytetracycline) have been found to be superior to most of the other antibiotics tested. These antibiotics were previously used in small amounts in the chilling tanks during poultry processing but are no longer approved for this purpose by the Food and Drug Administration. They extended the shelf life of the poultry and were destroyed in cooking.

Some experiments have combined antibiotics and heat treatments in foods in an effort to reduce the total heating time necessary for canning low-acid foods. Some antibiotics that have been tried without complete success are subtilin, nisin, and tylosin.

Some of the problems involved in the use of antibiotics in food preservation include the need to prove the nontoxicity of the substance and the possible developed resistance of microorganisms to antibiotics that are used over a period of time. The consumer may become sensitized to an antibiotic with undesirable results when it is present in a food he or she consumes. It is also possible that he or she may develop strains of microorganisms in his or her body that are resistant to the antibiotics used in the food so that when he or she needs an antibiotic for medical purposes it may not be effective. Many problems still must be solved in the area of the use of antibiotics for food preservation.

Economy of Preserved Foods

The preservation of foods makes possible the saving of food in times of plenty for use in times of scarcity. With the increasing complexity of our civilization, methods of food preservation will play an even more important role in feeding people all over the world. All foods are perishable to some degree and may begin to deteriorate immediately after harvest or gathering. Man's knowledge of the technology of food preservation, properly applied, has helped to control this deterioration and increase the general quality and economy of food.

Many of the foods commonly used in the home are preserved by such processes as canning, freezing, and dehydration. The decision as to whether or not these preserved foods are to be processed at home or purchased already processed is an individual family decision. Many factors may influence this decision, including the availability, cost, and quality of raw materials and equipment; storage space; the time and energy available; comparative palatability and family preferences for the various products; and the possible enjoyment derived from these types of do-it-yourself projects. If fruits and vegetables are grown in a family garden or are readily available and relatively inexpensive, the project of preserving them at home may be very economical and result in food budget savings. However, if fresh fruits and vegetables are relatively expensive and not readily available locally, they may actually be more expensive when home-processed than when purchased commercially in the processed form. Commercially canned and frozen foods may be more or less expensive in comparison with each other and with fresh products at various times of the year. The consumer should be aware of relative costs and comparative qualities and purchase accordingly.

Study Questions

1. List several basic causes of food spoilage.
2. Explain why it is important when considering food preservation to know something about the optimal conditions for growth of molds, yeasts, and bacteria.
3. For each of the conditions listed below, indicate optimal growth requirements for molds, for yeasts, and for bacteria:
   a. Oxygen or air
   b. Acidity or pH
   c. Temperature
   d. Moisture
4. Why are enzymes of some concern in preserving foods? Explain.
5. For each of the following general methods of food preservation, describe specific methods of preserving food that use this principle:
   a. Use of low temperatures
   b. Use of high temperatures
   c. Reduction of moisture
   d. Addition or development of acid
   e. Addition of large amounts of sugar
6. Discuss possible uses of ionizing radiation in preserving foods.

7. Discuss several factors that may affect the decision to preserve or not preserve foods at home.

References

1. Anderson, A. W. 1977. The significance of yeasts and molds in foods. *Food Technology* **31,** 47 (no. 2).
2. Frazier, W. C., and D. C. Westhoff. *Food Microbiology,* 3rd ed. New York: McGraw-Hill Book Company, 1978.
3. Gee, M., D. Farkas, and A. R. Rahman. 1977. Some concepts for the development of intermediate moisture foods. *Food Technology* **31,** 58 (no. 4).
4. Institute of Food Technologists' Expert Panel on Food Safety and Nutrition. 1983. Radiation preservation of foods. *Food Technology* **37,** 55 (no. 2).
5. Johnston, M. R., and R. H. Dougherty. 1978. Thermal processing of canned foods: Introductory Remarks. *Food Technology* **32,** 55 (no. 6).
6. Troller, J. A. 1980. Influence of water activity on microorganisms in foods. *Food Technology* **34,** 76 (no. 5).
7. Walker, H. W. 1977. Spoilage of food by yeasts. *Food Technology* **31,** 57 (no. 2).

27

Canning

Canning involves the application to foods of temperatures that are high enough to destroy essentially all microorganisms present, both vegetative cells and spores, plus airtight sealing in sterilized containers to prevent recontamination. The degree of heat and the length of time of heating vary with the type of food and the kinds of microorganisms that are likely to occur in it. Acid fruits and tomatoes that are sufficiently acid are successfully canned at the temperature of boiling water. The time of boiling will vary depending upon the degree of acidity, the consistency of the product, the method of preparation, and other factors. Vegetables and meats, which are relatively low in acid must be heated to temperatures higher than that of boiling water at atmospheric pressure. This involves the use of a pressure cooker. Because the bacterial spores that may be present are more resistant to heat under conditions of low acidity, the time of heating necessary to destroy them at the temperature of boiling water would likely be several hours. The food would be rather unpalatable after such a prolonged cooking period. Moist heat evidently destroys microorganisms by coagulating protein and destroys enzymes in a similar manner.

General procedures and principles involved in home canning are discussed in this chapter. Specific procedures and processing times to be followed for each food item can be found in U.S. Department of Agriculture bulletins listed as References 9 and 10.

Historical Highlights

The history of canning begins about 1795 when the French government offered a prize for the development of a new method of preserving food from one harvest to the next. Nicolas Appert, a Parisian confectioner, worked many years on such a process and finally, in 1809, he was successful in preserving some foods by sealing them with corks in glass bottles and heating them for various lengths of time [3]. Appert was awarded 12,000 francs for his accomplishment. From these crude beginnings, with contributions from many workers along the way, has come the modern canning industry with tin-plated steel cans being produced, filled, sealed, and processed by the millions. The tin cannister was first developed in England in about 1810; the retort for pressure canning was developed in Philadelphia around 1874 [7]; Pasteur's work with microorganisms in about 1860 began a study of the true causes of food spoilage; and canning was put on a scientific basis at about the turn of the twentieth century.

Commercial canning now also includes methods that employ higher temperatures and shorter time periods than are used in traditional commercial canning. In some cases, the cans are agitated during cooking to aid heat distribution and penetration into the food. Certain commercial methods of canning sterilize the food and containers separately before filling and sealing. With this process a more fresh flavor may be retained in the food than is possible with the usual long periods of heating in the container.

Much of our canned food is now produced commercially. However, many people still can or "bottle" foods at home for various reasons, which may include palatability, economy, and the enjoyment of doing something creative (Figure 27-1). A 1975 U.S. Department of Agriculture survey revealed that one out of three households canned fruits or vegetables [5]. Tomatoes were the most popular item to can.

Methods for Home Canning

High-quality products should be selected for canning. Recommended procedures should be followed to assure safe products that do not spoil on storage.

Methods of Packing

Foods may be packed into jars or cans either raw or hot. In the *raw pack method* of canning, the uncooked food is packed into the container and the container is then filled with boiling liquid. Some head space should be left in the top of the container before sealing. Usually ½ to 1 inch head space is suggested when glass jars are used

27-1 *Green beans that were bottled at home.* (Courtesy of Ball Brothers Co.)

and about ¼ inch head space is sufficient when using tin cans. Tin cans are available in some areas but are not generally used for home canning. Head space allows for the expansion of the jar contents during heating. If tin cans are used, the open can must be heated in a boiling water bath until the contents are at least 77° C (170° F) before the can is sealed (a process called *exhausting* the can). This process drives trapped air out of the can so that a partial vacuum may be formed after processing and cooling of the can. Glass jars are only partially sealed before processing at the necessary temperature for the recommended length of time.

In the *hot pack method* of canning, the food is heated in syrup, water, steam, or extracted juice before being packed into containers. With the hot pack method the temperature of the food should be at least 77° C (170° F) when it is packed in the container.

The raw pack method may have some advantages over the hot pack method in placing large pieces of fruit, such as peach halves, or fragile berries in jars so that they present an attractive appearance and are closely packed. The hot pack method may be advantageously used for some foods because it helps to drive out air, wilts or shrinks plant tissues, allows closer packing, and slightly shortens the processing time. The initial temperature of the food is relatively high and heat penetration is more rapid than when food is packed cold. Pears, apples, and pineapples have a more attractive translucent appearance when prepared by the hot pack than by the raw pack method and more fruit can be fitted into the container.

Methods of Processing

The processing of canned fruits, vegetables, and meats is done after these foods have been packed into containers by either hot or raw pack methods as described previously. The processing may be accomplished in a boiling water bath, for acid fruits and acid tomatoes, and in a pressure canner for vegetables, meat, fish, and poultry, which are low in acid and require higher temperatures for the complete destruction of bacterial spores.

Processing by a boiling water bath requires a large pan or other container to hold boiling water and a cover that fits fairly closely but permits the escape of some steam (Figure 27-2). A rack keeps jars an inch or less above the bottom thus avoiding breakage and allowing even circulation of heat underneath the jars. The boiling water is usually of sufficient depth to extend 2 inches above the top surface of the jars. Unless the bath has a removable holder for jars, a lifter of some kind is necessary for putting jars into the boiling water and for taking them out. Water should be boiling when jars are put into it and should be brought back to boiling before beginning to time the processing period. The water must boil continuously during the entire processing time.

In an alternative method for processing acid fruits and tomatoes a steamer especially designed for canning is employed (Figure 27-3). About 6 cups of water are placed in the bottom part of the processor,

27-2 *Processing by use of the boiling-water bath.* (Courtesy of Ball Brothers Co.)

Boiling water should extend 2 inches above the surface of the jars.

A lifter is desirable for putting jars into the boiling water and taking them out.

and a perforated metal plate covers the water and provides the platform on which the bottles of fruit are placed. A tall cover fits completely over the jars. Perforations at the bottom of the steamer allow the release of steam. The heating is similar to that achieved in a boiling water bath but less time is required to reach a boiling temperature. The jars are surrounded by steam during processing.

Some varieties of tomatoes now being grown in the United States, including Garden State, Ace, 55VF, and Cal Ace, are lower in acid content than tomatoes that were commonly produced in previous years. These tomatoes should be processed in a pressure canner instead of in a boiling water bath [11]. Some other local varieties may be too low in acid to be processed in a boiling water bath. State extension services should be contacted for the latest information on low-acid tomato varieties. Because of the possible danger of botulism, it is necessary to process low-acid tomatoes in a pressure canner.

If temperatures higher than 100° C (212° F) are necessary for processing, a pressure cooker must be used. The boiling point of a liquid such as water varies with the atmospheric pressure over its surface. As the atmospheric pressure is decreased with higher alti-

27-3 A specially designed steamer may be used in place of the boiling-water bath for processing acid fruits and tomatoes. Steam is produced from 6 to 8 cups of water placed in the bottom of the steamer; steam is retained in the high dome and surrounds the jars being processed; steam is released through small holes in the bottom part of the steamer so that pressure does not build up inside. The jars of food are placed on a perforated platform that is above the surface of the boiling water from which the steam is produced.

27-4 *A pressure cooker is necessary to obtain temperatures higher than 100° C (212° F).* (Courtesy of National Presto Industries, Inc.)

tudes, the boiling point of the liquid is decreased. In a pressure cooker the water vapor or steam that is produced when the water is heated to its normal boiling point is captured inside the pan with its tightly sealed cover, thus increasing the pressure over the surface of the water in the pressure cooker and raising the boiling point. Temperatures higher than the usual boiling point of water (100° C or 212° F) can thus be achieved. Pressure cookers are constructed of heavy metal and have tops that can be clamped on tightly (Figure 27-4). Although pressure cookers differ slightly, the essential features are a rack to hold jars off the bottom; a petcock, which is left open for a few minutes for the purpose of driving out air and filling the compartment with steam, after which it is closed; a safety valve through which steam may escape if too high a pressure is developed within the cooker; and a gauge that registers the amount of pressure developed within the cooker after the petcock is closed. The water in the pressure canner should be about 3 inches in depth in order that it may last throughout the processing time. Jars are spaced to permit the circulation of steam. Before the petcock is closed, the cooker should be heated for about 7 to 10 minutes while a steady stream of steam is coming from the opening. This *exhausts* the cooker (removes air) as completely as possible. If proper exhausting is not done and some air remains in the cooker, the remaining air will contribute a partial pressure that will be registered on the pressure gauge along with the steam pressure produced. The temperature inside the cooker will not be as high at a specified pressure if all of the pressure does not come from steam and the food may be underprocessed. Cookers are not usually equipped with thermometers that show the exact interior temperature, so it is very important that the cooker be properly exhausted. Table 27-1 shows temperatures that are obtainable in a pressure cooker at different pressures, provided that no air remains in the cooker. The pressure cooker is used primarily to provide a high temperature for the destruction of heat-resistant microorganisms and their spores in a shorter period of time than is possible at the boiling temperature of water. If glass jars or large tin cans are used, it is recommended that the pointer on the pressure gauge return to zero before the petcock is opened. Otherwise, liquid will be lost from the jars because of the sudden drop in pressure surrounding them [6]. If small tin cans are used, the petcock may be *very gradually* opened as soon as the processing time is completed. Immediately after processing in either the boiling water bath or pressure canner, jars that were not completely sealed before processing are sealed. A vacuum is gradually produced as the jars cool.

Pressure canners should be checked for accuracy at the beginning of each season. Checking is often done locally through the county extension service or the home service department of utility compa-

Table 27-1 *Temperatures Obtainable at Different Pressures in a Pressure Cooker*

Pounds Pressure	Temperature	
	°C	°F
5	109	228
10	116	240
15	121	250
20	126	259
25	131	267

nies. The amount and direction of error in the pressure gauge should be noted on a tag, which is tied to the cooker so that an adjustment will be made when the cooker is used.

Processing in a Pressure Saucepan. A pressure saucepan equipped with a gauge or weight for showing and controlling pressure and which is tall enough to hold pint jars on a rack, appears to be satisfactory for canning. Because pressure is reached and cooling occurs more rapidly in a pressure saucepan than in a pressure canner, about 20 minutes more processing time must be allowed after the proper pressure is reached. Canning instructions given by the manufacturer of the pressure saucepan should be followed.

Open Kettle Method of Processing. In the open kettle method of canning, food is cooked in an open kettle, after which it is transferred to sterile containers and sealed immediately. The open kettle method *must not* be used for vegetables or meats, which require a pressure cooker. The open kettle method should not, in general, be used for fruits, tomatoes, pickles, or jams because it usually does not result in complete sterilization by the end of the canning process. If insufficient heat has been applied to the food, or if the food is contaminated while transferring it from the kettle to the canning container, spoilage can result. Reinfection of food during open kettle canning may occur in several ways: air bubbles may be enclosed during the filling of the jar; a layer of unsterile air is always enclosed between the inside of the cover and the top of the food even when the jar has been filled completely (as it should be with this method); jars and tops may not be completely sterilized before being used. With this method, as with all methods, the failure to obtain a tight seal may permit microorganisms to enter the jar. The open kettle method is not generally recommended. However, a 1975 USDA survey revealed that 44 percent of the households who canned fruits used the open kettle method [5]. Approximately 25 percent of the households surveyed reported some spoilage in their home-canned fruits and vegetables.

Oven Processing Is Not Safe. Oven processing as a method of canning is not dependable, and is *not recommended for canning under any circumstances*. The method would be particularly dangerous if it were used for low-acid vegetables and meats because temperatures higher than the boiling point of water are not obtainable in oven processing. However, it is not a safe method to use for canning any product. Objections to oven processing include (1) the uncertainty of oven temperature because thermostats may not be operating properly; (2) different temperatures in various parts of the oven; (3) the loss of juice from the jars. However, the greatest objection to oven processing is (4) *the tremendous danger of explosion of jars resulting in serious injury* to the worker and the destruction of equipment. The reasons for explosions are not always clear and they are not always avoidable. In some cases, explosions may occur because the lids seal prematurely in the dry oven heat and pressure builds up in the glass jars.

Containers for Canning

Containers for canned foods may be made of tinplated steel (tin cans) or of glass. Tin cans are of two types: plain and lacquered tin. The latter may be coated with the bright, or R, lacquer suitable for all red-colored foods containing anthocyanin pigment, and for pumpkin and squash. If anthocyanins are canned in plain tin they fade and become bluish in color. Pumpkin and squash tend to corrode plain tin. The dull, or C, lacquer is best not used with acid foods or with meats that contain much fat as both acid and fat may cause the lacquer to peel off and make the food unsightly, although harmless. The dull, or C, lacquer is used for corn, succotash, and other sulfur-containing foods in order to prevent dark deposits of tin or iron sulfide on the food and on the can. Tin sulfide, which is brown in color, and iron sulfide, which is black, are not harmful but detract from the appearance of the food.

In order to use tin cans, a sealer is necessary, but canning in tin has a number of advantages. Breakage is eliminated; cans are always sealed before processing; heat penetration is more rapid than with glass; the cans may be rapidly cooled after processing by being plunged into cold water; and the cans are cheaper than glass and if reflanged can be used a second time. The cost of the sealer, however, offsets the lower costs of tin cans unless canning is done on a large scale. Most home canning is done in glass jars.

Most of the glass jars available in the United States today are those used with self-sealing lids (Figure 27-5). Some jars may also be used with glass tops, rubber sealing rings, and screw bands. The self-sealing closure for a canning jar has a composition ring in the lid that becomes soft when heated and then hardens, forming a seal on the edge of the jar top when it becomes cold. New lids are required for self-sealing jars each time the jars are used but the screw bands may be reused over a long period of time. The lids are placed briefly in boiling water prior to use according to the manufacturer's directions. The self-sealing lid is the type most commonly used for home canning.

For low-acid vegetables and for meats, jars no larger than quart size are recommended because of the danger of poor heat penetration in larger jars. The pint size is usually advised for corn, shell beans, and lima beans, in which heat penetration is slow.

Commercially, retort pouches (flexible laminated packages made of special materials that will withstand high-temperature processing in a commercial pressure canner called a retort) may be used as

27-5 *The most commonly used type of closure for canning jars includes a metal screw band and a metal self-sealing lid. Sealing occurs on the top edge of the jar.* (Courtesy of the U.S. Department of Agriculture)

containers. These packages are less expensive to process and ship, after the initial expense by the food processor for the necessary processing equipment or modification of conventional equipment [13,14].

Heat Penetration

Heat penetration during canning is affected by such factors as (1) the size of the container; (2) the material from which the container is made; (3) the initial temperature of the food when the processing is started; (4) the temperature used for processing; (5) the fullness of the pack; and (6) the character of the food. Heat penetration is more rapid in smaller containers and in tin than in glass. Starchy vegetables and closely packed leafy vegetables transmit heat poorly. Colloidal starch solutions retard heat penetration more than concentrated sugar solutions. Heat penetration is more rapid if the food is hot when the processing is started and if a higher temperature is used for processing. The length of time of heating is closely related to the temperature used for processing as well as to the character of the food and to the types of microorganisms present. The higher the temperature used the shorter is the required heating period.

Obtaining an Effective Seal

A good seal is fundamental in the preservation of foods. All jars should be examined for nicks or rough places on the sealing surfaces that might interfere with a good seal. Lids should fit well in order that they may form a good seal when the sealing material comes in contact with the glass surface. New screw bands are not necessary unless the old ones are defective (which includes bent edges) or unless the tops are corroded or otherwise unfit for use. Rubbers should be new stock and pliable because, if hardened, they will not form a good seal. Small bits of food should be removed carefully from the top of the jar before sealing as they interfere with a good seal.

Obtaining a Partial Vacuum

A partial vacuum in the sealed jar is important in the canning of food as it maintains an effective seal and inhibits oxidative changes. A partial vacuum is created when the air within the jar exerts less pressure outward than the atmosphere exerts upon the outside of the jar. A vacuum is produced as a result of several things that occur during the canning process. First, food is heated. The application of heat causes internal gases to expand. When the food is heated in the jar, the gases escape through the partially sealed lid. This process is called *venting*. The formation of an effective vacuum depends largely upon venting. After processing is completed and the jar is removed from the canner, the sealing of the jar occurs. With self-sealing devices the complete sealing takes place automatically as the softened sealing compound hardens on cooling. During cooling, the contents of the jar contract, leaving a space in the top that is less dense than the atmosphere pressing down on the outside of the lid. Thus, a partial vacuum is formed to aid in keeping the seal tight.

Handling After Processing

Proper handling and storage of canned food is important in maintaining its quality. When glass jars with self-sealing lids are thoroughly cool and have sealed, the screw bands should be removed and rinsed clean so that they can be used again. If left on the jars they may stick or rust, making removal difficult. The outside of the jars should be wiped clean of any residual syrup or other material. Containers should be labeled to show contents and date of processing.

Canned foods should be stored in a cool, dry, dark place. At cool storage temperatures the eating quality and nutritive value are better maintained. Glass jars, particularly, should be stored in a dark place since light causes fading and discoloration of plant pigments. Properly canned foods may be safely stored for several years but the quality of the food gradually decreases, especially if storage temperatures are relatively high.

Before home-canned low-acid vegetables and meats are used, it is generally recommended that they be boiled for at least 10 minutes in a covered pan. Spinach, corn, and meats should be boiled 20 minutes [9,10]. The heating period is a precaution to destroy any botulinum toxin that may be present since botulism has occurred most commonly from use of home-canned products.

Types of Spoilage in Canned Foods

Yeasts and Molds

Spoilage by yeasts and molds occurs only when canned foods are either grossly underprocessed or are recontaminated after packing. Recontamination may occur in open kettle canning while the container is being sealed or later because of a defective seal. If a can springs a tiny leak it may permit microorganisms from the cooling water to enter the can.

Flat Sour

This is a type of spoilage in which the food becomes highly acid but often appears normal and shows no gas formation. The bacteria responsible for flat sour spoilage are a species of *Bacillus* and may be found in sugar [2] and on unsterile equipment. The spoilage occurs chiefly in low acid foods such as peas or corn. Flat sour spoilage of acid foods, such as tomatoes, is caused by a special thermophilic species, *Bacillus coagulans*.

Botulinus Spoilage

The most dangerous of all forms of spoilage is that caused by the toxin formed by *Clostridium botulinum* as a result of improper processing of low acid foods (see Chapter 3, pp. 46–47 for a discussion of botulism).

Physical characteristics of canned foods that may indicate botulinus spoilage are (1) an odor of rancid cheese; (2) gas (although numerous other organisms cause gas); and (3) a soft, disintegrated condition of the food. However, cases of botulism have been reported from eating foods that had little or no abnormal appearance or odor.

Hydrogen Swells

When gas forms within tin cans, the ends bulge. Gas formation may accompany several types of spoilage, but substances in some fruits, such as prunes, apples, and berries, react, particularly during storage at warm temperatures, with the metal of the can to form hydrogen gas. The food is not adversely affected in cans that swell from hydrogen gas unless the can becomes punctured, thus permitting the entrance of bacteria from the outside. Bulging cans of fruits should be examined for signs of spoilage. If none are found, the fruit is safe to use. Bulging cans of meats and low-acid vegetables should always be discarded.

Metallic Salts

Tin cans are made of iron or steel with a coating of tin. Because the tin plating seldom, if ever, completely coats the iron, both iron and tin salts are formed when compounds in foods react with the can. Total lacquering of cans greatly decreases the accumulation of tin and iron in stored canned foods [8]. The safety of the food is not affected by such reactions. It has become a fairly common belief that foods must be removed from tin cans immediately on opening the can in order to prevent food poisoning. However, this is not true. Canned foods may *safely* remain in the cans after they are opened as long as they are properly refrigerated although a metallic flavor may develop. The appearance, especially the color, of some foods is also marred by standing in the tin can.

Discoloration

Discoloration may develop on storage of some canned foods. Discoloration in canned fruits may be caused by the oxidation of polyphenolic compounds or other substances in the fruits. This reaction, which is accelerated at warm storage temperatures, may be retarded by the addition of 125 milligrams ascorbic acid per pint jar of fruit. Other chemical reactions, possibly including nonenzymatic browning reactions, may produce discoloration in canned foods.

The pink discoloration of some canned pears has been found to be related to growing areas, soil types, heavy nitrogen fertilizer application, and skin blush [4]. Pears from certain growing areas have high acidity and a high content of phenolic compounds. These pears develop a pink color after canning, especially when excessive heating and delayed cooling processes are used [1,12].

Nutritive Value of Canned Foods

Because canned foods are essentially cooked foods, it is to be expected that the nutrients lost from cooked and canned foods will be similar. The extent of the loss, however, may differ. Canned vegetables, which require for safe preservation higher temperatures and longer heating periods than are required for cooking, tend to show greater losses of water-soluble nutrients than do cooked vegetables. Concentrating the liquor from canned vegetables and serving it with the vegetables results in a greater retention of nutrients than occurs when the vegetable and liquor are merely reheated and the liquor is discarded. The blanching of vegetables prior to canning results in the loss of water-soluble constituents if the blanching waters are not utilized. However, the practice of preheating foods before packing them in cans has, among other advantages, the advantage of driving off air, thus decreasing the extent of oxidation of certain nutrients during processing. Canning has only a slight destructive action on the vitamin A value of fruits and vegetables. The antioxidants in plant tissues are thought to exert some protective action on the vitamin A value.

The temperature of storage is a factor in nutritive loss in canned foods as well as in organoleptic changes. Storage slightly above freezing for extended periods of time results in a minor loss around 5 percent of most vitamins, but storage at warm temperatures may increase the loss from two to five times that amount. The reaction of acids in the food with tin in the can is lessened at low storage temperatures. The natural color of the food is retained better.

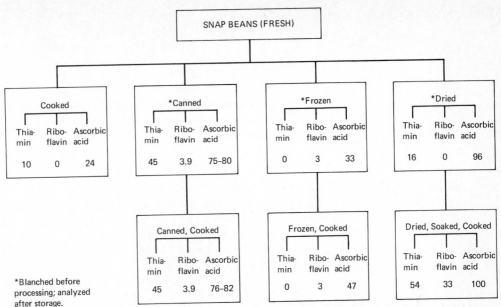

SNAP BEANS (FRESH)		

Cooked		
Thia-min	Ribo-flavin	Ascorbic acid
10	0	24

*Canned		
Thia-min	Ribo-flavin	Ascorbic acid
45	3.9	75–80

*Frozen		
Thia-min	Ribo-flavin	Ascorbic acid
0	3	33

*Dried		
Thia-min	Ribo-flavin	Ascorbic acid
16	0	96

Canned, Cooked		
Thia-min	Ribo-flavin	Ascorbic acid
45	3.9	76–82

Frozen, Cooked		
Thia-min	Ribo-flavin	Ascorbic acid
0	3	47

Dried, Soaked, Cooked		
Thia-min	Ribo-flavin	Ascorbic acid
54	33	100

*Blanched before processing; analyzed after storage.

27-6 *Vitamin losses in processing and cooking snap beans. Losses are expressed as percentages of the vitamins originally present in the fresh beans. (Courtesy of the U.S. Department of Agriculture, Misc. Pub. 536)*

Figure 27-6 shows the effect of canning snap beans on losses of some vitamins. These losses are also compared to those occurring in cooking fresh beans and in preserving them by freezing and drying. Losses in canning were greater than in freezing or in cooking the fresh vegetable.

The high acidity of a food, such as acid tomatoes or citrus fruits, provides some protection from the loss of ascorbic acid. Canned orange and grapefruit juices prepared under well-controlled conditions have been found to retain their ascorbic acid content well, although canned orange juice does not retain the characteristic flavor of the fresh juice. Because canned tomato juice contains the entire fruit except the seeds and skins, it is a good source of vitamin A value as well as ascorbic acid. Canned tomato cocktails retain little ascorbic acid because of the long cooking with seasonings. If the flavor of tomato cocktail is desired, it may be had by cooking a small amount of the juice with the seasonings and later adding the flavored juice to plain tomato juice either before canning or immediately before serving.

Study Questions

1. Describe some pertinent events in the history of canning that are associated with each of the following names and dates:
   a. Appert, 1809
   b. 1810

c. 1874

d. Pasteur, 1860s

2. Distinguish between the raw pack and the hot pack methods of packing canned foods and discuss advantages of each.

3. Why should filled tin cans be heated to a temperature of 77° C (170° F) before the cans are sealed? Explain.

4. Explain why fruits and high-acid tomatoes may be safely canned in a boiling water bath while vegetables and meat products must be canned in a pressure canner. What may botulism have to do with your explanation?

5. a. Describe the essential parts of a pressure canner and explain their functions.

    b. Why is it important to completely *exhaust* a pressure canner before closing the petcock and building up pressure?

    c. Suggest a possible explanation for the loss of liquid from jars being processed in a pressure canner.

6. Why is the open kettle method of canning not generally recommended? Explain.

7. Why is oven processing *not* recommended for canning?

8. a. Of what are "tin" cans made? Why may their inside surfaces be lacquered with R or C enamel?

    b. Describe self-sealing lids commonly used on "bottled" produce and explain how they work.

    c. What steps should be taken to ensure that an effective seal will be formed in "bottled" produce?

9. List several factors that may affect the rate of heat penetration as canned foods are processed.

10. Explain how a partial vacuum is formed in canned foods. Why is it important that this occurs?

11. Describe several types of spoilage that may occur in canned foods.

12. Compare the nutritive value of canned foods, in general, to that of similar foods freshly prepared.

References

1. Chandler, B. V., and K. M. Clegg. 1970. Pink discoloration in canned pears. I. Role of tin in pigment formation. *Journal of the Science of Food and Agriculture* **21,** 315.

2. Clark, F. M., and F. W. Tanner. 1937. Thermophilic canned food spoilage organisms in sugar and starch. *Food Research* **2,** 27.

3. Corcos, A. 1975. A note on the early life of Nicolas Appert. *Food Technology* **29,** 114 (no. 5).

4. Czerkaskyj, A. 1970. Pink discoloration in canned Williams' Bon Chretien pears. *Journal of Food Science* **35,** 608.

5. Davis, C. A., and L. Page. 1979. Practices used for home canning of fruits and vegetables. *Home Economics Research Report No. 43.* U.S. Department of Agriculture.

6. Esselen, W. B., and C. R. Fellers. 1948. Effect of different processing procedures on venting and loss of liquid from home canning jars. *Food Technology* **2,** 222.

7. Goldblith, S. A. 1972. Controversy over the autoclave. *Food Technology* **26,** 62 (no. 12).
8. Greger, J. L., and M. Baier. 1981. Tin and iron content of canned and bottled foods. *Journal of Food Science* **46,** 1751.
9. *Home Canning of Fruits and Vegetables.* Home and Garden Bulletin No. 8. Washington, DC: U.S. Department of Agriculture, 1983.
10. *Home Canning of Meat and Poultry.* Home and Garden Bulletin No. 106. Washington, DC: U.S. Department of Agriculture, 1977.
11. Institute of Food Technologists' Expert Panel on Food Safety and Nutrition and the Committee on Public Information. 1977. Home canning. *Food Technology* **31,** 43 (no. 6).
12. Luh, B. S., S. J. Leonard, and D. S. Patel. 1960. Pink discoloration in canned Bartlett pears. *Food Technology* **14,** 53.
13. Roop, R. A., and P. E. Nelson. 1982. Processing retort pouches in conventional sterilizers. *Journal of Food Science* **47,** 303.
14. Williams, J. R., J. F. Steffe, and J. R. Black. 1981. Economic comparison of canning and retort pouch systems. *Journal of Food Science* **47,** 284.

28
Preservation of Food by Freezing

Food preservation by freezing is a relatively new technology. The consumer oriented frozen food industry was developed by Birdseye and others between the 1930s and the 1950s [5]. Since that time there has been increased understanding of factors that contribute to frozen food quality and stability. This knowledge, along with the development of equipment for rapid freezing and the increased availability of home freezers, has led to considerable growth in the frozen food industry and the marketing of a wide assortment of frozen foods. These foods may be stored briefly in the freezing compartment of the household refrigerator. Those refrigerators equipped with dual temperature controls maintain a colder temperature in the freezer compartment than may be had in the ordinary freezing unit of a refrigerator, but even the dual-temperature refrigerators are not as efficient for freezing or holding frozen foods as are separate freezers that maintain temperatures of $-18°$ C ($0°$ F) or below.

The extent to which home freezing is practiced depends upon individual circumstances and desires. Produce must be available at advantageous prices in the market to make home freezing an economical practice. However, the home freezer contributes to efficient management in meal planning, allowing the advantages of quantity buying and less frequent shopping. It also provides convenience in the temporary storage of prepared foods made in larger quantities than will be consumed immediately.

Freezing is the change of physical state of a substance from liquid to solid. This occurs when heat or energy is removed from the substance, causing the molecules to reduce their motion and form an organized pattern [4]. The liquid substance in food that freezes is water and the solid phase of water is ice. Three intervals in the freezing process may be:

1. The temperature of the food is lowered to freezing.
2. Ice crystals begin to form. This is the freezing point and the temperature required varies with the product to be frozen. For water the freezing temperature is 0° C (32° F). As ice crystals form from water, the remaining water becomes more concentrated with solute, lowering the freezing point still further. This is a continuous process but the zone of maximum crystal formation in frozen foods is −4° to −0.5° C (25° to 31° F).
3. After ice formation ceases, the temperature of the frozen product is gradually lowered to the necessary storage temperature.

In freezing preservation, the low temperatures used check the life activities of plant and animal tissues. The action of microorganisms and of enzymes present in the food is negligible although some enzymatic changes do occur. Fast freezing and low storage temperatures are favorable for holding enzyme action at a minimum and for the best retention of nutrients. After defrosting, the growth of microorganisms may occur at a rapid rate.

The first commercial method of freezing foods was the slow freezing process sometimes called *sharp-freezing*. In this method, foods are placed in refrigerated rooms at temperatures ranging from −4° to −29° C (25° to −20° F). Large pieces of food or large containers of food require many hours or days to freeze. Quick-freezing methods have been developed. When lower temperatures are used, −32° to −40° C (−25° to −40° F), the time of freezing is greatly reduced over that required in sharp-freezing. Other factors that aid in hastening the freezing are small masses of foods, contact with freezing coils or metal plates, and rapidly moving currents of frigid air. One commercial method involves the direct or indirect contact of the food with refrigerated brine. Figure 28-1 shows the relative differences in time of freezing by the quick- and slow-freezing methods. It also shows that in slow freezing the food remains for a longer period of time in the zone of maximum crystal formation. Home freezing of food is a relatively slow process.

The process of freezing rapidly at very low temperatures is called *cryogenic freezing*. In cryogenic freezers the food is cooled so quickly that many tiny ice crystals form simultaneously rather than slowly forming a smaller number of large crystals. The fine ice crystals have a lesser effect on breaking up plant or animal cells. An addi-

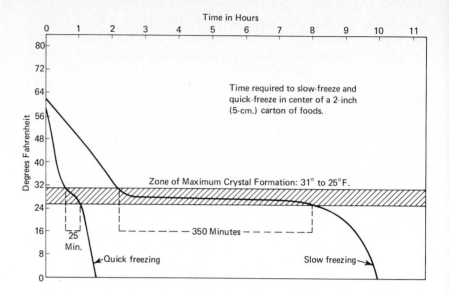

28-1 *Diagram showing the difference between quick and slow freezing.* (Courtesy of Frosted Foods Sales Corp.)

Time in Hours

Degrees Fahrenheit

Time required to slow-freeze and quick-freeze in center of a 2-inch (5-cm.) carton of foods.

Zone of Maximum Crystal Formation: 31° to 25°F.

25 Min.

— — — — 350 Minutes — — — — —

Quick freezing

Slow freezing

tional advantage of quick freezing for the commercial producer is the large quantity of food that can be frozen in a short period of time.

Changes During Freezing, Storage, and Thawing

If foods are harvested at the optimal stage of maturity and frozen before the sugar content is reduced or undesirable enzyme activity or fermentation can occur, the chances are good for a high quality product. Nevertheless, a number of changes occur on freezing food, holding it in frozen storage, and thawing it.

Formation of Ice Crystals

Ice crystal formation and later thawing affect the texture of many frozen foods. Injury to texture may be more than the mechanical rupture of the tissues by ice crystals. In meats that are slowly frozen, water leaves the cells and freezes between them. The fibers become desiccated and tend not to reabsorb all of the moisture on thawing. If freezing is rapid, ice is not formed between the cells but only in them. One result of desiccation is a toughening of the cells. Desiccation increases if the storage temperatures fluctuate and if the storage temperatures are too high.

Slow freezing of apple tissue has been shown to cause separation of the cells with crushing and rupturing of the cell walls. The thawed tissues are less firm than the raw tissue [17]. Similar processes appear to occur in vegetable tissues on freezing. The tearing of the tissues is probably responsible for part of the decrease in firmness with freezing and thawing. The loss of water held in the cells, or *turgor,* as the cells are killed in freezing is probably responsible for much of the loss of firmness from tissues. The water released from the cells of vegetables and fruits in freezing is not usually reabsorbed on thawing. Too high a temperature of holding frozen foods and too long a time of holding tend to increase drip on thawing.

Enzyme Action

Enzymes are present in all living tissue. Respiration, catalyzed by many enzymes, goes on in fruits and vegetables after they are severed from the growing plant. It reduces sugar content, which accounts for loss of sweetness in such vegetables as peas and corn. It is well known that even in the fresh state peas and corn are sweetest and have the best flavor immediately after they are picked, and that if they are held long they deteriorate markedly. Unless the enzymes responsible for respiration and other undesirable chemical changes are destroyed before foods are frozen, the foods will show various color, flavor, and texture changes during freezing, storage, and thawing. Freezing may inhibit enzyme action somewhat but it does not destroy the enzymes. To inactivate enzymes, vegetables are blanched before freezing. Both from the standpoint of overcooking and of the loss of nutrients, the blanching operation should be as short as possible. The blanching operation must, however, accomplish the purpose for which it is applied. The destruction of catalase in the tissues has been found to be an index to the destruction of other enzymes that are responsible for changes in the food. Vegetables should be chilled immediately after blanching.

Polyphenoloxidases in plant tissues may catalyze the oxidation of polyphenol substances to produce brown-colored compounds. Light fruits, such as peaches and apples, are particularly susceptible to enzymatic oxidative browning in both the fresh and frozen states. The addition of sugar or syrup to the fruit before freezing aids in the retention of color although darkening may occur if the fruits are held too long. Sugar also aids in preventing marked flavor changes and loss of the natural aroma. The addition of ascorbic acid helps to prevent browning, evidently because the ascorbic acid acts as an antioxidant. Citric and other organic acids may also be effective for some fruits by lowering the pH enough to interfere with the activity of the browning enzymes.

Oxidation Reactions

Nonenzymatic oxidation of fatty materials in frozen foods may also occur. Residual oxygen is usually present in frozen foods. The fat of pork is particularly susceptible to oxidation and the development of rancidity. Bacon does not freeze well. Antioxidants may be added to some products commercially to control unwanted oxidation.

Desiccation

If food products to be frozen are not properly packaged with moisture-vapor-proof packaging material close around them, they tend to lose moisture by sublimation. Some of the ice changes directly to water vapor without going through the liquid state and the water vapor collects as frost inside the package and/or inside the freezing compartment.

The term *freezer burn* as applied to frozen foods is dehydration resulting in discoloration, change in texture, and off flavors. This condition is often observed in frozen poultry and other flesh foods. Proper packaging is important in the control of freezer burn.

Activity of Microorganisms

Microorganisms are usually present in frozen foods. Although blanching lowers the microbial content and the activity of the microorganisms remaining in frozen fruits and vegetables is negligible so long as the storage temperature of the food remains at a temperature as low as $-9°$ to $-12°$ C ($16°$ to $10°$ F), the microorganisms become active at warmer temperatures and multiply rapidly. They attack the food as soon as defrosting occurs. It is highly important that frozen foods be held at optimal, nonfluctuating storage temperatures and be used as soon as they are defrosted. Many vegetables that have been partially defrosted and refrozen are bitter and disagreeable in flavor even though they may not be spoiled from a microbial standpoint.

Selection of Foods for Freezing

Success in freezing depends on the selection of the kinds and varieties of foods that are most adaptable to freezing as well as on the use of suitable methods, containers, and temperatures of freezing and holding. Local agricultural experiment stations are usually able to furnish advice concerning the kinds and varieties of locally grown fruits and vegetables that are best adapted to freezing preservation.

The proper stage of maturity of fruits and vegetables is highly important in affecting the quality of the frozen products. Vegetables should be harvested while they are young and tender, and fruits should be at their optimal stage of ripeness for best flavor, color, and texture. The fruits that are least changed in freezing preservation include red tart cherries, cranberries, currants, gooseberries, blueberries, and raspberries. Strawberries and peaches yield frozen products superior to those preserved by other methods. Loganberries, boysenberries, blackberries, dewberries, pineapple, melons, apples, and plums also yield good frozen products.

Although citrus fruits do not freeze well, their juices freeze very satisfactorily, as do apple cider and other fruit juices. Some fruit juices are concentrated by partial freezing, the ice crystals being removed by straining. Some vegetables do not freeze satisfactorily. These include green onions, lettuce and other salad greens, radishes, and raw tomatoes. Meats to be frozen should be of high quality. Beef and lamb are improved if the meat is allowed to hang in the cooler for ripening for a week or 10 days before freezing. Pork may be frozen within 1 or 2 days after slaughtering. Fish deteriorates so rapidly that it is best frozen as soon as possible after it is caught. Poultry should be thoroughly chilled after dressing and should be held 24 hours before freezing.

Freezing Fruits and Vegetables

Detailed steps in the preparation of fruits and vegetables for freezing are given in the U.S. Department of Agriculture bulletin listed in Reference 11. The procedures for preparing sliced peaches packed in syrup and for preparing snap beans are shown in Figures 28-2 and 28-3.

Fruits. Mixing juicy fruits with dry sugar, which draws out the juices to form a syrup, or the covering of the packed fruit with a syrup prepared from sugar or corn syrup has two advantages over a procedure for freezing fruit without added sugar: (1) protection against oxidation, which results in changes of color and flavor as well as vitamin inactivation; (2) retardation of other enzymatic changes during storage. Most fruits require sugar or syrup treatment because blanching to destroy enzymes changes the fresh flavor and texture characteristics of the fruits and is thus not commonly practiced. Blueberries and cranberries yield satisfactory products when frozen without sugar or syrup or scalding. Strawberries may be frozen whole but retain their best color and flavor in sliced form in sugar packs. Slicing results in better ascorbic acid retention than does crushing because all bruising of tissue results in a rapid loss of ascorbic acid.

Freezing Various Types of Foods

28-2 *Steps involved in the freezing of peaches at home.* (Courtesy of the U.S. Department of Agriculture)

(1) Select mature peaches that are firm-ripe, with no green color in the skins. Allow 1 to 1½ pounds for each pint to be frozen. Wash them carefully and drain.

(2) Pit the peaches and peel them by hand for the most attractive product. Peaches peel more quickly if they are dipped first in boiling water then in cold, but they may have ragged edges after thawing.

In preparing sugar packs the sugar is usually spread over the fruit in a large shallow pan, after which it is gently mixed with the fruit before it is packed into containers. Sugar packs may require inverting a few times to prevent sugar from settling to the bottom. When syrups are used, they are prepared and chilled prior to packing. The fruit is packed in the container before the syrup is added, more head space being required with liquid than with dry packs. Syrup concentrations vary from about 40 to 70 percent sugar, although some lower concentrations are sometimes preferred from a flavor standpoint (see Table 28-1). Fruits frozen for later use in jams and preserves or fruits that are to be held for short periods only are often satisfactorily frozen without sugar or syrup. Sugar and syrup packs of fruits may stand just long enough to allow the sugar to dissolve and the syrup to penetrate the fruit, but during this period

Table 28-1 *How to Make Sugar Syrup for Freezing Fruits**

Sugar Percentage of Syrup	Amount of Sugar to Be Added per Quart of Water	Pints of Water to Add to 4 Pints of White Corn Syrup†
40	1 lb. 6 oz	5
50	2 lb. 1 oz	3
60	3 lb. 2 oz	1½
65	3 lb. 14 oz	½
70	4 lb. 14 oz	¼

Method: Dissolve sugar in boiling water or mix syrup with warm water. Cool to 21°C (70°F) or lower before using.

*Courtesy of Dr. Donald K. Tressler.
†A high-grade corn syrup should be used.

(3) Pour about ½ cup of cold syrup into each pint container. Slice the peaches directly into the container.

(4) Add syrup to cover the peaches. Leave ½ inch of head space at the top of wide-mouth containers like these, to allow for expansion of the fruit during freezing.

(5) Put a small piece of crumpled parchment paper on top of the fruit to keep it down in the syrup. The syrup should always cover the fruit to keep the top pieces from changing color and flavor.

they should be held at temperatures just above the freezing point. In commercial practice, pectin substances used as a coating for fruits before freezing have resulted in the improved appearance and texture of the product and have decreased leakage after defrosting.

To prevent the browning of frozen fruits on defrosting, 150 milligrams of crystalline ascorbic acid may be used for each pound of finished pack (fruit plus sugar syrup), or ½ teaspoon (1,000 milligrams) crystalline ascorbic acid may be used in each 4 cups cold syrup. A number of commercial products containing ascorbic acid are available to retard the browning of frozen fruits.

Fruits may be frozen as purées for use as flavoring in ice creams or as toppings for sundaes.

Vegetables. Most vegetables yield products of the best quality and flavor when they are frozen on the day they are harvested. If immediate freezing is impossible, excellent refrigeration is necessary, but the speed at which the vegetables go from garden to freezer is one of the most important of all principles of freezing preservation. The stage of maturity is also important. For those vegetables, such as peas, corn, snap beans, lima beans, soybeans, and asparagus, that change rapidly in maturity, 1 or 2 days may mean the difference between a young tender vegetable and one that is tough and of poor quality. Leafy and root vegetables and squash do not require such exact timing although they should not be allowed to become too mature.

(6) Wipe all sealing edges clean for a good seal. Screw the lid on tight. Label with the name of the fruit and the date of freezing. Put the sealed containers in the coldest part of the freezer. Leave a little space between containers so that air can circulate freely. Store the frozen fruit at $-18°$ C ($0°$ F) or below.

565

(1) Select young, tender, stringless beans that snap when broken. Allow ⅔ to 1 pound for 1 pint frozen. Wash thoroughly.

(2) Cut the beans into 1- or 2-inch pieces, or slice them lengthwise.

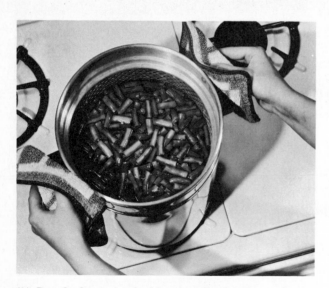

(3) Put the beans in the blanching basket, lower the basket into boiling water, and cover. Heat for 3 minutes. Keep heat high under the water.

(4) Plunge the basket of heated beans into cold water to stop the cooking. It takes about as long to cool vegetables as to heat them. When the beans are cool, remove them from the water and drain.

The preparation of vegetables for freezing is similar to that required for canning. Washing, draining, and sorting usually precede trimming and cutting. In order to avoid undesirable enzymatic changes, which adversely affect color, flavor, and texture during freezing and frozen storage, all vegetables require blanching or scalding to destroy or inactivate enzymes. Blanching may be done in boiling water or in steam. Water-soluble constituents are better retained in steam blanching but efficient steaming equipment is sometimes more difficult to provide for home use. What is necessary is a tightly closed container that holds enough rapidly boiling water to form steam and a rack to hold the vegetable above the water level. If boiling water is used, the water should be of such a volume that the boiling does not stop when the vegetable is placed in the water. Wire racks are desirable containers to hold the vegetable. At least 1 gallon of water per pound of vegetable is needed and more might be desirable.

Important as the blanching process is, it should not be overdone. The shortest possible time needed to inactivate enzymes should be used to avoid both actual cooking and the loss of water-soluble nutrients, such as ascorbic acid, the B vitamins, certain minerals, and sugar. Small quantities of vegetable should be blanched at one time in order that all pieces of vegetable may be quickly, thoroughly, and

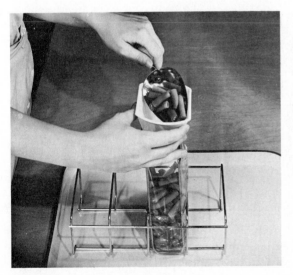

(5) Pack the beans into bags or other containers. A stand to hold the bags makes filling easier. A funnel helps keep the sealing edges clean.

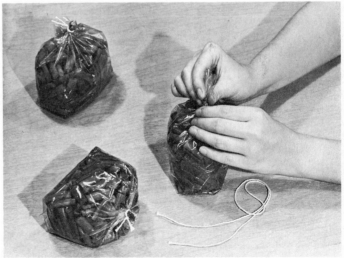

(6) Leave ½ inch of head space, and seal by twisting and folding back the top of the bag and fastening it. Freeze the beans at once. Store at a temperature of −18° C (0° F) or below. If the bags used are of materials that become brittle at low temperatures, they need an outside carton for protection.

uniformly heated. More than one large kettle or steamer may be used to hasten the scalding operation.

In addition to the inactivating of enzymes, other advantages result from blanching: the vegetable shrinks and becomes softer, which conserves space and promotes ease in handling; further cleansing of the product is accomplished; many but not all microorganisms are destroyed; in some vegetables, green color is intensified; and in some vegetables certain bitter and astringent flavor substances are eliminated and some objectionable odors are removed. After blanching, the vegetable must be cooled *quickly* in cold running water or ice water to a temperature of about 10° C (50° F). Chilling is necessary to check vitamin loss and maintain quality. Fully as much time is required for thorough chilling as for blanching.

Promptness in freezing is one of the most important of all conditions involved in the freezing preservation of foods, particularly for vegetables. The sooner vegetables are frozen after blanching the better the product is likely to be.

Freezing Meat, Fish, and Poultry

Meats are usually cut into pieces of a suitable size for cooking. Pieces may be steaks, chops, roasts, ground meat, cubes for stews, or other forms as desired. Removal of the bone conserves freezer space. Fish may be boned and packed as fillets or steaks. Poultry may be dressed and left whole for roasting, cut into pieces, or split down the back. Giblets are usually wrapped in parchment and put inside roasters and broilers. Only high quality, fresh products should be frozen.

Careful wrapping or packaging with recommended packaging materials is essential in protecting the products from oxidation and from drying out. More information on the home freezing of meat, fish, and poultry is given in U.S. Department of Agriculture bulletins listed in References 8, 12, and 13.

Freezing Eggs

Frozen egg whites seem to lose none of the quality needed for culinary uses, but yolks become gummy and gelled on thawing because of an irreversible change involving the lipoproteins. In order to be usable yolks must have a stabilizer added, such as sugar, syrup, or salt. Mixed whole eggs usually have a little of the stabilizer added because they contain the yolk, but these eggs have been successfully frozen without a stabilizer. When freezing eggs at home, about 1 tablespoon of sugar or corn syrup or ½ teaspoon of salt may be blended with 1 cup of egg yolks before freezing. The use of a small container that makes possible the thawing of only the amount of egg needed is recommended. Defrosted eggs usually have a relatively high bacterial count and deteriorate very rapidly after defrosting. The most sanitary practices fail to yield sterile frozen eggs.

Frozen eggs of a good quality result from the selection of eggs of good grade and sound quality. Unfit eggs can be found by candling or by breaking eggs singly in order to examine each egg before mixing it with the other stock. Shells require washing to remove dirt and bacteria. All processing equipment should be sterile.

Freezing Prepared Foods

Tremendous advancement has been made in the past few years in developing frozen prepared foods and meals that require only reheating. The microwave oven is ideal for reheating many of these products. Many boil-in-the-bag frozen products are available. They require only the heating of the bag and its contents in boiling water or in a microwave range. Materials used for packaging these products withstand both freezing and boiling temperatures.

Baked and unbaked pies, including both fruit and cream pies, cakes, pastries of several varieties, cookies and cooky doughs, bread and bread doughs are all available in the frozen food sections of many markets in the United States. Frozen bread doughs may be made from the usual formulations, provided that the level of yeast is increased to 4 or 5 percent. A fermentation period is recommended before freezing. It should probably be less than 15 minutes, however [14]. Sufficient yeast viability must be maintained during freezing and freezer storage to produce adequate amounts of carbon dioxide if a satisfactory product is to result. After fermentation, yeast appears to be more susceptible to destruction during freezing than if it has not undergone fermentation. The continuous mixing process, sometimes used for the commercial production of bread doughs, has been reported to give doughs the best freezer storage life. Doughs mixed by conventional processes are better for freezing if they are slightly stiff [15]. Buying frozen bread dough gives the consumer the advantages of baking fresh bread at home without the time involved in mixing and kneading. Time must still be allowed for thawing and rising, however. Baked bread may be very satisfactorily frozen at home.

Many prepared foods may also be frozen at home for convenience and efficiency. Instructions for freezing combination main dishes are given in the U.S. Department of Agriculture bulletin listed in

Reference 7. Freezing pie fillings as a convenience has been suggested [16]. Many baked products may be frozen at home either before or after baking. The storage life of unbaked batters and doughs is usually less than the already baked products. If frosted or iced cakes are to be frozen, they might be frozen first without wrapping to avoid the problem of the wrapping material sticking to the frosting, then wrapped and placed back in the freezer.

Certain foods do not freeze well at home. Cooked egg whites toughen and become rubbery, mayonnaise tends to separate as the emulsion breaks, starch-thickened sauces tend to weep as starch retrogradation occurs, and fried foods often change in flavor when reheated. However, materials and technical procedures to which the consumer does not have access are available commercially and research is constantly developing new ways of producing improved frozen products. Ultrafast freezing has been reported to give a good quality of cooked egg whites and of fried eggs, which tend to be wet and porous when frozen by conventional procedures [2]. Salad dressings stable to freezing have been developed using an oil that does not solidify at the storage temperature used. Frozen cooked chicken parts may be cooked before coating to allow for shrinkage and waxy cereal thickening agents may be used in the coatings for a better quality of product. Antioxidants delay off flavors that may result from the oxidation of fats [10].

Containers

Containers for freezing foods may be made of glass, metal, plastic materials, paper or fiber board, and certain moisture-vapor-proof transparent materials and should have tight-fitting lids or closures. A container that is ideal for home freezer use has been described as one that is both airtight to prevent oxidation and moisture-vapor-proof to prevent dehydration. Liquid tightness is necessary for use with sugar and syrup packs for fruits and brine packs for vegetables. Freezer space is usually such that a cubic shape of the containers permits the most efficient use of storage space. It is obvious that rigidity in a container prevents the crushing of products. If containers are of such a material as to permit sterilization by heat, they may be reused. Moisture-vapor-proof bags are satisfactory if little handling is required.

The materials available for wrapping meats include moisture-vapor-proof cellophane, vegetable parchment paper, heavy waxed paper, heavy wrapping paper, and special laminated papers made for wrapping frozen foods. Some papers have antioxidants applied to the surface to retard the rancidity of fat and possibly to improve the keeping quality of the meat. Double wrapping may be desirable, particularly if the wrapping is not completely moisture-vapor-proof.

Pliable moisture-vapor-proof bags should have as much air as possible removed from them and should be twisted and tightly closed. Immersing the lower part of the bag and its contents in water while packaging such irregularly shaped items as whole poultry may aid in removing air by the pressure of the water on the bag. Boil-in-the-bag containers are available for home use in freezing prepared foods. These bags may be heat sealed before freezing.

The size of the container used is important because many frozen foods should not be held after defrosting (see Table 28-2). Containers larger than ½ gallon or 5 pounds are not recommended because of the slow rate of freezing.

For dry packs, the cartons may be almost completely filled before freezing, but syrup or brine packs, or juicy products, such as sliced strawberries mixed with sugar, should have about 10 percent head space to allow for expansion of the contents during freezing.

Table 28-2 *Size of Container in Relation to Number of Servings*

Servings	Size of Container
1 or 2	½ pt.
4	1 pt.
8	1 qt.

Use and Management of the Home Freezer

A home freezer may prove a convenience in many ways but careful planning should go into its selection and use. Each family's needs differ, and freezer use should be adapted to individual conditions and preferences. A freezer is a large investment and should be kept full or nearly full all of the time to minimize the cost per unit of food stored. As the stock of home frozen fruits and vegetables diminishes it may be possible to buy large quantities of commercially frozen products at a discount. Suggested maximum home storage periods for maintaining good quality in commercially frozen foods are given in Table 28-3.

Time may be saved by doubling or tripling recipes when they are being prepared if they are suitable for freezing. The frozen products can be conveniently served on busy days. Advance planning in meal preparation and entertaining may be simplified with the use of a freezer. An accurate inventory of frozen foods should be kept. All foods should be stored at temperatures no higher than $-18°$ C ($0°$ F) to maintain palatability and nutritive value. Accurate and effective temperature control is, therefore, very important in a home freezer.

Sanitary Quality of Frozen Foods

Because frozen foods normally contain some microorganisms, they may become highly perishable when they are defrosted and held at warmer temperatures that allow more rapid growth and development of microbes. This is especially true of foods such as meats, fish, fruits, and vegetables that contain relatively large amounts of moisture. Promptness in using defrosted foods is highly important. De-

Table 28-3 *Suggested Maximum Home-storage Periods to Maintain Good Quality in Commercially Frozen Foods**

Food	Approximate Holding Period at −18° C (0° F) (months)	Food	Approximate Holding Period at −18° C (0° F) (months)	Food	Approximate Holding Period at −18° C (0° F) (months)
Fruits and vegetables		Pies (unbaked)		Cooked chicken and turkey	
Fruits		Apple	8	Chicken or turkey dinners	
Cherries	12	Boysenberry	8	(sliced meat and gravy)	6
Peaches	12	Cherry	8	Chicken or turkey pies	12
Raspberries	12	Peach	8	Fried chicken	4
Strawberries	12			Fried chicken dinners	4
Fruit juice concentrates		*Meat*			
Apple	12	Beef		*Fish*	
Grape	12	Hamburg or chipped (thin)		Fillets	
Orange	12	steaks	3	Cod, flounder, haddock,	
Vegetables		Roasts	12	halibut, pollack	6
Asparagus	8	Steaks	12	Mullet, ocean perch,	
Beans	8	Lamb		sea trout, striped bass	3
Cauliflower	8	Patties (ground meat)	3	Pacific Ocean perch	2
Corn	8	Roasts	12	Salmon steaks	2
Peas	8	Pork, cured	2	Sea trout, dressed	3
Spinach	8	Pork, fresh		Striped bass, dressed	3
		Chops	4	Whiting, drawn	4
Frozen desserts		Roasts	8		
Ice cream	1	Sausage	2	*Shellfish*	
Sherbet	1	Veal		Clams, shucked	3
		Cutlets, chops	4	Crabmeat	
Baked goods		Roasts	8	Dungeness	3
Bread and yeast rolls		Cooked meat		King	10
White bread	3	Meat dinners	3	Oysters, shucked	4
Cinnamon rolls	2	Meat pie	3	Shrimp	12
Plain rolls	3	Swiss steak	3		
Cakes				*Cooked fish and shellfish*	
Angel	2	*Poultry*		Fish with cheese sauce	3
Chiffon	2	Chicken		Fish with lemon butter	
Chocolate layer	4	Cut-up	9	sauce	3
Fruit	12	Livers	3	Fried fish dinner	3
Pound	6	Whole	12	Fried fish sticks, scallops,	
Yellow	6	Duck, whole	6	or shrimp	3
Danish pastry	3	Goose, whole	6	Shrimp creole	3
Doughnuts		Turkey		Tuna pie	3
Cake type	3	Cut-up	6		
Yeast raised	3	Whole	12		

frosting is not necessary for many foods that are to be cooked. They may be cooked directly from the frozen state.

Questions have arisen regarding the possibility of the existence of bacterial toxins in low acid vegetables that are frozen. Foods that are frozen before bacterial action has had a chance to occur, and cooked in the frozen state or immediately after defrosting, are thought to be safe from the standpoint of the presence of bacterial toxins, such as that of *Clostridium botulinum.*

Experiments with the quick-freezing of pork have shown that lowering the temperature rapidly to $-35°$ C $(-31°$ F) destroys *Trichinella* larvae. Earlier work has shown that chilling pork to a temperature of $-18°$ C $(0°$ F) and holding it at that temperature for 20 days renders the pork safe from trichina.

The flavor, color, texture, and vitamin value of frozen foods are impaired by defrosting and refreezing and spoilage may occur if the defrosted food is held too long at too high a temperature. The frozen food industry continues to work at improving the frozen food transport and distribution systems so that frozen foods will be constantly maintained at low temperatures [1, 3]. In retail stores great care is required to avoid unnecessary temperature rises.

If the home freezer stops running and will be off for an extended period of time, several alternatives are possible to keep the food from spoiling. If it is available, enough dry ice may be added to the freezer to maintain below freezing temperatures for a few days. Or, the food may be put into insulated boxes or wrapped in newspapers and blankets and rushed to a freezer-locker plant. If the freezer will be off only a few hours, it should simply be kept tightly closed.

Sometimes frozen foods are partially or completely thawed before it is discovered that the freezer is not operating. Although partial thawing and refreezing reduces the quality of most foods, partially thawed foods that still contain ice crystals or foods that are still cold (about $4°$ C or $40°$ F) may usually be safely refrozen. However, ground meats, poultry, and seafood should not be refrozen if they have thawed completely since bacteria multiply rapidly in these foods. Each package of meat, vegetable, or cooked food should be carefully examined. If the food is thawed and the color or odor is questionable, the food should be discarded since it may be dangerous.

Nutritive Value of Frozen Foods

Most studies of frozen foods, particularly vegetables, relate to vitamin content. Vitamins, as well as other nutrients, may be lost as a result of peeling and trimming, loss of exudate on thawing, leaching during water blanching, and chemical oxidation or breakdown [6]. The vitamin A precursors, which are not water soluble substances, are retained well in fruits and vegetables during processing and freezing. The water soluble vitamins tend to suffer some loss, particularly during the blanching and cooling of vegetables before freezing and in the leakage or drip after defrosting. Long storage, especially at fluctuating temperatures or temperatures that are too high, may result in further losses. The cooking of frozen vegetables results in additional loss, depending partly upon the method of cooking.

The effects of various steps in the home-processing of frozen vegetables on ascorbic acid retention have been studied [9]. The pattern of retention varied greatly from one vegetable to another but in each vegetable the combined effects of blanching, freezing, and frozen storage for 6 months were such that the percentage of retention of ascorbic acid in the cooked frozen vegetable was significantly less than in a similar fresh cooked vegetable. It should be noted that ascorbic acid or vitamin C is the most unstable of the vitamins. Greater losses were noted in most vegetables for blanching than for freezing and frozen storage. However, the blanching is a necessary process for frozen vegetables because it aids in the retention of vitamins during freezing and freezer storage as well as improving palatability of the vegetables as they are eaten.

Large variability in nutrient loss can occur in processed foods, depending upon the product and the conditions of processing. However, the water soluble vitamins are retained substantially better in frozen fruits and vegetables than they are in canned fruits and vegetables [6].

Study Questions

1. Discuss differences in methods, rate and time of freezing, and size of resulting ice crystals between sharp freezing and quick freezing.
2. Describe several undesirable changes that may occur during freezing, frozen storage, or thawing of frozen foods.
3. a. Explain why vegetables should be blanched before freezing.
   b. Give several suggestions for carrying out the blanching process to ensure that it will accomplish its purpose satisfactorily.
4. What is *freezer burn* and how may it be prevented in frozen foods?
5. How does freezing control the causes of food spoilage and thus preserve foods?
6. Discuss several points that should be considered in selecting foods for freezing.
7. What are two important roles, in addition to sweetening, that are played by sugar or syrup packs in freezing fruits?
8. What general procedures should be followed in the freezing of meat, fish, and poultry?
9. What differences are there between the procedures for freezing egg whites and egg yolks? Why are these different procedures necessary?

10. a. Why should containers and wrappers used on frozen foods be mois-
       ture-vapor-proof? Explain this in detail.
    b. Describe several types of containers and wraps that are appropriate
       for frozen foods.
    c. Why should head space be left in containers when freezing foods?
11. List several things that should be considered if one is to make the most
    effective use of a home freezer.
12. How does the nutritive value of frozen foods generally compare with
    that of similar fresh foods?

References

1. Ashby, B. H. 1981. Developments in frozen food transport. *Food Technology* **35,** 67 (no. 3).
2. Bengtsson, N. 1967. Ultrafast freezing of cooked egg white. *Food Technology* **21,** 1259.
3. Bramsnaes, F. 1981. Maintaining the quality of frozen foods during distribution. *Food Technology* **35,** 38 (no. 4).
4. Brown, M. S. 1976. Effects of freezing on fruit and vegetable structure.
   Food Technology **30,** 106 (no. 5).
5. Farkas, D. F. 1981. New concepts for expanding and improving frozen
   preservation techniques. *Food Technology* **35,** 63 (no. 3).
6. Fennema, O. 1977. Loss of vitamins in fresh and frozen foods. *Food
   Technology* **31,** 32 (no. 12).
7. *Freezing Combination Main Dishes*. Home and Garden Bulletin No. 40.
   Washington, DC: U.S. Department of Agriculture, 1976.
8. *Freezing Meat and Fish in the Home*. Home and Garden Bulletin No. 93.
   Washington, DC: U.S. Department of Agriculture, 1977.
9. Gordon, J., and I. Noble. 1959. Effects of blanching, freezing, freezing-
   storage, and cooking on ascorbic acid retention in vegetables. *Journal of
   Home Economics* **51,** 867.
10. Hanson, H. L. 1964. Recent research on prepared frozen foods. *Journal
    of the American Dietetic Association* **45,** 523.
11. *Home Freezing of Fruits and Vegetables*. Home and Garden Bulletin No.
    10. Washington, DC: U.S. Department of Agriculture, 1980.
12. *Home Freezing of Poultry and Poultry Main Dishes*. Home and Garden
    Bulletin No. 70. Washington, DC: U.S. Department of Agriculture,
    1975.
13. *How to Buy Meat for Your Freezer*. Home and Garden Bulletin No. 166.
    Washington, DC: U.S. Department of Agriulture, 1980.
14. Kline, L., and T. F. Sugihara. 1968. Frozen bread doughs. I. Prepared by
    the straight dough method. *Baker's Digest* **42,** 44 (no. 5).
15. Lorenz, K., and W. G. Bechtel. 1964. Frozen bread dough. *Baker's Digest*
    38, 59 (no. 6).
16. Snow, P. R., and A. M. Briant. 1960. Frozen fillings for quick lemon
    meringue pies. *Journal of Home Economics* **52,** 350.
17. Sterling, C. 1968. Effect of low temperature on structure and firmness
    of apple tissue. *Journal of Food Science* **33,** 577.

29

Drying and Pickling

Drying

Nature has used drying as a means of preservation in cereal grains, legumes, and nuts, all of which mature and dry on the plants. The sun-drying of fruits and vegetables has been practiced in homes for many years. Meat has also been dried in the form of *jerky*. In sunny climates, such as that of California, commercial producers of dried fruits continue to use the less expensive method of sun-drying although it has been shown that a better product with higher vitamin value is obtained by artificial heat and circulating air. A solar drier with shade provided has been shown to improve the retention of ascorbic acid and carotene (vitamin A value) over use of the same drier without shade from the direct rays of the sun [6].

The word *dehydration* sometimes implies the use of controlled conditions of heating with the forced circulation of air as compared with the use of the sun. Freeze-drying is a more recently developed method of drying involving freezing and then the sublimation of the ice under vacuum. This process is described below.

Preservation by Drying

Principles involved in the removal of moisture from foods include (1) surrounding the food with warm air, which has the capacity for holding more moisture than does cool air; (2) circulating air, which constantly brings a fresh supply of air into contact with the food; (3) heating in a vacuum, which increases water loss at very low temperatures, thus better retaining the natural characteristics of the food;

(4) dividing the food into small pieces, which exposes more surface to the action of heat and air; (5) lye-dipping, as in the case of prunes, to make skins more permeable to water; and (6) treating the food with the fumes of burning sulfur, which, in addition to inactivating enzymes that cause a darkening of color, also affects cell membranes in a way that accelerates the movement of water from the interior to the surface of the food. Not all of these principles are used in every method of drying.

Dried foods are preserved because the available moisture level is so low that microorganisms cannot grow. Enzyme activity is controlled in vegetables by blanching before drying and in some fruits by treatment with sulfur dioxide or sulfites. Because of their reduction in weight, dried foods are more easily transported and stored than are the fresh or canned products. Dehydration processes are used commercially for many foods, including dried milks, eggs, coffee, tea, fruit drinks, dessert mixes, whipped toppings, and flavor-base mixes as well as the more traditional dried fruits, vegetables, meat, and fish. Liquids may be spray-dried or drum-dried. Foam-mat drying may be used commercially with orange and tomato juices. In this process, a small amount of edible foam stabilizer, such as a monoglyceride or a modified soy protein with methylcellulose, is added to the liquid and a stiff foam is produced by whipping. The foam is spread in a thin layer and dried in a stream of hot air. The product separates easily into small particles on cooling. A process of osmotic dehydration of fruits has also been reported [8]. The method involves the partial dehydration of fruits by osmosis in a concentrated sugar solution or syrup. The fruit is reduced to about 50 percent of its original weight, after which it is drained and either frozen or dried further. The sugar protects color and flavor throughout the entire dehydration process.

Microwaves have been used in the finish-drying of potato chips [9]. This allows the desired removal of moisture from the potato chips without producing a dark brown color from frying for too long a period of time. The use of microwave dehydration for several food products on a commercial basis has been reported [4].

New technologies continue to be developed for the production of dried foods, such as explosion puffing. In this process, food pieces are air-dried in a conventional manner to 15 to 35 percent moisture and are then quickly heated with steam under pressure. Their remaining water becomes superheated relative to atmospheric pressure. When the food is suddenly discharged to the atmosphere, the rapid pressure drop causes some of the water within the pieces to flash into steam, causing channels and fissures that give a porous structure to the food. This makes finish drying and then rehydration much faster [3]. Processes have been developed for drying fruits and vegetables, such as blueberries, apples, potatoes, sweet potatoes, and carrots in this manner [11]. Much of the food used during space travel has been dehydrated. Some of the developments in space foods are discussed on pp. 30–32.

Some drying of foods is still practiced in homes in the United States, particularly in the southern part of the country where sun rays are plentiful. Fruits and vegetables, such as peaches, apricots, apples, onions, and corn, are commonly dried. A number of dryers for home use are available on the market.

Freeze-drying. In the usual process of freeze-drying, the preliminary preparation of food is carried out as for other methods of drying and then the prepared food is frozen, placed in a vacuum chamber, and a small amount of heat is applied. The ice in the frozen food, under the reduced pressure of the vacuum, changes directly to water vapor (sublimes) and is carried away by the circulating heated air, thus reducing the moisture content of the food. The food remains frozen through most of the drying period and does not get warm as does food that is subjected to ordinary drying processes. Fresh flavors and textures are, therefore, better preserved by freeze-drying than by sun-drying or other procedures of artificial drying without vacuum. Microwave freeze-drying is also possible on a commercial basis and may be less costly than conventional freeze-drying [12].

The freeze-drying of food is relatively expensive and is used only by commercial firms. Drying time depends on the product and its thickness. Freeze-drying usually requires 10 to 20 hours and the moisture content of the final product is 1 to 4 percent. Oxidation during freeze-drying is curbed by the low oxygen tension maintained and sometimes by the breaking of the vacuum with an inert gas rather than air.

By conventional drying methods, the satisfactory drying of meat is limited to ground or extremely thin strips, whereas by freeze-drying steaks and chops ½ to 1 inch thick can be processed. Roasts require a longer drying period, thus presenting cost and technical problems.

Freeze-dried products are similar in size and shape to the original fresh products. Low-temperature drying minimizes the loss of volatile constituents and tends to prevent appreciable chemical, enzymatic, and microbial action. The food industry is interested in freeze-drying for two principal reasons: (1) the saving in transportation and storage costs (the weight of the dried product is about one-third that of the original food); and (2) the fact that refrigeration is not required. Sir Edmund Hillary took 300 pounds of freeze-dried items on his Himalayan expedition. The products reconstituted to 1,200 pounds and included ham, chicken, chops, steaks, fruits, and vegetables. Although refrigeration is not required, the product does tend to deteriorate with long storage unless it is properly packaged. The best packaging is probably a metal container or a special film pouch with air removed or filled with inert gas. Low-temperature storage is advantageous but adds to the cost.

Some fruits are very successfully freeze-dried to 5 to 8 percent moisture. Apricots are light in color, hydrate rapidly, and have a fresh flavor. Some strawberries have been held for long periods of time without a change in flavor. The browning of fruits can be prevented by treatment with sulfur dioxide.

Freeze-dried coffee, dried by either conventional or microwave methods, is on the market. Freeze-dried fish salad mixes are available for institutional use. A number of freeze-dried foods for individual use are sold in some sporting goods outlets and are used by campers and hikers.

The present quality of freeze-dried meats is very similar to fresh meat in flavor and color but they may be somewhat tougher and drier. Tenderness is improved if the meat is hydrated in a 2 percent brine or if proteolytic enzymes are added to the hydrating liquid. Poultry cooked after freeze-drying has been reported to have better texture, tenderness, and juiciness than poultry cooked before freeze-drying [1].

Drying Fruits and Vegetables

General principles of drying are discussed here. Specific methods and information on equipment for home drying are included in the U.S. Department of Agriculture bulletin listed in Reference 2.

Preparation of Vegetables. Vegetables that are to be used for drying should be young and tender and in prime condition. Because deterioration starts immediately after gathering, promptness of drying is one of the most important considerations.

Vegetables require a thorough washing, after which they are blanched or scalded. Blanching destroys the enzymes that are responsible for the changes in flavor, color, and texture as well as those that inactivate vitamins during drying and storage. Blanching may be done in boiling water or in steam. Steam may be preferable to water as it results in smaller losses of soluble nutrients.

Cubing is a favorite method of preparing beets and carrots for drying. Green beans are left whole or cut into pieces. Lima beans and other fresh shell beans and peas are shelled before blanching and are dried whole. Corn is blanched on the cob and cut off whole-grain style. Tough stems and roots are trimmed from green leafy vegetables. After blanching, vegetables are piled one layer deep on trays. Particular care should be used to pile leafy vegetables loosely.

Preparation of Fruits. All fruits require washing and some may be pared. Small fruits need not be cut, but larger fruits dry more quickly if they are cut into halves, quarters, or slices of ¼-inch thickness. To avoid discoloration and to make cell membranes more permeable to water, fruits may be sulfured. Some practices in drying include steam blanching for fruits but sulfuring is more effective. A tight frame with trays is necessary for exposing fruits to the fumes of burning sulfur out of doors.

Procedures for Drying. After preliminary preparation, food that is to be dried should be placed on drying trays. The trays should not be overloaded and may require shifting from top to bottom as drying progresses in order to achieve a greater uniformity of drying. The source of heat may be the sun, an oven, or a specially built dehydrator or drying chamber [2].

The optimal temperatures for drying are between 52° and 60° C (125° and 140° F). Slightly higher temperatures may be used at the beginning of drying to drive off moisture more rapidly and to prevent the souring of the food that dries too slowly, but lower temperatures for a longer time yield a better quality of dried product and one with better retention of vitamin content. The length of time for drying varies and will depend on the type of food, the size of the food pieces, and the type of drier, but usually varies from 6 to 15 hours for vegetables and 6 to 24 hours for fruits. Vegetables are dried until they are brittle but fruits feel leathery when they are dried.

Drying of Meat

Meat may be dried at home if it is cut into thin strips. It is commonly called jerky. Lean meat should be cut, with the grain, into strips ¼ to ½ inch thick, 1 to 1½ inches wide, and 4 to 12 inches long. The sliced meat is salted and flavored or marinated for 6 to 12 hours before being dried in the sun, the oven, or a dehydrator [2]. Finished jerky is chewy and leathery, not brittle.

Packaging and Storing Dried Foods

Immediately after the dried food is cooled, it should be packed in insect-proof and moisture-proof containers, such as tin cans, plastic containers, glass jars, heavy waxed cartons, or heavy cloth bags coated with paraffin. Dried foods are sufficiently hygroscopic to absorb moisture from the air. If the product must be held for a time before packaging, it is safer to return it to the drier and reheat it 10 to 15 minutes at a temperature of about 57° C (135° F) before packaging. The dried food is cooled before storing. Storing dried foods in quantities that can be used relatively soon after opening is preferable to storing in large quantities that may deteriorate before being used. Storage conditions that favor the deterioration of dehydrated foods are air, moisture, and heat.

DRYING AND PICKLING   *581*

Use of Dried Foods

Many dried fruits can be eaten without rehydration if they have not been dried to an extremely low moisture level. If fruits are to be rehydrated, this can be done by covering them with water and allowing them to stand from 30 minutes up to several hours, depending upon the kind of fruit and size of pieces. Using hot water hastens the rehydration process. Dried fruits may be cooked in the soaking water. Sugar, if used to sweeten, should be added at the end of the cooking process so that it will not interfere with the absorption of moisture.

Most dried vegetables should be soaked in cold water for 20 minutes to 2 hours to begin the rehydration process. They should then be simmered in the soaking water until tender, allowing excess water to evaporate. Greens, cabbage, tomatoes, and herbs do not require preliminary soaking before they are cooked [2].

Nutritive Value of Dried Foods

The blanching and sulfuring of fruits and vegetables improves the flavor and appearance of the dried products and aids somewhat in vitamin retention by inactivating enzymes responsible for oxidation. This is especially pertinent for carotenes and ascorbic acid, which are easily inactivated by oxidation. However, dehydrated foods are uncertain or negligible sources of ascorbic acid. Although fruits are not important sources of thiamin, sulfuring has a destructive effect on this vitamin. Thiamin losses from dehydrated vegetables are apparently small and probably occur mainly during the preliminary blanching and cooling operations.

Pickling

Pickling is the preservation of vegetables, fruits, or meats by the use of acid (usually vinegar). The acid is generally supplemented by relatively large amounts of salt or sugar. Spices also are commonly used both for flavor and for the slight preservation action that some spices have. Some products, such as fermented pickles and sauerkraut, are preserved by the lactic acid formed by fermentation. Lactic acid, in addition to its preservative action, imparts a characteristic flavor.

Pickles may be classified as brined pickles and fresh-pack pickles. Brined pickles undergo a fermentation or curing process in brine for several weeks. During this time changes occur in appearance and texture. Green vegetables change to an olive- or yellow-green and become uniformly translucent. The texture becomes firm and crisp but tender. Characteristic flavors are developed. Fresh-pack pickles are placed in brine for a few hours or overnight. They are then drained and combined with a boiling hot mixture of vinegar and spices. They are not fermented or cured.

Brine

Most vegetables used for pickling are more than four-fifths water. Water may be removed from the vegetables chiefly by brining. In fresh-pack or quick-process pickles the whole vegetables may be soaked overnight in the brine or the vegetable may be chopped or sliced and covered with brine or salt. If dry salt is used, it is sprinkled over layers of the sliced or chopped vegetable and by extraction of water forms its own brine. If vegetables are rather finely chopped, the water will be removed if the vegetables are drained in a cheesecloth bag for several hours without the use of salt. The concentration of brine used for pickling varies with the use of the brine. Weak brines permit fermentation by acid-forming types of bacteria, chiefly lactic acid-formers, while stronger brines check or prevent fermentation.

When fairly concentrated brines are used, vegetables require some freshening by soaking in clear water before being made into pickles. It is always desirable to wash off surface brine whether or not freshening is needed in order to avoid too salty a taste.

Pickles are generally high in salt (sodium chloride). However, an evaluation of commercially processed dill pickles indicated that the level of sodium chloride in dill pickles could be significantly reduced from presently used levels without affecting sensory preference [5].

Processing

Hot pickling solutions are generally added after the product has been either brined overnight or fermented for several weeks. The fruits or vegetables may be heated in the pickling mixture or the boiling pickling mixture may be poured over the food which has been placed in jars. Pickled products require heat treatment to destroy microorganisms that can cause spoilage and to inactivate enzymes that can adversely affect flavor, color, and texture. Heating the filled jars in a boiling water bath is recommended. Methods of processing may affect the quality of pickles [10].

In preparing pickling solutions it is important to use vinegar that contains 5 to 6 percent acetic acid (50 to 60 grain) and vinegar should not be diluted unless the recipe so specifies. It is particularly important to maintain a high degree of acidity in pickled vegetables such as beets, peppers, and pimientos when they are processed with a boiling water bath. Spores of *Clostridium botulinum* may be present in these vegetables and, if the pickling solution is not very acid, these spores may survive processing in a boiling water bath. Botulism resulting from eating improperly processed pickled beets has caused several deaths in the United States.

Figure 29-1 shows the steps that are involved in the preparation of brined or fermented dill pickles. Specific procedures and recipes for making pickles at home can be found in the U.S. Department of Agriculture bulletin listed in Reference 7.

Equipment Used for Pickling

Aluminum utensils, being hardly affected by acid, are suitable for use in pickling. Enameled ware, in which the base metal is well covered with enamel, is also suitable, as are stainless steel and glass utensils. Iron, tin, brass, copper, and some other metals are affected by acid sufficiently to impart a metallic taste or unwholesome salts to the pickles. Aluminum, stainless steel, enamel, or wooden spoons are preferable for stirring pickles. For fermenting or brining, a lead-free crock or stone jar, an unchipped enamel-lined pan, or a large glass jar or bowl is appropriate.

Quality Characteristics of Pickles

Texture. Crispness rather than flabbiness is a desirable characteristic of pickles. Some conditions that increase flabbiness in pickles are too strong a brine, too long an application of brine, and overcooking in the pickling solution. Shriveling of pickles may result from using too strong a pickling solution at the beginning of the pickling process. If a strong pickling solution is desired, it is best to start with a dilute solution and increase the strength gradually.

Slippery or soft pickles usually indicates microbial spoilage. Microbial growth may be caused by too little salt or acid in the pickling solution, insufficient heat treatment, or lack of a tight seal on the jar.

Color. Because both heat and acid are destructive to chlorophyll,

29-1 *Steps involved in making brined dill pickles.* (Courtesy of the U.S. Department of Agriculture)

(1) Wash cucumbers thoroughly with a brush. Use several changes of cold water. Take care to remove all blossoms. Drain on rack.

(2) Place half of the spices and a layer of dill on the bottom of a 5-gallon jar or crock. Fill with cucumbers to 3 or 4 inches from the top. Cover with the remaining dill and add the rest of the spices. Add the mixed salt, vinegar, and water.

a bright green color is generally not expected in home-prepared pickles. At one time, copper kettles were used for cooking pickles in order to impart a bright green color but the copper salts formed were found to be unwholesome. The olive-green color of pickled green vegetables is commonly accepted as typical of the product. The use of overmature, poor quality cucumbers in the making of pickles may result in a product with particularly dull or faded color. Undesirable darkness in pickles may be caused by the use of ground spices, iodized salt, overcooking, and minerals, especially iron, in the water.

Study Questions

1. State and explain several principles that are involved in the process of removing moisture from food.
2. a. Explain why drying is an effective method of food preservation.
   b. Why are vegetables blanched before drying?
   c. Why are some fruits sulfured?
3. a. What basic steps are involved in the process of freeze-drying?
   b. Discuss advantages and possible disadvantages of the use of freeze-drying for preserving a variety of foods.
4. Describe a satisfactory procedure for drying vegetables; for drying fruits; and for drying meats. Explain why the various steps in the procedures are required.
5. How should dried foods be packaged and stored, and why?
6. a. Describe two general types of pickles.
   b. Explain the role played by brining for each type of pickle.

(3) Use a heavy plate or glass lid that fits inside the container. A glass jar filled with water makes a good weight to hold the cover down and keep the cucumbers under the brine.

(4) Bubbles and the formation of scum indicate active fermentation. Scum should be removed daily.

(5) After 3 weeks of fermentation the dills are ready for processing. Cloudiness of the brine results from yeast development during fermentation. Strain the brine before using.

(6) Pack pickles firmly into clean, hot quart jars. Do not wedge tightly. Add several pieces of the dill to each jar. Cover with boiling brine to ½ inch from top of jar; adjust lids. Place the jars in boiling water and process for 15 minutes.

(7) Remove the jars from the canner and complete the seals if necessary. Set the jars upright, several inches apart, on a wire rack to cool. Cloudiness of brine is typical when the original fermentation brine is used as the covering liquid.

c. How should pickles generally be processed in the final stages of preparation?
d. What type of equipment should be used for pickling and why?
e. Describe desirable characteristics of pickles.

References

1. Bele, L. M., H. H. Palmer, A. A. Klose, and T. F. Irmiter. 1966. Evaluation of objective methods of measuring differences in texture of freeze-dried chicken meat. *Journal of Food Science* **31**, 791.

2. *Drying Foods at Home.* Home and Garden Bulletin No. 217. Washington, DC: U.S. Department of Agriculture, 1977.
3. Heiland, W. K., J. F. Sullivan, R. P. Konstance, J. C. Craig, Jr., J. Cording, Jr., and N. C. Aceto. 1977. A continuous explosion puffing system. *Food Technology* **31,** 32 (no. 11).
4. Huxsoll, C. C., and A. I. Morgan, Jr. 1968. Microwave dehydration of potatoes and apples. *Food Technology* **22,** 47.
5. James, C., and R. Buescher. 1983. Preference for commercially processed dill pickles in relation to sodium chloride, acid and texture. *Journal of Food Science* **48,** 641.
6. Maeda, E. E., and D. K. Salunkhe. 1981. Retention of ascorbic acid and total carotene in solar dried vegetables. *Journal of Food Science* **46,** 1288.
7. *Making Pickles and Relishes at Home.* Home and Garden Bulletin No. 92. Washington, DC: U.S. Department of Agriculture, 1978.
8. Ponting, J. D., G. G. Watters, R. R. Forrey, R. Jackson, and W. L. Stanley. 1966. Osmotic dehydration of fruits. *Food Technology* **20,** 1365.
9. Porter, V. L., A. I. Nelson, M. P. Steinberg, and L. S. Wei. 1973. Microwave finish drying of potato chips. *Journal of Food Science* **38,** 583.
10. Sistrunk, W. A., and J. Kozup. 1982. Influence of processing methodology on quality of cucumber pickles. *Journal of Food Science* **47,** 949.
11. Sullivan, J. F., J. C. Craig, Jr., E. D. Dekazos, S. M. Leiby, and R. P. Konstance. 1982. Dehydrated blueberries by the continuous explosion-puffing process. *Journal of Food Science* **47,** 445.
12. Sunderland, J. E. 1982. An economic study of microwave freeze-drying. *Food Technology* **36,** 50 (no. 2).

30

Fruit Jellies and Preserves

Jelly is a product made from fruit juice. An ideal jelly is stiff enough to hold its form when it is removed from the mold, yet sufficiently delicate in texture to quiver. Jelly is transparent, and has the characteristic flavor and color of the fruit from which it is made. Jelly is tender, cuts easily, and yet is firm enough to retain the sharp angles produced by cutting. It is not gummy, sticky, or syrupy (Figure 30-1).

Essential Constituents of Jelly

The essential constituents for making jelly are (1) pectin, (2) acid, (3) sugar, and (4) water or fruit juice. Pectin is the basic gelling agent in fruit jellies.

The pectic substances that are present in many plant tissues include (1) protopectin, the parent substance which is relatively insoluble and has no jelly-making power; (2) pectin or pectinic acid, which is the soluble form needed for making jelly; and (3) pectic acid, which is formed from pectin by enzymes that hydrolyze a methyl ester group from the pectin molecule. Pectic acid has no jelly-making power. Pectin may be formed from protopectin by ripening enzymes and by boiling in dilute acid. If the fruit used for making jelly is slightly underripe, only part of the protopectin will

30-1 *A good quality jelly is stiff enough to hold its shape yet is delicate and tender.*

have been converted into pectin by ripening. The remainder can be converted into pectin by boiling the fruit in the presence of the natural acid. Some ripening of the fruit is necessary in order that the fruit may have a desirable color and characteristic flavor. If the fruit is overripe, too much of the pectic substance occurs as pectic acid.

The pectic substances of fruit are located (1) in the middle lamella (the area between cells), where their chief function appears to be as a cementing material, and (2) in the cell walls. In general, it is the pulp and not the juice of fruits that contains the pectin. Some juices, however, may show an appreciable amount of pectin. Fruits such as quince and apple contain abundant pectin in their cores and skins. In the preparation of such fruits, the cores and skins are cooked with the pulp for pectin extraction. In citrus fruits, the pectin is chiefly in the white part of the rind.

A certain degree of acidity is necessary in a jelly mixture in order for the pectin to form a gel structure. An optimum pH for gel formation is about 3.2. Acid also contributes to flavor.

Fruits differ widely in their pectin content and in acidity. From years of practical experience in making jelly as well as from scientific studies of the fruits suitable for making jelly, it is evident that only certain fruits contain sufficient pectin and acid to make good jelly without the addition of purified pectin and/or an acid substance. Some fruits may be rich in pectin but deficient in acid and vice versa. If fruit lacks pectin, it may be combined with another fruit that has abundant pectin or with a commercial pectin product. Lemon juice or citric acid may be added to fruit juices that are deficient in acid. Approximately ⅛ teaspoon of crystalline citric acid may be substituted for 1 tablespoon of lemon juice.

Fruits that are naturally suitable for making jelly include tart apples, crabapples, red currants, loganberries, blackberries, gooseberries, grapes, sour plums, and cranberries. Examples of fruits that are rich in pectin but deficient in acid are unripe figs, unripe bananas, sweet apples, unripe pears, and some varieties of ripe quinces. Apricots and strawberries are rich in acid but deficient in pectin. Peaches are usually considered to be deficient in both acid and pectin. However, much depends on the stage of ripeness of the fruit and on the quantity of water used in making extractions. Strawberries selected under the fully ripe stage for making preserves may show a distinct jellylike consistency of syrup, and some lots of raspberries will make an acceptable jelly.

Sugar is necessary for gel formation with pectin. Most homemade jellies will contain about 60 percent sugar. Sugar at this high concentration acts as a preservative and it also contributes to flavor.

Fruit juices furnish the water in jellies. They also contribute characteristic flavors. Some or all of the pectin and acid is naturally contained in the fruit juices.

Pectin Concentrates

Commercial pectins are prepared from cull apples, peels, and cores and from cull lemons. They are marketed as liquid or powder but because liquid pectins deteriorate after opening, they must be used promptly. Commercial pectins have no pronounced flavor to change the fruit flavors with which they may be combined. Acceptable jelly may be made from almost any fruit juice by using a pectin concentrate. Manufacturers' instructions should be followed.

Most of the pectin on the market is regular or high-sugar pectin requiring about 50 to 65 percent sugar to form a gel. Another type of pectin, however, is available for certain products where less or no sugar is desirable. This type of pectin is called *low-sugar pectin*. The molecular structures of the two pectins differ somewhat. The building blocks of the large pectin molecules (which may be classified as polysaccharides) are galacturonic acid. Galacturonic acid is a derivative of the sugar, galactose. The galacturonic acid units in the pectin may combine with methyl alcohol to form some methyl esters. Regular pectin has formed more methyl esters, or is said to have a higher degree of esterification with methyl alcohol, than has the low-sugar pectin. A gel may be formed by the low-sugar pectin in the presence of a small amount of a divalent ion such as calcium (Ca^{++}), but sugar is not necessary for gel formation as it is with regular pectin. The low-sugar pectin may be used in the preparation of vegetable and fruit salads and in artificially sweetened puddings and sauces. It is also used in the manufacture of dietetic jellies that contain artificial sweetening agents. The word *pectin* used without any other designation usually refers to regular pectin.

Testing for Pectin

A test that has commonly been used to determine the amount of pectin in juices that have been extracted from fruits is the alcohol precipitation test. Although other substances besides pectin are precipitated by alcohol, the test is nevertheless valuable in showing the relative amounts of pectin in various extractions. To apply the test, 1 tablespoon of cool or cold fruit juice is combined with 1 to 3 tablespoons of alcohol. A thick jellylike precipitate indicates abundant pectin. If the precipitate is somewhat broken, a medium amount of pectin is present, whereas a fine, flocculent precipitate indicates an extraction of fruit juice that is poor in pectin.

Another method of testing for pectin content involves the use of a simple pipette, called a *jelmeter*. The jelmeter measures the relative viscosity or thickness of the fruit extraction by determining the rate of flow of the juice through the pipette. The viscosity of a fruit juice is related to its content of pectin. Because viscosity varies with the temperature of the mixture, juices should be tested at approximately room temperature. The jelmeter is marked in terms of cups of sugar, indicating the amount of sugar to be used per cup ot extracted juice. Other substances than pectin in the solution affect viscosity just as other substances than pectin are precipitated by alcohol, yet comparisons of extractions are possible.

Through measurements of pectin content in fruit juices it has been shown that:

1. The maximum quantity of pectin is extracted in an acid solution.
2. High viscosity of the solution is closely related to good jellying power.
3. Heated extractions contain more pectin than raw juices.
4. If fruits are rich in pectin but low in acidity, acidifying the solution before heating increases the viscosity of the extraction.
5. Short periods of heating (usually 10 to 20 minutes) yield extractions of better jellying power than does long boiling. The long boiling of pectin in acid decomposes the pectin, giving pectic acid, which does not form jelly.
6. Fruit extractions lose viscosity on standing. This loss is more rapid at warm temperatures but occurs at cold temperatures.
7. The extra heating required to can fruit extractions for later use in making jelly lowers the viscosity although the extraction may still be usable for jelly.

Pectin, Acid, and Sugar in Jelly Formation

If pectin, acid, and sugar are present in the necessary proportions, the pectin is partially precipitated to form jelly. The effects of both acid and sugar are necessary.

The optimal amount of pectin required for a good jelly varies with its quality, but from 0.5 to 1.0 percent pectin usually gives a satisfactory product. The greater the concentration of pectin, the firmer is the jelly obtainable. Too low a concentration of pectin results in too soft a jelly to hold its form, but good homemade jellies do not require as high a percentage of pectin as do commercial jellies, which must be firm enough to withstand shipment. Pectins from different plant sources yield jellies of varying degrees of firmness. Cranberries tend to yield too firm a jelly to quiver when unmolded or to spread well. Citrus pectins yield jellies that tend to break easily into small masses, whereas apple pectins yield more elastic jellies.

A degree of acidity represented by a pH of 3.2 to 3.4 (where 7.0 is neutral and 1.0 is most acid) is desirable for good gel formation in fruit jellies. Juices of higher acidity, within an acceptable range, yield firmer jellies than do juices of lower acidity when both have similar pectin contents.

Fruit juice extractions have been boiled with no sugar and with varying amounts of sugar in a classic jelly experiment [1]. Fruit extractions boiled with no sugar did not form a true jelly but rather a small amount of a dark, opaque, tough substance. With the use of even a small amount of sugar (¼ cup per cup of juice) the volume increased, the color became lighter, the jelly clearer, and the texture less tough. When the amount of sugar was increased still further, the optimum amount was found that yielded an ideal jelly. Further additions of sugar gave a still larger volume and greater clearness but a soft syrupy consistency (see Figure 30-2). The finished volume tended to run parallel to the amount of sugar used.

One of the most uncertain factors in connection with jelly-making procedures is that of knowing how much sugar to add to various fruit extractions. It is particularly important to test the juice for pectin content as an aid in making this decision. Most fruit extractions yield better jellies with ¾ cup of sugar per cup of extraction than with 1 cup or more of sugar. Partly ripe currants, gooseberries, and grapes may require 1 or more cups of sugar but much depends on the stage of ripeness of the fruit and on the amount of water used to cook the fruit. As the pectin and acid in the fruit juice are more diluted, less sugar may be used.

Boiling pectin dispersions without sugar decomposes some of the pectin and produces weak jellies. If the sugar is added before the juice is boiled the boiling process has less effect on the hydrolysis of pectin and on jelly strength. A long boiling of sugar-fruit mixtures often produces a strong flavor and darkened color, but one can prevent excessive boiling by avoiding too great a dilution of the fruit extraction and by making small lots of jelly (using not over 4 to 6 cups of juice for one cooking).

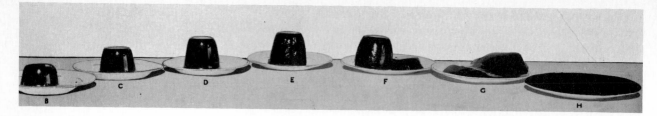

30-2 *Jellies made with various proportions of sugar for 1 cup of juice. The following table gives the amont of sugar per cup of juice used in samples B to H:*

Sample B: ¼ cup sugar.   Sample F: 1¼ cups sugar.
Sample C: ½ cup sugar.   Sample G: 1½ cups sugar.
Sample D: ¾ cup sugar.   Sample H: 1¾ cups sugar.
Sample E: 1 cup sugar.

With an increase in sugar the jelly increases in volume and becomes increasingly tender. Adding more than the optimum amount of sugar gives a soft jelly. Samples D and E gave the best jellies. Samples G and H have become so syrupy that they have lost all appearance of jelly. (Courtesy of Colorado Agricultural Experiment Station)

Pectin, acid, and sugar interact in the formation of a gel. Apparently the pectin molecules are stabilized, so that they remain dispersed in the fruit juice, by the negative charge that is on each molecule and also by the many molecules of water that are attracted to and held closely by the pectin molecules. The presence of a high concentration of sugar pulls much of the closely held water away from the pectin molecules because sugar is very hygroscopic (it loves water). At the same time, the acid, as hydrogen ions (H^+), neutralizes or reduces some of the negative charge on the pectin molecules. Thus the sugar and the acid together destabilize the pectin molecules so that they do not remain as separated or dispersed but move closer together. These pectin molecules then form some bonds with each other and establish a brush-heap type of structure. This three-dimensional structure traps water in its meshes so that rigidity develops, thus producing a gel.

Sugar Concentration in Finished Jelly

The finished homemade jelly may contain a sugar concentration that varies from 40 to 70 percent including that present in the fruit extraction. The optimum is probably somewhat lower than 70 percent. Some fruit extractions, such as gooseberry, that have a high acidity and a high pectin content give jellies of a better texture if the final sugar concentration does not exceed 60 percent. Jellies that tend to be too stiff, such as cranberry, have been improved in texture when the cooking was stopped at a sugar concentration somewhat below 60 percent. The optimum sugar concentration in the finished jelly, therefore, varies somewhat with the juice from which the jelly is made. A concentration of more than 75 percent sugar in the finished jelly may crystallize from that jelly because a saturated sugar solution has been produced. Crystallization of sugar from a jelly might be expected at less than 75 percent except for the fact that some inversion of sucrose to glucose and fructose occurs on boiling the acid fruit juice-sugar mixture. Invert sugar is more soluble than sucrose. Sugar may crystallize more readily from jellies made with added pectin and large amounts of sugar because the short boiling period is not sufficient to bring about much inversion of sucrose.

A federal standard of identity for fruit jelly requires that the soluble solids content (chiefly sugar) of a finished jelly be not less than 65 percent. Fruit jelly must be made from a mixture of not less than forty-five parts by weight of fruit juice ingredients to each fifty-five parts by weight of sweetening ingredients. Flavor substances, pectin, acids, and salts may be added as optional ingredients.

Procedures for Making Jelly

The procedures discussed here are those employed in making jelly from a fruit extraction that contains sufficient pectin and acid to allow the formation of a satisfactory gel.

Selecting the Fruit. In addition to the kind of fruit, the stage of ripeness is important in selecting it for jelly making. Fruits sufficiently ripe to have good flavor and color but sufficiently underripe to have maximum pectin content and good acidity will yield the best results. Some of the complex protopectin in immature fruit may be broken down to pectin during the heating process.

Extracting the Juice. Specific instructions for preparing fruit and extracting juice are given in the U.S. Department of Agriculture bulletin listed in Reference 2. Initial heating of the crushed or sliced fruit is usually necessary. Different amounts of water are required for heating soft and hard fruits. Only enough water should be added to soft fruits to start the cooking (about ¼ of a cup per pound of fruit). If the fruit is very watery and none too high in pectin and acid (as for example, red and black raspberries) crushing alone may be sufficient. The time for boiling soft fruits may range from 8 to 15 minutes, depending on the amount of water added and on how rapidly the fruit cooks to the pulpy state. Hard fruits should be sliced thin and should include cores and skins. Water to cover (or about 1 cup per pound of fruit) is usually necessary because about 20 minutes may be required to cook the fruit until it is soft. Mashing with a wooden spoon will hasten the disintegration of the fruit. Although recommendations that only one extraction be made seem justified on the basis of research, experience seems to show that some fruits, such as currants, contain sufficient pectin and acid to justify two extractions. A larger volume of jelly from a given lot of fruit is possible if more than one extraction can be made. A second extraction may be made by returning the drained pulp to the kettle, covering the pulp with water, and boiling it for 3 to 5 minutes.

A firmly woven cloth or several thicknesses of cheesecloth are necessary for draining or straining the fruit extraction in order to prevent the passage of pulp into the prepared juice. Squeezing the bag is not recommended since it may force pulp into the extraction and produce a cloudy juice. The use of cellulose pulp made by mixing uncolored unscented tissues (without wet-strength) with hot water and then draining off the water has been suggested as an aid in juice extraction. The pulp is mixed with the fruit after it has been heated and mashed and allows the squeezing of the bag for juice extraction without the production of cloudy juice.

Testing for Pectin and Adding Sugar. As previously described, the alcohol test or the jelmeter may be used to indicate the amount of pectin present in the extracted fruit juice. The character of the precipitate obtained with alcohol or the result of a jelmeter test helps to determine the quantity of sugar required by the extracted juice. However, these tests for pectin may not be accurate over a wide range of fruit extractions. Probably the best test is to make ½ to 1 cup of a test jelly with the amount of sugar that seems to be appropriate. By evaluating this test jelly the optimum amount of sugar can be ascertained.

In general, the larger the amount of pectin in the juice the larger is the amount of sugar that should be used. Less boiling is necessary with larger amounts of sugar as the jelly is cooked to a certain sugar concentration. Extractions of low pectin content may require only ½ cup of sugar per cup of juice. Sugar should be added when the jelly is put on to cook.

Cooking the Jelly. Cooking small lots of fruit juice (4 to 6 cups) is more rapid and yields jelly of a better color, flavor, and texture than cooking large lots. As soon as scum collects in firm enough masses, it may be removed from the surface. Rapid boiling accomplishes rapid evaporation and avoids a strong flavor and darkened color. It also prevents too great an inversion of sucrose.

The Sheeting Test for Doneness. When the sugar and fruit extraction are boiled together, the solution first drips from the spoon in several places. As the concentration increases, 2 or more drops may run together but continue to drip. Finally, several drops appear to run together and cut sharply from the edge of the spoon or 1 or 2

long hanging drops appear on the edge of the spoon (see Figure 30-3). The sheeting test in a boiling jelly mixture is an indication of doneness.

The Temperature Test for Doneness. A thermometer may be used to test the boiling jelly solution but, as in candy making, the bulb of the thermometer must be in the solution rather than in the foam and the bulb must not rest on the bottom or the sides of the pan. The temperature reading should be taken with the thermometer held in an upright position and with the eye on a level with the end of the mercury column. Jellies are usually done when cooked to a temperature of 4° to 5° C (7° to 9° F) above the boiling temperature of water. Suggested temperatures are given in the table at the right. The thermometer should be calibrated in boiling water in advance so that the exact boiling temperature is known for the locality.

Juices of high acidity and high pectin content will form good jelly if cooked to a temperature of 104° C (219° F) at sea level. Juices of lower acidity and pectin content will yield jellies of better texture if heated to a temperature of about 105° C (221° F). Jellies cooked to these temperatures have a sugar concentration of 60 to 65 percent.

As soon as cooking is completed, the jelly may again be skimmed, if necessary, and should be poured at once into hot, sterilized glasses or canning jars. The sterilized glasses may be sealed by spooning ⅛ inch hot paraffin onto the hot jelly surface. A slight tipping of the glass into various positions permits the paraffin to adhere to the

Elevation	Degrees C	Degrees F
Sea level	105	221
1,000 feet	104	219
5,000 feet	99.5	211

glass and form a seal. Canning jars should be filled to ⅛ inch of top with hot jelly. The hot lid with sealing compound should be placed on the jar immediately and the metal band screwed down firmly to seal. In warm or humid climates, the jelly in canning jars may be processed in a boiling water bath for about 5 minutes. Processing in a boiling water bath is also recommended for jams, preserves, marmalades, conserves, and fruit butters.

Over- and Undercooking. The overcooking of jelly produces a gummy, sticky mass that may harden in the glass if sufficient overcooking has occurred. Sugar also caramelizes, producing a strong flavor and dark color. If jelly is undercooked, it is syrupy and will not set.

Crystal Formation in Jelly. Sugar crystals form in jelly from (1) too high a sugar concentration, or (2) too little inversion of sucrose. Another type of crystal forms from a high concentration of acid potassium tartrate (as in grape jelly). One can prevent the formation of acid potassium tartrate crystals by chilling the extraction at a temperature of 5° C (41° F) for about 24 hours and straining the crystals from the extraction; by canning the extraction and later making small lots of jelly that can be used before crystals appear; or by diluting the concentration of the salt by combining the extraction with another that does not contain it. Mixing grape and apple extractions in equal proportions usually will completely prevent any precipitation of crystals of acid potassium tartrate.

Storing the Jelly. Although the high concentration of sugar in jelly and the paraffin seal are usually adequate to prevent fermentation or molding, a cool storage room is an extra safeguard and aids in the preservation of color [4]. Protection from light is also desirable to avoid fading or other discoloration.

Syneresis. The term *syneresis* is applied to the loss of fluid from some jellies. Currant, cranberry, and some grape jellies often show marked syneresis. In some jellies that do not show syneresis in the mold, cutting or breaking the gel may cause some liquid to be lost.

Nutritive Value of Jellies and Preserves

Concentrated sugar foods, such as jams, jellies, and preserves, are not dependable sources of essential nutrients. They provide, in general, only kilocalories and are usually eaten in small amounts as an adjunct to other foods.

Other Preserved Products

Preserves

The term *preserves* applies to fruits cooked in syrup until they are tender and transparent. During cooking, the cells of the fruit take up syrup, and because the syrup should be taken up gradually, the fruit should not be placed in too dense a syrup at the beginning. The effect of too dense a syrup is the extraction of water from the fruit by diffusion, leaving the fruit shrunken, tough, even hard, in some instances. Hard fruits, such as melon rinds and quinces, should be cooked tender in water before being placed in the syrup or be placed in a dilute syrup, which may later be concentrated. Under such treatment the fruit will remain tender and plump.

The color of preserves should be bright and sparkling. Rapid boiling tends to preserve good color better than long, slow cooking. The latter almost invariably yields a dark-colored product of strong flavor, especially in fruits such as strawberries, cherries, and plums. The proportion of sugar to fruit used in the making of preserves is usually three-fourths to one part sugar by weight to one part fruit.

Marmalade

Marmalade consists of a jellylike base with fine fruit particles suspended in it. It may be made from one fruit or from a combination of fruits but pectin is necessary to form jelly. From the standpoint of the tenderness of the fruit particles, it is necessary that the fruit, especially citrus fruit with rind, be *very* finely sliced or run through a food chopper. The proportion of sugar to fruit is about the same as for preserves.

Jam

Jam differs from preserves in that the fruit in jam is crushed or ground and is cooked to a somewhat even consistency instead of retaining its form and identity as in preserves. If the fruit contains pectin, a sheeting test (not so distinct as in jelly) will aid in determining the necessary amount of cooking. The proportion of sugar to fruit is about three fourths to one by weight. Acceptable jams may also be prepared with less sugar and with artificial sweeteners [3].

Conserves

Conserves are jams that are made from a mixture of fruits, usually including citrus fruits. Sometimes raisins and nuts are added. Conserves are thicker with fruit than marmalade, and the fruit need not be so finely divided unless citrus fruit rinds or other fruits are used that tend to become hard when cooked in syrup.

Fruit Butters

Either small or large pulpy fruits may be made into butters. The fruit is cooked and run through a colander or strainer to reduce it to a smooth, uniform pulp before being combined with sugar. The amount of sugar may be less than for jams and preserves (usually one half to two thirds as much sugar as pulp). Spices are sometimes added and the mixture is cooked until a spoonful tested will hold up in slightly rounded form on the surface. Frequent stirring is necessary to prevent scorching.

Study Questions

1. What constituents are essential for making jelly? What role does each constituent play?
2. a. What is pectin and where is it found?
   b. How is it removed from plant tissues in jellymaking?
   c. Describe two tests for measuring the pectin content of juices.
   d. What is the source of commercial pectin concentrates and how may they be used in jellymaking?
   e. Describe differences between regular pectin and low-sugar pectin.
3. In jellymaking, what is the relationship between pectin and the amount of sugar added? Explain.
4. What is the usual concentration of sugar in finished jelly? Why does the sugar usually *not* crystallize out on storage?
5. Describe a step-wise procedure for preparing a fruit jelly and explain what is happening at each step.
6. Describe distinguishing characteristics for:
   a. Preserves
   b. Marmalade
   c. Jam
   d. Conserves
   e. Fruit butters

References

1. Goldthwaite, N. E. *Principles of Making Fruit Jellies.* Colorado Experiment Station Bulletin No. 298. Fort Collins, CO: Colorado Experiment Station, 1925.
2. *How to Make Jellies, Jams, and Preserves at Home.* Home and Garden Bulletin No. 56. Washington, DC: U.S. Department of Agriculture, 1977.
3. Hyvönen, L., and R. Törmä. 1983. Examination of sugars, sugar alcohols, and artificial sweeteners as substitutes for sucrose in strawberry jam. Product development. *Journal of Food Science* **48**, 183.
4. Spayd, S. E., and J. R. Morris. 1981. Influence of immature fruits on strawberry jam quality and storage stability. *Journal of Food Science* **46**, 414.

Weights and Measures

Symbols for Measurements

t = teaspoon   c = cup
T = tablespoon   fg = few grains

Common Measurements Used in Food Preparation

3 t = 1 T	12 T = ¾ c	4 c = 1 qt
16 T = 1 c	5⅓ T = ⅓ c	4 qts = 1 gal
4 T = ¼ c	10⅔ T = ⅔ c	2 T = 1 liquid oz. or ⅛ c
8 T = ½ c	2 c = 1 pt	8 oz = 1 c or ½ pt

Approximate Number Cups or Units in a Pound of Some Common Foods

2¼ c granulated sugar
  4 c all-purpose or bread flour
4½ c pastry flour

4 c grated cheese
2 c butter or other fat

Weights and Measures for Some Food Ingredients

All purpose flour, sifted	1 lb = 4 c	115 g per c
Whole wheat flour, stirred	1 lb = 3⅓ c	132 g per c
SAS-phosphate baking powder	14 oz = 2½ c	3.2 g per t
Baking soda	1 lb = 2⅓ c	4 g per t
Granulated sugar	1 lb = 2¼ c	200 g per c
Brown sugar, packed	1 lb = 2¼ c	200 g per c
Salt	1 lb = 1½ c	288 g per c
Margarine	1 lb = 2 c	224 g per c
Hydrogenated fat	1 lb = 2⅓ c	188 g per c
Oil	1 lb = 2⅙ c	210 g per c
Eggs, fresh whole	1 lb = 1¾ c	248 g per c

Standard Can Sizes

Can Sizes	Contents, cups	Average Net Weight
8 oz.	1	8 oz
Picnic	1¼	11 oz
No. 300	1¾	15 oz
No. 303	2	16 oz
No. 2	2½	1 lb 4 oz
No. 2½	3½	1 lb 13 oz
No. 3 cylinder	5¾	46 fl oz
No. 10	13	6 lb 10 oz

Equivalent Metric and Avoirdupois Weight Units

$$1 \text{ kilogram} = 2.21 \text{ pounds}$$
$$= 1000 \text{ grams}$$
$$453.59 \text{ grams} = 1 \text{ pound}$$
$$28.35 \text{ grams} = 1 \text{ ounce}$$
$$1 \text{ pound} = 0.454 \text{ kilograms}$$

Equivalent Liquid Measures

1 liter = 1.06 quarts
= 1000 milliliters
1 quart = 0.946 liters
= 946 milliliters
1 cup = 236.6 milliliters

½ cup = 118 milliliters
⅓ cup = 79 milliliters
¼ cup = 59 milliliters
1 tablespoon = 14.8 milliliters

CONVERSIONS

English to Metric

pounds × 0.454 = kilograms
ounces × 28.35 = grams
quarts × 0.946 = liters
cups × 236.6 = milliliters
inches × 2.5 = centimeters

Metric to English

kilograms × 2.2 = pounds
grams × 0.035 = ounces
liters × 1.056 = quarts
centimeters × 0.4 = inches

Temperature Control

Temperatures for cooking can be most accurately controlled when a thermostat or a thermometer is used. Modern ovens have thermostat-controlled heat. They may be checked occasionally with a portable oven thermometer if there is some question about the accuracy of the thermostatic control.

Temperature Range for Ovens

Low	250° to 325° F
Moderate	350° to 375° F
Hot	400° to 425° F
Very hot	450° to 525° F

Thermometers are available for reading the temperature of deep fats, sugar syrups, and meats. In taking the temperature of hot fats or of boiling sugar syrups, the bulb of the thermometer should be fully submerged but should not touch the bottom of the utensil. In reading the scale, the eye should be on a level with the top of the mercury column.

Meat thermometers have a short scale (up to about 100° C or 212° F). The bulb is small and the thermometer is inserted so that the bulb rests in the center of the roast or the muscle being roasted. The thermometer should be inserted so that the position in the oven is convenient for reading the scale.

Converting Celsius or Centigrade Temperatures to Fahrenheit

Formulas To Use

$$1.8 \times °C = °F - 32$$

OR

$$°C = (°F - 32) \times \tfrac{5}{9}$$
$$°F = (°C \times \tfrac{9}{5}) + 32$$

The first formula given for temperature conversion may be used either for changing Celsius to Fahrenheit or Fahrenheit to Celsius simply by inserting the *known* temperature in the appropriate place in the formula and then solving the equation for the unknown.

Conversion Table

°F	°C	°F	°C
50	10.0	200	93.3
60	15.6	210	98.9
70	21.1	212	100.0
80	26.7	215	101.7
90	32.2	220	104.4
100	37.8	230	110.0
110	43.3	235	112.8
120	48.9	240	115.6
130	54.4	245	118.3
140	60.0	248	120.0
150	65.6	250	121.1
160	71.1	252	122.2
170	76.7	255	123.9
180	82.2	260	126.7
190	87.8	270	132.2

APPENDIX C

Nutritive Value of Selected Foods*

Vegetables

Vegetable	Approxi-mate Measure	Weight (gm)	Food Energy (kcal)	Water (%)	Protein (gm)	Carbo-hydrate (gm)	Calcium (mg)	Iron (mg)	Vitamin A Value (IU)	Thiamin (mg)	Ribo-flavin (mg)	Ascorbic Acid (mg)
Leaves												
Cabbage, raw, finely shredded	1 cup	90	20	92	1	5	44	0.4	120	0.05	0.05	42
Lettuce, raw, crisphead	¼ head	135	20	96	1	4	27	0.7	450	0.08	0.08	8
Spinach, frozen, cooked	1 cup	190	45	92	6	7	200	4.8	15,390	0.15	0.27	53
Vegetable-fruits												
Peppers, green, sweet, raw	1 pod	74	15	93	1	4	7	0.5	310	0.06	0.06	94
Squash, winter, baked	1 cup	205	130	81	4	32	57	1.6	8,610	0.10	0.27	27
Tomatoes, raw	one	135	25	94	1	6	16	0.6	1,110	0.07	0.05	28
Flowers and stems												
Asparagus, cooked	1 cup	145	30	94	3	5	30	0.9	1,310	0.23	0.26	38
Broccoli, cooked	1 cup	155	40	91	5	7	136	1.2	3,880	0.14	0.31	140
Cauliflower, cooked, buds	1 cup	125	30	93	5	5	26	0.9	80	0.11	0.10	69
Celery, raw, outer stalk	1 stalk	40	5	94	Trace	2	16	0.1	110	0.01	0.01	4
Bulbs, roots, and tubers												
Beets, cooked, diced	1 cup	170	55	91	2	12	24	0.9	30	0.05	0.07	10
Carrots, cooked, diced	1 cup	155	50	91	1	11	51	0.9	16,280	0.08	0.08	9
Potatoes, peeled, boiled	one	135	90	83	3	20	8	0.7	Trace	0.12	0.05	22
Sweet potatoes, boiled	one	151	170	71	3	40	48	1.1	11,940	0.14	0.09	26
Seeds and pods												
Snap beans, cooked	1 cup	125	30	92	2	7	63	0.8	680	0.09	0.11	15
Sweet corn, cooked	1 ear	140	70	74	2	16	2	0.5	310	0.09	0.08	7
Green peas, frozen, cooked	1 cup	160	110	82	8	19	30	3.0	960	0.43	0.14	21
Dry peas, split, cooked	1 cup	200	230	70	16	42	22	3.4	80	0.30	0.18	—
Dry beans, red, canned	1 cup	255	230	76	15	42	74	4.6	10	0.13	0.10	—

*From *Nutritive Value of Foods*. Home and Garden Bulletin No. 72. Washington, D.C.: U.S. Department of Agriculture, 1981.

Fruit	Approximate Measure	Weight (gm)	Food Energy (kcal)	Water (%)	Protein (gm)	Carbo-hydrate (gm)	Vitamin A Value (IU)	Ascorbic Acid (mg)
Apples, raw, unpeeled	1 medium	138	80	84	Trace	20	120	6
Apricots, raw	3 apricots	107	55	85	1	14	2,890	11
Avocados, raw, California	1 avocado	216	370	74	5	13	630	30
Bananas, raw, without peel	1 banana	119	100	76	1	26	230	12
Blueberries, raw	1 cup	145	90	83	1	22	150	20
Cantaloupe, raw	½ med. melon	477	80	91	2	20	9,240	90
Grapefruit, medium								
White	½ grapefruit	241	45	89	1	12	10	44
Pink or red	½ grapefruit	241	50	89	1	13	540	44
Grapefruit juice, frozen concentrate diluted with 3 parts water	1 cup	247	100	89	1	24	20	96
Grapes, raw, Thompson	10 grapes	50	35	81	Trace	9	50	2
Oranges, raw	1 orange	131	65	86	1	16	260	66
Orange juice								
Fresh	1 cup	248	110	88	2	26	500	124
Canned, unsweetened	1 cup	249	120	87	2	28	500	100
Frozen concentrate diluted with 3 parts water	1 cup	249	120	87	2	29	540	120
Dehydrated, prepared with water	1 cup	248	115	88	1	27	500	109
Peaches, raw	1 medium	100	40	89	1	10	1,330	7
Pears, raw	1 pear	164	100	83	1	25	30	7
Pineapple, raw, diced	1 cup	155	80	85	1	21	110	26
Raspberries, red, raw	1 cup	123	70	84	1	17	160	31
Strawberries, raw, capped	1 cup	149	55	90	1	13	90	88
Tangerines, raw	1 medium	86	40	87	1	10	360	27
Watermelon, raw, wedge, with rind and seeds	4 × 8 inches	926	110	93	2	27	2,510	30

Meat	Approximate Measure (Ounces)	Weight (gm)	Food Energy (kcal)	Water (%)	Protein (gm)	Fat (gm)	Iron (mg)	Thiamin (mg)
Beef: trimmed, cooked								
Cuts braised, simmered, or pot roasted								
Lean and fat	3	85	245	53	23	16	2.9	.04
Lean only	2.5	72	140	62	22	5	2.7	.04
Ground beef, broiled								
Lean with 10% fat	3	85	185	60	23	10	3.0	.08
Lean with 21% fat	2.9	82	235	54	20	17	2.6	.07
Roast, oven-cooked, no liquid added								
Relatively fat, such as rib								
Lean and fat	3	85	375	40	17	33	2.2	.05
Lean only	1.8	51	125	57	14	7	1.8	.04
Relatively lean, such as heel of round:								
Lean and fat	3	85	165	62	25	7	3.2	.06
Lean only	2.8	78	125	65	24	3	3.0	.06
Lamb: trimmed, cooked								
Leg, roasted								
Lean and fat	3	85	235	54	22	16	1.4	.13
Lean only	2.5	71	130	62	20	5	1.4	.12
Liver: beef, fried	3	85	195	56	22	9	7.5	.22
Pork: fresh, trimmed, cooked								
Chop, loin with bone, lean and fat	2.7	78	305	42	19	25	2.7	.75
Roast, oven-cooked, no liquid added:								
Lean and fat	3	85	310	46	21	24	2.7	.78
Lean only	2.4	68	175	55	20	10	2.6	.73
Veal: cooked, bone removed								
Roast, rib, medium fat	3	85	230	55	23	14	2.9	.11
Poultry								
Chicken, breast, fried								
Flesh and skin only	2.8	79	160	58	26	5	1.3	.04
Chicken, drumstick, fried								
Flesh and skin only	1.3	38	90	55	12	4	0.9	.03
Chicken, canned, boneless	3	85	170	65	18	10	1.3	.03
Turkey, roasted, without skin								
Dark meat	3	85	175	61	26	7	2.0	.03
Light meat	3	85	150	62	28	3	1.0	.04
Fish								
Haddock, breaded, fried	3	85	140	66	17	5	1.0	.03
Tuna, canned in oil								
Drained solids	3	85	170	61	24	7	1.6	.04

Product	Approx-imate Measure	Weight (gm)	Food Energy (kcal)	Water (%)	Protein (gm)	Fat (gm)	Carbo-hydrate (gm)	Calcium (mg)	Vit-amin A (I.U.)
Fluid milk									
Whole, 3.3% fat	1 cup	244	150	88	8	8	11	291	310
Nonfat (skim)	1 cup	245	85	91	8	trace	12	302	500
Low-fat, 2% fat nonfat milk solids added, 10 or more grams protein per cup	1 cup	246	135	88	10	5	14	352	500
Buttermilk	1 cup	245	100	90	8	2	12	285	80
Canned									
Evaporated, unsweetened whole	1 cup	252	340	74	17	19	25	657	610
Condensed, sweetened	1 cup	306	980	27	24	27	166	868	1000
Dry, nonfat, instant	1 cup	68	245	4	24	trace	35	837	1610
Yogurt, plain (from partially skimmed milk with added milk solids)	1 cup	227	145	85	12	4	16	415	150
Cream									
Half-and-half	1 cup	242	315	81	7	28	10	254	260
Light, coffee or table	1 cup	240	470	74	6	46	9	231	1730
Heavy whipping	1 cup	239	700	64	5	74	7	166	2690
Cheese									
Cheddar	1 ounce	28	115	37	7	9	trace	204	300
Creamed cottage, 4% fat (curd not pressed down), large curd	1 cup	225	235	79	28	10	6	135	370

Product	Approx-imate Measure	Weight (gm)	Energy (kcal)	Water (%)	Protein (gm)	Carbo-hydrate (gm)	Iron (mg)	Thi-amin (mg)	Ribo-flavin (mg)	Nia-cin (mg)
Wheat										
Bulgur, canned	1 cup	135	245	56	8	44	1.9	.08	.05	4.1
Farina, quick-cooking, enriched, cooked	1 cup	245	105	89	3	22	1.0–8.0	.12	.07	1.0
Whole-wheat flour	1 cup	120	400	12	16	85	4.0	.66	.14	5.2
All-purpose flour, enriched	1 cup	125	455	12	13	95	3.6	.80	.50	6.6
Cake or pastry flour, enriched	1 cup	96	350	12	7	76	2.8	.61	.38	5.1
Puffed wheat, added nutrients	1 cup	15	55	3	2	12	.6	.08	.03	1.2
Shredded wheat	1 biscuit	25	90	7	2	20	.9	.06	.03	1.1
Wheat flakes, added sugar and nutrients	1 cup	30	105	4	3	24	varies	.35	.42	3.5
Macaroni, cooked, hot tender Enriched	1 cup	140	155	73	5	32	1.3	.20	.11	1.5
Noodles (egg), cooked Enriched	1 cup	160	200	71	7	37	1.4	.22	.13	1.9
Corn										
Whole-ground cornmeal, unbolted, dry	1 cup	122	435	12	11	90	2.9	.46	.13	2.4
Degermed cornmeal, cooked										
Enriched	1 cup	240	120	88	3	26	1.0	.14	.10	1.2
Unenriched	1 cup	240	120	88	3	26	.5	.05	.02	.2
Corn (hominy) grits, degermed, cooked,										
Enriched	1 cup	245	125	87	3	27	.7	.10	.07	1.0
Unenriched	1 cup	245	125	87	3	27	.2	.05	.02	.5
Cornflakes, added nutrients										
Plain	1 cup	25	95	4	2	21	.6	.29	.35	2.9
Sugar-covered	1 cup	40	155	2	2	37	1.0	.46	.56	4.6
Puffed corn, presweetened, added nutrients	1 cup	20	80	4	2	16	2.3	.23	.28	2.3
Oats										
Oatmeal or rolled oats, cooked	1 cup	240	130	87	5	23	1.4	.19	.05	.2
Puffed oats, added sugar and nutrients	1 cup	25	100	3	3	19	2.9	.29	.35	2.9
Rice, white										
Enriched										
Cooked	1 cup	205	225	73	4	50	1.8	.23	.02	2.1
Instant, ready-to-serve	1 cup	165	180	73	4	40	1.3	.21	—	1.7
Puffed rice, added nutrients	1 cup	15	60	4	1	13	.3	.07	.01	.7

Glossary

Terms Used in Cookery

Baste. To spoon liquid over food as it cooks; the liquid may be drippings from the food itself.

Beat. To make a mixture smooth using a brisk motion that has an up and down movement.

Blanch. To apply boiling water or steam for a few minutes.

Blend. To mix two or more ingredients thoroughly.

Boil. To cook in water at boiling temperature.

Braise. To cook meat or poultry slowly in a covered utensil in a small amount of liquid or in steam.

Bread. To roll in bread crumbs before cooking.

Broil. To cook by direct exposure to radiant heat.

Brown. To produce a brown surface on a food by use of relatively high heat.

Caramelize. To heat sugar until a brown color and characteristic flavor develop.

Chop. To cut into pieces using a sharp knife or other tool

Cream. To mix one or more foods until smooth and creamy; usually applied to mixing fat and sugar.

Crumb. To coat or top with crumbs, such as topping a casserole dish.

Cut in. To distribute solid fat throughout dry ingredients using two knives or a pastry blender.

Dice. To cut into small cubes.

Dot. To place small particles at intervals on a surface, as to dot with butter.

Dredge. To sprinkle or coat with flour or other fine substance.

Fold. To combine by using two motions, cutting vertically through the mixture and turning mixture over and over.

Fricassee. To cook by braising; usually applied to fowl, rabbit, or veal cut into pieces.

Fry. To cook in fat; pan-fry is to cook in a small amount of fat while deep-fat frying is cooking in a deep layer of fat.

Grind. To reduce to small particles by cutting or crushing mechanically.

Knead. To manipulate by pressure alternated with folding and stretching, as in kneading a dough.

Lard. To place on top or insert strips of fat in uncooked lean meat or fish to give flavor and prevent drying of the surface.

Leaven. To make light by use of a gaseous agent such as air, water vapor, or carbon dioxide.

Level off. To move the level edge of a knife or spatula across the top edge of a container, scraping away the excess material.

Marinate. To let lie in a prepared liquid for a period of time for tenderizing and seasoning purposes.

Melt. To liquefy by use of heat.

Mince. To divide into very small pieces by chopping or cutting.

Mix. To combine ingredients.

Oven spring. The rapid increase in volume of yeast bread during the first few minutes of baking.

Pan-broil. To cook uncovered on a hot surface, pouring off fat as it accumulates.

Panning. To cook a vegetable in a tightly covered skillet, using a small amount of fat but no added water.

Pare. To cut off an outside covering such as skins of vegetables.

Peel. To remove outside coverings.

Poach. To cook in a hot liquid. The food is carefully handled to retain its form as in poaching an egg.

Pot-roast. Cooking large pieces of meat by braising.

Proofing. The final rising period before baking for yeast doughs that have been molded.

Render. To melt fat and remove from connective tissue using low heat.

Roast. To cook, uncovered, by use of dry heat.

Roux. A thickening agent made by heating a blend of flour and fat. It may be white or brown and is used in making sauces and gravies.

Sauté. To cook in a small amount of fat. Synonymous with pan-fry.

Scald. To heat milk or other liquids just below the boiling point.

Sear. To coagulate or brown the surface of meat by the application of intense heat for a brief period.

Sift. To separate the fine parts of a material from the coarse parts by use of a sieve.

Simmer. To cook in liquid at a temperature of about 85° C (185° F). The liquid may show slight movement or bubbling but the bubbles tend to form slowly and to break below the surface.

Steam. To cook in direct contact with steam in a closed container. Indirect steaming may be done in the closed top of a double boiler.

Steep. To extract flavor or color at a temperature below the boiling point of water.

Stew. To simmer in a small to moderate quantity of liquid.

Stir. To mix food materials with a circular motion.

Toast. To brown by means of dry heat.

Truss. To secure the wings and legs of a bird with pins or twine.

Whip. To rapidly beat such mixtures as gelatin dishes, eggs, and cream in order to incorporate air and increase volume.

Acid. A sour-tasting compound containing hydrogen that may be ionized or replaced by positive elements to form salts.

Acrolein. An irritating substance formed by the decomposition of glycerol at high temperatures.

Alkali. A substance having the ability to neutralize an acid.

Amino Acid. An organic molecule containing both an amino group ($-NH_2$)

$$O$$
$$\parallel$$

and an acid group ($-C-OH$); constitutes the basic building block of proteins.

Amylase. An enzyme that breaks down or hydrolyzes starch.

Amylopectin. A highly branched chain fraction of starch.

Amylose. A straight chain fraction of starch.

Antioxidant. A substance that retards oxidative rancidity in fats by becoming oxidized itself and stopping a chain reaction.

Aroma. A distinctive fragrance or odor.

Astringent. Shrinking or contracting of tissues in the mouth to produce a puckery effect.

Boiling point. The temperature at which the atmospheric pressure is equal to the vapor pressure of a liquid and an equilibrium is established.

Buffer. A substance that resists change in acidity or alkalinity.

Carbohydrates. Organic compounds containing carbon, hydrogen, and oxygen; simple sugars and polymers of simple sugars.

Catalyst. A substance that affects the rate of a chemical reaction without being used up in the reaction.

Coagulation. Usually refers to a change or denaturation of protein that results in hardening or precipitation. Often accomplished by heat or mechanical agitation.

Colloid. Usually refers to the state of subdivision of dispersed particles; intermediate between very small particles in true solution and large particles in suspension. Proteins and pectins are usually colloidal.

Crystallization. The process of forming crystals that result from chemical elements solidifying with an orderly internal structure.

Denaturation. The changing of a protein molecule, usually by the unfolding of the chains, to a less soluble state.

Dextrinization. Breaking down of starch molecules to dextrins by dry heat.

Dextrins. Polysaccharides resulting from the partial hydrolysis of starch.

Disaccharide. A carbohydrate made up of two simple sugars (monosaccharides) linked together. Table sugar (sucrose) is a disaccharide.

Disperse. To distribute or spread throughout some other substance.

Dispersion. A system composed of dispersed particles in a dispersion medium.

Emulsifier. A surface-active agent that acts as a bridge between two immiscible liquids and allows an emulsion to form.

Emulsion. Dispersion of one liquid in another with which it is usually immiscible.

Enzyme. An organic catalyst produced by living cells that changes the rate of a reaction without being used up in the reaction.

Ester. The chemical combination of an alcohol and an organic acid. Fats are esters of glycerol and three fatty acids.

Fatty acids. Organic acids made up of chains of carbon atoms with a car-
$$\overset{O}{\underset{\|}{}}$$
boxyl group ($-C-OH$) on one end; three fatty acids combine with glycerol to make a triglyceride.

Fermentation. Transformation of organic substances into smaller molecules by the action of a microorganism; yeast ferments glucose to carbon dioxide and alcohol.

Foam. Dispersion of a gas in a liquid.

Gel. A colloidal dispersion that shows some rigidity and will keep the shape
of the container in which it has been placed.

Gelatinization. The swelling and consequent thickening of starch granules
when heated in water.

Glycerol. A three carbon organic compound (an alcohol) that combines with
fatty acids to produce fats (triglycerides).

Gluten. The elastic, tenacious substance formed from the insoluble proteins
of wheat flour during dough development.

Gram. Basic unit of weight in the metric system; 28.35 grams equal 1 ounce
and 453.59 grams equal 1 pound.

Gustatory. Having to do with the sense of taste.

Homogenize. To break up particles into small, uniform-sized pieces. Fat in
milk may be homogenized.

Hydrogenation. A process in which hydrogen is combined chemically with
an unsaturated compound such as an oil. Hydrogenation of oil produces
a plastic shortening.

Hydration. The process of absorbing water.

Hydrolysis. A chemical reaction in which a molecular linkage is broken
and a molecule of water is utilized. Starch is hydrolyzed to produce
glucose; water is a necessary component of the reaction.

Hydrophilic. Attracted to water.

Hygroscopic. The tendency to absorb water readily.

Immiscible. Not capable of being mixed.

Inversion. Breaking down of sucrose to its component monosaccharides,
glucose and fructose.

Irradiation. A process in which food is exposed to radiant energy.

Kilocalorie. The amount of heat required to raise the temperature of 1 kilo-
gram (1,000 grams) of water 1° C. A unit of energy.

Lecithin. A fatty substance containing two fatty acids esterified to glycerol
along with phosphoric acid and a nitrogen-containing compound. A
phospholipid.

Maillard reaction. A browning reaction involving the combination of an
$$\overset{H}{\underset{|}{}}$$
amino group ($-NH_2$) from a protein and an aldehyde group ($-C=O$)
from a sugar, which then leads to the formation of many complex substances.

Minerals. Inorganic substances; noncarbon compounds; ash.

Monoglyceride. Glycerol esterified to one fatty acid.

Monosaccharide. A simple sugar. Examples are glucose, fructose, and
galactose.

Olfactory. Having to do with the sense of smell.

Opaque. Not reflecting or giving out light; not clear.

Organic. Pertaining to carbon compounds.

Osmosis. The movement of water through a semipermeable membrane from an area of low concentration of solute to an area of higher concentration in order to equalize the osmotic pressure created by differences in concentration.

Oxidases. Enzymes that catalyze oxidation reactions.

Oxidation. A gain in oxygen or loss of electrons.

Pasteurization. Mild heat treatment to destroy vegetative microorganisms; not complete destruction of microbes.

Pectin. A polysaccharide composed of galacturonic acid subunits, partially esterified with methyl alcohol, and capable of forming a gel.

pH. An expression of degree of acidity. On a scale from 1 to 14, 7 is neutral, 1 is most acid, and 14 is most alkaline or least acid.

Plasticity. Ability to be molded or shaped.

Polyphenols. Organic compounds that include as part of their chemical structures an unsaturated ring with more than one —OH group on it. These compounds are implicated in certain types of oxidative enzymatic browning in foods.

Polysaccharide. Complex carbohydrates containing many simple sugars (monosaccharides) linked together. Starch and pectins are polysaccharides.

Polyunsaturated fatty acid. A fatty acid that has two or more double bonds between carbon atoms. A polyunsaturated fat is one that contains a relatively high proportion of polyunsaturated fatty acids.

Reduction. A gain of hydrogen or gain of electrons.

Rennet. A crude extract from calf stomach containing the enzyme rennin.

Rennin. Enzyme from the stomach that clots milk.

Retrograde. Close association of amylose molecules in a starch gel during aging.

Saturated fatty acid. A fatty acid that has no double bonds between its carbon atoms and is thus holding all of the hydrogen that it can hold. A saturated fat is one that contains a relatively high proportion of saturated fatty acids.

Saturated solution. A solution containing all of the solute that it can dissolve at that temperature.

Solubility. The amount of a substance that will dissolve in a specified quantity of another substance.

Solute. The substance to be dissolved in another substance that is called the solvent.

Solution. The resulting mixture when a solute is dissolved in a solvent.

Spore. An encapsulated, resistant form of a microorganism.

Sterilize. To destroy microorganisms by heating with steam, dry heat, or by boiling in a liquid for 20 to 30 minutes.

Supersaturated Solution. A solution that has dissolved more solute or dispersed substance than it can ordinarily hold at a particular temperature. The solution is formed by being heated and slowly cooled without disturbance.

Syneresis. The separation or weeping of liquid from a gel.

Tactile. Having to do with the sense of touch.

Toxin. A poison, usually a protein, formed by microorganisms.

Translucent. Shining or glowing through; partly transparent.

Viscosity. Resistance to flow.

Volatile. Readily forming a vapor or gaseous phase.

Volatilization. The process of becoming volatile.

Whey. The liquid portion of milk remaining after the curd, which is chiefly the protein casein, is precipitated.

Index